COPYRIGHT © 1966 BY
HORIZON PUBLISHERS

All rights reserved. Reproduction in whole or any parts thereof in any form or by any media without written permission is prohibited.

Second Printing   August 1973

INTERNATIONAL STANDARD BOOK NUMBER 0-88290-022-6

LIBRARY OF CONGRESS CATALOG CARD NUMBER 66-25508

PROPHETS & PROPHECIES OF THE OLD TESTAMENT

by
Duane S. Crowther

HORIZON PUBLISHERS
191 North 650 East
Bountiful, Utah 84010
292-1959

PROPHETS & PROPHECIES
OF THE OLD TESTAMENT

by

Duane S. Crowther

This book is dedicated
with love and appreciation

To My Parents

about whom the patriarch told me in my blessing,
"You have indeed been blessed with a wonderful
heritage, having been born of goodly parents,
whose faith and devotion to the cause of Jesus
Christ are an example before you, and whose
teachings have prepared you more fully to
meet the problems of life . . ."

For my thoughts are not your thoughts, neither are your ways my ways, saith the Lord.

For as the heavens are higher than the earth, so are my ways higher than your ways, and my thoughts than your thoughts.

For as the rain cometh down, and the snow from heaven, and returneth not thither, but watereth the earth, and maketh it bring forth and bud, that it may give seed to the sower, and bread to the eater:

So shall my word be that goeth forth out of my mouth: it shall not return unto me void, but it shall accomplish that which I please, and it shall prosper in the thing whereto I sent it.

Isaiah 55:8-11.

TABLE OF CONTENTS

TABLE OF CONTENTS	vii
LIST OF MAPS AND CHARTS	xiii
CHANGES MADE IN THE INSPIRED VERSION OF THE BIBLE	xiv
ABBREVIATIONS FOR SCRIPTURAL BOOKS	xv
DIACRITICAL MARKINGS USED IN THIS BOOK	xvii
PART I	1
I. THIS BOOK AND HOW TO USE IT	3
The Purposes of This Book	3
This Book Contains Useful Material for Study on Three Levels	4
Explanation of the Materials Presented About Each Prophet	7
How to Use the Book	10
Summary	12
II. HOW TO STUDY AND INTERPRET SCRIPTURE	15
Proper Tools Are Needed for Bible Study	15
A Recommended Basic Library for Studying the Old Testament Prophets	18
Some Suggestions for Bible Study	19
Some Suggestions for Marking the Scriptures	23
Some Suggestions on the Interpretation of Scripture	29
Summary	34
III. AIDS FOR UNDERSTANDING BIBLE HISTORY AND CHRONOLOGY	36
The Historical Background of the House of Israel	37
A Simplified Diagram of Old Testament History	42
An Analysis of the Books of Kings and Chronicles from the Death of Solomon to the Fall of Judah	43
Chronological List of the Kings of Judah and Israel and the Approximate Dates and Periods of Their Reigns	71
Summary	74

IV. SIX MAJOR DOCTRINES OF THE OLD TESTAMENT PROPHETS 75
The Nature of God and Godhood 76
God's Communication With Man 80
The Nature of Sin 83
The Nature of Man's Agency and God's Judgment 88
Counsel for Righteous Living 91
The Events of the Last Days 115
Summary 168

PART II 171

V. HISTORICAL SUMMARY: ASSYRIA AND THE FALL OF ISRAEL 173
Kings of Assyria 173
Kings of Israel 177
Kings of Judah 181
Summary 185

VI. THE EARLY PROPHETS AND THEIR MESSAGES 187
Doctrinal Analysis 224
Summary 245

VII. JONAH 247
Information About Jonah and His Times 247
Outline of the Book 250
Doctrinal Analysis 251
Critical Information About the Book of Jonah 252
Summary 256

VIII. AMOS 257
Information About Amos and His Times 257
Outline of the Book 260
Doctrinal Analysis 263
Critical Information About the Book of Amos 267
Summary 268

IX. HOSEA 270
Information About Hosea and His Times 270
Outline of the Book 273
Doctrinal Analysis 274
Critical Information About the Book of Hosea 278
Summary 280

X. MICAH 282
Information About Micah and His Times 282
Outline of the Book 284

TABLE OF CONTENTS ix

    Doctrinal Analysis 285
    Critical Information About the Book of Micah 293
    Summary 295
XI. **ISAIAH** 297
    Information About Isaiah and His Times 207
    Notes on the Study and Interpretation of the Book
       of Isaiah 301
    Periods of Prophetic Fulfillment 303
    The Book of Isaiah Divided, By Chapter, Into the
       Four Periods of Prophetic Fulfillment 303
    Section I—Chapters of Isaiah Pertaining to the First
       Period of Prophetic Fulfillment: The Fall of
       Israel to Assyria 307
    Doctrinal Analysis of Isaiah, Section I 315
    Summary of Isaiah, Section I 319
    Section II—Chapters of Isaiah Pertaining to the Second Period of Prophetic Fulfillment: The Fall of
       Judah, the Babylonian Captivity, and The Return
       from Exile 320
    Doctrinal Analysis of Isaiah, Section II 328
    Summary of Isaiah, Section II 336
    Section III—Chapters of Isaiah Pertaining to the
       Third Period of Prophetic Fulfillment: The Ministry of Christ in the Meridian of Time 337
    Doctrinal Analysis of Isaiah, Section III 344
    Summary of Isaiah, Section III 345
    Section IV—Chapters of Isaiah Pertaining to the
       Fourth Period of Prophetic Fulfillment: The
       Last Days 347
    Doctrinal Analysis of Isaiah, Section IV 365
    Summary of Isaiah, Section IV 373
    Critical Information About the Book of Isaiah 374
    Notes on the Literary Problem of Isaiah and Its
       Importance to Latter-day Saints 377
    Summary of the Book of Isaiah 399

PART III 401
XII. **HISTORICAL SUMMARY: THE RISE OF BABYLONIA AND THE FALL OF JUDAH** 403
    The Rise of Babylonia as a World Power 403
    Kings of Babylonia 404
    The Fall of Judah 405
    Kings of Judah 406
    Summary 410

XIII. ZEPHANIAH ... 412
Information About Zephaniah and His Times ... 412
Outline of the Book ... 415
Doctrinal Analysis ... 417
Critical Information About the Book of Zephaniah ... 419
Summary ... 419

XIV. NAHUM ... 421
Information About Nahum and His Times ... 421
Outline of the Book ... 421
Doctrinal Analysis ... 423
Critical Information About the Book of Nahum ... 423
Summary ... 424

XV. OBADIAH ... 425
Information About Obadiah and His Times ... 425
Outline of the Book ... 426
Doctrinal Analysis ... 427
Critical Information About the Book of Obadiah ... 427
Summary ... 428

XVI. HABAKKUK ... 429
Information About Habakkuk and His Times ... 429
Outline of the Book ... 429
Doctrinal Analysis ... 431
Critical Information About the Book of Habakkuk ... 432
Summary ... 432

XVII. JEREMIAH ... 434
Information About Jeremiah and His Times ... 434
Notes on the Study and Interpretation of the Book of Jeremiah ... 440
Finding List of the Chapters of Jeremiah ... 441
Section I—Chapters of Jeremiah Pertaining to the Reign of Kings Josiah and Jehoahaz ... 442
Section II—Chapters of Jeremiah Pertaining to the Reign of King Jehoiakim ... 449
Section III—Chapters of Jeremiah Pertaining to the Reign of King Zedekiah ... 452
Section IV—Chapters of Jeremiah Pertaining to the Final Period of the Prophet's Life ... 457
Section V—Chapters of Jeremiah Pertaining to the Last Days ... 459
Doctrinal Analysis ... 462
Critical Information About the Book of Jeremiah ... 473
Summary ... 479

TABLE OF CONTENTS   xi

XVIII. LAMENTATIONS 480
    Historical Background 480
    Outline of the Book 480
    Doctrinal Analysis 481
    Critical Information About the Book of Lamentations 483
    Summary 484

PART IV 485

XIX. HISTORICAL SUMMARY: THE FALL OF BABYLONIA, THE RISE OF MEDIA AND PERSIA AND THE BABYLONIAN EXILE OF THE JEWS 487
    The Decline and Fall of Babylonia 487
    The Rise and Fall of Media 490
    The Rise of Persia 492
    Judah During the Babylonian Captivity 493
    Summary 494

XX. DANIEL 496
    Information About Daniel and His Times 496
    Outline of the Book 499
    Doctrinal Analysis 521
    Critical Information About the Book of Daniel 524
    Summary 526

XXI. EZEKIEL 528
    Information About Ezekiel and His Times 528
    Outline of the Book 530
    Doctrinal Analysis 554
    Critical Information About the Book of Ezekiel 562
    Summary 564

PART V 567

XXII. HISTORICAL SUMMARY: PERSIA AND JUDAH FOLLOWING THE BABYLONIAN CAPTIVITY 569
    Persia 569
    Judah, Following the Babylonian Captivity 571
    Summary 573

XXIII. EZRA 574
    Historical Background 574
    Outline of the Book 574
    Doctrinal Analysis 576
    Critical Information About the Book of Ezra 577
    Summary 578

TABLE OF CONTENTS

XXIV. ESTHER 579
  Historical Background 579
  Outline of the Book 579
  Examples for Living 581
  Critical Information About the Book of Esther 582
  Summary 582

XXV. NEHEMIAH 583
  Historical Background 583
  Outline of the Book 583
  Doctrinal Analysis 586
  Critical Information About the Book of Nehemiah 588
  Summary 590

XXVI. HAGGAI 592
  Information About Haggai and His Times 592
  Outline of the Book 596
  Doctrinal Analysis 596
  Critical Information About the Book of Haggai 597
  Summary 597

XXVII. ZECHARIAH 598
  Information About Zechariah and His Times 598
  Outline of the Book 600
  Doctrinal Analysis 608
  Critical Information About the Book of Zechariah 610
  Summary 612

XXVIII. MALACHI 613
  Information About Malachi and His Times 613
  Outline of the Book 614
  Doctrinal Analysis 619
  Critical Information About the Book of Malachi 621
  Summary 622

XXIX. JOEL 623
  Information About Joel and His Times 623
  Outline of the Book 623
  Doctrinal Analysis 629
  Critical Information About the Book of Joel 629
  Summary 631

INDEX 633

LIST OF MAPS AND CHARTS

A Simplified Diagram of Old Testament History 42

An Analysis of the Books of Kings and Chronicles
    From the Death of Solomon to the Fall of Judah . . 43

    Beginning of the Divided Kingdom 43

    Elijah the Prophet 51

    Elisha the Prophet 55

    End of the Northern Kingdom 67

    Isaiah the Prophet 68

    The Fall of Jerusalem 70

Chronological List of the Kings of Judah and Israel and
    the Approximate Dates and Periods of Their Reigns . . 71

CHANGES MADE IN THE INSPIRED VERSION OF THE BIBLE

1. 1st Kings 241
2. 2nd Kings 242
3. 2nd Chronicles 243
4. Jonah 256
5. Amos 268
6. Hosea 280
7. Isaiah 380
8. Nahum 424
9. Jeremiah 475
10. Daniel 526
11. Ezekiel 563
12. Nehemiah 588
13. Zechariah 611
14. Joel 630

ABBREVIATIONS FOR SCRIPTURAL BOOKS

The following abbreviations are used for the books of the Bible:

Old Testament:

Gen.	Genesis	Eccles.	Ecclesiastes
Ex.	Exodus	Song.	Song of Solomon
Lev.	Leviticus	Is.	Isaiah
Num.	Numbers	Jer.	Jeremiah
Deut.	Deuteronomy	Lam.	Lamentations
Josh.	Joshua	Ezek.	Ezekiel
Judg.	Judges	Dan.	Daniel
Ruth	Ruth	Hos.	Hosea
1 Sam.	1 Samuel	Joel	Joel
2 Sam.	2 Samuel	Amos	Amos
1 Ki.	1 Kings	Obad.	Obadiah
2 Ki.	2 Kings	Jon.	Jonah
1 Chron.	1 Chronicles	Mic.	Micah
2 Chron.	2 Chronicles	Nahum	Nahum
Ezra	Ezra	Hab.	Habakkuk
Neh.	Nehemiah	Zeph.	Zephaniah
Esther	Esther	Hag.	Haggai
Job	Job	Zech.	Zechariah
Ps.	Psalms	Mal.	Malachi
Prov.	Proverbs		

New Testament:

Mt.	Matthew	1 Tim.	1 Timothy
Mk.	Mark	2 Tim.	2 Timothy
Lk.	Luke	Tit.	Titus
Jn.	John	Philem.	Philemon
Acts.	Acts of the Apostles	Heb.	Hebrews
Rom.	Romans	Jas.	James
1 Cor.	1 Corinthians	1 Pet.	1 Peter
2 Cor.	2 Corinthians	2 Pet.	2 Peter
Gal.	Galatians	1 Jn.	1 John
Eph.	Ephesians	2 Jn.	2 John
Phil.	Philippians	3 Jn.	3 John
Col.	Colossians	Jude	Jude
1 Thess.	1 Thessalonians	Rev.	Revelation
2 Thess.	2 Thessalonians		

The following abbreviations are used for the books of the Book of Mormon:

1 Ne.	1 Nephi	Al.	Alma
2 Ne.	2 Nephi	He.	Helaman
Jac.	Jacob	3 Ne.	3 Nephi
Enos	Enos	4 Ne.	4 Nephi
Jar.	Jarom	Morm.	Mormon
Om.	Omni	Eth.	Ether
W. of Morm.	Words of Mormon	Moro.	Moroni
Mos.	Mosiah		

The Doctrine and Covenants is abbreviated D & C.

The following abbreviations are used for the books of the Pearl of Great Price:

Moses	Moses
Abra.	Abraham
JS 1	Writings of Joseph Smith, part I
JS 2	Writings of Joseph Smith, part II
A. of F.	The Articles of Faith

Thus (Is. 1:1) means Isaiah chapter 1 verse 1.

Other common abbreviations used in this book are:

v.	verse.
Cf.	Certify or compare. This is used as a cross reference indication.
f. or ff.	This means to read the verse or verses following the reference cited.
c.	"circa" or about. This is used in reference to dates to show that they are uncertain.
B. C.	Before Christ. This is used as a time indicator.
A. D.	Anno Domini (in the year of our Lord). This is used as a time indicator.
DEN	*Deseret Evening News*
HC	*History of The Church*
JD	*Journal of Discourses*
JI	*Juvenile Instructor*

DIACRITICAL MARKINGS USED IN THIS BOOK

In this book, the words of which the pronunciation is marked are divided into syllables by short hyphens (-). The syllable on which most stress is to be laid in reading is marked ('). In compound names two accents are often introduced. The following is a key to the symbols used:

ä as in ah, arm, father.
ă as in abet, hat, dilemma.
ā as in tame.
â as in fare.
ạ as in call.
ĕ as in met, her, second.
ē as in mete.
ë the same as a in tame.
ī as in fine.
ĭ as in him, fir, plentiful
î as in machine.
ị as in peculiar.
ō as in alone.
ŏ as in on, protect.
ô as in nor.
ọ as in son.
ū as in tune.
û as in rude.
ŭ as in us.
ù as in turner.
ȳ as in lyre.

y̆ as in typical, fully.
aā the same as a of am.
aâ the same as a of fare.
aē $\Big\}$ as in mediæval.
æ
aî as in aisle.
aị as in hail.
aō the same as o of alone.
aû as in maul.
eê as in heed.
eî the same as i of fine.
eû as in neuter.
eᴡ as in lewd.
oî as in oil.
ç as in celestial.
ch as in character.
c̱i as in delicious.
ġ as in giant.
ṣ as in his.
s̄i as in adhesion.
T̄h as in Thomas.
ṯi as in attraction.

PART I

Suggestions on How to Use the Book

Explanation of the Materials Presented

Tools for Bible Study

Suggestions for Effective Study

Suggestions for Scripture Marking

Suggestions for Scripture Interpretation

Aids for Understanding Bible History and Chronology
- Summary and Diagram of Previous Bible History
- Analysis of the Books of Kings and Chronicles
- Chronological Charts

Doctrinal Listings
- The Nature of God and Godhood
- God's Communication with Man
- The Nature of Sin
- The Nature of Man's Agency and God's Judgment
- Counsel for Righteous Living
- The Events of the Last Days

CHAPTER I

THIS BOOK AND HOW TO USE IT

The Purpose of This Book

Prophets and Prophecies of the Old Testament has been written to accomplish six specific purposes:

1. **To provide a useable study guide** to the prophetic section of the Old Testament for individuals and classes who wish to study the Bible from the interpretive viewpoint of the doctrine of The Church of Jesus Christ of Latter-day Saints. Its scope has been expanded to include the historical books of the period also. Thus it includes 1st and 2nd Kings, 2nd Chronicles, Lamentations, Ezra, Nehemiah, and Esther. Rather than follow the divisions of the Old Testament as suggested in the Hebrew listings, the book is designed to consider the history of the Old Testament from the times of the divided kingdoms to the end of the Old Testament. The books are considered in the light of the times the Biblical accounts and Jewish tradition assert that the events took place, rather than the time Bible critics assert that they were written.

2. **To analyze and publish the major doctrinal contributions** of Old Testament prophets to a more definitive level than has previously been published within the L. D. S. Church.

3. **To assemble and categorize the prophetic teachings concerning the last days,** which were uttered by Old Testament prophets, on a more comprehensive scale than has previously been published by Mormon students of the scriptures.

4. **To provide penetrating interpretive comment** in certain chosen areas of pertinent scriptural study.

5. **To assemble important historical information** which makes the Old Testament prophets more interesting and more easily understood.

6. **To suggest techniques for more effective study and interpretation** of the Bible and of all the Standard Works.

The Book Contains Useful Material for Study on Three Levels

It is intended that this book will help to fill the needs of three groups of people within the Church:

1. **For the beginning student** of the Old Testament it offers a variety of useful aids. It provides a useful reading guide. Each chapter or section of scripture is outlined to increase the reader's understanding. A variety of maps and charts is provided to aid him in his awakening awareness to the Old Testament drama. The material is arranged in outline form in a consistent manner throughout the book so that items can be quickly located. A summary and listing of items the reader should know is presented at the end of each chapter. The aids combine to make the book a helpful tool for the beginning student. **Prophets and Prophecies of the Old Testament helps to make the Old Testament understandable.**

2. **For the advanced student** the book presents an additional array of useable aids. The style and technique of the prophets is analyzed. All the known scriptural information concerning each prophet is listed in convenient form. Exhaustive information concerning author, date of authorship, textual transmission, and Bible criticism is

clearly summarized. The religious, political, social, and economic backgrounds of the countries to whom the prophets speak are detailed. The political interplay of the time is set forth in concise listings of the various kings and nations. Of special interest are the definitive listings of doctrinal passages which are found in each book. These are combined into a series of thought-provoking studies of the major themes of the Old Testament prophets. **The major contribution of Prophets and Prophecies of the Old Testament to the advanced student is that it makes a wide variety of information available and the material is assembled into a concise, useable form that will save him many hours of time and effort.**

3. **For the teacher** this book serves as a useful text and reading guide. It is organized and designed to help students recognize what they should know and aid them to learn effectively. The summaries at the end of each chapter serve an important purpose. If the student learns only the material listed in the summaries, he will have a grasp of the history, geography, doctrine, and message of the Old Testament prophets as complete as most students who have completed college courses on the subject. Yet the summaries are written on a level that they can be used in Sunday School and Seminary classes. Another important feature is that it provides a useable reading plan for the major prophets. Where the length and lack of order of these books was previously a major obstacle to the motivation of many students, they are presented in this book in shorter, more concise sections which are grouped in unified subject divisions. The study of doctrine is facilitated by the doctrinal analysis at the end of each prophetic section or book. Such an arrangement allows the

instructor to intermix or separate important doctrinal themes from the historical material to meet the needs and personality of his classes. A variety of useable maps is included, and pronunciation guides are given for many proper names. Of special value as an aid to interpretation is the parallel-columns listing of the changes Joseph Smith made in the Inspired Version of the Bible as compared with the King James translation. The teacher will recognize the importance of the sections on study aids, how to mark the scriptures, the suggestions for a basic Bible library, the aids on interpreting the scriptures, and the historical and chronological listings and charts. All these will combine to increase his success as a teacher. **Prophets and Prophecies of the Old Testament will be a valuable tool for the teacher because of its organization as a teaching and study aid.**

The reader will note, however, that the book is not intended to serve in certain capacities. It is not a complete commentary on the prophets, yet it clearly expounds the most vital data. It is not a Bible dictionary, yet it defines many terms for the beginning student. It is not an infallible guide to interpretation, yet it provides the key which will unlock many doors of discovery to the diligent student. It is not a "scholarly work" in the stuffy, name-dropping, academic sense of the term, yet it will aid every student who truly wants to be a Bible scholar. It is not a criticism of traditional interpretations within the Church, yet it will challenge the validity of some interpretations which violate the principles of meaningful interpretation. It is not a book designed for pleasurable reading, yet it is an outline which will bring the student greater enjoyment from some of the world's finest literature.

Explanation of the Materials Presented About Each Prophet.

The following materials are presented for each prophet:

1. **Prophet's Name:** The name, pronunciation of the name, and its meaning are given.
2. **Scriptural Information About the Prophet:** In most cases all the known information recorded in the scriptures concerning the prophet is listed. Occasionally certain items have been deemed more suitable for introduction later in the chapter.
3. **Date of Mission:** The date of the prophet's ministry is given, together with the basis on which it is determined.
4. **Prophesied To:** The recipients of the prophecy are indicated.
5. **Contemporary Prophets:** The other prophets whose ministries coincided with the prophet under consideration, together with their dates and to whom they prophesied, are given.
6. **Contemporary Prophets Contrasted:** A short statement concerning the most significant similarities and differences of the contemporary prophets is given.
7. **Contemporary Kings:** The name, dates of rule, and significant events of each king are listed. Kings are shown for each country which had influence on the prophet and his message.
8. **National Conditions:** The current political, economic, social and religious conditions of the prophet's country and/or the nation to which he prophesied are listed.
9. **Outline of the Book:** An outline and study guide of each prophetic book is given. Interpretive notes are included to clarify items of significance.

10. **Doctrinal Analysis:** The verses which hold major doctrinal significance are categorized in summary form.
11. **Style of the Book:** A listing of the major comments of Bible critics concerning the prophet's writing style is given.
12. **Textual Transmission:** The books of the Bible have been copied and recopied by numerous scribes over a period of hundreds of years. In some of the Hebrew manuscripts numerous errors and alterations crept in. Manuscripts which were altered in this manner are said to have been transmitted poorly. In many cases the existence of errors is speculative and alterations are merely suspected by various Bible critics.
13. **Author and Date of Authorship:** The opinion of Bible scholars concerning the identity of the author and the date of his writing is given. Again, this is an item which is greatly affected by the theories of various Bible critics.
14. **Bible Criticism:** Critics of the Bible have followed two major trends in Bible study and are thus called "higher critics" and "lower critics." Higher criticism is concerned mainly with attempts to determine the identity of the authors of the books, the time of their writing, and their historical validity. Lower criticism deals more with the language and messages of the books themselves.

    Bible criticism has taken on a spirit of irreverence and doubt which makes it incompatible with L. D. S. beliefs in many instances. Bible critics generally reject any element of a miraculous nature. They often disregard the ability of a prophet to foretell events far into the future and assert that the book was written as history rather than prophecy, at a much later time than the prophet's ministry. They attempt to determine the periods that doctrines became established and their determinations conflict with the additional evidence which Latter-day Saints have available in other books of scripture. They have proposed theories and now regard and state their theories as fact. There are few areas of science which are so speculative as the science of Bible criticism.

The study of Bible criticism is beyond the scope of this volume. Yet the assertions of critics are given in detail in several instances as a pattern (See Jonah, Amos, and Isaiah), and for each book they are briefly summarized. The study of the Old Testament prophets should be the study of the Bible, not the study of the theories of Bible critics.

15. **Changes Made in the Inspired Version:** Acting upon a commandment of the Lord (D & C 35:20; 42:56-57, 60-61), the Prophet Joseph Smith undertook a revision of the Bible. This was not done on the basis of ancient manuscripts, nor a knowledge of Biblical languages, but through the process of inspiration and revelation. Rather than reading through the book, he apparently went through the Bible topic by topic. It appears that his work was never completed although he made certain comments concerning his concluding of the work.[1] Two copies of his manuscript were made. Following the prophet's death, one copy came into the possession of the Saints in Utah while the other was given to the Reorganized Church of Jesus Christ of Latter Day Saints. The manuscript was published by the latter group in 1867 and has gone through several editions since that time. The

---
[1] See *HC* 1:324, 368.

Church of Jesus Christ of Latter-day Saints regards the book as unfinished and therefore has refrained from publishing it or canonizing it as the scripture of the Church. If the version made by Joseph Smith is inspired, then it is undoubtedly the most correct and complete version of the Bible currently available. Though the prophet's work on it may have been incomplete, it gives in its present form certain understandings which are of interest and value to Latter-day Saint Bible students.

The revised passages from the Inspired Version are presented in parallel columns with their King James Translation equivalents at the end of the chapter for each prophet.[2] No changes of a substantial nature were made for the books of Lamentations, Obadiah, Micah, Habakkuk, Zephaniah, Ezra, Esther, Haggai, and Malachi.

16. **Summary:** Important facts concerning each book are set forth in summary form for each of the books considered.

How to Use the Book

The following suggestions will aid the teacher and student in making the most effective use of this book to meet their needs:

1. **Get an overview.** Turn to the table of contents and note that the book is organized in five sections: this preliminary section, and four sections

---

[2]The changes shown are only those of a substantive nature—where a change in meaning is involved. There are numerous minor changes, such as in the spelling of words, e. g. ye for you, the article a for an before words beginning with an "h", show for shew, astonished for astonied, thoroughly for throughly, razor for rasor, loathe for lothe, cherubim for cherubims, portray for pourtray, music for musick, honor for honour, plaster for plaister, counsellors for counsellers, steadfast for stedfast, besides for beside, establisheth for stablisheth, etc. Such minor changes are **not** detailed in this study as they have little effect on meaning.

on the lives and messages of the Old Testament prophets.

2. **Scan the first four chapters.** Some teachers and students may then wish to begin right with the prophets and return intermittently to consider the items of these preliminary chapters.

3. **Use this book as a supplement to the Old Testament only.** This book is an aid to the reading of the Old Testament prophets. It does not substitute for the Bible. Lengthy quotations from the Bible have purposely been omitted from this book to focus attention on the Holy Scriptures themselves. This book must be the supplement. The Bible is the text.

4. **Do not feel compelled to use all the material in this book.** Be selective. One should choose from the material the items which will best meet his needs and the needs of his class. Use the chosen material in a manner which is appropriate to the level of preparation of the class, the degree of challenge for which the class is designed, and the time available.

5. **Make use of the historical reference chapters.** These chapters are designed as sources of reference rather than lessons in and of themselves. Yet without an understanding of the material they contain, no student can effectively grasp the message and meaning of the Old Testament prophets. It is suggested that the material listed in the summary of each historical chapter be thoroughly learned before consideration of the prophets of the section begins.

6. **Learn the material listed on the section dividers.** These materials will give important keys to understanding the material found in the section. Be

sure, especially, to learn in order the lists of the prophets.

7. **Use the summaries.** They give meaning and direction to the material. Refer to them consistently. Review them often.

8. **Mix history with doctrine.** Vary the teaching and reading approach. Change the order of presentation and stress the most important aspects of each prophetic book. This will help maintain interest.

9. **Do not dwell on Bible criticism.** The reader will note that rather extensive information is given in the critical background of several of the prophetic books. The others have only short statements concerning the general tenor of Bible criticism as it pertains to them. The course of study should be the Old Testament, not the criticism of it. Studying the scriptures leads towards the desired goals; most Bible criticism leads away from them.

10. **Keep the goal in focus at all times.** The Old Testament is being studied to help the students to return to the presence of God. They are to find within its pages the clues which will show them the path to God. The teacher's major task is to motivate them and help them to apply these clues in their lives.

Summary:

1. This book is written to be used as a study supplement to the Old Testament prophets. It also includes the historical books of the Bible of the period from about 950 to 400 B.C.

2. The book is designed to be used by beginning students as a study guide, by advanced students as a reference manual, and by teachers as a course outline.

3. The book has numerous features which will make it of value to student and teacher alike:

    A. Concrete suggestions on study methodology, building a basic Old Testament library, scripture marking, and the process of interpreting scripture.

    B. Historical data which shows the major events of each prophetic period.

    C. Chronological charts showing the varying datings of Bible scholars.

    D. A comprehensive array of maps which reveals the growth and decline of the nations of late Old Testament times.

    E. A detailed listing and analysis of the major doctrinal themes of the Old Testament prophets.

    F. A listing and ordering of the events of the last days as foreseen by the Old Testament prophets.

    G. A useable approach to the study of the major prophets which adds clarity and meaning to their history and message.

    H. A crisp, definitive style which presents the material in a concise outline form.

    I. Effective chapter summaries which define and highlight the essential items for learning.

    J. A comparison of the King James translation with the Inspired Version of Joseph Smith for each book where variations exist.

    K. Chapter and verse outlines for each of the prophets.

    L. Interpretive comment on many items of doctrinal interest.

4. The student should keep the major goal of scripture study in mind at all times: His objective is to find the references which outline the pathway back to the presence of God and to apply them by ordering his life to walk in that path.

CHAPTER II

HOW TO STUDY AND INTERPRET SCRIPTURE

Proper Tools Are Needed for Bible Study

Many members of the Church have a desire to study the Old Testament but fail to obtain the proper tools to make the study enjoyable and profitable. Trying to understand the Bible without proper study tools is like trying to fix a car without a wrench—it can be done, possibly, but the job will be tedious, the workmanship poor, and the outcome uncertain!

Those who study the scriptures are usually the teachers of others. They have an obligation to be well prepared and well equipped for the task of teaching the gospel. There are few people who would risk the life of their loved ones by attempting to perform a medical operation on them without proper training and proper tools. Yet many are willing to risk the spiritual life of those whom they hold dear by teaching without proper preparation and without the proper tools for learning and teaching.

The tools necessary for Bible study are easily obtained. They are relatively inexpensive, but are almost indispensable. The following are suggested:

1. **A Bible**—the King James translation is the Bible accepted by the Church. The Bible which is used should have:
    A. Large readable print.
    B. Margins sufficiently large to allow notations to be made.
    C. Center references which indicate alternate translations, cross references, etc.

D. Diacritical markings so that an acceptable pronunciation can be determined for the names and places mentioned. (How can people and events be discussed and remembered without the student being able to say their names?)

E. A thumb index for ease in locating passages.

2. **A Bible Concordance.** A concordance tells the location of each word used in the Bible. There are several available, with varying degrees of completeness. It is advantageous to choose the concordance which gives the longest portion of the sentence for each word.

3. **A Bible Atlas.** The Bible student is unable to understand many of the most important events of the Bible unless he can envision the localities involved. Many prophecies, especially, are references to particular localities and cannot be interpreted without the aid of a Bible atlas. In choosing an atlas, the student should insist on one which gives a location index so that he can find places mentioned in the Bible text. The atlas should also indicate both ancient and modern names.

4. **A Bible Dictionary.** It is difficult to understand the Bible unless one can understand the people and practices to which it refers. Several good ones are available at most religious book stores. How can the student choose the best dictionary for him? He could try picking several subjects and Bible personalities in which he is interested and looking them up in each of the Bible dictionaries offered. It will soon be obvious which one will best meet his needs.

These four tools, a good Bible, a Bible Concordance, a Bible Atlas, and a Bible Dictionary, are absolute essentials to effective Bible study. They are listed in the order the student will probably wish to obtain them, if he can't procure them all at once.

Other books are helpful and the reader may wish to obtain them for his library, namely:

1. A good **Bible handbook, textbook, or guide to reading the scriptures.** Such books serve as study guides for the material under consideration and help to organize the study approach. The books chosen should present a reasonable outline of the material and should provide a guide to interpretation. Care should be exercised to choose books which correspond with the general interpretive viewpoint of the Church. This book is intended as a representative volume in this category.

2. A good **Bible Commentary.** A commentary gives explanations of specific passages but offers little guidance to overall doctrinal patterns. Its value lies in aiding the reader in the understanding of difficult wordings, vague allusions, etc.

3. A good **history of Bible times.** Such a book will help the reader to understand the secular history of Bible times and will correlate it with the Biblical account.

4. A good compilation of **Biblical criticism and analysis.** This type of book will reveal what scholars have set forth pertaining to the history, authorship, and literary content of the books of the Bible. Although they are often lacking in the attitude of faith and reverence for God's word, they raise many points of scholarship which must be considered.

A Recommended Basic Library for Studying the Old Testament Prophets

The above outline is not intended as a recommendation for particular books, yet it may be helpful for the reader to know what books the author has found most helpful in the study of the Old Testament prophets. An extensive bibliography would probably be of little value in this context. Rather, the following group of 13 books is offered as a suggested **basic** list on the Old Testament prophets[1] which would be suitable[2] for a personal library.

Bible Concordance

Cruden, Alexander—*Cruden's Complete Concordance*, (The John C. Winston Co., Philadelphia.)

Bible Atlases

Pictorial Atlas of the Bible World, (C.S. Hammond & Co., Maplewood, N. J.)

Wright, George Ernest and Filson, Floyd Vivian —*The Westminster Historical Atlas of the Bible*, (The Westminster Press, Philadelphia.)

Keyes, Nelson Beecher—*Story of the Bible World*, (The Reader's Digest Association, Pleasantville, N. Y.)

Bible Dictionary

Smith, William—*Bible Dictionary*, (The John C. Winston Co., Philadelphia.)

Bible Handbooks and Interpretive Guides

Sperry, Sidney B.—*The Voice of Israel's Prophets*, (Deseret Book Co., Salt Lake City, Utah.)

---

[1]Almost all of these books are not limited to the prophets but treat the entire Bible.
[2]The final four on the list, plus the book by Dr. Sperry, have been used as textbooks by the Brigham Young University.

Halley, Henry H.—*Bible Handbook*, (Zondervan Publishing, Grand Rapids, Michigan.)

Bible Commentary

Dummelow, J. R.—*A Commentary on the Holy Bible*, (The Macmillan Co., N. Y.)

Bible Histories

Daniel-Rops—*Israel and the Ancient World*, (Eyre & Spottiswoode, London.)

Anderson, Bernhard W.—*Understanding the Old Testament*, (Prentice-Hall, Inc., Englewood Cliffs, N. J.)

Bible Criticism

Pfeiffer, Robert H.—*Introduction to the Old Testament*, (Harper & Brothers, Publishers, N. Y.)

Driver, S. R.—*An Introduction to the Literature of the Old Testament*, (Meridian Books, N. Y.)

Some Suggestions for Bible Study

Different methods must be used in studying the scriptures than would be used in ordinary study. This is because the scriptures are not written in the same, highly organized form as a textbook or article. The scriptures are a collection of books with each book having a different purpose and viewpoint. The student isn't able to merely read from cover to cover and in this manner gain an effective understanding of the message of any of the Standard Works. The books do not follow a definite system. They are not arranged properly from a chronological standpoint. Certainly they are not grouped by subject. The problem of not being in a readable order exists with all four of the Standard Works, but especially with the Bible.

The following are some specific suggestions that will aid in all types of scripture study, but especially in studying the prophetic section of the Old Testament.

Suggestion 1—Make Your Style of Reading Fit Your Needs and the Bible Book You Are Reading. Try reading in one of five different ways:

A. **Read the Stories.** Many of the books of the Bible have a story to tell, such as Jonah, Ezra, Nehemiah, and Esther. Read these books as a story or novel. Much of their message is found in the story itself. Books like Isaiah, or Ezekiel, however, are poison if read in this way.

B. **Read for Historical Understanding.** Bible history is fascinating! It is full of strategy, statesmanship, intrigue, violence, and passion. The plots for a thousand unwritten novels still lie within its pages. Read to understand the history in two ways: as a key to the doctrine of the Bible, and as a pattern whereby one can understand the actions of nations and individuals today.

C. **Read Chronologically.** Another useful method is to read and sort out the messages or events of the book chronologically. Don't just read the book from beginning to end. Obtain or make a systematic outline which will allow the book to be read in chronological order. This approach is especially helpful with the larger books. Jeremiah is very difficult to understand, for instance, unless it is read in the order the events took place in the prophet's life. Chronological reading is especially useful in considering prophetic sections like the last days prophecies of Isaiah. Placing them in the order in which they will come to pass provides a challenge which makes them far more interesting and understandable.

D. Read the Doctrinal "Fine Print." Try reading some books slowly and methodically, and attempt to group every doctrinal detail. The messages for most of the books of the Old Testament prophets are the same: that Israel is wicked, that it will be punished, and that it will be restored in the last days. Most readers know this before they start. If they find nothing more than this, the Bible will prove to be very dull reading. The exciting aspect of the Bible is that it answers man's basic questions, such as, Who is God? What kind of a person is He? What does He expect of His children? Does He control the lives of men? How can man communicate with Him? What is the program for happiness He has set up for man? What is sin? What is righteousness? How will God judge mankind? The answers to these questions are scattered throughout the Bible. Almost always they are found in very short but highly meaningful statements. These statements are often isolated commentaries mixed in with historical materials and speeches. They are the most meaningful part of the Bible. Read the "fine print" carefully to find them.

E. Skim Read for One or Two Ideas Only. One of the most rewarding experiences one can have is to skim the entire Bible (or all the Standard Works, for that matter) and look only for material pertaining to one or two subjects. What one may regard as a minor and little-known subject may suddenly blossom into a major doctrinal theme. Try this type of reading to explore such subjects as covenants, the Holy Ghost, the doctrine of sanctification, God's dealings with His prophets, etc.

Suggestion 2—Have an Organized Study Plan with Goals. Random reading of the Bible usually does little good. It needs to be read for a purpose. As soon as study is serving to meet a goal it becomes meaningful and effective. Set goals in terms of study projects to be completed, not just pages to be read. Organize your reading so it is methodical. Read parallel accounts together, etc.

Suggestion 3—Do Not Study Without Writing. This rule is basic to any kind of study. It is particularly important with Bible study. Much of the challenge in the study of the Bible consists in effective collecting of passages and their organization into meaningful patterns. This is not the type of work that is done well without writing. Few people have memories capable of doing the job effectively without written help. Make doctrinal subject lists, charts of the kings, chronological charts, marginal notations in your Bible—whatever interests you, but write it down.

Suggestion 4—Continually Summarize and List the Major Meanings of Bible Chapters. Long, repetitious, and detailed passages become more meaningful with this treatment. Form the habit of summarizing the major idea of each chapter in your notes or on the top margin of the Bible with a short (one phrase or sentence) statement. It is surprising how this will consolidate one's ideas on a passage and make it more meaningful the next time it is read.

Suggestion 5—Never Forget that the Purpose of Bible Study is to Bring the Student Nearer to God. The Lord gave man the scripture so he could learn the nature of God and discover the path back to the presence of the Creator. Never forget this! The Bible is to be read from a standpoint of faith and a desire to conform to God's will. To study the Bible without this attitude will only condemn man and lead him away from God.

Suggestion 6—Look for the Teachings Modern Man Can Apply in His Life. Bible study does little good until the student begins to find the items which he can use and apply. He is to use the principles set forth in the Bible as models and directives for his own growth and development. Without this application Bible study is fruitless and sterile.

Some Suggestions for Marking the Scriptures

A Bible is a book to be used! The student should make it his, by marking it and cross referencing it. The marking should be done neatly and carefully. Remember, the Standard Works are tools which are to be used for a lifetime. Just as the woodsman gives special and constant care to his axe, the student of the scriptures should give special care to his Sacred Books.

Every individual should develop his own style of marking the scriptures. There is no necessity for adopting the author's marking style. Some general suggestions, however, might be useful.

1. **Be neat.** Just as one should show reverence for the Holy Scriptures by not laying them on the floor, he should also respect the inside of his books by marking carefully and neatly.
2. **Use a good quality red pencil and a fine-pointed ball point pen.** Choose a good quality red pencil. Cheap ones will smear badly. Ball point pens also smear badly unless fine points are used. Use blue or black pens only. Other color inks tend to

soak through the pages of most Bible papers over the years. It is suggested that the same brands of ball point pens which are recommended for genealogy work be used for greatest permanency.

3. **Don't color extensive passages red.** To color long passages with a red pencil is time consuming. It places so much red on the pages that it smears on the adjoining leaves. It prohibits any emphasis markings within the passages. Instead, try marking the top line, mark down the center column(s), and the bottom line.

4. **Avoid color reference codes.** The use of many types of colored pencils is impractical. Many colors smear badly, but worse, the color codes are usually forgotten over the years. One color code is suggested. The use of blue pencil for the marking of all historical matters is suggested. This leaves red free for all items of doctrinal significance.

5. **Don't underline; color the line itself in red.** This suggestion will do much to preserve the neatness of the book.

6. **Make all marginal notes with a ball-point pen.** Over the years the pencil notations will fade.

7. **Keep summary notes and lengthy notations on the top and bottom margins.** Leave the side margins free for short notes and cross references.

Scripture marking serves eight purposes, and each purpose suggests a particular type of marking. These purposes and accompanying marking suggestions are as follows:

1. **To indicate the length of important passages.** Teachers and missionaries have especial need for this type of marking. They need to know at a glance where to begin and end the passages they cite. Such marking is a means of saving time for

them and of aiding the smoothness of their lesson presentations.

Marking suggestion:

A. Color the top line, color down the center column mark(s), and color the bottom line.

B. Some find it preferable to color about ⅜″ of the passage along the inside border.

> the God of judgment?
>
> 928]   CHAPTER 3
>
> ^oBEHOLD, I will send ^pmy messenger, and ^rhe shall prepare the way before me: and the Lord, whom ye seek, ^sshall suddenly come to his temple, even ^tthe messenger of the covenant, whom ye delight in: behold, he shall come, saith the LORD of hosts.
>
> 2 But who may abide ^wthe day of his coming? and who shall
>
> 8 ¶ Will a man rob God? Yet ye have robbed me. But ye say, Wherein have we robbed thee? In ^ttithes and offerings.
>
> 9 Ye *are* cursed with a curse: for ye have robbed me, *even* this whole nation.
>
> 10 Bring ye all the tithes into the storehouse, that there may be ^umeat in mine house, and ^vprove me now herewith, saith the LORD of hosts, if I will not open you the windows of heaven, and ⁸pour you out a
>
> 1183

2. To emphasize important passages. Certain words of significance should be marked as an aid to drawing special emphasis from important passages. This type of marking is especially useful in marking lengthy discussions of doctrinal themes.

Marking suggestions:

A. For short isolated items mixed in with other **unmarked** material, color the entire item.

B. For short items mixed in with other **marked** items, mark only the key words. Use marginal notes, if necessary.

> nations, ⁱas when he fought in the day of battle.
>
> 4 ¶ And his feet shall stand in that day upon ^jthe mount of Olives, which *is* before Jerusalem on the east, and the mount of Olives shall cleave in the midst thereof toward the east and toward the west, *and there* shall be ^ha very great valley; and half of the mountain shall remove toward the north, and half of it toward the south.
>
> 5 And ye shall flee *to* the val-
>
> it, and there shall be no more utter destruction; but Jerusalem ²shall be safely inhabited.
>
> 12 ¶ And this shall be the plague wherewith the LORD will smite all the people that have fought against Jerusalem; Their flesh shall consume away while they stand upon their feet, and their eyes shall consume away in their holes, and their tongue shall consume away in their mouth.
>
> 13 And it shall come to pass in

3. **To indicate a number of significant points in list form.** Often a passage lists a number of items which revolve around a central theme.

Marking suggestions: Mark the key word(s) of each item in red, then number them in the margin in ball-point pen so it is obvious that a list is given.

4. **To cross reference to similar passages quoted elsewhere.** This type of referencing is useful in studying the parallel accounts in Kings and Chronicles, the duplicate accounts in the four gospels, etc.

Marking suggestions: Write the cross reference in the margin with ball-point pen, but precede it with two parallel dashes to indicate that it is a parallel account.

HOW TO STUDY AND INTERPRET SCRIPTURE 27

5. **To cross reference to other passages with doctrinal or historical relationships.** This is the type of marking which is of particular use to missionaries and students of doctrine. They need a guide to the most significant passages which are related to the particular doctrinal theme they have marked.

Marking suggestions:

A. For **doctrinal** cross references, write the reference only. Use a word for clarification if needed. Cross reference to notes or reference books also if desired.

B. For **historical** cross references, write the reference only. Underline in blue pencil or mark with an (H) for historical. Use names if necessary.

> *Virgin Birth* / *Alma 7:10 ; Mt. 1:18-23*
>
> will ye weary my God also?
> 14 Therefore the Lord himself shall give you a sign; °Behold, ᵖa virgin shall conceive, and bear a son, and ⁸shall call his name ᵍIm-măn'-ū-ĕl.
> 15 ʳButter and honey shall he eat, ˢthat he may know to refuse the evil, and choose the good.
> 16 ᵗFor before the child shall know to refuse the evil, and choose the good, the land tha'
>
> o Mt. 1.23.
> p Ge. 3. 15.
> 8 Or, *thou,* O virgin, *shalt call.*
> q ch. 8. 8, 10. r ver. 22.
> s Lk. 2. 40, 52.
> t ch. 8. 4.
> u ch. 27. 10.
>
> shall be, where there were a thousand vines at a thousand silverlings, it shall *even* be for briers and thorns.
> 24 With arrows and with bows shall *men* come thither; because all the land shall become briers and thorns.
> 25 And *on* all hills that shall be digged with the mattock, there shall not come thither the fear of briers and thorns: but ᵘit shall be for the sending forth
>
> *(H) 2 Ki. 17:1-6*
>
> 879

6. **To call attention to the notations in the center column.** Much of the important work of cross-referencing has already been done. The student only needs a signal to alert him that a particular reference is especially meaningful to him.

Marking suggestions: Color the reference letter in the text red, then color the cross reference in the center column.

7. **To label passages so they will not be lost or overlooked.** A one-word note of the subject in the

margin will prove invaluable in years to come. This will make the locating process easier when all one can remember is that "Isaiah or Jeremiah said it...." This type of marking is often used on first readings.

Marking suggestions: Write the subject description in the margin. Be sure to leave room for other notes to be added later.

8. **To summarize lengthy passages.** Long, detailed passages, such as many found in Ezekiel, are best treated with a summary statement.

Marking suggestions:

    A. Do not attempt to bracket the passages if they are too long.

    B. If the summary provided by the Bible agrees with your summary, color it red.

    C. If you desire a more accurate summary, write it in ball-point pen at the top.

How to Study and Interpret Scripture 29

(handwritten annotations:)
(v.3) great eagle = Nebuchadnezzer.
(v.3) highest branch = Jehoiachin.
(v.5) seed = Zedekiah.
(v.7) another great eagle = King of Egypt.
(v.22) tender twig = Mulek (See Omni 15-17; Moses 25:2; Hel. 6:10 + 8:21)

The parable of two great eagles and a vine — EZEKIEL 16, 17

thy ways, and be ashamed, when thou shalt receive ᵃthy sisters, thine elder and thy younger: and I will give them unto thee for daughters, but not by thy covenant.

62 And I will establish my covenant with thee; and thou shalt know that I *am* the LORD:

a ver. 45, 46.
1 Heb. field.

forth her branches toward him, that he might water it by the furrows of her plantation.

8 It was planted in a good ¹soil by great waters, that it might bring forth branches, and that it might bear fruit, that it might be a goodly vine.

9 Say thou, Thus saith the Lord GOD; Shall it prosper?

Some Suggestions on the Interpretation of Scripture

The process of interpreting scripture is a challenging task which must be conducted with wisdom and understanding. Think of the vast divergence of belief which exists among Christendom today because of the variance in the interpretations of the Bible! Surely there must be a way to better understand the scriptures and more fully grasp the meaning of God's word than is common in the world today. How can one interpret the scriptures correctly?

This text makes no claim to having all the answers to these questions. The following suggestions on the proper manner of interpreting scripture, however, may be in order.

1. **One Should Gain His Own Interpretation of Scriptural Passages First.** Perhaps the most basic rule one should follow is to gain his own personal understanding and interpretation of the scriptures before attempting to learn the interpretations of other people. Undoubtedly this is a horrifying thought to many theologians, yet it is the key to a successful search for scriptural knowledge. **It is only by making a fresh beginning in the field of theological interpretation that one can gain the necessary basis for comparison to evaluate the beliefs and interpretations of others.** This is the pattern that has fostered our Church. Why did

the Lord choose Joseph Smith, an uneducated teenager, as an instrument through which to restore His Gospel? Certainly one reason was that Joseph had not yet been tainted by the theological ideas of his day. He was to gain his own interpretation of the scriptures, with the help of the Lord.

2. **One Should Seek Revealed Aid in Interpreting Scripture.** The scriptures are not to be interpreted merely according to one's opinion. As Peter taught, "No prophecy of the scripture is of any private interpretation, . . ."[3] What is interpretation which is not private interpretation? It is interpretation which is guided and inspired by the Lord. Such inspiration is **almost always personal in its nature.** It will come to the individual who is seeking, if he meets the necessary qualifications of worthiness, etc.[4] A revelation to Oliver Cowdery emphasized that inspiration is granted concerning scriptural interpretation:

> Oliver Cowdery, verily, verily, I say unto you, that assuredly as the Lord liveth, who is your God and your Redeemer, even so surely shall you receive a knowledge of whatsoever things you shall ask in faith, with an honest heart, believing that you shall receive a knowledge concerning the engravings of old records, which are ancient, which contain those parts of my scripture of which has been spoken by the manifestation of my spirit.
>
> Yea, behold, I will tell you in your mind and in your heart, by the Holy Ghost, which shall come upon you and which shall dwell in your heart.
>
> Now, behold, this is the spirit of revelation; behold, this is the spirit by which Moses brought the children of Israel through the Red Sea on dry ground.
>
> Therefore this is thy gift; apply unto it, and blessed art thou. . . . (D & C 8:1-4)

3. **Find a Pattern of Interpretive Scripture.** A major

---
[3] 2 Pet. 1:20.
[4] The author's book, *Gifts of the Spirit*, examines this matter in detail.

objective of scriptural study is to determine a pattern of scripture which will make the interpretation plain. How many scriptures are needed for a pattern? As Paul testified, "In the mouth of two or three witnesses shall every word be established."[5] Yet on almost all matters of doctrinal importance there is an abundance of information revealed from numerous witnesses. The **objective should be to let one passage interpret another, without need for interpretive comment by the student.**

4. **Determine the Relative Strength of a Doctrinal Interpretation.** The validity of doctrinal statements and interpretations can perhaps be measured according to a descending scale of value, as follows:

A. Doctrinal statements from numerous scriptural witnesses[6] which need no external interpretation. They are clearly and emphatically stated.

B. Doctrinal statements from only one scriptural witness which need no external interpretations.

C. Doctrinal statements from numerous scriptural witnesses which still are subject to various interpretations.

D. Doctrinal statements from only one scriptural witness which still are subject to various interpretations.

E. Doctrinal teachings from numerous authorized Church leaders which need no external interpretation, based on their interpretation of the scriptures.

F. Doctrinal teachings from only one author-

---
[5] 2 Cor. 13:1. See also Deut. 19:15.
[6] Such as Isaiah, Jeremiah, Peter, Paul, etc.

ized Church leader which need no external interpretation, based on his interpretation of the scriptures.

    G. The interpretive opinions of sectarian Bible students and scholars.

Thus the validity of doctrinal interpretations from scriptural and non-scriptural sources may to some extent be evaluated.

5. **Determine the Chronological Relationship of the Passage to Aid in Fixing the Interpretation.** This is particularly necessary in interpreting prophecy. Ask such questions as—

    A. Who was prophesying?
    B. To whom was he prophesying?
    C. Who is to fulfill the prophecy?
    D. Where is it to be fulfilled?
    E. Was this prophecy fulfilled in Bible times or is it a prophecy of the last days? What evidence supports this interpretation?
    F. What clues are given to indicate the order of events into which its fulfillment will fall? What must precede its fulfillment? What must follow its fulfillment?
    G. Is the determined chronological fulfillment of the prophecy supported by other prophecies and scriptural clues? What?

Failure to ask these questions pertaining to chronology has been the cause of some highly questionable interpretations being made in the past by Bible students, including some Latter-day Saints.

6. **Glean the Interpretive Clues from the Context.** Never be guilty of separating a passage or prophecy from its context. The passage is being said

or given at a particular time for a reason. Determine what the reason is and how it will influence the interpretation.

7. **Have a Hypothesis.** As one begins to discover a pattern of scriptures about a subject, he should write down a basic idea which he feels will be verified by other related passages as they are found. Then he should ask himself questions about his basic idea and write down the questions. These will serve as guides to his study and help him to recognize the significance of items which might otherwise be bypassed.

8. **Contrast Varying Interpretations.** Some passages may have alternative interpretations which may both seem possible and plausible. Write them both down and contrast them. Look for evidence which will substantiate or eliminate one of them. **Attempt to determine which interpretation the speaker intended** when he gave the passage.

9. **Continually Propose Alternative Interpretations.** This serves as a counterbalance and helps to maintain proper perspective. Never reject an interpretation, however, unless there is a better alternative to put in its place.

10. **Be Consistent.** One should not bend the scriptures to make them fit his point of view from one passage to another. Consistency can be overdone, however. Remember that words and terms often had more than one meaning and/or connotation in Bible days, just as they have today. Do not demand a consistency from the scriptures which they do not have.

11. **Look for Key Words.** Be alert for key words and phrases which will provide important interpretive clues.

12. **Check Interpretations with Other Scriptures.** One should verify the interpretations he has made from Biblical passages by comparing the message of other Standard Works.

13. **Check Interpretations With the Position of the Church.** One should verify his interpretations with the established views of the Church. It will be surprising to many to discover that the Church has relatively little stated doctrine. On many matters there is no stated position of the Church. There are many areas where significant contributions in the area of scriptural study can be made. One should not be hesitant to seek knowledge in new areas of Gospel learning. The commandment still remains to "Seek, and ye shall find."[7] But Gospel study must always be conducted with the major objective of bringing God's children back into His presence.

14. **Compare Interpretations with the Findings of Sectarian Scholars.** For hundreds of years learned professors at established divinity schools and noted theological seminaries have studied the scriptures and have written penetrating studies concerning them. Their findings in many cases are significant and meaningful. Yet many of them have treated the Bible with irreverence and have led their flocks away from God. They have rejected the very scriptural basis from which Mormonism draws its strength. One should be aware of their interpretations, but be willing to challenge them on the basis of revealed knowledge and inspired interpretation.

Summary:

After considering this chapter the student should:

---
[7] Mt. 7:7.

1. Acquire the basic tools for effective Bible study.

2. Organize a program for his personal acquisition of a basic Bible library.

3. Know five different reading approaches and be able to adapt them to his study of the scriptures.

4. Develop an organized Old Testament study plan with appropriate goals.

5. Know that the basic purpose for scripture study is to enable man to bring himself back into the presence of God.

6. Develop a personal style of marking the scriptures and evaluate and revise it from time to time.

7. Have a clear concept of the proper method of interpreting scriptural passages.

8. Seek divine guidance in the study of the Old Testament prophets.

CHAPTER III

AIDS FOR UNDERSTANDING BIBLE HISTORY AND CHRONOLOGY

This chapter is a reference chapter. It holds important tools for understanding the Old Testament prophets but it is not designed to be read as a chapter. Rather, it is a collection of reference sources to which the student will do well to refer as he considers the other chapters in the book. These sources are as follows:

1. **The Historical Background of the House of Israel** is a brief discussion of the history of God's chosen people from Abraham to the scattering of the Jews by the Romans in 71 A.D.

2. **A Simplified Diagram of Old Testament History** is a very basic reduction of the Old Testament story. It should be studied thoroughly until it can be duplicated from memory. The diagram serves as a simplified key to remembering the history of the Old Testament.

3. **An Analysis of the Book of Kings and Chronicles From the Death of Solomon to the Fall of Judah** is a study aid which corrolates the accounts of 1st and 2nd Kings and 2nd Chronicles. The books are summarized in parallel columns to aid the student in following the duplicate accounts. It should be noted that the books of Kings tell the history of both Israel and Judah, while the book of Chronicles reports only the history of Judah.

4. **Historical Maps.** A set of twelve historical maps depict the size and status of the house of Israel from the time of the divided kingdom to the inter-

testament period. Frequent reference to these maps will aid the student in understanding the events of the times and in grasping the messages of the prophets.

5. **Time Charts of Bible History.** These charts depict the rise and fall of nations during Bible times. On them are recorded many of the important events which shaped ancient history.

6. **The Kings of Judah and Israel** is a compilation of twelve Old Testament chronologies which pertain to the era of the divided kingdom. Perhaps the most important lesson to be learned from the chart is that scholars and historians do not know the exact dates of Biblical events. Beware of anyone who asserts any date during this period with undo certainty—he cannot substantiate his correctness. Each of the chroniclers shown have attempted to reconcile the Biblical accounts with the very few historical records of the times. Until more information is unearthed, these records will remain irreconcilable. Bible students must be content with the knowledge that all Bible dates are approximate and show little more than a general relationship to other events. In this book the Cambridge revised chronology has been followed. Although it shows several obvious inconsistencies, it seems to be as accurate or more so than the other chronologies listed.

THE HISTORICAL BACKGROUND OF THE HOUSE OF ISRAEL

Abraham lived approximately 1900 B.C. and was the father of **Isaac** who was the father of **Jacob**. (Genesis 12 - 25) The descendants of these three patriarchs are referred to as the "covenant people" because of the promises the Lord made to them.

Jacob was given the name of **Israel.** (Genesis 32:28) He had the following twelve sons: Reuben, Simeon, Levi, **Judah,** Zebulun, Issachar, Dan, Gad, Asher, Naphtali, **Joseph** and Benjamin. Joseph, who was sold into Egypt, had two sons: **Manasseh** and **Ephraim.** Although Ephraim was the younger son, he received the greater blessing and was also given the birthright over all the sons of Israel. (Genesis 48:18-20, I Chron. 5:1-2) Manasseh, however, was also listed as one of the "sons" of Israel. (Gen. 48:5) The tribes of Israel were called after the names of the sons of Jacob, with the exceptions that Levi was not listed as a separate tribe and Joseph's two sons were included in the place of Levi and their father (Numbers 1:4-16).

The descendants of Israel were in bondage in Egypt from c. 1700 B.C. to 1490 B.C. During this period they were greatly influenced by the cultural life of Egypt and many of them learned to speak and write Egyptian. Finally they were delivered by the power of God through **Moses.** (Exodus 13, 14) After forty years in the wilderness (c. 1490-1450 B.C.) they entered the promised land. For about 350 years (c. 1450-1095 B.C.) they were governed by at least thirteen **judges,** with Samuel being the last judge. (I Sam. 8:5-10) Then the people demanded a king and the **United Kingdom** was established, which lasted for approximately 120 years. (c. 1095-975 B.C.) Three kings reigned during this period: **Saul, David,** and **Solomon.**

Dissension developed in the kingdom, and about 975 B.C. the kingdom was divided. The northern kingdom, or **Kingdom of Israel,** led by descendants of Ephraim, consisted of most of the tribes of Israel. The southern kingdom, or **Kingdom of Judah,** ruled over by descendants of Judah, consisted of most of the tribe of Benjamin and the tribe of Judah, plus many descendants of Levi and a few individuals from most or all of the other tribes. (Note: Judah controlled the southern part of the land, including the city of Jerusalem; thus individuals from all of the tribes undoubtedly lived in Jerusalem among the tribe of Judah, particularly if they were merchants, traders, etc.)

About 722 B.C. the Kingdom of Israel was conquered by **Shalmaneser** and **Sargon II of Assyria,** and the **ten tribes** of the Kingdom of Israel were led away into captivity. (II Kings 17) About a year after this, these tribes mysteriously escaped and fled toward the north. Since then, they have been referred to as the "ten lost tribes" of Israel.

For more than a century the southern kingdom continued a troubled and uncertain existence. Then in the year 608 B.C.—which marks the era immediately preceding the opening of the Book of Mormon —Judah faced its crucial hour. **Necho,** Pharaoh of Egypt, had dispatched an army against Assyria, and the path of the Egyptian advance lay through Palestine. **Josiah,** king of Judah, resolved to resist the approaching army and went out to meet it at the head of a plucky little Judean force. In the battle that followed might prevailed over right. The Hebrews were beaten, and King Josiah was slain in the conflict. The Jews then chose one of Josiah's sons, **Jehoahaz** by name, for their king, but after a three month term of office the Egyptians replaced him with another of Josiah's sons, whose name was **Jehoiakim.** For three years the Pharaoh of Egypt exercised political control of the Kingdom of Judah through the puppet ruler Jehoiakim. Then in the memorable year 605 B.C. the **Babylonians** marshalled a mighty army and crushed the Pharaoh's cohorts in the Battle of Carchemish and, in so doing, took the Jewish nation out of Egypt's grasp. (The Biblical account of this era is found in II Kings, chapter 23-25, II Chronicles, chapter 36, and Jeremiah, chapters 26-39).

But the Jewish people did not gain their freedom. Instead of Egyptian foreigners ruling their country, Babylonian foreigners merely took their place. Southern Palestine became a Babylonian vassal state. Unfortunately for all concerned, they allowed the quisling Jehoiakim, Jewish appointee of Egypt, to retain his throne. Before long the new monarch and his subjects were in revolt. In response, King **Nebuchadnezzar** moved an army to Jerusalem and laid seige against the rebellious city. About this time Jehoiakim died or else was taken captive by the enemy, for **Jehoiachin,** his son, presently is spoken of in the Biblical account as surrendering to the Babylonians.

These struggles between Assyria, Babylonia and Egypt took place before the Book of Mormon record opens but during the lifetime of its early leading characters. When the account commences, twenty-one-year-old **Zedekiah,** the well-meaning but utterly weak uncle of the ill-fated King Jehoiachin is spoken of as being in the first year of his reign. According to the book of Second Kings he was appointed to the throne by Nebuchadnezzar of Babylon. It was a time of great wickedness. Immorality and corruption were rampant. Dishonesty, false swearing, and idolatry were common vices of the day. As if the sins of the people were not already enough to invite God's judgments, Zedekiah chose to follow the disastrous course of Jehoiakim in seeking an alliance with Egypt and scheming a break from Babylon. It was at this point that the prophet **Jeremiah,** whose gloomy prophecies had already brought him notoriety in Jehoiakim's day, now thundered forth anew the ominous pronouncement that Jerusalem and its temple were doomed for destruction and that the entire nation would be led into captivity except they repent and heed the admonitions of the Lord. But the declaration that God would not protect his chosen people and allow his sacred temple and his holy city to be destroyed was considered an outrage. To the incensed priests and princes the prophecy was traitorous and bordered on blasphemy. Jeremiah's arrest and imprisonment were ordered.

At length, on the promise of support from Egypt, Zedekiah revolted; but before Egyptian help materialized, Nebuchadnezzar's army invaded Jerusalem. Ruthlessly the Babylonians burned out Zedekiah's eyes and enslaved his people. Nebuchadnezzar also removed the treasures of the temple and the palace and carried them to his own capital; and thus the words of the prophets of God were fulfilled.

However, the prophets had also prophesied concerning the restoration of the people of Judah and some fifty years later (c. 538 B.C.), after Babylonia had been conquered by **Persia,** they were allowed to return to their lands by **Cyrus,** king of Persia. They rebuilt the temple and lived in the Holy Land for over five hundred years under the rule of four separate groups: the **Persians, Greeks, Asmonaeans,** and **Romans.** Finally about 71 A.D. the Romans under Nero destroyed the city of Jerusalem and the temple and dispersed the people of the kingdom of Judah throughout the Roman Empire. These people were later scattered among many of the other nations of the world.

A SIMPLIFIED DIAGRAM OF OLD TESTAMENT HISTORY

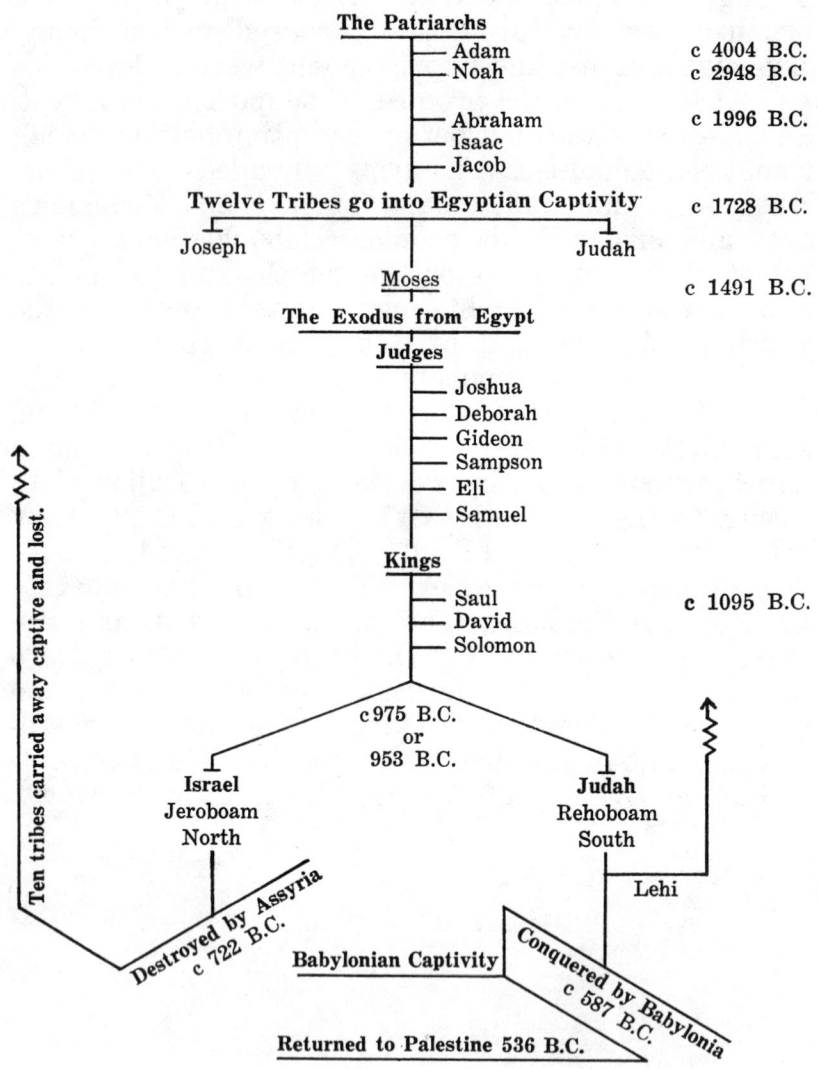

AN ANALYSIS OF THE BOOKS OF KINGS AND CHRONICLES FROM THE DEATH OF SOLOMON TO THE FALL OF JUDAH

ISRAEL

1 Ki.	2 Chron.	
11:43	9:31	Solomon died and was buried in the city of David. His son, **Rehoboam**, reigned in his stead.
12:1	10:1	Rehoboam went to Shechem to be crowned King by all Israel.
12:2-14	10:2-14	Rehoboam was challenged by **Jeroboam**, son of Nebat, who had returned from exile in Egypt, as to whether his rule would be easier than Solomon's. Rehoboam asked for 3 days to decide. Among his counselors the elder statesmen advised kindness; the younger men harshness. Rehoboam told the council he would be harsh.

JUDAH

		Rehoboam continued to reign over the cities of Judah.

ISRAEL

12:16, 19	10:16, 19	Israel rebelled against **Rehoboam** and the House of David.
12:17	10:17	
12:18	10:18	The Israelites killed **Hadoram** (**Adoram** in Kings), Rehoboam's embassary.
12:18	10:18	Rehoboam fled to Jerusalem.
12:20 & 14:20		Israel made **Jeroboam** King. He reigned 22 years. Only the tribe of Judah followed the House of David.

1 Ki.	2 Chron.	ISRAEL	JUDAH
12:15	10:15	This fulfilled the prophecy made by the prophet Ahijah to Jeroboam that he would be ruler over 10 tribes of Israel (1 Ki. 11:29-39) because of **Solomon's** wickedness (1 Ki. 11:9-13)	
12:21	11:1		Rehoboam gathered an army from Judah and Benjamin to fight against Israel and unite his Kingdom again.
12:22-24	11:2-4		**Shemaiah**, a man of God, warned **Rehoboam** not to go to war against **Jeroboam**, for the division was "from me." **Rehoboam** harkened unto his word.
12:25		**Jeroboam** built Shechem in Mount Ephraim and Penuel.	
14:21	12:13		Rehoboam was 41 years old when he began to reign. He reigned 17 years.
	11:5-12		Rehoboam dwelt in Jerusalem and built many cities of defense in Judah. He fortified the cities with arms and food.

12:26-31		Jeroboam built up places of worship at Bethel and Dan to keep the people from returning to Jerusalem to worship. He set up idols and two golden calves and made priests of the "lowest people."
	11:14-15	Jeroboam cast off the Levites and they deserted Israel.
	11:13-17	The Levites came to Rehoboam in Jerusalem because Jeroboam ignored them and made his own priests.
		The Kingdom of Judah was strengthened by the Levites and followed the Lord for three years.
12:32-33		Jeroboam made changes in worship including offerings to the calves and devising new feast days.
	11:18-21	Rehoboam took 18 wives. He loved Maachah, the daughter of Absalom, best. She bore him Abijah who became the next king.
13:1-6		A man of God came from Judah and prophesied to Jeroboam that his priests would be burned on their own altars at Bethel.

46 PROPHETS AND PROPHECIES OF THE OLD TESTAMENT

1 Ki.	2 Chron.	ISRAEL	JUDAH
(2 Ki. 23: 4-25)	(34:3-7)	(Prophecy later fulfilled by Josiah) This prophet caused **Jeroboam's** arm to be withered and when threatened with capture, he restored it.	
13:7-34		A prophet of Bethel invited the "man of God" into his home. The man of God disobeyed the Lord by accepting the invitation. He was killed for his disobedience.	
	11:22		**Rehoboam** made his son, **Abijah,** "the chief."
	11:23		**Rehoboam** dealt wisely with Judah.
	12:1		**Rehoboam** forsook the law of the Lord.
14:25	12:2-4		In **Rehoboam's** fifth year as king, **Shishak,** king of Egypt, came up against Judah with "people without number" and took all the fenced cities of Judah.
	12:5-6		**Shemaiah,** the prophet, told **Rehoboam** that **Shishak** had come because they had forsaken the

14:26-28		Lord. **Rehoboam** and the princes of Judah humbled themselves.
12:7-12		**Shishak** took away the treasures of the temple and the 12 shields of gold **Solomon** had made. **Rehoboam** was made to pay tribute. He replaced the shields with shields of brass and humbled himself before the Lord. The Lord turned away his wrath and things went well in Judah for a while.
14:1-18		**Abijah**, the son of **Jeroboam**, became sick and died as **Ahijah** the prophet had foretold.
14:30 & 15:6	12:15	**Jeroboam** was at war continually with **Rehoboam** during their reigns.
		Rehoboam was at war continually with **Jeroboam** during their reigns.
14:31 & 15:1-7	12:16	**Rehoboam** died. His son, **Abijah**, (**Abijah** in Chron.; **Abijam** in Ki.) reigned in his stead. **Abijah** reigned for 3 years, beginning in the 18th year of **Jeroboam**, king of Israel. He walked in all the sins of his father.

48 Prophets and Prophecies of the Old Testament

1 Ki.	2 Chron.	ISRAEL	JUDAH
	13:3-19		Abijah (Abijam) smote Jeroboam and the Lord delivered Israel into his hand. He took the cities of Bethel and others from Israel.
15:8-12	14:1		Abijah (Abijam) died. His son, Asa, reigned for 41 years, beginning in the 20th year of Jeroboam, king of Israel. He walked with the Lord.
14:20 & 15:25-26	13:20	Jeroboam died. His son, Nadab, reigned in his stead. He reigned for 2 years, beginning in the 2nd year of Asa, king of Judah. He did evil in the sight of God.	
	14:1-8		Asa did that which was good. Judah was quiet for 10 years. He broke down idols and the evil places of worship.
15:13	15:16		Asa removed his mother, Maachah, from being queen because she made an idol.
	14:9-15		Asa fought with Zerah, the Ethiopian, and won.

15:27-29		Nadab was killed by Baasha, son of Ahijah, of the house of Issachar. He killed all of the house of Jeroboam.
15:33-34		Baasha reigned as King. He reigned for 24 years, beginning in the 3rd year of Asa, king of Judah. He did evil in the sight of God.
	16:1-4	Jehu, the son of Hanani, prophesied the doom of Baasha and his house because of their wickedness.
15:16, 32		There was war between Baasha and Asa all their days.
	16:1	There was war between Asa and Baasha all their days.
15:17		Baasha laid siege to Jerusalem.
15:18-22	16:3-7	Asa sent gold and silver to Benhadad, king of Syria, to break the siege of Baasha. Benhadad was successful in breaking the siege, but Baasha escaped him.
	16:7-10	Wars began in Judah because Asa relied on Syria rather than the Lord.

1 Ki.	2 Chron.	ISRAEL	JUDAH
16:6-8		Baasha died. His son, Elah, reigned in his stead. Elah reigned 2 years, beginning in the 26th year of Asa, king of Judah.	
	15:1-15		Azariah, the son of Oded, prophesied to Asa. Asa humbled himself and repented.
	15:19		There was no more war until the 35th year of Asa's reign.
16:9-15		Elah was killed by Zimri, his captain of half his chariots. Zimri killed all of the house of Baasha in fulfillment of Jehu's prophecy. Zimri reigned 7 days, beginning in the 27th year of Asa, king of Judah.	
16:16-18		Israel declared Omri, captain of the hosts, King. Zimri killed himself.	
16:21		Tibni, son of Ginath, was supported by half the people against Omri for the kingship.	
16:22-26		Omri won. He reigned for 12 years, beginning in the 31st year of Asa, king of Judah.	

UNDERSTANDING BIBLE HISTORY AND CHRONOLOGY 51

16:28-30   **Omri** died. His son, **Ahab**, reigned in his stead. **Ahab** reigned 22 years, beginning in the 38th year of **Asa**, king of Judah. He did evil in the sight of God.

16:31   **Ahab** married **Jezebel**, daughter of **Ethbaal**, king of the Zidonians, and they both became Baal worshippers.

22:41-42   **Asa** died. His son, **Jehoshaphat**, reigned in his stead. **Jehoshaphat** began when he was 35 years old and reigned for 25 years. He began in the 4th year of **Ahab**, king of Israel. He walked in the ways of the Lord and established teachers in all the cities.

17:1-9 & 20:31

17:1-7   **Elijah**, the Tishbite, began his work in Israel. He prophesied a drought in Israel to **Ahab** the King.

17:9-24   **Elijah** lived by the brook Cherith.

17:1   **Elijah** lived with the widow of Zarephath and restored her son to life.

1 Ki.	2 Chron.	ISRAEL	JUDAH
18:1-16		Obadiah, governor of Ahab's house, arranged a meeting between Elijah and Ahab.	
18:17-40		Elijah challenged the priests of Baal, and called down fire from heaven.	
18:41-46		Elijah prayed for the drought to cease and received rain.	
19:1-14		Elijah escaped from the wrath of Jezebel into the wilderness where he talked with God.	
19:15		Elijah was told to anoint Hazael to be king of Syria.	
19:16		Elijah was told to anoint Jehu, son of Nimshi, to be king of Israel. Elisha, the son of Shaphat of Abelmeholah, was to become a prophet.	
19:19-21		Elijah called Elisha.	
20:1-43		Benhadad, king of Syria, went to battle against Israel. Through the Lord's intervention, Israel defeated Syria.	

UNDERSTANDING BIBLE HISTORY AND CHRONOLOGY 53

	17:10-11		No war was made against Jehoshaphat for many years. The Philistines and Arabians paid him tribute.
21:1-29		Ahab coveted Naboth's vineyard. Jezebel arranged Naboth's death. The Lord prophesied through Elijah of the end of Ahab's house.	
22:1-29	18:1-34	Ahab and Jehoshaphat went to war as allies against Syria. They inquired of the Lord about whether to fight at Ramoth-gilead. Some 400 of Ahab's prophets recommended it. The prophet Micaiah warned against it.	Jehoshaphat and Ahab went to war as allies against Syria. They inquired of the Lord about whether to fight at Ramoth-gilead. Some 400 of Ahab's prophets recommended it. The prophet Micaiah warned against it.
22:34-53 2 Ki. 1:1	18:33-34	Ahab was killed in the battle of Ramoth-gilead. His son, Ahaziah, reigned in his stead. Ahaziah reigned for 2 years, beginning in the 17th year of Jehoshaphat, king of Judah. He did evil in the sight of God.	
	20:1-34		Jehoshaphat went to war against Syria, Moab and Ammon. Judah's enemies were overthrown.

54 PROPHETS AND PROPHECIES OF THE OLD TESTAMENT

		ISRAEL	JUDAH
2 Ki.	2 Chron.		
	20:35-37	Ahaziah and Jehoshaphat joined forces to form a navy. Prophets foretold the doom of the alliance; the ships broke up and sank.	Jehoshaphat and Ahaziah joined forces to form a navy. Prophets foretold the doom of the alliance; the ships broke up and sank.
1:2-17		Ahaziah became sick after a fall. He sent for Elijah. Ahaziah died.	
1:17 & 3:1-2		Jehoram (Joram), son of Ahab, reigned in Ahaziah's stead because he had no son. He reigned 12 years beginning in the 18th year of Jehoshaphat, king of Judah. He did evil in the sight of God.	
1:1 & 3:4-27		Moab rebelled against Israel. Jehoram (Joram) and Jehoshaphat allied together against the Moabites. The Lord, through Elisha the prophet, helped them win the victory.	Jehoshaphat formed an alliance with Jehoram (Joram) against the Moabites.
1 Ki. 22: 50, 2 Ki. 8:16-18	21:1-7		Jehoshaphat died. His son, Jehoram, reigned in his stead. Jehoram was 32 years old and reigned 8 years, beginning in the 5th year of Jehoram

21:16-17	(Joram), king of Israel. He married Ahab's daughter, killed his brothers so they could not become king, and did much evil in the sight of God.
	Elijah wrote a letter to **Jehoram** and prophesied that a great plague would come upon **Jehoram's** house and he would be stricken with a disease.
	Edom revolted against Judah.
21:12-17	The Philistines and Arabians attacked Judah. They carried away all of the royal family except **Jehoahaz (Ahaziah)**, **Jehoram's** youngest son.
2:1-18	Elijah the prophet was taken up into heaven by a chariot of fire. Elisha took up his mantle and began his work.
8:20-22	
2:19-22	Elisha sweetened the water at Jericho with salt.

2 Ki.	2 Chron.	ISRAEL	JUDAH
8:25-26	21:18-20 & 22:1-4		Jehoram died, unloved by his people, of a hideous disease. His son, Ahaziah (Jehoahaz), reigned in his stead. He reigned 1 year, beginning in the 12th year of Joram (Jehoram), king of Israel. He was 22 (42) years old and walked in the way of evil.
8:28-29		Benhadad, king of Syria, attacked Judah and Israel. They united against him.	Benhadad, king of Syria, attacked Israel and Judah. They united against him.
8:7-15		Elisha prophesied the death of Benhadad. He was killed by his servant, Hazael, who became king in his stead.	
8:28-29	22:5-6	The Syrians attacked. They wounded Joram (Jehoram).	Ahaziah went to war with Joram (Jehoram) against Syria.
8:28-29	22:6-7		Ahaziah went to Jezreel to visit Joram (Jehoram) who was wounded.
9:1-13		Elisha kept the Lord's commandment to Elijah and had one of the prophets anoint Jehu, captain of the hosts, King at Ra-	

moth-gilead. **Jehu** was accepted by the army.

9:7-37

Jehu was commanded to kill **Jezebel** and **Joram (Jehoram)**. He fought with **Ahaziah**, king of Judah, and killed him also.

22:6-12

Ahaziah was killed by **Jehu**. His mother, **Athaliah**, reigned in his stead. She was an evil woman and killed all her grandchildren who were heirs to the throne. She reigned for 6 years. **Jehosheba (Jehoshabeath)**, **Ahaziah's** sister and her husband, **Jehoiada**, a priest, succeeded in saving **Ahaziah's** baby son, **Joash**, and hid him in the House of God for 6 years.

4:1-7

Elisha caused oil to appear for the widow of a prophet.

4:8-37

Elisha promised the lady of Shunem who accepted him that she should have a son. He later restored that boy to life.

4:38-44

Elisha purified a pot of food for the sons of the prophets during a famine.

5:1-27

Naaman of Syria was cured of leprosy by **Elisha**.

58   PROPHETS AND PROPHECIES OF THE OLD TESTAMENT

2 Ki.	2 Chron.	ISRAEL	JUDAH
6:1-7		Elisha caused an axe head to float in water.	
11:4-20	23:1-21		Jehoiada, the priest, gathered all the Levites together. They proclaimed Joash king. They killed Athaliah and covenanted to serve the Lord.
11:21 & 12:1-6	24:1-14		Joash (Jehoash) was 7 years old when he began to reign. He reigned 40 years, beginning in the 7th year of Jehu, king of Israel. Jehoiada served as his adviser. He collected funds and repaired the temple.
6:24-25		Syria attacked Israel and besieged Samaria.	
6:25-30 & 7:1		There was a great famine in the land. Elisha prophesied the end of the famine.	
7:2-20		The Syrians fled because the Lord made a great noise of many chariots and men and they were afraid of attack by Israel and its allies. The people of Samaria	

13:1-3	sacked their camp and got their food.	
	Jehoahaz, son of Jehu, began to reign in the 23rd year of Joash and reigned 17 years. He did evil in the sight of God.	
24:15		Jehoiada, the priest, died when he was 130 years old.
24:17-22		Joash forsook God. He killed Zechariah, Jehoiada's son, who came to warn him.
13:3-7, 22	The Lord allowed Hazael, king of Syria, and his son, Benhadad, to attack Jehoahaz all his days because of his wickedness. Jehoahaz did repent for a time and he was relieved of war with Syria.	
12:17-18		Hazael, king of Syria, came up against Jerusalem to plunder. Joash bribed him with the treasures of the temple and the Holy things.

2 Ki.	2 Chron.	ISRAEL	JUDAH
13:9-11		Jehoahaz died. His son, **Joash**, (**Jehoash**), reigned in his stead. He reigned for 16 years, beginning in the 37th year of Joash, king of Judah. He did evil in the sight of God.	
13:14-20		Elisha became sick. Joash (Jehoash) visited him. Elisha prophesied more war with Syria. Elisha died. Bands of Moabites invaded Israel.	
12:20-21 & 14:1-3	24:25-27 & 25:1		Joash was murdered by his servants. His son, **Amaziah**, reigned in his stead. He was 25 years old and reigned 29 years, beginning in the second year of Joash (Jehoash), king of Israel. He walked in the way of the Lord.
14:5-6	25:3-4		**Amaziah** killed the servants who murdered his father.
13:24-25		**Hazael**, king of Syria, died. His son, **Benhadad**, reigned in his stead. Joash won some battles from Benhadad.	

14:7	25:5-12	Amaziah smote the children of Seir (Edom) after following a prophet's advice to break his alliance with Israel.
	25:13	An army of Israel that Amaziah sent home, after breaking the alliance, killed 3000 of Judah on their way home.
	25:14-15	Amaziah set up the gods of the children of Seir to be his Gods. The Lord was angry.
14:11-14	25:17-24	Judah and Israel went to battle. Israel won. Jerusalem was sacked.
13:13 & 14:16-17, 23-24		Israel and Judah went to battle. Israel won. Jerusalem was sacked. Joash died. His son, Jeroboam II, reigned in his stead. He reigned 41 years, beginning in the 15th year of Amaziah, king of Judah. He did evil in the sight of God.
14:17		Amaziah lived 15 years after Joash.
14:19-21 & 15:1-4	26:1-4	Amaziah was killed by a conspiracy. His son, Azariah (Uzziah), reigned in his stead. He was 16 years old and reigned 52 years, beginning in the 27th year of

2 Ki.	2 Chron.	ISRAEL	JUDAH
			Jeroboam II, king of Israel. He walked in the way of the Lord.
14:25-28		Jeroboam II restored the coast of Israel as was foretold by **Jonah**, the son of **Amittai**.	
14:29 & 15:8-9		Jeroboam II died. His son Zachariah reigned in his stead. He reigned 6 months, beginning in the 38th year of **Azariah** (**Uzziah**), king of Judah. He did evil in the sight of God.	
	26:5		Uzziah (Azariah) sought God in the days of **Zechariah** and prospered.
15:10-13		Zachariah was killed by **Shallum**, son of **Jabash**, who became king. (This fulfilled the prophecy that Jehu's sons would reign unto the fourth generation.) **Shallum** reigned one month.	
15:14-18		Menahem, the son of Gadi of Tirzah, killed **Shallum** and others who opposed his claim to the throne. He reigned 10 years, beginning in the 39th year of	

26:6-15	Azariah (Uzziah), king of Judah. He did evil in the sight of God.	Azariah (Uzziah) warred with the Philistines, the Arabians, the Ammonites, and even went into Egypt. He strengthened Judah militarily.
26:16-21		Azariah (Uzziah) was lifted up in his pride and strength and tried to burn incense in the temple. The Lord smote him with leprosy. He appointed his son, **Jotham**, to be judge and to be "over his house."
15:5		
15:19-20		**Pul**, king of Assyria, came up against Israel. **Menahem** gave him 1000 talents of silver, which he exacted from the people, and **Pul** turned back.
15:22-24		**Menahem** died. His son, **Pekahiah**, reigned in his stead. He reigned 2 years, beginning in the 50th year of **Azariah (Uzziah)**, king of Judah. He did evil in the sight of God.

2 Ki.	2 Chron.	ISRAEL	JUDAH
15:25-28		Pekah, the son of **Remaliah**, killed Pekahiah, and reigned in his stead. He reigned for 20 years, beginning in the 52nd year of **Azariah (Uzziah)**, king of Judah. He was evil in the sight of God.	
15:7, 32-35	26:23 & 27:1-2		Azariah (Uzziah) died. His son, Jotham, became king in his stead. **Jotham** was 25 years old and reigned 16 years, beginning in the 2nd year of **Pekah**, king of Israel. He walked in the way of the Lord.
15:29		**Tiglath-pileser III**, king of Assyria, attacked Israel and carried many away into Assyria.	
15:37	27:1-4	The Lord sent **Rezin**, king of Syria, against Israel and Judah.	The Lord sent **Rezin**, king of Syria, against Judah and Israel.
	27:5-6		Jotham built many fortresses. Jotham fought the Ammonites. He was mighty in war.
16:1-4	27:9 & 28:1-4		Jotham died and his son, **Ahaz**, reigned in his stead. **Ahaz** was 20 years old and reigned 16

16:5-6	28:5-7	years, beginning in the 17th year of **Pekah**, king of Israel. He did evil in the sight of God and worshipped Baal. The kings of Syria and Israel attacked. **Pekah** killed 120,000 in one day including the son of **Ahaz**. **Pekah** captured many thousands.
		Rezin, king of Syria, joined with **Pekah** to attack Judah.
	28:8-15	**Pekah** was advised by **Oded** the prophet to send the captives from Judah home. He treated them well and then did so.
16:7-8	28:16-19	**Ahaz** sent to King **Tiglath-pileser III**, of Assyria, to help him against the Syrians, Edomites and Philistines.
16:9		Assyria came and took Damascus and killed **Rezin**, king of Syria.
	28:20-21	Assyria also distressed Jerusalem, even though **Ahaz** bribed them with the treasures of the temple.
16:10-19	28:22-25	**Ahaz** met with **Tiglath-pileser III** at Damascus. He made himself gods like he saw there, because he felt those gods had helped

2 Ki.	2 Chron.	ISRAEL	JUDAH
			their people but his god had not helped him. He changed the altars in the temple to accommodate the gods of Damascus.
15:30		Hoshea, son of Elah, killed Pekah and reigned in his stead. He began in the 20th year of Jotham, king of Judah. (Note: Jotham only reigned 16 years. See 2 Ki. 15:33)	
17:1-2		Hoshea reigned 9 years, beginning in the 12th year of Ahaz, king of Judah. He did evil in the sight of God.	
16:20 & 18:1-3	28:27 & 29:1-2		Ahaz died. His son, **Hezekiah**, reigned in his stead. **Hezekiah** was 25 years old and reigned for 29 years, beginning in the 3rd year of **Hoshea**, king of Israel. He walked in the way of the Lord.
17:3		Hoshea gave tribute to Shalmaneser, king of Assyria.	

Understanding Bible History and Chronology

17:4	Shalmaneser found that Hoshea tried to make an alliance with Egypt. He imprisoned Hoshea.
17:5	Shalmaneser besieged Israel for three years.
17:6 & 18:1-11	In the 9th year of Hoshea, Assyria took Samaria and carried Israel away to Assyria.
18:10	Shalmaneser came upon Israel in the 4th year of Hezekiah, king of Judah.
17:24	The Assyrians replaced the Israelites with men from Babylon and other places.
	END OF NORTHERN KINGDOM (ISRAEL)
29:3-36	Hezekiah opened the temple and repaired it. He offered sacrifices and began to worship the Lord.
30:1-27	Hezekiah proclaimed a solemn passover.
31:1	Hezekiah broke down the idols and all the "high places."
18:4	
18:5-6	Hezekiah trusted in the Lord the most of all the Kings of Judah.
18:7	Hezekiah rebelled against Assyria and did not serve it.
18:8	Hezekiah went to war against the Philistines and smote them.
32:1-8	
18:13	In the 14th year of Hezekiah, Sennacherib, king of Assyria, took the fenced cities of Judah.
32:9	Assyria besieged Jerusalem.

JUDAH

2 Ki.	2 Chron.	
18:14-16		Sennacherib asked for a heavy tribute. **Hezekiah** stripped the treasures from the Temple.
18:17-37 & 19:1-37	32:10-21	Through the intervention of the Lord, the Assyrians were defeated. God caused the soldiers to die overnight. **Sennacherib** returned to Nineveh where he was killed by his own sons.
20:1-11	32:24	Isaiah told **Hezekiah** that he, the king, would die. **Hezekiah** pled with the Lord. His life was extended for 15 more years.
	32:25-29	Hezekiah was lifted up in his power and wealth.
20:12-13		**Merodach-baladan**, a prince of Babylon, sent presents to **Hezekiah**. **Hezekiah** showed all his treasures to the Babylonian emissaries.
20:14-19		Isaiah reproved King **Hezekiah** for the foolishness of this move and prophesied of the eventual defeat of Judah by Babylon.
21:1-9	32:33 & 33:1-8	Hezekiah died. His son, **Manasseh**, reigned in his stead. He was 12 years old and reigned 55 years. He was very evil and built up the idols and the high places. He was a Baal worshipper.
21:9	33:9	Manasseh made Judah the most wicked it had ever been.
21:12-15		The Lord promised he would forsake Judah.
	33:11-13	**Manasseh** was carried away to Babylon by Assyria. He humbled himself there. The Assyrians brought him back to Judah.
	33:13-17	Manasseh repented.
21:18-22	33:20-23	Manasseh died. His son, **Amon**, reigned in his stead. He was 22 years old and reigned 2 years. He did evil in the sight of God.

UNDERSTANDING BIBLE HISTORY AND CHRONOLOGY 69

21:23-26 & 22:1-2	33:24-25 & 34:1-2	**Amon** was killed by his servants. The people of the land killed the servants and set up **Amon's** son, **Josiah**, as king. He was 8 years old and reigned 31 years. He walked in the way of the Lord.
23:4-25	34:3-7	In **Josiah's** 8th year as king, he began to seek the Lord. In his 12th year as king he began to purge Judah of its idols. He burned Baal images, broke down the temples, and killed the priests of Baal.
22:3-20 & 23:1-3, 23	34:8-33 & 35:1-19	In his 18th year as king, the book of the law of the Lord was found. Josiah read it and had it read to the people. They all made covenants with God. They had a great passover.
23:29-32	35:20-24 & 36:1-2	**Josiah** went up against **Pharaoh Necho** of Egypt. He was killed at Megiddo. His son, **Jehoahaz**, reigned in his stead for 3 months. He walked in evil ways.
	35:25	**Jeremiah** lamented for Josiah.
23:33-37	36:3-4	**Pharaoh Necho** captured Jehoahaz. He made **Eliakim** (Jehoahaz's brother) king and changed his name to **Jehoiakim**. **Jehoahaz** died in Egypt.
	36:5	**Jehoiakim** was 25 years old and reigned 11 years. He walked in evil ways.
24:7		Egypt was driven out by Babylon.
24:1		**Jehoiakim** became Nebuchadnezzar's servant. He rebelled against him.
24:2		**Jehoiakim** fought with the Chaldeans, Syrians, Moabites, and Ammonites, which were all sent by the Lord to destroy Judah.
	36:6-7	**Nebuchadnezzar** had Jehoiakim carried to Babylon in fetters. He took the vessels of the temple.

JUDAH

2 Ki.	2 Chron.	
24:6-9	36:9	**Jehoiakim** died. His son, **Jehoiachin**, reigned in his stead. He was 8 years old (18 according to 2 Kings). He reigned 3 months.
24:10-11		The Babylonians laid siege to Jerusalem.
24:13-16	36:10	Nebuchadnezzar carried away **Jehoiachin** to Babylon.
		Nebuchadnezzar carried away all the treasures and the noblemen.
24:17-19	36:10-12	Nebuchadnezzar made Mattaniah, **Jehoiakim's** brother, king and changed his name to **Zedekiah**. He was 22 years old and reigned 11 years. He was a weak king.
24:20	36:13	**Zedekiah** rebelled against Babylon.
25:1-2		Nebuchadnezzar came up and besieged Jerusalem for a year-and-a-half until the 11th year of **Zedekiah**.
25:3		There was a great famine.
25:4-7		**Zedekiah** tried to escape but was captured. His sons were killed before his eyes. He was blinded and taken to Babylon.
25:8	36:17-20	In the 19th year of Nebuchadnezzar, Jerusalem was burned and the people were either killed or taken away to Babylon.
25:27		In the 37th year of his captivity **Jehoiachin**, the former king of Judah, was taken out of prison and allowed to live quietly in Babylon.
	36:22-23	In the 1st year of his reign, Cyrus, king of Persia, fulfilled **Jeremiah's** prophecy by letting the people go back and rebuild Jerusalem.

CHRONOLOGICAL LIST OF THE KINGS OF JUDAH AND ISRAEL AND THE APPROXIMATE DATES AND PERIODS OF THEIR REIGNS

The year (B.C.) in which the king's reign began, as indicated in the chronologies prepared by the following Bible scholars or organizations:

Kings of Judah	Years reigned	Years from the accession of the kings of Israel[1]	Keil	Winer	Ewald	Clinton	Ussher	Browne	Watchtower	Cambridge (standard)	Cambridge (revised)	Westminster	Dummelow	Daniel-Rops	Years reigned	Years from the accession of the kings of Judah[1]	Kings of Israel
Rehoboam	17	1	975	975	985	976	975	935?	997	975	953	926	937	935			
Abijam	3	18	957	957	968	959	958	923?	980	957	932	910	920	915			
Asa	41	20	955	955	965	956	955	920?	978	955	929	908	917	913			
			953	954	963	955	954	918?	977	954	927	907	915	911	22	1	Jeroboam
			952	953	961	954	953	915?	976	953	925	906	914	910	2	2	Nadab
			930	930	937	930	930	891?	953	930	901	883	900		24	3	Baasha
			929	928	935	930	929	888?	952	929	899	882	899		2	26	Elah
			929	928	935	930	929	888?	952	929	897	882	899		7da.27		Zimri
									948	925					4	47	Omri (at war with Tibni)
Jehoshaphat	25	4	925	924	919	919	918	876?	941	918	875	871	875	875	8	31	Omri (sole king)
			918	918	917	915	914	874?	938	914	873	872	876	873	22	38	Ahab
			914	914	897	896	898	853?	922	898	853	852	853		2	17	Ahaziah
			897	897	895	895	896	852?	921	897	851	851	852	852	12	18	Jehoram (Joram)
Jehoram (co-regent?)	2	5	896														
Jehoram (sole ruler)	6		891	889	893	891	892	849?	917			852	851	849			
Ahaziah	1	12	884	885	885	884	885	844?	910	885	844	845	843				

[1] This column indicates the year the king's reign began in relation to the reign of the contemporary king of the other kingdom. For example: The Judean king, Abijam began his reign in the 18th year of the reign of Jeroboam, king of Israel; the Israelite king, Ahab, took office in the 38th year of King Asa of Judah.

72 — Prophets and Prophecies of the Old Testament

The year (B.C.) in which the king's reign began, as indicated in the chronologies prepared by the following Bible scholars or organizations:

Kings of Judah	Years reigned	Years from the accession of the kings of Israel	Keil	Winer	Ewald	Clinton	Usher	Browne	Watchtower	Cambridge (standard)	Cambridge (revised)	Westminster	Dummelow	Daniel-Rops	Years reigned	Years from the accession of the kings of Judah	Kings of Israel
Athaliah	6		883	884	883	883	884	842?	909	884	843	845	842	842			
Joash (Jehoash)	40	7	877	878	877	877	878	836?	903	878	837	839	836	836	28		Jehu
			856	856	855	855	856	814?	881	856		818	815		17	22?	Jehoahaz
			840	840	839	839	841	798?	867	842	798	802	798	799	16	37	Joash (Jehoash)
Amaziah	29	2	838	838	837	837	839	797?	866	841	797	800	796				
			824	825	823	823	825	783?	852	826	790	787	782	784	41	15	Jeroboam II
Uzziah (Azariah)	52	15?	810	809	808	808	810	778?	826	811	792	785	789	789			
			783	784					837						11		Interregnum (no king)
			772	772	770	771	773	743	789	773	749	747	741		6 mo.	38	Zachariah
			771	771	770	770	772	743	788	772	748	747			1 mo.	39	Shallum
			771	771	769	770	772	740?	788	772	748	746	740	744	10	39	Menahem
									778								Interregnum (no king)
			760	760	759	759	761	737?	777	761	737	736	736		2	50	Pekahiah
Jotham	16	2	759	758	757	757	759	736	775	759	735	734	735	733	20	52	Pekah
Ahaz	16	17	758	758	756	756	758	740?	774	758	740	758					
			742	741	740	741	742	736?	759	742	734	742	734	733	7	4	Interregnum (no king)
			739	738					755								

UNDERSTANDING BIBLE HISTORY AND CHRONOLOGY

The year (B.C.) in which the king's reign began, as indicated in the chronologies prepared by the following Bible scholars or organizations:

Kings of Judah	Years reigned	Years from the accession of the kings of Israel	Keil	Winer	Ewald	Clinton	Usher	Browne	Watchtower	Cambridge (standard)	Cambridge (revised)	Westminster	Dummelow	Daniel-Rops	Years reigned	Years from the accession of the kings of Judah	Kings of Israel
Hezekiah	29	3	730	729	728	730	730	730?	748	730	733	732	729	718	9	12	Hoshea
			727	725	724	726	726	727?	745	726	728	725	722	722		6	DESTRUCTION OF ISRAEL
			722	721	719	721	721	722	740	721	722	721	722				
Manasseh	55		698	696	695	697	698	685?	716	697	697	696	692	689			
Amon	2		643	641	640	642	643	641?	661	642	642	641	641				
Josiah	31		641	639	638	640	641	639?	659	640	640	639	639	639			
Jehoahaz	3 mo.		610	609	608	609	610	608	628	609	609	609	608				
Jehoiakim (Eliakim)	11		610	609	607	609	610	608	628	609	609	609	608				
Jehoiachin	3 mo.		599	598	597	598	599	597	618	598	598	598	597	597			
Zedekiah	11		599	598	596	598	599	597	617	598	598	598	597	597			
DESTRUCTION OF JERUSALEM			588	588		587	588	586	607	587	587	587	586	586			
Gedaliah (Babylonian Gov.)	2 mo.		588	588				586									
LAST DEPORTATION OF THE JEWS			584	584													

Summary:

After considering this chapter the student should know:

1. The basic history of the Old Testament to the extent that he could draw and label the chart from memory.
2. The historical account of the period of the Old Testament prophets is found in 1st and 2nd Kings and 2nd Chronicles.
3. Kings gives an account of both Israel and Judah. Chronicles is a record of Judah only.
4. The chronology of the Old Testament is extremely vague and inaccurate. No date can be asserted with finality. All dates should be considered as relative to other dates.
5. Many dating inconsistencies will be found in comparing the writings of various authors pertaining to the Old Testament.

CHAPTER IV

SIX MAJOR DOCTRINES OF THE OLD TESTAMENT PROPHETS

The most important reason for studying the scriptures is to determine the basic teachings which man can use and apply to enrich his life. There is little justification for scriptural study unless applications can be found to improve man's spiritual lot today. The history revealed in scriptural study is also interesting and important, but a knowledge of it is useless unless it can be applied in some manner. As Nephi said concerning the writings of Isaiah, "I did liken all scriptures unto us, that it might be for our profit and learning."[1] The application of eternal principles found in the scriptures to man's present life is a rewarding process. Indeed, the abundance of "spiritual food" in the scriptures is what makes them of such great value to man. It is also the reason why they are so enjoyable to read.

Certain doctrines tend to be revealed in greater abundance in some portions of the scriptures than do others. Yet the most important doctrinal themes will be found in all the Standard Works of the Church. Six doctrines comprise the predominant themes of the Old Testament prophets. They are vital to every man who seeks to understand the workings of God and who desires to comprehend his own relationship with Deity. These doctrines are:

1. The nature of God and Godhood.
2. The manner in which God communicates with man.
3. The nature of sin.

---
[1] 1 Ne. 19:23.

4. The nature of man's agency and God's judgment.

5. God's program to aid man in living righteously.

6. God's program to prepare the world for His coming in the last days.

This chapter does not propose to analyze these doctrines in detail. As was stated previously, this book is intended only as an aid to the study of the Bible itself. These listings are assembled in this chapter to show that a pattern of scripture exists which gives ample evidence of the teaching. The listing will also provide a basic outline upon which other studies can be based. Each of the six doctrinal themes will be presented with an outline of its major sub-divisions. This list does not represent a complete coverage of the pertinent passages found in the writings of the Old Testament prophets, but most important passages are included. Those judged to be major passages are marked with an asterisk (*).

The Nature of God and Godhood:

This doctrine is concerned with the many qualities, attributes, and emotions of God. It is believed that man must understand God to effectively love Him, serve Him, and seek Him in prayer. It becomes obvious that God desires man to know Him and understand His nature and personality, for one can scarcely read a chapter of scripture without finding information which He has revealed about Himself.

In the passages that follow, no effort has been made to differentiate between the Father and the Son. It should be observed, however, that almost all of the verses are references to God the Son, Jehovah.

1. **God is Accessible and Should be Sought:** (2 Chron. 14:4; 14:7; 15:2*; 26:5; Amos 5:4-5, 8; Hos. 5:15; Is. 8:19; 55:6; Jer. 23:23; 29:12-13*)

SIX MAJOR DOCTRINES 77

2. **God is All-powerful (Omnipotent):** (Is. 40:13, 14, 15-17, 22, 25-26*, 28; 42:13; Jer. 32:27)
3. **God Allows Man a Choice:** (2 Chron. 13:12; 15:2*; 24:20; Is. 1:19-20*)
4. **God May Feel Anger, Indignation, Fury, and Wrath:** (1 Ki. 11:9; 15:30; 16:2, 7, 13, 26; 22:53; 2 Ki. 22:17; 23:19, 26; 24:20; 23:26*; 2 Chron. 28:11, 25; Mic. 7:8-9; Is. 12:1; 27:4; 42:25*; 51:20; 60:10; 66:14; Nahum 1:2, 6; Hab. 3:2, 8, 12; Jer. 3:12; 4:4, 26; 6:11; 7:18-20; 8:19; 12:13; 18:23; 21:5; 23:20; 25:7, 15-16, 37-38; 44:6; Lam. 1:12; 2:6; 4:11; 5:22; Ezek. 5:15; 7:3; Zech. 10:3.
5. **God May Appear unto Man:** (1 Ki. 11:9; 22:19-23; 2 Chron. 18:18-22; Amos 9:1; Is. 1:1-5; Ezek. 1:1, 26-28; 3:23-24; Dan. 3:25)
6. **God May be Astonished:** (Jer. 8:21)
7. **God May Avenge or Take Vengeance:** (Jer. 5:9, 29; 9:9; 50:15; Nahum 1:2)
8. **God has Beauty:** (Zech. 9:17)
9. **God May Give Comfort and Compassion:** (2 Ki. 13:23; Is. 12:1; 49:13; Jer. 12:15; 31:3; Lam. 3:22, 23)
10. **God Controls the Actions and Fate of Individuals:** (1 Ki. 11:14, 21, 34*, 36; 12:15; 20:42; 22:20-3; 2 Ki. 3:10*; 9:7; 10:30; 15:5, 12; 19:7; 24:20; 2 Chron. 10:15; 11:4; 13:20; 15:6-7; 16:7, 8; 18:31; 21:18; 25:16, 20; 26:16-20; 28:19; 33:11; 36:22; Mic. 7:8-9; Is. 29:10; 63:17; Ezek. 24:16-18; Ezra 7:6; Dan. 1:9, 17; 2:37; 4:17, 25, 32; Zech. 8:10)
11. **God Controls the Actions and Fate of Nations:** (1 Ki. 12:24; 14:14; 20:13, 23; 2 Ki. 3:18; 8:19; 10:32; 13:5; 15:37*; 17:20*; 19:34; 21:14; 24:2*, 3*; 2 Chron. 13:15-16*; 20:6-7, 27; 24:24*; 29:8; 30:12; 32:21; 36:17; Mic. 1:6; Is. 3:1-3; 7:20; Obad. 2, 4, 8; Jer. 5:15-17; 6:8; 7:3-7; 12:12, 17; 14:12; 15:4; 19:7; 20:5; 21:4-6, 7*; 22:7; 25:9, 12; 27:8; 32:3; 46:26; Ezek. 20:18-26; 29:19; 30:23-24; 38:16; 39:1-2; Dan. 1:1-2; 2:21)
12. **God Controls Nature and the Elements:** (2 Ki. 8:1; Jon. 1:4, 17; 4:6, 8; Amos 4:7-10*, 13; 5:8; 8:9; 9:5, 6; Is. 23:11; 29:6*; 42:15; 43:16; 44:3; 50:2; 51:10, 15; Nahum 1:3, 4; Hab. 3:6-11; Jer. 3:3;

5:22, 24; 10:10, 13*; 14:22; Dan. 2:22; Neh. 9:11; Joel 2:23)
13. **God Covenants With His People:** (2 Ki. 11:17; 2 Chron. 21:7*; Is. 54:10; 61:8; Dan. 9:4; Neh. 1:5; 9:32)
14. **God is a Creator:** (Jon. 1:9; Amos 4:13; 5:8; Is. 37:16*; 40:12; 41:19-20; 42:5*; 43:15; 44:2, 24*; 45:7, 12; 48:13; 51:13; 64:8; Jer. 10:12; 27:5; 32:17; Neh. 9:6; Zech. 12:1)
15. **God is Eternal:** (Is. 40:8; 51:6, 8; Lam. 5:19; Dan. 4:3, 34; 6:26-27)
16. **God is Faithful:** (Is. 49:7)
17. **God is the Father of Man:** (Is. 63:16; Jer. 3:19; Mal. 1:6; 2:10)
18. **God Never Forgets Men's Works:** (Amos 8:7)
19. **God Forgives and Pardons:** (2 Chron. 12:7, 12; 32:26; Mic. 7:18-20*; Is. 1:18*; 38:17; 43:25; 44:22; 55:7; Jer. 31:34; 33:8; Lam. 3:42; Dan. 9:9; Neh. 9:17)
20. **God Gives His Servants Power to Perform Miracles:** (1 Ki. 13:4-6; 18:36-38; 2 Ki. 1:9-12; 2:8, 14; 2:11; 4:18-37; 13:21)
21. **God has Glory:** (Is. 6:3; 42:8; 66:1; Hag. 1:8)
22. **God is Good:** (Ezra 3:11; Zech. 9:17)
23. **God is Gracious:** (2 Ki. 13:23; 2 Chron. 30:9; Jon. 4:2; Neh. 9:17, 31; Joel 2:13)
24. **God May Feel Grief:** (Jer. 10:19)
25. **God Guides Man:** (Is. 11:2-3*; 48:17; 49:10; 50:4; 55:3, 10-11; 61:8*; Jer. 14:9; Ezek. 2:2; Neh. 9:20)
26. **God May Hate:** (Mal. 1:2-3)
27. **God Hears and Answers Prayers:** (2 Ki. 20:5; 2 Chron. 33:11-13; Jon. 2:2, 7; Mic. 7:7; Is. 38:2-3, 5-8; 41:14; Lam. 3:57)
28. **God is Helpful:** (2 Chron. 14:11; 32:7-8; Is. 41:10, 13*, 14)
29. **God is Holy:** (Is. 5:16, 6:3; 43:3)
30. **God May be Hurt:** (Jer. 8:21; 10:19)
31. **God May be Jealous:** (1 Ki. 14:22; Nahum 1:2; Joel 2:18)

SIX MAJOR DOCTRINES 79

32. **God Will Judge and Bring Judgment:** (Mic. 4:3-4; Is. 16:5; 61:8; Jer. 1:16; 9:24; Lam. 3:59)
33. **God is Kind:** (Jon. 4:2; Is. 43:20; 54:8, 10; 63:7; Jer. 9:24; Neh. 9:17; Joel 2:13)
34. **God Knows Man's Thoughts and Acts:** (2 Ki. 19:27; 2 Chron. 16:9*; Jon. 1:2; 3:10; Amos 4:13; 5:12*; 9:8; Mic. 1:2; Is. 37:28*; 66:18; Nahum 1:7; Jer. 2:2, 34; 5:3; 12:3; 16:17*; 17:10; 21:10; 23:24; 29:23; 32:19*; Zech. 4:10)
35. **God Loves:** (Is. 38:17; Jer. 9:24; 31:13; 32:18; Mal. 1:2-3)
36. **God is Merciful:** (2 Chron. 20:21; 30:9*; Jon. 4:2; Mic. 7:18-20*; Is. 14:1; 16:5; 49:10, 13; 54:7, 8, 10; 55:7; 60:10; Hab. 3:2; Jer. 3:12; 31:20; 33:11; 42:12; Lam. 3:22, 23; Ezra 3:11; 9:9; Dan. 9:9; Neh. 1:5; 9:17, 31; Zech. 1:16; Joel 2:13)
37. **God is No Respecter of Persons:** (2 Chron. 19:7)
38. **God is the Only God With Whom Man is to be Concerned:** (Hos. 13:4; Is. 37:16; 41:4; 42:8; 43:10-11, 13; 44:6, 8; 45:18, 22; 46:9; 48:11-12)
39. **God May Feel Pain:** (Jer. 4:19)
40. **God May Praise:** (Jer. 33:9)
41. **God has Purpose:** (Is. 43:7; 45:18, 23)
42. **God is a Redeemer of Man:** (Is. 43:1, 3; 44:22; 47:4; 49:26; 53:5-6, 8, 9, 10, 11, 12; 63:9, 16; Jer. 14:8; Lam. 3:58)
43. **God Provides Refuge:** (Is. 8:13-14; 25:4; Nahum 1:7)
44. **God is a Revelator:** (1 Ki. 19:12; 22:14; 2 Ki. 17:13; 21:10; Jon. 1:2; 3:2; Amos 3:6-8; 7:14-15; Hos. 12:10; Is. 6:8; 43:12; 44:26; 45:11; 46:9-11; 48:3, 4-5, 16; Jer. 33:6; Ezek. 1:3; 2:6-7; 3:11; 3:18-22; 12:21-25; Dan. 2:18-19, 20-22, 28, 29, 45; Neh. 9:13-14)
45. **God is a Rewarder of Good and Evil:** (2 Ki. 17:25; 21:14; 2 Chron. 13:12; Amos 9:2, 3, 4; Hos. 4:9*; 14:9; Is. 3:10; 13:11*; 48:22; 64:4; Nahum 1:3; Jer. 25:14; 32:19*; Lam. 1:5; 2:2; 3:64; Ezek. 7:3, 4, 27; 11:21; 14:23; 22:31; 24:14; 44:12-13; Zech. 1:6)

46. **God is Righteous:** (2 Chron. 19:7*; Hos. 14:9; Mic. 6:3-5*; 7:8-9; Is. 5:16; 16:5; 33:5; 45:19*; 46:13; 63:1; Jer. 4:2; 12:1; 9:24*; Lam. 1:18; Ezra 9:15; Dan. 9:7, 14; Neh. 9:8, 33; Zech. 8:8)
47. **God is Slow To Anger:** (Jon. 4:2; Nahum 1:3; Neh. 9:17; Joel 2:13)
48. **God is the Source of Salvation:** (Jon. 2:9; Is. 45:17; Hab. 3:13)
49. **God is the Source of Strength:** (Is. 41:10, 13; 49:5; Hab. 3:19; Joel 3:16)
50. **God is a Stumbling Stone to the Wicked:** (Is. 9:14-15)
51. **God Tests Men:** (2 Chron. 32:31; Is. 48:10; Zech. 13:9)
52. **God Requires True Religion:** (Hos. 6:6; Mic. 6:6-8)
53. **God Speaks Truth:** (Is. 16:5; Jer. 4:2; 10:10; Zech. 8:8)
54. **God is Unchangeable:** (Mal. 3:6)
55. **God Shows Visions to His Servants:** (2 Ki. 2:11; 6:17; 13:14; Hab. 2:2-3; Ezek. 1:1, 4-25, 26-28; 3:23-24; 8:1-3; 8:4-11:24; Dan. 3:25; 5:5; 6:22; 7:13-14; 9:20-27; 10:5-7, 10-21)
56. **God May be Weary:** (Jer. 6:11)
57. **God's Ways Differ From Man's:** (Hos. 11:9; Is. 55:8-9)
58. **God Withdraws From Man Because of Man's Wickedness:** (Mic. 3:6-7; Is. 54:7, 8; 60:10; 63:10; 64:7; Jer. 7:16; 11:14; 14:11; 15:1; Ezek. 20:1-3, 31; 14:7-8)

An examination of the above outline reveals a God who is possessor of the many attributes of man. He may be regarded as a Being who knows and understands man's thoughts, feelings, and actions, and who is endowed with all the qualities one would hope to attain in his own quest for eventual perfection. God is man's pattern and model for growth.

God's Communication With Man:

The second of the major doctrines of the Old

SIX MAJOR DOCTRINES 81

Testament prophets deals with the manner in which God manifests His will to mortals. To comprehend the method of God's communication with man, one must fully understand the functions of God's servants, the prophets. The Old Testament gives a comprehensive view of the manner in which prophets serve as spokesmen and agents for the Lord. In addition, it becomes clear that prophets and other individuals received revelation for their personal needs through the Holy Ghost.

—The Prophetic Functions:

1. **Prophets are Spokesmen and Agents for God:** (1 Ki. 22:14, 28; 2 Ki. 3:11, 15; 17:13; 18:40; 21:10; 2 Chron. 18:13, 27; Jon. 1:2; 3:2; Hos. 12:10; 12:13; Is. 48:16; Jer. 1:7, 9, 17; 2:1; 3:15; 7:2; 11:2-3, 6; 19:1-2; 27:1-4; 22:1-2; 26:2; 7:25; 25:4, 13; 26:5; 28:9; Dan. 9:10)
2. **Prophets are Witnesses for God:** (2 Ki. 17:13; Amos 3:3-15; Neh. 9:30)
3. **Prophets are Writers and Compilers of Revelation:** (Hab. 2:2-3; Jer. 36:1-4, 27-32; 30:2; Dan. 7:1; 12:4, 9)
4. **God Reveals His Mysteries to the Prophets:** (Amos 3:7; Is. 45:11; Jer. 33:3; Dan. 2:18-19, 20-22, 28, 45; 5:12)
5. **Prophets are a Channel Through Which People May Inquire of the Lord:** (2 Ki. 3:11; Is. 45:11; Jer. 42:1-6; 21:2; 37:3; 37:17; 42:2; Ezek. 7:25-26)
6. **Prophets Must Speak the Lord's Will:** (1 Ki. 22:14; 2 Chron. 18:13; Amos 3:6-8; Jer. 1:7, 9, 17; 2:1; 7:2; 22:1-2; 26:2*; 15:16; 17:16; 29:9*; Ezek. 33:1-8; 2:4; 3:26-27*)
7. **God Chooses the Men Who are to be His Prophets:** (Amos 2:11; 7:14-15; Is. 6:8; Jer. 1:4-5; Ezek. 1, 2, 3)
8. **Prophets and Prophecies Should be Verified by the Spirit of Discernment:** (1 Ki. 13:11-32; 22:6-28; 2 Chron. 18:5-27; Is. 44:26)

9. **Fulfillment of His Prophecy is the Test of a Prophet:** (1 Ki. 22:28; 2 Chron. 18:27; Jer. 28:6-9)
10. **Prophets Receive Visions and Revelations from God:** (Hos. 12:10; Dan. 2, 7, 8, 10-12; Ezek. 1-3, 8, 9, 10; Neh. 9:13-14)

—The Nature of Revelation and Prophecy:

11. **Much Revelation is Received Through the Holy Spirit:** (1 Ki. 18:12; 19:12; 2 Ki. 2:9, 16; 2 Chron. 15:1; 20:14; 24:20; Is. 32:15; 44:3; 42:5; 11:2-3; 63:11, 14; 32:15; Ezek. 1:12, 20; 2:2; 3:12-14; 8:3; 11:1; 11:24; 11:4-5*; 37:1; Neh. 9:20; Hag. 1:14; 2:5; Joel 2:28-29; Zech. 4:6; 7:12)
12. **Prophecy Serves to Prove the Lord is God:** (Is. 46:9-11; 44:26; 48:3; 55:10-11; Hab. 2:2-3; Jer. 40:21; 42:9)
13. **The Lord Brings to Pass the Fulfillment of His Prophecies:** (2 Chron. 10:15; 36:21; 36:22-23; Is. 46:9-11; 44:26; 48:3; 55:10-11; Hab. 2:2-3; Jer. 25:13; 1:12; 25:13*; Lam. 2:17; Ezek. 33:30-33; 2:5; 5:13; 12:21-25*; Ezra 1:1; Neh. 9:8)
14. **Prophecy is Specific and Accurate and Receives Literal Fulfillment:** (2 Ki. 10:10; 17:23; 24:2; Examples: 1 Ki. 11:29-12:20; 14:1-18 & 15:25-30; 1 Ki. 13:1-10 & 2 Ki. 23:1-18; 1 Ki. 13:11-32; 13:1-13; 19:1-21 & 2 Ki. 8:13-29 & 9:15-10:30 & 13:14-25; 1 Ki. 21:17-29 & 2 Ki. 9:22-10:11; 2 Chron. 21:12-20; 1 Ki. 20:13-21; 20:28-30; 20:31-43 & 22:34-38; 2 Chron. 20:14-30; 2 Ki. 6:24-7:20; 8:7-29; 9:1-10 & 9:22-10:11; 21:1-16 & chapters 24, 25)
15. **Prophecy is Not Predestination. When Situations Change, the Outcome of Prophecy May Change:** (2 Chron. 12:2-12; 1 Ki. 22:6-38; 2 Chron. 18:5-27; 25:1-12; 2 Ki. 22:13-23:30; 2 Chron. 34:22-28; Jon. 3:5-10; 4:10-11; Amos 7:1-3; 7:4-6; Is. 38)
16. **Man's Life is Not Predestined. Man Himself Determines His Fate by Establishing in the Present a Cause-and-Effect Relationship With the Future. Prophecy Merely Pre-states What the Ultimate Effect of Present Actions Will Be:** (2 Chron. 16:7-10; 2 Ki. 1:1-4; 1 Ki. 20:31-43; 1 Ki. 22:6-28;

2 Chron. 18:5-27; 2 Ki. 5:1-19; 2 Ki. 6:24-7:20; 13:14-21; 2 Chron. 25:1-12; 25:15-28)

In addition to the information above, the student of this topic should examine the list of thirty-five lessons concerning the prophets and their calling in the summary to chapter six.

The Nature of Sin:

To understand the third basic doctrine of the Old Testament prophets, the nature of sin, one must understand the plans and purpose of a wise and loving God. A fundamental principle in God's master plan of creation is that man is to progress and strive for perfection. Indeed, the ultimate objective of mortal life is for man to attain the perfection of immortality and eternal life.

There are forces and influences which aid man in approaching his goal. There are also certain actions and influences which retard man in his progress toward exaltation. God has seen fit to reveal unto man many keys which will help him to progress toward perfection. As one of these keys He has indicated in detailed form the actions, attitudes, and thoughts which will retard man's progress toward his goal. When man does that which retards his progress, he does that which opposes God's plan. He does that which displeases God; he commits sin. Obstructions or hindrances to the progress of God's plan may be small or great, but they will always leave their mark upon man and those around him.

The nature of sin has remained constant. That which was wickedness in Old Testament times is still wickedness today. One of the most valuable contributions of the Old Testament is that it reveals to man the pitfalls which he should avoid. They are considered in this context as being divisible into five categories: 1. Perversion of religious truths and practices; 2. Apathy, lack of faith, and negative personal traits; 3. Rejection and opposition to God's plan; 4. Moral depravity, and 5. Social, economic and national wickedness.

—Perversion of Religious Truths and Practices:

1. **They Accept Corrupt Religious Leaders:** (Mic. 3:11; Zeph. 3:4)
2. **False Prophets and Precepts Lead People Astray:** (Mic. 3:5; Is. 29:13; 44:18, 20; Ezek. 13:2-4, 9, 22; 20:13, 16)
3. **Pagan Worship and Religious Harlotry is Practiced:** (Amos 4:4-5; Hos. 1:2; 4:13-19; 5:1-3; 6:10)
4. **They Practice Idolatry:** (1 Ki. 11:7-8, 33; 14:9; 2 Ki. 17:7-12, 16; 21:3-7; Amos 5:26; Hos. 8:4; 9:10; 11:2; 13:1-2; Mic. 1:7; Zeph. 1:4-5; Hab. 2:19; Jer. 1:16; 2:13; Ezek. 8:12-16; 16:17-19; 23:27; 33:25; Dan. 5:23; Zech. 10:2)
5. **The Pastors Transgress:** (Is. 43:27; Jer. 2:8; 10:21; 12:10-11; 23:1-2)
6. **The Religious Leaders Err:** (Zeph. 3:4; Jer. 2:8; 5:21; 7:9; 10:21; 12:10-11; 14:13-16; 20:6; 23:1-2, 11, 13, 16-17, 21-22, 25-40; 27:9-10, 14-18; 28:1-17; 29:8-9; Ezek. 13:2-4, 19; 22:26, 28; 34:2-4, 6, 8; Zech. 10:2; Mal. 2:8)
7. **Enchantments, Familiar Spirits, Wizards are Sought:** (2 Ki. 17:17; 21:6; 2 Chron. 33:6; Nahum 3:4)
8. **The False Clergy Corrupts and Labors for Money:** (Hos. 6:9; Mic. 3:11)
9. **They Offer Human Sacrifices:** 2 Ki. 16:3; 17:17; 21:6; 2 Chron. 28:2-4; 33:6; Jer. 7:21; 19:4-5; 32:35; Ezek. 16:20-21; 23:37)
10. **They Break the Sabbath:** (Ezek. 20:13, 16; 23:38)
11. **They Serve Other Gods:** (1 Ki. 11:4; 2 Ki. 17:7-8; Hab. 1:11; Jer. 1:16; 2:25-28; 7:9, 18-20; 13:10; 17:2; 18:15; 19:4-5; Ezek. 16:26-29)

—Apathy, Lack of Faith, and Negative Personal Traits:

12. **They Have Apathy:** (Amos 6:1; Zeph. 1:12; Mal. 1:13; 3:14)

13. **They Do Not Know God:** (Jer. 2:8; 4:22; 9:3)
14. **They Do Not Seek God:** (Hos. 7:10, 16; Zeph. 3:2; Jer. 2:8)
15. **They Do Not Trust God:** (Zeph. 3:2)
16. **They are Doubters:** (Is. 5:19)
17. **They Have No Knowledge; No Understanding:** (Amos 3:10; Hos. 4:1, 6, 14; Is. 1:3; 5:13; 44:19; Obad. 7; Jer. 4:22; 5:21; 9:23-24)
18. **They Have No Mercy:** (Hos. 4:1; Is. 47:6; Obad. 14)
19. **They are Not Valiant:** (1 Ki. 11:6; Jer. 9:3; Mal. 1:13)
20. **They Oppose Righteousness:** (2 Chron. 19:2; Amos 5:10; 6:12; Is. 5:23; Hab. 1:4; Jer. 11:21)
21. **They Have a Religion of Ritual Only:** (Amos 5:21-23; Hos. 7:14; Is. 1:10-14)
22. **They are Self-righteous and Self-justified:** (Is. 65:5; Jer. 7:10; Mal. 3:15)
23. **They Make Wrong Judgments:** (Amos 5:18-20; Mic. 3:11; Mal. 2:17; 3:15)

—**Rejection and Opposition To God's Plan:**

24. **They Commit Blasphemy:** (Is. 52:5; Ezek. 20:27)
25. **They Break God's Covenants and Laws:** (Hos. 6:7; 8:1; Is. 24:5; Jer. 11:10; 34:18; Ezek. 16:59)
26. **They Defile and Desecrate:** (Amos 2:8; Zeph. 3:4; Jer. 2:7; 3:9; 7:30; 32:34; Ezek. 5:11; 23:38; 28:18; 36:17)
27. **They are Disobedient:** (1 Ki. 11:10; 2 Chron. 33:10; Hos. 7:13; Is. 42:24; Jer. 3:25; 9:13; 44:23; Ezek. 3:7; 11:12; 20:13, 16; Dan. 9:6, 10; Zech. 1:4; Mal. 3:7, 8)
28. **They Have Forsaken God:** (1 Ki. 11:9, 33; 2 Ki. 17:9, 15, 16; 21:22; 2 Chron. 12:1; 29:6; Amos 4:6, 8, 9, 10, 11; Is. 1:4*; 5:24*; 17:10; 43:22; 66:4; Jer. 1:16; 2:5; 13*, 31, 32; 3:17, 21; 5:7, 19; 9:13; 13:25; 32:33)
29. **They are Headstrong and Stubborn:** (Is. 66:3*; Jer. 18:18; 19:15; 22:21; 32:33*; 37:2; 44:10, 16, 23; 48:26, 27; Ezek. 2:4*)

30. **Their Hearts are Not Right:** (1 Ki. 11:4; 2 Chron. 12:14; 20:33; 25:2)
31. **They are Irreverent:** (Amos. 2:8; Ezek. 36:23; Dan. 5:23; Mal. 2:11)
32. **They are Rebellious:** (2 Chron. 33:23; Hos. 7:14; Is. 1:2, 23; 3:8; 29:16; 65:2; Jer. 4:17; 8:6; 29:32; Ezek. 2:3; 5:6; 12:2; Dan. 5:22-23; 9:5; Zech. 7:11; Mal. 3:13)
33. **They Reject God and His Prophets:** (Amos 2:12; Mic. 2:6; Zeph. 1:6)
34. **They Scorn God's Servants:** (2 Chron. 13:9; 36:16; Zeph. 1:6)
35. **They Will Not Receive Correction:** (Amos 5:10; Is. 29:21; Zeph. 3:2; Jer. 5:3)

—**Moral Depravity:**

36. **They Commit Adultery:** (Amos 2:7; Hos. 4:2; 5:7; 7:4; Ezek. 23:37)
37. **They Eat Human Flesh:** (Jer. 19:9)
38. **They are Corrupters:** (Is. 1:4; Zeph. 3:7; Jer. 6:28; Mal. 2:8)
39. **They are Covetous:** (Mic. 2:2; Hab. 2:5, 9; Jer. 6:13; 22:17; Ezek. 33:31)
40. **They are Deceitful:** (2 Ki. 17:9; Is. 1:10-14; 5:20; 10:6; 29:15*; 47:10; 48:1; Jer. 5:27*; 6:13, 14; 7:9, 28; 8:5, 11; 9:3, 5, 6, 8*; 23:10, 14; 29:23; Ezek. 33:31)
41. **They are Drunken:** (Hos. 7:14; Is. 5:11, 22; Hab. 2:5, 15-16)
42. **They Make False Covenants:** (Hos. 10:4)
43. **They are Generally Evil:** (1 Ki. 21:20; 2 Ki. 17:17; Amos 5:7; Hos. 4:8; Mic. 2:1; 3:2; 7:2; Is. 1:4; 65:12; 66:4; Jer. 3:5; 6:10; 9:3, 5; 22:13, 17; 23:14; Ezek. 11:2)
44. **They Wear Improper Dress.** (Zeph. 1:8)
45. **They Lie:** (Hos. 4:2; 7:1; 11:12; Mic. 6:12; Nahum 3:1; Jer. 14:13-16; Ezek. 13:19; 22:28; 24:12)
46. **They are Morally Depraved:** (Nahum 3:4; Jer. 2:20; 3:1-6, 9; 5:8; 6:15; 8:11; 9:3; 13:27; 23:10, 14; 29:23; Ezek. 22:11; 33:26)

47. **They Commit Murder:** (2 Ki. 21:16; Hos. 4:2; 7:7; Is. 1:2; Jer. 4:31; 7:9; 22:17; Ezek. 7:23; 22:12)
48. **They Have Not Truth:** (Hos. 4:1)
49. **They Commit Robbery and Stealing:** (Amos 3:9-10; Hos. 4:2; 7:1; Nahum 3:1; Obad. 13; Jer. 7:9; Ezek. 22:29; Mal. 3:8)
50. **They are Shameless:** (Zeph. 3:5; Jer. 6:15; 8:11)
51. **They Spoil and Commit Violence:** (Hab. 1:3; 2:8, 10; Ezek. 7:23)
52. **They Swear:** (Hos. 4:2)

—**Social, Economic, and National Wickedness**

53. **They Betray Trust:** (Mic. 7:2, 5-6)
54. **They Give and Accept Bribes:** (Amos 5:12; Mic. 3:11; 7:3-4; Is. 1:23; Ezek. 22:12)
55. **They Employ Dishonest Business Practices:** (Amos 8:6; Mic. 6:11; Ezek. 22:12)
56. **They Follow Unwise Counsel:** (1 Ki. 12:8, 13-14; 2 Chron. 10:8; 22:3)
57. **They are Unpatriotic:** (Amos 6:6)
58. **They Live Luxuriously:** (Amos 3:15; 6:4-6)
59. **They Oppress the Poor and Just:** (Amos 2:6, 7; 4:1; 5:11, 12; 8:4, 6; Mic. 2:2, 9; 3:2-3; Is. 1:23; 3:15; 5:8; 10:2; Hab. 3:14; Ezek. 16:49; 22:29)
60. **They Pervert Justice:** (Is. 5:23; 10:2; 29:21; Hab. 1:4; Jer. 5:28; Ezek. 5:6)
61. **The Political Leaders Err:** (Jer. 2:8; 5:28; Ezek. 22:27; 28:2-6)
62. **They Practice Slavery:** (Jer. 34:11-16)
63. **They Have Undeserved Pride:** (Obad. 3, 12; Jer. 48:29; 49:16; Ezek. 16:49; 28:2-6, 17)
64. **They Practice Racial Intermarriage:** (Hos. 7:8-9; Mal. 2:11)
65. **They Rule Unrighteously:** (Is. 3:12; 10:1; Ezek. 34:4)
66. **They Set Up Kings Without Divine Approval:** (Hos. 8:4)
67. **They Slander:** (Jer. 6:28)
68. **They Seek Foreign Alliances Instead of Relying Upon God:** (Hos. 5:13; 7:11; 8:9-10; 9:3; 12:1; Is. 8:9-12)

69. **They Cause Strife and Contention:** (Hab. 1:3)
70. **They Practice Treachery:** (Is. 24:16; Jer. 3:20; 5:11, 26, 27; 6:13; 9:8; Mal. 2:10)
71. **They are Vain:** (Is. 5:18, 21; 10:13; 47:10; Zech. 10:2)
72. **They are Worldly Minded:** (Is. 3:16; 5:12; 47:8; Jer. 13:10; 48:7; Ezek. 16:15)

Each of the above items is regarded as sin in the scriptures. Each of them was displeasing in the eyes of God. Each of them will similarly retard man's progress and be displeasing to God if practiced today.

The Nature of Man's Agency and God's Judgment:

A fourth major doctrinal area of the Old Testament prophets concerns man's agency in relationship to God's eternal plan. The message of the Old Testament is that man has a sizeable degree of free agency. It appears, however, that God still maintains ultimate control of the fate of man, both individually and collectively. Man is given the freedom to choose his course in most situations, but God sometimes controls the choices which are available to him. Man has the agency to control his own relationship with God through obedience or disobedience to divine commandments. Thus he partially controls his fate. Actions and attitudes have a result, and God reveals Himself as the controller of future outcomes which are predicated on man's past and present activities and attitudes. The relationship between God and man appears to be very similar to that of a mortal parent with his young children. The parent gives the children choices and responsibilities to help them grow, but controls the limits, scope, and nature of their activities. In this way the activities function in the best interests of the children and operate in conformity with parental plans and objectives.

Divine reward and punishment is just. Many rewards or punishments, however, come as the direct result of righteousness or sin, and are not sent from God.

1. **Man is a Free Agent and Makes His Choices:** (2 Chron. 13:12; 15:2*; 24:20; Amos 5:1-9; Is. 1:18-20; Jer. 21:8*; Lam. 3:27-41; Mal. 2:2)
2. **Man's Life is Not Predestined. Man Himself Determines His Fate By Establishing in the Present a Cause-and-Effect Relationship With the Future. Prophecy Merely Pre-states What the Ultimate Effect of Present Actions Will Be:** (2 Chron. 16:7-10; 2 Ki. 1:1-4; 1 Ki. 20:21-43; 1 Ki. 22:6-28; 2 Chron. 18:5-27; 2 Ki. 5:1-19; 2 Ki. 6:24-7:20; 13:14-21; 2 Chron. 25:1-12; 25:15-28)
3. **Man's Attitude Toward God Influences God's Attitude Toward Man:** (2 Chron. 24:20; Hos. 4:6; Zech. 1:3, 15; 7:12, 13)
4. **God Tests Man:** (2 Chron. 32:31; Is. 48:10; Zech. 13:9)
5. **God Knows Man's Thoughts and Acts:** (2 Ki. 19:27; 2 Chron. 16:9*; Jon. 1:2; 3:10; Amos 4:13; 5:12*; 8:7; 9:8; Mic. 1:2; Is. 37:28*; 66:18; Nahum 1:7; Jer. 2:1, 34; 5:3; 12:3; 16:17*; 17:10; 21:10; 23:24; 29:23; 32:19*; Zech. 4:10)
6. **God Both Rewards and Punishes:** (2 Ki. 17:25; 21:14; 2 Chron. 13:12; Amos 9:2, 3, 4; Hos. 4:9*; 14:9; Is. 3:10; 13:11*; 48:22; 64:4; Nahum 1:3; Jer. 25:14; 32:19*; Lam. 1:5; 2:2; 3:64; Ezek. 3:18-21; 7:2, 4, 27; 11:21; 14:23; 18:21-29; 22:31; 24:14; 33:12-20; 44:12-13; Zech. 1:6)
7. **Man is Judged for His Own Deeds:** (Is. 3:10; 5:15; 13:11*; Jer. 2:19; 17:10; 21:14; 25:14; 31:30; 48:10; Ezek. 18:20*; Zech. 1:6)
8. **Punishment is the Result of Sin:** (2 Ki. 17:25; 2 Chron. 21:14; 36:16; Is. 3:10; 13:11; 3:9-11; Jer. 2:19; 5:25; 14:7; 17:11; 20:4; 23:36)
9. **Punishment May Be Avoided or Softened Through Repentance:** (2 Chron. 12:7*, 12; 19:2-11; 32:26; 33:11-13; 34:27-28; 1 Ki. 21:17-29; Jer. 18:7-10; 26:13; 31:34; 33:8; Ezek. 18:20-22*; 33:8-20)

10. **Punishment is Certain in the Absence of Repentance:** (Is. 50:1; Jer. 1:16; 2:22; 4:12; 5:3, 4; 6:19; 14:10, 16; 15:7; 16:18-21; 17:18; 22:22; 44:29; 51:56; Ezek. 7:27; 11:21; 14:23; 22:31; 24:14; 44:12-13; Zech. 1:6)

11. **God Withdraws His Spirit From the Wicked:** (Mic. 3:6-7; Is. 54:7-8; 60:10; 63:10; 64:7; Jer. 7:16; 11:14; 14:11; 15:1; Ezek. 14:7-11; 20:1-3, 31; Mal. 1:10)

12. **Kinds of Punishment Specified by the Old Testament Prophets:**

    A. **Captivity:** (Amos 5:5, 27; 7:11; Mic. 4:8-10)
    B. **Chastisement:** (Hos. 7:12; 8:7; 9:6; 10:8; Mic. 6:16)
    C. **Death (various circumstances):** (Amos 6:9-10; 7:17; 8:3, 14; Hos. 10:14)
    D. **Destruction, desolation, loss of lands:** (Amos 1:2; 3:11, 14, 15; 5:5; 6:10; 7:9, 17; 9:8; Hos. 4:5-6, 14; 5:9; 8:14; 9:2, 12; 10:8; Mic. 1:6, 7; 3:12; 6:16; Is. 1:7; 7:23-25; 8:4)
    E. **Elements to be Disturbed:** (Amos 8:9; 9:5)
    F. **Famine and Starvation:** (Amos 4:6; Hos. 4:10; 8:7; 9:2; Mic. 6:14)
    G. **Glory To Diminish:** (Hos. 9:11)
    H. **Lord's Name is Forbidden:** (Amos 6:10)
    I. **Nation Shall Fall:** (Hos. 1:4, 5; 10:15; Is. 7:8)
    J. **Nations Shall Afflict:** (Amos 6:14)
    K. **No Increase:** (Hos. 4:10; 9:14, 16)
    L. **Removal and Scattering:** (Amos 3:12; 4:2; 5:2-3; 9:9; Hos. 1:6; 8:3; 9:3, 17; Is. 3:1-3)
    M. **Shame:** (Hos. 4:7, 19; 10:6)
    N. **Sickness:** (Mic. 6:13)
    O. **Sorrow and Mourning:** (Amos 1:2; 5:16-17; 8:3, 10; Hos. 2:11; 4:3; 8:10)
    P. **Thirst:** (Amos 8:13; Hos. 2:3)
    Q. **Uncertain Crops:** (Amos 4:7-10; Hos. 2:12; 8:7; Mic. 6:15; Hag. 1:10)
    R. **War:** (Amos 7:9, 11, 17; Hos. 7:16; 8:3; 11:6; Mic. 5:1; 6:14; Is. 3:25; 7:20; 8:7-8; 10:5-6)
    S. **Weakness:** (Amos 2:14-16)
    T. **Withdrawal of God:** (Amos 8:2, 11-12; Hos.

SIX MAJOR DOCTRINES 91

>   4:6; 5:6, 15; 9:15; Mic. 2:6; 3:4, 6-7; Is. 1:15; Ezek.
>   20:1-3, 31; Mal. 1:10)
>   U. **Other Chastisements:** (Amos 9:1-4; 7:17; Is.
>   1:5; 3:4, 17-24; Hag. 2:17; Mal. 2:2)
> 13. **God Controls the Actions and Fate of Individuals:**
>   (1 Ki. 11:14, 31, 34*, 36; 12:15; 20:42; 22:20-23;
>   2 Ki. 3:10*; 9:7; 10:30; 15:5, 12; 19:7; 24:20; 2
>   Chron. 10:15; 11:4; 13:20; 15:6-7; 16:7, 8; 18:31;
>   21:18; 25:16, 20; 26:16-20; 28:19; 33:11; 36:22;
>   Mic. 7:8-9; Is. 29:10; 63:17; Ezek. 24:16-18; Ezra
>   7:6; Dan. 1:9, 17; 2:37; 4:17, 25, 32; Zech. 8:10)
> 14. **God Controls the Actions and Fate of Nations:** (1
>   Ki. 12:24; 14:14; 20:13, 28; 2 Ki. 3:18; 8:19; 10:32;
>   13:5; 15:37*; 17:20*; 19:34; 21:14; 24:2*, 3*; 2
>   Chron. 13:15-16*; 20:6-7, 27; 24:24*; 29:8; 30:12;
>   32:21; 36:17; Mic. 1:6; Is. 3:1-3; 7:20; Obad. 2, 4, 8;
>   Jer. 5:15-17; 6:8; 7:3-7; 12:12, 17; 14:12; 15:4;
>   19:7; 20:5; 21:4-6, 7*; 25:9, 12; 27:8; 22:7; 32:3;
>   46:26; Ezek. 20:18-26; 29:19; 30:23-24; 38:16;
>   39:1-2; Dan. 1:1-2; 2:21)

Counsel for Righteous Living:

The fifth of the major doctrines of the Old Testament prophets is a treatment of God's program to aid man in living righteously. Throughout the scriptures one encounters a continual series of precepts and examples which can guide man in his search for perfection. They are immediately applicable to man in his present circumstances and form the basis for righteous living. The prophetic section of the Old Testament is especially rich in such counsel and example.

Because of their applicability and importance for modern Christian living, the passages are given in summary form as a convenience to the reader:

> 1. **Accept Counsel:**
>   A. Take counsel, execute judgment. (Is. 16:3)
> 2. **Aid the Afflicted and Oppressed, Help Others:**
>   A. If thou wilt be a servant unto this people, and wilt serve them and answer them, and speak

good words to them, then they will be thy servants forever. (1 Ki. 12:7)

   B. Learn to do well; seek judgment, relieve the oppressed, judge the fatherless, plead for the widow. (Is. 1:17)

   C. Comfort ye my people, saith your God. (Is. 40:1)

   D. The Lord hath given me the tongue of the learned, that I should know how to speak a word in season to him that is weary. (Is. 50:4)

   E. Execute judgment in the morning, and deliver him that is spoiled out of the hand of the oppressor. (Jer. 21:12; 22:3)

   F. Execute true judgment, and show mercy and compassions every man to his brother: and oppress not the widow, nor the fatherless, the stranger, nor the poor; and let none of you imagine evil against his brother in your heart. (Zech. 7:9-10)

3. **Avoid Evil:**

   A. They that observe lying vanities forsake their own mercy. (Jon. 2:8)

   B. Hate the evil and love the good, and establish judgment in the gate. (Amos 5:15)

   C. Whoredom and wine and new wine take away the heart. (Hos. 4:11)

   D. Nehemiah avoids a compromising situation in which he could be accused of sin. (Neh. 6:1-13)

4. **Be Courageous and Strong:**

   A. Be ye strong therefore, and let not your hands be weak: for your work shall be rewarded. (2 Chron. 15:7)

   B. Deal courageously, and the Lord shall be with the good. (2 Chron. 19:11)

   C. He became mighty, because he prepared his ways before the Lord his God. (2 Chron. 27:6)

   D. Be strong and courageous, be not afraid nor dismayed; with him is an arm of flesh; but with us is the Lord our God to help us; and to fight our battles. (2 Chron. 32:7-8)

   E. I am full of power by the spirit of the Lord, and of judgment and of might to declare the sins of Jacob and Israel. (Mic. 3:8)

F. Take heed, and be quiet; fear not, neither be fainthearted . . . (Is. 7:4)

G. Let him take hold of my strength, that he may make peace with me; and he shall make peace with me. (Is. 27:5)

H. Strengthen ye the weak hands, and confirm the feeble knees. Say to them that are of a fearful heart, Be strong, fear not. (Is. 35:3-4)

I. Lift up thy voice with strength; lift it up, be not afraid. (Is. 40:9)

J. They that waiteth upon the Lord shall renew their strength; they shall run, and not be weary; and they shall walk, and not faint. (Is. 40:31)

K. Fear not, for I am with thee: be not dismayed; for I am thy God: I will strengthen thee and help thee and uphold thee with the right hand of my righteousness. (Is. 41:10, 13)

L. My God shall be my strength. (Is. 49:5)

M. The Lord God is my strength. (Hab. 3:19)

N. I was strengthened as the hand of the Lord my God was upon me. (Ezra 7:28)

O. Remember the Lord, and fight for your brethren, your sons, and your daughters, your wives and your houses. (Neh. 4:14)

P. Be strong, all ye people of the land, saith the Lord, and work: for I am with you. (Hag. 2:4)

Q. Fear not, but let your hands be strong. (Zech. 8:13)

5. **Be Diligent:**

A. My sons, be not now negligent: for the Lord hath chosen you to stand before him, to serve him, that ye should minister unto him . . . (2 Chron. 29:11)

B. In every work that he began in the service of the house of God, and in the law, and in the commandments, to seek his God, he did it with all his heart, and prospered. (2 Chron. 31:21)

6. **Be Humble:**

A. Because thine heart was tender, and thou hast humbled thyself before the Lord, I have heard thee. (2 Ki. 22:19)

B. They humbled themselves; and they said, the Lord is righteous. (2 Chron. 12:6)

C. When he was in affliction, he besought the Lord his God, and humbled himself greatly before the God of his fathers. (2 Chron. 33:12)

D. Be ye not stiffnecked, as your fathers were, but yield yourselves unto the Lord, and enter into his sanctuary, which he hath sanctified forever: and serve the Lord, your God, that the fierceness of his wrath may turn away from you. (2 Chron. 30:8)

E. Because thine heart was tender, and thou didst humble thyself before God, I have heard thee, saith the Lord. (2 Chron. 34:27)

F. What doth the Lord require of thee but to do justly, and to love mercy, and to walk humbly with thy God? (Mic. 6:6-8)

G. The meek shall increase their joy in the Lord. (Is. 29:19)

H. To this man will I look, even to him that is poor and of a contrite spirit, and trembleth at my word. (Is. 66:2)

I. Seek ye the Lord, seek righteousness, seek meekness. (Zeph. 2:3)

J. Seekest thou great things for thyself? seek them not. (Jer. 45:5)

K. My soul remembers my afflictions and is humbled in me. This I recall to my mind. Therefore I have hope. (Lam. 3:20-21)

7. **Covenant:**

A. They made a covenant between the Lord and the king and the people, that they should be the Lord's people. (2 Ki. 11:17)

B. He made a covenant before the Lord to walk after the Lord, and to keep his commandments and his testimonies and his statutes with all their heart and all their soul, to perform the words of this covenant that were written in this book (of scripture). (2 Ki. 23:3)

C. They entered into a covenant to seek the Lord God of their fathers with all their heart and with all their soul; that whosoever would not seek the Lord God of Israel should be put to death. (2 Chron. 15:12-13)

D. They rejoiced at the oath, for they had sworn with all their heart, and sought God with their whole desire; and he was found of them, and the Lord gave them rest round about. (2 Chron. 15:15)

E. Now it is in mine heart to make a covenant with the Lord God of Israel, that his fierce wrath may turn away from us. (2 Chron. 29:10)

F. The king made a covenant before the Lord, to walk after the Lord, and to keep his commandments, and his testimonies, and his statutes, with all his heart, and with all his soul, to perform the words of the covenant which are written in this book (of scriptures). (2 Chron. 34:31)

G. I will pay that that I have vowed. (Jon. 2:9)

H. Come let us join ourselves to the Lord in a perpetual covenant that shall not be forgotten. (Jer. 50:5)

I. Let us make a covenant with our God according to the counsel of my Lord and of those that tremble at the commandment of our God; and let it be done according to the law. (Ezra 10:3)

J. We make a sure covenant. (Neh. 9:38)

K. The covenant of righteousness is explained. (Neh. 10:29-39)

L. My covenant was with him of life and peace; and I gave them to him for the fear wherewith he feared me, and was afraid before my name. (Mal. 2:4-5)

8. **Do What Is Right:**

A. If thou wilt hearken unto all that I command thee, and wilt walk in my ways, and do that is right in my sight, to keep my statutes and commandments, I will be with thee, and build thee a sure house. (1 Ki. 11:38)

B. He did that which was right in the eyes of the Lord, and turned not aside from anything that he commanded him. (1 Ki. 15:5)

C. They dealt faithfully. (2 Ki. 12:15)

D. I beseech thee, O Lord, remember now how I have walked before thee in truth and with a perfect heart, and have done that which is good in thy sight. (2 Ki. 20:3)

E. They dealt faithfully. (2 Ki. 22:7)

F. Take heed what ye do: for ye judge not for man, but for the Lord, who is with you in the judgment. Wherefore now let the fear of the Lord be upon you, take heed and do it: for there is no iniquity with the Lord our God, nor respect of persons, nor taking of gifts (bribes). (2 Chron. 19:7)

G. He wrought that which was good and right and truth before the Lord his God. (2 Chron. 31:20)

H. I will pay that that I have vowed. (Jon. 2:9)

I. Hate the evil, and love the good, and establish judgment in the gate. (Amos 5:15)

J. Let judgment run down as waters, and righteousness as a mighty stream. (Amos 5:24)

K. Sow to yourselves in righteousness, reap in mercy: for it is time to seek the Lord. (Hos. 10:12)

L. The ways of the Lord are right, and the just shall walk in them; but the transgressors shall fall therein. (Hos. 14:9)

M. Is the spirit of the Lord straitened? Do not God's words do good to him that walketh uprightly? (Mic. 2:7)

N. What doth the Lord require of thee but to do justly, and to love mercy, and to walk humbly with thy God? (Mic. 6:6-8)

O. (Hezekiah's prayer) Remember now, O Lord, I beseech thee, how I have walked before thee in truth and with a perfect heart, and have done that which is good in thy sight. (Is. 38:3)

P. All ye that kindle a fire, that compass yourselves about with sparks: walk in the light of the fire, and in the sparks that ye have kindled. (Is. 50:11)

Q. In righteousness shalt thou be established. (Is. 54:14)

R. This is the heritage of the servants of the Lord, and their righteousness is of me, saith the Lord. (Is. 54:17)

S. May ye also do good, that are accustomed to do evil. (Jer. 13:23)

T. A man that is just, and does that which is lawful and right . . . He is just, he shall surely live, saith the Lord God. (Ezek. 18:5-9)

U. Remove violence and spoil, and execute judgment and justice, take away your exactions from my people, saith the Lord God. (Ezek. 45:9)

V. Ye shall have just balances. (Ezek. 45:10)

W. The people put away usury. (Neh. 5:1-13)

X. Speak ye every man the truth to his neighbour; execute the judgment of truth and peace in your gates: and let none of you imagine evil in your hearts against his neighbour; and love no false oath. (Zech. 8:16-17)

Y. The law of truth was in his mouth, and iniquity was not found in his lips: he walked with me in peace and equity, and did turn many away from iniquity. (Mal. 2:6)

Z. With righteousness shall he judge the poor, and reprove with equity for the meek of the earth. (Is. 11:4)

AA. Righteousness shall be the girdle of his loins, and faithfulness the girdle of his reins. (Is. 11:5)

BB. The way of the just is uprightness: thou, most upright, dost weigh the path of the just. (Is. 26:7)

CC. The work of righteousness shall be peace; and the effect of righteousness quietness and assurance for ever. (Is. 32:17)

DD. Who shall dwell with everlasting burnings? He that walketh righteously, and speaketh uprightly; he that despiseth the gain of oppressions; that shaketh his hands from holding of bribes, that stoppeth his ears from hearing of blood, and shutteth his eyes from seeing evil, he shall dwell on high. (Is. 33:14-16)

9. **Fast:**

A. Then I proclaimed a fast . . . that we might afflict ourselves before our God, to seek of him a right way for us, and for our little ones, and for all our substance. (Ezra 8:21)

B. The fasting of the Jews to seek divine aid. (Esther 4:3, 16)

C. A description of a day of fasting and worship. (Neh. 9:1-38)

D. When ye fasted and mourned, did ye at all fast unto me, even to me? (Zech. 7:5)

E. Sanctify ye a fast, call a solemn assembly, gather the elders and all the inhabitants of the land into the house of the Lord and cry unto the Lord. (Joel 1:14)

F. Sanctify a fast, call a solemn assembly: gather the people, sanctify the congregations. (Joel 2:15-16)

10. **Fear and Acknowledge God:**

　　A. Thy servant did fear the Lord. (2 Ki. 4:1)

　　B. The Lord: him shall ye fear, and him shall ye worship, and to him shall ye do sacrifice. (2 Ki. 17:36)

　　C. The Lord your God ye shall fear; and he shall deliver you out of the hand of all your enemies. (2 Ki. 17:39)

　　D. As for us, the Lord is our God, and we have not forsaken him. (2 Chron. 13:10)

　　E. They came to him out of Israel in abundance, when they saw that the Lord his God was with him. (2 Chron. 15:9)

　　F. Take heed what ye do: for ye judge not for man, but for the Lord, who is with you in the judgment. Wherefore now let the fear of the Lord be upon you, take heed and do it: for there is not iniquity with the Lord our God, nor respect of persons, nor taking of gifts. (2 Chron. 19:6-7)

　　G. Thus shall ye do in the fear of the Lord. faithfully, and with a perfect heart. (2 Chron. 19:9)

　　H. I fear the Lord, the God of heaven, which hath made the sea and the dry land. (Jon. 1:9)

　　I. I will not ask, neither will I tempt the Lord. (Is. 7:12)

　　J. It is a small thing for you to weary men, but will ye weary my God also? (Is. 7:13)

　　K. Sanctify the Lord of hosts himself; and let him be your fear, and let him be your dread, and he shall be for a sanctuary. (Is. 8:13-14)

　　L. Shall the axe boast itself against him that heweth therewith? (Is. 10:15)

M. They shall sanctify my name, and sanctify the Holy One of Jacob, and shall fear the God of Israel. (Is. 29:23)

N. Wisdom and knowledge shall be the stability of thy times, and strength of salvation: the fear of the Lord is his treasure. (Is. 33:6)

O. Hear, ye that are far off, what I have done; and, ye that are near, acknowledge my might. (Is. 33:13)

P. Woe unto him that striveth with his maker! Shall the clay say to him that fashioneth it, What makest thou? or thy work, He hath no hands? (Is. 45:9-10)

Q. Who is among you that feareth the Lord, that obeyeth the voice of his servant, that walketh in darkness, and hath no light? let him trust in the name of the Lord, and stay upon his God. (Is. 50:10)

R. Hold thy peace at the presence of the Lord God. (Zeph. 1:7)

S. The Lord is in his holy temple: let all the earth keep silence before him. (Hab. 2:20)

T. It is an evil thing and bitter, that thou hast forsaken the Lord thy God, and that His fear is not in thee. (Jer. 2:19)

U. Thou shalt swear, The Lord liveth, in truth, in judgment, and in righteousness. (Jer. 4:2)

V. Ought ye not to walk in the fear of our God because of the reproach of our enemies? (Neh. 5:9)

W. He was a faithful man, and feared God above many. (Neh. 7:2)

X. Be silent, O all flesh, before the Lord: for He is raised up out of His holy habitation. (Zech. 2:13)

11. **Gain Knowledge:**

    A. The word of the Lord is with him. (2 Ki. 3:12)

    B. He had understanding in the visions of God. (2 Chron. 26:5)

    C. Learn to do well; seek judgment, relieve the oppressed, judge the fatherless, plead for the widow. (Is. 1:17)

    D. Come now, and let us reason together, saith the Lord. (Is. 1:18)

E. He will teach us of his ways, and we will walk in his paths. (Is. 2:3)

F. Bind up the testimony, seal the law among my disciples. (Is. 8:16)

G. To the law and to the testimony: if they speak not according to this word, it is because there is no light in them. (Is. 8:20)

H. They that erred in spirit shall come to understanding, and they that murmured shall learn doctrine. (Is. 29:24)

I. Wisdom and knowledge shall be the stability of thy times, and strength of salvation: the fear of the Lord is his treasure. (Is. 33:6)

J. Seek ye out of the book of the Lord, and read. (Is. 34:16)

K. The Lord God hath given me the tongue of the learned, that I should know how to speak a word in season to him that is weary. (Is. 50:4)

L. That which they had not heard shall they consider. (Is. 52:15)

M. Be thou instructed . . . lest my soul depart from thee. (Jer. 6:8)

N. Amend your ways and your doings . . . (Jer. 7:3)

O. Amend your ways, execute judgment, oppress not, shed not innocent blood, do not walk after other gods. (Jer. 7:5-6)

P. If they will diligently learn the ways of my people, to swear by my name, the Lord liveth; then shall they be built in the midst of my people. (Jer. 12:16)

Q. After I was turned, I repented; and after that I was instructed. I was ashamed because I did bear the reproach of my youth. (Jer. 31:19)

R. Will ye not receive instruction to hearken to my words? (Jer. 35:13)

S. All my words that I shall speak unto thee receive in thine heart, and hear with thine ears. (Ezek. 3:10)

T. Hear the word of the Lord God. (Ezek. 6:3)

U. Ye shall know that I am the Lord. (Ezek. 6:7)

V. They shall know that I am the Lord, and that I have not said in vain. (Ezek. 6:10)

W. We make prayer before the Lord our God, that we might turn from our iniquities, and understand thy truth. (Dan. 9:13)

X. The ears of all the people were attentive unto the book of the law. (Neh. 8:3)

Y. They caused the people to understand the law. (Neh. 8:7-8)

Z. Should ye not hear the words which the Lord hath cried by the former prophets? (Zech. 7:7)

12. **Give Glory to God:**

    A. Praise the beauty of holiness. Praise the Lord; for his mercy endureth forever. (2 Chron. 20:21)

    B. Make offerings unto the Lord with rejoicing and singing. (2 Chron. 23:18)

    C. With joy shall ye draw water out of the wells of salvation. (Is. 12:3)

    D. Praise the Lord, call upon his name, declare his doings among the people, make mention that his name is exalted. (Is. 12:4)

    E. Sing unto the Lord; for he hath done excellent things. (Is. 12:5)

    F. O Lord, thou art my God, I will exalt thee, I will praise thy name. (Is. 25:1)

    G. Sing unto the Lord a new song, and his praise from the end of the earth. (Is. 42:10-12)

    H. I will greatly rejoice in the Lord, my soul shall be joyful in my God; for he hath clothed me with the garments of salvation, he hath covered me with the robe of righteousness. (Is. 61:10)

    I. Be ye glad and rejoice for ever in that which the Lord creates. (Is. 65:18)

    J. I will rejoice in the Lord, I will joy in the God of my salvation. (Hab. 3:18)

    K. Give glory to the Lord your God, before he cause darkness, and before your feet stumble. (Jer. 13:16)

    L. Their heart shall rejoice in the Lord. (Zech. 10:7)

13. **Have Faith:**

    A. The children of Judah prevailed, because they relied upon the Lord God of their fathers. (2 Chron. 13:18)

B. Help us, O Lord our God; for we rest on thee, and in thy name we go against this multitude. (2 Chron. 14:11)

C. Fear not, nor be dismayed, for the Lord will be with you. (2 Chron. 20:17)

D. Believe in the Lord your God, so shall ye be established; believe his prophets, so shall ye prosper. (2 Chron. 20:20)

E. Take heed, and be quiet, fear not, neither be fainthearted . . . (Is. 7:4)

F. If ye will not believe, surely ye shall not be established. (Is. 7:9)

G. I will not ask, neither will I tempt the Lord. (Is. 7:12)

H. Behold, God is my salvation; I will trust and not be afraid: for the Lord Jehovah is my strength and my song; he also is become my salvation. (Is. 12:2)

I. The Lord hath founded Zion, and the poor of his people shall trust in it. (Is. 14:32)

J. Thou wilt keep him in perfect peace, whose mind is stayed on thee: because he trusteth in thee. (Is. 26:3)

K. Trust ye in the Lord for ever: for in the Lord Jehovah is everlasting strength. (Is. 26:4)

L. Good is the word of the Lord which thou hast spoken. For there shall be peace and truth in my days. (Is. 39:8)

M. My God shall be my strength. (Is. 49:5)

N. Who is among you that feareth the Lord, that obeyeth the voice of his servant, that walketh in darkness, and hath no light? let him trust in the name of the Lord, and stay upon his God. (Is. 50:10)

O. Therefore wait ye upon me, saith the Lord, until the day that I rise up to the prey. (Zeph. 3:8)

P. The just shall live by faith. (Hab. 2:4)

Q. Cursed be the man that trusteth in man, and whose heart departeth from the Lord. (Jer. 17:5)

R. Blessed is the man that trusteth in the Lord, and whose hope the Lord is. (Jer. 17:7-8)

S. Thy God whom thou servest continually, he will deliver thee. (Dan. 6:16)

Six Major Doctrines

14. **Have Mercy:**

    A. For I desired mercy and not sacrifice, and the knowledge of God more than burnt offerings. (Hos. 6:6)

    B. Sow to yourselves in righteousness, reap in mercy: for it is time to seek the Lord. (Hos. 10:12)

    C. Turn thou to thy God: keep mercy and judgment, and wait on thy God continually. (Hos. 12:6)

    D. What doth the Lord require of thee but to do justly, and to love mercy, and to walk humbly with thy God? (Mic. 6:6-8)

    E. Break off thy sins by righteousness, and thine iniquities by showing mercy to the poor, if it may be a lengthening of thy tranquility. (Dan. 4:27)

    F. Execute true judgment, and show mercy and compassions every man to his brother: and oppress not the widow, nor the fatherless, the stranger, nor the poor; and let none of you imagine evil against his brother in your heart. (Zech. 7:9-10)

15. **Hope:**

    A. Be not a terror unto me: thou art my hope in the day of evil. (Jer. 17:17-18)

    B. My soul remembers my afflictions and is humbled in me. This I recall to my mind. Therefore I have hope. (Lam. 3:20-21)

    C. The Lord is my portion, saith my soul; therefore will I hope in him. (Lam. 3:24)

    D. The Lord is good unto them that wait for him, to the soul that seeketh him. (Lam. 3:25)

    E. It is good that a man should both hope and quietly wait for the salvation of the Lord. (Lam. 3:26)

16. **Keep Records:**

    A. A genealogy was kept. (2 Chron. 31:16-19)

    B. A book of remembrance was written before him for them that feared the Lord. (Mal. 3:16)

17. **Keep the Sabbath:**

    A. Hallow the Sabbath day. (Jer. 17:21-24)

    B. I gave them my sabbaths, to be a sign between me and them, that they might know that I am the Lord that sanctify them. (Ezek. 20:12)

C. Hallow my sabbaths; and they shall be a sign between me and you, that ye may know that I am the Lord your God. (Ezek. 20:20)

D. They shall keep my laws and my statutes in all mine assemblies; and they shall hallow my sabbaths. (Ezek. 44:24)

E. They should cleanse themselves and should come and keep the gates, to sanctify the sabbath day. (Neh. 13:15-22)

18. **Learn of God and Seek Him:**

A. He turned to the Lord with all his heart, and with all his soul, and with all his might, according to all the Law . . . (2 Ki. 23:25)

B. He commanded his people to seek the Lord God of their fathers, and to do the law and the commandment. (2 Chron. 14:4)

C. We have sought the Lord our God and he hath given us rest on every side. So they built and prospered. (2 Chron. 14:7)

D. The Lord is with you while ye be with him; and if ye seek him, he will be found of you; but if ye forsake him, he will forsake you. (2 Chron. 15:2)

E. Our eyes are upon thee. (2 Chron. 20:12)

F. All Judah stood before the Lord, with their little ones, their wives, and their children. (2 Chron. 20:13)

G. He sought the Lord with all his heart. (2 Chron. 22:9)

H. As long as he sought the Lord, God made him to prosper. (2 Chron. 26:5)

I. The good Lord pardon everyone that prepareth his heart to seek God, the Lord God of his fathers. (2 Chron. 30:19)

J. While he was yet young he began to seek after the God of David. (2 Chron. 34:3)

K. Seek the Lord and ye shall live. (Amos 5:4-5)

L. For I desired mercy and not sacrifice; and the knowledge of God more than burnt offerings. (Hos. 6:6)

M. Sow to yourselves in righteousness, reap in mercy: for it is time to seek the Lord, till he come and rain righteousness upon you. (Hos. 10:12)

N. Is the spirit of the Lord straitened? Do not God's words do good to him that walketh uprightly? (Mic. 2:7)

O. Search the past doings of God (examples given) that ye may know the righteousness of the Lord. (Mic. 6:3-5)

P. I will look unto the Lord; my God will hear me. (Mic. 7:7)

Q. He will teach us of his ways, and we will walk in his paths. (Is. 2:3)

R. I will wait upon the Lord, and I will look for him. (Is. 8:17)

S. Should not a people seek unto their God? for the living to the dead? (Is. 8:19)

T. The desire of our soul is to thy name, and to the remembrance of thee. (Is. 26:8)

U. With my soul have I desired thee in the night; yea, with my spirit within me will I seek thee early. (Is. 26:9)

V. Ye are my witnesses, saith the Lord, and my servant whom I have chosen that ye may know and believe me and understand that I am he. (Is. 43:10; 44:8)

W. Surely, shall one say, in the Lord have I righteousness and strength: even to him shall men come. (Is. 45:24)

X. Thou shalt know that I am the Lord: for they shall not be ashamed that wait for me. (Is. 49:23)

Y. Hearken to me, ye that follow after righteousness, ye that seek the Lord. (Is. 51:1)

Z. Hearken unto me, my people; and give ear unto me, O my nation. (Is. 51:4)

AA. Wherefore do ye spend money for that which is not bread? and your labour for that which satisfieth not? hearken diligently to me, and eat ye that which is good. (Is. 55:2)

BB. Incline your ear, and come unto me: hear, and your soul shall live. (Is. 55:3)

CC. Seek ye the Lord while he may be found, call ye upon him while he is near. (Is. 55:6)

DD. Seek ye the Lord, seek righteousness, seek meekness. (Zeph. 2:3)

EE. Let him that glorieth glory in this, that he understandeth and knoweth me. (Jer. 9:23-24)

FF. Thy father judged the cause of the poor and needy; was not this to know me? (Jer. 22:16)

GG. I will give them an heart to know me, that I am the Lord. (Jer. 24:7)

HH. Call upon me, ye shall go and pray unto me. Ye shall seek me and find me when ye shall search for me with all your heart. (Jer. 29:12-13)

II. The Lord is good unto them that wait for him, to the soul that seeketh him. (Lam. 3:25)

JJ. Let us lift our heart with our hands unto God in the heavens. (Lam. 3:41)

KK. Hear the word of the Lord God. (Ezek. 6:3)

LL. Ye shall know that I am the Lord. (Ezek. 6:7)

MM. They shall know that I am the Lord, and that I have not said in vain. (Ezek. 6:10)

19. **Live Harmoniously:**

A. Is it not good if peace and truth be in my days? (2 Ki. 20:19)

B. Doest thou well to be angry? (Jon. 4:4, 9)

C. Can two walk together, except they be agreed? (Amos 3:3)

D. Let no man strive, nor reprove another. (Hos. 4:4)

20. **Live Religion From the Heart, Not Ritualistically:**

A. He turned to the Lord with all his heart, and with all his soul, and with all his might, according to all the Law . . . (2 Ki. 23:25)

B. They entered into a covenant to seek the Lord God of their fathers with all their heart and with all their soul; that whosoever would not seek the Lord God of Israel should be put to death. (2 Chron. 15:12-13)

C. They rejoiced at the oath, for they had sworn with all their heart, and sought God with their whole desire; and he was found of them, and the Lord gave them rest round about. (2 Chron. 15:15)

D. For I desired mercy and not sacrifice; and the knowledge of God more than burnt offerings. (Hos. 6:6)

E. When ye fasted and mourned, did ye at all fast unto me, even to me? (Zech. 7:5)

F. Saith the Lord, turn ye even to me with all your heart, and with fasting, and with weeping, and with mourning, and rend your heart, and not your garments, and turn unto the Lord your God. (Joel 2:12-13)

21. **Marry According to God's Law:**

    A. The importance of proper marriage discussed. (Ezra, chapters 9 & 10)

    B. Nehemiah reproved the people for marrying outside of the Church. (Neh. 13:23-29)

22. **Pay Tithing:**

    A. The tithe of all things brought they in abundantly that they might be encouraged in the law of the Lord. (2 Chron. 31:4-5)

    B. Then brought all Judah the tithe. (Neh. 13:12)

    C. Bring ye all the tithes into the storehouse, and prove me now herewith, if I will not open you the windows of heaven. (Mal. 3:10-12)

23. **Prepare the Heart:**

    A. His heart was lifted up in the ways of the Lord. (2 Chron. 17:6)

    B. Thou hast prepared thine heart to seek God. (2 Chron. 19:3)

    C. The good Lord pardon everyone that prepareth his heart to seek God, the Lord God of his fathers. (2 Chron. 30:18-19)

    D. (Hezekiah's prayer) Remember now, O Lord, I beseech thee, how I have walked before thee in truth and with a perfect heart, and have done that which is good in thy sight. (Is. 38:3)

    E. I will give them an heart to know me, that I am the Lord. (Jer. 24:7)

    F. He proposed in his heart that he would not defile himself. (Dan. 1:8)

    G. Ezra had prepared his heart to seek the law of the Lord, and to do it, and to teach in Israel statutes and judgments. (Ezra 7:10)

24. **Pray and Seek Guidance:**

   A. Inquire at the word of the Lord today. (1 Ki. 22:5)

   B. Inquire of the Lord concerning the words of this book (of scripture). (2 Ki. 22:13)

   C. Inquire at the word of the Lord today. (2 Chron. 18:4)

   D. Judah fasted and gathered themselves together, to ask help of the Lord. (2 Chron. 20:4)

   E. If, when evil cometh upon us, as the sword, judgment, or pestilence or famine, we stand before this house, and in thy presence, (for thy name is in this house) and cry unto thee in our affliction, Then thou wilt hear and help. (2 Chron. 20:9)

   F. Their prayer came up to his holy dwelling place, even unto heaven. (2 Chron. 30:27)

   G. Arise, call upon thy God. (Jon. 1:6)

   H. Cry mightily unto God, let everyone turn from his evil way and from violence. (Jon. 3:8)

   I. Turn to the Lord: say unto him, take away all iniquity, and receive us graciously. (Hos. 14:2)

   J. I will look unto the Lord; my God will hear me. (Mic. 7:7)

   K. O Lord, by these things (God's answer to prayer) men live, and in all these things is the life of my spirit . . . (Is. 38:16)

   L. Heal me, O Lord, and I shall be healed; save me, and I shall be saved. (Jer. 17:14)

   M. Call upon me, ye shall go and pray unto me, Ye shall seek me and find me when ye shall search for me with all your heart. (Jer. 29:12-13)

   N. Seek the peace of the city, and pray unto the Lord for it: for in the peace thereof shall ye have peace. (Jer. 29:7)

   O. I called upon thy name, O Lord, out of the low dungeon. Thou hast heard my voice. (Lam. 3:55-56)

   P. They desired the mercies of the God of heaven concerning this secret. (Dan. 2:18)

   Q. He kneeled upon his knees three times a day, and prayed, and gave thanks before his God. (Dan. 6:10)

   R. We make prayer before the Lord our God,

that we might turn from our iniquities, and understand thy truth. (Dan. 9:13)

S. We do not present our supplications before thee for our righteousness, but for thy great mercies. (Dan. 9:18)

T. From the first day that thou didst set thine heart to understand, and to chasten thyself before thy God, thy words were heard. (Dan. 10:12)

U. O Lord, I beseech thee, to hear the prayer of thy servants who desire to fear thy name. (Neh. 1:11)

V. So I prayed to the God of heaven (for immediate help during a conversation). (Neh. 2:4)

W. Remember me, O my God, concerning this, and wipe not out my good deeds that I have done. (Neh. 13:14)

X. Let us go speedily to pray before the Lord, and to seek the Lord of hosts. (Zech. 8:21)

Y. Ask ye of the Lord rain in the time of the latter rain. (Zech. 10:1)

Z. Beseech God that he will be gracious unto us. (Mal. 1:9)

AA. Sanctify ye a fast, call a solemn assembly, gather the elders and all the inhabitants of the land into the house of the Lord and cry unto the Lord. (Joel 1:14)

BB. O Lord, to thee will I cry. (Joel 1:19)

25. **Repent:**

A. Turn ye from your evil ways, and keep my commandments and my statutes, according to all the law which I commanded your fathers and which I sent to you by my servants the prophets. (2 Ki. 17:13)

B. They gathered their brethren, and sanctified themselves. (2 Chron. 29:15)

C. They made confession to the Lord God of their fathers. (2 Chron. 30:22)

D. The people of Nineveh were saved because they repented in sackcloth and ashes. (Jon. 3:4-10)

E. Turn thou to thy God: keep mercy and judgment, and wait on thy God continually. (Hos. 12:6)

F. Turn to the Lord: say unto him, take away all iniquity, and receive us graciously. (Hos. 14:2)

G. Wash you, make you clean; put away the evil of your doings from before mine eyes; cease to do evil. (Is. 1:16)

H. Let the wicked forsake his way, and the unrighteous man his thoughts: and let him return unto the Lord, and he will have mercy upon him; and to our God, for he will abundantly pardon. (Is. 55:7)

I. Acknowledge thine iniquity, that thou hast transgressed against the Lord. (Jer. 3:13)

J. Wash thine heart from wickedness, that thou mayest be saved. How long shall thy vain thoughts lodge within thee? (Jer. 4:14)

K. May ye also do good, that are accustomed to do evil. (Jer. 13:23)

L. We acknowledge, O Lord, our wickedness. (Jer. 14:20-21)

M. After I was turned, I repented; and after that I was instructed. I was ashamed because I did bear the reproach of my youth. (Jer. 31:19)

N. Flee out of the midst of Babylon, and deliver every man his soul. (Jer. 51:6, 45)

O. Wherefore doth a living man complain for the punishment of his sins? Let us search and try our ways, and turn again to the Lord. (Lam. 3:39-40)

P. When a righteous man doth turn from his righteousness, and commit iniquity, his righteousness which he hath done shall not be remembered. (Ezek. 3:18-21)

Q. The son that sees the sins of his father and does not do them, he shall not die for the iniquity of his father, he shall surely live. (Ezek. 18:1-18)

R. If the wicked will turn from all his sins that he hath committed, he shall surely live, and his transgressions shall not be mentioned to him. But when a righteous man turneth away from his righteousness, and committeth iniquity, he shall surely die, and all his righteousness shall not be remembered. (Ezek. 18:20-29)

S. Repent, and turn yourselves from all your transgressions; so iniquity shall not be your ruin. Make you a new heart and a new spirit: for why will ye die? (Ezek. 18:30-32)

T. Thus saith the Lord God: Repent, and turn away your faces from all your abominations. (Ezek. 14:6)

U. The righteousness of the righteous shall not deliver him in the day of his transgression: as for the wickedness of the wicked, he shall not fall thereby in the day that he turneth from his wickedness. (Ezek. 33:8-20)

V. Break off thy sins by righteousness, and thine iniquities by showing mercy to the poor, if it may be a lengthening of thy tranquility. (Dan. 4:27)

W. We make prayer before the Lord our God, that we might turn from our iniquities, and understand thy truth. (Dan. 9:13)

X. From the first day that thou didst set thine heart to understand, and to chasten thyself before thy God, thy words were heard. (Dan. 10:12)

Y. He had prayed and confessed, casting himself down before the house of God. (Ezra 10:1)

Z. Nehemiah confesses his sins and the sins of his people. (Neh. 1:6-7)

AA. Saith the Lord, turn ye even to me with all your heart, and with fasting, and with weeping, and with mourning, and rend your heart, and not your garments, and turn unto the Lord your God. (Joel 2:12-13)

26. Respect Authority:

A. Unauthorized persons were denied the rights of the priesthood. (Neh. 7:64-65)

B. The priest's lips should keep knowledge, and they should seek the law at his mouth. (Mal. 2:7)

27. Serve and Obey God:

A. The Lord chose him because he kept the commandments and statutes. (1 Ki. 11:34)

B. If thou wilt hearken unto all that I command thee, and wilt walk in my ways, and do that is right in my sight, to keep my statutes and commandments, I will be with thee, and build thee a sure house. (1 Ki. 11:38)

C. They hearkened unto the word of the Lord. (1 Ki. 12:24)

D. He did that which was right in the eyes of the Lord and turned not aside from anything that he commanded him. (1 Ki. 15:5)

E. The statutes and the ordinances, and the law, and the commandment, which he wrote for you ye shall observe to do for evermore. (2 Ki. 17:37)

F. He trusted in the Lord God of Israel. He clave to the Lord, and departed not from following him, but kept his commandments, and the Lord was with him; and he prospered whithersoever he went forth. (2 Ki. 18:5-7)

G. We keep the charge of the Lord our God, and behold, God himself is with us for our captain. (2 Chron. 13:11-12)

H. He commanded his people to seek the Lord God of their fathers, and to do the law and the commandment. (2 Chron. 14:4)

I. Ye have consecrated yourselves unto the Lord. (2 Chron. 29:31)

J. Be ye not stiffnecked, as your fathers were, but yield yourselves unto the Lord, and enter into his sanctuary, which he hath sanctified forever: and serve the Lord, your God, that the fierceness of his wrath may turn away from you. (2 Chron. 30:8)

K. He will teach us of his ways, and we will walk in his paths. (Is. 2:3)

L. Come ye, and let us walk in the light of the Lord. (Is. 2:5)

M. See ye, when he lifteth up an ensign on the mountains; and when he bloweth a trumpet, hear ye. (Is. 18:3)

N. Lord, thou wilt ordain peace for us: for thou also hast wrought all our works in us. (Is. 26:12)

O. O that thou hadst hearkened to my commandments! then had thy peace been as a river, and thy righteousness as the waves of the sea. (Is. 48:18)

P. Surely my judgment is with the Lord, and my work with my God. (Is. 49:4)

Q. For Zion's sake will I not hold my peace, and for Jerusalem's sake I will not rest, until the righteousness thereof go forth as brightness, and the salvation thereof as a lamp that burneth. (Is. 62:1)

SIX MAJOR DOCTRINES   113

R. He who blesseth himself in the earth shall bless himself in the God of truth; and he that sweareth in the earth shall swear by the God of truth. (Is. 65:16)

S. All flesh shall come to worship before me. (Is. 66:23)

T. Obey my voice, and walk ye in all the ways that I have commanded you. (Jer. 7:23)

U. Obey the voice of the Lord, so it shall be well unto thee, and thy soul shall live. (Jer. 38:20)

V. Be not thou rebellious like that rebellious house. (Ezek. 2:8)

W. I am the Lord your God; walk in my statutes, and keep my judgments, and do them. (Ezek. 20:19)

X. They shall keep my laws and my statutes in all mine assemblies; and they shall hallow my sabbaths. (Ezek. 44:24)

Y. Make confession unto the Lord God of your fathers, and do his pleasure. (Ezra 10:11)

Z. The people obeyed the voice of their God and the words of their prophet. (Hag. 1:12)

AA. If thou wilt walk in my ways, and if thou wilt keep my charge, then thou shalt also judge my house, and shalt also keep my courts, and I will give thee places to walk among these that stand by. (Zech. 3:7)

28. **Teach and Warn Others:**

A. Ye shall even warn your brethren that they trespass not against the Lord. (2 Chron. 19:10)

B. They taught the good knowledge of the Lord. (2 Chron. 30:22)

C. He made all that were present in Israel to serve the Lord their God. (2 Chron. 34:33)

D. He encouraged the priesthood to the service of the house of the Lord. (2 Chron. 35:2)

E. Praise the Lord, call upon his name, declare his doings among the people, make mention that his name is exalted. (Is. 12:4)

F. The father to the children shall make known thy truth. (Is. 38:19)

G. Lift up thy voice with strength; lift it up, be not afraid. (Is. 40:9)

H. The Lord God hath given me the tongue of the learned, that I should know how to speak a word in season to him that is weary. (Is. 50:4)

I. How beautiful upon the mountains are the feet of him that bringeth good tidings of good, that publisheth salvation; that saith unto Zion, Thy God reigneth. (Is. 52:7)

J. All thy children shall be taught of the Lord; and great shall be the peace of thy children. (Is. 54:13)

K. Ye that make mention of the Lord, keep not silence. (62:6)

L. Son of man, I have set thee a watchman unto the house of Israel. (Ezek. 33:1-7)

M. They shall teach my people the difference between the holy and profane, and cause them to discern between the unclean and the clean. (Ezek. 44:23)

N. Ezra had prepared his heart to seek the law of the Lord, and to do it, and to teach in Israel statutes and judgments. (Ezra 7:10)

O. Group scripture reading. (Neh. 8:1-8)

P. Tell your children of it, and let your children tell their children, and their children another generation. (Joel 1:3)

29. **Work**

A. Woe to them that are at ease in Zion. (Amos 6:1)

B. Sow to yourselves in righteousness, reap in mercy: for it is time to seek the Lord, till he come and rain righteousness upon you. (Hos. 10:12)

C. Thy work shall be rewarded. (Jer. 31:16)

D. They furthered the people, and the house of God. (Ezra 8:36)

E. Nehemiah supports himself as governor instead of taxing the people. (Neh. 5:14-19)

F. Consider your ways. Ye have sown much and bring in little, ye eat but have not enough. Consider your ways. (Hag. 1:5-7)

G. Be strong, all ye people of the land, saith the Lord, and work: for I am with you. (Hag. 2:4)

The Events of the Last Days

The sixth major theme, the Lord's plan for His children in the last days, is undoubtedly the most predominant theme of the scriptures of the Church. Far more has even been said in them on this subject than concerning other such fundamental principles as faith, repentance, baptism, Church organization, etc. There can be little doubt that the Lord intends for man to understand His program and to recognize the significance of coming events as they transpire. The prophetic portion of the Old Testament makes an important contribution to the Church's understanding of future events. Indeed, it provides the nucleus around which the other prophecies center. Without understanding the Old Testament prophecies of the last days one can not hope to clearly envision the events of the future.

In other works[2] the author has attempted to compile prophetic evidence of the Master's program for the last days and to determine a proper chronology for these events. In those volumes extensive evidence is cited to verify the conclusions determined therein. Those conclusions are not reported as an indication of the author's personal views, but rather as a composite picture of the message of the scriptures and of the prophets of the Church in the latter days. The evidence reported in those studies will not be repeated here. Instead, the reader is invited to consider a predetermined list of fifty important events which prophecy indicates are to take place in the last days. With this list as an outline, the pertinent scriptural passages of the prophetic section of the Old Testament will be considered. It will be noted that some of the

---

[2]See *The Prophecies of Joseph Smith* and *Prophecy—Key To The Future*. The reader will note that this listing is far more extensive than the number of Old Testament passages cited in those works. They were designed to determine key interpretations. This list is prepared in an effort to place all of the pertinent scriptural passages in the area where they should be considered.

prophesied events will show few or no Old Testament references. They are documented from prophecies found in other of the four standard works or in prophecies of L.D.S. General Authorities. They are included in this context, however, because it would be impossible to understand the ordering of last days events without giving them proper consideration.

A listing and allocation of scriptures such as is being presented here of necessity involves considerable interpretation. The author is well aware that there are many people of other faiths who would disagree with the interpretations given for two reasons: (1) they may regard these Biblical passages as being uninspired, and therefore not applicable as a pattern for the future, or (2) they may regard them as prophecies which were fulfilled in the days of their prophets. Being a Latter-day Saint, the author feels willingly compelled to regard the scriptures from the same general viewpoint as the leaders of his Church, with the same eschatological[3] direction as that which is expressed in the tenth Article of Faith:

> We believe in the literal gathering of Israel and in the restoration of the Ten Tribes; that Zion will be built upon this [the American] continent; that Christ will reign personally upon the earth; and, that the earth will be renewed and receive its paradisiacal glory.

Several factors should be kept clearly in mind while considering a list such as this one. First, extreme difficulty exists in showing the continuation of time in any list, and this list is no exception. The list indicates when continuing processes begin, but the reader must be alert to determine when some processes end. The proper interpretation of many passages is dependent on the chronological setting of the events they report. Second, many prophecies are so general that they cannot be connected to only one event. Thus the

---
[3]means of or pertaining to the last days.

SIX MAJOR DOCTRINES   117

reader will find them cited under several topic headings where they may prove applicable. Third, some passages may be open to other lines of interpretation. An attempt will be made to distinguish such passages by placing a question mark before the quotation. It is deemed valuable to have all such passages listed, as an invitation to consideration, however, and so some passages which are subject to varying interpretations are indicated on the list. Fourth, it should be noted that many passages which have been posted to the list do not stand by themselves, but must be understood in the light of their context. The reader should investigate the context thoroughly with all such passages.[4] Fifth, some passages are merely allusions to future events. While they carry little importance in and of themselves, they are significant because they contribute their weight to the pattern of scripture pertaining to the subject and indicate that the prophet was conversant with the coming event.

This listing is a beginning study guide. It is certainly not the final word that will be set forth on this important subject. The list is prepared in anticipation that new areas of contemplation may be opened to those who are interested in the field of Old Testament study.

1st Event: The Apostasy.

Latter-day Saints generally regard the apostasy as having begun during the time of the apostles in the first century A.D. With the end of that generation the apostasy became complete and continued until the restoration of the Church in 1830. In reality, the apostasy still continues among many people of the world and will extend in part to the end of the millen-

---

[4]If the meaning of the passage listed is not immediately clear to the reader, he will do well to consult the treatment of the passage in this book under the appropriate prophet.

nium. (See 1 Tim. 4:1-3; 2 Tim. 4:3-4; 2 Thess. 2:1-4; Gal. 1:6-8)

Micah:

    1. The Lord will give up his goings forth until the time that she which travaileth hath brought forth (the restoration of Israel). (5:1-4)

Isaiah:

    2. The Lord hath covered your prophets and seers. (29:9-10; see 2 Ne. 27:4-5, Morm. 1:13-19)

2nd Event: The Coming Forth of the Book of Mormon.

The Book of Mormon was revealed, translated, and published between 1823 and 1830. This section also contains prophetic references pertaining to the content of that book. (See JS 2:30-75; D & C 2; 3; 5; 6; 8; 9; 10; 17)

Isaiah:

    1. The fall of the Nephites. Thou shalt speak out of the ground. Thy voice shall be as one that hath a familiar spirit. (29:1-4; See 2 Ne. 26:14-18; 30:4-6; Morm. 6:1-15)
    2. The vision of all is become unto you as the words of a book that is sealed. (29:11)
    3. The words of the book shall be delivered to one that is learned, saying, Read this, I pray thee: and he saith I cannot, for it is sealed. (29:11-12; See 2 Ne. 27:9-10; 15-22; JS 2:64-65)
    4. The deaf shall hear the words of the book, and the eyes of the blind shall see out of darkness. (29:18)

Ezekiel:

    5. Ezekiel's explanation of the prophecy of the two sticks: The sticks will be in thine hand before their eyes, (therefore tangible objects). (37:18-20)
    6. A tender one will be cropped off of the young twigs of the cedar. The Lord will plant it upon an high mountain and it shall bring forth boughs, and bear

Six Major Doctrines 119

  fruit, and be a goodly cedar. (the Mulekites) (17: 22-24)

3rd Event: The Restoration of the Church.

This section includes references to the specific messengers and events of the restoration as well as to the coming forth of the Church itself. The restoration took place from 1820 to 1836. (See D & C 20; 21; 110)

Isaiah:

1. Wherefore the Lord said, the people draw near me with their mouth but have removed their heart far from me . . . (29:13; see 2 Ne. 27:25; JS 2:19)
2. I will do a marvelous work and a wonder among this people. (29:14; See 2 Ne. 27:26)

? 3. There shall be a root of Jesse, which shall stand for an ensign; to it shall the Gentiles seek. (11:10)

Daniel:

4. The stone is a kingdom which shall be set up by the God of heaven. (2:44-45)
  A. It will come in the time of the divided kingdoms represented by the image's feet.
  B. It shall never be destroyed.
  C. The kingdom shall not be left to other people.
  D. The kingdom shall break in pieces and consume all the other kingdoms.
  E. The kingdom shall stand forever.
  F. The dream is certain, and the interpretation thereof sure. (See also event #18.)

Malachi:

5. A messenger will prepare the way before the Lord suddenly comes to His temple. When the Lord comes He will be like refiner's fire to purify the sons of Levi. (3:1-3)
6. Elijah the prophet shall come before the coming of the great and dreadful day of the Lord. He shall come and turn the hearts of the fathers to the children and the hearts of the children to the fathers, lest I come and smite the earth with a curse. (4:5-6)

4th Event: The Beginning of the Times of the Gentiles.

This event represents the beginning of L.D.S. missionary work, immediately following the restoration of the Church. The present missionary work among the Gentiles is considered as event #7. (See D & C 45:28; JS 2:41) (No references in the Prophetic Section of the Old Testament)

5th Event: War Poured Out Upon All Nations.

This period began with the U.S. Civil War in 1861 and will continue to the coming of Christ in glory. (See D & C 87:1-8) (No References in the Prophetic Section of the Old Testament)

6th Event: The Period of Preparatory Wars.

This event began in conjunction with the U.S. Civil War (5th event). It will continue until the times of the Gentiles are fulfilled (11th event). Early Church leaders explained that during the period of preparatory wars, warfare would tend to overthrow governments which were unfriendly to the L.D.S. missionary effort. New governments would then be formed which would accept our missionary efforts. These wars would thus prepare the way for the spread of the gospel. (See JD 7:186, 188; 18:63-64) (No References in the Prophetic Section of the Old Testament.)

7th Event: The Fulness of the Times of the Gentiles.

This period represents the present missionary work of the Church and the first of four periods of missionary labor. It began following the restoration (4th event) and will continue until the Gentiles (primarily the people of Europe and the Americas) reject the Church and persecute its members (10th event). Then the missionaries will be called home and the Gentiles will lose their opportunity to hear the gospel. This will be the fulfilling of the times of the Gentiles (11th event). (See D & C 45:26-33; JS 2:41)

Isaiah:

    1. He shall bring forth judgment to the Gentiles. (42:1)

    2. He will be a light to the Gentiles. (42:6; 49:6)

8th Event: The Rising of Slaves Against Their Masters.

This is being fulfilled as many colonies throughout the world are throwing off the control of their masters. Witness the number of independent states formed since the second world war. Fulfillment can also be seen in the rise of the status of minority groups in the United States. (See D & C 87:4-5; *Conference Report*, October 1958, p. 33) (No References in the Prophetic Section of the Old Testament.)

9th Event: The Third World War.

This is a conflict which is expected to take place between the communist forces and the nations of the free world. Reference to it is found primarily in the writings and discourses of certain L.D.S. General Authorities. It is expected to result in the eventual overthrow of Communism. (See Mosiah Lyman Hancock, *Life Story of Mosiah Lyman Hancock*, p. 29;[5] JI, March 15, 1890, p. 162) (No References in the Prophetic Section of the Old Testament)

10th Event: The Saints to Suffer Persecution.

Numerous prophecies by General Authorities have detailed a period of persecution in which the Church and its members will endure great hardships. (See JD

---

[5] A typewritten copy of the original manuscript is available in the B.Y.U. library.

7:185-187; 20:146; *Prophetic Sayings of Heber C. Kimball to Amanda H. Wilcox*)

Daniel:

? 1. There came up among them another little horn. which made war with the saints, and prevailed against them. (7:21, 25; See also event #25)

11th Event: The Fulfilling of the Times of the Gentiles.

This event will mark the end of concentrated missionary labor among the nations of Europe and the Americas. Events 11, 12, 13, and 14 are expected to take place concurrently. (See JD 18:176-77; 18:64; 8:123) (No References in the Prophetic Section of the Old Testament.)

12th Event: The Saints in Foreign Lands Will Gather to the Americas.

Statements and prophecies by early General Authorities foresaw the re-centralization of the Church within the Americas as persecution mounts against it in foreign lands. This is regarded as the time for the call to "come out of Babylon." Events 11, 12, 13, and 14 are expected to take place concurrently. (See D & C 45:69; JS 1:27; D & C 115:6; JD 18:64) (No References in the Prophetic Section of the Old Testament.)

13th Event: The Gospel Will Be Taken from the Gentiles and Later Given to Israel.

This period is expected to be the era in which the missionary effort will turn from the Gentiles (as their times are fulfilled) and increase in intensity to the house of Israel. The gospel will apparently go first to the Lamanites, then to the Ten Tribes, and then to the scattered house of Judah. Events 11, 12, 13, and 14 are expected to take place concurrently. (See JD

18:177; Mt. 20:16; *Doctrines of Salvation* III, 258-59) (No References in the Prophetic Section of the Old Testament.)

14th Event: God Will Pour Out His Judgments Upon the Earth.

Prophecies pertaining to this period include world-wide destruction from the Lord's desolating scourge, earthquakes, famine and drought, and the sweeping clean of Jackson County, Missouri. These destructions are foreseen as substitutes for the missionary labors among the Gentile nations. Events 11, 12, 13, and 14 are expected to take place concurrently. (See JS 2:45; D & C 88:88-91; JD 8:123; D & C 45:30-33)

Isaiah:

    1. Woe to the land shadowing with wings. They shall be cut off and left for the fowls and the beasts to eat. (18:1-6)

Haggai:

    2. I will shake the heavens and the earth, and the sea, and the dry land, and all nations. (2:6-7)

15th Event: Internal Wars in the United States.

Internal wars and mobocracy are expected to bring about the collapse of local, state and national government in the United States. (See HC 3:390-91; 5:394; 6:116; JD 12:344; 8:143) (No References in the Prophetic Section of the Old Testament.)

16th Event: World-Wide Revolutions and Deterioration of Governments as the Period of Wars of Total Destruction Begins.

In contrast to the warfare during the period of preparatory wars, the wars during this era will not better the condition of mankind. Instead, it appears that this period will encompass a series of wars and revolutions which will greatly decrease the populations and well-being of the nations of the world. The period of wars of total destruction will continue until the coming of Christ in glory. This period will begin with the internal warfare in the United States (15th event). (See JD 18:341; 21:301)

Micah:
1. I will make thine horn iron and thy hoofs brass: and thou shalt beat in pieces many people. (4:13; For interpretive context see 3 Ne. 20:15-22)
2. The remnant of Jacob shall be in the midst of many people among the Gentiles. They will tread down and tear in pieces the cities and strongholds of their enemies. (5:7-15; For interpretive context see 3 Ne. 21:1-21)

Jeremiah:
? 3. The Lord has a controversy with the nations. The slain at that day shall be from one end of the earth to the other. (25:30-33)

17th Event: The Saints in America Will Gather to Places of Refuge in the Western Mountains.

As persecution continues against the Church, and as wars and strife rage in America and throughout the world, it is expected that the members of the Church will be summoned to protected areas in order to escape the mobocracy and chaos throughout the land. (See JD 12:345; HC 3:390-91; JD 3:16; 4:106) (No References in the Prophetic Section of the Old Testament)

18th Event: The Political Kingdom of God Will Be Established.

A political organization will be established among the Saints in their cities of refuge to govern them.

This organization, while secular in its nature, will be comprised mainly of Church members, who will carry out their duties under inspiration. The political kingdom of God will govern the Saints as they return to establish the New Jerusalem and as that center rises to world prominence. (See DEN, Vol. 8, No. 265, Oct. 2, 1875; HC 7:381-82)

Daniel:

1. The stone is a kingdom which shall be set up by the God of heaven.
    A. It will come in the time of the divided kingdoms of the image's feet.
    B. It shall never be destroyed.
    C. The kingdom shall not be left to other people.
    D. The kingdom shall break in pieces and consume all the other kingdoms.
    E. The kingdom shall stand forever.
    F. The dream is certain, and the interpretation thereof sure. (2:36-45; See also event #3)

19th Event: The Law of Consecration Will Be Established.

The great distress within the United States and the rapid gathering of the Saints to the cities of refuge will create a need for the renewal of the principles of the United Order and the Law of Consecration. A preliminary introduction of the principle of unity and sharing is expected while the Saints are still in the west. It appears that the principle will not be renewed in its entirety until the Saints return to Jackson County, Missouri. (See DEN 8:265, Oct. 2, 1875; JD 2:57; JD 16:276)

Micah:

1. I will consecrate their gain unto the Lord, and their substance unto the Lord of the whole earth. (4:13)

20th Event: The New Jerusalem and Its Temple Will Be Built in Missouri.

A selected group of the Saints will be summoned to journey to Missouri from the West and establish the city of the New Jerusalem in Jackson County. They will be joined during the growth of the city by a huge influx of Indians from North, Central, and South America, by the Ten Tribes who will come from the north, and by increasing numbers of Gentiles who will be drawn to the peace and progress of the city. The city will continue to grow into the millennium. (See DEN 8:265, Oct. 2, 1875; JD 24:156-57; 24:23)

Isaiah:

1. The Lord will lay thy stones with fair colours, and thy foundations with sapphires. (54:11-12; For interpretive context see 3 Ne. 21; 22)

21st Event: The Conversion of the Lamanites.

In the early days of the New Jerusalem the major period of conversion of the Lamanites, or Indians, is expected to take place. Prophecy depicts these people as gathering to the New Jerusalem area by the millions. They will participate in the building of the city and the temple. (See JD 3:18; 17:301-02; 3 Ne. 21:23-22:3) (No References in the Prophetic Section of the Old Testament.)

22nd Event: The Ten Tribes of Israel Will Come From the North to Missouri.

As the New Jerusalem grows, the Ten Tribes of Israel are expected to come from the north to that city. Their coming will somehow be associated with a great earthquake. It is believed that they will stay temporarily in the Missouri area and then move to the land

SIX MAJOR DOCTRINES 127

of Israel (31st event). (See *Messenger and Advocate*, Oct. 1835; D & C 133:26-34)

Isaiah:

1. In that time the nation scattered and peeled shall be brought unto Mount Zion. (18:7)
2. The children of the desolate are more than the children of the married wife. (54:1; For interpretive context see 3 Ne. 21; 22)
3. Thy seed shall inherit the desolate cities of the Gentiles. (54:2-3; For interpretive context see 3 Ne. 21; 22)
4. Though the Lord has hidden his face from Israel for a moment, He will remember and comfort His people in that day. (54:4-10; For interpretive context see 3 Ne. 21; 22)
5. The Lord will raise up the tribes of Jacob and restore the preserved of Israel. (49:6)
6. The Lord will also be a light of the Gentiles and the salvation for all the earth. (49:6)
7. The Lord will cause them to inherit the desolate heritages. (49:8)
8. The Lord will lead his people. He will make all his mountains a way, and his highways shall be exalted. (49:9-11; See D & C 133:26-29)
9. These shall come from far from the north and from the west, and from the land of Sinim (location unknown). (49:12-13)
10. Thy destroyers and they that made thee waste shall go forth of thee. (49:17; See D & C 133:28)
11. The waste and desolate places they inherit will be too crowded. They will object to them and the people there. (49:18-21)
12. A Prayer: Return for thy servant's sake, the tribes of thine inheritance. (63:15-19)

Jeremiah:

13. The people will say, The Lord liveth which led the tribes from the north and from all the countries. (23:7-8; See also #30-31)
14. The Lord will gather them from the north country. (31:8-9; See also #30-31)

23rd Event: Christ Will Come to the New Jerusalem Temple.

A visit of the Savior to the temple in Jackson County is anticipated either shortly before or just after the coming of the Ten Tribes from the north. (See *Millennial Star*, Oct. 22:1845; D & C 97:15-16; 3 Ne. 21:23-25)

Isaiah:

1. Thy children shall be taught of the Lord. Thou shalt not fear. (54:13-14; For interpretive context see 3 Ne. 21; 22)

24th Event: 144,000 High Priests Will Be Called.

A group of 144,000 high priests, 12,000 from each of the tribes of Israel, will be called and sent to search out the scattered members of the house of Israel. Their ministry will extend beyond the major period of gathering to the land of Israel (30th and 31st events) and probably beyond the Battle of Armageddon (35th event). See Rev. 7:1-8; D & C 77:7-11; JD 15:365-66; 16:325-26)

Isaiah:

1. Put on thy strength, O Zion. (52:1; See D & C 113:7-8; also #38)
2. How beautiful upon the mountains are the feet of him that bringeth good tidings by telling Zion thy God reigneth. (52:7; See Mos. 15:13-18)

25th Event: A Period of Great Plagues and Destruction.

As the 144,000 are gathering the scattered people of Israel to their homeland, the earth will undergo a great period of destruction from plagues and warfare. Events 25, 26, 27, and 28 are expected to take place concurrently. (See Rev. 8-11; D & C 29:14-20)

SIX MAJOR DOCTRINES 129

Isaiah:

1. Enemies will gather against them, but not by the Lord. No weapon that is formed against them shall prosper. (54:15-17; For interpretive context see 3 Ne. 21; 22)

Daniel:

2. There came among them another little horn. (7:8; 20-25) (See also #10.)
    A. Before the little horn three of the first horns were plucked up by the roots.
    B. In this horn were eyes like the eyes of man, and a mouth speaking great things, whose look was more stout than his fellows.
    C. The little horn made war with the saints, and prevailed against them until the Ancient of days came.
    D. He shall speak great words against the most High.
    E. He shall wear out the saints of the most High.
    F. He shall think to change times and laws.
    G. The saints shall be given into his hand until a time and times and the dividing of time.

26th Event: A Universal Conflict, or Fourth World War, Will Take Place.

Another terrible conflict is to take place, according to prophecy. This war will be the most extensive of the Wars of Total Destruction. Events 25, 26, 27, and 28 are expected to take place concurrently. (See JD 20:150-51; 7:188; 18:339-40; 15:72-73)

Daniel:

1. Thrones were cast down. (7:9)
2. The (fourth) beast was slain, and his body destroyed, and given to the burning flame. (7:11)
3. The rest of the beasts had their dominion taken away, yet their lives were prolonged for a season and a time. (7:12)

? 4. The king of the south shall push at the north. (11:40)

? 5. The king of the north shall come against him with chariots, horsemen, and with many ships. He shall enter into the countries, overflow, and pass over.
    A. He shall enter into the glorious land.
    B. Many countries shall be overthrown.
    C. Edom, Moab, and Ammon shall escape.
    D. Egypt shall not escape. He shall possess Egypt's precious things. The Libyans and the Ethiopians shall be at his steps.
    E. Tidings out of the east and north shall trouble him. He shall go forth to destroy, and utterly to make away many.
    F. He shall plant the tabernacles of his palace between the seas in the glorious holy mountain.
    G. He shall come to his end, and none shall help him.
    H. It shall be at a time when
      (1). Michael shall stand up.
      (2). There shall be a time of trouble worse than any previous.
      (3). Thy people shall be delivered.
      (4). Many that sleep in the dust shall awake, both righteous and wicked. (11:41-12:2)

6. There shall be a time of trouble such as never there was since there was a nation even to that same time. (12:1)

7. Daniel saw heavenly beings and one inquired, "How long shall it be to the end of these wonders?" The reply was "It shall be for a time, times, and a half; and when he shall have accomplished to scatter the power of the holy people, all these things shall be finished." (12:5-7)

8. From the time that the daily sacrifice shall be taken away and the abomination that maketh desolate set up, there shall be a thousand two hundred and ninety days. (12:11)

Haggai:

? 9. The Lord will overthrow thrones, and destroy the strength of the kingdoms of the heathens. Their horsemen will come down, every one by the sword of his brother. (2:22)

27th Event: The Coming to the Ancient of Days and the Savior to the Council at Adam-ondi-Ahman.

During the universal conflict a huge assembly will convene at Adam-ondi-Ahman, Missouri. Adam (the Ancient of Days) will preside, and will be visited by Christ. Judgment will be held on the nations of the earth, and the kingdom of the earth will be given to the Savior. Events 25, 26, 27, and 28 are expected to take place concurrently. (See HC 3:386-87; 4:207-09; JD 18:338-39; 17:185-86)

Daniel:

1. The Ancient of days did sit and judgment was given to the saints of the most High.
    A. Ten thousand times ten thousand (100,000,-000) stood before him.
    B. The judgment was set, and the books were opened.
    C. The judgment shall sit, and the saints will take away the dominion of the little horn, to consume and destroy it unto the end.
    D. The Son of Man came to the Ancient of Days, and they brought him near before him. There was given him dominion, and glory, and an everlasting kingdom. (7:9-10, 13-14, 22, 26)
2. Michael shall stand up. (12:1)
3. Many of them that sleep in the dust of the earth shall awake, some to everlasting life and some to shame and everlasting contempt. (12:2-3)

? 4. Blessed is he that waiteth, and cometh to the thousand three hundred and five and thirty days. (12:12)

28th Event: The Fall of the Great and Abominable Church.

The great and abominable church is expected to fall, but not become extinct, during the period of universal conflict. It will collapse along with the Christian nations of Europe and the Americas during the universal conflict. Its fall is to take place just before the major period of the gathering of the house of Israel. (See 1 Ne. 14:17 & 22:11-12; 22:13-14; Rev. 17:12-17; 2 Ne. 28:18-20)

Daniel:

? 1. The judgment shall sit, and the saints will take away the dominion of the little horn, to consume and destroy it unto the end. (7:26)
? 2. At that time thy people shall be delivered. (12:1)

29th Event: The Gathering to the New Jerusalem and Its Rise As a World Center of Influence.

The period of world destruction of the universal conflict will serve to diminish the prestige and dominion of many nations. As they decline, the influence of the New Jerusalem will grow. That city will be known for its beauty and righteousness and will gain world prominence as people seek shelter there. (See JD 22:36; 24:31-32)

Daniel:

1. The kingdom (the stone cut out without hands) shall break in pieces and consume all the other kingdoms. (2:44)

30th Event: The Gathering to the Land of Israel of the Scattered Remnants of Judah.

Through the efforts of the 144,000 the scattered members of the house of Judah will be sought out and gathered to their homeland from throughout the world. This will be the second major period of missionary labor. Their gathering will take place before, during, and after the universal conflict, but it is expected to reach its height during the rule of David the Prince. Events 30, 31, and 32 are expected to take place concurrently. The gathering of Judah and the restoration of the Ten Tribes to their homeland are frequent themes in the Old Testament. It is often impossible to determine whether the passage is speaking of just Judah or just Israel, or whether it refers to both. Those passages which seem to refer to both are shown as 30-31 in this listing. References which speak specifically of the gathering of Judah are shown as the 30th event. Specific references to the gathering of the tribes of Israel are shown as the 31st event. (See D & C 45:25; 3 Ne. 20:28-29; 21:28-29)

Isaiah:
1. Loose thyself from the bands of thy neck, O captive daughter of Zion. (52:2; See D & C 113:9-10)
2. The Lord will redeem the waste places of Jerusalem and all the nations shall see His salvation together. (52:8-10)

Zephaniah:
3. The remnant of the house of Judah will inhabit the sea coast when it returns from captivity. (2:6-7; See also #4)

Jeremiah:
4. The Lord will bring one of a family and two of a city back to Zion. They shall have righteous pastors, and will not need to remember the ark of the covenant. (3:14-16)
5. The Lord will send fishers and hunters to find Israel. (16:16)
6. Judah shall be called the mountain of holiness. (31:22-26)
7. The dimensions of the holy city in the last days are given. (31:38-40)

Ezekiel:
1. The Lord will gather His people out of the countries where they are scattered with a mighty hand and with fury poured out. (20:33-44)
2. He will plead with them face to face in the wilderness. (20:35)

3. He will purge out the rebels from among them. He will bring them out of the country where they sojourn, and they shall not enter into the land of Israel. (20:38)
4. Ye shall know He is the Lord when He brings you into the land of Israel. (20:42)

Zechariah:

5. The Lord shall inherit Judah his portion in the holy land, and shall choose Jerusalem again. (2:12)
6. The governors of Judah shall say in their heart, The inhabitants of Jerusalem shall be my strength in the Lord. In that day the governors of Judah shall devour the people round about, and Jerusalem shall be inhabited again. (12:5-6)
7. Jerusalem shall be inhabited from Benjamin's gate unto the place of the first gate, unto the corner gate, and from the tower of Hananeel unto the king's winepresses. (14:10-11)

30th and 31st Events: General References to the Gathering of the House of Israel.

There are numerous passages which refer to the gathering process but which do not indicate with clarity whether they are speaking of Israel or Judah or both. These have been combined into a special grouping and have been indicated throughout the book as (30-31). This section also includes the passages which specifically establish the return of both Judah and Israel.

Amos:

1. God will restore his people to their land and they shall build the waste cities. (9:14-15)

Hosea:

2. They shall be like the sands of the sea, and known as the sons of the living God. Judah and Israel shall be gathered together and appoint themselves one head, for great shall be the day of Jezreel. (1:10-11)

3. God will speak comfortably to Israel and give her the valley of Achor for a door of hope. God will give them safety and betroth them to Himself, and will show mercy. (2:14-23)
4. Israel shall return and seek God and David their king. (3:5)
5. Israel will grow as the lily, his branches shall spread. (14:4-9)

Micah:
6. A restoration in the last days is predicted. (2:12-13)
7. I will surely gather the remnant of Israel; their king shall pass before them, and the Lord on the head of them. (2:12-13)
8. God will make those that were cast off a strong nation and the Lord will reign over them in Mount Zion. (4:5-7)

Isaiah:
9. The Lord shall be gracious to his people when they dwell in Zion at Jerusalem. He shall make the ground increase. (30:18-24)
10. The light of Israel will be a flame which will devour the land of Assyria in the day that the remnant of Israel (the ten tribes) and those that are escaped of Jacob (the scattered Jews) shall return and shall rely upon the Lord. (10:20-22)
11. God will lift up an ensign to the nations from far and will hiss unto them from the end of the earth. (5:26; see 2 Ne. 29:1-2)
12. Israel will thresh the mountains. God will open up rivers in high places and fountains in the valleys so people will know God has helped Israel. (41:15-20; cf. 30:25-26)
13. The Lord will gather the seed of Israel from the east, west, north, and south. (43:5-7)
14. The Lord will make a way in the wilderness, and rivers in the desert for his chosen people. (43:18-21)
15. He will raise up the tribes of Jacob. (49:6)
16. He will restore the preserved of Israel. (49:6)
17. Lebanon shall be a fruitful field. (29:15-17)
18. Israel will be called out of wickedness and God will protect her in her return. (52:11-12)

19. The desert shall rejoice, and blossom as the rose. (35:1-2)
20. The weak will be strengthened in their journey (to Zion). (35:3-6)
21. Waters and streams will break out in the desert. (35:6-7)
22. A highway shall be there, called the way of holiness, and the ransomed of the Lord shall return to Zion. (35:8-10)
23. Israel and Judah shall be gathered to Palestine. (11:11-12)
24. The Lord will comfort Zion, and make her waste places fertile. (51:3)
25. The Lord will help Israel to return with joy and singing. (51:11-16)
26. Cast up the highway, lift up a standard for the people. (62:10)
27. The Lord will send a message throughout the world to Israel that his salvation cometh. (62:11)
28. They shall build the old waste and desolate cities, while strangers tend their flocks. (61:3-5)
29. Israel travailed and brought forth a man child before her pain came. (66:7-8)
30. A seed will inherit the mountains. (65:8-10)

Obadiah:

31. The children of Israel shall possess the lands of their neighbors. (19-20)

Jeremiah:

32. Israel will be saved and will return from the lands of her captivity. (46:27-28)
33. God will gather the people back out of all countries and make them His people. (32:37-42)
34. Fields shall be purchased in the land. (32:43-44)
35. Judah and Israel will come together to the land of their inheritance. (3:18)
36. The children of Israel will be gathered back into their land. (16:15)
37. The Lord will gather them from the north country, and from the coasts of the earth. They shall walk by the rivers in a straight way. (31:8-9)

SIX MAJOR DOCTRINES 137

38. They shall come and sing in the height of Zion, and shall flow together to the goodness of the Lord. (31:10-14)
39. Set up waymarks, and set thine heart toward the highway. (31:21)
40. Judah and Israel will be built up. Men shall be punished for their own iniquity, not another's. (31:27-30)
41. At present, no one desires the house of Israel, but she shall be restored and Jerusalem will be rebuilt. (30:13-18)
42. The Lord will gather the remnant of his flock. They shall increase and fear no more. (23:3-4)
43. People will say, "The Lord liveth which led the tribes from the north and from all the countries. (23:7-8)

Ezekiel:

44. The Lord will gather the people and assemble them out of the countries where they have been scattered, and give them the land of Israel. (11:17-20)
45. When Sodom and Samaria shall return to their former estate, then Jerusalem will return to its former estate. (16:53-55)
46. When the Lord has gathered the house of Israel from the people among whom they are scattered they will dwell safely in their land. They will build houses and plant vineyards. (28:25-26)
47. The Lord will seek out his sheep, and will deliver them out of all places where they have been scattered, and bring them to their own land, and feed them upon the mountains of Israel. (34:11-15)
48. The Lord will multiply man upon the mountains of Israel. The cities shall be inhabited and the waste places shall be builded. (36:8-12)
49. Ezekiel was shown a valley of dry bones. He saw them regain their flesh and life and become an exceeding great army. The Lord said the bones are the whole house of Israel. They will know that He is the Lord when He causes them to come out of their graves and places them in their own land. (37:1-14)

50. Ezekiel's explanation of the prophecy of the two sticks: The sticks will be in thine hand before their eyes, (therefore tangible objects.) (37:18-20)
51. The children of Israel will gather from among the heathen to their own land. (37:21-22)
52. The borders of Israel in the last days are given. (46:13-23)

Zechariah:

53. Israel is to flee from the land of the north and deliver herself from Babylon. (2:6-7)
54. The Lord will save His people from the east and the west and will bring them to Jerusalem. (8:7-8)
55. The Lord will strengthen the house of Judah, and will save the house of Joseph, and will bring them again to place them. (10:6)
56. In that day there shall be a fountain opened to the house of David and to the inhabitants of Jerusalem for sin and for uncleanness. (13:1)
57. False prophets will be thrust through when they prophesy. (13:2-5)

31st Event: The Removal of the Ten Tribes from America to the Land of Israel.

After the Ten Tribes have come from the north to the New Jerusalem and have dwelt in the Americas for a period of time, they are expected to move as a unit to the land of Israel and inherit portions of the land as outlined by Ezekiel. They will join with the house of Judah and form a single, unified government. This section contains prophecies pertaining to their removal from America to Israel and also prophecies which speak of the gathering of Ephraim, the Ten Tribes, or Israel but do not specify from where they will be gathered. (See JD 18:25; 14:349-50; 20:153)

Jeremiah:

1. The Lord will bring Israel to feed on Carmel and Bashan, Mount Ephraim and Gilead. The iniquity of Israel and Judah will not be found in that day. (50:19-20; See #38)

2. The Lord will build the people. They shall yet plant vines on the mountains of Samaria. (31:2-5)
3. The watchmen upon Mount Ephraim shall cry, "Arise ye, and let us go up to Zion unto the Lord our God." (31:6-7)
4. The Lord will remember Ramah and Ephraim and restore their children. (31:15-20)

Zechariah:

5. They of Ephraim shall be like a mighty man. The Lord will gather them, and they shall increase as they have increased. They shall remember the Lord in far countries and turn again. (10:7-9)
6. The Lord will gather Ephraim out of Egypt and Assyria and they will settle in Gilead and Lebanon, and place shall not be found for them. (10:10)
7. Ephraim shall pass through the sea with affliction, and shall smite the waves in the sea, and all the deeps of the river shall dry up. (10:11-12)

32nd Event: The Rule of David the Prince.

As the House of Israel returns to their homeland they will combine under the rule of a descendant of the house of David, David the prince. He will oversee the construction of the temple and will govern during the Battle of Armageddon and on into the millennium. (See HC 6:253 & D & C 132:38-39)

Hosea:

? 1. Judah and Israel will be gathered together and appoint themselves one head. (1:11)
2. After many days Israel will return and seek the Lord their God and David their king. (3:5)

Isaiah:

3. Prince David will rule. (55:3-5)
    A. He will be a witness to the people.
    B. He will be a leader and commander.
    C. He shall call a nation he does not know.
    D. Nations which do not know him shall run to him.

    E. The Lord will glorify him.
? 4. A rod and branch shall come out of the stem of Jesse. (11:1-5)
    A. He shall have the spirit of the Lord. (11:2)
    B. He shall judge the poor and meek with righteousness. (11:3-4)
    C. He shall slay the wicked. (11:4)
  5. In that day (when there will be those of Israel who will have escaped) shall the branch of the Lord be beautiful. (4:2)

Jeremiah:

  6. The Lord will raise up a righteous Branch. (23:5-6)
    A. A king who shall reign and prosper.
    B. He shall execute judgment and justice.
    C. In his days Judah shall be saved, and Israel shall dwell safely.
    D. He shall be called "The Lord Our Righteousness."
  7. They shall serve the Lord and David their king. (30:9)
  8. The Lord will cause the Branch of righteousness to grow up unto David; David shall never want for a man to sit upon the throne of the house of Israel. (33:15-18)
  9. The covenant that the seed of David will reign on the throne will not be broken unless the day and night cease to come in their order. (33:19-26)

Ezekiel:

  10. The Lord will set His servant, David, over them. (34:23-24)
  11. One king shall be king to them all: David. (37:22-25)
  12. The east gate of the sanctuary will be reserved for the prince. (44:1-3)
  13. The sacrifices to be offered by the prince are defined. (45:14-25)
  14. The prince shall worship at the threshold of the east gate of the inner court. (46:1-3)
  15. Regulations regarding the prince are given. (46:4-18)

SIX MAJOR DOCTRINES 141

Haggai:
>? 16. In that day, I will take thee, O Zerubbabel, and will make thee as a signet, for I have chosen thee. (2:23)

Zechariah:
> 17. Speak unto Joshua saying (6:12-13)
>   A. Behold the man whose name is The Branch,
>   B. He shall grow up out of his place,
>   C. He shall build the temple of the Lord,
>   D. He shall bear the glory, and shall sit and rule upon his throne.
>   E. He shall be a priest upon his throne.
>   F. The counsel of peace shall be between them both.

33rd Event: The Construction of the Temple in Jerusalem.

As the house of Israel returns to its homeland in large numbers, it is anticipated that the Jerusalem temple will again be built. Sacrificial worship will also be restored. (See JD 24:215; HC 4:211-12)

Amos:
> 1. God will raise up the tabernacle of David and raise up his ruins. (9:11)

Micah:
> 2. The glory of Judah in the last days is predicted. (4:1-7; See #41)
> 3. The house of the Lord shall be established in the tops of the mountains. Many nations shall come to learn of God, and the law shall go forth of Zion. (4:1-2)

Isaiah:
> 4. Wood from Lebanon will be brought to adorn the sanctuary. (60:13-17)
> 5. The Lord's house shall be established in the tops of the mountains, and all nations shall flow unto it. (2:1-3)

Ezekiel:

6. The Lord will place His sanctuary and tabernacle in the midst of them for evermore. (37:26-27)
7. The dimensions and description of the latter-day temple are given. (40:3-49)
8. More dimensions are given. (43:13-17)
9. The ordinances for offering sacrifices are given. (43:18-27)
10. The rules and ordinances for the temple are given. (44:4-31)
11. The division of the land for the temple and priests is defined. (45:1-5)
12. The division of the land for the prince is defined. (45:7-8)
13. The measuring system is defined. (45:9-13)
14. Water will come out from the temple, and will flow into the Dead Sea, and fish will flourish there. (47:1-12)

Zechariah:

15. The Lord is returned to Jerusalem with mercies: his house shall be built in it. (1:16)

34th Event: Israel's Political Affairs.

Rather than being a specific event, this is a general category dealing with the relationships of Israel and other countries in the last days. Most of the prophecies concerning this period are without identifying chronological clues and so cannot be placed in order with exactness. They seem to take place in the period when Israel exists as a nation and before the Battle of Armageddon. It is sometimes difficult to determine whether events should be classed in this category or as a reference to the Battle of Armageddon.

Amos:

1. Israel will possess the remnant of Edom and of all the heathen which are called by the Lord's name. (9:12; see #41)

Isaiah:

    2. The leaders of Egypt are not wise, but make their people err. (19:11-14)
    3. In that day the Lord will heal Egypt and the Egyptians shall know and worship the Lord. (19:16-22)
    4. In that day there will be a highway from Egypt to Assyria and Israel will be a blessing in the Lord. (19:23-25)
    5. The light of Israel will be a flame which will devour the land of Assyria. (10:16-19)
    6. Israel and Judah will unite and stand together against their enemies. (11:13-16)
?   7. The pride of Moab will be brought down. (25:9-12)

Zephaniah:

    8. Moab and Ammon shall be destroyed by the residue of the Lord's people and the remnant of His people shall possess them. (2:9-10)

Obadiah:

    9. The house of Israel will be as a flame and burn Esau as stubble. (18)
  10. The children of Israel shall possess the lands of their neighbors. (19-20; See also #30-31)

Jeremiah:

  11. The Lord will bring again (restore) Moab in the latter days. (48:47)
  12. The Ammonites will be restored afterward. (49:6)
  13. Elam will be restored in the latter days. (49:39)

Joel:

  14. Egypt shall be a desolation, and Edom shall be a desolate wilderness. (3:19)

35th Event: The Battle of Armageddon.

This great war which is to take place in the land of Israel is one of the most prophesied about events of the scriptures. It draws its name from the city of Megiddo in the plain of Esdraelon in north-western

Israel. It appears that the surrounding nations, motivated by greed, will attempt to conquer and plunder Israel. The attacking army, Magog, will be led by its general, Gog. As the covenant people are about to succumb to their attack the Lord will appear on the Mount of Olives. His appearance will rally the people of Israel and they will emerge victorious. Events 35, 36, 37, and 38 are expected to take place concurrently. (See JD 7:188-89; Rev. 11:1-12; D & C 45:48-52)

Hosea:

1. They shall be like the sands of the sea, and known as the sons of the living God. Judah and Israel shall be gathered together and appoint themselves one head, for great shall be the day of Jezreel. (1:10-11)
2. God will speak comfortably to Israel and give her the valley of Achor for a door of hope. God will give them safety and betroth them to himself, and will show mercy. (2:14-23)

? 3. God will heal us. After two days will he revive us: in the third day he will raise us up. (6:1-3)

Isaiah:

4. In that day the Lord will heal Egypt and the Egyptians shall know and worship the Lord. (19:16-22)
5. The Lord will sift the nations with destruction through devouring fire, scattering, tempest, and hailstones. (30:27-30)
6. There shall be water on every high mountain and the light of the sun shall be sevenfold in the day the towers fall and the Lord heals the wound of his people. (30:25-26)
7. In that day the Lord will give his people the spirit of judgment and strength in battle. (28:5-6)
8. When the enemy shall come in like a flood, the Spirit of the Lord shall lift up a standard against him and the Redeemer shall come to Zion. (59:19-21)
9. The Lord shall make a consumption in the midst of all the land. (10:23)
10. The Lord will ease himself of his enemies and will purge the dross of Israel. (1:24-25)

SIX MAJOR DOCTRINES   145

   11. Israel shall be powerful and lay hold of the prey.
       (5:27-29)
   12. In that day there will be darkness and sorrow in the
       land. (5:30; See Joel 3:12-15)
   13. Those who have warred against Israel shall not be
       found. (41:11-14)
? 14. He shall slay the wicked. (11:4)
   15. Jerusalem will drink the cup of the Lord's fury.
       (51:17-18)
   16. These two things are come unto thee: Thy sons will
       lie in the streets of Jerusalem, who have been full
       of fury of the Lord. (51:19-20; See 2 Ne. 8:19-20;
       Rev. 11:1-13)
   17. The Lord will take His fury from Israel and place it
       on those who afflict her. (51:22-23)
   18. The Lord will purge Jerusalem. (4:3-4)
   19. The Lord will show His indignation upon His ene-
       mies, and the slain of the Lord shall be many.
       (66:14-17)
   20. Men will see the carcasses of those who have trans-
       gressed against the Lord. (66:24)
   21. At the lifting up of the Lord the nations were scat-
       tered. His spoil shall be gathered. (33:2-4)
   22. The highways lay waste, the earth mourneth and
       languisheth. (33:7-8)
   23. The Lord has destroyed cities but has aided the poor
       and the needy. (25:1-5)

Zephaniah:

   24. The Lord will assemble the nations to pour his indig-
       nation upon them. (3:8)
   25. The Lord will take away the haughty and shall leave
       an afflicted and poor people, but they will be free
       from pride and iniquity. (3:11-13)
   26. The Lord will cast out enemies and undo those that
       afflict Israel. (3:15, 19)

Obadiah:

   27. The day of the Lord is near upon all the heathen.
       (15-16)
   28. There shall be deliverance and holiness upon Mount
       Zion, and the house of Jacob shall possess their
       possessions. (17)

Jeremiah:

29. The Lord will make a full end of the nations where she has been driven. (46:28)
30. The house of Israel will not go wholly unpunished. (46:28)
31. At first the Lord will recompense their iniquity double. (16:17-18)
? 32. They shall know the Lord's hand and his might. (16:21)
33. The Lord will break the bonds off Israel and Judah in the time of Jacob's trouble. (30:1-8)
? 34. The Lord will make a full end of the nations in which Israel is scattered but will not make a full end of Israel. (30:10-11; cf. Jer. 46:27-28)
? 35. The Lord will correct Israel and not leave her altogether unpunished. (30:11-12)

Daniel:

? 36. A king of fierce countenance will be raised up. (8:23-25)
   A. His power shall be mighty, but not by his own power.
   B. He shall prosper and practice.
   C. He shall destroy the mighty and holy people.
   D. He shall cause craft to prosper in his hand.
   E. He shall magnify himself in his heart.
   F. By peace he shall destroy many.
   G. He shall stand up against the Prince of princes.
   H. He shall be broken without hand.

Ezekiel:

37. The Lord will be sanctified in them before the heathen. (20:41)
? 38. Fire will devour every green tree in the south forest, and faces from the south to the north shall be burned therein. And all flesh shall see that I the Lord have kindled it: it shall not be quenched. (20:45-48)
39. The Lord will be sanctified among his people in the sight of the heathen and will execute judgments upon all those that despise His people round about them. (28:25-26)

Six Major Doctrines

? 40. The Lord will judge His flock. He will judge between cattle and cattle. He will destroy the fat and the strong and feed them with judgment. (34:16-22)
41. They shall be safe in their land when the Lord has broken the bands of their yoke, and delivered them out of the hand of those that served themselves of them. They shall no more be a prey to the heathen. (34:27-28)
42. The mountains shalt devour men no more, neither will the Lord cause men to hear in thee the shame of the heathen any more. (36:13-15)
43. The Lord will sanctify His great name which was profaned among the heathen and the heathen shall know that I am the Lord, when He shall be sanctified in Israel before their eyes. (36:21-23)
44. The general, Gog, is identified: (38:2, 3; 39:1)
    A. From the land of Magog.
    B. The chief prince of Meshech and Tubal.
45. The Lord will turn back his (Gog's) army of horses and horsemen, bucklers, shields and swords. (38:3-4)
46. Persia, Ethiopia, Libya, Gomer, Togarmah and many people will be with him. (38:5-6)
47. Israel is to be prepared when it is brought forth out of the nations. (38:7-8)
48. They shall come to take a spoil. (38:9-13)
49. They will come on horseback from the north parts, a great company. (38:14-16)
50. The Lord will bring them against His land that the heathen may know Him when He is sanctified in Gog before their eyes. (38:16)
51. When Gog comes against Israel there will be a great shaking in that land; and the mountains and walls shall be thrown down. (38:17-20)
52. The Lord will call for a sword against him throughout the mountains. (38:21)
53. The Lord will rain pestilence, rain, hailstones, fire and brimstone upon them. Thus He will magnify and sanctify Himself before the heathens. (38:22-23; See D & C 29:16-21)
54. The Lord will turn Gog back and leave but a sixth part of his army. (39:1-2)
55. Gog will come up from the north parts to the mountains of Israel. (39:2)

56. Gog will fall with his bands upon the open field. (39:3-5)
57. The Lord will send fire on the army of Magog so the heathen shall know that he is the Lord. (39:6-8)
58. The people from the cities of Israel shall burn their weapons for seven years and shall spoil and rob those that robbed them. (39:9-10)
59. The valley of the passengers on the east of the sea will be the burial place for Gog and his multitude. It will take seven months to bury them. (39:11-16)
60. The fowls and beasts will devour the dead. (39:17-20; See D & C 29:18-20)

Zechariah:

61. The Lord will shake his hand upon the nations that spoil Israel, and they shall be a spoil to the servants, and ye shall know that the Lord of hosts hath sent me. (2:8-9)
? 62. The two olive branches are the two anointed ones, that stand by the Lord of the whole earth. (4:12-14; See Rev. 11:4)
63. The Lord has made Judah as His goodly horse in the battle, and they shall be as mighty men. They shall fight, because the Lord is with them. (10:3-5)
64. The pride of Assyria shall be brought down, and the sceptre of Egypt shall depart away. (10:11)
65. They will lay siege both against Judah and against Jerusalem. (12:1-2)
66. All that burden themselves with Judah in that day shall be cut in pieces, though all the people of the earth be gathered together against it. (12:3)
67. In that day the Lord will smite every horse with astonishment and blindness and his rider with madness. (12:4)
68. The governors of Judah shall say in their heart, The inhabitants of Jerusalem shall be my strength in the Lord. In that day the governors of Judah shall devour the people round about, and Jerusalem shall be inhabited again. (12:5-6)
69. The Lord shall save the tents of Judah first, that the glory of the house of David and the inhabitants of Jerusalem do not magnify themselves against Judah. (12:7)

SIX MAJOR DOCTRINES 149

70. In that day shall the Lord defend the inhabitants of Jerusalem; and he that is feeble among them at that day shall be as David. The Lord will seek to destroy all the nations that come against Jerusalem. (12:8-9)
71. In that day shall there be a great mourning in Jerusalem, as the mourning of Hadadrimmon in the valley of Megiddon. (12:11-14)
72. The spoil will be divided in the midst of thee. (14:1)
73. The Lord will gather all nations against Jerusalem to battle. The city shall be taken, and half the city shall go into captivity, and the residue of the city shall not be cut off from the city. (14:2)
74. In all the land, two parts therein shall be cut off and die; but the third shall be left therein and shall be refined as silver is refined. (13:7-9)
75. Ye shall flee to the valley of the mountains. (14:5)
76. It shall come to pass in that day that the light should not be clear, nor dark, not day, nor night; at evening time it shall be light. (14:6-7)
77. The land shall be turned as a plain from Geba to Rimmon. (14:10)
78. This will be the plague wherewith the Lord will smite all the people that have fought against Jerusalem: Their flesh, eyes and tongue shall consume away. (14:12)
79. A great tumult from the Lord shall be among them, and Judah also shall fight at Jerusalem. (14:13-14)
80. The wealth of all the heathen round about shall be gathered together. (14:14)
81. And so shall be the plague of the horse, mule, camel, ass, and all the beasts that shall be in these tents, as this plague. (14:15)

Joel:

82. A strong nation has come and laid the countryside bare. (1:6-7)
83. The offering is cut off from the house of the Lord and the priests mourn. (1:8-9)
84. The field is wasted and the harvest is perished. (1:10-12)
85. The priests howl for the drink offering is withheld. Call a solemn assembly and gather the elders into the house of the Lord. (1:13-14)

86. The day of the Lord is at hand. As a destruction from the Almighty shall it come. (1:15)
87. Fire hath devoured the wilderness and the rivers of water are dried up. (1:16-20)
88. Blow the trumpet and sound the alarm in Zion, the holy mountain, for the day of the Lord is nigh at hand. (2:1)
89. A day of darkness, gloominess, clouds, and thick darkness in the morning. (2:2)
90. A great people and a strong. There shall not be another people like it for many generations. (2:2)
91. A flame burns before and behind them. They leave the land desolate. (2:3)
92. A description of the approaching army. (2:4-9)
    A. As horsemen, so shall they run.
    B. Like the noise of chariots in the tops of mountains shall they leap.
    C. They shall run like mighty men.
    D. They shall climb the wall like men of war.
    E. They shall not break their ranks.
    F. When they fall upon the sword they shall not be wounded.
    G. They shall run to and fro in the city. They shall enter in at the windows like a thief.
93. The earth shall quake before them; and the heavens shall tremble. (2:10)
94. The sun and the moon shall be dark, and the stars shall withdraw their shining. (2:10; See D & C 29: 14; 8-13)
95. The Lord shall utter his voice before his army: for his camp is very great: for he is strong that executeth his word. (2:11)
96. The day of the Lord is great and very terrible; and who can abide it? (2:11)
97. Repent and rend your hearts. (2:12-14)
98. Let the priests pray that the heathen shall not rule over them. (2:15-17)
99. Then the Lord will pity his people and send them corn. (2:18-19)
100. The Lord will remove far off the northern army and drive him to a barren land where his face is toward the east sea and his back toward the utmost sea. (2:20)

SIX MAJOR DOCTRINES 151

101. The army's stink and ill savour shall come up. (2:20)
102. The Lord will restore the rain and the food which has been lost. (2:21-26)
103. The Lord will be in the midst of Israel, and His people will know he is their God. (2:27)
104. The Lord will show wonders in the heavens and in the earth: blood, and fire, and pillars of smoke. The sun shall be turned into darkness and the moon into blood, before the great and terrible day of the Lord come. (2:31)
105. In the time when the Lord shall bring again the captivity of Judah and Jerusalem the Lord will gather all nations and bring them down into the valley of Jehoshaphat and will plead with them there. (3:1-2)
106. The nations have sold and scattered Israel. The Lord will recompense His enemies and Judah will sell their children to the Sabeans. (3:3-8)
107. Proclaim war among the Gentiles, and beat your plowshares into swords. (3:9-10)
108. Assemble the heathen. Let them come up to the valley of Jehoshaphat, for there the Lord will sit to judge all the heathen round about. (3:11-13)
109. Multitudes, multitudes in the valley of decision. (3:14)
110. The day of the Lord is near in the valley of decision. (3:14)
112. The sun, moon, and stars shall be darkened. (3:15)

36th Event: The Fall of Rome.

John the Revelator describes the destruction of the great city which sits on seven mountains or hills and is close enough to the sea that the smoke of its destruction can be seen from ships. He shows it as being destroyed at the time of the earthquake during the Battle of Armageddon. Events 35, 36, 37, and 38 are expected to take place concurrently. (See Rev. 16:12-21; 18:1-24) (No References in the Prophetic Section of the Old Testament.)

37th Event: The Appearance of Christ on the Mount of Olives.

The Savior will appear on the Mount of Olives as the Battle of Armageddon is raging in Jerusalem and throughout Israel. His appearance will rally the distressed forces of Israel and will enable them to successfully repel their oppressors. He will demonstrate the wounds which have been inflicted upon him to show that he is the crucified Jesus. His appearance will be accompanied by a great earthquake. Events 35, 36, 37, and 38 are expected to take place concurrently. (See Rev. 19:11-16; D & C 45:47-53; *Millennial Star*, 21:583, Sept. 19, 1859)

Isaiah:

1. When the enemy shall come in like a flood, the Spirit of the Lord shall lift up a standard against him and the Redeemer shall come to Zion. (59:19-21; See #35)
2. The Lord shall appear to your joy. There will be noise from the city and the temple as the Lord renders recompense to his enemies. (66:5-6)

Zechariah:

3. One shall say unto him, What are these wounds in thine hands? Then He shall answer, Those with which I was wounded in the house of my friends. (13:6; See also D & C 45:48-54; See #38)
4. The Lord shall stand in that day upon the mount of Olives and the mount shall cleave in the midst thereof toward the east and toward the west, and there shall be a very great valley. (14:4; See D & C 45:48-49; 133:20)
5. The Lord my God shall come, and all the saints with thee. (14:5)
6. The Lord shall be king over all the earth in that day. (14:9)

38th Event: The Conversion of the House of Israel.

The conversion of the house of Israel is to be culminated with the Savior's appearance on the Mount of Olives. Many of Israel will already have been converted, however, including the Ten Tribes who will have dwelt in the American Zion and many who will have been converted by the 144,000. Events 35, 36, 37, and 38 are expected to take place concurrently. (See D & C 45:51-52)

Hosea:

1. God will speak comfortably to Israel and give her the valley of Achor for a door of hope. God will give them safety and betroth them to himself, and will show mercy. (2:14-23; See Zech. 14:1-5; #30-31; #35)

Isaiah:

2. Jacob shall sanctify the name of the Lord and learn doctrine. (29:22-24)
3. Put on thy strength, O Zion. (52:1; See Moro. 10:31; D & C 113:7-8; See #24)
4. He that is left in Jerusalem (after the Lord has purged its filth by judgment and burning) shall be called holy. (4:3)

Jeremiah:

5. The Lord will bring Israel to feed on Carmel and Bashan, Mount Ephraim and Gilead. The iniquity of Israel and Judah will not be found in that day. (50:19-20; See #31)
6. Judah and Israel shall call God "My Father," and shall not turn away from Him. (3:19)
7. The Lord will be the God of all the families of Israel. (31:1)
8. God will make a new covenant with the house of Israel. He will put his law in their hearts. He will be their God, and they shall be his people. They all shall know the Lord. (31:31-37)

Ezekiel:
9. He will bring them into the bond of the covenant. (20:37)
10. In his holy mountain shall all of them in the land serve the Lord, and he will accept them. (20:40)
11. Ye shall remember your doings wherein ye have been defiled, and ye shall loathe yourselves. (20:43)
12. His people shall know the Lord is their God. (28:26)
13. They shall no more be consumed with hunger. Thus shall they know that the Lord their God is with them. (34:29-31)
14. The Lord will give Israel a new spirit and a new heart, and He will be their God. (36:24-28)
15. The waste cities shall be filled with flocks of men: and they shall know that I am the Lord. (36:37-38)
16. The heathen will see the judgment the Lord has executed. The house of Israel shall know the Lord is their God from that day forward. (39:21-24)
17. When the Lord has gathered His people out of their enemies' lands, and is sanctified in them in the sight of many nations, then shall they know that He is the Lord their God. (39:25-28)

Zechariah:
18. They shall be the Lord's people, and He shall be their God. (8:8)
19. The Lord will pour upon the house of David and upon the inhabitants of Jerusalem the spirit of grace and of supplication, and they shall look upon me whom they have pierced. (12:10; See Jn. 19:37)
20. One shall say unto him, What are these wounds in thine hands? Then he shall answer, Those with which I was wounded in the house of my friends. (13:6; see also D & C 45:48-54; #37)

Malachi:
21. Then shall the offering of Judah and Jerusalem be pleasant unto the Lord. (3:4)

39th Event: Christ Will Come to the Jerusalem Temple and Place His Glory upon Zion.

It is prophesied that the Savior will come to the

Six Major Doctrines 155

Jerusalem temple and will visit with David the prince. This appears to take place after the Battle of Armageddon but evidence is not conclusive on this point.

Hosea:

    1. I will be thy king. (13:9-10)

Isaiah:

?   2. The Lord will place his salvation and glory in Zion. (46:12-13)
    3. The Lord will place his glory (smoke or fire) upon Zion as a defense. (4:5-6)
    4. The Lord will not rest until the righteousness of Jerusalem goes forth as brightness, and the salvation thereof as a lamp that burneth. (62:1)
    5. The glory of the Lord is upon Israel, yet gross darkness covers the people of the earth. (60:1-2)
    6. The glory of the Lord shall be there and provide light. (60:19-20)

Ezekiel:

    7. The Lord will not hide His face from them any more, for He has poured out His spirit upon the house of Israel. (39:29)

Haggai:

    8. I will fill this house with glory, and in this place I will give peace. (2:7-9)

Zechariah:

    9. The Lord will come and dwell in the midst of Israel. (2:10)

Joel:

    10. The Lord also shall utter his voice out of Jerusalem. So shall ye know that He dwells in Zion. (3:16-17)
    11. Judah shall dwell forever, for the Lord dwelleth in Zion. (3:20-21)

40th Event: A Mission to the Heathen Nations.

The Battle of Armageddon will open the way for a third major missionary effort, in which the gospel message will be carried among the heathen nations. This will seemingly be of relatively short duration, and then will blend into the 4th period of missionary effort, a final mission to all mankind in preparation for Christ's coming in glory.

Isaiah:

1. In that day the Lord will heal Egypt and the Egyptians shall know and worship the Lord. (19:16-22; #34; See #35)
2. The conversion of Egypt: (19:18-25)
    A. Five cities of Egypt shall speak the language of Caanan and shall swear unto the Lord of Hosts.
    B. There shall be an altar to the Lord in Egypt and a pillar to the Lord at the border.
    C. The Lord shall send Egypt a great savior, and he shall deliver them.
    D. The Egyptians shall know the Lord and shall do sacrifice and vows unto Him.
    E. The Lord shall smite Egypt and then heal it, and they shall return even to the Lord.
    F. There shall be a highway out of Egypt to Assyria, even a blessing in the midst of the land.
3. Men will call the people of Israel the ministers of God; their seed will be known among the Gentiles. (61:6-9; See #41)
4. The Lord will cause righteousness and praise to spring forth before all the nations. (61:10-11)

Ezekiel:

5. The heathen shall know that the Lord sanctifies Israel. (37:28)

Zechariah:

6. Many nations shall be joined to the Lord in that day. (2:11)

41st Event: Israel's Growth Following the Battle of Armageddon and The Final Mission To All Mankind.

There is to be a final missionary labor conducted throughout the world. It is distinguished from the third period of missionary labor by including the Gentiles (Christian nations) as well as the Heathens (Non-Christian nations). This will be the fourth period of missionary labor. During this period Israel will be increasing in glory and prestige as the world at large reaches the height of its wickedness. This gathering process will be a final call to come out of wickedness. This missionary period will extend into the millennium. References cited in this category deal with the missionary effort and with the rise and glory of Israel following the Battle of Armageddon. It is difficult to distinguish with certainty whether some of the passages deal with pre-millennial or with millennial conditions, since the scriptures give no indication as to what event begins the millennium.

Amos:

1. Israel will possess the remnant of Edom and of all the heathen which are called by the Lord's name. (9:12; See #34)

Micah:

2. The glory of Judah in the last days is predicted. (4:1-7; See #33)

Isaiah:

3. The Lord which gathereth the outcasts of Israel will gather others to him, beside those that are gathered unto him. (56:8)
4. Afterward thou shalt be called the city of righteousness, the faithful city. Zion shall be redeemed with judgment. (1:26-27)
5. The good things of Palestine will no longer be given to enemies. (62:8-9)

6. They shall call them the Holy People, the redeemed of the Lord. (62:12)
7. The Gentiles and kings shall come to thy light. (60:3-4)
8. The abundance of the sea shall be given to Israel; the surrounding nations will bring their treasures. (60:5-7)
9. The sons of strangers shall build up thy walls, and their kings shall minister unto thee. (60:10-11)
10. The nation and kingdom that will not serve thee shall perish. (60:12)
11. Those that despised Israel and the sons of those that afflicted her will bow down to her. (60:14)
12. Thou shalt suck the milk of the Gentiles and kings. (60:16)
13. Violence shall no more be heard in the land. (60:18)
14. A little one shall become a thousand, and a small one a strong nation. (60:21-22)
15. The Lord will cause righteousness and praise to spring forth before all the nations. (61:10-11; See #40)
16. Jerusalem shall be comforted. She shall have peace like a river and the glory of the Gentiles like a flowing stream. (66:9-13)
17. The nations will gather to Jerusalem to see the Lord's glory. Those that have escaped will be sent to the nations to declare the glory of God among the Gentiles. (66:18-19)
18. The nations will help bring the remaining members of Israel as an offering to the Lord. (66:19-21)
19. Israel's seed and all flesh will come up to worship him. (66:22-23)
20. A song of praise unto God when his goodness is known throughout all the earth. (12:1-6)
21. The Lord's house shall be established in the tops of the mountains, and all nations shall flow unto it. (2:1-3; See also 11:6-9; 65:25; #33)
22. We have a strong city where only the righteous may enter. (26:1-4)
? 23. The Lord has made the nation increase. (26:12-18; See #40)
24. Thou art glorified: thou hadst removed the nation far unto all the ends of the earth. We have not wrought any deliverance in the earth, neither have

SIX MAJOR DOCTRINES   159

   the inhabitants of the world fallen. (26:15-18)
25. The Lord is exalted and has filled Zion with judgment and righteousness. (33:4-6)

Zephaniah:

26. Men shall worship the Lord, every one from his place, even all the isles of the heathen. (2:11)
27. The Lord will give the people a pure language. (3:9)
28. The dispersed will return from beyond the rivers of Ethiopia. (3:10)

Jeremiah:

29. Jerusalem shall be called the throne of the Lord, and all nations shall be gathered unto it. (3:17)
30. The gentiles will come and acknowledge that they had inherited lies (which kept them from recognizing God). (16:19-20)
31. Israel will multiply, their rulers will draw near the Lord, and He shall be their God. (30:19-22)

Ezekiel:

32. The Lord will make them a covenant of peace. The shower will come down in its season and the earth shall yield her increase. (34:25-27)
33. The Lord will multiply the food, and there will be no more famine. (36:29-31)
34. In the day that I shall have cleansed you from all your iniquities, I will also cause you to dwell in the cities, and the wastes shall be builded and the desolate land shall be tilled. Then the heathen that are left round about you shall know that I the Lord build the ruined places. (36:32-36)

Haggai:

35. The desire of all nations shall come. (2:7)

Zechariah:

36. Old people and young children will dwell happily in Jerusalem. (8:4-6)
37. People from many cities and nations will come to seek the Lord in Jerusalem. (8:20-22)

38. Ten men of all nations shall take hold of a Jew, saying, we will go with you, for we have heard that God is with you. (8:23)
39. Living waters shall go out from Jerusalem; half of them toward the former sea, and half of them toward the hinder sea. (14:8)
40. Everyone that is left of all the nations which came against Jerusalem shall even go up from year to year to worship the King. Upon those that do not come up to worship, there shall be no rain. (14:16-17)
41. If Egypt does not come up to worship there shall be the plague. (14:18-19)
42. In that day shall there be upon the bells of the horses, Holiness Unto the Lord. The pots shall be like the bowls before the altar. All they that sacrifice shall come and take of them, and seethe therein. (14:20-21)
43. In that day there shall be no more the Canaanite in the house of the Lord of hosts. (14:21)

Malachi:

44. The Lord's name will be great among the Gentiles and among the heathen. (1:11)

Joel:

45. It shall come to pass afterward that the Lord will pour out His spirit on all flesh. Your sons and daughters shall prophesy, old men will dream dreams and young men shall see visions. (2:28-29; See Acts 2:14-21; JS 2:41)
46. Deliverance shall be in Mount Zion and in Jerusalem and in the remnant whom the Lord shall call. (2:32)
47. The hills shall flow with milk, the rivers of Judah shall flow with waters, and a fountain shall come forth of the house of the Lord and shall water the valley of Shittim. (3:18)

42nd Event: Christ's Coming in Glory.

Christ will come in glory, accompanied by the hosts of heaven. His coming will be visible to all mankind. The righteous living will be caught up to descend with Him and the righteous dead will come forth from their graves. The earth will be burned and the wicked will be destroyed at His coming. (See *Millennial Star*, 21:583, Sept. 10, 1859; D & C 88:95-110; 29:9-13; 133:46-52; 133:21-25; 101:24-25)

Amos:
1. All the hills shall melt. (9:13)

Micah:
2. Prophecies of coming judgment to all the world. (1:2-4)
3. The Lord will tread upon the high places of the earth and the mountains shall be molten under him. (1:3-4)

Isaiah:
4. The destruction of the transgressors and of the sinners shall be together; they shall be burned and consumed. (1:28-31)
5. The day of the Lord is at hand. (13:6-13)
    A. Men shall be afraid.
    B. The day of the Lord is cruel both with wrath and with fierce anger.
    C. The sun, moon, and stars shall not give their light.
    D. The Lord will punish the world.
    E. A man will be more precious than fine gold.
    F. The Lord will shake the heavens, and the earth shall remove out of her place.
6. The terrible one is brought to naught, and the scorner is consumed, and all that watch for iniquity are cut off. (29:19-21)
7. The wicked shall be destroyed, but the Lord's righteousness shall be forever. (51:6-8)
8. Every valley shall be exalted, and every mountain and hill shall be made low. (40:3-4)
9. The glory of the Lord shall be revealed, and all flesh shall see it together. (40:5)
10. Temporal things shall wither but the word of God shall stand forever. (40:6-8)

11. Fear and a terrible earthquake will come when Christ is exalted. (2:10-21)
12. The Lord will come in His glory, dressed in red apparel, and tread down the wicked. (63:1-6; See D & C 133:46-52)
13. A prayer that the Lord will cleanse the earth with fire. (64:1-3)
14. The Lord will destroy the wicked because they will not learn righteousness. (26:5-11)
15. The Lord will come to punish the inhabitants of the earth for their iniquity. (26:20-21)
16. The earth is desolate, with few men left. (24:1-12)
17. The earth is cleansed because the people have transgressed the laws, changed the ordinances, and broken the everlasting covenant. (24:5-6)
18. The fires of that day will cause the righteous to sing praises to the Lord. (24:13-15)
19. The earth, in this day shall (24:19-20)
    A. Be utterly broken down.
    B. Be clean dissolved.
    C. Be moved exceedingly.
    D. Reel to and fro like a drunkard.
    E. Be removed like a cottage.
    F. Fall and not rise again.
20. The wicked shall be cast into the (spirit) prison, and shall not be visited for many days. (24:21-22)
21. The Lord has destroyed the armies of all nations. Their dead stink. (34:1-3)
22. The host of heaven shall be dissolved, and the heavens shall be rolled together as a scroll. (34:4)
23. The land shall be turned into unquenchable burning, for it is the day of the Lord's vengeance. (34:5-10)
24. The nobles will be removed and thorns will come up in the palaces. (34:11-15)
25. The treacherous spoiler will be spoiled. (33:1)
26. The Lord is exalted, the wicked are burned with fire. (33:10-13)
27. He will rend the veil and reveal himself to the people. (25:7; See D & C 67:10; 38:8)

Nahum:

28. The Lord will take vengeance on his adversaries. (1:2-3)

29. The Lord will dry up the sea and the rivers. (1:4)
30. The mountains quake, the hills melt and the world and all that dwell therein is burned at his presence. (1:5-7)

Habakkuk:

31. God's glory covered the heavens. (3:3-4)
32. He measured the earth, drove asunder the nations, and scattered the everlasting mountains. (3:5-6)
33. Affliction was seen among the people of Cushan (Ethiopia) and Midan. (3:7)
34. The mountains trembled, the overflowing water passed by, the sun and the moon stood still. (3:8-11)
35. The Lord threshed the heathen and the wicked in anger. (3:12-16)

Jeremiah:

36. The Lord will punish the wicked: in the latter days ye shall consider it. (30:23-24)

Zechariah:

37. The Lord will remove the iniquity of that land in one day. (3:9)
38. The roll is a record of those that steal and swear. Those that commit those crimes shall be cut off. (5:3-4)

Malachi:

39. The Lord will come in judgment upon the wicked, but the sons of Jacob will not be consumed. (3:5-6)
40. The day cometh when all that do wickedly shall be as stubble. (4:1; See also JS 2:36-37, 40; JS 2:37; D & C 29:9, 24; and 133:64)

43rd Event: The First Resurrection, or Resurrection of the Righteous.

Many of the righteous dead will be resurrected at the time of Christ's coming in glory. Some of the dead may also be resurrected long before his advent. (See D & C 88:95-110; JD 25:33-34; 9:27)

Hosea:

    1. I will ransom them from the power of the grave; I will redeem them from death. (13:14)

Isaiah:

    2. He will swallow up death in victory. (25:8)

Zechariah:

? 3. As for thee also, by the blood of thy covenant I have sent forth thy prisoners out of the pit wherein is no water. The Lord will render double unto thee. (9:11-12; See D & C 128:22; Is. 14:15; 24:22; Ezek. 31:16; 32:21-30 etc.)

Malachi:

    4. A book of remembrance was kept for them that feared the Lord. They will be spared when the Lord makes up his jewels. Then shall ye return, and discern between the righteous and the wicked. (3:16-18; See Esther 6:1-11; Moses 6:5-6)

44th Event: The Millennium.

The millennium is to be a thousand years of peace and prosperity during which the Savior will rule here upon the earth. The scriptures do not clearly define what event will begin the millennial era, but it is generally regarded as beginning with Christ's coming in glory. (See D & C 63:50-52; Rev. 20:1-3; D & C 101:32-34)

Amos:

    1. Agriculture will be simpler and year around. The mountains shall drop sweet wine. (9:13)

Micah:

    2. The Lord shall judge among many people and rebuke strong nations afar off. They shall beat their spears into pruning hooks. Nation shall not lift up a sword against nation, neither will they learn war any more, and none shall make them afraid. (4:3-4)

SIX MAJOR DOCTRINES   165

   3. The Lord shall reign over them in mount Zion from henceforth, even for ever. (4:7)
   4. The Lord shall be great unto the ends of the earth. (5:1-4)

Isaiah:

   5. Of the increase of his government and peace there shall be no end, upon the throne of David, and upon his kingdom, to order it, and to establish it with judgment, and with justice from henceforth even for ever. (9:7)
   6. He shall set judgment in the earth unto truth. (42:3-4)
   7. Peace during the millennium. (11:6-9)
 ? 8. In that day there shall be a root of Jesse, which shall stand for an ensign; to it shall the Gentiles seek. (11:10)
   9. The Lord will create a new heaven and a new earth. (66:22)
  10. The Lord God will rule from Jerusalem. (40:9-11)
  11. Out of Zion shall go forth the law, and the word of the Lord from Jerusalem. (2:3)
  12. Nation shall not lift up the sword against nation. (2:4)
  13. The Lord shall reign in mount Zion, and in Jerusalem. (24:23)
  14. The Lord will punish the wicked among the people of Israel. (65:11-16)
  15. A child shall live to one hundred. (65:18-20)
  16. They shall build and enjoy the work of their hands. (65:21-24)
  17. They shall not hurt or destroy; there shall be peace. (65:25)
  18. A king shall reign in righteousness, and princes shall rule in judgment. (32:1-4)
  19. No longer will the vile person be honored as good, nor be allowed to destroy the poor with lying words. (32:5-8)
  20. The spirit shall be poured out from on high and the righteous will dwell in quietness and assurance for ever. (32:15-20)
  21. He will give the people a feast of fat things. (rich blessings) (25:6)

Obadiah:

    22. Saviors shall come upon mount Zion to judge the mount of Esau and the kingdom shall be the Lord's. (21)

Zechariah:

    23. In that day shall ye call every man his neighbor under the vine and under the fig tree. (3:10)

? 24. The Lord will speak peace to the heathen, and His dominion shall be from sea even to sea, and from the river even to the ends of the earth. (9:10)

45th Event: The Battle of Gog and Magog.

At the end of the millennial era wickedness will again break out and Satan will be loosed. A struggle will take place between the forces of good and the hosts of evil. The evil forces are personified as Gog and Magog. They are expected to encompass the saints in the "beloved city" and then be destroyed by fire from heaven. (See Rev. 20:7-10; HC 5:298; JD 16:119-20, 322; D & C 88:111-116; 43:31-33)

Isaiah:

    1. The wicked shall be destroyed, but the Lord's righteousness will be forever. (51:7-8; See #42, #48)

46th Event: The Second Resurrection, or Resurrection of the Unrighteous.

A second resurrection will take place in which the remainder of the dead will regain their bodies. These are the people who will inherit the telestial kingdom or will become sons of perdition. (See D & C 76:81-85; 88:100-102; 29:26-30; Rev. 20:13)

Isaiah:

    1. He will bring prisoners from the (spirit?) prison. (42:7)

    2. He shall release prisoners. (49:9)

SIX MAJOR DOCTRINES   167

47th Event: The Final Judgment.

A final judgment will be held in which all mankind will come before the Savior to be judged for their works. (See D & C 19:1-3; 38:5; Rev. 20:12-15; Mos. 27:31; 2 Ne. 9:13-16; JD 17:182)

Isaiah:

1. The Lord has sworn that every knee shall bow and every tongue shall acknowledge Him. (45:23-25)

48th Event: The Crowning and Exalting of Christ and the Saints.

At the end of the judgment Christ will present the kingdom of the earth to the Father and in turn be crowned with power and glory. (See D & C 76:106-108; 1 Cor. 15:22-26, 28; D & C 130:9; D & C 76:54-62)

Isaiah:

1. The heavens shall vanish and the earth shall wax old like a garment, but the Lord's salvation will continue forever. (51:4-6; See #49)
2. The wicked shall be destroyed, but the Lord's righteousness shall be forever. (51:7-8; See #42; #45)
3. The righteous shall dwell (with God) in everlasting burnings. (33:14-17)
4. Jerusalem shall be a quiet habitation with a tabernacle. It shall not be removed. (33:18-24)

49th Event: The Dissolution of the Earth and its Heaven.

After the final judgment and the crowning of the Savior the earth is to return to its elemental state and pass away into space. The cities of the old and New Jerusalem and their occupants will be caught up into the air until the earth is restored. (See D & C 88:25-26; JD 1:331; 18:346-47)

Isaiah:

1. The heavens shall vanish and the earth shall wax old like a garment, but the Lord's salvation will continue forever. (51:6; See #48)

50th Event: The Re-creation of the Earth as a Celestial World.

The earth is to be re-created as a celestialized sphere. The old and the New Jerusalem will descend upon it and will also become sanctified and immortal. (See Rev. 21:1-27; JD 18:322; D & C 88:17-20; 29:23-25)

Daniel:

1. The kingdom shall stand forever. (2:44)
2. The saints of the most High shall take the kingdom, and possess the kingdom for ever. (7:18, 27)

Summary: After studying this chapter the student should know:

1. The six most predominant doctrinal themes of the prophetic section of the Old Testament are
    A. the nature of God,
    B. God's communication with man,
    C. the nature of sin,
    D. the relationship of man's agency to God's judgment,
    E. counsel for righteous living, and
    F. prophecies of the last days.
2. God reveals Himself as possessing many qualities and attributes known to humans.
3. Prophets are spokesmen and agents for God. Their prophecies are specific and accurate and receive literal fulfillment.
4. The prophets clearly portray the nature of sin. The numerous sins may be classed into five categories:

SIX MAJOR DOCTRINES 169

    A. perversion of religious truth and practices,
    B. apathy and lack of faith,
    C. rejection and opposition to God's plan,
    D. moral depravity, and
    E. social, economic and national wickedness.

5. Man is a free agent and makes his own choices. His attitude toward God controls God's attitude toward him. Though man's life is not predestined, God still maintains ultimate control of the fate of individuals and nations and shapes man's life and activities.

6. Extensive counsel for righteous living is given by the Old Testament prophets. Their counsel is the same as that found in the New Testament and in the teachings of the prophets in the latter days.

7. Prophecies concerning the last days are the largest single doctrinal item found in the scriptures.

8. The Old Testament prophets discussed or alluded to thirty-seven of a selected group of fifty important happenings which are prophesied to take place in the last days. They prophesied extensively concerning fourteen events in particular:

    A. the restoration of the Church,
    B. the coming of the ten tribes from the north to Missouri,
    C. a universal conflict, or fourth world war,
    D. the gathering of Judah to the land of Israel,
    E. the removal of the ten tribes from America to the land of Israel,
    F. the rule of David the Prince,
    G. the construction of the temple in Jerusalem,
    H. Israel's political affairs in the last days,

I. the Battle of Armageddon,
J. the conversion of Judah and Israel to Christ,
K. Christ's rule as king in Israel,
L. missionary work to the heathens and gentiles following the Battle of Armageddon,
M. Christ's coming in glory, and
N. the millennium.

9. The purpose of scriptural study is to understand doctrine and to apply it for the betterment of one's life.

PART II

The History
- The Syro-Ephraimite War
- The Fall of Israel To Assyria
- Assyrian Attacks on Judah

The Prophets
- Early prophets, including Elijah and Elisha
- Jonah
- Amos
- Hosea
- Micah
- Isaiah

The Doctrine
- The Nature of God
- God's Communication with His Prophets
- Man's Agency and God's Judgment
- The Sins of Israel and Judah
- God's Punishments upon Israel

- Four Periods of Prophetic Fulfillment
- Important Events of the Last Days
- Counsel for Righteous Living

CHAPTER V

HISTORICAL SUMMARY
ASSYRIA AND THE FALL OF ISRAEL

Kings of Assyria

The ancient empire of Assyria began to rise from an extended period of decline about the same time that Judah and Israel were separated into separate nations. By Jonah's day it had been a predominant world power for almost a century. Assyria continued to rise in power and dominion, and reached the peak of its control over neighboring territories in the same era as it conquered the kingdom of Israel. A struggle for power between the two sons of Esarhaddon, however, so weakened the empire that it collapsed half a century after reaching its highest glory. Its activity is reflected in the following outline with particular emphasis on its relationship to Israel and Judah.

Kings of Assyria (Later kingdom).

    Previous Kings of the Late Assyrian Empire

(First phase—late kingdom)

Adad-nirari II	c. 911-891 B.C.
Tukulti-Ninurta II	c. 890-884 B.C.
Ashur-nasirpal II	c. 883-859 B.C.
Shalmaneser III	c. 858-824 B.C.
Shamshi-Adad V	c. 823-811 B.C.

1. **Adad-nirari III**—c. 810-783 B.C.

    A. For four years was under the control of the queen-regent Sammuramat.

    B. After he was freed from his mother's control he began a great program of conquest, which brought many States, including Syria and Israel (but not Judah) into vassal status. He also conquered Babylonia and Media (as far as the Caspian Sea).

C. Something apparently interrupted the advance of Assyrian arms in the middle of his reign. All his recorded victories of consequence took place in the first half of his reign. From 797 B.C. his records tell virtually nothing of any further exploits.

D. His reign is the period of the prophet Jonah. Some believe that it was Jonah's mission which changed the policies of Adad-nirari III.

2. **Shalmaneser IV**— c. 783-771 B.C.
3. **Assur-Dayan III**— c. 771-753 B.C.
4. **Asshur-Lush**— c. 753-745 B.C.

Under these three kings no policy of aggression was pursued. Their laxity allowed many vassal states to throw off Assyrian domination. Revolts took place in Assyria and abroad and Assyria suffered a rapid decline in prestige.

(Second phase—late kingdom)

5. **Tiglath-Pileser III**—c. 745-727 B.C. Also known as **Pul.**

A. Brought to the throne by a rebellion in the city of Calah.

B. Probably not of royal blood, for later kings were hostile to his memory.

C. A ruler of extraordinary ability. He restored Assyrian prestige and founded the last and greatest phase of the Assyrian Empire.

D. Resubjugated vassals in Babylonia and western Media.

E. In 743 B.C. he fought a decisive battle with Sarduris of Urartu (Armenia) and began the reconquest of Syria. Uzziah of Judah apparently masterminded the resistance but died during the campaign.

F. He overran the northern area of Israel in 734 B.C. (during the reign of Pekah of Israel) and conquered Damascus, capital of Syria, two years later.

G. He began the Assyrian policy of moving conquered populations to other areas.

HISTORICAL SUMMARY: ASSYRIA — FALL OF ISRAEL 175

6. **Shalmaneser V**—c. 726-722 B.C.

   A. Son of Tiglath-Pileser III.

   B. Laid siege to Samaria, capital of Israel, dur-the reign of Israel's king Hoshea, but died before Samaria fell.

7. **Sargon II**—c. 721-705 B.C.

   A. An Assyrian army general.

   B. In 721 B.C. he completed the siege of Samaria and deported the ten tribes of Israel to the northern and eastern provinces of the Assyrian Empire.

   C. He defeated the remaining major states of Syria in 720 and 717 B.C.

   D. The major campaign of his career was his invasion, in 714 B.C., of Urartu (Armenia) and the conquest of that nation.

   E. He was troubled by the activities of a Babylonian prince, Merodach-baladan, who made an alliance with Hezekiah, king of Judah, against Assyria. (2 Ki. 20:12; 2 Chron. 32:31; Is. 39:1)

   F. He moved the capital of Assyria from Calah to a new site called Dur-Sharrukin (Khorsabad). Excavations here have been of great value to the history of civilization because archaeological artifacts can be dated to his reign.

8. **Sennacherib**—c. 704-681 B.C.

   A. Son of Sargon II.

   B. Troubled by many rebellions throughout his rule.

   C. In 701 B.C. he invaded the west and exacted heavy tribute from Hezekiah, king of Judah.

   D. In 698 B.C., apparently because he was defeated by the Babylonians and Elamites in the battle of Khalule, new rebellions broke out. Hezekiah, king of Judah, rebelled and Sennacherib attacked Judah. His army was suddenly smitten (by plague?) and he was compelled to retire to his own territory.

9-10. **Sennacherib's two sons**—c. 681 B.C.

   A. They assassinated their father but were immediately driven into exile in Armenia by their brother, Esarhaddon.

11. **Esarhaddon**—c. 681-669 B.C.

   A. One of the greatest kings of Assyria.

   B. He rebuilt Babylon, made it one of his chief capitals, and consolidated Assyrian control of Babylonia.

   C. He invaded Egypt and conquered Memphis.

   D. He repelled the Cimmerians and Scythians near the Caucasus Mountains and, though Assyria lost much territory, saved Assyria from what could have been a disastrous barbarian invasion.

12. **Ashurbanipal**—c. 668-633 B.C.

   A. Son of Esarhaddon.

   B. The last great king of Assyria.

   C. Completed his father's conquest of Egypt.

   D. Defeated the forces of his brother, Shamash-shum-ukin, who had become king of Babylon (Esarhaddon had divided the kingdom between his two sons). The four-year war greatly weakened the Assyrian empire.

   E. Rebellions broke out once again and Assyria crushed Elam and the Arabs. (The collapse of Elam opened the way for the new Aryan state of Persia, which rose to world power by conquering Babylonia in 539 B.C.)

   F. Ashurbanipal was very much interested in scholarship and culture. He had his scholars collect rare tablets and records from throughout the kingdom. To his scholarly interest the world is much indebted for its present-day knowledge of Assyrian and Babylonian literature, history, and higher culture.

Rapid Decline of Assyria Through a Struggle for Power by the Successors to the Throne—633-606 B. C.

Nabopolassar, a general in the Assyrian army and Chaldean governor of Babylonia, declared his independence and entered into an alliance with the Median king **Cyaxares**, and the Medes and Babylonians rapidly devastated the Assyrian armies.

HISTORICAL SUMMARY: ASSYRIA — FALL OF ISRAEL   177

Three final battles:
1. The Medes destroyed the ancient capital of Asshur in 614 B.C.
2. The Medes destroyed Nineveh in 612 B.C.
3. The Medes destroyed the emergency capital of Haran in 608-606 B.C. and the Assyrian empire collapsed completely.

Kings of Israel (the Northern Kingdom)

The divided kingdom of Israel had nineteen kings. Most of these were wicked men who brought about a rapid decline in the moral integrity of their nation and led their country to a rapid collapse. In the following outline, details of the lives of the kings are included only for those kings who lived during and after the ministry of Elijah.

Early Kings:

1. Jeroboam   c. 953-927 B.C.
2. Nadab   c. 927-925 B.C.
3. Baasha   c. 925-901 B.C.
4. Elah   c. 901-899 B.C.
5. Zimri   c. 899-882 B.C.
6. Omri   c. 897-875 B.C.

Kings During the Ministry of Elijah and Elisha:

7. Ahab—c. 875-853 B.C. (1 Ki. 16:29-17:1; 18:1-19:2; 20:1-22:40; 2 Chron. 18:33-34)

   A. Son of Omri, captain of the hosts.

   B. He was the most wicked of all the kings of Israel.

   C. He married Jezebel, daughter of Ethbaal, King of the Zidonians. They both became Baal worshippers.

   D. He attempted to kill the prophets of Jehovah.

   E. He was guided by the Lord in twice defeating Benhadad (Bĕn-hā'-dăd) and the Syrian army which had surrounded Samaria. It was prophesied that he would die for releasing Benhadad.

F. He coveted Naboth's vineyard. Jezebel arranged Naboth's death. Elijah prophesied an end to Ahab's house in the days of his sons.

G. He made an alliance with Syria against Assyria. They were defeated by Shalmaneser III.

H. He imprisoned the prophet Micaiah.

I. Ahab was killed in the battle of Ramoth-gilead, where he was allied with Judah against Syria.

8. **Ahaziah**—c. 853-851 B.C. (1 Ki. 22:40, 49, 2 Ki. 1: 2-17, 2 Chron. 20:35-37)

 A. Son of Ahab.

 B. Conducted a joint maritime venture with Jehoshaphat, king of Judah, which was unsuccessful.

 C. He fell through a lattice and was injured. Elijah promised him he would die.

9. **Jehoram**—c. 851-843 B.C. (2 Ki. 1:17; 3:1-27; 5:7; 6:8-10, 21-23; 8:16, 25, 28-29; 9:14-26, 29; 2 Chron. 22:5-8)

 A. Son of Ahab. (Ahaziah had no son.)

 B. Also known as Joram.

 C. He did evil, but he put away the image of Baal his father had made.

 D. Moab rebelled against Israel. Israel and Judah won with the help of Elisha.

 E. He was wounded by the Syrians under Hazael in the battle of Ramoth-gilead.

 F. Killed by Jehu.

10. **Jehu**—c. 843-815 B.C. (1 Ki. 19:16-17; 2 Ki. 9, 10; 2 Chron. 22:6-9, 25:17)

 A. Son of Jehoshaphat, the son of Nimshi.

 B. He was anointed by a prophet at Ramoth-gilead and told to smite the house of Ahab. The army accepted him as king.

 C. He killed Joram, king of Israel; Ahaziah, king of Judah, and Jezebel.

 D. He forced the people of Israel to slay the seventy sons of Ahab.

 E. He slew forty-two of the brethren of Ahaziah, former king of Judah.

HISTORICAL SUMMARY: ASSYRIA — FALL OF ISRAEL   179

   F. He slew all the worshippers of Baal in Israel.
   G. The Lord promised him that his children would occupy the throne of Israel unto the fourth generation.
   H. He took no heed to walk in the law of the Lord with all his heart.
   I. Hazael, king of Syria, began to attack Israel all along its frontiers.
   J. He ruled 28 years.
21. **Jehoahaz**—c. 815-798 B.C. (2 Ki. 10:35; 13:1-9, 25; 14:1, 8, 17)
   A. Son of Jehu.
   B. He reigned 17 years.
   C. He was an evil king.
   D. Syria continually harassed Israel during his reign.
   E. Most of his army was smitten by Syria.
12. **Joash**—c. 798-790 B.C. (2 Ki. 13:10-13, 25; 14:8-16; 2 Chron. 25:17-25)
   A. Son of Jehoahaz.
   B. Also known as Jehoash.
   C. He reigned 16 years.
   D. He was an evil king.
   E. On three occasions he defeated Benhadad of Syria and recovered the cities which his father had lost.
   F. He overcame Amaziah and the army of Judah, and broke down a portion of the wall of Jerusalem.

Kings of Israel During the Ministry of Jonah, Amos, Hosea, Micah, and Isaiah.

13. **Jeroboam II**—c. 790-749 B.C. (2 Ki. 13:13; 14:16, 23, 27-29; 15:1, 8)

   A. Son of Joash (also known as Jehoash) of the dynasty of Jehu.
   B. He reigned 41 years.
   C. He was the ablest of the kings of Israel, and the most successful in war.

D. He conquered Damascus and Hamath.
E. His reign enjoyed great prosperity.

14. **Zachariah**—c. 749 B.C. (2 Ki. 14:29; 15:8-12; 18:2)
    A. Son of Jeroboam II.
    B. An evil king.
    C. Reigned six months.
    D. Slain by Shallum.

15. **Shallum**—c. 749-748 B.C. (2 Ki. 15:10, 13-15)
    A. Son of Jabesh. He killed Zachariah to become king.
    B. An evil king.
    C. Reigned one month.
    D. Slain by Menahem.

16. **Menahem**—c. 748-737 B.C. (2 Ki. 15:14-20)
    A. Son of Gadi.
    B. He reigned for 10 years.
    C. An evil king: he was unspeakably cruel.
    D. Kept Pul (Tiglath-Pileser), king of Assyria, from conquering Israel by paying a tribute of 1,000 talents of silver.

17. **Pekahiah**—c. 737-735 B.C. (2 Ki. 15:22-26)
    A. Son of Menahem.
    B. He reigned for 2 years.
    C. An evil king.
    D. Slain by Pekah, son of Remaliah (Pekahiah's captain).

18. **Pekah**—c. 735-733 B.C. (2 Ki. 15:25-32, 37; 16:1, 5; 2 Chron. 28:6; Is. 7:1)
    A. An evil king.
    B. During his reign Tiglath-Pileser III, king of Assyria, attacked Israel and carried the northern section (Galilee and above) into captivity.
    C. He allied with Rezin, king of Syria, and they together attacked Judah in an effort to force Judah to ally itself with them against Assyria.
    D. Slain by Hoshea.
    E. There is much difficulty in determining the chronology of Pekah's reign.

19. **Hoshea**—c. 733-722 B.C. (2 Ki. 15:30; 17:1-6; 18:1-10)
   A. Son of Elah.
   B. Paid tribute and served as a puppet king under Shalmaneser V, king of Assyria.
   C. Tried to form an alliance with Egypt to throw off Assyria.
   D. Assyria learned of Hoshea's alliance with Egypt and put him in prison.
   E. Israel fell captive to Assyria after a three-year siege. The siege was begun by the Assyrian king, Shalmaneser V, who died during the siege. The conquest was completed by the Assyrian general, Sargon II, who ascended to the throne of Assyria.

Kings of Judah (the Southern Kingdom)

Judah was ruled by a total of twenty-one kings (including Gedeliah, a provisional governor). Thirteen of these kings are considered in this chapter; the remainder are considered in the outline of Chapter XII. Six of the kings ruled during the era of Elijah and Elisha. Four kings ministered to Judah during the missions of Jonah, Amos, Hosea, Micah, and Isaiah.

Early Kings:

1. Rehoboam   c. 953-932 B.C.
2. Abijah   c. 932-929 B.C.
3. Asa   c. 929-873 B.C.

Kings During the Ministry of Elijah and Elisha:

4. **Jehoshaphat**—c. 873-848 B.C. (1 Ki. 15:24; 22; 2 Ki. 1:17; 3:1, 14; 8:16; 12:18; 1 Chron. 3:10; 2 Chron. 17:1-12; 18; 19; 20; 21:1, 2, 12; 22:9)
   A. Son of Asa.
   B. He fortified and strengthened the cities of Judah.
   C. He removed the pagan high places from Judah.
   D. The land was prosperous and at peace during much of his reign.

E. He united with Ahab, king of Israel, against Syria, to recapture Ramoth-gilead. Ahab was mortally wounded in the battle.

F. He was a righteous king.

G. He entered into an unsuccessful sailing venture with Ahaziah, king of Israel.

H. During his reign Judah was attacked by the Ammonites, Edomites, and Moabites. Judah was saved when the invaders fought among themselves.

5. **Jehoram**—c. 848-840 B.C. (1 Ki. 22:50; 2 Ki. 8:16-24; 12:18; 1 Chron. 3:11; 2 Chron. 21; 22:1, 6, 11)

    A. Son of Jehoshaphat.

    B. He killed his brothers and the princes of Israel.

    C. He married the daughter of Ahab, king of Israel.

    D. He was an evil king.

    E. Edom rebelled from being ruled by Judah.

    F. Libnah also rebelled.

    G. He built high places and compelled Judah to worship there.

    H. During his reign the Philistines and Arabians sacked Jerusalem.

    I. In fulfillment of prophecy, he died of a terrible disease.

6. **Ahaziah**—c. 844-843 B.C. (2 Ki. 8:25-29; 9:16-29; 10:13; 12:18; 1 Chron. 3:11; 2 Chron. 22:1-11; Called Azariah 2 Chron. 22:6 and Jehoahaz 2 Chron. 21:17)

    A. Son of Jehoram and Athaliah, the daughter of Ahab, king of Israel.

    B. He was an evil king.

    C. He allied with Israel and fought against Syria at Ramoth-gilead.

    D. He visited Jehoram, king of Israel, who was recovering from a wound incurred while fighting against the Syrians.

    E. He was slain by Jehu.

    F. His mother attempted to destroy all his children but Joash escaped and was hidden for six years.

HISTORICAL SUMMARY: ASSYRIA — FALL OF ISRAEL 183

7. **Athaliah**—c. 843-837 B.C. (2 Ki. 8:18, 26-27; 11:1-3, 13-20; 2 Chron. 18:1; 21:6; 22:2, 10-12; 23:12-21; 24:7; 1 Chron. 8:26; Ezra 8:7)
    A. Daughter of Ahab, king of Israel.
    B. She was the mother of Ahaziah.
    C. When Ahaziah was killed she attempted to kill all his children so she could rule. His son, Joash, escaped.
    D. After six years Joash was acclaimed as king and she was slain.

8. **Joash**—c. 837-797 B.C. (2 Ki. 11, 12, 14:1)
    A. Son of Ahaziah.
    B. Saved from Athaliah's attempt to murder him by his aunt.
    C. Hidden for six years.
    D. Established on the throne by Jehoiada the priest.
    E. Also called Jehoash.
    F. He had the house of the Lord repaired.
    G. He paid tribute to Hazael, king of Syria.
    H. He was killed by his servants after reigning forty years.

9. **Amaziah**—c. 797-792 B.C. (2 Ki. 12:21; 13:12; 14:1-23; 15:1, 3; 1 Chron. 3:12; 2 Chron. 24:27-26:4)
    A. Son of Joash.
    B. He slew the servants who had killed his father.
    C. He conquered Edom, but brought their gods home and worshipped them.
    D. He challenged Jehoash, king of Israel, to war. Israel defeated Judah and plundered Jerusalem.
    E. He was murdered in Lachish.

Kings of Judah during the Ministry of Jonah, Amos, Hosea, Micah, and Isaiah:

10. **Uzziah**—c. 792-740 B.C. (2 Ki. 14:21-22; 15:5; 2 Chron. 26:1-23; Zech. 14:5; Is. 6:1)
    A. Son of Amaziah.
    B. Also called Azariah (2 Ki. 14:21) and Azias (Mt. 1:8).
    C. Built Elath and restored it to Judah.
    D. Defeated the Philistines and Arabians.

E. Fortified Jerusalem and maintained a strong army.

F. A good and righteous king. Increased Judah's agricultural capacities.

G. Smitten with leprosy when he tried to usurp priestly authority.

H. Earthquake in his reign.

11. **Jotham**—c. 749-734 B.C. (2 Ki. 15:5, 32-38; 2 Chron. 27; Is. 1:1, 7:1; Hos. 1:1; Mic. 1:1)

　　A. Son of Uzziah.

　　B. A good and righteous king. During much of his reign he was co-regent with Uzziah.

　　C. Built cities and fortifications.

　　D. Defeated the Ammonites.

12. **Ahaz**—c. 734-728 B.C. (2 Ki. 16; 2 Chron. 28; Is. 7)

　　A. Son of Jotham.

　　B. An evil king. He turned to idol worship.

　　C. His kingdom was defeated by Pekah (of Israel) and Rezin (of Syria) but the captors were prevented from keeping their hostages by the prophet Oded.

　　D. He was told by Isaiah not to fear Israel and Syria.

　　E. Formed an alliance with Assyria against Israel and Syria while the latter were attacking him.

　　F. Was forced to pay tribute to Tiglath-Pileser III of Assyria to keep Assyria from conquering Judah.

　　G. Copied heathen altars and worship forms.

13. **Hezekiah**—c. 728-697 B.C. (2 Ki. 18-21; 2 Chron. 29-33; Is. 36-38)

　　A. Son of Ahaz.

　　B. A righteous king who was a great religious and political reformer.

　　C. Fought against the idolatry his father had introduced.

　　D. Defeated the Philistines.

　　E. The first part of his reign was prosperous.

　　F. Refused to pay tribute to Assyria.

　　G. During his reign Israel fell to the Assyrians under Sargon II.

H. The Assyrians under Sennacherib attacked Judah along with other nearby Mediterranean states. Hezekiah was compelled to pay heavy tribute. (701 B.C.)

I. Through prayer he gained a 15-year extension to his life. (Is. 38)

J. Hezekiah and Judah again rebelled against Sennacherib and Assyria in 698 B.C.

K. Assyria attacked Judah and demanded complete surrender. Jerusalem was miraculously saved when 185,000 Assyrians died in one night in fulfillment of a prophecy of Isaiah. (2 Ki. 18-19, Is. 37-38)

Summary:

While studying the period of the decline and fall of Israel, the student should know:

Assyria

1. The three most important kings of Assyria were:

    A. Tiglath-Pileser III—carried away northern Israel into captivity.

    B. Sargon II—captured Samaria and carried the rest of Israel into captivity.

    C. Sennacherib—invaded Judah but lost 185,000 men.

Israel

2. The divided kingdom of Israel had nineteen kings, most of whom were wicked.
3. Israel's most important kings were:

    A. Ahab—the most wicked; opposed by Elijah.

    B. Jeroboam II—extended the boundaries and prosperity of Israel to its greatest extent.

    C. Pekah—fought in the Syro-Ephraimite war against Judah; northern Israel went into captivity during his reign.

    D. Hoshea—Israel's last king. Israel went into captivity to end his reign.

Judah

4. The kingdom of Judah had twenty-one kings, most of whom were wicked.

5. Judah's most important kings of this period were:
    A. Jehoshaphat—a righteous king who was aided by the Lord.
    B. Ahaz—a wicked king; his alliance with Assyria brought about the fall of Israel.
    C. Hezekiah—his life was extended 15 years because of righteousness; Sennacherib lost his 185,000 men during his reign.

Important Dates

6. c. 734 B.C.—the Syro-Ephraimite War.[1]
7. c. 734 B.C.—Fall of northern Israel (the Galilee captivity).
8. c. 722 B.C.—Fall of Samaria.
9. c. 698 B.C.—The Lord defeats Sennacherib outside of Jerusalem.

---

[1]Discussed in the Chapter on Isaiah, Section I, pp. 307-308.

CHAPTER VI

THE EARLY PROPHETS AND THEIR MESSAGES

This chapter is different from the others in this book because it does not deal with just one prophet. This is a consideration of over five hundred prophets of the Lord who are recognized in the Old Testament as living during the period of the divided kingdom. Most of them had their ministry in the early part of that era. Most of these prophets left no record or book by which they can be easily remembered. The names of most of them are even unknown. The record of these men is fragmentary. If one were to study them in a disconnected manner, most of their messages would be regarded as minor and as having little bearing on the mainstream of history. Yet when they are studied collectively they provide the most definitive picture available in the Bible of the manner in which the Lord shapes the destinies of men through His prophetic spokesmen. This chapter will briefly consider each prophet or group in his order of appearance in Bible history.

1. **Ahijah, the Shilonite** (A-hī'-jăh the Shī'-lō-nīte).
   A. **Prophecy of the Division of the kingdom.** (1 Ki. 11:29-39)

   Situation: Jeroboam, a servant of King Solomon, was stopped on the road out of Jerusalem by Ahijah.

   The prophecy:
   (1). Ahijah tore his new garment into twelve pieces and gave ten pieces to Jeroboam.
   (2). The Lord will divide the kingdom of Solomon and will make Jeroboam ruler over ten of the tribes of Israel.
   (3). The kingdom will be divided because of idolatry.

(4). The kingdom will be divided in the days of Solomon's son.
(5). Jeroboam will be king over Israel. Solomon's son will have one tribe and Jerusalem.
(6). Walk in God's commandments.

Fulfillment: Jeroboam took the kingdom from Rehoboam. (1 Ki. 12:1-20; 2 Chron. 10:1-19)

The Lessons:
(1). God reveals the future to His prophets.
(2). Prophecy is specific and accurate.
(3). Prophecy is literally fulfilled.

B. **Prophecy of the Fall of the House of Jeroboam.** (1 Ki. 14:1-18)

Situation: Jeroboam had led the people into idolatry and had ruled wickedly. His son, Abijah, had fallen sick. Jeroboam sent his wife in disguise to Ahijah in Shiloh to inquire if his son would die. The Lord revealed that she would come in disguise to Ahijah before she arrived.

The prophecy:
(1). Jeroboam has been evil and has introduced idolatry.
(2). The Lord will cut off the house of Jeroboam and leave him no remnant.
(3). Jeroboam's relatives who die in the city will be eaten by the dogs; those who die in the fields will be eaten by the fowls.
(4). When Jeroboam's wife enters the city her child shall die.
(5). The child of Jeroboam is the only one of his descendants who will be buried in a grave.
(6). A king will be raised up who will cut off the house of Jeroboam.
(7). Israel will be rooted up and scattered beyond the river.

Fulfillment: The child died and was buried. (1 Ki. 14:17-18) Baasha was raised up and destroyed the rest of the house of Jeroboam. (1 Ki. 15:25-

The Early Prophets and Their Messages

30) Israel went into captivity across the rivers of Assyria.

The lessons:
(1). God warns His prophets of approaching challenges and dangers.
(2). God reveals the future to His prophets.
(3). Prophecy is specific and accurate.
(4). Prophecy is literally fulfilled.

2. **Shemaiah, the Man of God.** (Shĕm-ai'-ăh)

A. **Judah prevented from attacking Israel.** (1 Ki. 12:21-24; 2 Chron. 11:1-4)

Situation: Rehoboam, king of Judah, formed a force of 180,000 men to attack Israel and restore the ten tribes to his kingdom. The Lord sent Shemaiah to prevent the attack.

His Message:
(1). Do not fight against your brethren.
(2). The division into the two kingdoms was caused by the Lord.

The Lessons:
(1). God directs people, through his prophets, as to how they should conduct their lives.
(2). God rules the destinies of nations.
(3). God will not allow man to disturb his plans.

B. **Prophecies of the Fall of Judah to Shishak.** (2 Chron. 12:2-12)

Situation: After the kingdom had been divided five years, Judah was attacked by an army of Egyptians under Pharaoh Shishak because of its wickedness. Shemaiah came to the princes of Judah with his prophecy.

The Prophecy: The Lord has left Judah in the hand of Shishak.

Situation Altered: The princes of Judah humbled themselves and acknowledged the righteousness of God.

Second Prophecy:
- (1). They have humbled themselves so they won't be destroyed.
- (2). The Lord's wrath will not be poured out on them by Shishak.
- (3). They still will become servants of Egypt.

Fulfillment: Jerusalem was looted but Rehoboam humbled himself before Shishak and turned away his wrath. (2 Chron. 12:9-12)

The Lessons:
- (1). God reveals the future to his prophets.
- (2). When situations change, the outcome of prophecy may change.
- (3). When God changes a prophetic outcome, He reveals the change to his prophet. (See Is. 38)
- (4). Man can avert or soften a prophecy of the Lord's punishment against him by truly repenting and manifesting humility.

3. **A Man of God from Judah.**
4. **An Old Prophet in Bethel.**

A. A Prophecy that the Bones of Pagan Priests Will Be Burned By Josiah. (1 Ki. 13:1-10)

Situation: Jeroboam had set up pagan altars and two golden calves in Israel and was burning incense by one of the altars in Bethel. A man of God from Judah came and addressed a prophecy to the altar.

His Prophecy:
- (1). A child named Josiah will be born unto the house of David.
- (2). He will offer the priests of the high places upon that altar.
- (3). He will burn men's bones upon that altar.
- (4). As a sign, the altar would be rent and the ashes poured out.

Situation: When Jeroboam attempted to seize the man of God his hand withered and the altar broke and spilled out the ashes. The king asked the prophet to heal his hand. The prophet prayed and the hand was restored. Jeroboam invited the prophet to come and eat with him but the man of God declined, saying that the Lord had instructed him not to eat or drink in Bethel and to return by a different route.

Fulfillment: The sign was given immediately. The remainder of the prophecy was fulfilled about 330 years later by Josiah, king of Judah, who slew the pagan priests and dug up human bones and burned them on the altar to pollute it. (2 Ki. 23:1-18, 2 Chron. 34:3-7)

The Lessons:
   (1). God reveals the future to His prophets.
   (2). Prophecy is specific and accurate.
   (3). Prophecy is literally fulfilled.
   (4). A prophet can foresee events hundreds of years into the future, and in differing national situations. (Josiah, for instance, lived after the kingdom of Israel had ceased to exist.)
   (5). God sometimes shows the truthfulness of a prophecy by giving a sign which receives immediate fulfillment.
   (6). A prophet can call upon the power of God to smite and curse his enemies.
   (7). A prophet can call upon the powers of God to heal and remove curses.
   (8). God demands that His prophets be treated with respect and reverence.

Note: This is an extremely significant prophecy because the fulfillment (1) looks far into the future, (2) foresees an event which takes place under far different national conditions, and (3) actually specifies the name of the fulfiller. Bible critics who scoff at Isaiah's naming of Cyrus would do well to take heed. (See Is. 44:28; 45:1)

B. **The Man of God Is Killed For Disobedience.** (1 Ki. 13:11-32)

Situation: As the man of God returned to Judah, word of his prophecy came to an old prophet living in Bethel. He apparently desired the association and companionship of the man of God and went after him. He invited the man of God to return to his home and eat with him. The man of God refused, saying that he had been specifically commanded to eat and drink nothing in Bethel. The old prophet, still desiring his company, lied to him, telling him that an angel had commanded him to go back to Bethel and eat. The man of God returned to Bethel and broke his fast. Then the word of the Lord came to the old prophet of Bethel:

His Prophecy:

(1). The man of God has disobeyed the Lord by returning to Bethel and breaking his fast.

(2). His carcass will not come unto the sepulchre of his fathers.

Fulfillment: The man of God was killed by a lion on the way home. The old prophet of Bethel went and retrieved his body and buried him in Bethel instead of Judah. (1 Ki. 13:23-32)

The Lessons:

(1). God may use a man as a prophet even though the man is not free from sin.

Note: The old prophet of Bethel received revelation even though he had lied to the man of God. Apparently when there is a message to be delivered the Lord uses whatever means is available. Jonah is another example of a prophet who disobeyed the laws of God and still received prophecy to be delivered. Certainly this incident should not be interpreted as an authorization for sin among the prophets. Anyone conversant with the promptings of the Spirit of the Lord well knows that "the powers of heaven cannot be controlled nor handled only upon the principles of righteousness."[1] Yet while sin removes man's power to control the

---

[1] D&C 121:36.

things of the Spirit, yet God is not prohibited from using whoever He chooses as the spokesman for His word.

Some might attempt to escape from the small dilemma raised by this account by asserting that the old prophet of Bethel was actually a false or hireling prophet. Such an interpretation is untenable. Note that the word of the Lord actually came to him (verses 20 and 21) and that his prophecy came true.

(2). God demands strict obedience from His prophets.

Note: Some might regard the sudden death of the man of God as an overly harsh punishment. It is not man's prerogative to judge God. Apparently the man of God was guilty of two sins. Not only did he return to Bethel and break his fast, he also failed to use the spirit of discernment with which he was endowed as an authorized representative of God to determine which of the conflicting commandments he should follow. His sin was thus greatly increased.

(3). Man should test the prophets and their prophecies by the spirit of discernment.

(4). Prophecy is specific and accurate.

(5). Prophecy is literally fulfilled.

5. **Azariah the son of Oded** (az-ă-rī'ăh).

A. **God Will Reward Judah.** (2 Chron. 15:1-8)

Situation: Asa (third king of Judah) had been a righteous king. He was approached by the prophet Azariah.

His Prophecy:

(1). The Lord is with you while ye be with him. If ye forsake him, he will forsake you.

(2). Israel has long been without the true God and has suffered.

(3). Be strong and your work shall be rewarded.

The Lessons:
- (1). God directs people as to how they should conduct their lives through His prophets.
- (2). Revelation serves for commendation as well as reproof.

6. **Hanani the Seer** (Hă-nā'-nī).

    A. **A Prophecy that Judah Will Have Wars.** (2 Chron. 16:7-10)

    Situation: Baasha (the third king of Israel) built the city of Ramah to prevent Israelites from going to Jerusalem. To stop the building of the city Asa (the third king of Judah) bribed Syria to break its truce with Israel and attack it. Syria's army came against Israel and the work at Ramah stopped. Then Hanani prophesied to Asa.

    His Prophecy:
    - (1). Since you relied on the king of Syria instead of on the Lord the Syrian host has escaped out of your control.
    - (2). The reliance on Syria was foolish.
    - (3). From henceforth thou wilt have wars.

    Fulfillment: War with Syria continued intermittently down to the Syro-Ephraimite war in 634 B. C. (See 1 Ki. 22:29-32; 2 Ki. 8:25-28; 16:5; 2 Chron. 28:5-15)

    The Lesson:
    - (1). Man's life is not predestined. Man himself determines his fate by establishing in the present a cause-and-effect relationship with the future. Prophecy merely pre-states what the ultimate effect of present actions will be.

7. **Jehu, Son of Hanani.**

    A. **A Prophecy of the End of the House of Baasha.** (1 Ki. 16:1-7)

    Situation: Baasha (the third king of Israel) was the king who destroyed the house of Jeroboam. After

The Early Prophets and Their Messages

rising in power he continued in the idolatry of his predecessors. Jehu spoke this prophecy.

His Prophecy:
  (1). Baasha's idolatry has provoked God's anger.
  (2). The Lord will take away his posterity and destroy his line as he did Jeroboam's.
  (3). His posterity shall be eaten by the dogs and the fowls.

Fulfillment: When Baasha's son, Elah, came to the throne he was assassinated by an army captain, Zimri, who ascended to the throne and then destroyed all the house of Baasha. (1 Ki. 16:8-13)

The Lessons:
  (1). God reveals the future to His prophets.
  (2). Prophecy is specific and accurate.
  (3). Prophecy is literally fulfilled.

B. Reproof From the Lord upon Jehoshaphat. (2 Chron. 19:2-3)

Situation: Jehoshaphat (the fourth king of Judah) had allied himself with Israel in a war with Syria. After the battle had ended he was approached by Jehu who delivered this message:

His Prophecy:
  (1). Shouldest thou help the ungodly, and love them that hate the Lord?
  (2). The wrath of God is upon you.
  (3). Nevertheless there are good things found in thee, for thou hast destroyed the groves and hast prepared thine heart to seek God.

The Result: Jehoshaphat went among his people and caused them to return to God. (2 Chron. 19:4-11)

The Lessons:
  (1). God directs people as to how they should conduct their lives through His prophets.
  (2). Man can avert or soften a prophecy of the Lord's punishment against him by truly repenting and manifesting humility.

8. **One Hundred Prophets in Israel** (1 Ki. 18:4, 13).

Situation: Ahab (the seventh king of Israel) married Jezebel, a princess from Zidon. Both of them were wicked, but Jezebel attempted to stamp out Jehovah-worship and completely convert Israel to idolatry. She ordered all the prophets of Jehovah killed.

At this time, Obadiah, a servant to king Ahab, "took an hundred prophets, and hid them by fifty in a cave, and fed them with bread and water."

The Lessons:
(1). God often uses many prophets at the same time.
(2). A calling as prophet did not necessarily require that the person with this calling stand at the head of the Church.

9. **Elijah the Tishbite** (ē-lī'-jăh the Tish'-bīte).

A. **Prophesied of a Drought in Israel.** (1 Ki. 17:1-7)

Situation:
(1). Because of the evil which Ahab brought to Israel, Elijah told him "there shall not be dew nor rain these years, but according to my word."
(2). The Lord told Elijah to hide by the brook Cherith.
(3). The ravens brought him food in response to a commandment of the Lord.

The Lessons:
(1). God gives His prophets control over nature to further His work.
(2). God protects His prophets and supplies their needs.

B. **Miracles at Zarephath** (Zăr'-ĕ-phăth). (1 Ki. 17:8-24)

Situations:
(1). God commanded Elijah to go into the Phoenician village of 'Zarephath and be sustained by a widow there.

The Early Prophets and Their Messages

(2). Elijah increased the barrel of meal and the cruse of oil so they had supplies till the rains came.

(3). Elijah restored the life of the widow's son.

The Lessons:

(1). Prophets have the power to perform miracles.

(2). Some miracles are performed by the powers already vested in the prophet. For other miracles he must call upon God.

C. God versus Baal on Mount Carmel. (1 Ki. 18:1-46)

Situation:

(1). Elijah came out of hiding and confronted Ahab. The prophet told the King to gather the people of Israel and the priests of Baal to Mt. Carmel.

(2). On Mt. Carmel Elijah challenged the people to commit themselves to either Baal or the Lord.

(3). Elijah challenged the prophets of Baal to call down fire from heaven for their sacrifice. They could not.

(4). He laid a sacrifice, then called on the Lord to show that He is the true God and that Elijah was His servant.

(5). Fire came down from heaven and consumed the sacrifice. The people acknowledged Jehovah as God.

(6). Elijah had the prophets of Baal taken away and he slew them.

(7). Rain came.

(8). The hand of the Lord was on Elijah and he ran before Ahab to the entrance of Jezreel. (about 30 miles down the side of Mt. Carmel and across the plain of Esdraelon.)

The Lessons:

(1). Miracles are often used to establish the divinity of Jehovah and the authority of His prophets.

(2). On special occasions God gives His servants strength beyond the normal limits of endurance.

D. A Revelation To Anoint Kings and a Prophet. (1 Ki. 19:1-21)

Situation:
  (1). Elijah fled from Jezebel south beyond Beersheba.
  (2). An angel brought him food and drink in the wilderness.
  (3). He went "in the strength of that meat forty days and forty nights unto Horeb the mount of God."
  (4). The Lord spoke to Elijah by the still small voice and commanded him to
    a. anoint Hazael to be king of Syria.
    b. anoint Jehu to be king of Israel, and
    c. anoint Elisha to replace himself as prophet.

His Prophecy:
  (1). Those that escape the sword of Hazael shall be slain by Jehu.
  (2). Those that escape the sword of Jehu shall be slain by Elisha.

Fulfillment:
  (1). Hazael killed Benhadad and became king of Syria. He fought against Israel and Judah at Ramoth-gilead and his army wounded Jehoram (Joram, the ninth king of Israel). (2 Ki. 8:13-29)
  (2). Jehu killed Jehoram and Ahaziah (the sixth king of Judah) and their families and friends. He killed all the house of Ahab. (2 Ki. 9:15-10:30)
  (3). Perhaps the latter portion of the prophecy finds its fulfillment in the death-bed prophecy of Elisha: that Israel would smite Syria thrice. (2 Ki. 13:14-25)

Resulting Situation: Elijah called Elisha.

The Lessons:
- (1). God protects His prophets and supplies their needs.
- (2). On special occasions God gives His servants strength beyond the normal limits of endurance.
- (3). God rules the destiny of nations.
- (4). Prophecy is literally fulfilled.

E. A Prophecy of the Fall of the House of Ahab. (1 Ki. 21:17-29)

Situation:
- (1). Ahab desired the vineyard of Naboth in Jezreel but the latter refused to sell it.
- (2). Jezebel had false accusations made against Naboth. He was convicted and stoned to death.
- (3). Ahab went to possess the vineyard. Elijah was sent by the Lord to confront him there.

His Prophecy:
- (1). In the place where the dogs licked the blood of Naboth they shall lick thy blood.
- (2). Ahab's posterity shall be cut off.
- (3). The dogs shall eat Jezebel by the walls of Jezreel.

Situation Altered: Ahab fasted and humbled himself.

Second Prophecy: Because Ahab humbled himself the evil will not be brought in Ahab's day but in his son's day.

Fulfillment:
- (1). Jehu killed Ahab's son, Jehoram (Joram), and his family. Jehoram's body was thrown into Naboth's vineyard to fulfill the prophecy. (2 Ki. 9:22-26)
- (2). Jezebel was thrown from the wall of Jezreel and her body was devoured by dogs. (2 Ki. 9:30-37)
- (3). The seventy sons of Ahab were killed by frightened rulers in Samaria. (2 Ki. 10:1-11)

The Lessons:
- (1). Prophecy is specific and accurate.
- (2). Prophecy is literally fulfilled.
- (3). Man can avert or soften a prophecy of the Lord's punishment against him by truly repenting and manifesting humility.
- (4). When situations change, the outcome of prophecy may change.
- (5). When God changes a prophetic outcome, He reveals the change to His prophet.

F. A Prophecy of a Plague Upon Jehoram. (2 Chron. 21:12-15)

Situation: Jehoram (the fifth king of Judah) had killed his brothers and had married the wicked daughter of Israel's king Ahab. He established the idolatry of Israel in Judah. Elijah sent him a prophetic letter:

His Prophecy:
- (1). Because Jehoram had killed his brothers and established idolatry,
- (2). His people will be smitten with a great plague.
- (3). He will have a great sickness of the bowels until they fall out.

Fulfillment: Jehoram suffered with such a disease for two years and then died. (2 Chron. 21:16-20)

The Lessons:
- (1). God reveals the future to His prophets.
- (2). Prophecy is specific and accurate.
- (3). Prophecy is literally fulfilled.

G. A Prophecy of the Death of Ahaziah. (2 Ki. 1:1-4)

Situation: Ahaziah (the eighth king of Israel) fell through a lattice in his upper chamber at Samaria and was badly injured. He sent servants to the Philistine city of Ekron to inquire of the god Baalzebub if he would live. An angel sent Elijah to intercept the messengers and prophesy the fate of Ahaziah:

His Prophecy: Ahaziah shalt not come down from his bed but shalt surely die.

Second Situation: The king sent soldiers to find Elijah (see section H). Elijah finally went to the king and repeated his prophecy, telling him that his death would be because he had inquired of a pagan god rather than the true God of Israel.

Fulfillment: Ahaziah died. (2 Ki. 1:17)

The Lesson: Man's life is not predestined. Man himself determines his fate by establishing in the present a cause-and-effect relationship with the future. Prophecy merely pre-states what the ultimate effect of present actions will be.

H. Elijah Calls Down Fire On the Soldiers. (2 Ki. 1:9-15)

Situation:

(1). King Ahaziah sent soldiers to find Elijah. They approached the prophet, who sat on the top of a hill, and challenged him to come down.

(2). Elijah replied, "If I be a man of God, then let fire come down from heaven, and consume thee and thy fifty." Fire came down and consumed them.

(3). The situation was repeated with another group of fifty.

(4). A third group came, but their leader pled for their lives.

(5). An angel of the Lord advised Elijah not to fear the soldier but to go with him.

The Lessons:

(1). A prophet can call upon the powers of God to smite and curse his enemies.

(2). Miracles are often used to establish the divinity of Jehovah and the authority of His prophets.

(3). God protects His prophets and supplies their needs.

I. **Elijah Is Taken Into Heaven.** (2 Ki. 2:8-11. See also under Elisha)

Situation:
(1). Elijah and Elisha crossed the Jordan River. Elijah separated the waters so they crossed on dry ground.
(2). A chariot of fire and horses of fire separated the two.
(3). Elijah went up by a whirlwind into heaven.

The Lessons:
(1). Many miracles are designed for the convenience of God's servants.
(2). Some servants of God are apparently transferred from this earth to another. They become translated beings.[2]

10. **A Prophet Unto Ahab.**

A. **A Prophecy that The Syrians Will Be Delivered to Israel.** (1 Ki. 20:13-14, 22)

Situation: Benhadad, king of Syria, besieged Samaria, and demanded tribute of Ahab (the seventh king of Israel). During the siege an unnamed prophet approached Ahab with this prophecy:

His Prophecy:
(1). The Lord will deliver the Syrian multitude into his hand this day.
(2). Ahab will know Jehovah is the Lord.
(3). The young princes of the provinces will fight the battle.
(4). Ahab is to order the battle.

Fulfillment: The young princes of the provinces with their small band slaughtered the Syrians. (1 Ki. 20:15-21)

His Second Prophecy:
(1). Strengthen thyself.
(2). At the return of the year the king of Syria will come up against thee.

---

[2]For further information on later appearances of Elijah see Chapter 28 on Malachi.

THE EARLY PROPHETS AND THEIR MESSAGES

Fulfillment: The Syrians returned but the Israelites were prepared and slew 100,000 footmen in one day. (1 Ki. 20:23-30)

The Lessons:
  (1). God reveals the future to His prophets.
  (2). Prophecy is specific and accurate.
  (3). Prophecy is literally fulfilled.
  (4). God rules the destiny of nations.

11. **A Man of God.**

    A. **A Prophecy that the Syrians will be Delivered to Israel.** (1 Ki. 20:28)

    Situation: The Syrians returned to make war on Israel (in fulfillment of second prophecy, number 10 above). Israel was badly outnumbered. While the two armies were camped and preparing for the battle Ahab was approached by an unnamed man of God.

    His Prophecy:
      (1). The Syrians (who previously were defeated by Israel in the mountains and had now attempted to draw the Israelite army onto the plains) had said, The Lord is God of the hills, but he is not God of the valleys.
      (2). All the Syrian multitude will be delivered into thine hand.
      (3). Ye shall know that I am the Lord.

    Fulfillment: In spite of their small numbers, Israel defeated Syria. (1 Ki. 20:29-30)

    The Lessons:
      (1). God reveals the future to His prophets.
      (2). Prophecy is specific and accurate.
      (3). Prophecy is literally fulfilled.
      (4). God rules the destiny of nations.

12. **A Certain Man of the Sons of the Prophets.**

    A. **A Prophecy That Ahab's Life Will Be Given for Benhadad's Life.** (1 Ki. 20:31-43)

    Situation: When Israel defeated Syria (see number 11 above) Ahab spared the life of the Syrian king, Benhadad. A certain man of the sons of the prophets, wanting to emphasize the prophecy he was going to make to Ahab, told his neighbor in the word of the Lord, "Smite me, I pray thee." The neighbor refused.

His Prophecy to the Neighbor:
(1). Because thou hast not obeyed the voice of the Lord,
(2). As soon as thou art departed from me, a lion shall slay thee.

Fulfillment: The neighbor was killed by a lion. (1 Ki. 20:36)

Second Situation: The prophet was successful in getting another man to smite and wound him. Then the prophet disguised himself and waited along the way for king Ahab. He told Ahab that he was responsible for a prisoner with the instruction that if the prisoner were missing that his life would be forfeited for the prisoner's. The prisoner had escaped. Ahab judged him, saying, "So shall thy judgment be, thyself hast decided it." The prophet removed his disguise and made his prophecy to Ahab:

His Prophecy to Ahab:
(1). Because he let go out of his hand a man God had appointed for utter destruction (Benhadad),
(2). Ahab's life would be taken for Benhadad's and his people for the Syrians.

Fulfillment: Ahab was killed in battle against Syria at Ramoth-gilead. (1 Ki. 22:34-38). The Israelite army was beaten. Benhadad escaped unharmed.

The Lessons:
(1). God reveals the future to His prophets.
(2). Prophecy is specific and accurate.
(3). Prophecy is literally fulfilled.
(4). Man's life is not predestined. Man himself determines his fate by establishing in the present a cause-and-effect relationship with the future. Prophecy merely pre-states

The Early Prophets and Their Messages

what the ultimate effect of present actions will be.

13. **Four Hundred Prophets**
14. **Micaiah, the Son of Imlah** (Mī-cai'-ăh the son of Im'-läh)

   A. **Conflicting Prophecies of the Outcome of A Battle with Syria.** (1 Ki. 22:6-28; 2 Chron. 18:5-27)

   Situation: Jehoshaphat, (the fourth king of Judah) and Ahab (the seventh king of Israel) united to drive the Syrians from Ramoth-gilead. They sought counsel of four hundred prophets of the Lord.

   Their Counsel: Go up, for the Lord shall deliver it into the hand of the king.

   Second Situation: Since the kings were still uncertain of their fate, they called for Micaiah. This was done over Ahab's protestations, for he complained that Micaiah always prophesied against him. The servant who summoned Micaiah admonished him to prophesy good concerning the kings. Micaiah's reply was, "What the Lord saith unto me, that will I speak."
   During the interlude in which Micaiah was being summoned, the two kings established themselves by the gate to Samaria and allowed other prophets to prophecy before them. Zedekiah, son of Chenanah, who later proved to be a false prophet, made him horns of iron and said "With these shalt thou push the Syrians, until thou have consumed them."

   Micaiah's First Prophecy: Go, and prosper, for the Lord shall deliver it into the hand of the king.

   Third Situation: The king challenged him to tell the truth.

   Micaiah's Second Prophecy:
   (1). I saw all Israel scattered upon the hills, as sheep that have not a shepherd.
   (2). These have no master: let them return every man to his house in peace.

Fourth Situation: Ahab complained that Micaiah always prophesied evil concerning him. Micaiah replied by relating a vision to explain the conflicting prophecies.

Micaiah's Vision:
(1). He saw the Lord sitting on His throne, surrounded by the hosts of heaven.
(2). The Lord said, "Who shall persuade Ahab, that he may go up and fall at Ramoth-gilead?" The matter was discussed.
(3). A spirit stood before the Lord and said, I will persuade him.
(4). The Lord questioned how, and the spirit replied, "I will go forth, and I will be a lying spirit in the mouth of all his prophets."
(5). The Lord replied, "Thou shalt persuade him, and prevail also: go forth, and do so."
(6). Micaiah's explanation:
   a. The Lord hath put a lying spirit in the mouth of all these thy prophets. (See 2 Thess. 2:11-12)
   b. The Lord hath spoken evil concerning thee.

Fifth Situation: The false prophet, Zedekiah, came up and struck Micaiah, saying, "Which way went the Spirit of the Lord from me to speak unto thee?"

Micaiah's Prophecy To Zedekiah: Thou shalt see in that day, when thou shalt go into an inner chamber to hide thyself.

Sixth Situation: Ahab ordered that Micaiah be imprisoned.

Micaiah's Prophecy to Ahab: If thou return at all in peace, the Lord hath not spoken by me.

Fulfillment: Ahab was killed in the battle and the hosts of Israel returned to their homes. (1 Ki. 22:29-38)

Note: This passage is one of the most difficult to interpret in all the Bible because of the theological questions it raises. No Biblical help is available outside of the account itself. The only course possible is to take the passage at face value and apply the clues it provides:

(1). **Were the 400 prophets authorized spokesmen for Jehovah or were they false prophets?**
   a. They lived in the period after Elijah had slain the false prophets of Baal. It is known that Obadiah had protected one hundred prophets of Jehovah from annihilation by queen Jezebel.
   b. Jehoshaphat had specifically requested that the prophets of Jehovah (the term LORD written in capital letters in the Bible text indicates that it is the translation for Jehovah) be brought. These were apparently men who had been accepted in that area as being representatives of Jehovah.
   c. In Micaiah's vision they were depicted as being instructed by a spirit sent from the Lord. They prophesied the message the Lord sent them. Is authorization indicated in their receiving messages from the Lord and having the responsibility to deliver them faithfully? Note that Micaiah, who clearly was authorized, delivered the same message until he was challenged and given the opportunity to say more. Note also that he gave the false message immediately after asserting his determination to speak what the Lord would guide him to speak.

(2). **Did the prophets intentionally deceive Ahab, or did they merely show obedience to the Lord and repeat what they were prompted to say?**
   a. "Now therefore, behold, the LORD hath put a lying spirit in the mouth of all these thy prophets." (2 Chron. 18:22; See also Inspired Version.)

b. This was, apparently, to accomplish the Lord's ultimate purpose, of bringing Ahab to his death. "And the Lord said, who shall persuade Ahab, that he may go up and fall at Ramoth-gilead?"

(3). **Did the Lord deceive Ahab?** While the Lord did allow the large group of prophets to strengthen Ahab's desire for battle, it certainly could not be asserted that He deceived the king. He sent Micaiah, who clearly prophesied and explained what would happen in the battle. He gave Micaiah a choice vision of the proceedings of the heavenly councils in which the true nature of the four hundred prophets' message was explained, and He allowed this vision to be repeated to Ahab. Rather than deceive Ahab, the Lord gave the king all the facts of the case and allowed him to choose his own future.

The Lessons:
(1). When situations change, the outcome of prophecy may change.
(2). When God changes a prophetic outcome, He reveals the change to His prophet.
(3). Man's life is not predestined. Man himself determines his fate by establishing in the present a cause-and-effect relationship with the future. Prophecy merely pre-states what the ultimate effect of present actions will be.
(4). God often uses many prophets at the same time.
(5). Man should test the prophets and their prophecies by the spirit of discernment.

15. **Jahaziel, Son of Zechariah** (Jă-hā'-zi-ĕl, Son of Zĕch-ă-rī'-ăh)

A. **A Prophecy That God Will Deliver Judah from Ammon, Moab and Edom.** (2 Chron. 20:14-18)

Situation: Jehoshaphat (fourth king of Judah) was attacked by a coalition of Ammon, Moab, and

The Early Prophets and Their Messages

Edom. Jehoshaphat declared a fast and gathered the people of Judah to a meeting in the court of the Jerusalem temple. During the meeting "came the Spirit of the Lord in the midst of the congregation" upon Jahaziel, who spoke this prophecy:

His Prophecy:
  (1). The battle is not yours, but God's.
  (2). Go against them tomorrow and you will find them at the end of the brook before the wilderness of Jeruel.
  (3). Ye shall not need to fight in this battle.
  (4). Stand ye still, and see the salvation of the Lord.

The Fulfillment: Judah went out to the battlefield and watched as the Ammonites and Moabites turned on the Edomites and destroyed them, and then turned on each other and were smitten. (2 Chron. 20:19-30)

The Lessons:
  (1). God reveals the future to His prophets.
  (2). Prophecy is specific and accurate.
  (3). Prophecy is literally fulfilled.
  (4). God directs people as to how they should conduct their lives through His prophets.
  (5). God rules the destiny of nations.

16. **Eliezer, the Son of Dodavah** (ĕl-i-ē′-zĕr, the son of Dō′-dă-văh)

    A. **A Prophecy Against Jehoshaphat's Shipping Venture.** (2 Chron. 20:37)

    Situation: Jehoshaphat (4th king of Judah) combined in a shipping venture with Ahaziah (eighth king of Israel). They undertook to build ships to sail to Tarshish (southern Spain?).

    His Prophecy:
      (1). Because thou hast joined thyself with Ahaziah
      (2). The Lord hath broken thy works.

    Fulfillment: 2 Chron. 20:37; 1 Ki. 22:48-49.

    The Lesson: God directs people as to how they should conduct their lives through His prophets.

17. **Elisha, the Son of Shaphat** (ē-lī'-shă the son of Shā'-phăt)

   A. **His Call to the Ministry. (1 Ki. 19:19-21)**

   Situation: Elijah came (from mount Horeb?) and found Elisha plowing with twelve yoke of oxen. He called him by casting his mantle over him. Elisha went and ministered to Elijah.

   B. **Elisha Receives A Double Portion of the Spirit of Elijah as They Part. (2 Ki. 2:1-8)**

   Situation: Elisha refused to leave Elijah as they traveled from Gilgal to Bethel to Jericho and across the Jordan. Before Elijah was taken up into heaven he asked if there was anything he could do for Elisha. Elisha requested a double portion of the prophet's spirit. Elijah replied that if Elisha saw him when he was taken up, that his wish would be granted. He saw Elijah's ascension and obtained his mantle. He used the mantle to part the waters of the River Jordan and crossed over to the sons of the prophets, who accepted him as the new prophet.

   The Lessons:

   (1). God often shows the truthfulness of a prophecy by giving a sign which receives immediate fulfillment.

   (2). God gives his prophets control over nature to further His work.

   (3). Prophets have the power to perform miracles.

   (4). Many miracles are designed for the convenience of God's servants.

   C. **Elisha Heals the Waters of Jericho.** (2 Ki. 2:19-22)

   Situation: The men of Jericho pointed out to Elisha that the poor water made the ground barren. He cast salted water into the spring and pronounced it healed by the word of the Lord.

The Early Prophets and Their Messages

The Lessons:
  (1). God gives His prophets control over nature to further His work.
  (2). Prophets have the power to perform miracles.

D. Elisha Curses the Mocking Children. (2 Ki. 2:23-25)

Situation: While going from Jericho to Bethel a group of small children mocked him for his baldness. Elisha cursed them in the name of the Lord. Two she bears came out of the woods and tore forty-two of the children. Elisha went on to Mt. Carmel and back to Samaria.

The Lessons:
  (1). A prophet can call upon the powers of God to smite and curse his enemies.
  (2). God demands that His prophets be treated with reverence and respect.

E. A Prophecy of Victory Over Moab. (2 Ki. 2:11-19)

Situation: The king of Moab rebelled against Israel. Israel, Judah, and Edom united to subdue him. As they were marching to battle through Edom all the water holes were dry. Jehoshaphat fourth king of Judah) called for a prophet and Elisha was summoned.

His Prophecy:
  (1). Fill the valley with ditches.
  (2). Though it will not rain, the valley will be filled with water.
  (3). The Lord will deliver the Moabites into your hands.
  (4). Ye shall smite every fenced and choice city.

Fulfillment: The ditches filled with water. The Moabites saw it from afar and thought it was blood and that the armies had slain each other. The Israelites smote the Moabites. (2 Ki. 3:20-27)

The Lessons:
   (1). God reveals the future to His prophets.
   (2). Prophecy is specific and accurate.
   (3). Prophecy is literally fulfilled.

F. Elisha Multiplies the Oil. (2 Ki. 4:1-7)

Situation: A widow of one of the sons of the prophets sought help from Elisha because her creditors were attempting to take her two sons as slaves. The prophet had her borrow many empty vessels. He then had her pour oil from her one jar into all the others. The oil increased until it filled all the containers. Elisha then commanded her to sell the oil and pay her debts.

The Lesson: Prophets have the power to perform miracles.

G. Elisha Helps The Shunammite Woman. (2 Ki. 4:18-37)

Situation: Elisha often passed by the village of Shunem, where a generous woman provided him with food and lodging. Elisha chose to reward her.

His Prophecy: Even though she is old she shall give birth to a son.

Second Situation: The boy was born and grew up. One day the child fell and hit his head, and soon died. The mother found Elisha on Mt. Carmel. He went to her home, prayed to the Lord, and restored life to the child.

The Lessons:
   (1). Prophets have the power to perform miracles.
   (2). Some miracles are performed by the powers already vested in the prophet. For other miracles he must call upon God.

H. Elisha Heals the Poison Pottage. (2 Ki. 4:38-41)

Situation: Elisha came to Gilgal and ate with the sons of the prophets. Wild gourds were put into the pot which poisoned the pottage. Because of the dearth of food they did not want to waste it. Elisha healed the pottage by casting meal into it.

The Lesson: Prophets have the power to perform miracles.

I. Elisha Multiplies the Food. (2 Ki. 4:42-44)

Situation: There was a dearth (famine) in the land. Elisha was with a hundred of the sons of the prophets when a man brought a small quantity of food. Elisha commanded that the food be divided among the people, for the Lord said they would all be able to eat of it and have food left over.

The Lessons:
(1). Prophets have the power to perform miracles.
(2). Many miracles are designed for the convenience of God's servants.

J. Elisha Heals Naaman the Syrian and Curses Gehazi. (2 Ki. 5:1-19)

Situation: The Syrian captain, Naaman, was a leper. His wife's servant girl was an Israelite slave. She let it be known that Elisha could heal Naaman. Naaman came to Elisha and was told to wash in the Jordan River seven times. He at first refused, then obeyed and was healed. He offered gifts to Elisha, who refused them. Elisha's servant, Gehazi, secretly accepted some of the gifts. Elisha discerned Gehazi's duplicity and cursed him by letting him be stricken by Naaman's leprosy.

The Lessons:
(1). Prophets have the power to perform miracles.
(2). Miracles are often used to establish the divinity of Jehovah and the authority of His prophets.
(3). Prophets have the power to discern the thoughts and deeds of others.

(4). A prophet can call upon the powers of God to smite and curse others.

(5). God demands strict obedience from His prophets and servants.

(6). Man's life is not predestined. Man himself determines his fate by establishing in the present a cause-and-effect relationship with the future. Prophecy merely pre-states what the ultimate effect of present actions will be.

K. Elisha Makes Iron Swim. (2 Ki. 6:1-7)

Situation: The sons of the prophets decided to move to the Jordan River area. While felling trees in that area one of the sons of the prophets lost his axe head in the water. Elisha inquired where it fell, cut a stick and threw it in the water, and the axe head swam to the top.

The Lessons:

(1). Prophets have the power to perform miracles.

(2). Many miracles are designed for the convenience of God's servants.

L. Elisha Blinds the Syrians and Turns Them Away. (2 Ki. 6:8-23)

Situation: Syria made war on Israel and set up a camp to capture the Israelite king. Elisha sent word to the king of Israel and saved him from being captured. The Syrian king learned that Elisha was working against him and sent a band of spies to Dothan to capture him there. When Elisha and the people of Dothan awoke, they found they were surrounded. Elisha told his servant not to be afraid and showed him that they were surrounded by chariots and horses of fire. Elisha asked the Lord to smite the Syrians with blindness and it was done. Elisha then offered to lead them to the city where they could find "the man ye seek" but he led them to Samaria. There Elisha prayed for the return of their eyesight and they were again able to see.

Then he fed them and sent them away. The bands of Syria no more came upon Israel.

The Lessons:
 (1). A prophet can call upon the powers of God to smite and curse his enemies.
 (2). Prophets have the power to perform miracles.
 (3). Some miracles are performed by the powers already vested in the prophet. For others, he must call upon God.

M. A Prophecy of the End of the Famine in Samaria. (2 Ki. 6:24-7:2)

Situation: Benhadad, king of Syria, again waged war against Israel. He besieged Samaria and caused a great famine there. The king of Israel held Elisha responsible for not ending the famine and vowed to cut off his head. He sent a messenger to capture Elisha. The prophet, however, foresaw the mission of the messenger and had his friends hold him till the king came to his house. Elisha made this prophecy to the king and his nobles:

His Prophecy:
 (1). Tomorrow food will be plentiful and cheap in Samaria.
 (2). (To a nobleman who doubted) Thou shalt see it with thine eyes but shalt not eat thereof.

Fulfillment: Four lepers who were dying at the gate decided to go over to the Syrians. They discovered that the Lord had caused the Syrians to hear a great noise and flee, leaving their camp unattended. The people of Samaria looted the Syrian camp and food was plentiful. The doubting nobleman was assigned to guard the gate and was trampled by the crowd and killed. (2 Ki. 7:3-20)

The Lessons:
 (1). God reveals the future to His prophets.
 (2). Prophecy is specific and accurate.

(3). Prophecy is literally fulfilled.
(4). God warns His prophets of approaching challenges and dangers.
(5). Man's life is not predestined. Man himself determines his fate by establishing in the present a cause-and-effect relationship with the future. Prophecy merely pre-states what the ultimate effect of present actions will be.

N. A Prophecy of Seven Years of Famine. (2 Ki. 8:1-6)

Situation: Elisha told the Shunammite woman and her son to move from their home and live elsewhere for seven years until the famine was over. She did so and then returned and reclaimed her home.

The Lessons:
(1). God reveals the future to His prophets.
(2). God directs people as to how they should conduct their lives through his prophets.

O. A Prophecy that Hazael Would Be King of Syria. (2 Ki. 8:7-15)

Situation: Elisha went to Damascus. Benhadad was sick, and sent Hazael to Elisha to inquire if he would die. Elisha instructed Hazael to return and tell Benhadad, "Thou mayest certainly recover" (from the disease).

The Prophecy:
(1). The Lord has showed me that he shall surely die.
(2). Hazael shalt be king over Syria.
(3). Hazael will burn and pillage Israel.

Fulfillment: Hazael murdered Benhadad and became king. He defeated the Israelites at Ramoth-gilead. (2 Ki. 8:14-29)

The Lessons:
(1). God reveals the future to His prophets.
(2). Prophecy is specific and accurate.

(3). Prophecy is literally fulfilled.
(4). God rules the destiny of nations.
(5). At times people perform specific actions to intentionally fulfill prophecies.

P. Elisha Arranges the Anointing of Jehu. (2 Ki. 9:1-3)

See under number 18, The Sons of the Prophets, Item B.

Q. Elisha's Deathbed Prophecy of Victories over Syria. (2 Ki. 13:14-21)

Situation: Elisha lay on his deathbed. Joash, the king of Israel, came and wept over him. Elisha had the king help him and together they shot an arrow out of the east window.

His Prophecy: Thou shalt smite the Syrians in Aphek, till thou have consumed them.

Second Situation: Elisha told the king to take the arrows and hit them on the ground. He did so three times. Elisha prophesied again:

His Prophecy:
(1). Thou shouldest have smitten five or six times; then hadst thou smitten Syria till thou hadst consumed it.
(2). Now thou shalt smite Syria but thrice.

Fulfillment: Not recorded in the Bible.

The Lessons:
(1). God reveals the future to His prophets.
(2). Man's life is not predestined. Man himself determines his fate by establishing in the present a cause-and-effect relationship with the future. Prophecy merely pre-states what the ultimate effect of present actions will be.
(3). The Bible does not record the fulfillment of some prophecies. This does not, however, make them untrue.

18. More than a Hundred of The Sons of The Prophets.

A. **Prophecies of the Ascension of Elijah.** (2 Ki. 2:1-18)

Situation: Elijah and Elisha traveled together on the day Elijah was taken up into heaven. They passed groups of the sons of the prophets in Bethel and Jericho. The sons of the prophets spoke (prophetically?) to Elisha:

Their Prophecy: Knowest thou that the Lord will take away thy master from thy head today?

Second Situation: Fifty of them went and searched for the body of Elijah, but were unable to find it.

The Lesson: God often uses many prophets at the same time.

B. **The Anointing of Jehu.** (2 Ki. 9:1-10)

Situation: Elisha called one of the children of the prophets and sent him to anoint Jehu. The young man found Jehu at Ramoth-gilead and anointed him King.

His Prophecy:
- (1). The Lord has anointed thee king over Israel.
- (2). Thou shalt smite the house of Ahab thy master.
- (3). The whole house of Ahab shall perish.
- (4). The dogs shall eat Jezebel in Jezreel.

Fulfillment: Jehu made himself king by destroying all the house of Ahab. (2 Ki. 9:22-10:11)

The Lessons:
- (1). God reveals the future to His prophets.
- (2). Prophecy is specific and accurate.
- (3). Prophecy is literally fulfilled.

C. **Miscellaneous Activities.**
- (1). Elisha multiplied oil for one of their widows. (2 Ki. 4:1-7)
- (2). Elisha healed their poisoned pottage. (2 Ki. 4:38-41)
- (3). Elisha miraculously fed a hundred of them. (2 Ki. 4:42-44)

THE EARLY PROPHETS AND THEIR MESSAGES 219

(4). Elisha helped them build a new home by the River Jordan. (2 Ki. 6:1-7)

(5). One of them prophesied that Ahab's life would be taken for Benhadad's. (1 Ki. 20:31-43—See number 12, item A.)

The Lesson: God often uses many prophets at the same time.

19. **Zechariah, the Son of Jehoiada.** (Zĕch-ă-rī'-ăh, the son of Jĕ-hoi'-ă-dă) (2 Chron. 24:19-22, 26:5)

Situation: During the early part of the reign of Joash (eighth king of Judah) the young king was guided by the priest, Jehoiada, in the way of righteousness. When Jehoiada died, however, Joash was led back into idolatry by the young princes of Judah. Zechariah, Jehoiada's son, was guided to call them to repentance. His message was rejected, however, and they stoned him at the command of king Joash.

His Prophecy:

(1). Why transgress ye the commandments of the Lord, that ye cannot prosper?

(2). Because ye have forsaken the Lord, he hath also forsaken you.

The Lesson: At times prophets must suffer martyrdom for their testimony.

20. **A Man of God—Unto Amaziah.** (2 Chron. 25:7-9)

Situation: Amaziah (the ninth king of Judah) prepared to make war against the Edomites. He formed the troops of Judah, and hired 100,000 men of Israel to fight with them. Then there came a man of God to him:

His Prophecy:

(1). Let not the army of Israel go with thee, for the Lord is not with the children of Ephraim.

(2). If you take them with you, God shall make thee fall before the enemy.

(3). God hath power to help, and to cast down.

(4). Do not worry about the one hundred talents of silver paid to Israel; the Lord is able to give thee much more than this.

Fulfillment: Amaziah heeded the counsel of the man of God and left the troops of Israel behind. He defeated the Edomites and his life was spared. (2 Chron. 25:1-12)

The Lessons:
  (1). God directs people, through His prophets, as to how they should conduct their lives.
  (2). God rules the destiny of nations.
  (3). When situations change, the outcome of prophecy may change.
  (4). Man's life is not predestined. Man himself determines his fate by establishing in the present a cause-and-effect relationship with the future. Prophecy merely pre-states what the ultimate effect of present actions will be.

21. **A Prophet—Unto Amaziah.** (2 Chron. 25:15-16)

Situation: When Amaziah defeated the Edomites he seized their idol Gods and brought them back to Judah. He bowed down to them and worshipped them. The Lord sent a prophet to him, who told him his message and was then forbidden to say more by the king:

His Prophecy:
  (1). Why hast thou sought after the gods of the people, which could not deliver their own people out of thine hand?
  (2). God hath determined to destroy thee, because thou hast done this, and hast not hearkened unto my counsel.

Fulfillment: Amaziah unwisely challenged Israel to war[3] and saw his army scattered, Jerusalem plundered, and the wall of Jerusalem partially destroyed. Then a conspiracy arose against the king and he was murdered at Lachish. (2 Chron. 25:17-38)

---
[3]This "came of God." (2 Chron. 25:20)

The Early Prophets and Their Messages

The Lessons:
  (1). Man's life is not predestined. Man himself determines his fate by establishing in the present a cause-and-effect relationship with the future. Prophecy merely pre-states what the ultimate effect of present actions will be.
  (2). God rules the destiny of nations.

22. **Jonah, the Son of Amittai** (Jō'-năh, the son of ă-mĭt'-tai) (2 Ki. 14:25-27)

  Situation: This is merely an allusion to a prophet Jonah, who is believed to be the same prophet who prophesied to Nineveh. He prophesied in the reign of Jeroboam II (the thirteenth king of Israel). Jonah's prophecy was apparently instrumental in causing Jeroboam to extend the borders of Israel.

  His Prophecy: Jeroboam would restore the coast of Israel from the entering of Hamath unto the sea of the plain.

  The Lesson: At times people perform specific actions to intentionally fulfill prophecies.

23. **Oded** (ō'-dĕd) (2 Chron. 28:9-11.)

  Situation: During the Syro-Ephraimite War (c. 734 B.C.) Syria and Israel captured many of the troops of Judah. These troops, plus 200,000 women, sons, and daughters, were carried into Samaria. The army was challenged as it made its victorious return by the prophet Oded.

  His Prophecy:
  (1). Because God was wroth with Judah He delivered them into your hand.
  (2). You have also sinned by trying to keep slaves.
  (3). Release the captives, for the fierce wrath of the Lord is upon you.

  Fulfillment: The captives were released at Jericho. Israel still fell because of its wickedness. (2 Chron. 28:12-15; 2 Ki. 17)

The Lesson: At times people perform specific actions to intentionally fulfill prophecies.

24. **Prophets who Spoke Against Manasseh.** (2 Ki. 21:1-16)

   Situation: Manasseh (the fourteenth king of Judah) was especially wicked. He led his country into idolatry, and even offered his son as a human sacrifice. Judah never recovered from the wickedness he initiated. Unknown prophets were called to cry against him:

   Their Prophecy:
   (1). Because of Manasseh's wickedness, the Lord will bring such evil upon Judah it will make one's ears tingle to hear of it.
   (2). The Lord will wipe Jerusalem and turn it upside down.
   (3). The Lord will forsake them and deliver them into the hands of their enemies.
   (4). They shall become a prey and a spoil to all their enemies.

   Fulfillment: Judah fell to Babylonia. (2 Ki. 24, 25)

   The Lesson:
   (1). God reveals the future to His prophets.
   (2). Prophecy is literally fulfilled.
   (3). God rules the destiny of nations.
   (4). A prophet can foresee events hundreds of years into the future, and in differing national situations.

25. **Isaiah's Wife, the Prophetess.** (Is. 8:3)

   The Lesson: Women can also speak the Lord's will, as prophetesses.

26. **Huldah the Prophetess.** (2 Ki. 22:13-20; 2 Chron. 34:22-28)

   Situation: During the reign of Josiah (the sixteenth king of Judah) the high priest, Hilkiah, found the book of the law of the Lord. Josiah sent his servants to inquire of the Lord concerning the book. They went and sought revelation from Huldah the prophetess. This event is significant for in this instance, the high priest could not, apparently, obtain such revelation. It is also significant because it is known that Jeremiah was actively prophesying at this time, and Zephaniah may have been also. Their word, however, was not sought. It appears that Huldah held the king's and high priest's regard as the most effective spokesman for the Lord.

Her Prophecy:
   (1). The Lord will bring evil upon this place, even all the words of the book.
   (2). They have forsaken me and burned incense to other gods.
   (3). Because the king has humbled himself before the Lord, (when he read the book) the Lord has heard his tears.
   (4). He shall go to his grave in peace, and his eye shall not see the evil which will come upon this place.

Fulfillment: Josiah achieved many reforms in Judah and died before the destruction of Jerusalem. (2 Ki. 23:1-30)

The Lessons:
   (1). God reveals the future to His prophets.
   (2). Prophecy is specific and accurate.
   (3). Prophecy is literally fulfilled.
   (4). When situations change, the outcome of prophecy may change.
   (5). When God changes a prophetic outcome, He reveals the change to His prophet.
   (6). Man can avert or soften a prophecy of the Lord's punishment against him by truly repenting and manifesting humility.
   (7). Women can also speak the Lord's will, as prophetesses.

Doctrinal Analysis: (1 Ki. 11 - 2 Ki. 25; 2 Chron. 10-36)

The Nature of God:

1 Kings.

1. The Lord was angry with Solomon. (11:9)
2. Judah provoked the Lord to jealousy. (14:22)
3. He provoked the Lord God to anger. (15:30; 16:2, 7, 13, 26; 22:53)

2 Kings.

1. He provoked the Lord God to anger. (22:17; 23:19; 24:20)
2. The Lord was gracious unto them, and had compassion on them, and had respect unto them. (13:23)
3. The Lord turned not away the fierceness of his great wrath. (23:26)

2 Chronicles.

1. He provoked the Lord God to anger. (28:25)
2. Lord, it is nothing with thee to help, whether with many, or with them that have no power. (14:11)
3. There is no iniquity with the Lord our God, nor respect of persons, nor taking of gifts (bribes). (19:7)
4. His mercy endureth forever. (20:21)
5. The Lord would not destroy the house of David, because of the covenant that he had made with David. (21:7)
6. The fierce wrath of the Lord is upon you. (28:11)
7. The Lord your God is gracious and merciful, and will not turn away his face from you, if ye return unto him. (30:9)

Appearances of God and Heavenly Hosts:

1 Kings.

1. The Lord appeared unto Solomon twice. (11:9)
2. I saw the Lord sitting on his throne, and all the hosts of heaven standing by him. (22:19-23; 2 Chron. 18:18-22)

2 Kings.

1. There appeared a chariot and horses of fire. (2:11)
2. The Lord opened the eyes of the young man; and he saw: and behold, the mountain was full of horses and chariots of fire. (6:17)

THE EARLY PROPHETS AND THEIR MESSAGES

3. (Elisha's deathbed vision) O my father, my father, the chariot of Israel, and the horsemen thereof. (13:14)

God Controls Nature:

2 Kings.

1. The Lord hath called a famine. (8:1)

Sins of Judah and Israel:

—They Follow Other Gods:

1 Kings.

1. His wives turned away his heart after other gods. (11:4)

2 Kings.

1. The children of Israel had sinned against the Lord and had feared other gods and walked in the statutes of the heathen. (17:7-8)

—They Worship Idols:

1 Kings.

1. They committed idolatry. (11:7-8, 33; 14:9)

2 Kings.

1. They committed idolatry. (17:7-12, 16; 21:3-7)

2 Chronicles.

1. They committed idolatry. (33:3-9)

—They Dealt With Enchantments, Familiar Spirits, and Wizards:

2 Kings.

1. They used divination and enchantments. (17:17)
2. He observed times, and used enchantments, and dealt with familiar spirits and wizards. (21:6)

2 Chronicles.

1. He observed times, and used enchantments, **and used** witchcrafts, and dealt with a familiar spirit, **and with wizards.** (33:6)

—They Are Not Valiant:

1 Kings.

1. He went not fully after the Lord. (11:6)

—They Are Disobedient:

1 Kings.

1. He kept not that which the Lord commanded. (11:10)

2 Chronicles.

1. The Lord spake unto him and his people, but they would not hearken. (33:10)

—They Followed Unwise Counsel:

1 Kings.

1. He forsook the counsel of the old men and consulted with the young men that were grown up with him. (12:8, 13-14)

2 Chronicles.

1. He forsook the counsel of the old men and took counsel with the young men. (10:8)
2. His mother was his counsellor to do wickedly. (22:3)

—They Turned Away From God:

1 Kings.

1. His heart was turned from the Lord God of Israel. (11:9)
2. They have forsaken me. (11:33)
3. They have not walked in my ways, to do that which is right in mine eyes, and to keep my statutes and my judgments. (11:33)

2 Kings.

1. They would not hear, but hardened their necks; they did not believe in the Lord their God. (17:14)
2. They rejected his statutes, and his covenant that he made with their fathers, and his testimonies . . . (17:15)
3. He forsook the Lord God of his fathers, and walked not in the way of the Lord. (21:22)

The Early Prophets and Their Messages

2 Chronicles.
1. They have turned away their faces from the habitation of the Lord, and turned their backs. (29:6)

—They Did Not Keep The Lord's Commandments:

2 Kings.
1. They left all the commandments of the Lord their God. (17:16)

2 Chronicles.
1. He forsook the law of the Lord. (12:1)

—They Caused Their Children To Pass Through The Fire:

2 Kings.
1. He made his son to pass through the fire. (16:3)
2. They caused their sons and daughters to pass through the fire. (17:17)
3. He made his son pass through the fire. (21:6)

2 Chronicles.
1. He burnt his children in the fire. (28:2-4)
2. He caused his children to pass through the fire. (33:6)

—They Were Guilty of Murder:

2 Kings.
1. He shed innocent blood very much. (21:16)

—They Did Not Accept The Lord's Servants:

2 Chronicles.
1. They cast out the priests of the Lord. (13:9)
2. They mocked the messengers of God, and despised his words, and misused his prophets. (36:16)

—Their Hearts Were Not Right:

1 Kings.
1. His heart was not perfect with the Lord his God. (11:4)

2 Chronicles.
1. He did evil, because he prepared not his heart to seek the Lord. (12:14)

2. The people had not prepared their hearts unto the God of their fathers. (20:33)
3. He did what was right in the sight of the Lord, but not with a perfect heart. (25:2)

—Other Sins:

1 Kings.

1. Thou hast sold thyself to work evil in the sight of the Lord. (21:20)

2 Kings.

1. The children of Israel did secretly those things that were not right against the Lord their God. (17:9)
2. They sold themselves to do evil in the sight of the Lord. (17:17)

2 Chronicles.

1. They help the ungodly, and love them that hate the Lord. (19:2)
2. He humbled himself not before the Lord. (33:23)

Judgments:

—Punishment Is the Result of Sin:

2 Kings.

1. They feared not the Lord; therefore the Lord sent lions among them, which slew some of them. (17:25)

2 Chronicles.

1. With a great plague will the Lord smite thy people, and thy children, and thy wives, and all thy goods, because of idolatry. (21:14)
2. They mocked the messengers of God, and despised his words, and misused his prophets, until the wrath of the Lord arose against his people, till there was no remedy (36:16)

—God Knows Man's Thoughts and Deeds:

2 Kings.

1. I know thy abode, and thy going out, and thy coming in, and thy rage against me. (19:27)

—God Removes His Wrath From The Repentant:

2 Kings.
1. I have heard thy prayer, I have seen thy tears: behold I will heal thee. (20:5)

2 Chronicles.
1. When the Lord saw that they humbled themselves, he said, They have humbled themselves; therefore I will not destroy them, but I will grant them some deliverance. (12:7)
2. When he humbled himself, the wrath of the Lord turned from him, that he would not destroy him altogether. (12:12)
3. Hezekiah and his people humbled themselves for the pride of their heart, so the wrath of the Lord came not upon them in the days of Hezekiah. (32:26)
4. Manasseh humbled himself greatly before the God of his fathers, and prayed unto him: and God heard his supplication and brought him out of captivity to Jerusalem to his kingdom. (33:11-13)
5. Because of his humility, he shall not see all the evil the Lord shall bring upon this place. (34:27-28)

—Man May Choose Or Reject God:

2 Chronicles.
1. Ye have forsaken me, and therefore have I also left you in the hand of the Egyptians. (12:5)
2. O children of Israel, fight ye not against the Lord God of your fathers, for ye shall not prosper. (13:12)
3. The Lord is with you, while ye be with him, and if ye seek him, he will be found of you; but if ye forsake him, he will forsake you. (15:2)
4. The eyes of the Lord run to and fro throughout the whole earth, to show himself strong in the behalf of them whose heart is perfect toward him. (16:9)
5. The Edomites and Libnah revolted from Jehoram because he had forsaken the Lord God of his fathers. (21:10)
6. Why transgress ye the commandments of the Lord, that ye cannot prosper? Because ye have forsaken the Lord, he hath also forsaken you. (24:20)
7. He was marvelously helped, till he was strong. But when he was strong, his heart was lifted up to his destruction, for he transgressed against the Lord his God. (26:15-16)

—God Tests Man:

2 Chronicles.

1. God left him, to try him, that he might know all that was in his heart. (32:31)

—God Controls The Actions and Fate of Individuals:

1 Kings.

1. The Lord stirred up an adversary unto Solomon. (11:14)
2. God stirred him up another adversary. (11:23)
3. I will rend the kingdom out of the hand of Solomon. (11:31)
4. I will make Solomon a prince all the days of his life for David my servant's sake. (11:34)
5. Unto Solomon's son the Lord will give one tribe, that David will always have a light before the Lord in Jerusalem. (11:36)
6. Wherefore the king hearkened not unto the people, for the cause was from the Lord, that he might perform his saying . . . (12:15)
7. Thy life shall go for his life, and thy people for his people. (20:42)
8. The Lord said, Who shall persuade Ahab, that he may go up and fall at Ramoth-gilead? (22:20-23)

2 Kings.

1. The Lord hath called these three kings together, to deliver them into the hand of Moab. (3:10)
2. Thou shalt smite the house of Ahab, that I may avenge the blood of my servants the prophets, and the blood of all the servants of the Lord. (9:7)
3. Because thou hast done well in executing that which is right in mine eyes, thy children of the fourth generation shall sit on the throne of Israel. (10:30; 15:12)
4. The Lord smote the king, so that he was a leper unto the day of his death. (15:5)
5. The Lord said, I will send a blast upon the king of Assyria, and he shall hear a rumor, and shall return to his own land; and I will cause him to fall by the sword in his own land. (19:7)
6. For through the anger of the Lord it came to pass in Jerusalem and Judah, until he had cast them out from his presence, that Zedekiah rebelled against Babylon. (24:20)

THE EARLY PROPHETS AND THEIR MESSAGES

2 Chronicles.

1. So the king hearkened not unto the people: for the cause was of God, that the Lord might perform his word, which he spoke by the hand of his prophet. (10:15)
2. The word of the Lord came unto him, saying, Ye shall not fight against your brethren, for this thing is done of me. (11:4)
3. The Lord struck him, and he died. (13:20)
4. He had no war in those years, because the Lord had given him rest. (15:15, 19)
5. Because thou hast relied on Syria, and not relied on the Lord thy God, therefore is the host of the king of Syria escaped out of thine hand. (16:7)
6. Because thou didst rely on the Lord, he delivered your enemies into your hand. (16:8)
7. They compassed about him to fight, and Jehoshaphat cried out, and the Lord helped him; and God moved them to depart from him. (18:31)
8. The Lord smote him in his bowels with an incurable disease. (21:18)
9. God hath determined to destroy thee, because thou hast not hearkened unto my counsel. (25:16)
10. Amaziah challenged Israel to war. Israel told him there was no need for battle, but Amaziah would not hear; for it came of God, that he might deliver them into the hand of their enemies. (25:20)
11. The Lord smote Uzziah with leprosy for offering to the Lord without authority. (26:16-20)
12. For the Lord brought Judah low because of Ahaz king of Israel; for he made Judah naked, and transgressed sore against the Lord. (28:19)
13. God had given him substance very much. (32:29)
14. The Lord brought upon Manasseh the Assyrians. They bound him with fetters and carried him to Babylon. (33:11)
15. Josiah hearkened not unto the words of Necho from the mouth of God, and came to fight in the valley of Megiddo. (35:22)
16. The Lord stirred up the spirit of Cyrus, that he made a proclamation. (36:22)

—God Controls the Actions and Fate of Nations:

1 Kings.

1. Rehoboam was told not to pursue Israel; for this thing is from God. (12:24)
2. The Lord shall raise him up a king over Israel who shall cut off the house of Jeroboam. (14:14)
3. I will deliver the multitude into thine hand this day, and thou shalt know that I am the Lord. (20:13)
4. Because the Syrians think my power is limited, I will deliver this great multitude into thine hand and ye shall know that I am the Lord. (20:28)

2 Kings.

1. The Lord will deliver the Moabites into your hand. (3:18)
2. The Lord had made the host of the Syrians to hear a noise of chariots and horses, even the noise of a great host. (7:6)
3. Yet the Lord would not destroy Judah for David's sake, as he promised him to give him always a light, and to his children. (8:19)
4. In those days the Lord began to cut Israel short. (10:32)
5. The Lord gave Israel a saviour, so that they went out from under the hand of the Syrians. (13:5)
6. In those days the Lord began to send against Judah the kings of Syria and Israel. (15:37)
7. The Lord rejected all the seed of Israel, and afflicted them, and delivered them into the hand of spoilers, until he had cast them out of his sight. (17:20)
8. I will defend Jerusalem to save it, for mine own sake, and for my servant David's sake. (19:34)
9. I will deliver Jerusalem into the hand of their enemies. (21:14)
10. The Lord sent against him bands of the Chaldees, Syrians, Moabites, and Ammonites to Judah to destroy it. (24:2)
11. Surely at the commandment of the Lord came this upon Judah, to remove them out of his sight, for the sins of Manasseh ... (24:3)

2 Chronicles.

1. God smote Jeroboam and all Israel before Abijah and Judah, and God delivered them into their hand. (13:15-16)
2. O Lord God, rulest not thou over all the kingdoms of the heathen? (20:6-7)

THE EARLY PROPHETS AND THEIR MESSAGES

3. The Lord had made them to rejoice over their enemies. (20:27)
4. The Lord delivered a very great host into the hands of the Syrians because they had forsaken the Lord God of their fathers. (24:24)
5. God did vex them with all adversity. (15:6)
6. The wrath of the Lord was upon Judah and Jerusalem, and he hath delivered them to trouble, to astonishment, and to hissing. (29:8)
7. In Judah the hand of God was to give them one heart to do the commandment of the king and of the princes, by the word of the Lord. (30:12)
8. The Lord sent an angel, which cut off all the mighty men of valour, and the leaders and captains in the camp of the king of Assyria. (32:21)
9. The Lord brought upon Judah the king of the Chaldees. (36:17)

God's Dealings With His Prophets:

—Prophets Act As Spokesmen and Agents for God:

1 Kings.

1. Elijah slew the false priests of Baal. (18:40)
2. What the Lord saith unto me, that will I speak. (22:14)
3. If thou return at all in peace, the Lord hath not spoken by me. (22:28)

2 Kings.

1. Is there not here a prophet of the Lord, that we may inquire of the Lord by him? (3:11)
2. Bring me a minstrel. When the minstrel played, the hand of the Lord came upon him. (3:15)
3. The Lord testified against Israel, and against Judah, by all the prophets, and all the seers. (17:13)
4. Turn ye from your evil ways, and keep my commandments and my statutes, according to all the law which I commanded your fathers, and which I sent to you by my servants the prophets. (17:13)
5. The Lord spake by his servants the prophets. (21:10)

2 Chronicles.

1. As the Lord liveth, what my God saith, that will I speak. (18:13)

2. If thou certainly return in peace, then hath not the Lord spoken by me. (18:27)
3. The king humbled not himself before Jeremiah the prophet speaking from the mouth of the Lord. (36:12)

—Prophets Can Perform Miracles:

1 Kings.

1. The man of God had power to wither Jeroboam's hand and restore it. (13:4-6)
2. Elijah calls down fire from heaven. (18:36-38)

2 Kings.

1. Elijah calls down fire which consumes one hundred soldiers. (1:9-12)
2. Elijah and Elisha divide the waters. (2:8, 14)
3. Elijah was taken to heaven in a whirlwind. (2:11)
4. Elisha restored a boy to life. (4:18-37)
5. A dead man revived when he touched the bones of Elisha. (13:21)

—Prophets Have the Power of Discernment:

2 Kings.

1. Elisha, the prophet that is in Israel, telleth the king of Israel the words that thou speakest in thy bedchamber. (6:12)

—Prophecy Is Fulfilled:

2 Kings.

1. Know now that there shall fall to the earth nothing of the word of the Lord. (10:10)
2. The Lord removed Israel out of his sight, as he had said by all his servants the prophets. (17:23)
3. God sent bands of enemies against Judah to destroy it, according to the word of the Lord, which he spake by his servants the prophets. (24:2)

2 Chronicles.

1. So the king hearkened not unto the people, for the cause was of God, that the Lord might perform his word which he spoke by the hand of his prophet. (10:15)
2. The Lord brought upon Judah the king of the Chaldees to fulfill the word of the Lord by the mouth of Jeremiah. (36:21)

THE EARLY PROPHETS AND THEIR MESSAGES

3. The Lord stirred up the spirit of Cyrus to make a proclamation that the word of the Lord spoken by Jeremiah might be accomplished. (36:22-23)

—Personal Revelation and Actions of the Spirit:

1 Kings.
1. The Spirit of the Lord shall carry thee. (18:12)
2. Elijah heard the still small voice. (19:12)

2 Kings.
1. Let a double portion of thy spirit be upon me. (2:9)
2. The Spirit of the Lord hath taken him up. (2:16)

2 Chronicles.
1. The Spirit of God came upon Azariah. (15:1)
2. Upon Jahaziel came the Spirit of the Lord in the midst of the congregation. (20:14)
3. The Spirit of God came upon Zechariah. (24:20)

Counsel for Righteous Living:

—Obedience to the Commandments:

1 Kings.
1. The Lord chose him because he kept the commandments and statutes. (11:34)
2. If thou wilt hearken unto all that I command thee, and wilt walk in my ways, and do that is right in my sight, to keep my statutes and commandments, I will be with thee, and build thee a sure house. (11:38)
3. They hearkened unto the word of the Lord. (12:24)
4. He did that which was right in the eyes of the Lord, and turned not aside from anything that he commanded him. (15:5)

2 Kings.
1. The statutes, and the ordinances, and the law, and the commandment, which he wrote for you ye shall observe to do for evermore. (17:37)
2. He trusted in the Lord God of Israel. He clave to the Lord, and departed not from following him, but kept his commandments, and the Lord was with him; and he prospered whithersoever he went forth. (18:5-7)

2 Chronicles.

1. We keep the charge of the Lord our God, and behold, God himself is with us for our captain. (13:11-12)
2. He commanded his people to seek the Lord God of their fathers, and to do the law and the commandment. (14:4)

—Serve Others:

1 Kings.

1. If thou wilt be a servant unto this people, and wilt serve them, and answer them, and speak good words to them, then they will be thy servants forever. (12:7)

—Fear and Serve God:

1 Kings.

1. How long halt ye between two opinions? If the Lord be God, follow him. (18:21)

2 Kings.

1. Thy servant did fear the Lord. (4:1)
2. The Lord: him shall ye fear, and him shall ye worship, and to him shall ye do sacrifice. (17:36)
3. The Lord your God ye shall fear; and he shall deliver you out of the hand of all your enemies. (17:39)
4. He turned to the Lord with all his heart, and with all his soul, and with all his might, according to all the Law . . . (23:25)

2 Chronicles.

1. As for us, the Lord is our God, and we have not forsaken him. (13:10)
2. They came to him out of Israel in abundance, when they saw that the Lord his God was with him. (15:9)
3. Thus shall ye do in the fear of the Lord, faithfully, and with a perfect heart. (19:9)
4. Ye have consecrated yourselves unto the Lord. (29:31)

—Seek Guidance and Help:

1 Kings.

1. Inquire at the word of the Lord today. (22:5)

2 Kings.

1. Inquire of the Lord concerning the words of this book (of scripture). (22:13)

2 Chronicles.
1. Inquire at the word of the Lord today. (18:4)
2. Judah fasted and gathered themselves together, to ask help of the Lord. (20:4)
3. If, when evil cometh upon us, as the sword, judgment, or pestilence or famine, we stand before this house, and in thy presence, (for thy name is in this house) and cry unto thee in our affliction, then thou wilt hear and help. (20:9)
4. Their prayer came up to his holy dwelling place, even unto heaven. (30:27)

—**Covenant:**

2 Kings.
1. They made a covenant between the Lord and the king and the people, that they should be the Lord's people. (11:17)
2. He made a covenant before the Lord to walk after the Lord, and to keep his commandments and his testimonies and his statutes with all their heart and all their soul, to perform the words of this covenant that were written in this book (of scripture). (23:3)

2 Chronicles.
1. They entered into a covenant to seek the Lord God of their fathers with all their heart and with all their soul; that whosoever would not seek the Lord God of Israel should be put to death. (15:12-13)
2. They rejoiced at the oath, for they had sworn with all their heart, and sought God with their whole desire; and he was found of them, and the Lord gave them rest round about. (15:15)
3. Now it is in mine heart to make a covenant with the Lord God of Israel, that his fierce wrath may turn away from us. (29:10)
4. The king made a covenant before the Lord, to walk after the Lord, and to keep his commandments, and his testimonies, and his statutes, with all his heart, and with all his soul, to perform the words of the covenant which are written in this book (of scripture). (34:31)

—**Have Faith:**

2 Chronicles.
1. The children of Judah prevailed, because they relied upon the Lord God of their fathers. (13:18)

2. Help us, O Lord our God; for we rest on thee, and in thy name we go against this multitude. (14:11)
3. Fear not, nor be dismayed, for the Lord will be with you. (20:17)
4. Believe in the Lord your God, so shall ye be established; believe his prophets, so shall ye prosper. (20:20)

—Be Honest:

2 Kings.

1. They dealt faithfully. (12:15)
2. They dealt faithfully. (22:7)

2 Chronicles.

1. Take heed what ye do: for ye judge not for man, but for the Lord, who is with you in the judgment. Wherefore now let the fear of the Lord be upon you, take heed and do it: for there is no iniquity with the Lord our God, nor respect of persons, nor taking of gifts (bribes). (19:6-7)

—Repent:

2 Kings.

1. Turn ye from your evil ways, and keep my commandments and my statutes, according to all the law which I commanded your fathers, and which I sent to you by my servants the prophets. (17:13)

2 Chronicles.

1. They gathered their brethren, and sanctified themselves. (29:15)
2. They made confession to the Lord God of their fathers. (30:22)

—Do Good:

2 Kings.

1. I beseech thee, O Lord, remember now how I have walked before thee in truth and with a perfect heart, and have done that which is good in thy sight. (20:3)

2 Chronicles.

1. He wrought that which was good and right and truth before the Lord his God. (31:20)

The Early Prophets and Their Messages

—Be Humble:

2 Kings.

1. Because thine heart was tender, and thou hast humbled thyself before the Lord, I have heard thee. (22:19)

2 Chronicles.

1. They humbled themselves; and they said, the Lord is righteous. (12:6)
2. When he was in affliction, he besought the Lord his God, and humbled himself greatly before the God of his fathers. (33:12)
3. Be ye not stiffnecked, as your fathers were, but yield yourselves unto the Lord, and enter into his sanctuary, which he hath sanctified forever: and serve the Lord, your God, that the fierceness of his wrath may turn away from you. (30:8)
4. Because thine heart was tender, and thou didst humble thyself before God, I have heard thee, saith the Lord. (34:27)

—Seek God:

2 Chronicles.

1. He commanded his people to seek the Lord God of their fathers, and to do the law and the commandment. (14:4)
2. We have sought the Lord our God and he hath given us rest on every side. So they built and prospered. (14:7)
3. The Lord is with you while ye be with him; and if ye seek him, he will be found of you; but if ye forsake him, he will forsake you. (15:2)
4. Our eyes are upon thee. (20:12)
5. All Judah stood before the Lord, with their little ones, their wives, and their children. (20:13)
6. He sought the Lord with all his heart. (22:9)
7. As long as he sought the Lord, God made him to prosper. (26:5)
8. While he was yet young he began to seek after the God of David. (34:3)

—Be Courageous and Strong:

2 Chronicles.

1. Be ye strong therefore, and let not your hands be weak: for your work shall be rewarded. (15:7)

2. Deal courageously, and the Lord shall be with the good. (19:11)
3. He became mighty, because he prepared his ways before the Lord his God. (27:6)
4. Be strong and courageous, be not afraid nor dismayed; with him is an arm of flesh; but with us is the Lord our God to help us; and to fight our battles. (32:7-8)

—Prepare the Heart:

2 Chronicles.

1. His heart was lifted up in the ways of the Lord. (17:6)
2. Thou hast prepared thine heart to seek God. (19:3)
3. The good Lord pardon everyone that prepareth his heart to seek God, the Lord God of his fathers. (30:19)

—Teach and Warn Others:

2 Chronicles.

1. Ye shall even warn your brethren that they trespass not against the Lord. (19:10)
2. They taught the good knowledge of the Lord. (30:22)
3. He made all that were present in Israel to serve the Lord their God. (34:33)
4. He encouraged the priesthood to the service of the house of the Lord. (35:2)

—Praise God:

2 Chronicles.

1. Praise the beauty of holiness. Praise the Lord; for his mercy endureth forever. (20:21)
2. Make offerings unto the Lord with rejoicing and singing. (23:18)

—Gain Knowledge:

2 Kings.

1. The word of the Lord is with him. (3:12)

2 Chronicles.

1. He had understanding in the visions of God. (26:5)

—Be Diligent:

2 Chronicles.

1. My sons, be not now negligent: for the Lord hath chosen you to stand before him, to serve him, that ye should minister unto him . . . (29:11)

THE EARLY PROPHETS AND THEIR MESSAGES 241

2. In every work that he began in the service of the house of God, and in the law, and in the commandments, to seek his God, he did it with all his heart, and prospered. (31:21)

—Pay Tithing:

2 Chronicles.

1. The tithe of all things brought they in abundantly that they might be encouraged in the law of the Lord. (31:4-5)

—Keep Records:

2 Chronicles.

1. A genealogy was kept. (31:16-19)

Miscellaneous:

1 Kings.

1. Thou shalt reign according to all that thy soul desireth. (11:37)

2 Kings.

1. The Lord pardon thy servant in this thing. (5:18)
2. Is it not good if peace and truth be in my days? (20:19)

Changes made in the Inspired Version of the Bible—1 Kings.

King James Translation	Inspired Version
13:18 He said unto him, I am a prophet also as thou art; and an angel spake unto me by the word of the Lord, saying, Bring him back with thee into thine house, that he may eat bread and drink water. But he lied unto him.	13:18 He said unto him, I am a prophet also, **even as** thou, and an angel spake unto me by the word of the Lord, saying, Bring him back with thee into thine house, that he may eat bread and drink water, **that I may prove him;** and he lied **not** unto him.
14:8 And rent the kingdom away from the house of David, and gave it thee: and yet thou hast not been as my servant David, who kept my commandments and who fol-	14:8 And rent the kingdom away from the house of David and gave it thee, **because he kept not my commandments. But thou hast not been as my servant David, when he fol-**

King James Translation	Inspired Version
lowed me with all his heart, to do that only which was right in mine eyes.	lowed me with all his heart only to do right in mine eyes.
15:3 ... and his heart was not perfect with the Lord his God, as the heart of David his father.	15:3 ... and his heart was not perfect with the Lord his God, **as the Lord commanded** David his father.
15:5 Because David did that which was right in the eyes of the Lord, and turned not aside from any thing that he commanded him all the days of his life, save only in the matter of Uriah the Hittite.	15:5 Because David did right in the eyes of the Lord, and turned not aside from **all** that he commanded him, **to sin against the Lord; but repented of the evil** all the days of his life, save only in the matter of Uriah the Hittite, **wherein the Lord cursed him.**
15:11 And Asa did that which was right in the eyes of the Lord, as did David his father.	15:11 And Asa did right in the eyes of the Lord, as **he commanded** David his father.
15:12 And he took away the sodomites out of the land, and removed all the idols that his fathers had made.	15:12 And he took away the sodomites out of the land, and removed all the idols that his fathers had made; **and it pleased the Lord.**
18:37 Hear me, O Lord, hear me, that this people may know that thou art the Lord God, and that thou hast turned their heart back again.	18:37 Hear me, O Lord, hear me, that this people may know that thou art the Lord God, and **thou mayest turn** their heart back again.

Changes made in the Inspired Version of the Bible—2 Kings.

King James Translation	Inspired Version
8:10 And Elisha said unto him, Go, say unto him, Thou mayest certainly recover: howbeit the Lord hath shewed me that he shall surely die.	8:10 And Elisha said unto him, **Thou wilt** go, and say unto him, Thou mayest certainly recover; howbeit, the Lord hath showed me that he will surely die.

THE EARLY PROPHETS AND THEIR MESSAGES

19:35 And it came to pass that night, that the angel of the Lord went out, and smote in the camp of the Assyrians an hundred forescore and five thousand: and when they arose early in the morning, behold they were all dead corpses.

19:35 . . .
. . . and when they **who were left** arose early in the morning . . .

Changes made in the Inspired Version of the Bible—2 Chronicles.

King James Translation

2:4 . . . This is an ordinance for ever to Israel.

2:5 And the house which I build is great; for great is our God above all gods.

2:7 Send me now therefore a man . . . that can skill to grave with the cunning men . . .

2:8 . . . for I know that thy servants can skill to cut timber in Lebanon; and, behold, my servants shall be with thy servants.

2:18 . . . and six hundred overseers to set the people a work.

6:17 . . . let thy word be verified . . .

7:22 . . . therefore hath he brought all this evil upon them.

13:3 . . . with eight hundred thousand chosen men . . .

Inspired Version

2:4 . . . And this ordinance **shall be kept in Israel for ever.**

2:5 And the house which I build **shall be a great house;** for great is **the Lord our God** above all gods.

2:7 Send me now therefore a man . . . that **has** skill to grave with the cunning men . . .

2:8 . . . for I know that thy servants **have** skill to cut timber in Lebanon; and, behold, **I will send my servants** with thy servants.

2:18 . . . and six hundred overseers to set the people **at** work.

6:17 . . . let **the** word be verified . . .

7:22 . . . therefore hath he brought evil upon them.

13:3 . . . with eight hundred thousand men . . .

18:21 . . . go out, and do even so.

18:22 Now therefore, behold, the Lord hath put a lying spirit in the mouth . . .

20:2 . . . and, behold, they be in Hazazon-tamar, which is En-gedi.

20:6 And said, O Lord God of our fathers, art not thou God in heaven? and rulest not thou over all the kingdoms of the heathen? and in thine hand is there not power and might, so that none is able to withstand thee?

20:7 Art not thou our God, who didst drive out the inhabitants of this land before thy people Israel, and gavest it to the seed of Abraham thy friend for ever?

20:11 Behold, I say, how they reward us, to come to cast us out of thy possession, which thou hast given us to inherit.

20:17 Ye shall not need to fight in this battle: set yourselves . . .

22:2 Forty and two years old was Ahaziah when . . .

24:22 . . . And when he died, he said, The Lord look upon it, and require it.

25:18 . . . The thistle that was in Lebanon sent to the cedar that was in Lebanon . . .

18:21 . . . go out, and do even so; **for all these have sinned against me.**

18:22 Now therefore, behold, the Lord hath **found** a lying spirit in the mouth . . .

20:2 . . . and, behold, they **are** in Hazazon-tamar, which **was called** En-gedi.

20:6 And said, O Lord God of our fathers, thou God who art in heaven; and rulest over all the kingdoms of the heathen; and in thy hand thou hast power and might, so that none is able to withstand thee;

20:7 Thou our God didst drive out the inhabitants of this land before thy people Israel, and gavest it to the seed of Abraham thy friend for ever.

20:11 Behold, they reward us **not,** but have come to cast us out of thy possession, which thou hast given us to inherit.

20:17 Ye shall not go to fight in this day; set yourselves . . .

22:2 **two and twenty** years old was Ahaziah when . . .

24:22 . . . And when he died he said, The Lord look upon **me,** and require **me.**

25:18 . . . The thistle that **grew** in Lebanon sent to the cedar that **grew** in Lebanon . . .

The Early Prophets and Their Messages 245

Summary: After studying the early prophets and their messages the reader should know:

1. The books of 1st and 2nd Kings and 2nd Chronicles are valuable because:
    A. They record the history of Israel during the era of the divided kingdoms.
    B. They show that man has his agency to choose righteousness or wickedness. God will govern the outcome of his life, based on his choice. He may change his life's course through repentance.
    C. They show that God governs the fate of men and of nations.
    D. They give the most penetrating indication of the nature of prophets and their calling which is found in all scripture.

2. The many references concerning the prophets emphasize and repeat thirty-five basic conclusions about the nature of the prophetic gift, as follows:
    A. God reveals the future to His prophets.
    B. Prophecy is specific and accurate.
    C. Prophecy is literally fulfilled.
    D. God warns His prophets of approaching challenges and dangers.
    E. God directs people, through His prophets, as to how they should conduct their lives.
    F. God rules the destiny of nations.
    G. God will not allow men to disturb His plans.
    H. When situations change, the outcome of prophecy may change.
    I. When God changes a prophetic outcome, He reveals the change to His prophet.
    J. Man can avert or soften a prophecy of the Lord's punishment against him by truly repenting and manifesting humility.
    K. A prophet can foresee events hundreds of years into the future, and in differing national situations.
    L. God often shows the truthfulness of a prophecy by giving a sign which receives immediate fulfillment.
    M. A prophet can call upon the powers of God to smite and curse his enemies.
    N. A prophet can call upon the powers of God to heal and remove curses.

O. God demands that His prophets be treated with reverence and respect.

P. God can use a man as a prophet even though the man is not free from sin.

Q. God demands strict obedience from His prophets.

R. Man should test the prophets and their prophecies by the spirit of discernment.

S. Revelation serves for commendation as well as reproof.

T. Man's life is not predestined. Man himself determines his fate by establishing in the present a cause-and-effect relationship with the future. Prophecy merely pre-states what the ultimate effect of present actions will be.

U. God often uses many prophets at the same time.

V. A calling as a prophet did not necessarily require that the person with this calling stand at the head of the Church.

W. God gives His prophets control over nature to further His work.

X. God protects his prophets and supplies their needs.

Y. Prophets have the power to perform miracles.

Z. Some miracles are performed by the powers already vested in the prophet. For other miracles he must call upon God.

AA. Miracles are often used to establish the divinity of Jehovah and the authority of His prophets.

BB. On special occasions God gives His servants strength beyond the normal limits of endurance.

CC. Many miracles are designed for the convenience of God's servants.

DD. Some servants of God are transferred from this earth to another. They become translated beings.

EE. Prophets have the power to discern the thoughts and deeds of others.

FF. At times people perform specific actions to intentionally fulfill prophecies.

GG. The Bible does not record the fulfillment of some prophecies. This does not, however, make them untrue.

HH. At times prophets must suffer martyrdom for their testimony.

II. Women can also speak the Lord's will, as prophetesses.

CHAPTER VII

JONAH

Prophet's Name: Jonah (Jō'-năh) means "dove."

Scriptural Information About the Prophet:

1. He was the son of Amitai (ă-mit'-tai). (Jon. 1:1, 2 Ki. 14:25)
2. He was born in Gath-hepher (Găth-hē'-phĕr). (It is 3 miles n.e. of Nazareth. According to monastic tradition this is the present Arab village of El-Meshed.) (2 Ki. 14:25)
3. He was of the tribe of Zebulun (Zĕ-bū'-lun) (because of his birthplace, Cf. Josh. 19:10-15, especially v. 13.) (2 Ki. 14:25)
4. He prophesied to Jeroboam II, king of Israel, of the recovery from Syria of the northern border possessions of Israel. (2 Ki. 14:25)
5. Jesus referred to the account of Jonah's mission. (Mt. 12:38-41; see also 16:4, Luke 11:29-30)

Date of Jonah's Mission: 788 B. C. ? (2 Ki. 14:23-27)

1. He lived during the reign of Jeroboam II, who ruled as king of the northern kingdom (Israel) for 41 years, from 790-749 B. C.
2. He probably lived during the early part of the reign of Jeroboam II for he prophesied good concerning the king's affairs. Later in the king's reign Amos was reproving Israel and warning that Israel would be conquered by Assyria.

Prophesied to: Assyria. (Also to Israel, though not mentioned in the book of Jonah. See 2 Ki. 14:25)

Contemporary Prophets: None.

Contemporary Kings:

Israel:	Jeroboam II 790-749 B. C.
Judah:	Uzziah 792-740 B. C.
Assyria:	Adad-nirari III 810-783 B. C.

National Conditions:

1. Assyria had been a strong empire since about 900 B. C. It had a powerful military machine which loomed as a potential threat to Israel. In 853 B. C. the Assyrian king Shalmaneser III had met a coalition of eleven kings including "Ahab the Israelite" in the battle of Karkar (about 250 miles north of Samaria, near the Orontes River in Syria). The battle was not a clear victory for either side, but it turned the Assyrian invasion back and caused them to return to their homeland. Later, in 841 B. C., the Assyrian king, Shalmaneser III, had extracted tribute from Jehu, king of Israel.
2. Following these conquests Assyria was shaken by a rebellion of one of the sons of Shalmaneser III, which greatly weakened the empire and caused the loss of many of its recently conquered vassals around the periphery of the empire. It had made some progress towards recovery in the time of Jonah.
3. The Assyrians were regarded as being extremely ruthless and cruel.

Archaeological and Historical Evidence:

1. Natives in Gath-hepher point out several Moslem tombs which they claim to be the tomb of Jonah.
2. One of the archaeological mounds left in Nineveh is the "Nebi Yunus" mound, which occupies approximately 40 acres and is 100 feet high. Local legends assert that this is the tomb of the prophet Jonah. The mound is covered by a modern village with a mosque and cemetery so little excavation has been possible.
3. **Description of Nineveh:**

    Greater Nineveh, to which Jonah apparently had reference when he called it an "exceedingly great city of three days' journey," comprised a triangle which included Khorsabad (ten miles north-east) and Calah (twenty miles south-east). Nineveh's fortifications extended to the triangle formed by the Tigris and Great Zab rivers. The dimensions of greater Nineveh were thus about thirty miles long by ten miles wide. Jonah's mention of 120,000 babies would indicate that the population of the city may have been as much as one million.

For many hundreds of years after its destruction in 612 B. C. at the hands of the Medes and Babylonians, Nineveh was barren and desolate. Its site was even forgotten. The site was not identified until 1845 when Sir Austin Henry Layard began his work there. The archaeological site has been described as follows:

> The mounds which mark its ruins are situated on the east bank of the Tigris opposite the modern city of Mosul in northern Iraq (Upper Mesopotamia). It has been excavated intermittently by British expeditions over a period of more than 100 years. Nineveh has yielded magnificent Assyrian sculpture (since deposited in the British Museum), as well as the greatest library of cuneiform tablets ever found.
>
> . . . The city walls, clearly visible in outline, are eight miles long and enclose two important mounds. One is called Nebi Yunus and, according to local legend, is the tomb of the prophet Jonah. It is covered by a modern village with cemetery and mosque; consequently only very superficial excavation has been possible. The northern and larger mound, Kuyunjik, is one of the largest in Mesopotamia; it is estimated that over 14 million tons of earth would have to be moved to excavate it completely.
>
> The main buildings thus far discovered are three royal palaces and two temples. At the southern end is the palace of Sennacherib; at the northern end, the palace of Ashurbanipal. In between is the palace of Ashurnasirpal II, the temple of Ishtar, goddess of love and war, and the temple of Nabu, god of writing. Parts of other buildings have been found and more remain to be discovered. The lower levels of the mound are as yet largely unexplored. A sounding made in depth disclosed that Nineveh was an important site already in prehistoric times. The oldest pottery belongs to a type called Hassuna ware, one of the earliest found in Mesopotamia. Sennacherib, in his inscriptions, relates that prior to building his own palace, he raised the height of the mound on the southwest side, filling in the "old Palace."[1]

---

[1] "Nineveh," *The Encyclopedia Americana*, XX, 1957 Edition, p. 368.

Outline of the Book:

Chapter 1

1. Jonah was called by the Lord to go to Nineveh, a major city of Assyria, and cry against it. (1-2)
2. He decided to avoid the mission by fleeing to Tarshish (believed to be the city of Tartessus, in southern Spain). He boarded a ship at Joppa and set sail. (3-4)

   Note: Many reasons have been expressed why Jonah may have chosen to flee from the Lord. These include a hatred for Assyria, lack of faith, desire to escape an unpleasant experience, etc. Many fail to note the reason for his flight which Jonah himself expresses in 4:2, that he fully expected the Lord to spare the city and so he saw no reason for his going to proclaim its doom.

3. The Lord caused a storm to arise and the ship was in danger of breaking up. When the storm continued, the mariners cast lots to see who had caused the storm and the lot fell upon Jonah. (4-10)
4. The sailors challenged Jonah, who finally had them cast him into the sea. The storm abated. (11-16)
5. The Lord had prepared a great fish which swallowed Jonah. He was in the belly of the fish three days and three nights. (17)

Chapter 2

6. Jonah offered a prayer of repentance to the Lord from out of the belly of the fish. (1-9)
7. The fish cast Jonah out upon land. (10)

Chapter 3

8. God again called Jonah to go to Nineveh. (1-2)
9. Jonah went to Nineveh and prophesied that the city would be overthrown in forty days. (3-4)
10. The king and inhabitants of Nineveh repented in sackcloth and ashes so God did not destroy them. (5-10)

Chapter 4

11. Jonah was displeased that God did not fulfill his prophecy and asked God to end his life. (1-4)

JONAH

12. Jonah went out and waited by the side of the city. The Lord taught him a lesson by causing a gourd to grow and give him shade, and then sending a worm the next day which caused it to wither. (5-7)
13. As the sun beat down upon him, Jonah was first angry and then had pity on the fallen gourd. (8-10)
14. God challenged Jonah, saying that if Jonah could pity the gourd, should not God pity the people of Nineveh and spare them? (10-11)

Doctrinal Analysis:

Counsel for Righteous Living:

1. Arise, call upon thy God. (1:6)
2. They that observe lying vanities forsake their own mercy. (2:8)
3. I will pay that that I have vowed. (2:9)
4. The people of Nineveh were saved because they repented in sackcloth and ashes. (3:4-10)
5. Cry mightily unto God, let everyone turn from his evil way and from violence. (3:8)
6. Doest thou well to be angry? (4:4, 9)

Nature of God:

1. I fear the Lord, the God of heaven, which hath made the sea and the dry ground. (1:9)
2. Salvation is of the Lord. (2:9)
3. Thou art a gracious God, merciful, slow to anger, and of great kindness. (4:2)

God Hears and Answers Prayers:

1. I cried by reason of my affliction unto the Lord, and he heard me. (2:2)
2. When my soul fainted within me I remembered the Lord, and my prayer came in unto thee, into thine holy temple. (2:7)

God Knows Man's Thoughts and Acts

1. Their wickedness is come up before me. (1:2)
2. God saw their works, that they turned from their evil way. (3:10)

God Governs Nature

1. The Lord sent out a great wind into the sea, and there was a mighty tempest. (1:4)
2. The Lord had prepared a great fish to swallow up Jonah. (1:17)
3. The Lord prepared a gourd so that its shadow would cover Jonah and deliver him from his grief. (4:6)
4. The Lord prepared a vehement east wind. (4:8)

God Reveals Specific Messages To His Prophets:

1. Arise, go to Nineveh, and preach unto it the preaching that I bid thee. (3:2, 1:2)

Major Lessons of the Book of Jonah: Bible scholars have found numerous meanings and interpretations as to the aim and purpose of the book of Jonah. These include:

1. **God's love and grace are universal.** They are not limited to the Jews but are available to all mankind.
2. **God requires obedience** of his servants.
3. **Prophecy is conditional.** Prophetic outcomes may be altered if a given situation changes.
4. **Only true repentance can bring the salvation of God.**
5. Jonah is considered by some to be **an allegorical figure symbolizing Israel's apostasy and return** to the Lord.

Style of the Book:

1. It is almost entirely a narration; it does not contain the discourses and sermons found in most of the prophetic books. It is not a prophecy but a story about a prophet.
2. It is written in the 3rd person, unlike most of the **prophetic books.**
3. It resembles the biographical narratives of Elijah and Elisha. (1 Ki. 17-19, 2 Ki. 4-6)
4. It has a distinctly didactic (teaching) aim.
5. It is written in prose, except for the psalm (2:1-9) which is poetry. The poetry is spirited and forceful.
6. It is simple and straightforward.

Textual Transmission: The text of the book has been preserved in good order and condition.

Author: Unknown. Most scholars believe the book was written by an unknown individual in the post-exilic period, about the 5th or 4th century B. C.

Bible Criticism:

Higher Criticism: There can be no doubt that a prophet named Jonah lived and labored during the reign of Jeroboam II. Most higher critics doubt, however, that he was swallowed by a fish and that he ever went to Nineveh. They hold that instead of being a true account of Jonah's experience, the book is, rather, a fictitious story with a didactic purpose which was written several centuries later. The criticisms they offer, in keeping with the spirit of higher criticism, which rejects items of a miraculous nature, are as follows:

1. Such coincidences as the cessation of the tempest when Jonah was cast overboard seldom occur in real life.
2. A man's survival for three days and three nights in the belly of a fish (or whale, which is the only marine animal of sufficient size known today) is physiologically improbable.
3. The instantaneous and general conversion of the city of Nineveh to Jehovah is considered highly improbable by historians of antiquity. Certainly any alleged conversion had no lasting effect on the nation of Assyria. There is no record of such a conversion anywhere else in the Old Testament or in any contemporary writings.

   Note: No inscriptions of Jonah's mission have been found in Assyrian records. There are indications, however, that Adad-Nirari III made certain reforms, as did Amenophis IV in Egypt. During the reigns of the three succeeding kings of Assyria there was a lull in the Assyrian conquests which allowed Israel and other nations to recover territory they had previously lost.

4. The story contains historical inaccuracies, such as

   A. No Assyrian king would be called the "King of Nineveh" (3:6) but rather the king of Assyria. Nineveh was not even the capital city in Jonah's day.

   B. Nineveh was never "an exceeding great city of three days' journey" (3:3). It is known that the circuit of its walls in the time of Sennacherib, ninety years later, measured about eight miles.

Note: For their purposes, the critics refuse to recognize the dimensions of "Greater Nineveh," the circumference of which was probably from sixty to seventy miles.

5. It is considered improbable that heathen sailors would admonish an Israelite to call upon a non-pagan God. (1:6)
6. It is doubtful that an Assyrian king would respond immediately to a foreign, unknown prophet who was preaching unannounced in his city. (3:4-9)
7. There are none of the casual allusions to time, place, or persons which would normally be expected in a man's account of his own experiences.
8. That Jonah is nowhere mentioned as the author and is always referred to in the third person, except when the author places words in his mouth, is held to be significant.

Lower Criticism: Lower critics have endeavored to show that the book of Jonah is a fictional account written three or four centuries after the time of the prophet Jonah, which has been shaped by influences which became prominent after the eighth century. They cite the following evidence:

1. The text contains several Aramaisms or other marks of a supposedly later age, such as

   A. The title "God of heaven" (1:9) which appears in Nehemiah 1:5 and other post-exilic writings but not before;

   B. Approximately six other Hebrew words or expressions which seemingly show Aramic influence.

2. The psalm (2:1-9) seemingly consists of reminiscences of other psalms, some of which apparently had not been written in Jonah's day (compare verse 2:2 with Ps. 18: 5-6, 120:1; verse 2:3 with Ps. 18:4, 42:7; verse 2:4 with Ps. 31:22, Lam. 3:54; verse 2:5 with Ps. 18:4, 116:3, 69:1; verse 2:6 with Ps. 30:3; verse 2:7 with Ps. 142:3, 18:6; verse 2:8 with Ps. 31:6; verse 2:9 with Ps. 50:14, 116:17f, 3:8). It is asserted that a Psalm of Jonah's age would certainly have been more original, as it would also have shown a more antique coloring.

3. The general thought and tenor of the book allegedly presupposed the teaching of the great prophets (Cf. especially 3:10 with Jer. 18:7f).

JONAH

4. The strange instruction that domestic animals, as well as human beings, should fast and wear sackcloth as a sign of repentance, finds a parallel in Judith 4:10 and is said to be a Persian custom. Herodotus wrote (9:24) that not only the soldiers but also the horses and oxen were shaved in mourning for Masistius.
5. The miraculous elements, such as the storm calming, the big fish, the gourd and the worm are said to be the major elements of the story, which is characteristic of Oriental fiction in general, in which miracles are extremely prominent.
6. Some critics believe that the story is an allegory which protests against the Jews' religious pride following the canonization of the law of Moses (about 400 B. C.) and their expectation that Jehovah would soon annihilate the heathen for the benefit of the Jews.

Rebuttal of the Literalists Against the Higher and Lower Critics:

Those who hold to absolute literal interpretation of the scriptures believe that Jonah travelled to Nineveh, experienced the happenings reported in the book, and that the book was recorded in Jonah's day. They point out that

1. All criticisms regarding miraculous elements are invalid if God is truly a God of miracles.
2. Criticisms concerning Aramaisms and Hebrew expressions, stylistic characteristics, and third person authorship are no criteria that a book containing them is late, or fictional.
3. Arguments concerning theological beliefs being characteristic of certain periods are too subjective to be of value.
4. Historical criticisms, it is said, cannot be decisive, for Jonah was a Hebrew who probably did not know Assyrian history and customs very well.
5. Precise historical details ought not to be expected in an account whose main interest is religion.
6. Jesus referred to Jonah's mission as an actuality, saying,

> An evil and adulterous generation seeketh after a sign; and there shall no sign be given to it, but the sign of the prophet Jonas:
>
> **For as Jonas was three days and three**

nights in the whale's belly; so shall the Son of man be three days and three nights in the heart of the earth.

The men of Nineveh shall rise in judgment with this generation, and shall condemn it: because they repented at the preaching of Jonas; and, behold, a greater than Jonas is here. (Mt. 12:39-41)

Position of The Church of Jesus Christ of Latter-day Saints: So far as the author has been able to determine, the Church has no official position as to whether the book of Jonah should be interpreted literally or regarded as a didactic story. Throughout its history, however, it has tended to follow a literal interpretation of such passages. This is in keeping with the 8th Article of Faith:

"We believe the Bible to be the word of God as far as it is translated correctly; we also believe the Book of Mormon to be the word of God."

Changes Made in the Inspired Version of the Bible— Book of Jonah:

King James Translation	Inspired Version
3:10—And God saw their works that they turned from their evil way; and God repented of the evil, that he had said that he would do unto them; and he did it not.	3:10—And God saw their works that they turned from their evil way **and repented; and God turned away the evil** that he had said he would bring upon them.

Summary. After studying the book of Jonah, the student should know:

1. The story of Jonah.
2. The three major lessons of the book:
   A. God loves the people of all nations.
   B. God requires obedience.
   C. Prophecy is conditional.
3. The book contains extensive teachings concerning the nature of God.
4. The geographical location of Assyria and Nineveh.
5. The major question raised by Bible critics: Is this a true experience or a teaching story?

CHAPTER VIII
AMOS

Prophet's Name: Amos (A'-mos) means "burden-bearer" or "burdened." He is not Amoz, the father of the prophet Isaiah.

Scriptural Information About the Prophet:

1. He was among the herdsmen of Tekoa. Therefore he was probably of the tribe of Judah. (Tekoa is a desolate site about six miles south of Bethlehem.) (1:1)
2. He was a herdsman and a dresser of sycamore trees. (7:14)

   Note: The sycamore is a poor quality fig tree, actually a cross between a fig and a mulberry tree. These trees do not grow in Tekoa, but further to the west. To dress them meant to make a small incision in the fruit so that insects which formed inside could come out. This also aided the fruit to ripen.

3. He lived during the reign of Uzziah, king of Judah, and Jeroboam II, king of Israel. (1:1, 7:9-11)
4. He preached two years before the earthquake. (The date of the earthquake, however, is unknown.) (1:1)

   Note: Josephus says that the earthquake happened at the same time Uzziah was smitten with leprosy (see 2 Chron. 26:16-21).

5. He was called from his flock by the Lord and sent to preach to Israel. (7:15)
6. He disclaimed being a prophet by inheritance, profession or education. (7:14)

Date of Amos' Mission: c. 750 B. C.

1. It must be between 790-749 B. C., the period in which the reign of Uzziah (792-740 B. C.) and the reign of Jeroboam II (790-749 B. C.) overlapped.
2. Internal evidence indicates that he must have preached in the later portion of the reign of Jeroboam II, after that king had achieved most of his successes:

A. The nation was reposing in opulence and ease. (6:1-5)

B. The ritual of calf-worship was being splendidly maintained at Bethel and Gilgal. (4:4-5, 5:21-23, 7:13)

C. The people of Israel were proud and felt capable of meeting any opponent. (6:13)

Prophesied to: Israel (though called from Judah).

Contemporary Prophet: Hosea c. 760-720 B. C. to Israel.

Note: The mission of Amos was one of short duration while the labors of Hosea continued over a period of years.

Contemporary Prophets Contrasted:

Amos was a discerning observer of the people of his times. He thought methodically and was able to clearly define the sins of the people and foretell the destruction and tribulation they would bring to Israel. Although he was only a shepherd and drew images from his rural background, his writing is beautifully expressed, and indicates that he was a person of refinement and culture. He knew the history of his people and thoroughly understood their religious laws.

Hosea gives a more intimate understanding of his personal affairs in his writing than any of the other prophets except Jeremiah. Hosea was a man of patience, who suffered many hardships to keep the commandments of God. His writing does not have the polished dignity or careful organization that the book of Amos shows. It is more emotional and less objective than that of Amos.

Contemporary Kings:

Israel: Jeroboam II 790-749 B. C.
Israel reached its greatest extent during his ministry.

Judah: Uzziah 792-740 B. C.

Assyria: Asshur-Lush 753-745 B. C.

Conditions of Surrounding Nations:

Israel and Judah

—Political

1. Both nations had risen to positions of power and wealth.

AMOS

2. Their boundaries had been restored, and they were relatively free from threat of war.
3. There seemed to be two political parties in Israel near the end of that kingdom. One favored alliance with Assyria; the other favored alliance with Egypt and resistance to Assyria. Israel's political situation varied as the two parties rose or diminished in power.
4. Edom was conquered by Judah and trade was resumed in the Red Sea area.
5. Syria was troubled by palace intrigues and Israel was able to regain the border territory it had lost during the reign of Jehu.
6. Assyria, the world power of the day, was not showing any territorial interest in the Mediterranean area during this period.

—Economic

1. Their leaders had become rich, haughty and proud. Trade had been revived and the kingdoms had also grown richer from booty taken in conquest.
2. The middle classes were rapidly disappearing. The rich were creating large estates by foreclosing mortgages on small landowners and taking their properties.
3. Rents and food prices were exorbitant, and served to bring greater economic distress upon the lower classes. The poor were oppressed on every hand. Slums and squalor had developed in contrast to the vast estates of the rich.

—Social

1. The governments were filled with the graft and corruption of self-seeking politicians.
2. Family life had degenerated and there was little family cohesiveness.
3. The exorbitant rents and foreclosures on land had made the practice of parents selling their children as slaves in payment of debts very common.

—Religious

1. The worship of Jehovah had degenerated into a religion of form. People offered sacrifices, paid tithes, and care-

fully observed the laws concerning the Sabbath day; yet their lives showed little evidence of true social morality and love for their neighbors.

2. The pagan rites and idolatry of the fertility cults were still common in Israel and Judah, especially among the lower classes. This took the form of ritual fornication[1] with the representatives of Baal, Astarte, Ashtoreth, etc. Such rites did much to destroy the moral influence of the law of Moses.

Assyria

1. Assur-Dayan III and Asshur-Lush were weak kings who allowed the might of Assyria's empire to decline from the unparalleled conquests of Adad-nirari III (810-783 B. C. —Jonah's day). Their laxness allowed the various states of Palestine and Syria to grow in power and wealth.
2. When Tiglath-Pileser III came to the throne he immediately endeavored to restore Assyria's prestige in these and other areas. He conquered northern Israel and Damascus (capital of Syria).

Outline of the Book:

Section I. Prologue: Threats of Judgments Against Eight Surrounding Nations (Chapters 1-2).

1. God will punish Syria. (1:3-5)
2. God will punish Philistia. (1:6-8)
3. God will punish Phoenicia. (1:9-10)
4. God will punish Edom. (1:11-12)
5. God will punish Ammon. (1:13-15)
6. God will punish Moab. (2:1-3)
7. God will punish Judah. (2:4-5)
8. God will punish Israel. (2:6-16)

Section II. The Reasons for God's Approaching Judgments upon Israel. (Chapters 3-6).

1. Israel will be singled out for judgment because she has failed to honor her position as God's chosen people. (3:2)
2. Prophets have warned her of her wickedness. (3:3-15)

---

[1] Sexual intercourse between the worshipper and the priest or priestess of the pagan god.

Amos

3. The ruling classes have oppressed the needy. (4:1-3)
4. The Israelites have followed pagan worship forms. (4:4-5)
5. Israel has failed to heed God's corrective measures. (4:6-13)
6. Israel had a choice: Seek God and live, or serve idols and go into captivity. (5:1-9)
7. Israel had rebuked those that speak mightily. She had afflicted the just. (5:10-13)
8. The rich have sought ease and comfort instead of being grieved for the afflictions of their people. (6:1-6)
9. Israel will be afflicted and go into captivity. (6:7-14)

Section III. Visions of the Lord's Judgments Upon Israel (Chapters 7-9).

1. **1st vision**—Grasshoppers (locusts?) devour the grass. The prophet intercedes and the destruction is cancelled. (7:1-3)
2. **2nd vision**—Fire (drought?) devours the great deep. The prophet intercedes and the destruction is cancelled. (7:4-6)
3. **3rd vision**—The plumbline: God will rise against the house of Jeroboam with the sword. (7:7-10)
4. **Interlude**—The priest of Bethel demands that Amos return to the land of Judah. (7:10-17)
5. **4th vision**—The basket of summer fruit: the end is come upon the people of Israel. (8:1-3)
6. **Interlude**—The Lord will send a famine from hearing his word.[2] (8:4-14)

---

[2]Commentary on Amos 8:11-12. This passage has been used in some L.D.S. missionary plans and dialogues as a reference to the universal apostasy from Christianity (c. A. D. 100-1830). While it is a very suitable description of the lack of revelation which occurred during that period, there is little basis for the assertion that Amos was intentionally speaking of that era, rather than of the time of the fall of Israel, in his prophecy. It is suggested that the prophecy be cited only when comparing the apostate condition of Israel following Amos' day with the apostasy which followed the New Testament period. To support this contention, it should be noted that

   A. This period of apostasy (100-1830 A.D.) is a period which is almost entirely bypassed by Old Testament prophets. It would appear that the Lord chose to bring forth prophecies of this era in New Testament times, when there would be less confusion concerning their interpretation. (See for example, 2 Thess. 2:1-4, 11:12; 2 Tim. 4:3-4; Rev. 13:4-8; 1 Tim. 4:1-3, etc.)

   B. A sudden abrupt change to a period 850 years in advance for

262   PROPHETS AND PROPHECIES OF THE OLD TESTAMENT

7. **5th vision**—The smitten sanctuary: though the wicked may flee, they cannot escape their just condemnation. (9:1-6)
8. **Epilogue**—Though Israel shall be scattered, it shall return. (9:7-15)

---

two verses, then an immediate return to his original subject is definitely not typical of the style of careful transitions and full exposition of the theme characteristic of the book of Amos.

C. Amos, in earlier chapters, prophesies the same lack of availability of the Lord's word, in contexts which undeniably refer to the time of the fall of Israel.
   (1). While carrying out the dead, men will say, "Hold thy tongue: for **we may not make mention of the name of the Lord.**" (6:10)
   (2). Speaking of a time when there would be many dead bodies in every place, the Lord told Amos, "The end is come upon my people of Israel; **I will not again pass by them any more.**" (8:2-3)

D. Hosea, the contemporary of Amos, made similar predictions while foretelling the fall of Israel:
   (1). "They shall go with their flocks and with their herds to seek the Lord; but **they shall not find him; he hath withdrawn himself from them.**" (Hos. 5:6; see also 5:15)
   (2). "All their wickedness is in Gilgal: for there I hated them: for the wickedness of their doings **I will drive them out of mine house, I will love them no more** . . ." (Hos. 9:15)
   (3). "**My God will cast them away,** because they did not hearken unto him: and they shall be wanderers among the nations." (Hos. 9:17)

E. It should be noted that, according to Amos' prophecy, the time of the famine from hearing the words of the Lord will happen in the same period as an actual famine and drought. (Compare Amos 8:11-12 with 8:13: **In that day** shall the fair virgins and young men faint for thirst.) Both Amos and Hosea foresaw that the fall of Israel would be accompanied by conditions of famine and drought. (See Amos 4:6, Hos. 2:3, 12, 4:10, 9:2, 8:7.)

This explanation of the author's views should in no manner be taken as an indication that he rejects the doctrine of the universal apostasy. Certainly there is overwhelming prophetic and historical evidence that such a falling away took place. The author merely questions the wisdom of some L.D.S. expositors of the scriptures who have, in his view, forced the interpretation of this passage with gross disregard for context and the true intent of the prophet Amos.

May it be suggested that those who quote this passage in connection with any discussion of the period of apostasy which followed New Testament times introduce the passage in a manner similar to the following:

"There have been many periods of apostasy in the history of God's dealings with men. Perhaps a comparison could be made between this period when men did not receive revelation and the period when the nation of Israel was conquered by Assyria. Of that period the prophet Amos had prophesied to the people, 'Behold, the days come, saith the Lord God, that I will send a famine in the land, . . .'"

AMOS

Doctrinal Analysis

The Sins of Israel

1. They sold the righteous and the poor into slavery. (2:6, 8:6)
2. They turn aside the way of the meek. (2:7)
3. Adultery, fornication and incest are committed. (2:7)
4. They desecrate the house of God. (2:8)
5. They cause holy men (Nazarites) to break their vows. (2:12)
6. They command the prophets not to prophesy. (2:12)
7. The rich store up violence and robbery in their palaces. (3:9-10)
8. They oppress the poor and crush the needy. (4:1, 5:11)
9. They practice pagan worship. (4:4-5)
10. Ye have not returned unto God. (4:6, 8, 9, 10, 11)
11. They turn judgment to wormwood and leave off righteousness. (5:7)
12. They hate those that rebuke them and abhor those who speak uprightly. (5:10)
13. They afflict the just. (5:12)
14. They take bribes. (5:12)
15. They turn the poor out of their rightful possessions. (5:12, 8:4)
16. Their offerings are meaningless and unacceptable. (5:21-23)
17. They have made images of idols: Moloch and Chiun. (5:26)
18. They have false pride and security. (6:1, 13)
19. They live luxuriously. (6:4-6)
20. They are not grieved by the afflictions of their nation. (6:6)
21. They made judgment and righteousness bitter. (6:12)
22. They falsify the balances by deceit. (8:5)
23. They sell the refuse of the wheat. (8:6)

The Judgments upon Israel

1. Habitations of the shepherds shall mourn. (1:2)
2. The top of (Mt.) Carmel shall wither. (1:2)
3. The strong and the swift shall not have strength. (2:14-16)
4. An adversary shall be round about the land. (3:11)
5. Thy palaces shall be spoiled. (3:11)

6. The people of Israel shall be taken out. (3:12)
7. The heathen altars shall be broken. (3:14)
8. The great houses shall fall and have an end. (3:15)
9. God will take you away with hooks, your posterity with fishhooks. (4:2)
10. You will have famine. (4:6)
11. You will have unpredictable rainfall. (4:7-8)
12. Mildew and worms will ruin the crops. (4:9)
13. You will have pestilence. (4:10)
14. Only a tenth of the people shall be left. (5:2-3)
15. Gilgal shall go into captivity; Bethel shall come to nought. (5:5)
16. There shall be wailing and mourning in the streets. (5:16-17)
17. You will go into captivity beyond Damascus. (5:27, 7:11)
18. Those who remain behind shall die. (6:9-10)
19. It will be forbidden to mention the name of the Lord. (6:10)
20. The houses will be smitten with breaches and clefts. (6:11)
21. A nation shall afflict you from the entering in of Hamath unto the river of the wilderness. (6:14)
22. Your high places and sanctuaries will be made desolate. (7:9)
23. God will rise against the house of Jeroboam with the sword. (7:9, 11)
24. Your wife shall be a harlot in the city. (7:17)
25. Your sons and daughters shall fall by the sword. (7:17)
26. Israel's land shall be divided by line. (7:17)
27. Thou shalt die in a polluted land. (7:17)
28. God will not pass by the people any more. (8:2)
29. The songs of the temple shall be howling. (8:3)
30. There shall be many dead bodies in every place; they shall cast them forth with silence. (8:3)
31. God will cause the sun to go down at noon and will darken the earth in the clear day. (8:9)
32. God will bring sackcloth and make the day of mourning a bitter day. (8:10)
33. There will be a famine from hearing the words of the Lord. (8:11-12)
34. The youth shall faint for thirst. (8:13)
35. The wicked shall fall and never rise up again. (8:14)
36. He that flees shall not escape. (9:1-4)
37. The land shall melt and rise up like a flood. (9:5)

AMOS 265

38. The Lord will destroy the sinful kingdom from off the face of the earth. (9:8)
39. God will sift the house of Israel among all nations. (9:9)

The Last Days

1. (33)[3] God will raise up the tabernacle of David and raise up his ruins. (9:11)
2. (34, 41) Israel will possess the remnant of Edom and of all the heathen which are called by the Lord's name. (9:12)
3. (44) Agriculture will be simpler and year around. The mountains shall drop sweet wine. (9:13)
4. (42) All the hills shall melt. (9:13)
5. (30, 31) God will restore his people to their land and they shall build the waste cities. (9:14-15)

God Controls Nature and the Affairs of Men:

1. I have withholden the rain from you, sent you mildew and pestilence. (4:7-10)
2. He that formeth the mountains, and createth the wind ... The Lord, The God of Hosts, is his name. (4:13)
3. Seek God that maketh the stars, that sends the night and sends the rain; the Lord is his name. (5:8)
4. I will cause the sun to go down at noon, and I will darken the earth in the clear day. (8:9)
5. Though the wicked be hid from my sight in the bottom of the sea, thence will I command the serpent and he shall bite them. (9:3)
6. The Lord is he that toucheth the land, and it shall melt. (9:5)
7. The Lord buildeth his stories in heaven, and hath founded his troop in the earth, he poureth the waters of the sea upon the face of the earth. (9:6)
8. He declareth unto man what is his thought. (4:13)
9. I know your manifold transgressions and your mighty sins. (5:12)
10. I will never forget any of their works. (8:7)
11. Though the wicked dig into hell or climb into heaven, thence shall mind hand take them. (9:2)
12. I will set mine eyes upon the wicked for evil, not for good. (9:4)

---

[3]Numbers in parentheses at the beginning of items refer to the list of fifty events of the last days found in Chapter IV.

13. The eyes of the Lord are upon the sinful kingdom, he will destroy it. (9:8)

God's Dealings with His Prophets

1. I raised up your sons for prophets, and of your young men for Nazarites. (2:11)
2. Shall there be evil in a city and the Lord not sound the warning trumpet through his prophets? (3:6-8)
3. Surely the Lord God will do nothing, but he revealeth his secret unto his servants the prophets. (3:7)
4. I was no prophet, neither was I a prophet's son. The Lord took me from following the flock and said unto me: Go, prophesy unto my people, Israel. (7:14-15)

Vision of the Lord

1. I saw the Lord standing upon the altar. (9:1)

Racial Equality before God

1. Are ye not as children of the Ethiopians (Negroes) unto me, O children of Israel? (9:7)

   Note: This is a passage often cited by those who are interested in the racial issues of the day. They sometimes fail to grasp its significance. Here the Lord is including Israel in a list of sinful people who are to be destroyed. Yet note that even in destruction the house of Israel is accorded special recognition. (see verse 8). Many commentators find meanings that are foreign to the true intent of this passage.

Calls to Repentance

1. Seek the Lord and ye shall live. (5:4-5)
2. Seek good and not evil, that ye may live, and so the Lord shall be with you. (5:14)

Counsel for Righteous Living:

1. Can two walk together, except they be agreed? (3:3)
2. Hate the evil and love the good, and establish judgment in the gate. (5:15)
3. Woe unto you that desire the day of the Lord! to what end is it for you? (5:18-20)
4. Let judgment run down as waters, and righteousness as a mighty stream. (5:24)
5. Woe to them that are at ease in Zion. (6:1)

AMOS   267

Style of the Book:
1. The book of Amos is regarded as being the best Hebrew writing (perhaps with the exception of some portions of Isaiah) in the Old Testament.
2. The book is all in prose.
3. It is finished and refined.
4. It has balanced, regular structure. His is one of the best arranged of the prophetic books.
5. The themes are carefully introduced and developed.
6. It has regular, flowing sentences with balanced clauses (as contrasted to the short, abrupt clauses of Hosea).
7. It uses well-chosen imagery (though his imagery is not considered as grand or picturesque as that of Isaiah). Amos uses many images derived from rural life.
8. It shows a clear knowledge of Mosaic law and the history of Israel.
9. It has vigorous, direct, animated thought.
10. His classical Hebrew is pure and simple.
11. The writing style is bold.

Textual Transmission: The Hebrew text has been well preserved.

Author and Date of Authorship: Most critics acknowledge that Amos was the author and assume that the book was written at the time of his ministry. He is the earliest of the prophets whose writings are of undisputed date.

Bible Criticism: Little disagreement exists. This is one of the few books which has not been subject to heavy critical controversy. Some critics believe that certain glosses and additions were made by Jews of Jerusalem between 500 and 200 B. C. These supposedly include:
1. Specific references to Judah and David. (1:1, 1:2, 2:4-5, 6:1 [Zion], 6:5, 9:11-12)
2. Prophecies against Tyre and Edom (1:9-12), Judah (2:4-5), and Gaza (1:6-8).
3. Three later visions of Amos. (7:7-9, 8:1-3, 9:1-4)
4. Explanatory glosses. (3:7 explains 3:8 and 5:20)
5. Glosses referring to stories in the Pentateuch. (4:11, 3:1b, 4:10, 5:25)
6. Calneh and Hamath are believed to be references to Assyrian conquests later than Amos' time.
7. Many of the threats of Amos are believed to have been

intensified and given an apocalyptic slant. Apocalyptic blessings are promised. (9:8b, 9:15)
8. Pious exhortations characteristic of the post exilic community are said to have been added. (4:12b, 5:4b, 13-15)
9. Doxologies may have been inserted for the purpose of public reading. (4:13, 5:8-9, 9:5-6)

Note: A doxology is a hymn or statement which praises God.

Changes Made in the Inspired Version of the Bible—Book of Amos:

King James Translation	Inspired Version
3:7—Surely the Lord God will do nothing, but he revealeth his secret unto his servants the prophets.	3:7—Surely the Lord God will do nothing, **until** he revealeth the secret unto his servants the prophets.
4:3—And ye shall go out at the breaches, every cow at that which is before her; and ye shall cast them into the palace, saith the Lord.	4:3—And ye shall go out at the breaches, every **one before his enemy; and ye shall be cast out of your palaces,** saith the Lord.
4:5—. . . and publish the free offerings: for this liketh you, O ye children of Israel . . .	4:5—. . . and publish the free offerings; for **thus do ye,** O ye children of Israel . . .
7:3—The Lord repented for this: It shall not be, saith the Lord.	7:3—**And the Lord said, concerning Jacob, Jacob shall repent for this, therefore I will not utterly destroy him,** saith the Lord.
7:6—The Lord repented for this: This also shall not be, saith the Lord God.	7:6—**And the Lord said, concerning Jacob, Jacob shall repent of his wickedness; therefore I will not utterly destroy him,** saith the Lord God.

Summary: After studying the book of Amos, the student should know:
1. Amos prophesied to Israel about 750 B. C.
2. Israel reached its greatest extent and then began its decline under the king of this period, Jeroboam II.
3. The four major lessons of the book are:
   A. Israel has sinned and is corrupt.

B. The Lord warns his people of the results of evil through prophets.
C. Israel will be punished for its wickedness.
D. God is powerful and controls both man and nature.
4. The book of Amos is one of the best examples of Hebrew literature in the Old Testament. It is orderly, balanced, and refined.
5. The location of
    A. Israel
    B. Judah
    C. Syria
    D. Ammon
    E. Moab
    F. Edom
    G. Philistia
    H. Phonicia

CHAPTER IX

HOSEA

Prophet's Name: Hosea (Hō-sē'-ă) means "help, deliverance, salvation." This name is derived from the same Hebrew root as the names Joshua and Jesus.

Scriptural Information About the Prophet:
1. He was the son of Beeri (1:1).
2. He lived during the reign of four kings of Judah: Uzziah, Jotham, Ahaz and Hezekiah (1:1).
3. He lived during the reign of Jeroboam II, king of Israel (1:1).

Date of Hosea's Mission: c. 760-720 B. C.

This is determined by the dates of the rule of the kings during whose time he lived (see Hos. 1:1). Uzziah, Jotham, Ahaz and Hezekiah, kings of Judah, ruled from 792-697 B. C. with the reign of the final king beginning in 728 B. C. Jeroboam II, king of Israel, ruled from 790-749 B. C. The maximum period in which Hosea could have prophesied during the reign of these kings would have been from 792-697 B. C. The minimum period would have been from 750-725 B. C. If we assume that his ministry extended into a considerable part of the reigns of both Jeroboam II and Hezekiah, we could place his ministry at about 760-720 B. C.

> **Note:** Some critics regard the list of kings of Judah in the superscription (Hos. 1:1) as a Jewish interpolation which stretches the period of his ministry to make him a contemporary of Isaiah and Micah.

Prophesied to: Israel.
1. He speaks of the king of Israel as "our" king (7:5).
2. He often refers to localities within its borders (see 1:4, 4:15, 5:1, 6:8, 12:11).

Contemporary Prophets:

1.	Amos	c. 750 B. C.	To Israel.
2.	Micah	c. 740-697 B. C.	To Israel and Judah.
3.	Isaiah	c. 740-697 B. C.	To Israel and Judah.

HOSEA

Contemporary Prophets Contrasted:

Hosea gives a more intimate view of his personal affairs in his writing than any of the other prophets except Jeremiah. He is a man who suffered many hardships to keep the Lord's commandments. His writing is highly emotional and less objective than the writing of his contemporaries. His fervor substitutes for stylistic dignity.

Amos was a discerning observer of the people of his times. He thought methodically and was able to clearly define the sins of the people and foretell the destruction and tribulation they would bring to Israel. Although he was only a shepherd, and drew images from his rural background, his writing is beautifully expressed, and indicates that he was a person of refinement and culture. He knew the history of his people and thoroughly understood their religious laws.

Micah is a product of the open hills and shows dislike for the cities (see 1:5, 5:11, 6:9). As a member of the oppressed peasantry he speaks for the common people and defends them against the nobles and rich landlords of Judah. He is primarily an ethical and religious teacher and shows little knowledge or interest in political matters.

Isaiah is a statesman and a member of Jerusalem's ruling class. He is well acquainted with the society and political intrigues of the capital city of Jerusalem and shows much interest in the political events of his time. He is a capable author and speaker. His writing reflects his culture and refinement.

Contemporary Kings:

Israel: Jeroboam II   c. 790-749 B. C.
Israel reached its greatest extent during his reign.
Zachariah   c. 749 B. C.
Shallum   c. 749-748 B. C.
Menahem   c. 748-737 B. C.
Paid tribute to Tiglath-Pileser III to save Israel.
Pekahiah   c. 737-735 B. C.
Pekah   c. 735-733 B. C.
Israel and Syria attacked Judah in 734 B. C.
Hoshea   c. 733-722 B. C.
Fall of the Kingdom of Israel 722 B. C.

Judah: Uzziah c. 792-740 B. C.
Jotham c. 749-734 B. C.
Ahaz c. 734-728 B. C.
  Formed an alliance with Assyria against Israel and Syria. Judah was defeated by Israel and Syria in 734 B. C. but the captives were returned.
Hezekiah c. 728-697 B. C.
  Attacked by Sennacherib in 701 B. C. but was saved when 185,000 Assyrians died.

Assyria: Assur-Dayan III c. 771-753 B. C.
Asshur-Lush c. 753-745 B. C.
Tiglath-Pileser III c. 745-727 B. C.
  Overran northern Israel in 733 B. C.

Conditions of Surrounding Nations:

Israel and Judah

—Political

1. Both nations had risen to positions of power and wealth.
2. Their boundaries had been restored, and they were relatively free from the threat of war.
3. There seemed to be two political parties in Israel near the end of that kingdom. One favored alliance with Assyria; the other favored alliance with Egypt and resistance to Assyria. Israel's political situation varied as the two parties rose or diminished in power.
4. Edom was conquered by Judah and trade was resumed in the Red Sea area.
5. Syria was troubled by palace intrigues and Israel was able to regain the border territory it had lost during the reign of Jehu.
6. Assyria, the world power of the day, was not showing any territorial interest in the Mediterranean area during this period.

—Economic

1. Their leaders had become rich, haughty and proud. Trade had been revived and the kingdoms had also grown richer from booty taken in conquest.
2. The middle classes were rapidly disappearing. The rich were creating large estates by foreclosing mortgages on small landowners and taking their properties.

HOSEA

3. Rents and food prices were exorbitant, and served to bring greater economic distress upon the lower classes. The poor were oppressed on every hand. Slums and squalor had developed in contrast to the vast estates of the rich.

—Social

1. The governments were filled with the graft and corruption of self-seeking politicians.
2. Family life had degenerated and there was little family cohesiveness.
3. The exorbitant rents and land foreclosures had made the practice common of parents selling their children as slaves in payment of debts.

—Religious

1. The worship of Jehovah had degenerated into a religion of form. People offered sacrifices, paid tithes, and carefully observed the laws concerning the Sabbath day; yet their lives showed little evidence of true social morality and love for their neighbors.
2. The pagan rites and idolatry of the fertility cults were still common in Israel and Judah, especially among the lower classes. This took the form of ritual fornication with the representatives of Baal, Astarte, Ashtoreth, etc. Such rites did much to destroy the moral influence of the law of Moses.

Assyria

1. Assur-Dayan III and Asshur-Lush were weak kings who allowed the might of Assyria's empire to decline from the unparalleled conquests of Adad-nirari III (810-783 B. C.—Jonah's day). Their laxness allowed the various states of Palestine and Syria to grow in power and wealth.
2. When Tiglath-Pileser III came to the throne he immediately endeavored to restore Assyria's prestige in these and other areas. He conquered northern Israel and Damascus (capital of Syria).

Outline of the Book:

Section I—Hosea's Symbolic Marriage (Chapters 1-3)

1. Hosea was commanded of God to take a wife of "whoredoms." He married Gomer. (1:2-3)
2. They had three children, for whom God revealed prophetic names:

      A. A son, Jezreel (Jĕz'-reel), whose name referred to the valley where Israel would soon be defeated. (1:4-5)
      B. A daughter, Loruhamah (Lo-ru-ha-măh), whose name meant "no more mercy." (1:6-7)
      C. A son, Loammi (Lō-ăm'-mī), whose name meant "not my people." (1:8-9)
3. Gomer was an adulteress. She left her husband and went after other lovers because of the luxuries they offered her. (2:1-5)
4. Finally Gomer's lovers left her and she became a slave. (2:6-13)
5. Hosea resolved to recover his wife and to bring her back. (2:14-23)
6. Hosea went and brought her back. In spite of the wicked things she had done, he restored her to all she had had before and more, because of his love for her. (3:1-5)

The Symbolism:
1. Hosea—The Lord.
2. Gomer—Israel.
3. Children's names—Prophecies of what would happen to Israel.
4. Gomer's other lovers and adultery—Idol worship and wickedness.
5. Gomer's slavery—Israel's fall and captivity to Assyria.
6. Gomer's restoration—The gathering and restoration of Israel in the last days. God still loves his people.

Section II—Discourses and Prophecies of Israel's Wickedness and Fate (Chapters 4-14)
Part A, Chapters 4-8—Israel's Guilt.
Part B, Chapters 9-13:4—Israel's Punishment.
Part C, Chapters 13:5-14:9—Promise of Redemption.

Doctrinal Analysis

The Sins of Israel
1. There is no truth. (4:1)
2. There is no mercy. (4:1)
3. There is no knowledge. (4:1, 6)
4. They swear. (4:2)
5. They lie. (4:2, 7:1, 11:12)
6. They kill. (4:2)
7. They steal. (4:2, 7:1)
8. They commit adultery. (4:2, 5:1-3, 6:10, 7:4)

HOSEA

9. Their heart is set on iniquity. (4:8)
10. They practice idolatry and participate in the rites of pagan fertility cults. (4:13-19, 8:4, 9:10, 11:2, 13:2)
11. They have begotten strange children (children out of wedlock). (5:7)
12. Israel sought alliances with Assyria and Egypt, instead of relying on the Lord. (5:13, 7:11, 8:9-10, 9:3, 12:1)
13. They transgressed the covenant. (6:7, 8:1)
14. The priests consent to murder. (6:9)
15. All their kings are fallen (four kings of Israel were assassinated in quick succession). (7:7)
16. Ephraim has mixed himself among the people (racial mingling and intermarriage have taken place). (7:8-9)
17. They do not seek God. (7:10, 16)
18. They have spoken lies against God. (7:13)
19. They have not cried unto God from their hearts. (7:14)
20. They become drunken on corn and wine. (7:14)
21. They rebel against God. (7:14)
22. They have trespassed against God's law. (8:1)
23. They have set up kings without divine approval. (8:4)
24. They have sworn falsely in making covenants. (10:4)

Judgments Upon Israel

1. The kingdom of the house of Israel shall cease. (1:4)
2. God will break the bow of Israel in the valley of Jezreel. (1:5)
3. Israel will be taken away. (1:6)
4. God will slay Israel with thirst. (2:3)
5. God will cause her mirth, her Sabbaths and religious celebrations to cease. (2:11)
6. God will destroy Israel's vines and fig trees. (2:12)
7. The land shall mourn. (4:3)
8. The people and animals shall languish. (4:3)
9. The people shall fall and be destroyed. (4:5-6, 14)
10. They shall suffer shame. (4:7, 19, 10:6)
11. They shall suffer starvation. (4:10, 9:2)
12. They shall have no increase. (4:10, 9:14, 16)
13. They shall not find the Lord when they seek Him. (5:6, 15)
14. The land shall be desolate. (5:9, 9:12)
15. God will chastize them. (7:12)
16. Their princes shall fall by the sword. (7:16)
17. The enemy shall pursue Israel. (8:3)

18. They shall be among the Gentiles as a vessel wherein is no pleasure. (8:8)
19. They shall reap the whirlwind. (8:7)
20. Their crops will not yield. (8:7)
21. If there is food, strangers will eat it. (8:7)
22. They shall sorrow. (8:10)
23. Fire shall devour the cities and palaces. (8:14)
24. They shall not dwell in the Lord's land. (9:3)
25. Nettles and thorns shall possess them. (9:6, 10:8)
26. Their glory shall fly away. (9:11)
27. God will drive them out of His house. (9:15)
28. God will love them no more. (9:15)
29. They shall be wanderers among the nations. (9:17)
30. Their altars and images shall be broken down. (10:2, 8)
31. Mother shall be dashed in pieces upon her children. (10:14)
32. In a morning shall the king of Israel be cut off. (10:15)
33. The sword shall abide on their cities. (11:6)

The Last Days

1. (30, 31, 38, 32?, 35)[1] They shall be like the sands of the sea, and known as the sons of the living God. Judah and Israel shall be gathered together and appoint themselves one head, for great shall be the day of Jezreel. (1:10-11)

    Note: The valley of Jezreel is the plain of Esdraelon in Northwest Palestine. This is the area from which the battle of Armageddon will draw its name.

2. (30-31, 35, 38) God will speak comfortably to Israel and give her the valley of Achor for a door of hope. God will give them safety and betroth them to Himself, and will show mercy. (2:14-23)

    Note: The valley of Achor is a valley about six miles east of the Mt. of Olives. This may be the area through which the Israelites will flee during the Battle of Armageddon. (See Zech. 14:1-5.)

3. (30-31, 32) Israel shall return and seek God and David their king. (3:5)

    Note: There is to be a king who will rule in Palestine over Judah and Israel. He will be called David and will rule

---

[1]Numbers in parentheses at the beginning of an item refer to the list of fifty events of the last days found in Chapter Four.

from before the Battle of Armageddon until after Christ's coming in glory.
4. (35?) God will heal us. After two days will he revive us: in the third day he will raise us up. (6:1-3)
   Note: This may be a reference to the two prophets who will lie in the streets of Jerusalem during the Battle of Armageddon. (See Rev. 11:1-12.)
5. (39) I will be thy king. (13:9-10)
6. (43) I will ransom them from the power of the grave. I will redeem them from death. (13:14)
7. (30-31) Israel will grow as the lily, his branches shall spread. (14:4-9)

God's Methods of Working
1. My people are destroyed for lack of knowledge; seeing thou hast forgotten the law of thy God, I will also forget thy children. (4:6)
2. I will punish them for their ways, and reward them their doings. (4:9)
3. I will go and return to my place, till they acknowledge their offense, and seek my face: in their affliction they will seek me early. (5:15)
4. I am God, and not man . . . (11:9)
5. I have spoken by the prophets, and I have multiplied visions. (12:10)
6. By a prophet the Lord brought Israel out of Egypt, and by a prophet was he preserved. (12:13)
7. I am the Lord thy God, and thou shalt know no God but me, for there is no savior beside me. (13:4)

Prophecy of Christ in the Meridian of Time?
1. Called my son out of Egypt. (11:1)
   Note: A careful reading of Hosea, Chapter 11, will make it clear that the dear son to which Hosea referred was the house of Israel, not Jesus. Note that the son was called out of Egypt when **Israel** was a child (Moses' day, not the meridian of time) and that the son was not to return to Egypt but was to be ruled by Assyria. This description clearly fits Israel in its day but not Jesus, who lived 600 years after Assyria's collapse. (See 11:1, 5.) The gospel writer, Matthew, however, applied the passage in reference to the flight from Herod into Egypt which was undertaken by Joseph, Mary and the baby Jesus: "When he arose, he took

the young child and his mother by night, and departed into Egypt: And was there until the death of Herod: that it might be fulfilled which was spoken of the Lord by the prophet, saying, Out of Egypt have I called my son." (Mt. 2:14-15) Thus this passage came to be regarded as a prophecy of Christ.

Admonitions to Repentance
1. Turn thou to thy God: keep mercy and judgment, and wait on thy God continually. (12:6)
2. Turn to the Lord: say unto him, take away all iniquity, and receive us graciously. (14:2)

Counsel for Righteous Living
1. Let no man strive, nor reprove another. (4:4)
2. Whoredom and wine and new wine take away the heart. (4:11)
3. For I desired mercy and not sacrifice; and the knowledge of God more than burnt offerings. (6:6)
4. Sow to yourselves in righteousness, reap in mercy: for it is time to seek the Lord, till he come and rain righteousness upon you. (10:12)
5. The ways of the Lord are right, and the just shall walk in them; but the transgressors shall fall therein. (14:9)

Important Contributions of Hosea:
1. Hosea is the first to use the metaphor of the marriage relation to characterize the intimate relationship between God and those who worship him.
2. He is the first to shift the basic concept of religion from the "fear of God" to that of "knowledge of God," loyalty to Him, and partaking of His mercy. (See 6:6, 4:1, 12:6, 10:12, 14:9.)

Style of the Book:
1. The book is entirely in prose. It appears to be a compilation of little oracles delivered at different times.
2. Hosea's style is unique among the prophets because of his short, abrupt sentences.
3. Each sentence is full of force, compressed feeling and meaning.
4. The thought of some sentences is so condensed as to be obscure or ambiguous.
5. His style is the expression of deep emotion, as contrasted with the great objectivity of Amos.

Hosea

6. His figures of speech are very suggestive. They are often expressed in a single word rather than a phrase.
7. In several instances he uses words with double meanings.
8. The sentences and sections are often poorly connected with the context. He passes from mood to mood and from topic to topic without transitional phrases.

Textual Transmission:

1. This book has suffered seriously in the process of transmission and is generally regarded as being more corrupt than any other Old Testament book.
2. Certain portions of the book, especially chapters 4-14, have supposedly been altered so much that any present translation requires a great deal of guess work.
3. The style and text are so broken that it is difficult to make logical divisions for purposes of analysis.

Author: Hosea is generally acknowledged to be the author.

Bible Criticism:

—Higher Criticism

1. The higher critics generally accept the authorship of Hosea.
2. The only major area of conflict among higher critics is the interpretation of Hosea's marriage in chapters 1-3. The major interpretative assertions are:

    A. **The literal theory.** The story is assumed to be a literal account of Hosea's marital experience. This was the common view of most ancient interpreters.

    B. **The modified literal theory.** Believers in this theory assume that Hosea's wife (Gomer) was guilty of spiritual harlotry because she was a Baal worshiper, rather than that she was a common harlot. They claim that what Hosea did was meet Gomer's obligation to the pagan shrine where she worshipped and then brought her home and isolated her.

    C. **The allegorical theory.** The story is assumed to be a parable or allegory which symbolizes the relationship between Jehovah and his people, Israel. This is supported by these arguments:

    (1). For God to command Hosea to actually take a wife of whoredoms would be inconsistent with his holy nature.

(2). For Hosea to take an immoral wife would make it difficult for him to expose the immoralities of the day, for his family would also be guilty of them.

D. **The virtuous theory.** Many modern scholars set forth the opinion that Gomer was a pure woman at the time of her marriage and remained so until after the birth of her first child. While this avoids the problem of God commanding his prophet to marry an adulterous woman, it would seem to be in direct conflict with the text in which Hosea is told to "Go take unto thee a wife of whoredoms and children of whoredoms."

—Lower Criticism

1. Lower criticism asserts that Hosea was a prophet only to Israel and that all references to the kingdom of Judah are emendations or interpolations of Judean editors who attempted to adapt the book for readers from the southern kingdom. (See 4:15, 5:5, 10, 12, 13, 14, 6:4, 11, 8:14, 10:11, 11:12, 12:2.)
2. Most critics believe that the reassurances at the end of the book (14:2-10) were not written by Hosea.

Changes Made in the Inspired Version of the Bible— Book of Hosea

King James Translation	Inspired Version
11:8—. . . mine heart is turned within me, my repentings are kindled together.	11:8—. . . **my heart is turned toward thee, and my mercies are extended to gather thee.**

Summary

After studying the book of Hosea, the student should know:
1. The story of Hosea's marriage and the six points of symbolism which explain it.
2. The three major lessons of the book:
    A. God was displeased with the many sins of Israel.
    B. Israel would be punished by being conquered and scattered among the gentiles.
    C. God will restore Israel to her former home and prominence in the last days.
3. Hosea was the first Old Testament prophet through whom the Lord introduced the ideas of:

A. The metaphor of a marriage relationship between God and Israel, and
　　　B. Knowing about God and serving Him rather than fearing Him.
4. The location of
　　　A. The plain of Esdraelon (the valley of Jezreel of Battle of Armageddon significance).
　　　B. Samaria—capital of Israel.
　　　C. Bethel ⎫
　　　D. Dan　　⎬ Four cities which were centers of idolatry and wickedness during much of Israel's history.
　　　E. Gilgal　⎪
　　　F. Shechem ⎭

CHAPTER X

MICAH

Prophet's Name: Micah (Mī'-căh) is an abbreviated form of Mikayahu—"Who is like unto Jehovah?" He was not the elder prophet, Micaiah, the son of Imlah. (1 Ki. 22:8-28)

Scriptural Information About the Prophet
1. He was a native of Moreshath, or Moresheth-gath (Mō'-rĕsh-ĕth-găth), a dependency of Gath. (1:1, 14) This is a small town in the maritime plain, a low hilly region about 20 miles southwest of Jerusalem.
2. He preached in the days of Jotham, Ahaz, and Hezekiah, kings of Judah. (1:1)
3. He is mentioned as having taught the message found in 3:12 during the reign of Hezekiah, king of Judah. (Jer. 26:17-19)

Date of Micah's Mission: c. 740-697 B. C.
1. He preached in the days of Jotham (749-734 B. C.), Ahaz (734-728 B. C.), and Hezekiah (728-697 B. C.). (1:1)
2. He preached before the fall of Israel in 722 B. C. (1:6)
3. Thus his ministry could have been as long as fifty-two years (749-697 B. C.) or as short as six years (734-728 B. C.).
4. Micah is considered by most scholars as being a younger contemporary of Isaiah.

Prophesied to: Israel and Judah.

Contemporary Prophets:

1. Hosea   c. 760-720 B. C.   To Israel.
2. Isaiah   c. 740-697 B. C.   To Israel and Judah.

Contemporary Prophets Contrasted:

Micah is a product of the open hills and shows dislike for the cities (See 1:5, 5:11, 6:9). As a member of the oppressed peasantry he speaks for the common people and defends them against the nobles and rich landlords of Judah. He is primarily an ethical and religious teacher and shows little knowledge or interest in political matters.

MICAH

Hosea gives a more intimate view of his personal affairs in his writing than any of the other prophets except Jeremiah. He was a man who suffered many hardships to keep the Lord's commandments. His writing is highly emotional and less objective than the writing of his contemporaries. His fervor substitutes for stylistic dignity.

Isaiah is a statesman and a member of Jerusalem's ruling class. He is well acquainted with the society and political intrigues of the capital city of Jerusalem and shows much interest in the political events of his time. He is a capable author and speaker. His writing reflects his culture and refinement.

Contemporary Kings:

Israel: Menahem   c. 748-737 B. C.
Paid tribute to Tiglath-Pileser III to save Israel.
Pekahiah   c. 737-735 B. C.
Pekah   c. 735-733 B. C.
Israel and Syria attacked Judah in 734 B. C.
Hoshea   c. 733-722 B. C.
Fall of Israel c. 722 B. C.

Judah: Jotham   c. 749-734 B. C.
Ahaz   c. 734-728 B. C.
Formed an alliance with Assyria against Israel and Syria. Judah was defeated by Israel and Syria in 734 B. C. but the Jewish captives were returned.
Hezekiah   c. 728-697 B. C.
Attacked by Sennacherib in 701 B. C. but was saved when 185,000 Assyrians died overnight.

Assyria: Tiglath-Pileser III   c. 745-727 B. C.
Overran northern Israel in 733 B. C.
Shalmaneser V   c. 726-722 B. C.
Laid siege to Samaria, capital of Israel, in 722 B. C. He died during the siege.
Sargon II   c. 721-705 B. C.
Completed the conquest of Israel. Deported the Ten Tribes in 721 B. C.
Sennacherib   c. 704-681 B. C.
Attacked Judah in 701 B. C. He withdrew when 185,000 of his men died.

284   PROPHETS AND PROPHECIES OF THE OLD TESTAMENT

National Conditions—Israel and Judah:
(Review conditions listed in the chapter on Amos)

—Political
1. Political decay was even more in evidence in Micah's time than noted previously.
2. Power had become concentrated in Jerusalem.
3. The city rulers oppressed the rural population with heavy taxation to support their policy of paying tribute to Assyria and to fortify the city of Jerusalem.
4. Corrupt judges aided their friends in robbing the poor. Bribes and intrigue were characteristic of most governmental and judicial decisions.

—Economic
1. Greater social and moral decay than at previous times was found in Judah and Israel.
2. There was increased effort on the part of large landowners to evict small property owners and enlarge their estates.
3. High and unequal taxation and foreclosures on credit were the tools by which the poor were oppressed by the rich.

—Religious
1. Following the early reforms of Hezekiah men began to turn against the worship of Jehovah and assert that their religion had promised more than it could give.
2. Worshippers of Jehovah began to worship other Gods. Their national impotence against Assyria seemed to indicate that other national gods existed and that they should seek the favor of these foreign gods.
3. National misfortunes were mistakenly interpreted as indications of Jehovah's anger. They attempted to appease this anger by observing pagan worship forms such as offering their children as sacrifices.
4. The terror of approaching destruction led the people to persecute those who worshipped only Jehovah and who would not seek the aid of pagan deities.

Outline of the Book:

Section I—Prophecies of Coming Judgment (Chapter 1)
1. To all the world. (1:2-4)
2. To Israel and Judah. (1:5-7)
3. To Judah. (1:8-16)

MICAH

Section II—Contrast Between the Present and Future State of Judah (Chapters 2-5).

1. Judah's present sins are described. (2:1-11)
2. A restoration in the last days is predicted. (2:12-13)
3. Judah's present sins are described. (3:1-12)
4. The glory of Judah in the last days is predicted. (4:1-7)
5. Judah's Babylonian captivity is predicted. (4:8-10)
6. The overcoming of the gentiles in the last days is predicted. (4:11-13)
7. The birth of the Savior in Bethlehem is predicted. (5:2-4)
8. The Assyrian invasion is predicted. (5:5-6)
9. The overcoming of the gentiles in the last days is again predicted. (5:7-15)

Section III—The Lord's Controversy with Judah (A dialogue) (Chapters 6-7)

1. The Lord: Remember my blessings to Israel in the past. (6:1-5)
2. Israel: How can I worship God? (6:6-7)
3. Micah: True religion is justice, mercy, and humility. (6:8)
4. The Lord: Israel shall be smitten. (6:9-16)
5. Israel: A confession. (7:1-6)
   A declaration of faith in the Lord. (7:7-10)
6. The Lord: A promise of restoration from Babylonian captivity. (7:11-13)
7. Micah: A plea that the Lord's promise will be fulfilled. (7:14-17)
   A doxology of praise to the Lord. (7:18-20)

Doctrinal Analysis:

The Sins of Judah and the House of Israel

1. Idolatrous offerings were gathered by harlots (pagan officials of the fertility cults). (1:7)
2. They devise iniquity and work evil upon their beds. (2:1)
3. They covet fields and houses and take them away by violence and oppression. (2:2)
4. They tell the prophets not to prophesy. (2:6)
5. They have cast women and children from their pleasant houses. (2:9)
6. They accept false, lying and drunken prophets. (2:11)
7. They hate the good and love the evil. (3:2)
8. They eat the people's flesh and flay the skin from off them (through economic persecution). (3:2-3)

9. False prophets make the people err by crying peace. (3:5)
10. The heads judge for reward. (3:11)
11. The priests and prophets labor for money (as political hirelings). (3:11)
12. They assume that the Lord is among them and is protecting them. (3:11)
13. They use wicked balances and deceitful weights. (6:11)
14. The inhabitants have spoken lies. (6:12)
15. The good man is perished out of the earth, and there is none upright among men. (7:2)
16. They hunt every man his brother with a net. (7:2)
17. The princes and judges seek bribes and great men pay them. (7:3-4)
18. Friends and relatives can't be trusted; a man's enemies are the men of his own house. (7:5-6)

Judgments on Israel and Judah:
1. God will make Samaria as a heap of the field and will discover the foundations thereof. (1:6)
2. The graven images will be beaten to pieces. (1:7)
3. The offerings of idol shrines (hires) shall be burned with fire. (1:7)
4. The idols will lay desolate. (1:7)
5. The prophets will not prophesy to them. (2:6)
6. They shall cry unto the Lord, but he will not hear them. (3:4)
7. Ye shall not have a vision; the seers and diviners shall be confounded for there is no answer of God. (3:6-7)
8. Zion shall be plowed and Jerusalem shall become heaps. (3:12)
9. Enemies will lay siege. (5:1)
10. I will make thee sick in smiting thee. (6:13)
11. Thou shalt eat but not be satisfied. (6:14)
12. Thou shalt take hold but not deliver; that which thou deliverest God will give up to the sword. (6:14)
13. Thou shalt sow but not reap. (6:15)
14. I shall make thee a desolation. (6:16)
15. Ye shall bear the reproach of my people. (6:16)

Judgments on Judah:
1. They shall rely on the Lord when the Assyrians invade the land. God shall deliver them from the Assyrian invasion. (5:5-6)

MICAH 287

2. The people of the stronghold of the daughter of Zion (Jerusalem) shall go even to Babylon. (4:8-10)
3. The people of Judah shall be redeemed from Babylon and be gathered as the sheaves into the floor. (4:11-13)
4. Judah's enemies will be ashamed in the day her people return and build the walls and recover the desolate land. (7:8-17)

Note: It is difficult to determine with finality whether this passage refers to the return of Judah from Babylon or the restoration of Israel in the last days. Several items seem to indicate that it refers to Judah's return from Babylon:
A. The walls are to be rebuilt (in Jerusalem). (v. 11)
B. It shall be in the day of the decree (of Cyrus the Persian) to return to Palestine. (v. 11)
C. The land shall be desolate because of them that dwell therein. (The Jews had to reclaim and rebuild Palestine). (v. 13)
D. People will be returned to Palestine from the fortified cities of Assyria which became Babylonia. (v. 12)
E. The return will be like Israel's escape from Egypt —on a group basis rather than the return of individual Jews typical of the last days. (v. 15)

The Last Days:

1. (42)[1] The Lord will tread upon the high places of the earth and the mountains shall be molten under him. (1:3-4)
2. (30-31) I will surely gather the remnant of Israel; their king shall pass before them, and the Lord on the head of them. (2:12-13)
3. (33) The house of the Lord shall be established in the top of the mountains. Many nations shall come to learn of God, and the law shall go forth of Zion. (4:1-2)

Note: This prophecy is often cited in reference to the Salt Lake Temple. It is questionable whether this is the interpretation intended by Micah or by Isaiah, who made a similar prophecy. However, the Salt Lake Temple may well be considered an appropriate parallel

---
[1]Numbers in parentheses at the beginning of items refer to the fifty events of the last days listed in Chapter Four.

fulfillment. The matter is discussed in detail under the outline for Isaiah, Chapter Two, pages 361-362.

4. (44) God shall judge among many people at a time when nations shall not learn war any more. (4:3-4)
5. (30-31, 44) God will make those that were cast off a strong nation and the Lord will reign over them in Mount Zion. (4:5-7)
6. (16, 19) The daughter of Zion shall beat in pieces many people, and their gain shall be consecrated unto the Lord. (4:12-13)

Note: Ordinarily this passage would be regarded as a general reference to the house of Israel in the last days without specific reference to time or place. However, a significant contribution to the interpretation of Micah 5:7-15 is found in the Book of Mormon. During the short interlude when Jesus ministered to the Nephites and Lamanites in the Americas following His resurrection, He taught them with approximately the same words He had revealed to the prophet Micah:

Micah 4:12-13	3 Ne. 20:15-22
	And I say unto you, that **if the Gentiles do not repent after the blessing which they shall receive, after they have scattered my people—**
	Then shall ye, who are a remnant of the house of Jacob, go forth **among them;** and ye shall be in the midst of them who shall be many; and ye shall be among them as a lion among the beasts of the forests, and as a young lion among the flocks of sheep, who, if he goeth through both treadeth down and teareth in pieces, and none can deliver.
	Thy hand shall be lifted up upon thine adversaries, and all thine enemies shall be cut **off.**

MICAH   289

But they know not the thoughts of the Lord, neither understand they his counsel: for he shall gather them as the sheaves into the floor.

Arise and thresh, O daughter of Zion: for I will make thine horn iron, and I will make thy hoofs brass: and thou shalt beat in pieces many people: and I will consecrate their gain unto the Lord, and their substance unto the Lord of the whole earth.

And I will gather my people together as a man gathereth his sheaves into the floor.

For I will make my people with whom the Father hath covenanted, yea, I will make thy horn iron, and I will make thy hoofs brass. **And thou shalt beat in pieces many people; and I will consecrate their gain unto the Lord,** and their substance unto the Lord of the whole earth. And behold, I am he who doeth it.

And it shall come to pass, saith the Father, that the sword of my justice shall hang over them at that day; and except they repent it shall fall upon them, saith the Father, yea, **even upon all the nations of the Gentiles.**

And it shall come to pass that I will establish my people, O house of Israel.

And behold, **this people will I establish in this land,** unto the fulfilling of the covenant which I made with your father Jacob; and **it shall be a New Jerusalem.** And the powers of heaven shall be in the midst of this people; yea, even I will be in the midst of you.

The interpretation of these verses will be considered below in connection with Mic. 5:7-15.

7. (1, 44) The Lord will give up his goings forth until the time that she which travaileth hath brought forth (the

restoration of Israel); then He shall be great unto the ends of the earth. (5:1-4)

8. (16) The remnant of Jacob shall be in the midst of many people—among the Gentiles—as a lion among the beasts of the forest. They will

    A. Tread down and tear in pieces.
    B. All their enemies shall be cut off.
    C. Horses and chariots will be cut off.
    D. Cities will be cut off.
    E. Strongholds will be thrown down.
    F. Witchcrafts and soothsayers will be cut off.
    G. Standing images and groves will be cut off, so that Gentiles will no longer worship the work of their hands.
    H. Cities will be destroyed.
    I. God will execute vengeance and anger upon the heathen. (5:7-15)

Note: This passage was also cited and amplified by the Savior in the Book of Mormon as follows:

Micah 5:7-15	3 Ne. 21:12-21
And the remnant of Jacob shall be in the midst of many people as a dew from the Lord, as the showers upon the grass, that tarrieth not for man, nor waiteth for the sons of men.	
And the remnant of Jacob shall be among the Gentiles in the midst of many people as a lion among the beasts of the forest, as a young lion among the flocks of sheep: who, if he go through, both treadeth down, and teareth in pieces, and none can deliver.	And my people who are a remnant of Jacob shall be among the Gentiles, yea, in the midst of them as a young lion among the beasts of the forest, as a young lion among the flocks of sheep, who, if he go through both treadeth down and teareth in pieces, and none can deliver.
Thine hand shall be lifted up upon thine adversaries, and all thine enemies shall be cut off.	Their hand shall be lifted up upon their adversaries, and all their enemies shall be cut off.

And it shall come to pass in that day, saith the Lord, that I will cut off thy horses out of the midst of thee, and I will destroy thy chariots:	Yea, wo be unto the Gentiles except they repent; for it shall come to pass in that day, saith the Father, that I will cut off thy horses out of the midst of thee, and I will destroy thy chariots;
And I will cut off the cities of thy land, and throw down all thy strong holds:	And I will cut off the cities of thy land, and throw down all thy strongholds;
And I will cut off witchcrafts out of thine hand; and thou shalt have no more soothsayers:	And I will cut off witchcrafts out of thy land, and thou shalt have no more soothsayers;
Thy graven images also will I cut off, and thy standing images out of the midst of thee; and thou shalt no more worship the work of thine hands.	The graven images I will also cut off, and thy standing images out of the midst of thee, and thou shalt no more worship the works of thy hands;
And I will pluck up thy groves out of the midst of thee: so will I destroy thy cities.	And I will pluck up thy groves out of the midst of thee; so will I destroy thy cities.
	And it shall come to pass that lyings, and deceivings, and envyings, and strifes, and priestcrafts, and whoredoms, shall be done away.
	For it shall come to pass, saith the Father, that at that day whosoever will not repent and come unto my Beloved Son, them will I cut off from among my people, O house of Israel;
And I will execute vengeance in anger and fury upon the heathen, such as they have not heard.	And I will execute vengeance and fury upon them, even as upon the heathen, such as they have not heard.

The Book of Mormon account is important because it defines (1) who the remnant of Jacob is which will smite the

Gentiles, (2) who the Gentiles will be who will be smitten, and (3) when this situation will take place among the events of the last days. The context of the Book of Mormon shows that

1. The people who will beat in pieces many people are to be the Lamanites or remnant of Jacob in the Americas.

    A. It is they who will be among the gentiles, who will have rejected the gospel and will have scattered the Indians. (v. 15-16, see also 3 Ne. 16:8-10, 15)

    B. It is they who will be established in the Americas and help build the New Jerusalem. (v. 22)

2. The Gentiles who are to be smitten would be those who live in the proximity to the Lamanites in the last days, primarily the Caucasian inhabitants of North, Central, and South America. (It would seem to be primarily in Central and South America, where the Lamanite population is so large, that the Lamanites or Indians will be able to do so much damage that they actually cut off and destroy cities.)

3. The fulfillment of these prophecies is to take place at a certain point in the Lord's timetable, as He outlined in 3 Ne. 21. The order of events to precede the revolutions of the Lamanites appears to be:

    A. The Gospel shall be made known unto the Gentiles. (3 Ne. 21:2)

    >(1). A servant of the Lord will do a great and marvelous work declaring the Gospel. (3 Ne. 21:9-11)

    B. The Gospel shall come to the Lamanites from the Gentiles. (3 Ne. 21:3-4)

    C. The Lamanite seed, after some have heard the gospel, shall begin to dwindle in unbelief because of iniquity. (3 Ne. 21:5)

    D. The Gentiles who will not believe the gospel will be cut off from the people of God's covenant. (3 Ne. 21:11)

At this time the prophecies of Micah 4:12-13 (3 Ne. 20: 15-21) and Micah 5:7-15 (3 Ne. 21:12-21) will be fulfilled.[2]

---

[2]The nature of these upheavals and their chronological position among the events of the last days is detailed in another study by the author. See *Prophecy—Key To The Future*, pp. 17-139.

MICAH

The order of events to follow the revolutions of the Lamanites appears to be:
1. The Gentiles who have repented and accepted the gospel will participate with the Lamanites in building the New Jerusalem. (3 Ne. 21:23)
2. The Lamanites will gather in to the New Jerusalem. (3 Ne. 21:24)
3. Christ will visit the New Jerusalem. (3 Ne. 21:25)
4. The gospel will be preached among the Ten Tribes. (3 Ne. 21:26)
5. Israel shall be gathered out of all nations. (3 Ne. 21:27-29)
6. The desolate cities of the Gentiles shall be inhabited. (3 Ne. 22:1-3)

The Nature of God:
1. Let the Lord God be witness against you. (1:2)
2. God will bring me forth to the light, and I shall behold his righteousness. (7:8-9)
3. God pardons iniquity and does not forever retain his anger because He delights in mercy. (7:18-20)

Prophecy of Christ in the Meridian of Time:
1. Out of Bethlehem will come forth he that is to be ruler in Israel. (5:2)

Counsel for Righteous Living:
1. Is the spirit of the Lord straitened? Do not God's words do good to him that walketh uprightly? (2:7)
2. I am full of power by the spirit of the Lord, and of judgment and of might to declare the sins of Jacob and Israel. (3:8)
3. What doth the Lord require of thee but to do justly, and to love mercy, and to walk humbly with thy God? (6:6-8)
4. Search the past doings of God (examples given) that ye may know the righteousness of the Lord. (6:3-5)
5. I will look unto the Lord; my God will hear me. (7:7)

Style of the Book:
1. The book of Micah is entirely in poetry except for the superscription.
2. It is in excellent Hebrew. The poetry is regular and in correct Hebrew style.
3. Micah's speech is bold and direct.

4. He uses much imagery and picturesque phraseology which makes his language beautiful and rich.
5. He shows strong emotions, both anger and tenderness.
6. The discourses show logical development.
7. The topics are rapidly developed.
8. The book is considered to be a number of short oracles which were spoken separately and later brought together.

Textual Transmission: The Hebrew text has been badly corrupted, causing some difficulties in interpretation.

Author and Date of Authorship: Most scholars accept Micah as the author of the first portion of the book (Chapters 1-3) but deny to him the authorship of Chapters 4-7. Their date for Micah's writing is usually given as either 722 or 701 B. C. They tend to believe that the latter portion was written by either an anonymous prophet writing in the days of Manasseh, by an anonymous prophet writing during the Babylonian captivity of Judah, or by an anonymous prophet immediately after Judah's return to Palestine from Babylonia. Some assert that when the definitive edition of the prophetic books was prepared about 200 B. C., certain anonymous prophecies (Mic. 6-7, Zech. 9-14, and Isaiah 40-66) were placed after the writings of the known prophets and later became regarded as integral portions of the books which immediately preceded them.

Bible Criticism:

—Higher Criticism: Most of the criticism referring to the book of Micah deals with theories as to date and sources of authorship. These dates of authorship are as follows:
1. 722 B. C.—shortly before the capture of Samaria by Sargon II.

    A. This is considered only because of 1:5-9.

    B. It is noted that 1:5-9 predicts not only the capture but the complete destruction of Samaria. Sargon II, the Assyrian conqueror, did not raze the city, and by his record he took only 27,290 Israelites into captivity.

    C. If it were to be inferred from Jer. 26:17-19 that Micah functioned only in the reign of Hezekiah, this date would be excluded.

    D. Verse 1:9 implies that Judah would be attacked when Israel fell to Assyria.

MICAH

2. 701 B. C.—shortly before Sennacherib besieged Jerusalem. 1:10-16 and chapter 3 refer to this episode. The use of the terms "Israel" and "Jacob" to indicate Judah (3:9, Cf. 2:7, 3:1) would be highly improbable if this was written before the fall of the kingdom of Israel in 722 B. C.

3. 697-642 B. C. (for Chapters 6-7) during the reign of Manasseh.
This portion is connected with the time of Manasseh because of the connection with the sacrifice of the firstborn in 6:7 with the practice of Moloch worship in Manasseh's rule.

4. c. 500 B. C.—shortly after Judah's return from Babylonia.

   A. 6:4f mentions Aaron, which is unknown to the J document or any writings except E before the century.[3]

   B. Omri and Ahab are singled out as being especially wicked. This is considered to be most unlikely if the book of Micah was written before Josiah's reforms in 621 B. C. and before the Deuteronomic edition of the book of Kings in 600 B. C.

   C. The people of Jerusalem are depicted as being faced with economic ruin (6:13-15) and as being socially disintegrated (7:1-6). This is supposedly an indication that the section was written when these conditions existed, or later in the Persian period following Judah's return from the Babylonian captivity.

   D. The summary of prophetic teachings found in 6:6-8 are considered more likely to be like a catechism lesson for the young (like Prov. 15:8; 21:3, 27; see 16:1-9) than like the inspired utterances of an ancient prophet.

Summary: After studying the book of Micah the student should know:

1. Micah, Isaiah and Hosea were the prophets when Israel fell to Assyria.
2. The books of Micah, Hosea, and Isaiah are similar because they all have the same major messages:

    A. God was displeased with the many sins of Israel.

---

[3]The J and E documents are two of the four documents which are assumed to have made up the original Pentateuch (the first five books of the Old Testament.)

B. Israel would be punished by being conquered and scattered among the gentiles.

C. God will restore Israel to her former home and prominence in the last days.

3. Micah and Isaiah were similar because they were the only two prophets who prophesied concerning all four periods of prophetic fulfillment:[4]
   A. The fall of Israel to Assyria.
   B. The fall of Judah to Babylonia.
   C. The Meridian of time (the Savior's ministry).
   D. The last days.

4. Important interpretations for Micah's prophecies about the last days are found in 3 Ne. Chapters 20-21.

---

[4]The four periods of prophetic fulfillment are the four eras when most of the events foretold in the prophecies of the Old Testament prophets were to come to pass. Three of these periods are now past. We are living in the fourth period, the last days. The periods of prophetic fulfillment are explained in detail in the chapter on Isaiah, p. 303.

CHAPTER XI

ISAIAH

Prophet's Name: Isaiah (is-ā'-iăh), means "Jehovah has saved."

Scriptural Information About the Prophet:
1. He was a son of Amoz (not Amos the prophet). (1:1)
2. He preached during the reigns of Uzziah, Jotham, Ahaz and Hezekiah, kings of Judah. (1:1)
3. He preached actively to the kings of Judah during two crises of Judah:
    A. **The Syro-Ephraimite war** (c. 734 B. C.) in which Pekah (king of Israel) and Rezin (king of Syria) attempted to force Ahaz (king of Judah) to ally Judah with them against Assyria. (Chapters 7-8)
    B. **The Assyrian attack under Sennacherib** (c. 701 B. C.). The Assyrian hosts were smitten by the Lord and departed with heavy losses. (Chapters 36-37)
4. Isaiah's family:
    A. Wife: Her name is not known. She was a prophetess. (8:3)
    B. Son: Maher-shalal-hash-baz (Mā'-hĕr-shăl'-ăl-hăsh'-băz), means "the spoil speedeth, the prey hasteth." (8:3)
    C. Son: Shear-jashub (Shē'-är-jăsh'-ub), means "a remnant shall return." (7:3)
    D. Family mission: "Behold, I and the children whom the Lord hath given me are for signs and for wonders in Israel from the Lord of hosts, which dwelleth in mount Zion." (8:18)
5. Isaiah received his call as a prophet in the last year of king Uzziah's reign. (6:1)
6. Other books were written by Isaiah which have not been preserved:
    A. A life of Uzziah. (2 Chron. 26:22)
    B. The Book of the Kings of Judah and Israel. (2 Chron. 32:32)

7. Book of Mormon references to Isaiah show his greatness as a prophet:

A. "I did read unto them that which was written by the prophet Isaiah; for I did liken all scriptures unto us, that it might be for our profit and learning." (1 Ne. 19:23)

B. "And now I, Nephi, write more of the words of Isaiah, for my soul delighteth in his words. For I will liken his words unto my people, and I will send them forth unto all my children, for he verily saw my Redeemer, even as I have seen him." (2 Ne. 11:2)

C. "Isaiah spake many things which were hard for my people to understand; for they know not concerning the manner of prophesying among the Jews." (2 Ne. 25:1)

D. ". . . because the words of Isaiah are not plain unto you, nevertheless they are plain unto all those that are filled with the spirit of prophecy." (2 Ne. 25:4)

E. ". . . in the days that the prophecies of Isaiah shall be fulfilled men shall know of a surety, at the times when they shall come to pass." (2 Ne. 25:7)

F. "Ye remember that I spake unto you, and said that when the words of Isaiah should be fulfilled—behold they are written, ye have them before you, therefore search them—And verily, verily, I say unto you, that when they shall be fulfilled then is the fulfilling of the covenant which the Father made unto his people, O house of Israel." (3 Ne. 20:11-12)

G. "And now, behold, I say unto you, that ye ought to search these things. Yea, a commandment I give unto you that ye search these things diligently; for great are the words of Isaiah. For surely he spake as touching all things concerning my people which are of the house of Israel; therefore it must needs be that he must speak also to the Gentiles. And all things that he spake have been and shall be, even according to the words which he spake." (3 Ne. 23:1-3)

H. "And I did rehearse unto them the words of Isaiah, who spake concerning the restoration of the Jews, or of the house of Israel: and after they were restored they should no more be confounded, neither should they be scattered again." (1 Ne. 15:20)

I. "Search the prophecies of Isaiah. Behold, I cannot write them . . ." (Morm. 8:23)

ISAIAH

8. There are two traditions about Isaiah:

   A. Rabbinic tradition says that Isaiah's father was a brother to king Amaziah. If this was true, then Isaiah was a cousin of king Uzziah and therefore of royal blood.

   B. A tradition in the Talmud says that Isaiah was martyred by being tied to two planks and then being sawed asunder with a wooden saw. (Heb. 11:37?)

Date of Isaiah's Mission: c. 740-697 B. C.

1. He began his ministry in the year King Uzziah (of Judah) died (c. 740 B. C.). (6:1)
2. He preached during the reign of Uzziah and Jotham (c. 740-734 B. C.); Ahaz (c. 734-728 B. C.); and Hezekiah (c. 728-697 B. C.). (1:1)

Prophesied to: Israel and Judah.

Contemporary Prophets:

   Hosea c. 760-720 B. C.   to Israel.
   Micah c. 740-697 B. C.   to Israel and Judah.

Contemporary Prophets Contrasted:

Isaiah is a statesman and a member of Jerusalem's ruling class. He is well acquainted with the society and political intrigues of the capital city of Jerusalem and shows much interest in the political events of his time. He is a capable author and speaker. His writing reflects his culture and refinement.

Hosea gives a more intimate view of his personal affairs in his writing than any of the other prophets except Jeremiah. He was a man who suffered many hardships to keep the Lord's commandments. His writing is highly emotional and less objective than the writing of his contemporaries. His fervor substitutes for stylistic dignity.

Micah is a product of the open hills and shows dislike for the cities. (See 1:5, 5:11, 6:9.) As a member of the oppressed peasantry he speaks for the common people and defends them against the nobles and rich landlords of Judah. He is primarily an ethical and religious teacher and shows little knowledge or interest in political matters.

Contemporary Kings:

Israel: **Menahem**   c. 748-737 B. C.
    Paid tribute to Tiglath-Pileser III to save Israel.
    Pekahiah   c. 737-735 B. C.
    Pekah   c. 735-733 B. C.
    Israel and Syria attacked Judah in 734 B. C.
    Hoshea   c. 733-722 B. C.
    Fall of the Kingdom of Israel c. 722 B. C.

Judah: **Uzziah**   c. 792-740 B. C.
    Jotham   c. 749-734 B. C.
    Ahaz   c. 734-728 B. C.
    Formed an alliance with Assyria against Israel and Syria. Judah was defeated by Israel and Syria in 734 B. C. but the Jewish captives were returned.
    Hezekiah   c. 728-697 B. C.
    Attacked by Sennacherib in 701 B. C. but was saved when 185,000 Assyrians died.
    Manasseh   c. 697-642 B. C.

Assyria: **Tiglath-Pileser III**   c. 745-727 B. C.
    Overran northern Israel in 733 B. C.
    Shalmaneser V   c. 726-722 B. C.
    Laid siege to Samaria, capital of Israel in 722 B. C. He died during the siege.
    Sargon II   c. 721-705 B. C.
    Completed the conquest of Israel. Deported the Ten Tribes in 721 B. C.
    Sennacherib   c. 704-681 B. C.
    Attacked Judah in 701 B. C. He withdrew when 185,000 of his men died.

National Conditions—Israel and Judah:

—Political

1. Political decay was even more in evidence in Isaiah's time than noted previously.
2. Power had become concentrated in Jerusalem.
3. The city rulers oppressed the rural population with heavy taxation to support their policy of paying tribute to Assyria and to fortify the city of Jerusalem.

ISAIAH   301

4. Corrupt judges aided their friends in robbing the poor. Bribes and intrigue were characteristic of most governmental and judicial decisions.

—Economic

1. Greater social and moral decay than at previous times was found in Judah and Israel.
2. There was increased effort on the part of large landowners to evict small property owners and enlarge their estates.
3. High and unequal taxation and foreclosures on credit were the tools by which the poor were oppressed by the rich.

—Religious

1. Following the early reforms of Hezekiah men began to turn against the worship of Jehovah and assert that their religion had promised more than it could give.
2. Worshippers of Jehovah began to worship other gods. Their national impotence against Assyria seemed to indicate that other national gods existed and that they should seek the favor of these foreign gods.
3. National misfortunes were interpreted as indications of Jehovah's anger. They mistakenly attempted to appease this anger by observing pagan worship forms such as offering their children as sacrifices.
4. The terror of approaching destruction led the people to persecute those who worshipped only Jehovah and who would not seek the aid of pagan deities.

Notes on the Study and Interpretation of the Book of Isaiah:

Isaiah is the largest book of the Bible. Its size and complexity make it very difficult to understand unless a systematic program for its study is adopted. The book is often given some form of the following general outline by Bible scholars.

General Outline of the Book of Isaiah

I. Chapters 1-12—Prophecies concerning Judah.
II. Chapters 13-23—Prophecies concerning Judah's neighbors.
III. Chapters 24-27—Prophecies concerning a judgment on the world in the last days.

IV. Chapters 28-33—Prophecies concerning the future of Israel and discourses concerning the current relationship of Judah to Assyria.
V. Chapters 34-35—Prophecies contrasting the future of Edom and Israel.
VI. Chapters 36-39—Historical section. Isaiah's activities during the reign of King Hezekiah.
VII. Chapters 40-66—Prophecies of Israel's future glory.

Such an outline is so broad that it offers little, if any, help to the student.

Most studies examine the writings of Isaiah from the standpoint of **when he talked.** While such an approach is useful for some purposes, it leaves many students in utter confusion. It would seem more logical to group Isaiah's writings for study purposes into categories determined by **to whom he talked** and **when his prophecies would come to pass.**

In this book the writings of Isaiah are considered in four different sections. Each section represents one of the four major periods of prophetic fulfillment into which almost all scriptural prophecy may be conveniently classified. Again, these periods do not represent the time when the prophet is speaking. Rather, they deal with the time when his teachings and prophecies are to come to pass. The four periods of prophetic fulfillment are as follows:

Periods of Prophetic Fulfillment

I. Events Before and During the Fall of Israel to Assyria—800-700 B.C.

   A. The reigns of—
   1. Jeroboam II, Zachariah, Shallum, Menahem, Pekahiah, Pekah, and Hoshea, kings of Israel.
   2. Uzziah, Jotham, Ahaz, and Hezekiah, kings of Judah.
   3. Adad-nirari III, Shalmaneser IV, Assur-Dayan III, Tiglath-Pileser III, Shalmaneser V, Sargon II, and Sennacherib, kings of Assyria.

   B. Prophecies which primarily concern—
   1. The above kings.
   2. Assyrian assaults on the Mediterranean States.
   3. Alliances with Egypt and Assyria.
   4. The Syro-Ephraimite War, c. 734 B.C.
   5. The fall of northern Israel, c. 733 B.C.
   6. The siege and fall of Samaria, c. 722 B.C.
   7. The deportation of the remainder of Israel, c. 721 B.C.
   8. Sennacherib's attacks on Judah in 701 B.C. and 698 B.C.

II. Events Before and During the Fall of Judah, The Babylonian Captivity and the Jewish Return to Palestine (Primarily 635-535 B.C.)

   A. The reigns of—
   1. Manasseh, Amon, Josiah, Ahaziah, Jehoiakim, Jehoiachin, Zedekiah, and Gedeliah, kings of Judah.
   2. Nabopolassar, Nebuchadnezzar, Evil-Merodach, Nabonidus, and Belshazzar, kings of Babylonia.
   3. Cyrus II, Cambyses, and Darius I, kings of Persia and Media.

   B. Prophecies which primarily concern—
   1. The above kings.
   2. The Battle of Carchemish, 605 B.C.
   3. The fall of Nineveh and Assyria, c. 612 B.C.
   4. The first surrender of Jerusalem, under Jehoiachin, c. 598 B.C.
   5. The fall of Jerusalem under Zedekiah, c. 588 B.C.
   6. The Babylonian captivity.
   7. The fall of Babylon and the coming of Cyrus, c. 538 B.C.
   8. The three returns from captivity, 536 B.C., 457 B.C., 444 B.C.

III. Events Related to the Ministry of Christ (in the Meridian of time)

IV. Events During the Last Days (Beginning with the restoration of the Gospel about 1820 A.D.)

304   Prophets and Prophecies of the Old Testament

The book of Isaiah is open to many different interpretations by those of differing backgrounds and religions. It is recognized that some will disagree with the interpretative criteria by which the Latter-day Saints understand his writings. Be that as it may. For the purposes of this book, the author has divided the chapters of Isaiah into a study outline consisting of four sections, based on the four periods of prophetic fulfillment. It will be noted that the chapters are classified by their major message into one of the four groups. When a chapter makes reference to more than one period of prophetic fulfillment, the periods of the secondary items are indicated in the chapter outlines only.

The Book of Isaiah Divided, By Chapter, Into the Four Periods of Prophetic Fulfillment

Chapter	Outlined on page	Period I Israel, Judah, and Assyria	Period II Judah, Babylon, and the Captivity	Period III The Ministry of Christ	Period IV The Last Days
1	321		1		
2	361				2
3	322		3		
4	357				4
5	323		5		
6	307	6			
7	307	7			
8	309	8			
9	311	9			
10	320		10		
11	354				11
12	360				12
13	324		13		
14	325		14		
15	309	15			
16	309	16			
17	310	17			
18	349				18
19	310	19			
20	310	20			

ISAIAH

The Book of Isaiah Divided, By Chapter, Into the Four Periods of Prophetic Fulfillment

Chapter	Outlined on page	Period I Israel, Judah, and Assyria	Period II Judah, Babylon, and the Captivity	Period III The Ministry of Christ	Period IV The Last Days
21	325		21		
22	312	22			
23	321		23		
24	363				24
25	365				25
26	362				26
27	353				27
28	312	28			
29	348				29
30	311	30			
31	311	31			
32	365				32
33	364				33
34	363				34
35	353				35
36	314	36			
37	314	37			
38	314	38			
39	324		39		
40	360				40
41	326		41		
42	340			42	
43	327		43		
44	327		44		
45	327		45		
46	326		46		
47	326		47		
48	328		48		
49	351				49
50	342			50	

The Book of Isaiah Divided, By Chapter, Into the Four Periods of Prophetic Fulfillment

Chapter	Outlined on page	Period I Israel, Judah, and Assyria	Period II Judah, Babylon, and the Captivity	Period III The Ministry of Christ	Period IV The Last Days
51	356				51
52	352				52
53	342			53	
54	350				54
55	353				55
56	313	56			
57	313	57			
58	313	58			
59	313	59			
60	358				60
61	359				61
62	358				62
63	362				63
64	362				64
65	364				65
66	359				66

SECTION I

CHAPTERS OF ISAIAH PERTAINING TO THE FIRST PERIOD OF PROPHETIC FULFILLMENT: THE FALL OF ISRAEL TO ASSYRIA

The following chapters of the book of Isaiah will be considered in this section: 6, 7, 8, 15, 16, 17, 19, 20, 9, 30, 31, 22, 28, 56, 57, 58, 59, 38, 36, 37. As a guide to the student each chapter is briefly outlined. It is suggested that they be read in the order as given above so that they may be understood as a chronology of Isaiah's life and times.

The Beginning of Isaiah's Ministry (c. 740 B.C.)

Chapter 6—Isaiah's Call to the Ministry.

> Note: This chapter is quoted in 2 Ne. 16.
1. Isaiah's vision of the Lord in heaven. (1-4)
2. Isaiah's confession of his sins and his cleansing. (5-7)
3. Isaiah's call to the ministry. (8-11)
4. The captivity of Israel is predicted. (12-13)

> Note: Verse 13 is difficult. A tenth was to remain and then it would be eaten. Apparently Judah (more or less a tenth of Israel, or one tribe out of twelve) would be left when Israel was taken captive, and then Judah would later be destroyed.

The Syro-Ephraimite War (c. 734 B.C.)

Chapter 7—To Ahaz (King of Judah): Do not fear Israel and Syria. The Signs of the Future Birth of Christ.

> Note: This chapter is quoted in 2 Ne. 17.
1. Background on the war. (1-2) (See also 2 Ki. 16, 2 Chron. 28.)

> Note: In 734 B.C., Rezin, king of Syria, and Pekah, king of Israel, attempted to force Judah to join them in an alliance against Assyria. Judah's king, Ahaz, refused, so Syria and Israel attacked Judah in an attempt to set a new king on the Jewish throne who would be sympathetic to their plan. (Is. 7:6) Although Syria suffered heavy casualties, she also inflicted heavy

losses on Judah and carried a "great multitude" of the Jews captive to Damascus. (2 Chron. 28:5) Israel killed one hundred twenty thousand men of Judah, and took two hundred thousand more to Samaria as captives. (2 Chron. 28:6-8) However the prophet Oded (O'-dĕd) was there and he, together with four of the important political figures of Israel, convinced the returning Israelite army that the captives should be freed and sent back to Judah. (2 Chron. 28:9-16) While Judah was in this weakened condition it was attacked by the Edomites and Philistines. (2 Chron. 28:17-19) To relieve the pressure, Ahaz appealed to Tiglath-pileser III of Assyria for help. (2 Chron. 28:20, 2 Ki. 16:7) The Assyrian king used his appeal as an excuse to conquer Syria (2 Ki. 16:9) and to carry a portion of Israel into captivity. For his service to Judah he required Ahaz to pay a heavy tribute to Assyria. (2 Ki. 16:8, 2 Chron. 28:20-21)

2. Isaiah's message to Ahaz at the beginning of the war:

A. Don't be afraid of Israel and Syria. (3-6)

B. Israel and Syria will not be able to depose Ahaz. (7)

C. Within 65 years Ephraim (Israel) shall be broken so it will no longer be a nation. (8)

Note: The 65 years is believed to cover the period from the first deportation of Israel (734 B.C.) to the settlement of foreigners in the land by Esarhaddon about 670 B.C. (See 2 Ki. 17:24, Ez. 4:2.)

D. If ye will not believe, surely ye shall not be established. (9)

E. (III[1]) The Lord's sign to Ahaz that these things would happen: the Immanuel prophecy. (10-16)[2]

F. Ahaz's plan for seeking foreign help will reap unforeseen consequences. Judah will become the arena of conflict between Egypt and Assyria, and will be desolated by Assyria. (17-25)

---

[1]The Roman numerals I, II, III which are used throughout Isaiah refer to the first three periods of prophetic development. Arabic numerals in parentheses at the beginning of a paragraph or item refer to one of the fifty events listed in connection with the fourth period of prophetic fulfillment, the last days, in Chapter Four.

[2]This prophecy is considered in section III of Isaiah.

ISAIAH—SECTION I 309

Chapter 8—To Ahaz (cont'd.): **Instead of Forming Foreign Alliances, Trust in the Lord.**

Note: This chapter is quoted in 2 Ne. 18.
1. Before Isaiah's newborn son (whose symbolic name, Maher-shal-al-hash-baz, means "the spoil speedeth, the prey hasteth") can talk, Assyria will have conquered Damascus (Syria) and Samaria (Israel). (1-4)

   Note: Damascus soon fell to Assyria because of Ahaz's request to Assyria for help. (2 Ki. 16:7-9) The Assyrians took the northern portion of Israel into captivity in 734 B.C. (2 Ki. 15:29)
2. Assyria will not only conquer Syria, it will also attack Judah. (5-8)

   Note: This was fulfilled thirty-three years later, in 701 B.C., when Sennacherib invaded Judah. (Is. 36, 37)
3. Alliance with foreign powers will bring Judah's downfall. (9-12)

   Note: Ahaz's request for help from Assyria resulted in Judah's becoming a vassal state, and increased Judah's idolatry which was the eventual cause of its downfall. (See 2 Ki. 16:7-18)
4. Instead of forming foreign alliances, trust in the Lord. (13, 14, 17)
5. Those who do not trust in the Lord shall fall and be taken. (14-22)

Burdens On Surrounding Nations

Chapters 15 and 16—**The Burdens of Moab.**
1. The nation shall be laid waste, and lions will come upon the remnant that escape. (15:1-9)
2. Isaiah advises Moab that it would be wise to send a messenger to Jerusalem and declare allegiance to Judah. (16:1-5)
3. The people of Moab shall mourn; their prayers in the high places shall not prevail. (16:6-13)
4. Moab shall fall within three years. (16:14)

   Note: The cities of Moab were sacked by three different Assyrian kings: Tiglath-Pileser III, in 734 B.C.; Sargon, whose army was led by his son, Sennacherib, in 713 B.C.; and Sennacherib, 701 B.C.

Chapter 17—The Burden of Damascus (Syria).

1. Syria will be made desolate. (1-14)

   Note: Syria fell to Tiglath-Pileser III of Assyria in c. 734 B.C.

Chapters 19 and 20—The Burden of Egypt.

1. (II) The Egyptians will be given into the hand of a cruel lord and will be set one against another. (19:1-4)

   Note: Sargon II defeated the Egyptians at Raphia in 720 B.C. and Sennacherib defeated them at Eltekeh in 701 B.C., but this does not seem to be the actual fulfillment of the prophecy. It was fulfilled by the Assyrian king Esar-Haddon, who conquered Egypt in 671 B.C. He divided it into a number of small vassal states, the governors of which plundered and spoiled their subjects.

2. Those who labor in Egypt will not be able to find work. (19:5-10, 15)
3. (IV) (34) The leaders of Egypt are not wise, but make their people err. (19:11-14)
4. (34, 35, 40) In that day the Lord will heal Egypt and the Egyptians shall know and worship the Lord. (19:16-22)

   Note: While many Jews did live in Egypt in the days of the Savior, primarily at Alexandria and Heliopolis, this would not seem to be the fulfillment of the prophecy. Theirs was not a time when—

   A. Judah was a terror unto Egypt. (17)
   B. Egypt swore allegiance to the Lord of hosts. (18)
   C. A savior came and delivered them from oppressors. (20)
   D. Egypt returned to the Lord. (22)
   E. The Lord regarded Egypt, Israel, and Assyria as equal. (24)
   F. Israel stood as the place of inheritance for the Lord's people. (25)

   These clues seem to combine as an indication that the fulfillment of the prophecy is yet future.

5. (34) In that day there will be a highway from Egypt to Assyria and Israel will be a blessing in the Lord. (19:23-25)

ISAIAH—SECTION I

6. The Lord commanded Isaiah to go naked and barefoot for three years. This was a sign that Egypt and Ethiopia would be led away prisoners by Assyria in the same condition. (20:1-6)
    Note: Tartan came to the Philistine city of Ashdod in 711 B.C.

First Invasion of Israel—The Galilee Captivity (c. 734 B.C.)

Chapter 9—To Ahaz (cont'd.): Israel's Imminent Sorrow Contrasted with its Joy at the Birth of Christ.
  Note: This chapter is quoted in 2 Ne. 19.
1. (III) The suffering of the Zebulun (Zĕ-bū'-lun) and Naphtali (Năph'-tă-lī) areas of Israel will someday be alleviated by a visit of Christ to that area. (1-2) (See Mt. 4:12-16.)
    Note: This area, the Galilee region, was the first to fall before the Assyrians in c. 734 B.C. (2 Ki. 15:29) yet it would have the honor of being the home of the Savior.
2. (III) The birth of Christ will serve to increase the joy and reduce the burden of the people. (3-7)
    Note: Isaiah 9:8 to 10:4 is a poem in four strophes, each with the same refrain: "For all this his anger is not turned away, but his hand is stretched out still."
3. The inhabitants of Samaria shall be devoured by their enemies. (8-12)
4. The Lord will cut off the men and leave only the children and widows. (13-17)
5. No man will spare his brother; they shall suffer hunger. (18-21)

Chapters 30 and 31—The Folly of an Alliance With Egypt.
1. Those who attempt to ally Judah with Egypt sin in so doing because they have not sought God's counsel. Egypt will not help Judah. (30:1-7)
2. The strength of Judah is to sit still and be confident. (30:7, 15-17)
3. Judah's sins are listed. (30:8-13)
4. (30-31) The Lord will be gracious unto His people when they dwell in Zion at Jerusalem. He shall make the ground increase. (30:18-24)

5. (35) There shall be water on every high mountain and the light of the sun shall be sevenfold in the day the towers fall and the Lord heals the wound of His people. (30:25-26)
6. (35) The Lord will sift the nations with destruction through devouring fire, scattering, tempest, and hailstones. (30:27-30)
7. The Assyrian shall be beaten down. (30:31-33)
8. The Egyptians are only men; they will not be able to help Judah like God will. (31:1-3)
9. The Lord will defend, deliver, and preserve Jerusalem. Turn ye to him. (31:4-6)
10. The Assyrians shall flee and be discomfited, and fear the ensign of Jerusalem. (31:7-9)
    Note: This seems to refer to Sennacherib's invasion in 698 B.C., in which 185,000 of his men died suddenly. He left Judah and did not return. (See Is. 37.)

Chapter 22—A Reproof of Jerusalem for Its Conduct During Sennacherib's Invasion.

1. The city is joyous because the men have not been slain in battle. (1-7)
2. The people had foolishly attempted to fortify Jerusalem (See also 2 Chron. 32:3-5) instead of trusting in God. (8-14)
3. Demote Shebna (Shĕb'-nă) (it would appear that he was an officer of the city of Jerusalem who may have led the people of the city in their foolish defense) and appoint Eliakim (e-lī'-ă-kim) to rule over the people of the city. The latter shall rule well for a while and then his burden shall be removed. (15-25)

Chapter 28—God's Judgment Upon the Rulers of Israel and Judah.

1. The drunken rulers of Ephraim (Israel) will be trodden under feet. (1-4)
2. (35) In that day the Lord will give his people the spirit of judgment and strength in battle. (5-6)
3. The priests and false prophets have erred through wine. They would not hear when God tried to teach them his precepts. (7-13)
4. The rulers of Judah have falsely assumed that they are righteous enough to escape the overflowing scourge, judgment and hell. They will not escape. (14-22)

ISAIAH—SECTION I 313

5. A parable of sowing and reaping: just as the farmer does not thresh various types of grain with the same degree of force, so God will not punish his people beyond what they deserve. (23-29)

The Fall of Israel (c. 722 B.C.)

Chapter 56—**The Nations are Summoned to Devour Israel.**

1. Blessed is the man who does justice and observes the sabbath. (1-2)
2. Those who keep the sabbaths and take hold of the covenant without polluting them will come into the Lord's holy mountain. (3-7)
3. (41) The Lord which gathers the outcasts of Israel will gather others to him, beside those that are gathered unto him. (8)
4. The nations (depicted as beasts) are summoned to devour Israel because her watchmen (false prophets), wealthy men (dogs), and rulers (shepherds) are ignorant, greedy, and without understanding. 9-12)

Chapter 57—**The Only Hope for Israel is to Trust God.**

1. The people have sinned and debased themselves with idol worship and heathen fertility rites. (1-8)
2. The only hope for Israel is to put its trust in God. (9-16)
3. The Lord will heal the wicked person and restore comforts to him. (17-21)

Chapter 58—**True Religious Observance is Required.**

1. The people observe the outward ordinances but do not observe the true spirit of worship. (1-4)
2. The Lord defines the proper method of fasting. (5-7)
3. If Israel will aid the hungry and afflicted, and observe the Sabbath properly, the Lord will guide her and aid her. (8-14)

Chapter 59—**Sin Separates Man From God.**

1. God can save Israel, but their sins have separated them from God. (1-2)
2. Israel's sins are listed. (3-8)
3. Israel's confession of guilt. (9-14)
4. The Lord saw man's need for an intercessor and judge and accepted the task. (15-18)
5. (35, 37) When the enemy shall come in like a flood, the Spirit of the Lord shall lift up a standard against him and the Redeemer shall come to Zion. (19-21)

Hezekiah's Life Is Extended

Chapter 38—Hezekiah's Life Is Extended 15 Years.
1. Isaiah tells the ailing Hezekiah that he is about to die. (1)
2. Hezekiah prays to the Lord. (2-3)
3. The Lord sends Isaiah to Hezekiah to say:
    A. God will extend his life 15 years. (4-5)
    B. God will deliver Hezekiah and Jerusalem out of the hands of the Assyrians. (6)
    C. As a sign, the sun will move 10 degrees backward on the sun dial. (7-8)
4. Hezekiah's hymn of thanksgiving. (9-22)

Sennacherib's Invasions of Judah (c. 713 B.C. and 701 B.C.)

Chapters 36 and 37—Sennacherib's Invasion of Judah.

> Note: Isaiah 36 and 37 seem to be a blending of the accounts of two invasions under Sennacherib. The first was in 713 B.C., the second in 701 B.C. It would appear that Hezekiah was able to buy off the Assyrians the first time (2 Ki. 18:14-16). This account appears to be primarily an account of the 701 B.C. invasion, yet it is ascribed to the 14th year of Hezekiah's reign (Is. 36:1), which would indicate the earlier invasion. If Hezekiah's 15-year extension of life preceded the invasion of Is. 36-37, then this is the 701 B.C. attack. If it followed the Is. 36-37 invasion, then this is the 713 B.C. incident. It is impossible to determine the matter since the order in the accounts conflict. Bible scholars and historians are not in agreement as to the events of this period. (See 2 Ki. 18:13-19:36; 2 Chron. 32.)

1. The Assyrian king, Sennacherib, attacked the defensed cities of Judah and conquered many of them. (36:1)
2. He sent an ambassador to Jerusalem while he laid siege to the city of Lachish. (2 Chron. 32:9) Rabshakeh (Răb'-shă-kĕh), the ambassador, confronted Eliakim (E-lī'-ă-kim), the governor of Jerusalem, outside of Jerusalem. (36:2-3) The Assyrian's message was that
    A. Judah has rebelled against Assyria because of an alliance with Egypt. Egypt will not protect Judah. (36:4-6)

B. You cannot rely on Jehovah to protect you. He has sent me to destroy Judah (a false claim). (36:7-10)

C. Give Assyria 2,000 hostages so it won't destroy Jerusalem. (36:8, 16-17)

D. Hezekiah (king of Judah) will not be able to deliver you. Don't let him deceive you and make you rely on God. (36:13-15)

E. Jehovah will not be able to save you. No local God has been able to save other nations from Assyria's might. (36:18-20)

3. When Hezekiah heard from Eliakim the message of Rabshakeh, he sent Eliakim to Isaiah for counsel. (36:21-37:5)
4. Isaiah's message:
    A. Do not be afraid of the blasphemous words of the Assyrians. (37:6)
    B. The Assyrians shall hear a rumor and shall return to their own land. (37:7)
5. The Assyrians heard rumors of an Ethiopian attack and left. (37:8-9)
6. The Assyrians sent a threatening letter to Hezekiah. (37:10-14)
7. Hezekiah's prayer for deliverance. (37:15-20)
8. Isaiah sent the Lord's answer to Hezekiah's prayer:
    A. A taunt-song against Sennacherib. (37:22-29)
    B. The king of Assyria will not come into Jerusalem nor attack it. (37:30-35)
9. The angel of the Lord killed 185,000 of the Assyrians during the night so Sennacherib and his army returned to Nineveh, leaving Jerusalem unharmed. (37:36-37)

    Note: Herodotus, in his writings two centuries later, speaks of the tradition of an invasion of rats which attacked Sennacherib's army when it reached the delta, bringing with them the plague.

Doctrinal Analysis of Isaiah, Section I

The Sins of the House of Israel and its Neighbors

1. Associate yourselves (in foreign alliances) and ye shall be broken in pieces. (8:9-12)
2. Thou hast forgotten the God of thy salvation, and hast not been mindful of the rock of thy strength. (17:10)

Punishments Upon Israel

1. In threescore and five years shall Ephraim be broken, that it be not a people. (7:8)
2. The land that thou abhorrest shall be forsaken of both her kings. (7:16)
3. The Lord will shave Israel with a rasor that is hired, by the king of Assyria. (7:20)
4. With arrows and with bows shall men come thither; because all the land shall become briars and thorns. (7:23-25)
5. Before Isaiah's child will be able to speak, the riches of Damascus and the spoil of Samaria shall be taken away before the king of Assyria. (8:4)

Punishments Upon Judah

1. The king of Assyria shall pass through Judah. He shall fill the breadth of thy land. (8:7-8)

The Last Days

(30-31) The Gathering

1. The Lord shall be gracious to his people when they dwell in Zion at Jerusalem. He shall make the ground increase. (30:18-24)

(34) Israel's Political and International Affairs

1. The leaders of Egypt are not wise. They cause Egypt to err and stagger. (19:11-15)
2. Egypt will be afraid and fear because of the shaking of the Lord of hosts. The Lord of Judah shall be a terror unto Egypt. (19:16-17)

(35) The Battle of Armageddon

1. There shall be rivers and streams of water on the mountains in the day of the great slaughter, when the towers shall fall, the light of the moon shall be as the light of the sun, and the light of the sun shall be sevenfold, as the light of seven days, in the day that the Lord bindeth up the breach of his people, and healeth the stroke of their wound. (30:25-26)
2. The Lord will sift the nations through devouring fire, scattering, tempest and hailstones. (30:27-30)
3. In that day the Lord shall be a crown of glory. He shall give strength to them that turn the battle to the gate. (28:5-6)

Isaiah—Section I

4. When the enemy shall come in like a flood, the Spirit of the Lord shall lift up a standard against him and the Redeemer shall come to Zion. (59:19-21)

(40) The Conversion of Egypt

1. Five cities of Egypt shall speak the language of Canaan and shall swear unto the Lord of hosts. (19:18)
2. There shall be an altar to the Lord in Egypt and a pillar to the Lord at the border. (19:19-20)
3. The Lord shall send Egypt a great savior, and he shall deliver them. (19:20)
4. The Egyptians shall know the Lord and shall do sacrifice and vows unto Him. (19:21)
5. The Lord shall smite Egypt and then heal it, and they shall return even to the Lord. (19:22)
6. There shall be a highway out of Egypt to Assyria. (19:23)
7. Israel shall be a third with Egypt and with Assyria, even a blessing in the midst of the land. (19:24-25)

(41) 4th Period of Missionary Labor

1. The Lord which gathers the outcasts of Israel will gather others to him, beside those that are gathered unto him. (56:8)

The Nature of God

1. Holy, holy, holy is the Lord of hosts: the whole earth is full of his glory. (6:3)
2. The Lord himself shall give you a sign. (7:14)
3. He shall be a stone of stumbling and for a rock of offense to both the houses of Israel. (8:14-15)
4. In mercy shall the throne be established: and he shall sit upon it in truth, judging, and seeking judgment, and hasting righteousness. (16:5)
5. Behold, the Lord rideth upon a swift cloud . . . (19:1)
6. I have heard thy prayer, I have seen thy tears: behold I will add unto thy days fifteen years. (38:2-3, 5-8)
7. The Lord hath both spoken unto me, and himself hath done it (answered Hezekiah's prayer). (38:15)
8. Thou hast in love to my soul delivered it from the pit of corruption: for thou hast cast all my sins behind thy back. (38:17)
9. O Lord that dwellest between the cherubims, thou alone art the God of all the kingdoms of the earth: thou hast made heaven and earth. (37:16)

God's Dealings With His Prophets
1. I heard the voice of the Lord saying, Whom shall I send, and who will go for us? Then said I, Here am I, send me. (6:8)

Vision of the Lord
1. I saw the Lord sitting upon a throne, high and lifted up. (6:1-5)

Prophecy of Christ in the Meridian of Time
1. Behold, a virgin shall conceive, and bear a son, and shall call his name Immanuel. (7:14-15)

God's Judgment Upon Man
1. Woe is me for I am undone: because I am a man of unclean lips, and I dwell in the midst of a people of unclean lips. (6:5)
2. (After an angel touches Isaiah's lips with a live coal) Thine iniquity is taken away, and thy sin purged. (6:7)
3. For the grave cannot praise thee, death can not celebrate thee: they that go down into the pit cannot hope for thy truth. (38:18)
4. I know thy abode, and thy going out, and thy coming in, and thy rage against me. (37:28)

Allusions to the Temple Service
1. I will fasten him as a nail in a sure place. (22:23, 25)
2. In mine house and within my walls I will give to those who take hold of my covenant an everlasting name, that shall not be cut off. (56:4-5)

Counsel for Righteous Living
1. Take heed, and be quiet; fear not, neither be fainthearted . . . (7:4)
2. If ye will not believe, surely ye shall not be established. (7:9)
3. I will not ask, neither will I tempt the Lord. (7:12)
4. It is a small thing for you to weary men, but will ye weary my God also? (7:13)
5. Sanctify the Lord of hosts himself; and let him be your fear, and let him be your dread, and he shall be for a sanctuary. (8:13-14)
6. Bind up the testimony, seal the law among my disciples. (8:16)
7. I will wait upon the Lord, and I will look for him. (8:17)

ISAIAH—SECTION I

8. Should not a people seek unto their God? for the living to the dead? (8:19)
9. To the law and to the testimony: if they speak not according to this word, it is because there is no light in them. (8:20)
10. Take counsel, execute judgment. (16:3)
11. (Hezekiah's prayer) Remember now, O Lord, I beseech thee, how I have walked before thee in truth and with a perfect heart, and have done that which is good in thy sight. (38:3)
12. O Lord, by these things (God's answer to prayer) men live, and in all these things is the life of my spirit . . . (38:16)
13. The father to the children shall make known thy truth. (38:19)

Summary of Isaiah—Section I:

After studying Section I of Isaiah the student should know:
1. Isaiah preached at the time of the fall of Israel.
2. He preached at the time of two major crises of Judah:
    A. The Syro-Ephraimite War.
    B. The Assyrian attack under Sennacherib.
3. Isaiah was mainly concerned with two kings of Judah:
    A. Ahaz
    B. Hezekiah
4. The three major messages of Section I of Isaiah were the same as for Micah and Hosea:
    A. God was displeased with the many sins of Israel.
    B. Israel would be punished by being conquered and scattered among the Gentiles.
    C. God will restore Israel to her former home and prominence in the last days.
5. The first period of prophetic fulfillment was before and during the fall of Israel to Assyria, (800-700 B.C.).
6. Twenty of the sixty-six chapters of Isaiah pertain to the first period of prophetic fulfillment.
7. Isaiah prophesied concerning all four periods of prophetic fulfillment.

SECTION II

CHAPTERS OF ISAIAH PERTAINING TO THE SECOND PERIOD OF PROPHETIC FULFILLMENT: THE FALL OF JUDAH, THE BABYLONIAN CAPTIVITY, AND THE RETURN FROM EXILE

This section of Isaiah is concerned with his prophecies which pertained to the second period of prophetic fulfillment. It deals primarily with the prophecies of Assyria's fall to Babylonia, the fall of Judah to Babylonia, the fall of Babylonia to the Medes and Persians, and the return of the Jews from the Babylonian captivity. The section includes sixteen chapters: 10, 23, 1, 3, 5, 39, 13, 14, 21, 46, 47, 41, 43, 44, 45, and 48. It is suggested that they be read in the above order so that they will follow in the same chronological order as the events of which they speak.

The Fall of Assyria to Babylon and Media (c. 606 B.C.)

Chapter 10—The Eventual Fall of Assyria.

> Note: Verses 1-4 are the final verse of a poem of four strophes which all have the same refrain: "For all this his anger is not turned away, but his hand is stretched out still." The poem begins in 9:8.
>
> Note 2: This chapter is quoted in 2 Ne. 20.

1. Woe to those who oppress the poor: they shall fall under the slain. (1-4)
2. (I) Assyria will tread down the nation of Israel as a tool of God's anger. (5-10)
3. The fate of Samaria will eventually come upon Jerusalem. (11)
4. Assyria will boast, not knowing that in its conquests the Lord has used it as a tool. God will punish Assyria and bring its downfall. (12-15)
5. (34) The light of Israel will be a flame which will devour the land of Assyria. (16-19)
6. (30-31) Item 5 will take place in the day that the remnant of Israel (the ten tribes) and those that are escaped of Jacob (the scattered Jews) shall return and shall rely upon the Lord. (20-22)

ISAIAH—SECTION II 321

7. (35) The Lord shall make a consumption in the midst of all the land. (23)
8. Do not be afraid of Assyria, for the time will come when it will be destroyed, and its yoke will be removed from Judah. (24-34)

Tyre to Be Destroyed

Chapter 23—**The Burden of Tyre.**
1. Tyre shall be desolate and forgotten. (1-12)
2. Behold the land of the Chaldeans (Babylonia). (13)
3. Tyre will be forgotten for 70 years and then shall be restored. (14-18)

   Note: Tyre was conquered by Nebuchadnezzar, king of Babylonia, after a thirteen-year siege (585-573 B.C.). (See also Ezek. 26-28.)

The Fall of Judah to Babylonia

Chapter 1—**"The Great Arraignment" of Judah and Jerusalem.**

Note: This chapter may best be understood as a court scene, with Jehovah as the judge and Judah as the defendant.

1. The Lord's charge:
   A. Judah has rebelled against me. (2-4)
   B. The land of Judah will be left desolate and only a small remnant shall remain. (5-9)
2. The Lord anticipates and rejects Judah's defense:
   A. Sacrifices, burnt offerings and other outward manifestations of worship are vain before God (because they are a sham which hides evil deeds and minds.) (10-15)
   B. Cease to do evil, learn to do well. (16-17)
3. The Lord offers to pardon Judah:
   A. If ye be willing and obedient, ye shall eat the good of the land. (18-19)
   B. If ye refuse and rebel, ye shall be devoured with the sword. (20)
4. The Lord's sentence of judgment:
   A. The sins of the people are itemized. (21-23, 29)
   Note: Verse 29 is seemingly a reference to the groves in which heathen fertility rites were practiced.

      B. The Lord will avenge himself of his enemies, and they that forsake the Lord shall be consumed. (24-25, 28-31)

  5. The Lord's judgment will make possible the eventual restoration of Judah:

      A. (35) The Lord will ease Himself of His enemies and will purge the dross of Israel. (24-25)

      B. (41) Afterward thou shalt be called the city of righteousness, the faithful city. Zion shall be redeemed with judgment. (26-27)

      C. (42) The destruction of the transgressors and of the sinners shall be together; they shall be burned and consumed. (28-31)

Chapter 3—**The Men of Judah to Fall.**

Note: This chapter is quoted in 2 Ne. 13.

1. The leaders of Judah will be taken away from Jerusalem. (1-3)
2. Judah will be ruled by children and women. (4-8, 12)
3. The wicked people have rewarded evil unto themselves. (9-11)
4. The Lord will punish the ancients ("wise" leaders) and princes of the people for oppressing the poor. (13-15)
5. The Lord will punish the haughty daughters of Zion, for their men shall fall by the sword, and their mighty in the war. (16-26)
6. Note: It would seem that verse one of chapter 4 might well be included with chapter 3, as a continuation of the explanation of how the men of Judah will fall and/or be carried away captive:

    Ch. 4:1—And in that day seven women shall take hold of one man, saying, We will eat our own bread, and wear our own apparel: only let us be called by thy name, to take away our reproach.

The question of whether Is. 4:1 belongs with chapter 3 or chapter 4 is an important one. If the verse belongs with the preceding chapter, then it is a prophecy of the suffering of the women of Judah when their men were carried into exile at the time of the fall of Jerusalem to the Babylonians. (See 2 Ki. 24:14-16, 25:8-12; Jer. 52.) **There can be little doubt that this situation offered ample**

ISAIAH—SECTION II 323

fulfillment, if this interpretation of the passage is correct. This seems to be the logical understanding of the passage.

On the other hand, if Is. 4:1 is connected with the thought of Is. 4:2-6, then it is a prophetic indication of a future imbalance of the sexes among God's people either (1) during a period of the establishment of the New Jerusalem in Jackson County, Missouri, or (2) during the era of the latter-day Jerusalem in Palestine. Again the matter rests on the interpretation of Is. Chap. 4.

Chapter 5—The Parable of the Vineyard—God's Judgment Upon Judah.

Note: This chapter is quoted in 2 Ne. 15.

1. The parable:
    A. The well beloved had a vineyard which he gave great care, but it brought forth wild grapes. (1-4)
    B. The Lord will make the vineyard barren. (5-6)
    C. The vineyard of the Lord of hosts is the house of Israel, and the men of Judah his pleasant plant. (7)

2. Six woes upon Judah:
    A. Woe unto them who acquire much property (by oppressing the poor). Many houses shall be desolate. (8-10)
    B. Woe unto them who are drunkards instead of considering the work of the Lord. The people are gone into captivity because they have no knowledge. (11-17)
    C. Woe unto them that mock the Lord and ask that He hasten His work. (18-19)
    D. Woe unto them that call evil good and good evil. (20)
    E. Woe unto them that are wise in their own eyes. (21)
    F. Woe unto them that justify the wicked for reward (take bribes). Their carcasses shall be torn in the midst of the streets. (22-25)

3. The gathering of the house of Israel in the last days:
    A. (30-31) God will lift up an ensign to the nations from far, and will hiss unto them from the end of the earth. (26)

Note: See 2 Ne. 29:1-2.

324   Prophets and Prophecies of the Old Testament

  B. (35) Israel shall be powerful and lay hold of the prey. (27-29)

  Note: This does not appear to be the same conflict of Micah 5:6-14, 3 Ne. 20:15-20, and 3 Ne. 21:12-21, which the Book of Mormon context shows as taking place in the Americas (See discussion in Chapter on Micah). This is apparently a reference to the Battle of Armageddon, in which Israel is victorious but sorrows for the loss of two-thirds of its people. (See Zech. 13:7-9.)

  C. (35) In that day there will be darkness and sorrow in the land. (30) (See Joel 3:12-15.)

Chapter 39—Judah's Treasures Shall Be Carried Into Babylon.

Note: Review Chapter 38.

1. Merodach-baladan (Mĕr'-ō-dăch-băl'-ă-dăn), the Babylonian prince, sent messengers carrying gifts to Hezekiah to celebrate his recovery from sickness. (1)
2. Hezekiah showed the messengers the treasures of Judah. (2)
3. Isaiah, upon learning what the messengers had seen, prophesied that the treasures of Judah would be carried into Babylon. (3-8)

The Fall of Babylonia to Persia

Chapter 13—The Burden of Babylon.

Note: This chapter is quoted in 2 Ne. 23.

1. God will call his sanctified ones (Cyrus the Persian) and mighty ones (the Medes and the Persians) to defeat the Babylonians. (1-3)
2. The kingdoms of nations will gather together (the Persians will combine with the Medes and other armies they conquered) and come from a far country (Persia) to attack. (4-5)
3. (42) The cruel destruction of Babylon is compared to the destruction at the coming of the Savior. (6-13)
   Note: The comparison begins in verse 6: "It shall come as a destruction from the Almighty."
4. The Medes will be stirred up against Babylon. (17-18)
5. Babylon shall be desolate and shall never be inhabited again. (19-22)

ISAIAH—SECTION II 325

Chapter 14—**The Fall of Babylon.**
   Note: This chapter is quoted in 2 Ne. 24.
1. Israel will return (from Babylon) to their own land, and strangers shall be joined with them. (1-3)
   Note: See the book of Ezra for the fulfillment of this prophecy.
2. Israel's taunt-song against Babylon. (4-21)
   A. The Babylonian king is pictured as dying and going to hell, where the other spirits mock him, asking if he is now as weak as they. (9-11)
   B. The fall of the king of Babylon is compared with the fall of Lucifer. (12-15) (See Rev. 12:3, 7-9; D&C 76:25-28; Jn. 8:44.)
   C. The Babylonian king will not even receive proper burial. (16-21)
3. The Lord will cut off from Babylon both its name and its posterity. (22-23)
4. The Assyrians will also be broken by the Lord. (24-28)
5. The burden of Philistia. (29-32)
   Note: a. "Philistia" is the name from which "Palestine" is derived.
   b. The serpent whose rod is broken (29) probably alludes to the death of Tiglath-Pileser III, king of Assyria, who had conquered many Philistine cities.
   c. The cockatrice and the flying serpent (29): Sargon II and his son, Sennacherib.
   d. Messengers (32)—probably Philistine ambassadors sent to Jerusalem soliciting help against the Assyrians.
   e. Other prophecies against the Philistines: Jer. 47, Amos 1:6-8, Zeph. 2:4-7, Zech. 9:5-7.
   A. The Philistines will be slain and dissolved. (29-32)

Chapter 21—**The Burden of Babylon, Edom, and Arabia.**
   Note: a. Desert of the sea (1)—Babylon. (See v. 9.)
   b. Elam (2)—Persia.
   c. Dumah (11)—A district south of Edom, of which Seir was the central area. Here used for Edom.
   d. Dedanim (13)—Arabic nomads.

1. Babylon will be besieged and spoiled by the Persians and Medes. (1-4) (See Dan. 5:30-31.)
2. The Lord's watchman will report that Babylon is fallen. (5-10)
3. The burden of Edom. (11-12)
4. (I) The burden of Arabia—within a year, all the glory of Kedar shall fail. (13-17)
   Note: Sargon II, king of Assyria, invaded Arabia c. 716 B.C.

Chapter 46—**The Fall of Babylon.**
1. Bel (the chief god of Babylon—See Jer. 50:2) and Nebo (the interpreter of the gods) will not be able to keep Babylon from going into captivity. (1-2)
2. Jehovah, who has supported his followers throughout their lifetime, is greater than the idols. (3-11)
3. The Lord will bring a ravenous bird from the east (Cyrus), who will execute His judgment. (11)
4. (39?) The Lord will place His salvation and glory in Zion. (12-13)

Chapter 47—**The Fall of Babylon**
1. Babylon will be brought down, for she will shew no mercy to the Lord's people. (1-15)
   Note: Chapter 47 is a taunt-song of four stanzas: 1-4, 5-7, 8-11, and 12-15.

Judah's Return from the Babylonian Captivity

Chapter 41—**Judah's Return from Babylonia.**
   Note: This chapter is one of the most difficult to interpret of Isaiah's prophecies.

1. Isaiah foresees the rising up of Cyrus the Persian (?). (1-3)

   Note: The individual is so identified by most Bible scholars because:
   A. He is from the east (Persia?),
   B. And from the north. This is often interpreted in either of two ways: (1) Cyrus, as head of the Persian armies, had conquered the Median armies and stood as leader of the combined forces; Media is north of Palestine; or (2) Armies from the east always entered Palestine **from the north.**

ISAIAH—SECTION II 327

      C. He was a righteous man, who ruled over kings. (2)

      D. Although Cyrus is not mentioned by name, the description is similar to Isaiah's description of him in 44:28 and 45:1.
2. God has chosen Israel and has not cast her away. (4-10)
3. (35) Those who have warred against Israel shall not be found. (11-14)
4. (30-31) Israel will thresh the mountains. God will open up rivers in high places and fountains in the valleys so people will know God has helped Israel. (15-20) (cf. Is. 30:25-26.)
5. The pagan gods are challenged to predict their future activities in advance. Only Jehovah can do so. (21-29)

Chapter 43—The Lord Will Claim His People When Babylon Falls.

1. The Lord redeemed Israel and will protect her. (1-4)
2. (30-31) The Lord will gather the seed of Israel from the east, west, north and south. (5-7)
3. The Israelites are the Lord's witnesses that he is God and the only Savior. (8-13)
4. The nobles of Babylon shall lie down together and be extinct. (14-17)
5. (30-31) The Lord will make a way in the wilderness, and rivers in the desert for his chosen people. (18-21)
6. Though Israel has sinned, the Lord will blot out her transgressions. (22-28)

Chapters 44 and 45—The Lord Will Raise Up Cyrus and Guide Him.

1. The Lord will bless Israel's crops and offspring. (44:1-5)
    Note: Jesurun means "upright." It is a symbolic name for Israel. (See Deut. 32:15.)
2. There is no God beside Jehovah. Worshipping idols is meaningless. (44:6-20)
3. The Lord has redeemed Israel. (44:21-27)
4. Cyrus (the Persian) will cause Jerusalem to be built. (44:28, 45:13)
5. The Lord will raise up Cyrus and guide him, though he will not know Him. (45:1-6)
6. Jehovah created the heavens and the earth. He is superior to idols. (45:7-22)

7. (47) The Lord has sworn that every knee shall bow and every tongue shall acknowledge Him. (45:23-25)

Chapter 48—The Lord Will Not Cast Off His People When Babylon is Destroyed.
  Note: This chapter is quoted in 1 Ne. 20. It is regarded as a recapitulation of Isaiah Chapters 40-47.
1. Hear this, you religious hypocrites who swear by the name of the Lord but are not righteous. (1-2)
2. The Lord has declared things from the beginning so when the prophecies came to pass they would know it was His work and not the work of idols. (3-8, 16-17)
3. To maintain His good name, the Lord will not cut off Israel. (9-13)
4. The Lord's arm shall be on Babylon. Go ye forth from there. (14, 20)
5. God provided water for his people as they came through the desert. (21-22)

Doctrinal Analysis of Isaiah, Section II

The Sins of Judah and Israel, Assyria and Babylon:
—They Rule Unrighteously:
1. Woe unto them that decree unrighteous decrees. (10:1)
2. They which lead thee cause thee to err, and destroy the way of thy paths. (3:12)

—They Pervert Justice:
1. They turn aside the needy from judgment. (10:2)
2. Woe unto them that justify the wicked for reward. (5:23)

—They Oppress the Unfortunate:
1. They take away the right from the poor people. (10:2)
2. They make widows their prey and rob the fatherless. (10:2)
3. They judge not the fatherless, neither doth the cause of the widow come unto them. (1:23)
4. Ye beat my people to pieces, and grind the faces of the poor. (3:15)
5. They join house to house and field to field, till there be no place. (5:8)

—They are Deceitful:
1. They are a hypocritical nation. (10:6)

ISAIAH—SECTION II

2. Burnt offerings, new moons and sabbaths, I am weary to bear them (because they are not performed in the spirit of true worship). (1:10-14)
3. Woe to them that call evil good and good evil. (5:20)
4. They mention the God of Israel, but not in truth, nor in righteousness. (48:1)

—They are Proud, Vain and Boastful:

1. He saith by the strength of my hand I have done it, and by my wisdom. (10:13)
2. Woe to them that draw iniquity with cords of vanity. (5:18)
3. Woe to them that are wise in their own eyes, and prudent in their own sight. (5:21)
4. Thy wisdom and thy knowledge, it hath perverted thee. (47:10)
5. Thou hast said in thy heart, I am, and none else beside me. (47:10)

—They are Rebellious:

1. I have nourished and brought up children, and they have rebelled against me. (1:2)
2. They have forsaken the Lord. (1:4)
3. Thy princes are rebellious and companions of thieves. (1:23)
4. Their tongue and their doings are against the Lord. (3:8)
5. They have cast away the law of the Lord of hosts, and despised the word of the Holy One of Israel. (5:24)

—They are Full of Iniquity:

1. They are a people laden with iniquity, a seed of evil doers, children that are corrupters. (1:4)
2. Jerusalem is full of murderers. (1:21)
3. They rise up early to follow strong drink; they continue until night till wine inflame them. (5:11)
4. Woe to them that are mighty to drink wine and mingle strong drink. (5:22)
5. Thy princes loveth gifts, and followeth after rewards. (1:23)

—They are Worldly Minded:

1. The daughters of Zion are haughty, and walk with stretched forth necks and wanton eyes, mincing as they go. (3:16)

2. They regard not the work of the Lord, neither consider the operation of his hands. (5:12)
3. Thou art given to pleasures and dwellest carelessly. (47:8)
4. Thou hast not called upon me, but thou hast been weary of me. (43:22)

—They are Without Knowledge:

1. Israel doth not know, my people doth not consider. (1:3)
2. My people are gone into captivity because they have no knowledge. (5:13)
3. None considereth in his heart, neither is there knowledge nor understanding. (44:19)

—They are Unmerciful:

1. Thou didst shew the Lord's people no mercy. (47:6)

—They are Guilty of Being Misled:

1. Idols have shut their eyes, that they cannot see, and their hearts, that they cannot understand. (44:18)
2. A deceived heart hath turned him aside, that he cannot deliver his soul. (44:20)

—Other Sins:

1. Woe to those that say, Let the Lord make speed, and hasten his work, that we may see it. (5:19)
2. They take away the righteousness of the righteous from him. (5:23)
3. Thou hast trusted in thy wickedness. Thou hast said, None seeth me. (47:10)
4. Thy teachers have transgressed against me. (43:27)

Punishments Upon Judah and Israel:

1. The Assyrian will be the rod of the Lord's anger. (10:5)
2. The Assyrian will take a spoil and a prey, and tread them down like mire in the streets. (10:6)
3. Your country is desolate, your cities are burned with fire, strangers devour your land in your presence. (1:7)
4. When ye spread forth your hands, I will hide mine eyes from you; yea, when ye make many prayers, I will not hear. (1:15)
5. The Lord doth take away from Jerusalem the man of war, the judge, the prophet, the captain, the honourable man, the counsellor, the cunning artificer. and the eloquent orator. (3:1-3)

Isaiah—Section II

6. I will give them children to be their princes, and babes shall rule over them. (3:4)
7. The people shall be oppressed, every one by his neighbor. (3:5)
8. The child shall behave himself proudly against the ancient. (3:5)
9. The Lord will take away the ornaments of the daughters of Zion, and give them baldness, sackcloth, and burning. (3:17-24)
10. Thy men shall fall by the sword. (3:25)

Judgment:
1. (There is a choice.) If ye be willing and obedient, ye shall eat the good of the land: but if ye refuse and rebel, ye shall be devoured with the sword. (1:19-20)
2. The shew of their countenance doth witness against them. (3:9)
3. They have rewarded evil unto themselves. (3:9:11)
4. Say ye to the righteous that it shall be well with him; for they shall eat the fruit of their doings. (3:10)
5. The mean man shall be brought down, and the eyes of the lofty shall be humbled. (5:15)
6. I will punish the world for their evil, and the wicked for their iniquity, and I will cause the arrogancy of the proud to cease, and will lay low the haughtiness of the terrible. (13:11)
7. Israel shall be saved in the Lord with an everlasting salvation. (45:17)
8. There is no peace, saith the Lord, unto the wicked. (48:22)

The Nature of God:
—God is Merciful and Forgiving:
1. Though your sins be as scarlet, they shall be as white as snow. (1:18)
2. The Lord will have mercy on Jacob. (14:1)
3. I am He that blotteth out thy transgressions for mine own sake, and will not remember thy sins. (43:25)
4. I have blotted out, as a thick cloud, thy transgressions, and, as a cloud, thy sins. (44:22)
5. Return unto me, for I have redeemed thee. (44:22)

—God is the Creator:
1. I will plant trees in the wilderness, that they may see and know that the Holy One of Israel hath created it. (41:19-20)

2. I will bring every one that is called by my name, for I have created him for my glory, I have formed him, yea, I have made him. (43:7)
3. I am the Lord, your Holy One, the creator of Israel, your king. (43:15)
4. Thus saith the Lord, that made thee, and formed thee from the womb ... (44:2)
5. Thus saith the Lord thy redeemer, and he that formed thee from the womb, I am the Lord that maketh all things; that stretcheth forth the heavens alone; that spreadeth abroad the earth by myself. (44:24)
6. I form the light, and create darkness: I make peace, and create evil: I the Lord do all these things. (45:7)
7. I have made the earth, and created man upon it, I have stretched out the heavens, and all their host have I commanded. (45:12)
8. Mine hand also hath laid the foundation of the earth ... (48:13)

—God is the Source of Good and of Help:
1. Fear not, for I am with thee: be not dismayed, for I am thy God: I will strengthen thee and help thee and uphold thee with the right hand of my righteousness. (41:10, 13)
2. I will help thee, saith the Lord, and thy redeemer, the Holy One of Israel. (41:14)
3. When the poor and needy seek water and there is none, I the Lord will hear them, I the Lord will not forsake them. (41:17)
4. I give waters in the wilderness, and rivers in the desert, to give drink to my people, my chosen. (43:20)
5. I will pour water upon him that is thirsty, and floods upon the dry ground. (44:3)
6. I am the Lord thy God which teacheth thee to profit, which leadeth thee by the way that thou shouldst go. (48:17)

—The Lord Is The Only God With Whom We are Concerned:
1. I am God, and there is none else; I am God, and there is none like me. (46:9)
2. I (am) the Lord, the first, and with the last. (41:4)
3. Before me there was no God formed, neither shall there be after me. I, even I, am the Lord; and beside me there is no savior. (43:10-11)
4. Before the day was I am he. (43:13)

ISAIAH—SECTION II

5. I am the first, and I am the last; and beside me there is no God. (44:6)
6. Is there a God beside me? yea, there is no God; I know not any. (44:8)
7. I am the Lord, and there is none else, there is no God beside me. (45:5)
8. I am the Lord, and there is none else. (45:18)
9. Look unto me and be ye saved, all the ends of the earth: for I am God, and there is none else. (45:22)
10. I will not give my glory unto another. (48:11)
11. I am he; I am the first, and also the last. (48:12)

—God Deflates Egotism:
1. The Lord turns wise men backward, and maketh their knowledge foolish. (44:25)

—God Must Be Sought to be Found:
1. Verily thou art a God that hidest thyself, O God of Israel, the Savior. (45:15)

—A God of Purpose:
1. Thus saith the Lord that created the heavens; God himself that formed the earth and made it, he formed it to be inhabited. (45:18)
2. I have sworn by myself, the word is gone out of my mouth in righteousness, and shall not return, that unto me every knee shall bow, every tongue shall swear. (45:23)

—A God of Righteousness and Holiness:
1. The Lord of hosts shall be exalted in judgment, and God that is holy shall be sanctified in righteousness. (5:16)
2. I bring near my righteousness; it shall not be far off, and my salvation will not tarry. (46:13)
3. I have not spoken in secret, in a dark place of the earth: I said not unto the seed of Jacob, Seek ye me in vain: I the Lord speak righteousness, I declare things that are right. (45:19)

—God Tests Men:
1. I have refined thee, but not with silver; I have chosen thee in the furnace of affliction. (48:10)

—The Lord is Man's Redeemer:
1. As for our redeemer, the Lord of hosts is his name, the Holy One of Israel. (47:4)

2. O Israel, Fear not, for I have redeemed thee. (43:1)
3. I am the Lord thy God, the Holy One of Israel, thy Savior. (43:3)
4. Return unto me, for I have redeemed thee. (44:22)

—**God Is Capable of Anger:**
1. They have provoked the Holy One of Israel unto anger. (1:4)
2. The anger of the Lord is kindled against his people, and he hath stretched forth his hand against them. (5:25)
3. I will take vengeance, and I will not meet thee as a man. (47:3)

—**God Controls the Earth:**
1. He stretched out his hand over the sea, he shook the kingdoms. (23:11)
2. Thus saith the Lord, which maketh a way in the sea, and a path in the mighty waters. (43:16)

—**God's Dealings With His Prophets—Revelation:**
1. I am God, declaring the end from the beginning, and from ancient times the things that are not yet done. I have spoken it, I will also bring it to pass; I have purposed it, I will also do it. (46:9-11)
2. Who hath wrought and done it, calling the generations from the beginning? I the Lord am he. (41:4)
3. I have declared, and have saved, and I have shewed ... therefore ye are my witnesses that I am God. (43:12)
4. I will pour my spirit upon thy seed, and my blessing upon thine offspring. (44:3)
5. And who, as I, shall call, and shall declare it, and set it in order for me, since I appointed the ancient people? and the things that are coming and shall come, let them shew unto them. (44:7)
6. The Lord confirms the word of his servant, and performeth the counsel of his messengers. (44:26)
7. Thus saith the Lord, Ask me of things to come concerning my sons, and concerning the work of my hands command ye me. (45:11)
8. I have declared the former things from the beginning; and they went forth out of my mouth, and I shewed them; I did them suddenly, and they came to pass. (48:3)
9. Because I knew that thou art obstinate, I have even from the beginning declared it to thee; before it came to pass

I shewed it thee, lest thou shouldst say, Mine idol hath done them. (48:4-5)
10. I have not spoken in secret from the beginning; from the time that it was, there am I: and now the Lord God, and his Spirit, hath sent me. (48:16)

The Last Days:
Shown in the chapter outline above.

Admonition to Repentance:
1. Wash you, make you clean; put away the evil of your doings from before mine eyes; cease to do evil. (1:16)

Counsel for Righteous Living:
1. Shall the axe boast itself against him that heweth therewith? (10:15)
2. Learn to do well; seek judgment, relieve the oppressed, judge the fatherless, plead for the widow. (1:17)
3. Come now, and let us reason together, saith the Lord. (1:18)
4. Good is the word of the Lord which thou hast spoken. For there shall be peace and truth in my days. (39:8)
5. The Lord hath founded Zion, and the poor of his people shall trust in it. (14:32)
6. Fear not, for I am with thee: be not dismayed; for I am thy God: I will strengthen thee and help thee and uphold thee with the right hand of my righteousness. (41:10, 13)
7. Ye are my witnesses, saith the Lord, and my servant whom I have chosen that ye may know and believe me and understand that I am he. (43:10, 44:8)
8. Put me in remembrance: let us plead together: declare thou, that thou mayest be justified. (43:26)
9. Woe unto him that striveth with his Maker! Shall the clay say to him that fashioneth it, What makest thou? or thy work, He hath no hands? (45:9-10)
10. Surely, shall one say, in the Lord have I righteousness and strength: even to him shall men come. (45:24)
11. O that thou hadst hearkened to my commandments! then had thy peace been as a river, and thy righteousness as the waves of the sea. (48:18)

Miscellaneous Choice Passages:
1. (There is life after death.) Hell is moved to meet thee at thy coming. It stirreth up the dead kings for thee,

and they shall speak and say unto thee, Art thou become weak as we? (14:9-11)
2. How art thou fallen from heaven, O Lucifer, son of the morning! Thou hast said I will exalt my throne above the stars of God, I will be like the most High. Yet thou shalt be brought down to hell. (14:12-15)
3. (God controls man from before birth.) Hearken unto me, O house of Jacob, which are borne by me from the belly, which are carried from the womb. Even to your old age and hoar hairs will I carry you. I have made, and I will bear; even I will carry and will deliver you. (46:3-4)

Summary of Isaiah—Section II:

After studying Section II of Isaiah the student should know:
1. The second period of prophetic fulfillment was before and during the fall of Judah, the Babylonian captivity and the Jewish return to Palestine (Primarily 635-535 B.C.).
2. Sixteen of the sixty-six chapters of Isaiah pertain to the second period of prophetic fulfillment.
3. The four major events of this period of which Isaiah prophesied were:
    A. The fall of Assyria to Babylon and Media.
    B. The fall of Judah to Babylonia.
    C. The fall of Babylonia to Persia.
    D. Judah's return from the Babylonian captivity.
4. One of Isaiah's most profound prophecies was his identification of Cyrus the Persian as the individual who would allow the Jews to return to Palestine.
5. This section contains numerous teachings in three major doctrinal areas:
    A. The nature of sin.
    B. The nature of God.
    C. The nature of revelation.

SECTION III

CHAPTERS OF ISAIAH PERTAINING TO THE THIRD PERIOD OF PROPHETIC FULFILLMENT: THE MINISTRY OF CHRIST IN THE MERIDIAN OF TIME

Most of Isaiah's prophecies concerning the earthly ministry of Christ do not stand as the major subject of his chapters. Rather, they are important insights into the Savior's ministry which are given in contrasting Isaiah's day with that of the Christ. Consequently, the pattern of considering the entire chapter in the context of the period of prophetic fulfillment of its major items will not be completely observed in this section. Instead, commentary on ten chosen passages plus three chapter outlines (Chapters 42, 50, 53) will be given.

The Birth of the Savior

Is. 7:14-16

Therefore the Lord himself shall give you a sign; Behold, a virgin shall conceive, and bear a son, and shall call his name Immanuel.

Butter and honey shall he eat, that he may know to refuse the evil, and choose the good.

For before the child shall know to refuse the evil, and choose the good, the land that thou abhorrest shall be forsaken of both her kings.

Explanation:

1. The entire chapter is outlined in Section I.
2. In the early days of the Syro-Ephraimite war Isaiah prophesied to Ahaz, king of Judah, that Israel and Syria would not be able to conquer Judah. Isaiah offered to show Ahaz a sign from the Lord to show that his prophecy was true, but Ahaz refused to ask for one. Isaiah insisted that a sign be given, saying that the Lord Himself would give it, and then he prophesied of the Lord's birth. His prophecy concerned an event which was to take place more than seven centuries later.
3. This passage was quoted to Joseph, the intended husband of Mary (the mother of Jesus) as evidence that Mary's

child-to-be was the result of God's will and that Mary still retained her virginity. (See Mt. 1:18-25)
4. See also Lu. 1:27, 1 Ne. 11:13, 15, 18, 20; 2 Ne. 17:14-16; Al. 7:10.

The Birth of the Savior

Is. 9:6-7

For unto us a child is born, unto us a son is given: and the government shall be upon his shoulder: and his name shall be called Wonderful, Counselor, The mighty God, the everlasting Father, The Prince of Peace.

Of the increase of his government and peace there shall be no end, upon the throne of David, and upon his kingdom, to order it, and to establish it with judgment and with justice (44) from henceforth even for ever. The zeal of the Lord of hosts will perform this.

Explanation:

1. The entire chapter is outlined in Section I.
2. This passage first tells of the birth of the Savior, and then describes the peace and order which will characterize the eternal reign of the Lord and those who rule under His direction on the throne of David in the last days.

The Savior's Labors in Galilee

Is. 9:1-2

Nevertheless the dimness shall not be such as was in her vexation, when at the first he lightly afflicted the land of Zebulun and the land of Naphtali, and afterward did more grievously afflict her by the way of the sea, beyond Jordan, in Galilee of the nations.

The people that walked in darkness have seen a great light: they that dwell in the land of the shadow of death, upon them hath the light shined.

Explanation:

1. The entire chapter is outlined in Section I.
2. This prophecy of the Savior, together with the messianic prophecy in Chapter 9, verses 6 and 7, were apparently given by Isaiah as words of comfort for the people taken by Assyria in the Galilean captivity. (c. 734 B. C.) He prophesied of Christ's early ministry in their area.
3. Matthew explained the fulfillment of the prophecy:

ISAIAH—SECTION III

Now when Jesus had heard that John was cast into prison, he departed into Galilee;

And leaving Nazareth, he came and dwelt in Capernaum, which is upon the sea coast, in the borders of Zabulon and Nephthalim;

That it might be fulfilled which was spoken by Esaias the prophet, saying

The land of Zabulon, and the land of Nephthalim, by way of the sea, beyond Jordan, Galilee of the Gentiles;

The people which sat in darkness saw great light; and to them which sat in the region and shadow of death light is sprung up. (Mt. 4:12-16)

A Stumbling Block to Israel
Is. 8:13-14

Sanctify the Lord of hosts himself; and let him be your fear, and let him be your dread.

And he shall be for a sanctuary; but for a stone of stumbling and for a rock of offence to both the houses of Israel, for a gin and for a snare to the inhabitants of Jerusalem.

Explanation:
1. The entire chapter is outlined in Section I.
2. Jesus truly was a stumbling stone for Judah. They crucified him and have reaped continual persecution for their deed for centuries.

A Sure Foundation Stone
Is. 28:16

Therefore thus saith the Lord God, Behold, I lay in Zion for a foundation a stone, a tried stone, a precious corner stone, a sure foundation: he that believeth shall not make haste.

Explanation:
1. The entire chapter is outlined in Section I.
2. Peter explained the passage when he wrote,

Ye also, as lively stones, are built up a spiritual house, an holy priesthood, to offer up spiritual sacrifices, acceptable to God by Jesus Christ.

Wherefore also it is contained in the scripture, Behold, I lay in Sion a chief corner stone, elect, precious: and he that believeth on him shall not be confounded. (1 Pet. 2:5-6)

Preceded by John the Baptist

Is. 40:3

The voice of him that crieth in the wilderness, Prepare ye the way of the Lord, make straight in the desert a highway for our God.

Explanation:
1. The entire chapter is outlined in Section IV.
2. The context of this passage clearly shows it to be a prophecy of a forerunner of Christ **in the last days** (see verses 4 and 5). Latter-day Saints believe this forerunner to be John the Baptist who restored the Aaronic Priesthood to Joseph Smith on May 15, 1829 (see Mal. 3:1-3 and Mt. 11:10-14; JS 2:26-72; D & C 84:27-28; D & C 27:7-8).
3. The New Testament writers, however, regarded John's ministry in their day as being the fulfillment of Isaiah's prophecy:

In those days came John the Baptist, preaching in the wilderness of Judea,

And saying, Repent ye: for the kingdom of heaven is at hand.

For this is he that was spoken of by the prophet Esaias, saying, The voice of one crying in the wilderness, Prepare ye the way of the Lord, make his paths straight. (Mt. 3:1-3) (See also Mk. 1:3; Lk. 3:5; Jn. 1:23.)

The First Servant Song—Christ's Characteristics and Deeds

Chapter 42:

Note: Verses 1-9 are the first of four "Servant Songs" in which Isaiah describes the Lord.

1. The Savior's characteristics and deeds are listed:
   A. **Characteristics**
      (1). He shall have God's spirit. (1)
      (2). He shall not cry, nor lift up (boast). (2)
      (3). He shall be gentle. (3)
      (4). He shall not fail nor be discouraged. (4)
      (5). He is the Lord. (8)
      (6). He will not give his glory to another. (8)
      (7). He will not praise graven images. (8)
      (8). He will declare new things before they come to pass. (9)

ISAIAH—SECTION III 341

    B. **Deeds**
        (1). (4) He shall bring forth judgment to the Gentiles. (1)
        (2). (44) He shall set judgment in the earth unto truth. (3-4)
        (3). He created the heavens and the earth. (5)
        (4). He gives breath and spirit to people. (5)
        (5). He will serve as a covenant for the people. (6)
        (6). (7) He will be a light unto the Gentiles. (6)
        (7). He will heal the blind. (7)
        (8). (46) He will bring prisoners from the (spirit?) prison. (7)
  2. A song of praise for God. (10-13)
  3. The Lord proclaims the mighty deeds He will do, causing those who have not trusted Him to be ashamed. (14-17)
  4. (I) Israel is the Lord's servant, but is blind. (18-22)
  5. (I) The Lord has given Israel to the robbers because it sinned against Him. (23-25)

The Second Servant Song—Christ's Characteristics and Deeds

Is. 49:1-13
1. The entire chapter is outlined in Section IV.
2. In this section the Savior seems to be speaking of his mission with scattered Israel. As in the first Servant Song, He lists both His characteristics and His deeds.

    A. **Characteristics**
        (1). He was called from the womb. (5)
        (2). He was known by name before birth. (1)
        (3). His judgment and work is with God. (4)
        (4). He is faithful. (7)
    B. **Deeds**
        (1). He has made Isaiah his servant so he may be glorified. (2-3)
        (2). (30-31) He will raise up the tribes of Jacob. (6)
        (3). (30-31) He will restore the preserved of Israel. (6)
        (4). (7) He will be a light to the Gentiles. (6)
        (5). He is the source of the earth's salvation. (6)
        (6). He will be a covenant for the people. (8)
        (7). (46) He shall release prisoners. (9)

(8). He will comfort His people. (13)
(9). He will have mercy upon the afflicted. (13)

The Third Servant Song—Christ's Suffering and Passion
Chapter 50

Note: This chapter is quoted in 2 Ne. 8.
1. (I) The Lord has not divorced Israel. You have sold yourselves through sin. (1)
2. The Lord still has power to deliver and redeem His people. (2-3)
3. The Servant Song: The Lord's Suffering and Passion. (4-11)
    A. He gave his back to the smiters. (6) (see Mk. 14:65)
    B. He hid not his face from shame and spitting. (6) (see Mk. 14:65)
    C. God will help Him. (7-9)
    D. Trust in the Lord. (10-11)

The Fourth Servant Song—Christ's Suffering and Passion
Chapter 53

Note: The "Servant Song" extends from 52:13 to 53:12. Chapter 53 is quoted in Mos. 14.
1. He shall grow up as a tender plant, and as a root out of dry ground. (2)
2. He hath no form nor comeliness, nor beauty that he should be desired. (2)
3. He is despised, not esteemed, and rejected of men. (3) (see Jn. 1:11)
4. He is a man of sorrows, and acquainted with grief. (3)
5. He has borne our griefs and carried our sorrows. (4) (see Mt. 8:16-17)
6. He was wounded for our transgressions and bruised for our iniquities. (5) (see Rom. 4:25)
7. With His stripes we are healed. (5) (See I Pet. 2:24)
8. He opened not His mouth. (7) (see Mt. 27:11-14)
9. He was taken from prison and from judgment. (8). (see Mk. 15:1-15)
10. He was cut off out of the land of the living. (8)
11. For the transgression of the people was He stricken. (8)
12. He made his grave with the wicked, He was numbered with the transgressors. (9, 12) (see Mt. 27:38)

ISAIAH—SECTION III 343

13. He was with the rich in his death. (9)
14. He bare the sin of many and made intercession for the transgressors. (10-12) (see Rom. 8:34)

An Intercessor
Is. 59:15-16

Yea, truth faileth; and he that departeth from evil maketh himself a prey: and the Lord saw it, and it displeased him that there was no judgment.

And he saw that there was no man, and wondered that there was no intercessor: therefore his arm brought salvation unto him; and his righteousness, it sustained him.

Explanation:
1. The entire chapter is outlined in Section 1.
2. One function Jesus fulfills is that of making intercession for man with the Father. (see Heb. 7:25; Rom. 8:27)

Christ Sent to Proclaim the Acceptable Year of the Lord
Is. 61:1-2

The Spirit of the Lord God is upon me; because the Lord hath anointed me to preach good tidings unto the meek; he hath sent me to bind up the brokenhearted, to proclaim liberty to the captives, and the opening of the prison to them that are bound;

To proclaim the acceptable year of the Lord, and the day of vengeance of our God; to comfort all that mourn; . . .

Explanation:
1. The entire chapter is outlined in Section IV.
2. Christ, while teaching in the synagogue in Nazareth, read this scripture from "the prophet Esaias" and then told the congregation, "This day is this scripture fulfilled in your ears." (see Lk. 4:16-21)

The Dead to Rise with Him
Is. 26:19

Thy dead men shall live, together with my dead body shall they arise. Awake and sing, ye that dwell in dust: for thy dew is as the dew of herbs, and the earth shall cast out the dead.

Explanation:
1. The entire chapter is outlined in Section IV.

2. Many of the righteous dead were resurrected and came out of their graves at the time Jesus was resurrected. (see Mt. 27:52-53)

Doctrinal Analysis of Isaiah—Section III:

The Sins of Israel:
1. They would not walk in his ways, neither were they obedient unto his law. (42:24)

The Price of Sin (Judgment):
1. For your iniquities have ye sold yourselves, and for your transgressions is your mother put away. (50:1)

The Nature of God:
1. Thus saith God the Lord, he that created the heavens, and stretched them out; he that spread forth the earth, and that which cometh out of it; he that giveth breath unto the people upon it, and spirit to them that walk therein . . . (42:5)
2. I am the Lord: that is my name: and my glory will I not give to another. (42:8)
3. The Lord shall go forth as a mighty man, he shall stir up jealousy like a man of war: he shall prevail against his enemies. (42:13)
4. I will make the rivers islands, I will dry up the pools. (42:15)
5. He hath poured upon him the fury of his anger, and the strength of battle. (42:25)
6. At my rebuke, I dry up the sea, I make the rivers a wilderness: Their fish stinketh, because there is no water, and dieth for thirst. (50:2)
7. He was wounded for our transgressions, he was bruised for our iniquities: with his stripes we are healed. The Lord hath laid on him the iniquity of us all. (53:5-6)
8. For the transgression of my people was he stricken. (53:8)
9. He had done no violence, neither was any deceit in his mouth. (53:9)
10. Thou shalt make his soul an offering for sin. (53:10)
11. By his knowledge shall my righteous servant justify many; for he shall bear their iniquities. (53:11)
12. He bare the sin of many, and made intercession for the transgressors. (53:12)

ISAIAH—SECTION III 345

God's Dealings With His Prophets:
1. Behold, the former things are come to pass, and new things do I declare: before they spring forth I tell you of them. (42:9)

The Last Days:
Shown in the chapter outline above.

Counsel for Righteous Living:
1. Sing unto the Lord a new song, and his praise from the end of the earth. (42:10-12)
2. The Lord is well pleased for his righteousness' sake; he will magnify the law, and make it honourable. (42:21)
3. The Lord God hath given me the tongue of the learned, that I should know how to speak a word in season to him that is weary. (50:4)
4. Who is among you that feareth the Lord, that obeyeth the voice of his servant, that walketh in darkness, and hath no light? let him trust in the name of the Lord, and stay upon his God. (50:10)
5. All ye that kindle a fire, that compass yourselves about with sparks: walk in the light of the fire, and in the sparks that ye have kindled. (50:11)

Summary of Isaiah—Section III:

After studying Section III of Isaiah the student should know:
1. Isaiah prophesied of many events in the mortal life of the Savior, including:
   A. His birth
      —A virgin shall conceive, and bear a son, and shall call his name Immanuel.
      —For unto us a child is born, unto us a son is given.
   B. His Galilean ministry
      —The people that dwelt in darkness have seen a great light.
   C. His forerunner, John the Baptist
      —The voice of him that crieth in the wilderness.
   D. His suffering
      —He gave his back to the smiters.
      —He hid not his face from shame and spitting.

  E. His death
   —He has borne our griefs and carried our sorrows.
   —He was wounded for our transgressions and bruised for our iniquities.
   —He bare the sin of many and made intercession for the transgressors.
  F. His resurrection
   —Thy dead men shall live, together with my dead body shall they arise.
2. Reference to many of Isaiah's prophecies concerning Christ is made in New Testament passages.
3. The third period of prophetic fulfillment deals with events pertaining to the ministry of Christ in the meridian of time.
4. Three of the sixty-six chapters of Isaiah, plus numerous other passages, refer to the third period of prophetic fulfillment.
5. These three chapters are "Servant Songs."

SECTION IV

CHAPTERS OF ISAIAH PERTAINING TO THE FOURTH PERIOD OF PROPHETIC FULFILLMENT: THE LAST DAYS

The chapters discussed in this section form the largest portion of the book of Isaiah and pertain to the most predominant theme of the Old Testament prophets. The prophecies of the last days are important to everyone, for in them modern man finds the future laid out in a pattern before him. In them he finds a pattern by which he can prepare for that which lies ahead. This pattern is the plan which God has devised for His children in the last days. These prophecies are subject to interpretation and the interpretation, like the prophecy itself, must be made under inspiration and through the spirit of prophecy.

The vast amount of prophetic material found in the Old Testament creates an almost overwhelming obstacle to the beginning student of prophecy. The material is interrelated and complicated and requires an extensive background for one to be able to fully understand it. To aid the reader in the consideration of the prophecies of the last days a chronological list of fifty events has been established,[3] and is explained in detail earlier in this book. Each major prophesied event has been placed in a numbered order.

The entire scope of the eschatological[4] prophecies made by Isaiah which are to be studied in this section is keyed with the number code which refers to these events. The author recognizes that all students will not agree in every instance with his relegation of the prophecies to the predetermined future event. (Wouldn't it be a drab world if everyone did agree on such matters?!) Nevertheless, it is his belief that the number key can serve as a helpful device to aid people in their study of Old Testament prophecies. Section IV of Isaiah is a consideration of twenty-seven chapters: 29, 18, 54,

---

[3]The ordered list has been adapted from the author's books *The Prophecies of Joseph Smith* and *Prophecy—Key to the Future*. Evidence for his ordering of the prophetic events will be found in those volumes. They also serve to give a fuller and more complete explanation of the prophesied events of the last days than is attempted in this volume.

[4]Means "of or pertaining to the last days."

49, 52, 35, 27, 55, 11, 51, 4, 62, 60, 61, 66, 12, 40, 2, 63, 64, 26, 24, 34, 33, 65, 32, and 25. As in the previous sections on Isaiah, the chapters of this section are also arranged in a chronological order according to when they will take place. It will be helpful to read and study them in this order.

Restoration of the Book of Mormon

Chapter 29—The Coming Forth of the Book of Mormon.

Note: This chapter would be one of the most difficult of all the prophecies in the Bible, if it were not for the aid of a passage from the Book of Mormon which clarifies it and gives it the necessary interpretation. In the Book of Mormon passage (2 Ne. 26-27) Nephi shows that the prophecy deals with eight items (numbers 2-9 below) which are connected with the Book of Mormon and the restoration of the gospel.

1. A change of subject. Verses 1 and 2 begin by talking about Ariel (Jerusalem) and the manner in which it will be distressed. Then the subject is changed with these words: and it shall be unto me as Ariel (1-2), and the prophecy speaks of events which were to take place in the Americas.

2. (2) The fall of the Nephites and the preserving of the Book of Mormon plates. (3-5)

    A. I will camp against thee round about. (3) The Nephites were to be surrounded. (See 2 Ne. 26:15; Morm. 6:1-5, 7-8.)

    B. Thou shalt be brought down. (4) The Nephites were to be defeated. (See 2 Ne. 26:15.)

    C. Thou shalt speak out of the ground. (4) The Nephite records would be preserved and would come forth out of the ground. (See 2 Ne. 26:16, Morm. 6:6, 14, Moro. 10:2, J.S. 2:59.)

    D. Thy voice shall be as one that hath a familiar spirit. (4) Those who heard the message of the Nephite records would recognize it as being something familiar to them. (See 2 Ne. 26:16, 30:4-6.)

    E. It shall be at an instant suddenly. (5) The battle will be of short duration. (See 2 Ne. 26:18, Morm. 6:9-15.)

3. Thou shalt be visited with thunder, earthquake, noise, storm, and fire. (6) The great destruction which came

ISAIAH—SECTION IV 349

to the Americas at the time of Christ's crucifixion. (See 3 Ne. 8.)

4. (1) The Lord hath covered your prophets and seers. (9-10) The apostate condition that befell the Lamanites and the world in general. (See 2 Ne. 27:4-5, Morm. 1:13-19.)

5. (2) And the vision of all is become unto you as the words of a book that is sealed. (11) The coming forth of the Book of Mormon in the last days. (See 2 Ne. 27:6-8, J.S. 2:34.)

6. (2) The words of the book shall be delivered to one that is learned, saying Read this, I pray thee: and he saith I cannot, for it is sealed. (11-12) The Professor Anthon incident. (See 2 Ne. 27:9-10, 15-22; J. S. 2:64-65.)

7. (3) Wherefore the Lord said, the people draw near me with their mouth, and with their lips do honour me, but have removed their heart far from me. (13) Christ's words to Joseph Smith in his first vision, in which he was warned not to join any of the churches then in existence. (See 2 Ne. 27:25, J. S. 2:19.)

8. (3) I will do a marvelous work and a wonder among this people. (14) The restoration of the gospel. (See 2 Ne. 27:26.)

9. (2) The deaf shall hear the words of the book, and the eyes of the blind shall see out of darkness. (18) The carrying of the words of the Book of Mormon to the deaf and blind. (See 2 Ne. 27:29.)

10. (30-31) Lebanon shall be a fruitful field. (15-17)
11. (42) The wicked will be cut off. (19-21)
12. (38) Jacob shall sanctify the name of the Lord and learn doctrine. (22-24)

God Will Pour Out His Judgments

Chapter 18—**Desolation in the Americas.**[5]

1. Woe to the land identified in this manner:

　　A. Shadowing with wings. (1) (The American continents form the image of two wings.)

　　B. Beyond Ethiopia. (1) (As seen from Palestine.)

　　C. That sends ambassadors by sea in vessels of bulrushes. (2) (Many pipes?)

---

[5]For further explanation and original sources for the interpretation of this prophecy, see *Prophecy—Key to the Future*, p. 38-39.

D. The messengers will go to a nation scattered and peeled. (2) (American missionaries will be sent to gather Israel.)

E. That lifts up an ensign. (3) (The Church was restored in America.)

F. The ensign is lifted up upon the mountains. (3)

2. (14) They shall be cut off and left for the fowls and the beasts to eat. (4-6) (Destruction in the Americas—the Lord's desolating scourge?)
3. (22) In that time the nation scattered and peeled shall be brought unto Mount Zion. (7) (See D & C 115:6.)

Chapter 54—The Coming of the Ten Tribes to the New Jerusalem (In America).

Note:

a. The chronological determination for the interpretation of this passage is found in 3 Ne. 21:14-22:1. This passage also shows that Is. 54 is to find its fulfillment in the Americas.

b. This chapter was quoted by the Savior to the Nephites. (See 3 Ne. 22.)

1. (22) The children of the desolate are more than the children of the married wife. (1) (When the ten tribes come to the New Jerusalem they will outnumber the members of the Church gathered there.)
2. (22) Thy seed shall inhabit the desolate cities of the Gentiles. (2-3) (The ten tribes will find vacated cities in the New Jerusalem area of Missouri and will occupy them.)
3. (22) Though the Lord has hidden His face from Israel for a moment, He will remember and comfort His people in that day. (4-10)
4. (20) The Lord will lay thy stones with fair colours, and thy foundations with sapphires. (11-12) (The ten tribes will aid in the construction of the beautiful New Jerusalem.)
5. (23) Thy children shall be taught of the Lord. Thou shalt not fear. (13-14) (The Lord will teach the people when He comes to the New Jerusalem temple.)
6. (25) Enemies will gather against them, but not by the Lord. No weapon that is formed against them shall prosper. (15-17)

ISAIAH—SECTION IV   351

Chapter 49—The Second "Servant Song"—The Coming of the Ten Tribes to the New Jerusalem and Their Removal to Palestine.

   Note: This chapter is quoted in 1 Ne. 21 and 2 Ne. 6:6-7. 1 Ne. 22 aids in its interpretation.

1. Though Israel be not gathered, yet shall I be glorious in the eyes of the Lord. (5)
2. (22) The Lord will raise up the tribes of Jacob and restore the preserved of Israel. (6)

   Note: Another clue—the people of whom the Lord is speaking are still associated together in tribes.

3. (22) The Lord will also be a light to the Gentiles and the salvation for all the earth. (6)

   Note: In addition to helping these tribes, the Lord will also be a light unto the Gentiles. When else do we know of a group of tribes being associated with the Gentiles except when they come and mingle with the converted Gentiles in the New Jerusalem? (See 3 Ne. 21:14, 22-26.)

4. The Lord shall be worshipped by kings and princes. (7)
5. (22) The Lord will cause them to inherit the desolate heritages. (8)

   Note: When the Ten Tribes come to the New Jerusalem area, they are to inherit the nearby cities which have been left desolate. (See Is. 54:22, 3 Ne. 21:26-22:3.)

6. (22) The Lord will lead his people. He will make all His mountains a way, and His highways shall be exalted. (9-11) (See D & C 133:26-29)
7. (22) These shall come from far: from the north and from the west, and from the land of Sinim (location unknown). (12-13)
8. (22) Thy destroyers and they that made thee waste shall go forth of thee. (17) (See D & C 133:28.)
9. (22) The waste and desolate places they inherit will be too crowded for them. They will object to them and the people there. (18-21)

   Note: Is this the reason why the Ten Tribes move from the New Jerusalem to Palestine?

The Gathering of Israel to Palestine

Chapter 52—The Return and Redemption of Israel.

Note: This passage is quoted in 3 Ne. 20 and Mos. 15:8-10.

1. (24, 38) Put on thy strength, O Zion. (1) (See Moro. 10:31.)

Note:

This passage is interpreted in the Doctrine and Covenants as follows:

What is meant by the command in Isaiah, 52nd Chapter, 1st verse, which saith: Put on thy strength, O Zion—and what people had Isaiah reference to?

He had reference to those whom God should call in the last days, who should hold the power of the priesthood to bring again Zion, and the redemption of Israel; and to put on her strength is to put on the authority of the priesthood, which she, Zion, has a right to by lineage; also to return to that power which she had lost. (D & C 113:7-8)

2. (30) Loose thyself from the bands of thy neck, O captive daughter of Zion. (2)

Note:

This passage is interpreted in the Doctrine and Covenants as follows:

What are we to understand by Zion loosing herself from the bands of her neck; 2nd verse?

We are to understand that the scattered remnants are exhorted to return to the Lord from whence they have fallen; which if they do, the promise of the Lord is that he will speak to them, or give them revelation. See the 6th, 7th, and 8th verses. The bands of her neck are the curses of God upon her, or the remnants of Israel in their scattered condition among the Gentiles. (D & C 113:9-10)

3. Since his people have been oppressed, the Lord will redeem them. (3-6)
4. (24) How beautiful upon the mountains are the feet of him that bringeth good tidings by telling Zion that God reigneth! (7) (See Mos. 15:13-18.)
5. (30) The Lord will redeem the waste places of Jerusalem and all the nations shall see His salvation together. (8-10)
6. (30-31) Israel will be called out of wickedness and God will protect her in her return. (11-12)
7. (III) The beginning of the fourth "Servant Song." (13-15)

ISAIAH—SECTION IV 353

Note: This passage is considered in Section III.

Chapter 35—The Desert Shall Blossom as the Ransomed of the Lord Returns.

Note: This prophecy is often interpreted as referring to the Saints in the United States. The use of the phrase "the desert shall rejoice, and blossom as the rose" has been especially common among members of the Church as a reference to the productivity of the valleys of Utah. Certainly a parallel can be drawn between the growth and development of the Utah area and the prophesied growth and development of Palestine. Yet Isaiah clearly had reference to the Palestine area when he made the prophecy. Note that the identifying places he mentions are areas in northern Palestine: "The glory of Lebanon **shall be given unto it**, the excellency of Carmel and Sharon, **they shall see the glory of the Lord** . . ." (35:2)

1. (30-31) The desert shall rejoice, and blossom as the rose. (1-2)
2. (30-31) The weak will be strengthened in their journey (to Zion). (3-6)
3. (30-31) Waters and streams will break out in the desert. (6-7)
4. (30-31) A highway shall be there, called the way of holiness, and the ransomed of the Lord shall return to Zion. (8-10)

Chapter 27—Israel Shall Be Gathered and Fill the World With Fruit.

1. (30-31) Israel shall blossom and bud, and fill the world with fruit. (1-6)
2. The Lord has not punished Israel with the same severity as He has other nations. (7-11)
3. (30-31) Israel shall be gathered and worship in Jerusalem. (12-13)

David The Prince

Chapter 55—The Rule of David the Prince.

Note: A portion of this chapter is quoted in 2 Ne. 26.
1. An invitation to Christ. (1-2)
2. (32) Prince David will rule. (3-5)
    A. He will be a witness to the people. (4)
    B. He will be a leader and commander. (4)

C. He shall call a nation he does not know. (4)
   D. Nations which don't know him, shall run unto him. (5)
   E. The Lord will glorify him. (5)
3. Seek the Lord. He will abundantly pardon. (6-7)
4. God's ways and thoughts are not the same as man's. (8-11)
5. (30-31) The land shall be fertile. (12-13)

Chapter 11—The Rod and Branch and the Gathering to Palestine.

Note: This chapter was quoted in its entirety by Moroni to Joseph Smith. Moroni told him that "it was about to be fulfilled." (JS 2:40) It is also quoted in 2 Ne. 21.

1. (32?) A rod and branch shall come out of the stem of Jesse. (1-5)
   A. He shall have the spirit of the Lord. (2)
   B. He shall judge the poor and meek with righteousness. (3-4)
   C. (35?) He shall slay the wicked. (4)

Note:

a. The rod and branch are probably the same person. This is probably synonymous parallelism.[6]
b. The Doctrine and Covenants gives these items of interpretation:
   (1) The stem is Christ. (D & C 113:1-2)
   (2) The rod is "a servant in the hands of Christ, who is partly a descendant of Jesse as well as of Ephraim, or of the house of Joseph, on whom there is laid much power." (D & C 113:3-4)
c. 2 Ne. 30:1-15 shed light on the passage. In the context it is shown that these events will precede the time in question: (1) the Book of Mormon will come forth from the Gentiles to the Lamanites (v. 3-4), (2) the Lamanites will accept the gospel (v. 5-6),[7] (3) the Jews will gather in and begin to believe in Christ (v. 7-8),[8] then the passage says:

---

[6]Synonymous parallelism is a common technic used in Hebrew poetry in which one line expresses a thought and the next line repeats the same thought in different words.
[7]Item 21 on the list of events of the last days.
[8]Item 30 on the list of events of the last days.

ISAIAH—SECTION IV 355

> And with righteousness shall the Lord God judge the poor, and reprove with equity for the meek of the earth. And he shall smite the earth with the rod of his mouth; and with the breath of his lips shall he slay the wicked. For the time speedily cometh that the Lord God shall cause a great division among the people, and the wicked will he destroy; and he will spare his people, yea even if it so be that he must destroy the wicked by fire. And righteousness shall be the girdle of his loins, and faithfulness the girdle of his reins. (2 Ne. 30:9-11)

Note that in the Book of Mormon passage it is the Lord, not the rod (the servant in the hands of Christ of D & C 113:3-4) who judges and smites, yet Isaiah clearly states that it is the rod who does this. (This is not a serious dilemma if we realize that the rod will be acting as Christ's agent so they will both judge and smite.)

2. (44) Peace during the millennium. (6-9) (See D & C 29:11.)
3. (44?) In that day there shall be a root of Jesse, which shall stand for an ensign; to it shall the Gentiles seek. (10)

Note:
a. The Doctrine and Covenants gives this interpretation:
   (1) The root is "a descendant of Jesse, as well as of Joseph, unto whom rightly belongs the priesthood, and the keys of the kingdom, for an ensign and for the gathering of my people in the last days." (D & C 113: 5-6)
b. Some interpretive questions with theoretical answers:
   (1) Is the **rod** of Is. 11:1 the same person as the **root** of Is. 11:10?
   Some say yes, pointing out that they are described as being descendants of both Jesse and Joseph in D & C 113.
   Some say no, asserting that the rod is a descendant of the root (Is. 11:1). Thus, their lineage is the same but they are different individuals.
   (2) Is the root Joseph Smith?
   Some say yes, and assert these bits of evidence in interpretation of Is. 11:10:
      a. Joseph Smith restored the Church which has stood as an ensign. (See D & C 64:37-42.)

      b. He brought in the fulness of the Gentiles and the Gentiles joined themselves to him. (See D & C 45:28.)

      c. He held the priesthood and the keys of the kingdom for the gathering in the last days. (See D & C 27:12-13, 110:11.)

    Some say no, **if the root and the rod are the same person,** because:

      a. The rod apparently smites his enemies. This was not characteristic of the Prophet Joseph.

      b. The rod apparently lives into the millennium, which Joseph Smith did not do.

      c. If the root lives on into the millennium, his time will be after the time of the Gentiles is fulfilled. Thus the Gentiles probably would not see him.

  (3) Could it be that the rod and the root are separate individuals; that the root is Joseph Smith and the rod is David, the prince who will rule in Palestine during the Battle of Armageddon?

    This is the answer that fits best. In this way Joseph Smith meets the qualifications set forth in question 2 above, and David meets the qualifications of the rod who judges in righteousness yet slays the wicked (in the Battle of Armageddon) and lives into the millennium.

4. (30-31) Israel and Judah shall be gathered to Palestine. (11-12)[9]

5. (34) Israel and Judah will unite and stand together against their enemies. (13-16)

The Battle of Armageddon

Chapter 51—The Battle of Armageddon and the Lord's Eternal Righteousness.

Note: This chapter is quoted in 2 Ne. 8.

1. Remember Abraham and Sarah. (Just as the Lord blessed this childless couple with a child, He will remember and bless Israel.) (1-2)

2. (30-31) The Lord will comfort Zion, and make her waste places fertile. (3)

---

[9]For a map identifying the nations mentioned here see *Prophecy—Key to the Future,* p. 136.

ISAIAH—SECTION IV

3. (48, 49) The heavens shall vanish and the earth shall wax old like a garment, but the Lord's salvation will continue forever. (4-6)
4. (42 or 45, 48) The wicked shall be destroyed, but the Lord's righteousness shall be forever. (7-8)
5. A plea for the Lord to aid Israel as He did when He brought them out of Egypt. (9-10)

Note:
"Rahab"—a poetical name for Egypt which means "proud".
"dragon"—probably a symbolic representation of Egypt.

6. (30-31) The Lord will help Israel to return with joy and singing. (11-16)
7. (35) Jerusalem will drink the cup of the Lord's fury. (17-18)
8. (35) These two things are come unto thee: Thy sons will lie in the streets of Jerusalem, who have been full of fury of the Lord. (19-20) (See 2 Ne. 8:19-20, Rev. 11:1-13.)
9. (35) The Lord will take His fury from Israel and place it on those who afflict her. (22-23)

Chapter 4—The Glory of Jerusalem During the Rule of David the Prince Following the Battle of Armageddon.
   Note: This chapter is quoted in 2 Ne. 14.
1. (I?) Seven women shall take hold of one man, seeking to be called by his name. (1)
   Note: It is doubtful that this verse is referring to a latter-day period, for it seems to fit into the context of Chapter 3, but not into that of Chapter 4. See discussion of the passage under Section II, pp. 322-323.
2. (32) In that day (the day when there will be those of Israel who have escaped) shall the branch of the Lord be beautiful. (2)
   Note: The branch is apparently the prince, David, who is to rule in Palestine in the last days. (See Is. 11:1-5, then D & C 113:4)[10]
3. (38) He that is left in Jerusalem (after the Lord has purged its filth by judgment and burning) shall be called holy. (3)
4. (35) The Lord will purge Jerusalem. (3-4)

---
[10]For a detailed discussion of the identity of the "branch", see *Prophecy—Key to the Future*, pp. 179-182.

5. (39) The Lord will place his glory (smoke or fire) upon Zion as a defense. (5-6)

Note:
a. The previous context of the chapter places this event as following the purge of Jerusalem, apparently in the interval between Christ's coming to the temple in Jerusalem and His coming in glory.
b. Some L.D.S. interpreters have cited this as reference to the city of New Jerusalem in Missouri, based on D & C 84:2. Though their interpretation may be valid, what purge is to take place in that city which will cause the people to escape? How do they understand the "branch" as being in the New Jerusalem instead of in Palestine?

The Third and Fourth Periods of Missionary Labor and the Glory of Israel

Chapter 62—The Righteousness of Jerusalem After Israel is Restored to Palestine.
1. (39) The Lord will not rest until the righteousness of Jerusalem goes forth as brightness, and the salvation thereof as a lamp that burneth. (1)
2. Israel will no longer be called Desolate, but will have a new name: Hephzibah (Hĕph'-zi-băh), meaning "my delight is in her." (1-5)
3. The Lord's servants (angels?) will give Him no rest till He make Jerusalem a praise. (6-7)
4. (41) The good things of Palestine will no longer be given to enemies. (8-9)
5. (30-31) Cast up the highway, lift up a standard for the people. (10)
6. (30-31) The Lord will send a message throughout the world to Israel that His salvation cometh. (11)
7. (41) They shall call them The Holy People, the redeemed of the Lord. (12)

Chapter 60—The Glory of Israel in Palestine Following Christ's Coming to the Jerusalem Temple.
1. (39) The glory of the Lord is upon Israel, yet gross darkness covers the people of the earth. (1-2)
2. (41) The Gentiles and kings shall come to thy light. (3-4)
3. (41) The abundance of the sea shall be given to Israel; the surrounding nations will bring their treasures. (5-8)

ISAIAH—SECTION IV 359

4. Thy sons shall come from far with treasure because the Lord hath glorified thee. (9)
5. (41) The sons of strangers shall build up thy walls, and their kings shall minister unto thee. (10-11)
6. (41) The nation and kingdom that will not serve thee shall perish. (12)
7. (33) Wood from Lebanon will be brought to adorn the sanctuary. (13-17)
8. (41) Those that despised Israel and the sons of those that afflicted her will bow down to her. (14)
9. (41) Thou shalt suck the milk of the Gentiles and kings. (16)
10. (41) Violence shall no more be heard in the land. (18)
11. (39) The glory of the Lord shall be there and provide light. (19-20)
12. (41) A little one shall become a thousand, and a small one a strong nation. (21-22)

Chapter 61—The Seed of Israel to Be Ministers Among the Gentiles.

1. (III) The Lord will proclaim the acceptable year of the Lord. (1:2) (See Lk. 4:16-21.)
   Note: This passage is considered in Section III.
2. (30-31) They shall build the old waste and desolate cities, while strangers tend their flocks. (3-5)
3. (40, 41) Men will call the people of Israel the ministers of God; their seed will be known among the Gentiles. (6-9)
4. (40, 41) The Lord will cause righteousness and praise to spring forth before all the nations. (10-11)

Chapter 66—Missionary Work Following the Battle of Armageddon.

1. The heaven is the Lord's throne, the earth His footstool; Where is His house for him here on the earth? (1-2)
2. (I) The outward sacrifices of Israel are an abomination before God. (3-4)
3. (37) The Lord shall appear to your joy. There will be noise from the city and the temple as the Lord renders recompense to his enemies. (5-6)
4. (30-31) Israel travailed and brought forth a man child before her pain came. (7-8)
   Note: Some interpret the man child as being the newly established nation of Israel. The nation of Israel is

established before the pain of her cleansing in the battle of Armageddon.
5. (41) Jerusalem shall be comforted. She shall have peace like a river and the glory of the Gentiles like a flowing stream. (9-13)
6. (35) The Lord will show His indignation upon His enemies, and the slain of the Lord shall be many. (14-17)
7. (41) The nations will gather to Jerusalem to see the Lord's glory. Those that have escaped will be sent to the nations to declare the glory of God among the Gentiles. (18-19)
8. (41) The nations will help bring the remaining members of Israel as an offering to the Lord. (19-21)
9. (44) The Lord will create a new heaven and a new earth. (22)
10. (41) Israel's seed and all flesh will come up to worship him. (22-23)
11. (35) Men will see the carcasses of those who have transgressed against the Lord. (24)

Chapter 12—**Praise to Jehovah.**
Note: This chapter is quoted in 2 Ne. 22.
1. (41) A song of praise unto God when his goodness is known throughout all the earth. (1-6)

Christ's Coming in Glory

Chapter 40—**The Incomparable Glory of the Lord Will Be Revealed.**
1. (42) Every valley shall be exalted, and every mountain and hill shall be made low. (3-4)
2. (42) The glory of the Lord shall be revealed, and all flesh shall see it together. (5)
3. (42) Temporal things will wither but the word of God shall stand forever. (6-8)
4. (44) The Lord God will rule from Jerusalem. (9-11)
5. The Lord has controlled the earth and has knowledge. (12-14)
6. There is no one that can be likened unto God. Men are insignificant beside Him. (15-25)
7. The Lord is all powerful. He does not faint nor is He weary. (26-28)
8. The Lord gives strength to those that serve Him; they shall run and not be weary, and they shall walk and not faint. (29-31) (cf. D & C 89:20.)

Chapter 2—**The Temple in Jerusalem, Christ's Coming in Glory.**

Note: This chapter is quoted in 2 Ne. 12.

1. (33, 41) The Lord's house shall be established in the tops of the mountains, and all nations shall flow unto it. (1-3)

Note:

This prophecy, together with Mic. 4:1-2, is often quoted by Latter-day Saints as pertaining to the Salt Lake Temple, which is also high in the mountains and has been visited by the people of many nations. While an interesting parallel can be drawn between the prophecy and the Salt Lake Temple, there is no scriptural evidence that Isaiah was speaking of it rather than the temple in Jerusalem. The reader should note that—

a. The preceding verse clearly defines this prophecy as the word of Isaiah concerning Judah and its capital, **Jerusalem.** (1)
b. The following verse, which is clearly a portion of the prophecy, gives a chronological clue as to when the prophecy will be fulfilled. This is to take place at a time when the Lord will (1) judge among the nations, (2) rebuke many people, and the people will (3) beat their swords into plowshares and (4) cease from waging war. (4)
It would seem that this is clearly a prophecy of events immediately preceding the millennial era and of the millennium (See Is. 11:6-9, 65:25), rather than of the past seventy years.
c. "Mountain(s) of the Lord's house" is a phrase which seemingly refers to the dwelling place of God. D & C 133:13 clearly uses the phrase in referring to Jerusalem: "And let them who be of Judah flee unto Jerusalem, unto the mountains of the Lord's house."
d. Isn't the Salt Lake Temple an arbitrary selection as the fulfillment of the prophecy? Why not the temples in Manti, Logan, St. George or Idaho Falls, which all have been visited by people of many nations and which are relatively high above sea level?

2. (44) Out of Zion shall go forth the law, and the word of the Lord from Jerusalem. (3)

> **Note:** This may be a prophecy which refers to the two centers of power in the last days, the New Jerusalem (as Zion) and the old Jerusalem. However, Isaiah consistently used the term Zion as referring to the

Palestine Jerusalem. (See Is. 1:26-27, 33:20, 40:9, 41:27, 52:1, etc.) The passage is probably synonymous parallelism, a common Hebrew poetry form in which one line asserts an idea and the next line repeats the same thought in different words. (For other examples see Ps. 15:1, 10:1, 2:1 and hundreds more.)
3. (44) Nation shall not lift up the sword against nation. (4)
4. (I) The sins of Israel are listed. (5-9)
5. (42) Fear and a terrible earthquake will come when Christ is exalted (His coming in glory). (10-21) (See Morm. 9:2-5.)

Chapter 63—The Lord's Coming in Glory.
1. (42) The Lord will come in His glory, dressed in red apparel, and tread down the wicked. (1-6) (See D & C 133:46-52.)
2. (I) The Lord with loving kindness blessed Israel, but they rebelled against Him. (7-10)
3. (I) Israel then remembered the way the Lord had helped them in days gone by. (10-14)
4. (22) A prayer: Return the tribes to their inheritance. (15-19)

Chapter 64—A Prayer Seeking the Lord's Coming.
1. (42) A prayer that the Lord will cleanse the earth with fire. (1-3)
2. (I) Israel's confession that the Lord does not hear her people because of their wickedness. (4-8)
3. (I) Wilt thou hold thy peace, O Lord, when Jerusalem is a desolation? (9-12)

Chapter 26—The Lord Will Punish the Inhabitants of the Earth For Their Iniquity.
1. (41) We have a strong city where only the righteous may enter. (1-4)
2. (42) The Lord will destroy the wicked because they will not learn righteousness. (5-11)
3. (40-41?) The Lord has made the nation increase. (12-18)
4. (41) Thou art glorified: thou hadst removed the nation far unto all the ends of the earth. We have not wrought any deliverance in the earth, neither have the inhabitants of the world fallen. (15-18)
5. (III) Thy dead men shall live, the earth shall cast out the dead. (19)

ISAIAH—SECTION IV 363

6. (42) The Lord will come to punish the inhabitants of the earth for their iniquity. (20-21)

Chapter 24—The Cleansing of the Earth At Christ's Coming.
1. (42) The earth is desolate, with few men left. (1-12)
2. (42) The earth is defiled because the people have transgressed the laws, changed the ordinances, and broken the everlasting covenant. (5-6)

   Note: This passage is often included in scripture lists pertaining to the apostasy which took place following New Testament times. While the people did break the laws and changed the ordinances and covenants at that time, there is no indication that Isaiah was prophesying concerning that period here. In chapter 24 the prophet is clearly speaking of another period of apostasy and wickedness which will be evident in the day the Lord cleanses the earth and leaves but few inhabitants—an event which is yet future. This passage should properly be used for purposes of comparison, not as a prophecy of the apostasy which followed New Testament times.

3. (42) The fires of that day will cause the righteous to sing praises to the Lord. (13-15)
4. (42) The earth, in this day shall—
   A. Be utterly broken down. (19)
   B. Be clean dissolved. (19)
   C. Be moved exceedingly. (19)
   D. Reel to and fro like a drunkard. (20)
   E. Be removed like a cottage. (20)
   F. Fall and not rise again. (20)
5. (42) The wicked shall be cast into the (spirit) prison, and shall not be visited for many days. (21-22)
6. (44) The Lord shall reign in mount Zion, and in Jerusalem. (23)

Chapter 34—The Burning of the Earth At Christ's Coming.
1. (42) The Lord has destroyed the armies of all nations. Their dead stink. (1-3)
2. (42) The host of heaven shall be dissolved, and the heavens shall be rolled together as a scroll. (4)
3. (42) The lands shall be turned into unquenchable burning, for it is the day of the Lord's vengeance. (5-10)

Note: These verses may refer to special punishments which will come upon the land of Edom (or Idumea) at the time of the Lord's coming, or they have reference to the entire world, with the term "Idumea" being used to refer to general wickedness. (See D & C 1:36.)

4. (42) The nobles will be removed and thorns will come up in the palaces. (11-15)
5. Read out of the book of the Lord: no one of these (prophecies) shall fail. (16-17)

Chapter 33—The Exaltation of the Lord and the People of Zion.

1. (42) The treacherous spoiler will be spoiled. (1)
2. (42) A prayer:

   A. (35) At the lifting up of the Lord the nations were scattered. His spoil shall be gathered. (2-4)
   B. (41) The Lord is exalted and has filled Zion with judgment and righteousness. (5-6)
   C. (35) The highways lay waste, the earth mourneth and languisheth. (7-9)
3. (42) The Lord is exalted, the wicked are burned with fire. (10-13)
4. (49) The righteous shall dwell (with God) in everlasting burnings. (14-17)
5. (49) Jerusalem shall be a quiet habitation with a tabernacle. It shall not be removed. (18-24)

The Millennium

Chapter 65—The Millennium.

1. Israel does not hear the Lord because of her wickedness. (1-7)
2. (30-31) A seed will inherit the mountains. (8-10)
3. (35) The Lord will punish the wicked among the people of Israel. (11-16)
4. (44) The Lord will create a new heaven and a new earth. (17) (See Rev. 21:1-5.)
5. (44) A child shall live to 100. (18-20)
6. (44) They shall build and enjoy the work of their hands. (21-24)
7. (44) They shall not hurt or destroy; there shall be peace. (25)

ISAIAH—SECTION IV

Chapter 32—The Peaceful Life of the Millennium.
1. (44) A king shall reign in righteousness, and princes shall rule in judgment. (1-4)
2. (44) No longer will the vile person be honored as good, nor be allowed to destroy the poor with lying words. (5-8)
3. (I) The careless women will be troubled because of their barrenness, the palaces shall be forsaken. (9-14)
4. (44) The spirit shall be poured out from on high and the righteous will dwell in quietness and assurance for ever. (15-20)

Chapter 25—A Hymn of the Lord's Greatness During the Millennium.
1. (35) The Lord has destroyed cities but has aided the poor and the needy. (1-5)
2. (44) He will give the people a feast of fat things (rich blessings). (6)
3. (42) He will rend the veil and reveal himself to the people. (7) (See D & C 67:10, 38:8.)
4. (43) He will swallow up death in victory. (8)
5. (34?) The pride of Moab will be brought down. (9-12)

Doctrinal Analysis of Isaiah—Section IV:

The Sins of the People:
1. This people draw near me with their mouth, and with their lips do honour me, but have removed their heart far from me, and their fear toward me is taught by the precept of men. (29:13)
2. Woe unto them that seek deep to hide their counsel from the Lord, and their works are in the dark. (29:15)
3. Shall the work say of him that made it, He made me not? or shall the thing framed say of him that framed it, He had no understanding? (29:16)
4. They make a man an offender for a word. (29:21)
5. They lay a snare for him that reproveth in the gate. (29:21)
6. They turn aside the just for a thing of nought. (29:21)
7. My name continually every day is blasphemed. (52:5)
8. They have chosen their own ways, and their soul delighteth in their abominations. (66:3)
9. When I called, none did answer, when I spoke, they did not hear. (66:4)

10. They did evil before mine eyes, and chose that in which I delighted not. (66:4)
11. They have transgressed the laws, changed the ordinance, broken the everlasting covenant. (24:5)
12. The treacherous dealers have dealt treacherously. (24:16)
13. They are a rebellious people which walketh in a way that was not good, after their own thoughts. (65:2)
14. The people say, I am holier than thou. (65:5)
15. Ye did evil before mine eyes, and did choose that wherein I delighted not. (65:12)

Judgment:

—God Knows Man's Thoughts and Acts:
1. For I know their works and their thoughts. (66:18)

—God Withdraws His Spirit From the Wicked:
1. They rebelled, and vexed his holy Spirit: therefore he was turned to be their enemy, and he fought against them. (63:10)
2. Thou hast hid thy face from us, and hath consumed us, because of our iniquities. (64:7)

—God Rewards the Righteous:
1. For since the beginning of the world men have not heard, nor perceived by the ear, neither hath the eye seen, O God, beside thee, what he hath prepared for him that waiteth for him. (64:4)

—God Governs The Actions and Fate of Man:
1. The Lord hath poured out upon you the spirit of deep sleep, and hath closed your eyes: the prophets and your rulers, the seers hath he covered. (29:10)
2. O Lord, why hast thou made us err from thy ways, and hardened our heart from thy fear? (63:17)

The Nature of God:

—God Controls Nature:
1. Thou shalt be visited of the Lord of hosts with thunder, and with earthquake, and great noise, with storm and tempest, and the flame of devouring fire. (29:6)
2. Art thou not it which hath dried the sea, the waters of the great deep? (51:10)
3. The Lord is the maker that hath stretched forth the heavens, and laid the foundation of the earth. (51:13)

ISAIAH—SECTION IV

4. I am the Lord thy God, that divideth the sea, whose waves roared: The Lord of hosts is his name. (51:15)
5. I plant the heavens, and lay the foundations of the earth. (51:16)
6. Who hath measured the waters in the hollow of his hand, and meted out heaven with the span, and comprehended the dust of the earth in a measure, and weighed the mountains in scales, and the hills in a balance? (40:12)

—The Lord Is Merciful:

1. For a small moment have I forsaken thee; but with great mercies will I gather thee. (54:7)
2. In a little wrath I hid my face from thee for a moment; but with everlasting kindness will I have mercy on thee, saith the Lord. (54:8)
3. My kindness shall not depart from thee, neither shall the covenant of my peace be removed, saith the Lord that hath mercy on thee. (54:10)
4. He that hath mercy on them shall lead them. (49:10)
5. The Lord hath comforted his people, and will have mercy upon his afflicted. (49:13)
6. The Lord will have mercy upon the repentant, and will abundantly pardon. (55:7)
7. In my wrath I smote thee, but in my favour have I had mercy on thee. (60:10)

—The Lord Is Kind:

1. In a little wrath I hid my face from thee for a moment; but with everlasting kindness will I have mercy on thee, saith the Lord. (54:8)
2. My kindness shall not depart from thee, neither shall the covenant of my peace be removed, saith the Lord that hath mercy on thee. (54:10)
3. I will mention the loving kindnesses of the Lord. He hath bestowed goodness on them according to his mercies, and according to the multitude of his loving kindnesses. (63:7)

—The Lord Is Faithful:

1. The Lord is faithful. (49:7)

—The Lord is Man's Redeemer:

1. I the Lord am thy Savior and thy Redeemer, the mighty one of Jacob. (49:26)

2. In all their affliction he was afflicted, in his love and in his pity he redeemed them. (63:9)
3. Doubtless thou art our father. Thou, O Lord, art our father, our redeemer; thy name is from everlasting. (63:16)

—The Lord and His Work Are Eternal:
1. My salvation shall be for ever, and my righteousness shall not be abolished. (51:6)
2. My righteousness shall be for ever, and my salvation from generation to generation. (51:8)

—The Lord Can Be Provoked to Anger and Wrath:
1. They are full of the fury of the Lord, the rebuke of thy God. (51:20)
2. In my wrath I smote thee, but in my favour have I had mercy on thee. (60:10)
3. The hand of the Lord shall be known toward his servants, and his indignation toward his enemies. (66:14)
4. Though thou wast angry with me, thine anger is turned away, and thou comfortedst me. (12:1)

—The Lord Is Righteous:
1. I the Lord love judgment, I hate robbery for burnt offering. (61:8)
2. The Lord speaks in righteousness and is mighty to save. (63:1)
3. The Lord is exalted; for he dwelleth on high: he hath filled Zion with judgment and righteousness. (33:5)

—The Lord Guides Man:
1. I will direct their work in truth, and I will make an everlasting covenant with them. (61:8)

—The Lord Is All-Powerful:
1. All nations before him are as nothing; and they are counted to him less than nothing and vanity. (40:15-17)
2. It is he that sitteth upon the circle of the earth, and the inhabitants thereof are as grasshoppers; that stretcheth out the heavens as a curtain, and spreadeth them out as a tent to dwell in: (40:22)
3. To whom then will ye liken me, or shall I be equal? saith the Holy One. Lift up your eyes on high, and behold who hath created these things, that bringeth out their host by

number: he calleth them all by names by the greatness of his might. (40:25-26)
4. The Lord, the Creator of the ends of the earth, fainteth not, neither is weary. There is no searching of his understanding. (40:28)

—The Lord Is The Creator:
1. O Lord, thou art our father; we are the clay, and thou our potter; and we are the work of thy hand. (64:8)

—Other Qualities of God:
1. Fury is not in me. (27:4)
2. For my thoughts are not your thoughts, neither are your ways my ways, saith the Lord. For as the heavens are higher than the earth, so are my ways higher than your ways, and my thoughts than your thoughts. (55:8-9)
3. The heaven is my throne, and the earth is my footstool. (66:1)
4. Who hath directed the Spirit of the Lord, or being his counsellor hath taught him? (40:13)
5. With whom took he counsel, and who instructed him, and taught him in the path of judgment, and taught him knowledge, and showed to him the way of understanding? (40:14)
6. Thou hast been a strength to the poor; a strength to the needy in distress, a refuge from the storm . . . (25:4)

Revelation:
1. The prophets and your rulers, the seers hath he covered. (29:10)
2. As the rain cometh down, and maketh the earth bring forth and bud, so shall my word be. It shall not return unto me void, but it shall accomplish that which I please, and it shall prosper in the thing where to I sent it. (55:10-11)
3. The word of our God shall stand for ever. (40:8)
4. The spirit of the Lord shall rest upon him, the spirit of wisdom and understanding, the spirit of counsel and might, the spirit of knowledge and of the fear of the Lord, and shall make him of quick understanding in the fear of the Lord. (11:2-3)
5. Where is he that put his Holy Spirit within him? (63:11)
6. The Spirit of the Lord caused him to rest. (63:14)
7. The spirit will be poured upon us from on high. (32:15)

Pre-mortal Life:

1. Have ye not known? have ye not heard? hath it not been told you from the beginning? have ye not understood from the foundations of the earth? (40:21)

Spirit World:

1. They shall be gathered together, as prisoners are gathered in the pit, and shall be shut up in the prison, and after many days shall they be visited. (24:22)

Resurrection:

1. Thy dead men shall live, together with my dead body shall they arise. (26:19)
2. He will swallow up death in victory. (25:8)

The Last Days:

Shown in the chapter outline above.

Counsel for Righteous Living:

—Learn of God:

1. They that erred in spirit shall come to understanding, and they that murmured shall learn doctrine. (29:24)
2. Thou shalt know that I am the Lord: for they shall not be ashamed that wait for me. (49:23)
3. That which they had not heard shall they consider. (52:15)
4. He will teach us of his ways, and we will walk in his paths. (2:3)
5. Seek ye out of the book of the Lord, and read. (34:16)
6. Wisdom and knowledge shall be the stability of thy times, and strength of salvation: the fear of the Lord is his treasure. (33:6)

—Fear and Serve God:

1. They shall sanctify my name, and sanctify the Holy One of Jacob, and shall fear the God of Israel. (29:23)
2. Surely my judgment is with the Lord, and my work with my God. (49:4)
3. For Zion's sake will I not hold my peace, and for Jerusalem's sake I will not rest, until the righteousness thereof go forth as brightness, and the salvation thereof as a lamp that burneth. (62:1)

ISAIAH—SECTION IV

4. They that wait upon the Lord shall renew their strength; they shall run, and not be weary; and they shall walk, and not faint. (40:31)
5. Come ye, and let us walk in the light of the Lord. (2:5)
6. Lord, thou wilt ordain peace for us: for thou also hast wrought all our works in us. (26:12)
7. He who blesseth himself in the earth shall bless himself in the God of truth; and he that sweareth in the earth shall swear by the God of truth. (65:16)
8. The liberal deviseth liberal things; and by liberal things shall he stand. (32:8)

—Seek God:
1. Wherefore do ye spend money for that which is not bread? and your labour for that which satisfieth not? hearken diligently to me, and eat ye that which is good. (55:2)
2. Seek ye the Lord while he may be found, call ye upon him while he is near. (55:6)
3. The desire of our soul is to thy name, and to the remembrance of thee. (26:8)
4. With my soul have I desired thee in the night; yea, with my spirit within me will I seek thee early. (26:9)

—Heed the Word of the Lord:
1. See ye, when he lifteth up an ensign on the mountains; and when he bloweth a trumpet, hear ye. (18:3)
2. Incline your ear, and come unto me: hear, and your soul shall live. (55:3)
3. Hearken to me, ye that follow after righteousness, ye that seek the Lord. (51:1)
4. Hearken unto me, my people; and give ear unto me, O my nation. (51:4)
5. Hear, ye that are far off, what I have done; and, ye that are near, acknowledge my might. (33:13)

—Be Righteous:
1. In righteousness shalt thou be established. (54:14)
2. This is the heritage of the servants of the Lord, and their righteousness is of me, saith the Lord. (54:17)
3. With righteousness shall he judge the poor, and reprove with equity for the meek of the earth. (11:4)
4. Righteousness shall be the girdle of his loins, and faithfulness the girdle of his reins. (11:5)
5. The way of the just is uprightness: thou, most upright, dost weigh the path of the just. (26:7)

6. Who shall dwell with everlasting burnings? He that walketh righteously, and speaketh uprightly; he that despiseth the gain of oppressions; that shaketh his hands from holding of bribes, that stoppeth his ears from hearing of blood, and shutteth his eyes from seeing evil, he shall dwell on high. (33:15-17)
7. The work of righteousness shall be peace; and the effect of righteousness quietness and assurance for ever. (32:17)

—Be Humble and Meek:
1. The meek shall increase their joy in the Lord. (29:19)
2. To this man will I look, even to him that is poor and of a contrite spirit, and trembleth at my word. (66:2)

—Teach the Gospel:
1. All thy children shall be taught of the Lord; and great shall be the peace of thy children. (54:13)
2. How beautiful upon the mountains are the feet of him that bringeth good tidings of good, that publisheth salvation; that saith unto Zion, Thy God reigneth. (52:7)
3. Ye that make mention of the Lord, keep not silence. (62:6)
4. Praise the Lord, call upon his name, declare his doings among the people, make mention that his name is exalted. (12:4)
5. Lift up thy voice with strength; lift it up, be not afraid. (40:9)

—Comfort Others:
1. Comfort ye my people, saith your God. (40:1)

—Rejoice in the Lord:
1. I will greatly rejoice in the Lord, my soul shall be joyful in my God; for he hath clothed me with the garments of salvation, he hath covered me with the robe of righteousness. (61:10)
2. With joy shall ye draw water out of the wells of salvation. (12:3)
3. Be ye glad and rejoice for ever in that which the Lord creates. (65:18)
4. O Lord, thou art my God, I will exalt thee, I will praise thy name. (25:1)

—Sing Unto the Lord:
1. Sing unto the Lord; for he hath done excellent things. (12:5)

—Worship God:
1. All flesh shall come to worship before me. (66:23)

—Be Courageous:
1. Strengthen ye the weak hands, and confirm the feeble knees. Say to them that are of a fearful heart, Be strong, fear not. (35:3-4)
2. Let him take hold of my strength, that he may make peace with me; and he shall make peace with me. (27:5)

—Have Faith:
1. My God shall be my strength. (49:5)
2. Behold, God is my salvation; I will trust and not be afraid: for the Lord Jehovah is my strength and my song; he also is become my salvation. (12:2)
3. Thou wilt keep him in perfect peace, whose mind is stayed on thee: because he trusteth in thee. (26:3)
4. Trust ye in the Lord for ever: for in the Lord Jehovah is everlasting strength. (26:4)

—Repent:
1. Let the wicked forsake his way, and the unrighteous man his thoughts: and let him return unto the Lord, and he will have mercy upon him; and to our God, for he will abundantly pardon. (55:7)

Summary of Isaiah—Section IV:

After studying section IV of Isaiah the student should know:
1. Isaiah prophesied of many events in the last days, including:
    - A. The coming forth of the Book of Mormon.
    - B. Destruction in the Americas.
    - C. The coming of the Ten Tribes to the New Jerusalem in America.
    - D. The removal of the Ten Tribes to Palestine.
    - E. The gathering of Judah to Palestine.
    - F. Israel's political affairs in the last days.
    - G. David the Prince.
    - H. The building of the Jerusalem Temple.
    - I. The Battle of Armageddon.
    - J. The Third and Fourth periods of missionary labor.
    - K. The glory of Israel.
    - L. Christ's Coming in Glory.

      M. The cleansing of the Earth at Christ's coming.
      N. The Millennium.
2. Isaiah's prophecies are important because they provide a basis for comparison and interpretation with other scriptural prophecies. They are a pattern of scripture with numerous references to most of the major prophetic themes concerning the restoration of Israel.
3. Many of Isaiah's prophecies of the last days are amplified and interpreted in other standard works of the Church.
4. The prophecies of Isaiah are sometimes difficult to assign to their period of prophetic fulfillment because he suddenly skips from one time to another without warning. A key to understanding these skips is to realize that he continually compares one period with another.
5. Care should be taken in interpreting scriptures. The student should be careful to

      A. Find a pattern of scriptures which support and explain each other.

      B. Determine the chronological relationship of the passage to aid in determining the interpretation.

      C. Glean the interpretive clues from the context.

      D. Propose alternative interpretations. Attempt to determine which interpretation the speaker intended when he made the prophecy.

      E. Check interpretations with other scriptures and with Church interpretations.

      F. Be aware of the tendency to "force" interpretations so that prophecies of future events are said to apply to present situations.
6. Prophecy of the last days is the most important theme of the book of Isaiah. Twenty-seven of the sixty-six chapters of the book have this as their major subject.
7. The fourth period of prophetic fulfillment is the last days.

Style of the Book:

1. Isaiah's writing is considered by many to be the finest in the Bible.
2. The book is partly in prose, and partly in poetry, as follows:

ISAIAH

Prose	Poetry	Prose	Poetry	Prose	Poetry
1:1			14:24-27	27:12-13	
	1:2-31	14:28			28:1-29:10
2:1			14:29-16:11	29:11-12	
	2:2-3:17	16:12-14			29:13-30:18
3:18-23			17:1-6	30:19-26	
	3:24-26	17:7-9			30:27-28
4:1-6			17:10-19:15	30:29-33	
	5:1-30	19:16-20:6			31:1-5
6:1-8			21:1-15	31:6-7	
	6:9-13	21:16-17			31:8-35:10
7:1-6			22:1-8a	36:1-37:22a	
	7:7-11	22:8b-11			37:22a-29
7:12-8:8			22:12-14	37:30-38:9	
	8:9-10	22:15-25			38:10-20
8:11-9:1			23:1-12	38:21-39:8	
	9:2-10:11	23:13			40:1-44:8
10:12			23:14	44:9-20	
	10:13-19	23:15			44:21-52:2
10:20-27			23:16	52:3-6	
	10:28-11:9	23:17-18			52:7-59:20
11:10-11			24:1-25:5	59:21	
	11:12-13:22	25:6-12			60:1-66:16
14:1-3			26:1-21	66:17-21	
	14:4-21	27:1			66:22-23
14:22-23			27:2-11	66:24	

3. His poetry is rhythmic and makes full use of the complete array of Hebrew poetic techniques and figures of speech including:

    A. Metaphor (see for example, 1:13; 5:18, 22; 8:8; 10:22; 28:17, 20; 30:28, 30).

    B. Paronomasia (play on words) (see for example, 5:7; 7:9).

    C. Antithesis (see for example, 1:18; 3:24).

    D. Alliteration (see for example, 17:10, 12).

    E. Hyperbole and parable (see for example, 2:7; 5:1-7; 28:23-29).

    F. Interrogation (see for example, 10:8).

    G. Dialogue (see for example, 6:8).

    H. Personification (see for example, 49:18-23; 51:17-23; 54:1-6; 60:1-5; 47:1-15).

4. He uses a full, rich vocabulary, but his writing is not artificial or stiff.

5. He uses many beautiful illustrations (see for example, 5:1-7; 12:3; 28:23-29; 32:2).

6. He is versatile in his methods of expression, and is worthy of high praise not only as a writer, but also as an

orator and as a poet.
7. His writing is marked by its grandeur and beauty.
8. His diction and choice of words is excellent.
9. His sentences are compact and forceful.
10. He presents a subject, then raises different aspects of the subject as subdivisions.
11. He is able to adapt his language to the occasion.
12. He has noble thoughts and can express them in beautiful and appropriate language.
13. Isaiah makes abrupt jumps and transitions from one period of prophetic fulfillment to another, making it difficult to identify the period about which he is speaking in every instance.

Author and Date of Authorship: c. 700 B. C. Most critics assert that the book of Isaiah was written by either two or three individuals. The critics are nearly united, at least, in conceding that Isaiah was the author of the first section of the book (chapters 1-39) and that the book was written near the end of his ministry, following Sennacherib's invasion. There is less unity among the critics concerning the time of "second" or "Deutero"-Isaiah and upon the possibility of the existence of a "third" or "Trito"-Isaiah.

The problem of the authorship of the book of Isaiah is of major importance to Latter-day Saints because it calls in question the divine origin of the Book of Mormon. The Book of Mormon quotes numerous passages from Isaiah which were found within the brass plates brought to the Americas by Lehi about 600 B. C. Many of the passages it quotes are from the passages the Bible scholars assign to the second and third Isaiahs which, according to their theories, were written long after 600 B.C.

If the theories of the Bible scholars are correct, then the Book of Mormon could not be quoting from the brass plates, and it is a false, or forged book of scripture. On the other hand, if the Book of Mormon is true, then it disproves the theories of the Bible scholars and invalidates the conclusions they have reached on many of the Old Testament books as a result of these same theories. The following information summarizes the matter which is often called the "literary problem of Isaiah" among the **Latter-day Saints.**

Notes On the Literary Problem of Isaiah and Its Importance To Latter-day Saints:

1. **What is the literary problem of Isaiah?** Bible scholars (Higher Critics) during the past 180 years have begun to teach that much of the book of Isaiah was not written by that prophet but was written by several men who lived several hundred years later. Each scholar has a slightly different arrangement, but in general the scholars break down the book into three sections:

   A. Isaiah: Chapters 1-39.
   B. Deutero-Isaiah (Second Isaiah): Chapters 40-55.
   C. Trito Isaiah (Third Isaiah): Chapters 56-66.

   The higher critics say that Deutero and Trito-Isaiah must have lived much later than the time of Isaiah (740-697 B. C.), at least after the time of Cyrus the Persian (540 B. C.)

2. **What are the major assumptions the higher critics make in studying the prophets?** The three major assumptions made by the higher critics are:

   A. A prophet speaks only to the people of his own generation, and only about his own time.

   B. A prophet speaks out of his own circumstances, and not out of future circumstances.

   C. A prophet may anticipate future events only as the current events of his day indicate the future events are to come about.

   These assumptions, which are obviously contradictory to the Latter-day Saint concept of prophecy and revelation, have formed the basis for a major portion of the scholarly criticism of Isaiah. By accepting these assumptions as fact, Bible critics have rejected the possibility of all the far-ranging prophecies of Isaiah having been made by only one man. According to their theories, a prophet can only speak about one period of prophetic fulfillment—not four, as Isaiah does. Their theories have become so strongly entrenched in modern scholarship that they are often presented as fact in modern textbooks.

3. **What other items of evidence do higher critics cite to demonstrate that the book of Isaiah had more than one author?**

   A. The **literary style** of Second and Third Isaiah is supposedly different from the part attributed to Isaiah. They say that certain images and phrases are common in the first portion of the book, but that they disappear in the latter portion and are replaced by entirely new images.

B. The **theological ideas** of the latter portion of the book are different than the ideas expressed in the early portion, according to the higher critics. They say, for instance, that the early chapters stress the man-like qualities of God, while the latter chapters stress His majesty and infinitude. Not only the theology of the sections attributed to Deutero- and Trito-Isaiah is challenged, however, but also certain teachings in the early portion of the book. Some theological ideas used by Isaiah which the higher critics say were not accepted until much later are

    (1). "The conversion of the heathen." (2:2-4)
    (2). "The picture of universal peace." (11:1-9)
    (3). "Universal judgment upon the whole earth." (14:26)
    (4). The apocalyptic character of chapters 24-27 are said to represent a phase of Hebrew thought found only after Ezekiel.
    (5). The return from captivity. (11:11-16)
    (6). Prophecies concerning the coming of the Messiah.

4. **Many great scholars through the years have held that the Book of Isaiah is a unity, and have shown that the "critical" hypothesis is far from being proved. What evidence do they cite?**

A. The Jewish and Christian Churches have until the last one hundred and fifty years unhesitatingly assigned the whole book to Isaiah.

B. The Septuagint and other ancient versions of scripture give absolutely no hint of the multiple authorship of Isaiah. The critics have assumed that ten or more prophets contributed to Isaiah's book. Those who doubt the critics question why the names of all these prophets have been forgotten when they lived much closer to the time of the collector than did Isaiah.

C. Christ and His Apostles assigned the book to Isaiah. The New Testament quotes from thirty-two chapters of Isaiah. Many of these chapters are quoted several times. Fourteen chapters are from chapters 1-25; eighteen chapters are from chapters 40-66.

ISAIAH 379

   D. Early historians such as Jesus Ben-Sirach (c. 180 B. C.) and Josephus accepted Isaiah as being the author.

The above are external evidences. Those which follow are internal evidences.

   E. Isaiah keeps his personality detached from his prophecies. This is characteristic of both the early and later portion of the book.

   F. Every chapter in the book is characterized by the majestic imagery in which the writer revels—the poetic elevation of style and the love of nature.

   G. Throughout the book there is the common tendency to repetition.

   H. Throughout the book the prophet tends to quote his own words. This habit is more common to Isaiah than to any other prophet. (see for example, 11:6-9; 65:25)

   I. Throughout the book there is an abundant use of alliteration (the repetition of the same sound). This can only be seen, of course, in the Hebrew.

   J. Throughout the book many expressions peculiar to Isaiah are repeated, such as "the Holy One of Israel," "the God of Jacob," "the Mouth of the Lord hath spoken it," "Set up an ensign," etc.

   K. Throughout the book Isaiah "piles up" ideas or imagery. (see for example, 2:10-17; 65:13-14)

5. **What is the Latter-day Saint attitude concerning the Isaiah problem, and why?** Latter-day Saints believe that the entire book of Isaiah was written by Isaiah and that the book was written during his lifetime. They deny that the latter portion was written after the time of Cyrus the Persian.

Their reason for this belief lies in the Book of Mormon. According to the Book of Mormon account, Lehi and his family obtained the brass plates of Laban about 600 B. C. and left Palestine at that time, yet the Book of Mormon quotes extensively from the sections the higher critics assign to Deutero and Trito-Isaiah and which, they say, were written after Cyrus' time (540 B. C.). The Book of Mormon quotes from the following chapters of Isaiah:[11]

   2-14   (2 Ne. 12-24)
   29   (2 Ne. 27)
   48-49   (1 Ne. 20-21)

---
[11]The items listed are major quotations. Minor references and allusions are not shown.

50-51	(2 Ne. 7-8)
52	(3 Ne. 20; Mos. 15:8-10)
53	(Mos. 14)
54	(3 Ne. 22)
55	(2 Ne. 26:25)

6. **How have critics of the Book of Mormon tried to use the Isaiah problem against the Church?** They have accepted the multiple-author hypothesis as a fact, and then they have insisted that Deutero- and Trito-Isaiah lived after the time that Lehi was to have left Jerusalem. This has been their basis for claiming that the Isaiah passages in the Book of Mormon were merely copied from the King James Version by Joseph Smith. They point out that the Isaiah passages in the Book of Mormon are in "King James English."

The Church answers this charge by pointing out that of the 433 Isaiah verses in the Book of Mormon, 234 of them differ from the King James Version. When the gold plates agreed in thought with the King James Version, Joseph Smith used that version, but where there was disagreement, he made the necessary changes in accordance with the Book of Mormon plates.

Textual Transmission: Most critics regard the text of Isaiah as having been poorly transmitted. Some parts are regarded as being textually corrupt, others as being fragmentary, and still others as being amended and altered by later editorials.

Changes Made in the Inspired Version of the Bible—Book of Isaiah

King James Translation	Inspired Version
2:2—And it shall come to pass in the last days, that the mountain of the Lord's house . . .	2:2—And it shall come to pass in the last days, **when** the mountain of the Lord's house . . .
2:5—O house of Jacob, come ye, and let us walk in the light of the Lord.	2:5—O house of Jacob, come ye, and let us walk in the light of the Lord; **yea, come, for ye have all gone astray, every one to his wicked ways.**

ISAIAH

King James Translation	Inspired Version
2:6—Therefore thou hast forsaken thy people the house of Jacob, because they be replenished from the east and are soothsayers like the Philistines . . .	2:6—Therefore, O Lord, thou hast forsaken thy people the house of Jacob, because they be replenished from the east, and **hearken unto the soothsayers** like the Philistines . . .
2:9—And the mean man boweth down, and the great man humbleth himself: therefore forgive them not.	2:9—And the mean man boweth **not** down, and the great man humbleth himself **not**; therefore forgive them not.
2:10—Enter into the rock, and hide thee in the dust, for fear of the Lord, and for the glory of his majesty.	2:10—**O ye wicked ones,** enter into the rock, and hide **ye** in the dust; for the fear of the Lord and **his majesty shall smite thee.**
2:11—The lofty looks of man shall be humbled, and the haughtiness of men shall be bowed down . . .	2:11—**And it shall come to pass that** the lofty looks of man shall be humbled, and the hautiness of **man** shall be bowed down . . .
2:12—For the day of the Lord of hosts shall be upon every one that is proud and lofty, and upon every one that is lifted up; and he shall be brought low:	2:12—For the day of the Lord of hosts **soon cometh upon all nations; yea, upon every one; yea,** upon the proud and lofty, and upon every one **who** is lifted up, and he shall be brought low.
2:13—And upon all the cedars of Lebanon, that are high and lifted up, and upon all the oaks of Bashan,	2:13—**Yea, and the day of the Lord shall come** upon all the cedars of Lebanon, **for they are** high and lifted up; and upon all the oaks of Bashan.
2:14—And upon all the high mountains, and upon all the hills that are lifted up,	2:14—And upon all the high mountains, and upon all the hills, **and upon all the nations** which are lifted up;
2:15—And upon every high tower, and upon every fenced wall,	2:15—**And upon every people,** and upon every high tower, and upon every fenced wall,
2:16—And upon all the ships of Tarshish, and upon all pleasant pictures.	2:16—**And upon all the ships of the sea,** and upon all the ships of Tarshish, and upon all pleasant pictures.

King James Translation	Inspired Version
2:19—... for fear of the Lord ...	2:19—... for **the** fear of the Lord ...
2:20—... and his idols of gold, which they made each one for himself to worship, ...	2:20—... and his idols of gold which **he hath made** for himself to worship, ...
2:21—... for fear of the Lord, and for the glory of his majesty, when he ariseth to shake terribly the earth.	2:21—... for **the** fear of the Lord **shall come upon them, and the majesty of the Lord shall smite them,** when he ariseth to shake terribly the earth.
3:1—... the stay and the staff, the whole stay of bread and the whole stay of water,	3:1—... The stay and the staff, the whole **staff** of bread, and the whole stay of water,
3:4—And I will give children to be their princes, and babes shall rule over them.	3:4—And I will give children **unto them** to be their princes, and babes shall rule over them.
3:6—... saying, Thou hast clothing, be thou our ruler, and let this ruin be under thy hand:	3:6—... **and shall say,** Thou hast clothing, be thou our ruler, and let **not** this ruin come under thy hand;
3:8—... their tongue and their doings are against the Lord, to provoke the eyes of his glory.	3:8—... their **tongues** and their doings **have been** against the Lord, to provoke the eyes of his glory.
3:9—The shew of their countenance doth witness against them; and they declare their sin as Sodom, they hide it not. Woe unto their soul!	3:9—The **show** of their countenance doth witness against them; and **doth declare their sin to be** even as Sodom, they cannot hide it. Woe unto their souls!
3:10—Say ye to the righteous that it shall be well with him: ...	3:10—Say **unto the** righteous, that it **is** well with **them**; ...
3:11—Woe unto the wicked! it shall be ill with him: for the reward of his hands shall be given him.	3:11—Woe unto the wicked! **for they shall perish;** for the reward of **their** hands shall be **upon them.**

ISAIAH

King James Translation	Inspired Version
3:12—... they which lead thee ...	3:12—... they who lead thee ...
3:14—... the spoil of the poor is in your houses.	3:14—... **and** the spoil of the poor is in your houses.
3:15—What mean ye that ye beat my people to pieces, and grind the faces of the poor? saith the Lord God of hosts.	3:15—What mean ye? ye beat my people to pieces, and grind the faces of the poor, saith the Lord God of hosts.
3:18—In that day the Lord will take away the bravery of their tinkling ornaments about their feet, and their cauls, and their round tires like the moon,	3:18—In that day the Lord will take away the bravery of tinkling ornaments, and cauls, and round tires like the moon.
3:26—... and she being desolate shall sit upon the ground.	3:26—... and she **shall be** desolate **and** shall sit upon the ground.
4:1—And in that day seven women shall take hold of one man ...	3:27—(The wording is identical with 4:1 in the King James Translation. The verse is made a part of Chap. 3.)
4:3—And it shall come to pass that he that is left in Zion, and he that remaineth in Jerusalem ...	4:2—And it shall come to pass, **they** that are left in Zion, and he that remaineth in Jerusalem ...
4:5—... for upon all the glory shall be a defence.	4:4—... for upon all the glory of Zion shall be a defence.
5:1—Now will I sing ...	5:1—**And then** will I sing ...
5:5—... and break down the wall ...	5:5—... and **I will** break down the wall ...
5:9—... many houses shall be desolate, even great and fair, without inhabitant.	5:9—... many houses shall be desolate, and great and fair **cities** without inhabitant.
5:11—... that they may follow strong drink; that continue until night, till wine inflame them!	5:11—... that they may follow strong drink, **and** that continue until night, **and** wine inflame them!

King James Translation	Inspired Version
6:9—. . . Hear ye indeed, but understand not; and see ye indeed, but perceive not.	6:9—. . . Hear ye indeed, but **they understood** not; and see ye indeed, but **they perceived** not.
6:12—. . . and there be a great forsaking in the midst of the land.	6:12—. . . **for** there **shall** be a great forsaking in the midst of the land.
6:13—But yet in it shall be a tenth, and it shall return, and shall be eaten:	6:13—But yet in it there shall be a tenth, and **they** shall return, and shall be eaten;
8:19—. . . should not a people seek unto their God? for the living to the dead?	8:19—. . . should not a people seek unto their God? for the living to **hear from** the dead?
9:1—. . . by the way of the sea . . .	9:1—. . . by the way of the **Red** sea . . .
9:3—Thou hast multiplied the nation, and not increased the joy:	9:3—. . . Thou hast multiplied the nation, and increased the joy;
9:7—Of the increase of his government and peace there shall be no end . . .	9:7—Of the increase of his government and peace there is no end . . .
9:17—. . . for every one is an hypocrite . . .	9:17—. . . for every one **of them** is a hypocrite . . .
10:7—. . . but it is in his heart to destroy and cut off nations not a few.	10:7—. . . but in his heart **it is** to destroy and cut off nations not a few.
10:10—As my hand hath found the kingdoms . . .	10:10—As my hand hath **founded** the kingdoms . . .
10:13—For he saith, By the strength of my hand I have done it, and by my wisdom; for I am prudent: and I have removed the bounds of the people . . .	10:13—For he saith, By the strength of my hand, and by my wisdom I have done **these things**; for I am prudent, and I have moved the **borders** of the people . . .
13:2—Lift ye up a banner . . .	13:2—Lift ye up **my** banner . . .
13:3—. . . I have also called my mighty ones for mine anger, even them that rejoice in my highness.	13:3—. . . I have also called my mighty ones, for mine anger **is not upon** them that rejoice in my highness.

ISAIAH   385

King James Translation

13:15—Every one that is found shall be thrust through; and every one that is joined unto them shall fall by the sword.

13:22—... and her days shall not be prolonged.

14:2—And the people shall take them, and bring them to their place: and the house of Israel shall possess them ...

14:3—And it shall come to pass in the day that the Lord shall give thee rest from thy sorrow, and from thy fear, and from the hard bondage wherein thou was made to serve,

14:4—That thou shalt take up this proverb against the king of Babylon, and say, How hath the oppressor ceased! the golden city ceased!

14:16—They that see thee shall narrowly look upon thee, and consider thee, saying, Is this the man ...

14:19—... and as the raiment of those that are slain, ...

16:6—We have heard of the pride of Moab; he is very proud: even of his haughti-

Inspired Version

13:15—Every one that is **proud** shall be thrust through; and every one that is joined **to the wicked** shall fall by the sword.

13:22—... and her days shall not be prolonged; **for I will destroy her speedily; yea, for I will be merciful unto my people, but the wicked shall perish.**

14:2—And the people shall take them, and bring them to their place: **yea, from far, unto the end of the earth, and they shall return to their land of promise,** and the house of Israel shall possess them ...

14:3—And it shall come to pass in **that** day that the Lord shall give thee rest from thy sorrow and from thy fear, and from the hard bondage wherein thou was made to serve.

14:4—**And it shall come to pass in that day** that thou shalt take up this proverb against the king of Babylon, and say, How hath the oppressor ceased! the golden city ceased!

14:16—They that see thee shall narrowly look upon thee, and **shall** consider thee, **and shall** say, Is this the man ...

14:19—.... and the **remnant** of those that are slain, ...

16:6—We have heard of the pride of Moab; of his haughtiness and his pride, for he is

King James Translation	Inspired Version
ness, and his pride, and his wrath: but his lies shall not be so.	very proud; and his wrath, his lies, and all his evil works.
23:10—. . . there is no more strength.	23:10—. . . there is no more strength **in thee.**
29:2—Yet will I distress Ariel and there shall be heaviness and sorrows; and it shall be unto me as Ariel.	29:2—Yet I will distress Ariel, and there shall be heaviness and sorrow; **for thus hath the Lord said unto me, It shall be unto Ariel:**
29:3—And I will camp against thee round about, and will lay siege against thee with a mount, and I will raise forts against thee.	29:3—**That I the Lord** will camp against **her** round about, and will lay siege against **her** with a mount, and I will raise forts against **her.**
29:4—And thou shalt be brought down and shalt speak out of the ground, and thy speech shall be low out of the dust, and thy voice shall be, as one that hath a familiar spirit, out of the ground, and thy speech shall whisper out of the dust.	29:4—And **she** shall be brought down, and shall speak out of the ground, and **her** speech shall be low out of the dust; and **her** voice shall be as of one that hath a familiar spirit, out of the ground, and **her** speech shall whisper out of the dust.
29:5—Moreover the multitude of thy strangers . . .	29:5—Moreover the multitude of **her** strangers . . .
29:6—Thou shalt be visited of the Lord of hosts . . .	29:6—**For they** shall be visited of the Lord of hosts . . .
29:8—It shall even be as when an hungry man dreameth, and, behold, he eateth; but he awaketh, and his soul is empty; or as when a thirsty man dreameth, and, behold, he drinketh; but he awaketh, and, behold he is faint, and his soul hath appetite: so shall the multitude of	29:8—**Yea, it shall be unto them even as unto** a hungry man who dreameth, and behold, he eateth, but he awaketh and his soul is empty; **or like unto** a thirsty man who dreameth, and behold, he drinketh, but he awaketh, and behold, he is faint, and his soul hath appetite. **Yea, even**

ISAIAH

King James Translation	Inspired Version
all the nations be, that fight against mount Zion.	so shall the multitude of all the nations be that fight against mount Zion.
29:9—Stay yourselves, and wonder; cry ye out, and cry: they are drunken, but not with wine; they stagger, but not with strong drink.	29:9—For, behold, all ye that do iniquity, stay yourselves, and wonder; for ye shall cry out, and cry: yea, ye shall be drunken, but not with wine; ye shall stagger, but not with strong drink.
29:10—For the Lord hath poured out upon you the spirit of deep sleep, and hath closed your eyes: the prophets and your rulers, the seers hath he covered.	29:10—For, behold, the Lord hath poured out upon you the spirit of deep sleep. For, behold, ye have closed your eyes, and ye have rejected the prophets, and your rulers; and the seers hath he covered because of your iniquities.
	29:11—And it shall come to pass that the Lord God shall bring forth unto you the words of a book; and they shall be the words of them which have slumbered.
	29:12—And behold, the book shall be sealed; and in the book shall be a revelation from God, from the beginning of the world to the ending thereof.
	29:13—Wherefore because of the things which are sealed up, the things which are sealed shall not be delivered in the day of the wickedness and abominations of the people. Wherefore, the book shall be kept from them.
	29:14—But the book shall be delivered unto a man, and he shall deliver the words of the

King James Translation	Inspired Version
	book, which are the words of those who have slumbered in the dust; and he shall deliver these words unto another, but the words that are sealed he shall not deliver, neither shall he deliver the book.

29:15—For the book shall be sealed by the power of God, and the revelation which was sealed shall be kept in the book until the own due time of the Lord, that they come forth; for, behold, they reveal all things from the foundation of the world unto the end thereof.

29:16—And the day cometh, that the words of the book which were sealed shall be read upon the housetops; and they shall be read by the power of Christ; and all things shall be revealed unto the children of men which ever have been among the children of men, and which ever will be, even unto the end of the earth.

29:17—Wherefore, at that day when the book shall be delivered unto the man of whom I have spoken, the book shall be hid from the eyes of the world, that the eyes of none shall behold it, save it be that three witnesses shall behold it by the power of God, besides him to whom the book shall be delivered; and they shall testify to

ISAIAH   389

King James Translation　　　**Inspired Version**

the truth of the book and the things therein.

29:18—And there is none other which shall view it, save it be a few according to the will of God, to bear testimony of his word unto the children of men; for the Lord God hath said, that the words of the faithful should speak as it were from the dead.

29:19—Wherefore, the Lord God will proceed to bring forth the words of the book; and in the mouth of as many witnesses as seemeth him good will he establish his word; and woe be unto him that rejecteth the word of God.

29:11—And the vision of all is become unto you as the words of a book that is sealed, which men deliver to one that is learned, saying, Read this, I pray thee: and he saith, I cannot; for it is sealed.

29:20—But, behold, it shall come to pass that the Lord God shall say unto him to whom he shall deliver the book, Take these words which are not sealed and deliver them to another, that he may show them unto the learned, saying, Read this I pray thee.

29:21—And the learned shall say, Bring hither the book and I will read them; and now because of the glory of the world, and to get gain will they say this, and not for the glory of God. And the man shall say, I cannot bring the book for it is sealed. Then shall the learned say, I cannot read it.

King James Translation	Inspired Version
29:12—And the book is delivered to him that is not learned, saying, Read this, I pray thee: and he saith, I am not learned.	29:22—Wherefore it shall come to pass, that the Lord will deliver again the book and the words thereof to him that is not learned; and the man that is not learned shall say I am not learned. Then shall the Lord God say unto him, The learned shall not read them, for they have rejected them, and I am able to do mine own work; wherefore thou shalt read the words which I shall give unto thee. 29:23—Touch not the things which are sealed, for I will bring them forth in mine own due time; for I will show unto the children of men that I am able to do mine own work. 29:24—Wherefore, when thou hast read the words which I have commanded thee, and obtained the witnesses which I have promised unto thee, then shalt thou seal up the book again, and hide it up unto me, that I may preserve the words which thou hast not read until I see fit in mine own wisdom to reveal all things unto the children of men. 29:25—For behold, I am God; and I am a God of miracles; and I will show unto the world that I am the same, yesterday, to-day, and for ever; and I work not among the children of men, save it be according to their faith.

ISAIAH 391

| King James Translation | Inspired Version |

29:13—Wherefore the Lord said, Forasmuch as this people draw near me with their mouth, and with their lips do honour me, but have removed their hearts far from me, and their fear toward me is taught by the precept of men:

29:26—And again it shall come to pass, that the Lord shall say unto him that shall read the words that shall be delivered him, Forasmuch as this people draw near unto me with their mouth, and with their lips do honor me, but have removed their hearts far from me, and their fear toward me is taught by the precepts of men, therefore I

29:14—Therefore, behold, I will proceed to do a marvellous work among this people, even a marvellous work and a wonder: for the wisdom of their wise men shall perish, and the understanding of their prudent men shall be hid.

will proceed to do a marvelous work among this people: yea, a marvelous work and a wonder; for the wisdom of their wise and learned shall perish, and the understanding of their prudent shall be hid.

29:15—Woe unto them that seek deep to hide their counsel from the Lord, and their works are in the dark, and they say, Who seeth us? and who knoweth us?

29:27—And woe unto them that seek deep to hide their counsel from the Lord. And their works are in the dark; and they say, Who seeth us and who knoweth us? And

29:16—Surely your turning of things upside down shall be esteemed as the potter's clay: for shall the work say of him that made it, He made me not? or shall the thing framed say of him that framed it, He had no understanding?

they also say, Surely your turning of things upside down shall be esteemed as the potter's clay.

29:28—But behold, I will show unto them, saith the Lord of hosts, that I know all their works. For, shall the work say of him that made it, He made me not? or shall the thing framed say of him that framed it, He had no understanding?

King James Translation	Inspired Version
	29:29—But behold, saith the Lord of hosts, I will show unto the children of men,
29:17—It is not yet a very little while, and Lebanon shall be turned into a fruitful field, and the fruitful field shall be esteemed as a forest.	that it is not yet a very little while, and Lebanon shall be turned into a fruitful field; and the fruitful field shall be esteemed as a forest.
29:18—And in that day shall the deaf hear the words of the book, and the eyes of the blind shall see out of obscurity, and out of darkness.	29:30—And in that day shall the deaf hear the words of the book; and the eyes of the blind shall see out of obscurity and out of darkness; and
29:19—The meek also shall increase their joy in the Lord, and the poor among men shall rejoice in the Holy One of Israel.	the meek also shall increase, and their joy shall be in the Lord; and the poor among men shall rejoice in the Holy One of Israel.
29:20—For the terrible one is brought to nought, and the scorner is consumed, and all that watch for iniquity are cut off:	29:31—For, assuredly as the Lord liveth, they shall see that the terrible one is brought to naught, and the scorner is consumed, and all that watch for iniquity are cut off, and they that make
29:21—That make a man an offender for a word, and lay a snare for him that reproveth in the gate, and turn aside the just for a thing of nought.	a man an offender for a word, and lay a snare for him that reproveth in the gate, and turn aside the just for a thing of naught.
29:22—Therefore thus saith the Lord, who redeemed Abraham, concerning the house of Jacob, Jacob shall not now be ashamed, neither shall his face now wax pale.	29:32—Therefore, thus saith the Lord who redeemed Abraham concerning the house of Jacob, Jacob shall not now be ashamed, neither shall his face now wax pale; but when
29:23—But when he seeth his children, the work of mine hands, in the midst of him, they shall sanctify my name,	he seeth his children, the work of my hands, in the midst of him, they shall sanctify my name, and sanc-

ISAIAH

King James Translation	Inspired Version
and sanctify the Holy One of Jacob, and shall fear the God of Israel.	tify the Holy One of Jacob, and shall fear the God of Israel. They also that erred in spirit shall come to understanding, and they that murmured shall learn doctrine.
29:24—They also that erred in spirit shall come to understanding, and they that murmured shall learn doctrine.	
32:14—Because the palaces shall be forsaken; the multitude of the city shall be left; . . .	32:14—Because the palaces shall be forsaken; the **houses** of the city shall be left **desolate**; . . .
34:7—And the unicorns shall come down with them, . . .	34:7—And the **reem** shall come down with them, . . .
34:16—Seek ye out of the book of the Lord, and read: no one of these shall fail, none shall want her mate: for my mouth it hath commanded, and his spirit it hath gathered them.	34:16—Seek ye out of the book of the Lord, and read **the names written therein;** No one of these shall fail; none shall want **their** mate; for my mouth it hath commanded, and **my** spirit it hath gathered them.
34:17—And he hath cast the lot for them, and his hand hath divided it unto them by line: . . .	34:17—And **I** have cast the lot for them, and **I** have divided it unto them by line; . . .
35:8—And an highway shall be there, and a way, and it shall be called The way of holiness; the unclean shall not pass over it; but it shall be for those: the wayfaring men, though fools, shall not err therein.	35:8—And a highway shall be there; **for a way shall be cast up,** and it shall be called the way of holiness. The unclean shall not pass over **upon** it; but it shall be **cast up** for those **who are clean,** and the wayfaring men, though **they are accounted** fools, shall not err therein.
36:5—I say, sayest thou, (but they are but vain words) I have counsel and strength for war: . . .	36:5—I say, thy words are but vain when thou sayest, I have counsel and strength for war. . . .

King James Translation	Inspired Version
37:17—. . . and hear all the words of Sennacherib, which hath sent to reproach the living God.	37:17—. . . and hear all the words of Sennacherib, which **he** hath sent to reproach the living God.
37:32—For out of Jerusalem shall go forth a remnant, and they that escape out of mount Zion: the zeal of the Lord of hosts shall do this.	37:32—for out of Jerusalem shall go forth a remnant; and they that escape out of **Jerusalem shall come up upon mount Zion;** the zeal of the Lord of hosts shall do this.
37:36—Then the angel of the Lord went forth, and smote in the camp of the Assyrians a hundred and fourscore and five thousand: and when they arose early in the morning, behold, they were all dead corpses.	37:36—Then the angel of the Lord went forth, and smote in the camp of the Assyrians a hundred and four-score and five thousand, and when they **who were left** arose, early in the morning, behold they were all dead corpses.
38:15—. . . he hath both spoken unto me, and himself hath done it: I shall go softly all my years in the bitterness of my soul.	38:15—. . . he hath both spoken unto me, and himself hath **healed me.** I shall go softly all my years, **that I may not walk** in the bitterness of my soul.
38:16—O Lord, by these things men live, and in all these things is the life of my spirit: so wilt thou recover me, and make me to live.	38:16—Oh Lord, **thou who art the life of my spirit, in whom I live;** so wilt thou recover me, and make me to live; **and in all these things will I praise thee.**
38:17—Behold, for peace I had great bitterness: but thou hast in love to my soul delivered it from the pit of corruption: . . .	38:17—Behold, **I had great bitterness instead of peace,** but thou hast in love to my soul, **saved me** from the pit of corruption, . . .
41:28—For I beheld, and there was no man; even among them, . . .	41:28—For I beheld, and there was no man; even among **men,** . . .
42:19—Who is blind, but my servant? or deaf, as my messenger that I sent? who is	42:19—**For I will send my servant unto you who are blind; yea, a messenger to**

ISAIAH

King James Translation	Inspired Version
blind as he that is perfect, and blind as the Lord's servant?	open the eyes of the blind, and unstop the ears of the deaf;

42:20—Seeing many things, but thou observest not; opening the ears, but he heareth not.

42:20—And they shall be made perfect notwithstanding their blindness, if they will hearken unto the messenger, the Lord's servant.

42:21—Thou art a people, seeing many things, but thou observest not; opening the ears to hear, but thou hearest not.

42:21—The Lord is well pleased for his righteousness' sake; he will magnify the law, and make it honourable.

42:22—The Lord is not well pleased with such a people, but for his righteousness' sake he will magnify the law and make it honorable.

42:22—But this is a people robbed and spoiled; they are all of them snared in holes, and they are hid in prison houses: they are for a prey, and none delivereth; for a spoil, and none saith, Restore.

42:23—Thou art a people robbed and spoiled; **thine enemies, all of them,** have snared thee in holes, and they have hid thee in prison houses; they have taken thee for a prey, and none delivereth; for a spoil, and none saith, Restore.

42:23—Who among you will give ear to this? who will hearken and hear for the time to come?

42:24—Who gave Jacob for a spoil, and Israel to the robbers? did not the Lord, he against whom we have sinned? for they would not walk in his ways, neither were they obedient unto his law.

42:24—Who among **them** will give ear unto **thee,** or hearken and hear **thee** for the time to come? And who gave Jacob for a spoil, and Israel to the robbers? did not the Lord, he against whom **they** have sinned?

42:25—Therefore he hath poured upon him the fury of

42:25—For they would not walk in his ways, neither were they obedient unto his law: therefore he hath poured upon **them** the fury of his anger, and the strength of

King James Translation	Inspired Version
his anger, and the strength of battle: and it hath set him on fire round about, yet he knew not; and it burned him, yet he laid it not to heart.	battle; and **they** have set **them** on fire round about, yet **they** know not, and it burned **them**, yet **they** laid it not to heart.
43:13—. . . I will work and who shall let it?	43:13—. . . I will work and who shall **hinder** it?
44:21—Remember these, O Jacob and **Israel**; . . .	44:21—Remember **thee**, O Jacob and Israel; . . .
50:1—Thus saith the Lord, Where is the bill of your mother's divorcement, whom I have put away? or which of my creditors is it to whom I have sold you? Behold, for your iniquities have ye sold yourselves, and for your transgressions is your mother put away.	50:1—**Yea, for thus saith the Lord, Have I put thee away, or have I cast thee off for ever?** For thus saith the Lord, Where is the bill of your mother's divorcement? To whom have I put thee away, or to which of my creditors have I sold you; yea, to whom have I sold you?
50:2—Wherefore, when I came, was there no man? when I called, was there none to answer? Is my hand shortened at all, that it cannot redeem? or have I no power to deliver? behold, at my rebuke I dry up the sea, I make the rivers a wilderness: their fish stinketh, because there is no water, and dieth for thirst.	50:2—Behold, for your iniquities have ye sold yourselves, and for your transgressions is your mother put away; wherefore, when I came there **was no man**; when I called **there was none to answer. O house of Israel,** is my hand shortened at all, that it cannot redeem; or have I no power to deliver?
	50:3—Behold, at my rebuke I dry up the sea, I make their rivers a wilderness; and their fish to stink, because the waters are dried up, and they die because of thirst. I clothe the heavens with blackness, and I make sackcloth their covering.
50:3—I clothe the heavens with blackness, and I make sackcloth their covering.	
50:4—. . . I should know how to speak a word in season to	50:4—. . . I should know how to speak a word in season

ISAIAH

King James Translation	Inspired Version
him that is weary: he wakeneth morning by morning, he wakeneth mine ear to hear as the learned.	unto thee, O house of Israel, when ye are weary. He waketh morning by morning, he waketh mine ear to hear as the learned.
50:5—The Lord God hath opened mine ear, . . .	50:5—The Lord God hath appointed mine ears, . . .
50:8—He is near that justifieth me; . . .	. . . and the Lord is near and he justifieth me.
. . . who is mine adversary? let him come near to me.	50:6—. . . Who is mine adversary? let him come near me, and I will smite him with the strength of my mouth; for the Lord God will help me; and all they which shall condemn me, behold all they shall wax old as a garment and the moth shall eat them up.
50:9—Behold, the Lord God will help me; who is he that shall condemn me? lo, they shall all wax old as a garment; the moth shall eat them up.	
50:11—Behold, all ye that kindle a fire, . . .	50:8—Behold all ye that kindleth fire, . . .
51:1—Hearken to me, ye that follow after righteousness, ye that seek the Lord: look unto the rock whence ye are hewn, and to the hole of the pit whence ye are digged.	51:1—Hearken unto me, ye that follow after righteousness; ye that seek the Lord, look unto the rock from whence ye were hewn, and to the hole of the pit from whence ye are digged.
51:7—. . . the people in whose heart is my law; . . .	51:7—. . . the people in whose heart I have written my law; . . .
51:11—. . . and everlasting joy shall be upon their head: . . .	51:11—. . . and everlasting joy and holiness shall be upon their heads; . . .
51:12—I, even I, am he that comforteth you: who art thou . . .	51:12—I am he, yea, I am he that comforteth you; behold, who art thou . . .
51:19—These two things are come unto thee; who shall be sorry for thee? desolation,	51:19—These two sons are come unto thee; they shall be sorry for thee, thy desolation,

King James Translation	Inspired Version
and destruction, and the famine, and the sword: by whom shall I comfort thee?	and destruction, and the famine, and the sword; **and** by whom shall I comfort thee?
51:20—Thy sons have fainted, . . .	51:20—Thy sons have fainted **save these two,** . . .
52:6—. . . therefore they shall know in that day that I am he that doth speak: . . .	52:6—. . . **yea, in that day** they shall know that I am he that doth speak: . . .
52:7—How beautiful upon the mountains are the feet of him that bringeth good tidings, that publisheth peace; that bringeth good tidings of good, . . .	52:7—**And then shall they say,** How beautiful upon the mountains are the feet of him that bringeth good tidings **unto them,** that publisheth peace; that bringeth good tidings **unto them** of good, . . .
52:15—So shall he sprinkle many nations; . . .	52:15—So shall he **gather** many nations; . . .
54:10—. . . the covenant of my peace . . .	54:10—. . . the covenant of my **people** . . .
54:15—Behold, they shall surely gather together, but not by me: . . .	54:15—Behold, they shall surely gather together **against thee,** but not by me; . . .
57:5—. . . under the clifts of the rocks?	57:5—. . . under the **clefts** of the rocks?
60:22—. . . I the Lord will hasten it in his time.	60:22—. . . I the Lord will hasten it in **my** time.
62:4—. . . but thou shalt be called Hephzibah, and thy land Beulah: . . .	62:4—. . . but thou shalt be called **Delightful,** and thy land **Union;** . . .
62:5—For as a young man marrieth a virgin, so shall thy sons marry thee . . .	62:5—For as a young man marrieth a virgin, so shall thy **God** marry thee; . . .
63:17—O Lord, why hast thou made us to err from thy ways, and hardened our heart from thy fear? . . .	63:17—O Lord, why hast thou **suffered us** to err from thy ways, and **to harden** our heart from thy fear? . . .
64:5—Thou meetest him that rejoiceth and worketh righteousness, those that remem-	64:5—Thou meetest him that **worketh righteousness, and rejoiceth him that remember-**

King James Translation	Inspired Version
ber thee in thy ways: behold, thou art wroth; for we have sinned: in those is continuance, and we shall be saved.	eth thee in thy ways; in righteousness there is continuance, and such shall be saved.
64:6—But we are all as an unclean thing, and all our righteousnesses are as filthy rags; . . .	64:6—But we have sinned; we are all as an unclean thing, and all our righteousnesses are as filthy rags; . . .
65:1—I am sought of them that asked not for me; I am found of them that sought me not: I said, Behold me, behold me, unto a nation that was not called by my name.	65:1—I am found of them who seek after me, I give unto all them that ask of me; I am not found of them that sought me not, or that inquireth not after me.
65:2—I have spread out my hands all the day unto a rebellious people, which walketh in a way that was not good, after their own thoughts;	65:2—I said unto my servant, Behold me, **look upon me; I will send you unto** a nation that is not called after my name, for I have spread out my hands all the day to a people who walketh not in my ways, and their works are evil and not good, and they walk after their own thoughts.
65:4—. . . which eat swine's flesh, and broth of abominable things is in their vessels;	65:4—. . . which eat swine's flesh, and broth of abominable **beasts, and pollute their vessels;**
65:20—There shall be no more thence an infant of days, . . .	65:20—**In those days** there shall be no more thence an infant of days, . . .

Summary of the Book of Isaiah:

After studying the Book of Isaiah the student should know:
1. Isaiah labored from c. 740-697 B. C. His contemporary prophets were Hosea and Micah.
2. Isaiah preached to both Israel and Judah. His prophecies encompassed the surrounding nations also.
3. The Book of Mormon makes significant comments about Isaiah and his writing:

A. I will liken his words unto my people . . .
   B. Isaiah's words are plain unto all those that are filled with the spirit of prophecy.
   C. In the days that the prophecies of Isaiah shall be fulfilled men shall know of a surety (of their fulfillment).
   D. Great are the words of Isaiah. He spake as touching all things concerning my people which are of the house of Israel.
   E. Search the prophecies of Isaiah.
4. The "Literary Problem of Isaiah" is a conflict between the multiple-authorship theories of Bible critics and the Book of Mormon quotations of Isaiah. The critics claim that much of Isaiah was written after the Book of Mormon people had his complete writings and left Jerusalem.
5. Bible critics have based many of their studies on three major assumptions which most informed Latter-day Saints regard as false:
   A. A prophet speaks only to the people of his own generation, and only about his own time.
   B. A prophet speaks out of his own circumstances, and not out of the future circumstances.
   C. A prophet may anticipate future events only as the current events of his day indicate the future events are to come about.

PART III

The History
- The Fall of Assyria and the Rise of Babylonia
- The Fall of Judah to Babylonia
- The Jewish Deportations

The Prophets
- Zephaniah
- Nahum
- Obadiah
- Habakkuk
- Jeremiah and Lamentations

The Doctrine
- The Sins of Judah
- God's Punishment upon Judah
- The Nature of God
- God's Communication with His Prophets
- Counsel for Righteous Living
- Important Events of the Last Days

CHAPTER XII

HISTORICAL SUMMARY:
THE RISE OF BABYLONIA AND
THE FALL OF JUDAH

The Rise of Babylonia as a World Power.

The Babylonian culture was one of the oldest cultures in the world. It had been influenced by invading tribes and had been known by several names. In this context we are only concerned with it as it existed at the zenith of its power.

Assyria controlled Babylonia from the late tenth century until the end of the reign of the Assyrian king Ashurbanipal (c. 668-633 B.C.) Esarhaddon (c. 681-669 B.C.), Ashurbanipal's father, divided his kingdom between his two sons. Ashurbanipal controlled the west (Assyria) and his brother, Shamash-shumukin, controlled the east (Babylon). The two brothers fought a bloody four-year long war to determine who had control. Though Ashurbanipal defeated his brother, the Assyrian kingdom became so weak that it soon collapsed under pressure from the east. Seeing Assyria's weakened condition, Media attacked Assyria in league with Babylonia. Ashurbanipal divided his army. He went to meet the Medes and placed the remainder of his army under his general, Nabopolassar. Nabopolassar broke faith with Ashurbanipal and established himself as king of Babylon. He allied himself with the Medes to the north, and they together destroyed the Assyrian empire. The fall of Assyria was completed when it suffered defeat at Asshur (614 B.C.), Nineveh (612 B.C.), and at the emergency capital, Haran (608-606 B.C.).

When Assyria fell, its vast territory was divided between the Medes and the Babylonians. Nabopolassar received the independence of Babylonia, plus southern Assyria, Syria, Palestine and Egypt. He maintained a strong alliance with Cyaxares, the king of Media, and the alliance was sealed by the marriage of Nabopolassar's son to the daughter of the Median king.

Kings of Babylonia:

1. **Nabopolassar**—c. 625-604 B.C.
    A. Established the Babylonian empire.
    B. Beautified the city of Babylon and improved its irrigation system.
    C. Acted as a peacemaker in a war between the Medes and the Lydians.
    D. In 610 B.C. the Egyptian Pharaoh died and was succeeded by his son, Necho.
    - (1). Necho declared his independence from Babylon and attacked Syria in an effort to support the dying kingdom of Assyria.
    - (2). Josiah, king of Judah, attempted to prevent the Egyptian army from crossing Palestine by blocking the Egyptians with the army of Judah. Necho defeated Josiah's army, killed the Jewish king, and marched on to the Euphrates.
    - (3). Necho ruled Syria for three years.
    - (4). Nabopolassar was too old to challenge him. He sent his son, Nebuchadnezzar, with the Babylonian army, to oust Necho.
    - (5). Nebuchadnezzar defeated the Egyptians in the battle of Carchemish,

fought at the Euphrates River in 605 B.C.

(6). Nebuchadnezzar was pursuing Necho into Egypt when he learned of his father's death. He made a hasty treaty with Necho and hurried back to Babylon to claim the throne.

2. **Nebuchadnezzar**—c. 604-562 B.C.

A. The greatest of the Babylonian kings.

B. Upon becoming king, he returned to Syria and completed the subjugation of that land. At that time he made Judah pay tribute.

C. In 598 B.C. he took Jehoiachin and 10,023 of the leading Jews into captivity in Babylon.

D. When Zedekiah, king of Judah, made a treaty with Egypt, Nebuchadnezzar took Zedekiah and the remaining Jews to Babylon in 586 B.C. He destroyed Jerusalem.

E. He laid siege to Tyre for 13 years before subjecting it to vassaldom. c. 572 B.C.

F. He conquered all of Egypt in 572 B.C.

G. Using slave labor he built Babylon into one of the largest and most beautiful cities of the world (larger than present day London).

The Fall of Judah.

The decline of Judah can be traced back more than a century to the Assyrian assaults at the time of Israel's fall. From this period the religious, economic, and political situations of the southern kingdom show a continuous downward trend with but few exceptions to the pattern of decline.

The idolatry introduced by King Manasseh was definitely a determining factor in the fall of Judah. Although idolatry was common before his reign, it received such strong encouragement during his period that the country was not able to escape from its grip in spite of the efforts of King Josiah and the prophets of this period.

Judah actually fell twice: during the reigns of kings Jehoiachin and Zedekiah. There were three deportations to Babylon: at the fall of Judah under Jehoiachin, at the end of the reign of King Zedekiah, and after the assassination of the governmental appointee, Gedeliah.

The details of the period are summarized in the following outline of the kings of Judah.

Kings of Judah (The Southern Kingdom):

1. **Manasseh**—c. 697-642 B.C. (2 Ki. 20:21-21:18; 23:12, 26; 24:3; 2 Chron. 32:33-33:20, 23; Jer. 15)
    A. Son of Hezekiah.
    B. Began to reign at 12 years of age.
    C. An evil king.
    D. Restored idol worship, particularly the Astral cults (worship of the sun, moon and stars) and even placed idols in the Jerusalem temple.
    E. Offered his son as a human sacrifice.
    F. Used enchantments, familiar spirits and wizards.
    G. Because of his wickedness the prophets foretold the fall of Judah.
    H. Shed much innocent blood. (Tradition says that he had Isaiah killed.)
    I. Was taken in chains to Babylon by the Assyrian captains but then was returned to Jerusalem.
    J. Supposedly repented and abolished his own idol worship, but the land continued in idolatry.

THE RISE OF BABYLONIA AND THE FALL OF JUDAH 407

2. **Amon**—c. 642-640 B.C. (2 Ki. 21:18-26; 1 Chron. 3:14; 2 Chron. 33:20-25; Jer. 1:2, 25:3; Zeph. 1:1)
    A. Son of Manasseh.
    B. An evil king.
    C. He worshipped idols.
    D. His servants conspired against him and killed him.
3. **Josiah**—c. 640-609 B.C. (2 Ki. 22-24; 2 Chron. 34-35; Jer. 22:10, 18; Zech. 12:11)
    A. Son of Amon.
    B. Came to the throne at the age of eight.
    C. A righteous king.
    D. Hilkiah (Hil-kī'-ah), the high priest, found the book of the law during his reign.
    E. He inquired of the Lord through Huldah (Hul'-dah) the prophetess.
    F. He and the people covenanted to keep the commandments of the Lord found in the book of the law of the Lord.
    G. He cast out the idols and the idolatrous priests.
    H. Killed by the Egyptian Pharaoh, Necho Nē'-chō) at Megiddo (Me-gid-dō) when he tried to keep the Egyptian army from marching through Palestine.
4. **Jehoahaz** (Je-hō'-a-haz)—c. 609 B.C. (2 Ki. 23:30-34; 2 Chron. 21:17; 25:17, 23, 25; Jer. 22:11; 1 Chron. 3:15; 2 Chron. 36:1-4)
    A. Son of Josiah.
    B. Also known as Shallum.
    C. An evil king.
    D. Ruled three months.
    E. Pharaoh Necho deposed him, putting him in chains in Egypt.

5. **Jehoiakim** (Je-hoi'-a-kim)—c. 609-598 B.C. (2 Ki. 23:34-36; 24:1-6; 1 Chron. 3:15-16; 2 Chron. 36:4, 5, 8; Jer. 1:3; 22:18, 24; 26:1, 21-23; 27:1, 20; 28:4; 35:1; 36:1, 9, 28-32, etc.)

   A. Son of Josiah, brother to Jehoahaz.

   B. Originally known as Eliakim (ē-lī-a-kim). His name was changed to Jehoiakim by Pharaoh Necho.

   C. Established on the throne of Judah by Pharaoh Necho.

   D. An evil king.

   E. Paid tribute to the Egyptian Pharaoh.

   F. Nebuchadnezzar carried more of the temple vessels to Babylon during his reign.

   G. Jehoiakim served Nebuchadnezzar as a vassal king for three years, then rebelled against him.

   H. He was attacked by bands of Chaldeans, Syrians, Moabites, and Ammonites.

   I. Killed the prophet Urijah (ū-rī'-jah).

   J. Burned the roll containing Jeremiah's prophecies.

6. **Jehoiachin** (Je-hoi'-a-chin)—c. 598 B.C. (2 Ki. 24:6-16; 25:27-30; 2 Chron. 36:9-10; Jer. 52:31-34; Ezek. 1:2)

   A. Son of Jehoiakim.

   B. Also known as Jeconiah, Joachin, and Coniah.

   C. Reigned three months.

   D. Placed on the throne at the age of eight years. (2 Chron. 36:9; 2 Ki. 24:8 says eighteen years old.)

   E. Nebuchadnezzar, king of Babylon, besieged Jerusalem. Jehoiachin and his court went out to him and surrendered.

F. Nebuchadnezzar carried Jehoiachin, the treasures of Jerusalem, and 10,023 of Judah's royalty, army, and skilled craftsmen into captivity in Babylonia in 598 B.C. **(First deportation of the Jews.)**

G. Evil-merodach, king of Babylon (son of Nebuchadnezzar), released Jehoiachin from prison after 37 years of captivity and allowed him to participate in the affairs of the Babylonian court.

7. **Zedekiah** (Zed-ē-kī'-ah)—c. 598-587 B.C. (2 Ki. 24:17-20; 25:1-7; 1 Chron. 3:15; 2 Chron. 36:10; Jer. 1:3; 21:1-7; 24:8; 27:3; 12; 28:1; 29:3; 32:1-5; 34:2-8, 21, 37-39; 44:30; 49:34; 51:59; 52)

    A. Son of Josiah, brother to Jehoahaz and Jehoiakim.

    B. Placed on the throne by Nebuchadnezzar when Jehoiachin was taken into captivity.

    C. Original name was Mattaniah (Mat-ta-nī'-ah). His name was changed to Zedekiah by Nebuchadnezzar.

    D. An evil king.

    E. He rebelled against Babylon.

    F. He rejected Jeremiah's advice and attempted to withstand Nebuchadnezzar's siege of Jerusalem instead of surrendering.

    G. After Jerusalem had been under siege for a year-and-a-half, he attempted to escape but was captured.

    H. Nebuchadnezzar killed his sons before his eyes, then put out his eyes, and carried him and the people of Judah to Babylon as captives in c. 586 B.C. **(Second deportation of the Jews.)**

8. **Gedeliah** (Ged-a-lī'-ah)—c. 586 B.C. (2 Ki. 25: 22-25; Jer. 39:14; 40; 41; 43:6)

A. Not a king, but a temporary governor established by Nebuchadnezzar.

B. He ruled for two months and encouraged the people to make themselves subject to the rule of Babylonia.

C. He was murdered by a group of the Jews who then fled.

Summary:

In studying the period of the rise of Babylonia and the fall of Judah, the student should know:

Babylonia

1. Babylonia became a country by rebelling against Assyria.
2. Although it became a great power, the Babylonian empire lasted only for 86 years, from 625 to 539 B.C.
3. Babylonia had only six kings. The two greatest kings lived during this early period:

    A. Nabopolassar—established the Babylonian Empire.

    B. Nebuchadnezzar—Babylonia's greatest king. He conquered Judah.

Assyria

4. Assyria collapsed during this period. It lost its final important battles from 614 to 606 B.C.

Egypt

5. Egypt lost a decisive battle to Babylonia, which kept it from regaining its influence as a world power. This was the battle of Carchemish in 605 B. C.

Judah

6. The last five kings of Judah were:
   A. Josiah—killed by Pharaoh Necho.
   B. Jehoahaz
   C. Jehoiakim
   D. Jehoiachin—taken to Babylon with the first Jewish deportation.
   E. Zedekiah—taken to Babylon with the second Jewish deportation.

Important Dates

7. c. 625 B. C.—Babylonia established.
8. c. 605 B. C.—Egypt defeated at the Battle of Carchemish.
9. c. 598 B. C.—First deportation of the Jews.
10. c. 588-86 B. C.—Siege and fall of Jerusalem. Second deportation of the Jews.

Important Places

11. Asshur ⎫
12. Nineveh ⎬ last Assyrian strongholds.
13. Haran ⎭
14. Carchemish—where Egypt was defeated.
15. Jerusalem—capital of Judah
16. Babylon—capital of Babylonia.
17. Extent of the Babylonian Empire.

Bible References

18. 2 Ki. 22-24—Record of the last five kings of Judah.
19. 2 Ki. 24—Record of the first deportation of the Jews.
20. 2 Ki. 25; Jer. 52—Record of the second deportation of the Jews.

CHAPTER XIII

ZEPHANIAH

Prophet's Name: Zephaniah (Zĕph-ă-nī'-ăh) means "Jehovah has hidden."

Scriptural Information About the Prophet:
1. He was the son of Cushi (Cū'-shī). (1:1)
2. He was the great, great grandson of Hezekiah, probably king of Judah. (1:1) (Zephaniah is the only prophet for whom extended genealogy is given in the superscription.)
3. He preached in the days of Josiah, king of Judah. (c. 640-609 B. C.) (1:1)
4. He probably lived in Jerusalem, for he refers to parts of that city with familiarity. (see "this place" [1:4], the "fish gate" [1:10], and his reference to the merchants' quarter, "Mactesh" [1:11])
5. If Zephaniah was a descendant of Hezekiah, king of Judah, he was of the royal line and would have been in a position in the court to greatly influence the boy king, Josiah.
6. He is not the Zephaniah that was referred to as the "second priest" (see 2 Ki. 25:18; Jer. 21:1; 29:25, 29; 37:3, 52:24) nor the Zephaniah of I Chron. 6:36 or Zech. 6:10, 14)

Date of Zephaniah's Mission: c. 626 B. C.
1. The only indication as to when in Josiah's reign Zephaniah labored is his constant reference to the poor condition of the morals and religion in Judah. (see 1:4-6, 8, 9, 12; 3:1-4, 7) It is known that Josiah brought about a great reformation (see 2 Chron. 34:3-33) and caused the people to covenant with God in the eighteenth year of his reign (c. 621 B. C.). The assumption is made that Zephaniah's labors preceded Josiah's reforms and probably coincide with the Scythian invasion of the Mediterranean coast (between 630 and 624 B. C.).

ZEPHANIAH

Prophesied to: Judah

Contemporary Prophets: Jeremiah c. 626-586 B. C. to Judah.

Contemporary Prophets Contrasted:

    Zephaniah was supposedly of royal blood, and is believed to have been influential in the royal court of Judah. It appears that he was closely connected with the young boy-king, Josiah, and was able to influence him for good. He seemingly was from Jerusalem and knew the city well. He would probably have been a young man in this period, judging by the time of generations from Hezekiah, king of Judah. The tone of his message indicates that he is of a bold, unflinching nature.

    Jeremiah was probably a descendant of the priestly line, and his forefathers apparently were from Israel rather than Judah. Unlike Zephaniah, Jeremiah had no political connections and was not influential in the affairs of the royal court during Josiah's time. Like Zephaniah, Jeremiah was a young man in the days of Josiah. The recorded ministry of Zephaniah was short, while Jeremiah's ministry extended over fifty years and during the reign of five kings of Judah. Jeremiah was of a more introspective and emotional temperament than was Zephaniah.

Contemporary Kings:

    Judah: Josiah (c. 640-609 B. C.)
    Assyria: This is the period shortly after the death of Ashurbanipal (c. 668-633 B. C.) when the successors to his throne were struggling for power.
    Babylonia: Nabopolassar had just betrayed his command as a general in the Assyrian army (c. 626 B. C.) and was in the process of establishing himself as king of Babylonia and defeating Assyria. His reign as king of Babylonia extended from 625-604 B. C.

National Conditions—Judah:

—Political:

1. Josiah's father, Amon, had been slain in his own house by his servants, who conspired against him. The people of Judah killed the conspirators and established Josiah on the throne.
2. When Josiah came to the throne he was only eight years of age.

3. It appears that Josiah's counsellors must have been men of righteousness who won him away from the idolatrous ways of his predecessors: Amon and the wicked king, Manasseh.
4. External pressure from Assyria had abated as that nation suffered a rapid decline through internal strife.
5. Many commentators assert that the approaching Scythian hordes, who were sweeping towards the Mediterranean area from southwestern Asia, were the instigation of Zephaniah's prophecy, and that he understood them to be the source of the judgment of which he spoke.
6. The same political corruption of Isaiah's day was apparent in Zephaniah's day. He saw that the nobility were all "clothed in strange apparel" rather than the garb designed to keep the people of Israel distinct from other peoples, that this was a day of hireling prophets, and that the homes of the nobility were filled with deceit.

—**Economic:**
1. The economy of Judah had been previously disrupted by payments of tribute to Assyria. Since that time Judah had received an influx of refugees from Israel and had been living in a continual state of economic unbalance because of the precarious condition of national and international affairs.
2. Corruption was common. The rich were still oppressing the poor, and even the servants filled the abodes of their masters with "violence and deceit."

—**Religious:**
1. King Josiah's two predecessors, Manasseh and Amon, had filled the land with idolatry. Pagan deities and their cults were well established in Judah, and had many followers.
2. Josiah, while still a young boy, undertook an extensive program to counter the idolatry which apparently was being carried on during Zephaniah's ministry. This undoubtedly brought sharp criticism upon the boy king from the pagan factions.
3. The followers of Jehovah were apathetic in their worship. Their religion had become a display of external righteousness designed to cover internal corruption. Religion had degenerated into meaningless ritual.
4. Professional prophets were prophesying falsely and were leading the people astray. The priests of the church were corrupting the teachings and the laws of the Lord.

ZEPHANIAH   415

Outline of the Book:

Section I—The Approaching Destruction of Judah and Her Neighbors. (1:2-3:8)

Interpretive Note: There is confusion as to whether part I of Zephaniah (1:3-3:8) is a prophecy of the impending judgment upon the nations of the Mediterranean area from the Scythian invasion and the rapidly approaching Babylonian invasions, or whether it is a prophecy of the cleansing of the earth in the last days at the time of the Lord's coming in glory. The nature of the judgments prophesied by Zephaniah indicate that he was speaking of his day rather than the latter-days. For instance,

1. He speaks of the removal of the idols and wicked priests (Chemarims [Chĕm'-ă-rims]) from Judah. (1:4-5) This is a common prophecy in connection with the fall of Israel and Judah, but not pertaining to the last days.
2. Some of the sins for which Judah will be punished are sins of that day, such as the wearing of "strange apparel" which failed to distinguish those of the House of Israel from the people of other nations, and also the indifference of the men that are "settled on their lees."
3. The destruction is related to scenes of localized warfare rather than a massive cleansing by fire which would melt the elements and completely destroy the wicked.
    A. The trumpet and alarm against fenced cities. (1:16)
    B. Their blood shall be poured out. (1:17)
    C. Their goods shall become a booty. (1:13)
    D. A great crashing from the hills. (1:10)
    E. Ye shall be slain by my sword. (2:12)
4. The result of the day of the Lord's wrath of which Zephaniah prophesies is the desolation of many of the cities and areas mentioned. Nineveh, in particular, is described as being desolate. That city was destroyed, abandoned and laid desolate in 612 B. C.

It is important to observe, however, that Zephaniah is seemingly using language characteristic of the final destruction of the wicked as he warned the people of his day. This includes statements such as

1. The great day of the Lord is near, it is near. (1:14)
2. The whole land shall be devoured by the fire of his jealousy. (1:18)

3. I will utterly consume all things from off the land. (1:2)

He apparently followed a common procedure among those who have labored in God's kingdom through the ages; he drew upon references to the Lord's eventual coming in glory to dramatize the need for immediate repentance. Others have done so. John the Baptist proclaimed, "Repent ye: for the kingdom of heaven is at hand" in a clear allusion to a prophecy by Isaiah with a last-days setting. (Compare Mt. 3:1-3 with Is. 40:3-5). Paul taught the need for repentance because of the nearness of the Lord's coming to the Thessalonians so vividly that it became necessary for him to write them again to instruct them that other events must precede the Lord's advent. (see 1 Thess. 4:13-5:28; 2 Thess. 1:4-2:12) The theme of the nearness of Christ's coming in glory has played a prominent role in the Church in the latter-days also. (See, for instance D & C 1:12; 35:15; 49:6; 106:4; 133:8-10; 133:17) While the time of the Lord's coming is approaching rapidly, the Savior has revealed a definite series of events which is to precede His advent. He will not deceive the faithful by coming before these events are fulfilled.

Just as Judah and her neighbors experienced their own day of the Lord's wrath, other individuals and nations have need to repent in preparation for their own day of judgment, which may come long before the final day of judgment when the Lord comes in all His glory.

1. The Lord will consume all things from off the land. (1:2-3)
2. The Lord will stretch out His hand on Judah and Jerusalem and remove the idolatry. (1:4-6)
3. The Lord will punish the wicked in Jerusalem and those that are indifferent. (1:7-13)

    Note: "Settled on their lees" (1:12)—this metaphor is a comparison to the sediment that settles to the bottom of wine containers.

4. The great day of the Lord is near. (1:14)
5. The land shall be devoured by fire, and the blood of the wicked shall be poured out. (1:15-18)
6. Seek righteousness: it may be ye shall be hid in the day of the Lord's anger. (2:1-3)
7. Judah's neighbors will be destroyed. (2:4-5)

ZEPHANIAH 417

8. (30)¹ The remnant of the house of Judah will inhabit the sea coast when it returns from captivity. (2:6-7)
9. (34) Judah's neighbors shall be destroyed and the remnant of Judah shall possess their lands. (2:8-12)
10. The Lord will destroy Assyria and make Nineveh a desolation. (2:13-15)
11. The sins of Jerusalem are listed. (3:1-7)

Section II—The Lord's Blessings Upon the House of Israel in the Last Days. (3:8-13)

1. (35) The Lord will assemble the nations to pour His indignation upon them. (3:8)
2. (41) The Lord will give the people a pure language. (3:9)
3. (41) The dispersed will return from beyond the rivers of Ethiopia. (3:10)
4. (35) The Lord will take away the haughty and shall leave an afflicted and poor people, who will be free from pride and iniquity. (3:11-13)
5. (39) The Lord will be in the midst of Israel. (3:14-17)
6. (35) The Lord will cast out enemies and undo those that afflict Israel. (3:15, 19)
7. (41) Israel will have fame and praise among the nations. (3:19-20)

Doctrinal Analysis:

The Sins of Judah and Her Neighbors:

1. Idolatry. (1:4-5)
2. Men have not sought the Lord, nor inquired for him. (1:6)
3. They are clothed in strange apparel. (1:8)
4. Servants fill their masters houses with violence and deceit. (1:9)
5. The people say in their heart that the Lord will do neither good nor evil. (1:12)
6. They have reproached my people. (2:8, 10)
7. She obeyed not the voice, she received not correction. (3:2)
8. She trusted not the Lord. (3:2)
9. She drew not near to her God. (3:2)
10. (Hireling) prophets are light and treacherous persons. (3:4)

---

¹Numbers in parentheses at the beginning of items have reference to the fifty events of the last days listed in Chapter Four.

11. Her priests have polluted the sanctuary, they have done violence to the law. (3:4)
12. The unjust knoweth no shame. (3:5)
13. They corrupted all their doings. (3:7)

The Last Days:

1. (30) The coast shall be for the remnant of the house of Judah, for the Lord their God shall visit them, and turn away their captivity. (2:6-7)
2. (34) Moab and Ammon shall be destroyed by the residue of the Lord's people and the remnant of His people shall possess them. (2:9-10)
3. (41) Men shall worship the Lord, every one from his place, even all the isles of the heathen. (2:11)
4. The Lord's blessings upon the House of Israel in the last days: (3:8-13)
    A. (41) The Lord will give the people a pure language. (3:9)
    B. (41) The dispersed will return from beyond the rivers of Ethiopia. (3:10)
    C. (35) The Lord will take away the haughty and shall leave an afflicted and poor people, but they will be free from pride and iniquity. (3:11-13)

Nature of God:

1. The just Lord is in the midst thereof; he will not do iniquity: every morning doth he bring his judgment to light, he faileth not. (3:5)
2. I said, Surely thou wilt fear me, thou wilt receive instruction; so their dwelling should not be cut off, howsoever I punished them. (3:7)

Counsel for Righteous Living:

1. Hold thy peace at the presence of the Lord God. (1:7)
2. Seek ye the Lord, seek righteousness, seek meekness. (2:3)
3. Therefore wait ye upon me, saith the Lord, until the day that I rise up to the prey. (3:8)

Author and Date of Authorship:

Most critics accept Zephaniah as the author of the book at the time of his ministry. Some, however, deny him as the

ZEPHANIAH 419

author of chapters two and three, mainly on the assumption that his description of the redeemed Israel is typical of a later period. No real evidence is advanced and their assertions are highly speculative.

Style of the Book:
1. With the exception of the superscription, the book is entirely in poetry.
2. The poetry lacks the poetic brilliance of Isaiah and Amos.
3. In the sections predicting the ruin of Judah, Moab, Ammon, Ethiopia and Assyria, the lamentation meter (a line with three beats followed by a line with two beats) is used.
4. Zephaniah's writing calls to mind vivid images.
5. He uses fewer figures of speech than his prophet predecessors.
6. His writing is forceful, direct and positive.

Textual Transmission: The Hebrew text, particularly of the first portion of the prophecy, has suffered considerably in transmission. The Greek version (the Septuagint) has been used to help restore the original text.

Bible Criticism:

Bible scholars have challenged the authorship of Zephaniah for almost all portions of chapters two and three. These differences of authorship are asserted on the basis of supposed stylistic and doctrinal differences.

Summary: After studying the book of Zephaniah the student should know:
1. The three major lessons of the book:

    A. Judah would be destroyed because of its wickedness.

    B. In addition to the final "day of the Lord," every nation and individual has its own day of judgment. All mankind must prepare to meet their Maker.

    C. Israel will be restored to its land and to glory in the last days.
2. It is probable that Zephaniah was instrumental in causing the boy king, Josiah, to work on important reforms in Judah.

3. Zephaniah prophesied at the beginning of Jeremiah's ministry.
4. The five last kings of Judah:
    A. **Josiah**—worked reforms; killed by Pharaoh.
    B. **Jehoahaz**—ruled three months, then deposed by Pharaoh.
    C. **Jehoiakim**—control of Judah changed back from Egypt to Babylonia.
    D. **Jehoiachin**—first Babylonian captivity.
    E. **Zedekiah**—second Babylonian captivity, Jerusalem destroyed.
5. Judah was deported in 598 and 586 B. C.

CHAPTER XIV

NAHUM

Prophet's Name: Nahum (Nā'-hum) means "comforter" or "consoler."

Scriptural Information About the Prophet: Nahum was born in Elkosh. (1:1) (The location of this area is now unknown. Various traditions place it in Babylon, Assyria, Galilee, and southern Judah.)

Date of Nahum's Mission: c. 620 B. C.? This can only be deduced from certain references in his book:
1. It was after the fall of No-Amon (the Egyptian city of Thebes) which fell to Ashurbanipal, king of Assyria in 663 B. C. (3:8-10)
2. It preceded the destruction of Nineveh in 612 B. C. Therefore it can only be safely said that his mission was between 663 and 612 B. C.

Prophesied to: Nineveh (capital of Assyria)

Contemporary Prophets: It is not known which prophets were his contemporaries since the date of Nahum's prophecy is so poorly established. Zephaniah, Habakkuk, and Jeremiah possibly labored in his day.

National Conditions: Review the history of the late Assyrian empire. See pp. 174-177.

Outline of the Book:

Section I—An explanation of how the Lord can destroy the wicked—The Lord's Coming in Glory. (1:2-10)
1. (42)[1] The Lord will take vengeance on his adversaries. (1:2-3)
2. (42) The Lord will dry up the sea and the rivers. (1:4)
3. (42) The mountains quake, the hills melt and the world and all that dwell therein is burned at his presence. (1:5-7)

---

[1]Numbers in parentheses at the beginning of items refer to the fifty events of the last days listed in Chapter Four.

Interpretive Note: What distinguishes this portion of the prophecy as a reference to Christ's final coming in glory, rather than the approaching destruction of Nineveh?

A. The method of destruction is that which is common to the final destruction of the last days, not to the fall of Nineveh at the hands of the Medes and Babylonians.
- (1). The mountains quake. (1:5)
- (2). The hills melt. (1:5)
- (3). The earth is burned **at his presence.** (1:5)
- (4). The rocks are thrown down **by him.** (1:6)

B. The scope of the prophecy encompasses the whole world, not just Nineveh:
- (1). The earth is burned at his presence, **yea, the world, and all that dwell therein.** (1:5)
- (2). The Lord dries up the rivers and the sea (1:4) yet Nineveh is far inland and there is no evidence of this being fulfilled when Nineveh was destroyed.
- (3). Bashan, Carmel, and Lebanon are to languish, yet they are far from Nineveh. (1:4)

C. These features of Nahum's prophecy can be easily contrasted with the local factors and limited destruction of Zephaniah's prophecy, which show the latter to be a reference to his day rather than to events of the Last days.

Section II—Words of comfort to Judah. (1:11-15)

1. Though Judah has been afflicted, the Lord breaks her oppressor's yoke and will afflict her no more. (1:11-13)
2. Judah's graven images must still be cut off. (1:14)
3. The wicked shall no more pass through thee; he is utterly cut off. (1:15)

Section III—The siege and fall of Nineveh.

1. The fall of the city. (2:1-10)
2. An allegory compares Assyria's soldiers to lions and shows that they shall die by the sword. (2:11-13)
3. Woe to Nineveh because of its slaughter of the people of foreign nations. (3:1-7)
4. Nineveh shall experience the same fate as the city of No **(the Egyptian city of Thebes).** (3:8-10)

NAHUM

5. The Gates of Nineveh shall be flung open and the people shall be scattered upon the mountains. (3:11-19)

Doctrinal Analysis:

The Sins of Nineveh:
1. The city is full of lies and robbery. (3:1)
2. There is a multitude of slain, they stumble over the corpses. (3:3)
3. They sell families through their witchcrafts. (3:4)
4. They selleth nations through her whoredom. (3:4)

Attributes of God:
1. God is jealous. (1:2)
2. The Lord will take vengeance on his adversaries. (1:2)
3. The Lord is slow to anger. (1:3)
4. The Lord will not at all acquit the wicked. (1:3)
5. The Lord controls the whirlwind, the storm, and the clouds. (1:3)
6. The Lord dries up the sea and the rivers. (1:4)
7. Who can stand before His indignation. (1:6)
8. The Lord is good, a stronghold in the day of trouble. (1:7)
9. The Lord knoweth them that trust in him. (1:7)

Author and Date of Authorship:

Nahum is accepted as the author of the latter portion of the book, but most critics assert that 1:2-10 is a later insertion. This section is regarded as a very corrupt form of an alphabetic acrostic, although only the first part of the acrostic arrangement can be discovered. Some critics challenge the belief that Nahum was a prophet, and regard him only as a poet. The date of the writing is, of course, dependent upon a correct determination of the date of Nahum's ministry.

Style of the Book:
1. The book is entirely in poetry, with the exception of the superscription and 2:13.
2. Nahum's poetry is excellent. He is ranked as the last of the great classical Hebrew poets.
3. His descriptions are especially vivid and concrete in detail.
4. His poetic dignity and force approaches more nearly that of Isaiah than do the words of most of the other prophets.

5. His thoughts are expressed compactly.
6. The parallelism is regular.

Textual Transmission: The text has been well preserved unless chapter 1:2-10 are a mutilated acrostic poem, as some critics have asserted.

Bible Criticism:

There is little criticism of importance concerning the book of Nahum except for the assertion that 1:2-10 is a mutilated acrostic. An acrostic is a poem in which each line starts with the succeeding letter of the alphabet. Some scholars assert that the first fifteen of the twenty-two verses of the acrostic psalm are found in 1:2a, 3b, 4a, 4b, 5a, 5b, 6a, 6b, 7, 8a, 9b, 9c, 9a, 2b, 10. The alphabetic arrangement, of course, can only be seen in Hebrew and is not evident in the English translation. Some critics also assert that Nahum was not even a prophet but only an accomplished poet.

Changes Made in the Inspired Version of the Bible— Book of Nahum:

King James Translation	Inspired Version
1:8—But with an overrunning flood will he make an utter end . . .	1:8—But with an **everrunning** flood he will make an utter end . . .

Summary: After studying the book of Nahum the student should know:
1. Nahum, like Jonah, prophesied to Nineveh.
2. The two major lessons of the book:
    A. Nineveh will fall because of its slaughter of the people of foreign nations.
    B. The Lord will not acquit the wicked. (1:3)
3. The four Assyrian kings important to Bible History:
    A. Tiglath Pileser III (Pul) ⎫ Brought about the fall
    B. Shalmaneser V ⎬ of Israel, the Northern
    C. Sargon II ⎭ kingdom.
    D. Sennacherib—His army was smitten while attacking Judah.
4. Nineveh fell in 612 B. C.
5. The collapse of the Assyrian Empire brought the rise of the Babylonian Empire.

CHAPTER XV

OBADIAH

Prophet's Name: Obadiah (ō-bă-dī'-ăh) means "Servant of the Lord" or "Worshipper of Jehovah."

Scriptural Information About the Prophet: Nothing is known of his personal history. He should not be confused with the twelve other Obadiahs of the Old Testament.

Date of Obadiah's Mission: c. 598-587 B. C.? Obadiah apparently prophesied just after Jerusalem was plundered. (v. 11) Four such plunderings took place:
1. By the Philistines and Arabians, in the reign of Jehoram c. 850-845 B. C. (2 Chron. 21:8, 16, 17; Amos 1:6)
2. By Israel, in the reign of Amaziah c. 797-792 B. C. (2 Chron. 25:11-12, 23-24)
3. By Edom and the Philistines, in the reign of Ahaz c. 734-728 B. C. (2 Chron. 28:16-21)
4. By the Babylonians, who destroyed Jerusalem c. 598-587 B. C. in the reign of King Zedekiah. (2 Chron. 36:11-21)

Scholars differ in their opinion of to which of these periods Obadiah belonged. Since he speaks of the **destruction** of Jerusalem, most scholars place him in the reign of Zedekiah, when Babylonia destroyed Jerusalem.

Prophesied to: Edom

Contemporary Prophets: If his date is properly established, Obadiah prophesied during the later period of Jeremiah's ministry.

National conditions:

—**Political:** Zedekiah was placed on the throne of Judah by the Babylonian king Nebuchadnezzar. This happened as Jehoiachin and 10,023 of the men of Judah were taken captive into Babylonia. This was a period of vassalage and of sorrow for Judah.

—**Judah's Relationship to Edom:**
1. Edom was a 100 mile long mountain range which lay south east of Judah.

2. The Edomites were descendants of Esau, and were always bitter enemies of the Jews. (See Gen. 25:23; 27:41; Num. 20:14-21)
3. The Edomites, with their well-protected fortresses and their strategic command of important trade routes, became wealthy. They were materialistic and lacked consciousness of the spiritual values. They became a symbol of the wickedness of the world to the Israelite prophets.

Outline of the Book:

Section I—The Approaching Destruction of Edom.

1. Edom shall be destroyed. (1-9)
    A. The heathen shall rise up against them in battle. (1-2)
    B. The nations which have been at peace with thee have deceived thee. (7)
    C. Thy wise and mighty men shall be slaughtered. (8-9)
2. Edom will be cut off forever because of its violence against Judah. (8-14)

    Interpretive Note: The prophecies against Edom in that day have by some been interpreted as a prophecy of the final destruction of the wicked. (See D & C 1:36. Edom has been known as Idumea since the days of the Maccabees.)

Section II—The Glory of Israel in the Last Days.

1. (35)[1] The day of the Lord is near upon all the heathen. (15-16)
2. (39) There shall be deliverance and holiness upon Mt. Zion, and the house of Jacob shall possess their possessions. (17)
3. (35) The house of Israel will be as a flame and burn Esau as stubble. (18)
4. (30-31) The children of Israel shall possess the lands of their neighbors. (19-20)
5. (44) Saviors shall come upon mount Zion to judge the mount of Esau and the kingdom shall be the Lord's. (21)

---

[1]Numbers in parentheses at the beginning of items refer to the fifty events of the last days listed in Chapter Four.

Obadiah

Note: For the statements made by Joseph Smith in which he interpreted the term "saviors of mount Zion" see HC 4:360; 6:183-84.

Doctrinal Analysis:

The Sins of Edom:

1. The pride of thine heart hath deceived thee. (3)
2. There is no understanding in him. (7)
3. Edom rejoiced over the destruction of Judah. (12)
4. Edom spoke proudly in the day of Judah's distress. (12)
5. Edom robbed Judah. (13)
6. Edom kept the people of Judah from escaping from their enemies. (14)

God Governs in the Affairs of Men:

1. I have made thee small among the heathen. (2)
2. I will bring Edom down, saith the Lord. (4)
3. The Lord shall destroy the wise men of Edom. (8)

The Last Days:

See outline on the Glory of Israel in the Last Days above.

Author and Date of Writing:

Critics usually assert that two authors wrote the book, with one writing 1-14, 15b about 460 B. C. and the other writing 15a, 16-21 about 400 B. C. This is based on interpretation of internal evidence concerned with whether the prophecy was made before or after Jerusalem fell to Babylonia and the relationship to Jer. 49.

Style of the Book:

1. The book is all in poetry.
2. This is the shortest of the Old Testament books.

Textual Transmission: The text has been transmitted poorly, with many corruptions.

Lower Criticism:

Much of the Bible study of this book has been concerned with the close similarity between the book and chapter 49 of Jeremiah. This similarity is as follows:

Obadiah	Jeremiah 49
1a	7a
1b, 2	14, 15
3, 4	16
5a	9b
5b	9a
6	10
8	7b
9	22

Apparently one of five possibilities explains the relationship:

1. The Lord revealed the same things to the two prophets and each prophet expressed them in his own thought pattern;
2. Jeremiah borrowed from Obadiah;
3. Obadiah borrowed from Jeremiah;
4. One of the passages is a late post-exilic interpolation; or
5. Both borrowed from a common original.

Most critics ignore the first possibility and quote varying reasons why each of the later explanations are untenable. The consensus seems to lie with the fifth possibility, that both borrowed from memory from a common original.

Summary: After studying the book of Obadiah the student should know:

1. Obadiah prophesied to Edom, Israel's traditional enemy.
2. The two major lessons of the book:
    A. Edom would be destroyed for its sins against Judah.
    B. When the House of Israel is restored in the last days it will overcome its neighbors and possess their territories.
3. Obadiah is the smallest book of the Old Testament.
4. The prophets who preached in the period of the fall of Judah:
    A. Zephaniah.   D. Habakkuk.
    B. Nahum.   E. Jeremiah.
    C. Obadiah.
5. The three prophets of this period whose dates are uncertain:
    A. Nahum.
    B. Obadiah.
    C. Habakkuk.

CHAPTER XVI

HABAKKUK

Prophet's Name: Habakkuk (Hă-băk'-kuk). The Hebrew root means "ardent embrace."

Scriptural Information about the Prophet: There is no scriptural reference to Habakkuk outside of his book, nor is there any reliable historical source or tradition which identifies the prophet.

Date of Habakkuk's Mission: c. 607? B. C. This date is highly speculative. Some have dated him during the period of Alexander the Great, 250 years later.

Prophesied to: Rather than being sent to a nation, Habakkuk is questioning the Lord.

Contemporary Prophets: Jeremiah c. 626-586 B. C. to Judah

Contemporary Prophets Contrasted:

Nothing is known of **Habakkuk's** personal life nor the duration of his ministry. In his book he is revealed as being more concerned with understanding the Lord's motives for His actions than merely being content to speak the word of the Lord. He was philosophical in his approach.

Jeremiah's ministry extended over fifty years and during the reign of five kings of Judah. Much of his record is historical in nature. Jeremiah was of an introspective and emotional temperament, but he was forthright in his approach to the problems of the day.

Outline of the Book:

Section I—Habakkuk's two questions and the Lord's Answers (1:2-2:4)

> **Note:** The first portion of the book of Habakkuk can best be understood if the prophet is envisioned by the reader as asking questions from the Lord and receiving God's revealed answers to his queries.

1. Habakkuk's first question: Why is the Lord leaving the wickedness (of Judah) unpunished? (1:2-4) (Compare with D & C 121:1-6)

2. The Lord's Answer: The Lord is not indifferent to their sins. He is raising the Chaldeans (Babylonians) to punish them. (1:5-11)
3. Habakkuk's second question: Why does the Lord use a more wicked nation (Babylonia) to punish a more righteous nation (Judah)? (1:12-21)
4. The Lord's Answer: The Chaldeans will soon be destroyed. The righteous shall live by faith and the earth will eventually be filled with the knowledge of the Lord. (2:2-20)

    A. A taunt-song over the destruction of the Chaldeans. (2:5-20)

        (1). The people will rise against the Chaldeans because of their greed. (2:5-8)

        (2). Woe to the Chaldeans for cutting off many people. (2:9-11)

        (3). Woe to the Chaldeans for using slave labor (from conquered nations) to build their cities. (2:12-14)

        (4). Woe to those who get their neighbor drunk, to uncover his nakedness. (2:15-17)

        (5). Woe to those who practice idolatry. (2:18-20)

Section II—The Prayer of Habakkuk: A Psalm (3:1-19)

1. Superscription. (3:1)

    Note: Shigionoth (Shig-i-ō'-nōth): variable songs or tunes.

2. Habakkuk's request of God: Do again thy wonders as in the days of old. (3:2)
3. A vision of the coming of the Lord. (3:3-15)

    Note: Selah: a musical sign, probably instruction for the singers to sing higher. (3:3, 9, 13)

    A. (42)[1] God's glory covered the heavens. (3:3-4)

    B. (42) He measured the earth, drove asunder the nations, and scattered the everlasting mountains. (3:5-6)

    C. (42) Affliction was seen among the people of Cushan (Ethiopia) and Midian. (3:7)

    D. (42) The mountains trembled, the overflowing water passed by, the sun and the moon stood still. (3:8-11)

---

[1]Numbers in parentheses at the beginning of items refer to the fifty events of the last days listed in Chapter Four.

HABAKKUK

    E. (42) The Lord threshed the heathen and the wicked in anger. (3:12-16)
4. Though the crops fail, yet I will rejoice in the Lord. (3:17-19)

Doctrinal Analysis:

The Sins of the People:
1. Spoiling and violence. (1:3)
2. Men raise up strife and contention. (1:3)
3. The law is slack, so judgment doth never go forth. (1:4)
4. The wicked compass about the righteous. (1:4)
5. Attribute the power of Jehovah to other Gods. (1:11)
6. He transgresseth by wine. (2:5)
7. He enlargeth his desire as hell, and cannot be satisfied. (2:5)
8. Thou hast spoiled many nations and cut off many people. (2:8, 10)
9. Woe to him that coveteth an evil covetousness to his house. (2:9)
10. Woe to him that makes his neighbor drunken to look on his nakedness. (2:15-16)
11. Idolatry. (2:18-19)
12. Their rejoicing was to devour the poor secretly. (3:14)

The Nature of God:
1. Thou art of purer eyes than to behold evil, and canst not look on iniquity. (1:13)
2. In wrath (O Lord) remember mercy. (3:2)
3. Was the Lord displeased against the rivers? (3:8)
4. Was thy wrath against the sea? (3:8)
5. He has power over the elements. (3:6-11)
6. Thou didst march through the land in indignation. (3:12)
7. Thou didst thresh the heathen in anger. (3:12)
8. Thou wentest forth for the salvation of thy people, even for salvation with thine anointed. (3:13)

God's Dealings with His Prophets:
1. Write the vision and make it plain; it will surely come. (2:2-3)

Counsel for Righteous Living:
1. The just shall live by his faith. (2:4)
2. The Lord is in his holy temple: let all the earth keep silence before him. (2:20)

3. I will rejoice in the Lord, I will joy in the God of my salvation. (3:18)

The Lord's Blessings to the Righteous:
1. The Lord God is my strength. (3:19)
2. He will make my feet like hinds' feet. (3:19)
3. He will make me to walk upon mine high places. (3:19)

Author and date of Authorship:

Because of the indefinite nature of the book, some critics have questioned whether it is the Jews who are the wicked who must be punished or whether the wicked ones are the Assyrians, the Chaldeans, or the Egyptians. The dating of the book is dependent upon the interpretation of this question. The entire matter of date and authorship is quite vague, but the book is most often placed between 630 and 600 B. C. Chapter three is regarded as a later addition by many critics.

Style of the Book:
1. The entire book is in poetry.
2. The book is rhetorical and majestic, dignified and sublime.
3. It lacks the simplicity of ancient Hebrew poetry at its best.
4. The parallelisms are usually regular and complete.
5. The descriptions are vivid and clear.

Textual Transmission—The Hebrew text has not been well preserved, thereby causing difficulty in translating and interpreting certain portions of the book.

Bible Criticism:

There is little agreement among the critics as to the authorship of the book and the date it was written. Many of them consider chapter three to be written by a different author. No evidence is available to support any theory but the line of reasoning is such as that followed by one critic, Robert H. Pfeiffer, who wrote, "There is no valid reason for attributing both parts of the book to the same author."

Summary: After studying the book of Habakkuk the student should know:
1. The proper spelling of Habakkuk. (one b, two k's)

HABAKKUK

2. Habakkuk was different from the other prophets. Instead of prophesying to a nation, he asked questions of the Lord. He was a philosopher.
3. Habakkuk's two questions and their answers:
    A. Q. Why is the Lord leaving the wickedness of Judah unpunished?
    A. The Babylonians will soon punish them.
    B. Q. Why does the Lord use a more wicked nation (Babylonia) to punish a less wicked nation (Judah)?
    A. The Babylonians will soon be destroyed too.
4. The two major lessons of the book:
    A. The Lord will punish the wicked.
    B. The righteous shall live by faith.

CHAPTER XVII

JEREMIAH

Prophet's Name: The meaning of the name Jeremiah (Jĕr-ĕ-mī'-ăh) is not clear. It may mean "Jehovah hurls."

The Life of Jeremiah: More is known about Jeremiah than any of the other prophets. Rather than presenting the few scriptural allusions to him, as in the case of the other prophets, it is possible to set forth an outline of his life, as depicted in the scriptures, which is as follows:[1]

The Reign of King Josiah (c. 640-609 B.C.)

1. His birth: c. 645 B.C.?
    A. He was the son of Hilkiah (Hil-kī'-ăh). (1:1) This was a priestly line. He was probably a descendant of Abiathar (ă-bī'-ă-thär) who was the priest of King David, but was banished by Solomon. Abiathar was a descendant of the prophet Eli.
    B. He came from Anathoth (ăn'-ă-thōth) in the land of Benjamin. (1:1) This is a small town about 2½ miles northeast of Jerusalem near what is now the Arab village of Anata.
2. His call to the ministry: c. 626 B. C.
    A. It was in the 13th year of Josiah's reign, about c. 626 B. C. (1:2-19)
3. Jeremiah's early teachings: The house of Israel had abandoned its God. (2, 3)
4. **The Scythian Invasion:** c. 630-624 B.C. Jeremiah warned of approaching danger from the north. (4, 5, 6)
5. **Discovery of the Book of the Law.** c. 621 B. C. (2 Ki. 22)
6. **Josiah's Reformation:** c. 621 B. C. (2 Ki. 22) He was called from Anathoth to Jerusalem to support the reform movement. (7)
7. Jeremiah's preaching in support of Josiah's reformation. (7, 8, 9, 10, 11)
8. Men in Anathoth plotted to take Jeremiah's life. (11)

---

[1]External events which did not directly involve Jeremiah are indicated in bold type. Chapter numbers are indicated in parentheses at the end of each item.

JEREMIAH

9. Jeremiah's complaint because the people did not heed him. (12)
10. He took a girdle to the Euphrates River and recovered it. (13)
11. **The Fall of Assyria:**
    A. **Asshur** (c. 614 B. C.)
    B. **Nineveh** (c. 612 B. C.)
    C. **Haran** (c. 608-606 B. C.)
12. **A Famine in Judah:** Jeremiah attempted to intercede for his people. (14, 15)
13. Jeremiah was commanded not to marry. (16)
14. Jeremiah preached about the Sabbath day on the temple steps. (17)
15. Jeremiah made the marred vessel from potters clay. (18)
16. A plot was made against Jeremiah's life. (18)
17. Jeremiah broke an earthen bottle by the east gate of Jerusalem. (19)
18. Pashur put Jeremiah in the stocks by the temple. (20)
19. **The death of King Josiah:** (At Megiddo, killed by troops of Pharaoh Necho) (2 Ki. 23)

The reign of King Jehoahaz (c. 609 B. C.)

20. Jeremiah prophesied of three kings in the palace of Jerusalem. (22)
21. **Jehoahaz was deposed by Pharaoh Necho** (2 Ki. 23)

The reign of King Jehoiakim (c. 609-598 B. C.)

22. Jeremiah was tried for prophesying the fall of the temple. c. 609 B. C. (26)
23. Jeremiah wore a yoke in Jerusalem. (27)
24. Jeremiah encountered the false priest Hananiah. (28)
25. Jeremiah prophesied against foreign lands. c. 605 B. C. (25, 46, 47, 48, 49:1-33)
26. **The Egyptians were defeated at the Battle of Carchemish.** c. 605 B. C.
27. Jeremiah offered wine to the Rechabites. (35)
28. Jeremiah dictated his book to Baruch. (36)
29. Jeremiah prophesied to Baruch. (45)
30. Jehoiakim cut up Jeremiah's book. (36)
31. Jeremiah and Baruch went into hiding. (36)
32. Jeremiah and Baruch rewrote Jeremiah's book. (36)

The reign of Jehoiachin (c. 598 B. C.)

33. **c. 598 B. C. Babylonia besieged Jerusalem. Jehoiachin surrendered. The First deportation of Jews to Babylon was made.** (2 Ki. 24)

The reign of Zedekiah: (c. 598-587 B. C.)
34. c. 598 B. C. Jeremiah wrote a letter to the exiles in Babylonia. (29)
35. c. 598 B. C. Jeremiah bought a field in Anathoth. (32)
36. c. 598 B. C. Jeremiah's prophecy against Elam. (49: 34-39)
37. c. 594 B. C. Jeremiah sent prophecies of the fall of Babylon to the exiles. (50, 51)
38. He contrasted two baskets of figs—the first and second deportation. (24)
39. Jeremiah prophesied of the restoration of Israel. (30, 31, 33)
40. c. 588 B. C. **Nebuchadnezzar besieged Jerusalem.** (2 Ki. 25)
41. Zedekiah inquired of Jeremiah. (21)
42. **The Babylonian army left Jerusalem to challenge the Egyptian Army.** (37)
43. **Zedekiah liberated the slaves.** (34)
44. Jeremiah left Jerusalem, was arrested and imprisoned in the house of Jonathan. (37)
45. Zedekiah again inquired of Jeremiah and had him imprisoned in Jerusalem. (37)
46. Jeremiah was placed in a mire-filled dungeon by the temple officials. He was saved by an Ethiopian eunuch. (38)
47. Zedekiah again inquired of Jeremiah. (38)
48. c. 587 B. C. **Jerusalem fell and Zedekiah was captured. The Second deportation of the Jews was made.** (39, 52)
49. Jeremiah was shown special favor by the Babylonians. (39)

The reign of Gedeliah (c. 586 B. C.)
50. c. 586 B. C. **Gedeliah was made Governor.** (40)
51. c. 586 B. C. Jeremiah was taken by mistake to Ramah, then released. (40)
52. c. 586 B. C. **Gedeliah was assassinated.** (41)
53. Johanan asked counsel from Jeremiah. (42)
54. Jeremiah was carried captive into Egypt. (43)
55. Jeremiah hid a stone as a symbol of the fall of Egypt. (43)
56. Jeremiah predicted the destruction of the Jewish remnant in Egypt. (44)

Date of Jeremiah's Mission: c. 626-586 B. C.
1. He was called in the 13th year of the reign of King Josiah, King of Judah. (1:2-19)

JEREMIAH

2. He continued preaching after he was carried into Egypt after the fall of Jerusalem. (44)

Prophesied To: Judah

Contemporary Prophets:
Zephaniah: to Judah. (c. 626 B. C.)

Three prophets who were probably contemporaries, but of unsure date:
- Nahum: to Nineveh.
- Obadiah: to Edom.
- Habakkuk: questioned the Lord.

Two prophets in Babylon:
- Daniel: to Babylon and Persia (c. 606-533 B. C.)
- Ezekiel: to the Jews in captivity in Babylonia. (c. 593-571 B. C.)

Contemporary Prophets Contrasted:

Jeremiah was probably a descendant of the priestly line, and his forefathers apparently were from Israel rather than Judah. Unlike Zephaniah, Jeremiah had no political connections and was not influential in the affairs of the royal court during Josiah's time. Like Zephaniah, Jeremiah was a young man in the days of Josiah. The recorded ministry of Jeremiah extended over fifty years and during the reign of five kings of Judah. Jeremiah was of an introspective and emotional temperament.

Zephaniah was supposedly of royal blood, and is believed to have been influential in the royal court of Judah. It appears that he was closely connected with the young boy king, Josiah, and was able to influence him for good. He seemingly was from Jerusalem and well knew the city. He would probably have been a young man in this period, judging by the time of the generations from Hezekiah, king of Judah. The tone of his message indicates that he is of a bold, unflinching nature.

(Nahum, Obadiah and Habakkuk are not contrasted because so little is known concerning their date and ministry. Daniel and Ezekiel will be considered in the next section of this book.)

Contemporary Kings:

Judah: **Josiah**   (c. 640-609 B. C.)
Brought about important reforms in Judah.
He was killed by the Egyptians at Megiddo under Pharaoh Necho.
Jehoahaz   (c. 609 B. C.)
He was deposed after three months by the Egyptian Pharaoh Necho.
Jehoiakim   (c. 609-598 B. C.)
Placed on the throne by the Egyptian Pharaoh Necho.
Persecuted Jeremiah and burned the roll of his prophecies.
Paid tribute first to Egypt, then to Babylonia.
Jehoiachin   (c. 598 B. C.)
An eight year old king who only ruled three months.
He surrendered to Babylonia and went into captivity.
First deportation of Judah to Babylon.
Zedekiah   (c. 598-587 B. C.)
A weak king who asked for advice from Jeremiah but would not accept the advice.
Jerusalem fell after a 1½ year siege. It was destroyed.
Second deportation of Judah to Babylon.
Gedeliah   (c. 586 B. C.)
A governor established by Babylonia. He ruled two months and then was assassinated.

Babylonia: **Nabopolassar**   (c. 625-604 B. C.)
Established the Babylonian Empire by defeating Assyria.
Sent his son, Nebuchadnezzar, who defeated the Egyptians at the Battle of Carchemish. c. 605 B. C.
Nebuchadnezzar   (c. 604-562 B. C.)
Took Jehoiachin and the Jews to Babylon.
First Deportation (c. 598 B.C.)
Took Zedekiah and more Jews to Babylon.
Second Deportation (c. 586 B.C.)
Destroyed Jerusalem. c. 586 B. C.

National Conditions:
—Political:
1. Jeremiah lived during a three-way struggle for supremacy between Assyria, Babylonia, and Egypt. In the middle of his ministry this struggle came to an end. Assyria, which had dominated the scene for approximately three centuries, fell to a coalition of Babylonia and Media. Babylonia, which had been a vassal state to Assyria, rose to power and conquered the Mediterranean states, including Judah. It controlled the Near East for seventy years. Egypt attempted to maintain the balance of power which would keep Assyria from falling to Babylonia, but was defeated in the battle of Carchemish in 605 B. C. and was soon overrun by Babylonia.
2. Jeremiah watched the continual disintegration of his government as it suffered repeated assaults from Egypt and then Babylonia. He held the formula for escape from impending devastations but could not win the necessary respect of the kings he counselled so they would heed his message.

—Economic:
1. Just as Judah disintegrated politically, it also collapsed economically. Jeremiah watched as the country was stripped of its wealth by the invaders and as the nobles and the rich were taken into captivity, leaving their estates uncontrolled and disorganized.
2. He saw the slaves freed and then forced back into slavery.
3. He watched the barter and trade which undoubtedly went on during the siege of Jerusalem as the people struggled to avert starvation.
4. He even bought a field in a conquered and desolated area as a testimony of his faith that the economy of all Israel would be restored.

—Religious:
1. As the distress of the country grew, the people attempted to gain relief from the various gods that they worshipped, and thus they plunged deeper into idolatry. Even after some of the Jews had fled into Egypt and their country lay desolate, some asserted that the problem arose because they hadn't been sufficiently diligent in worshipping the "queen of heaven." (the moon)

2. The worship of Jehovah had deteriorated into a hollow form. The ranks of Jehovah worshippers had shrunk also so that it was just one of many religions. Its priests and prophets were corrupt.
3. Hireling prophets, who were paid to preach that peace would soon come (apparently to aid some people in their financial dealings), did much to mislead the people and keep them from heeding the prophecies of the Lord's authorized servants.

Notes on the Study and Interpretation of the Book of Jeremiah:

Most of the book of Jeremiah can best be understood from a historical standpoint. If the reader will follow the chronology of Jeremiah's life he will be able to grasp the relationship of his prophecies to the historical developments of his time. To facilitate such a reading plan, the chapters of Jeremiah are presented in a study outline with a chronological grouping under the reigns of the various kings of Judah, as follows:

Section I—Chapters of Jeremiah Pertaining to the Reign of Kings Josiah and Jehoahaz.

1, 2, (3), 4, 5, 6, 7, 8, 9, 10, 11, 12, 13, 14, 15, (16), 17, 18, 19, 20, 22

Section II—Chapters of Jeremiah Pertaining to the Reign of King Jehoiakim.

26, 27, 28, (23), 25, 46, 47, 48, 49:1-33, 35, 36, 45

Section III—Chapters of Jeremiah Pertaining to the Reign of King Zedekiah.

29, 32, 49:34-39, 50, 51, 24, (30), (31), (33), 21, 34, 37, 38, 39, 52

Section IV—Chapters of Jeremiah Pertaining to the Final Period of the Prophet's Life.

40, 41, 42, 43, 44

If the reader will consider the chapters in the order given above, he will experience little difficulty in keeping track of the historical events of chronological significance in Jere-

JEREMIAH 441

miah's account. The above list is, of course, correlated with the outline of Jeremiah's life given earlier in the chapter.

There are six chapters of Jeremiah which contain significant passages concerning the last days. They have been separated into a special section for particular study as follows:

Section V—Chapters of Jeremiah Pertaining to the Last Days.

3, 16, 31, 30, 23, 33

The chronological order for these passages was indicated in sections I, II, and III by placing the chapter numbers in parentheses. The chapters, however, are actually outlined in Section V.

For the reader's convenience the following finding list of the chapters of Jeremiah is presented:

Chapter	Page	Section	Chapter	Page	Section
1	442	I	27	449	II
2	442	I	28	449	II
3	459	(I) V	29	452	III
4	442	I	30	460	(III) V
5	443	I	31	460	(III) V
6	443	I	32	452	III
7	443	I	33	461	(III) V
8	444	I	34	454	III
9	444	I	35	451	II
10	444	I	36	451	II
11	445	I	37	454	III
12	445	I	38	455	III
13	445	I	39	455	III
14	445	I	40	457	IV
15	445	I	41	457	IV
16	459	(I) V	42	457	IV
17	446	I	43	457	IV
18	446	I	44	458	IV
19	447	I	45	451	II
20	447	I	46	450	II
21	454	III	47	450	II
22	447	I	48	450	II
23	461	(II) V	49	451, 2	II, III
24	453	III	50	452	III
25	450	II	51	453	III
26	449	II	52	456	III

SECTION I
CHAPTERS OF JEREMIAH PERTAINING TO THE REIGN OF KINGS JOSIAH AND JEHOAHAZ.

Chapter 1—Jeremiah's Call to the Ministry.
1. Superscription. (1-3)
2. Jeremiah's call: he was ordained a prophet before birth. (4-5)
3. The purpose of his ministry: to root out and to destroy, to build and to plant. (6-10)
4. **Vision of the almond rod**: the Lord will hasten to perform his work. (11-12)
5. **Vision of the seething pot facing north**: an evil out of the north will encompass the cities of Judah. (13-16)
6. The Lord will protect Jeremiah so his enemies cannot prevail against him. (17-19)

Chapter 2—Judah's Wickedness Will Bring About Her Punishment.
1. Judah is depicted as the Lord's bride. He remembers her goodness as she came into the promised land. (1-4)
2. Though the Lord brought them into a plentiful country they disliked him and worshipped other gods. (5-8)
3. The Lord will still plead with his people unto the third generation. (9-10)
4. The nation has changed to false gods. They have forsaken the Lord. (11-13)
5. Judah's own wickedness will bring about its punishment. The cities will be without inhabitants. (14-19)
6. The nation has wandered into the harlotry of the idolatrous fertility rites and has turned to other gods. (20-35)
7. Judah will be sorry for treaties made with Egypt as it has been for those made with Assyria. (36-37)

Chapter 3—The Restoration of Israel in the Last Days.
This chapter is outlined in Section V. It is suggested that verses 1-11 be studied in connection with Section I.

Chapter 4—Destruction Will Soon Come From the North. (The Babylonians and/or the Scythians)
1. If Judah will return to the Lord she will not be removed (into captivity). (1-4)
2. The destroyer of the Gentiles is on his way from the north, and the whole land shall be desolate. (5-31)

JEREMIAH—SECTION I

> Note: Some scholars assert that chapters 4, 5, and 6, were originally written by Jeremiah to the remnant left in the northern kingdom, warning them of the Scythian invasion, and then rewritten with reference to the sins of Judah and the coming attacks by Nebuchadnezzar and the Babylonians.

Chapter 5—Judah will be Destroyed Because of Wickedness. (The Babylonians and/or Scythians)
1. There is no righteous man in Jerusalem so they shall be torn in pieces. (1-6)
2. Judah has been guilty of adultery; they have behaved like animals. (7-8)
3. The people have scoffed at the prophets' warnings of destruction by sword and famine. (9-14)
4. A nation will come upon Judah from afar which will eat their food and impoverish their cities, yet it will not make a full end of Judah. (15-19)
5. The wickedness of the people has turned them away from the Lord. Their sins have withheld good things from them. (20-25)
6. The people oppress the poor and the prophets prophesy falsely. (26-31)

Chapter 6—Destruction Will Soon Come from the North. (The Babylonians and/or the Scythians)
1. Evil and great destruction appears out of the north. (1)
2. The destruction of Jerusalem is described. (2-12)
3. The sins of the people have prevented them from walking in the path of the Lord. (13-17)
4. They will be punished for rejecting the law of the Lord. (18-21)
5. Jerusalem will be destroyed by an invader from the north. (22-26)
6. The people are wicked corrupters. (27-30)

Chapter 7—Only Righteousness Can Save Judah.
1. The people must live lives of good character. Proper living, rather than reliance on the temple rituals, is what will save them from captivity. (1-11)
2. Go to Shiloh and see how the Lord destroyed the place of worship there. (12-15)
3. The Lord's instruction to Jeremiah: Do not pray for the people or attempt to intercede for them. (16)

444   PROPHETS AND PROPHECIES OF THE OLD TESTAMENT

4. The idolatry of the people will cause the Lord to burn Jerusalem. (17-20)
5. The Lord commanded their forefathers: Obey my voice, and I will be your God, but Judah has rejected the Lord and his prophets. (21-28)
6. The abominations and idolatry of Jerusalem has caused the Lord to slay the people and make the city desolate. (29-34)

Chapter 8—The people have Refused to Repent.
1. The enemy will scatter the bones of the bodies of the slain of Judah. The living will choose death rather than captivity. (1-3)
2. The people have foolishly asserted that they are wise and that they are observing the law of the Lord instead of repenting. (4-9)
   Note: "the pen of the scribes is in vain": a reference to the scribes who wrote down the reforms brought about by King Josiah.
3. False priests and prophets have misled the people by prophesying peace (when the future will bring war and destruction). They shall be destroyed. (10-12)
4. The destruction of Jerusalem foreseen. (13-17)
5. The harvest (opportunity for repentance) is past. Judah is not saved. (18-22)

Chapter 9—Judah's Sins will bring Sorrow and Destruction.
1. Jeremiah weeps for his people. (1-2)
2. Their sins are listed, for which the Lord will punish them. (3-8)
3. The mountains and cities will be burned and desolate. (9-11)
4. Learn to wail, for sorrow approaches. They shall be scattered and slain. (12-22)
5. Do not glory in wisdom, might, or riches, but in understanding and knowing the Lord. (23-24)
6. Judah will be punished, along with her unrighteous neighbors. (25-26)

Chapter 10—Idols have No Power. Only the Lord Rules.
1. Idols do not speak, walk, or do good. Only the Lord has power. (1-16)
2. Judah will be cast out and distressed. Jeremiah grieves that they will be carried away to the north. (17-22)

JEREMIAH—SECTION I 445

3. Jeremiah's plea: O Lord, correct me, but with judgment. Not in thine anger. (23-25)

Chapter 11—Judah Refuses to Keep Her Covenant With God.
1. The man that does not obey his covenant with God shall be cursed. (1-5)
2. Jeremiah was commanded by the Lord to proclaim the covenant throughout Judah. (6-7)
3. The people have refused to obey the covenant. (8-10)
4. When trouble comes to Judah, the people will cry to false gods. (11-13)
5. The Lord's instruction to Jeremiah: Do not pray in behalf of the people; He will not hear their cry. (14)
6. The men of Anathoth plot to kill Jeremiah because he preaches against idolatry. (15-23)

Chapter 12—The Lord will Not Allow the Wicked To Prosper for Long.
1. **Jeremiah questions the Lord:** Why do the wicked prosper? (1-4)
2. **The Lord's answer:**
   A. If the wickedness of these individuals wearies you, how will you be able to withstand greater things? (5-6)
   B. The wicked will be punished. Judah shall be destroyed. (7-14)
   C. A group will be allowed to return, but if they will not be obedient, they will be destroyed as a nation. (15-17)

Chapter 13—The Pride of Judah Will be Marred Like Jeremiah's Girdle.
1. **The symbol of the Girdle:**
   A. Jeremiah was commanded to take a girdle and bury it by the Euphrates River. Many days later he was commanded to dig it up. It was marred and useless. (1-7)
   B. The girdle symbolized the pride of Judah, which would be marred and reduced to nothingness (in the Babylonian captivity). (8-11)
2. Judah will be brought down and carried into captivity because of her iniquities. (12-27)

Chapters 14 and 15—The Famine: A Punishment for Judah.
1. A terrible drought and famine existed in Judah. (14:1-6)
2. **Jeremiah's prayer for relief for his people:** (14:7-9)

3. **The Lord's reply:** He is punishing the people for their sins. Do not pray in their behalf. (14:10-12)
4. **Jeremiah:** Their prophets have misled them. (14:13)
5. **The Lord:** They listen to false prophets. The prophets and the people who listen to them will be destroyed by the famine and sword which they deny. (14:14-22)
6. **The Lord:** I am weary with (ineffective) repenting. I will give Judah to death, to the sword, to famine, and to captivity. (15:1-9)
7. **Jeremiah:** I have lived righteously but men curse me. (15:10)
8. **The Lord (to Jeremiah):** I will cause the enemy to treat thee well, but you will go into an unknown land. (15:11-14)
9. **Jeremiah:** I know that the rebuke I have suffered is for thy sake. Why am I still pained by this persecution? (15:15-18)
10. **The Lord:** I will make thee a fenced wall to the people. They shall not prevail against thee. (19-21)

Chapter 16—Judah's Approaching Destruction and Eventual Return.

This chapter is outlined in Section V. It is suggested that verses 1-13 be studied in connection with Section I.

Chapter 17—Judah must Repent and Trust in the Lord.

1. Because of idolatry Judah shall serve her enemies in an unknown land. (1-4)
2. Cursed be the man who trusteth in man; blessed is the man that trusteth in the Lord. (5-8) (See 2 Ne. 4:34)
3. The Lord searches the heart. (9-11)
4. Jeremiah pleads that the Lord will heal and save him and confound his enemies. (12-18)
5. The Lord sends Jeremiah to preach at the entrance of the temple: If you keep the Sabbath day holy, then shall the city not be destroyed. If the sabbath is not kept, Jerusalem will be destroyed. (19-27)

Chapter 18—God Can Discard Judah as a Potter's Vessel.

1. **The symbol of the potter's clay:**
    A. The Lord sent Jeremiah to the potter's house. He made a vessel of clay, but it was marred. Then he made another vessel. (1-4)

JEREMIAH—SECTION I 447

    B. **Interpretation:**
    The potter: The Lord.
    The clay: The House of Israel.
    If the Lord chooses, he can discard a marred vessel and raise up another. (5-10)
2. Because Judah has forgotten the Lord and walked after their own devices, they will be scattered before the enemy. (11-17)
3. A plot against Jeremiah: his words are rejected. (18)
4. Jeremiah's plea to the Lord for justice: Shall evil be recompensed for good? Deliver them up to the famine and the sword. (19-23)

Chapter 19—**Judah will be Broken like an Earthen Bottle.**
1. **The symbol of the earthen bottle:**
    A. The Lord commanded Jeremiah to take an earthen bottle (perhaps one of elegance) and break it in front of the people of Judah, and prophesy to them. (1-13)
    B. Jeremiah broke the bottle as instructed as a symbol that the people and city would be broken beyond repair. He prophesied that evil will come upon Judah. (14-15)

Chapter 20—**Though Persecuted and Discouraged, Jeremiah Finds He Still Must Teach.**
1. Pashur (Păsh'-ur) (a high officer of the temple?), heard Jeremiah's prophecy with the earthen vessel, and put him in stocks. (1-2)
2. When released, Jeremiah prophesied that Judah would be captured by Babylon and that Pashur would die a captive in Babylon. (3-6)
3. Discouraged, Jeremiah resolved he would no longer preach the word of the Lord, but he could not hold back. (7-9)
4. Jeremiah curses the day he was born, but asks the Lord to take vengeance upon his persecutors. (10-18)

Chapter 22—**Jeremiah's Prophecies Concerning Three Kings of Judah.**
1. The Lord sent Jeremiah to the king's palace to preach this message:
    A. If you will execute judgment in righteousness kings shall enter this house; if you do not, this house shall be a desolation. (1-5)

B. The Lord will make Judah uninhabited. Other nations will say it is because Judah forsook the Lord and worshipped other gods. (6-10)
2. Prophecies concerning the kings of Judah:
   A. **Jehoahaz** (Shallum): His many sins are listed. He shall die in captivity. (11-17)
   B. **Jehoiakim:** He refused to listen to Jeremiah. He shall be killed and cast before the gates of Jerusalem. (18-23)
   C. **Jehoiachin** (Coniah): He shall be given into the hands of Babylonians. He shall not return to his own country. No ruler shall prosper in Judah. (24-30)

SECTION II

CHAPTERS OF JEREMIAH PERTAINING TO THE REIGN OF KING JEHOIAKIM

Chapter 26—Jeremiah's Trial for Prophesying the Fall of the Temple.
1. Jeremiah prophesied the fall of the temple if the people would not repent. (1-7)
2. The priests and false prophets seized him and brought him before the princes, asserting that he should be put to death for prophesying the fall of the temple. (8-11)
3. Jeremiah told them the Lord had commanded him to prophesy. If they slew him, they would be taking innocent blood. (12-15)
4. The elders discussed Jeremiah's fate, recalling the prophecies of Micah and Urijah. Ahikam (ă-hī'-kăm) prevailed on his companions to spare Jeremiah's life. (16-24)

Chapter 27—Come Under the Yoke of Babylon and Live.
1. The symbol of the yoke:
    A. The Lord commanded Jeremiah to place a yoke on his neck and send yokes to nearby kings, with the message to: (1-4)
    B. Come under the yoke of Babylon, or be punished with famine, sword, and pestilence. (5-8)
    C. Do not listen to the false prophets, who say the nations will not have to serve Babylon. (9-18)
    D. The remainder of Judah's temple treasures will go into Babylon. (19-22)

Chapter 28—The False Prophecy of Hananiah Exposed.
1. Jeremiah's confrontation with the false prophet Hananiah (Hăn-ă-nī'-ah) in the temple. (1-17)
    A. Hananiah's prophecy: Within two years the yoke of Babylon will be broken, Jehoiachin and the temple vessels will be returned. (1-4)
    B. Jeremiah proposed the test of a true prophet: "When the word of the prophet shall come to pass, then shall the prophet be known, that the Lord hath truly sent him." (6-9)
    C. Hananiah took the yoke from Jeremiah's neck and broke it, as he repeated his prophecy. (10-11)

D. Jeremiah's prophecy: The people will be conquered by Babylonia; Hananiah will die within the year. (He died two months later.) (12-17)

Chapter 23—False Prophets Have Misled the People.
This chapter is outlined in Section V. It is suggested that verses 9-40 be studied in connection with Section II.

Chapter 25—Seventy Years of Captivity.
1. Jeremiah and the other prophets have called the people to repentance, but the people have not listened. (1-7)
2. Nebuchadnezzar and his followers will destroy Judah and her neighbors and make their lands desolations. These nations shall serve Babylon seventy years. (8-11)
3. In seventy years the Lord will destroy Babylon. (12-14)
4. Jeremiah is commanded to drink wine as a symbol of the cup of the Lord's fury that will be poured out on more than twenty countries and cities. They will fall and rise no more. (15-29)
5. (16?) The Lord has a controversy with the nations. The slain at that day shall be from one end of the earth to the other. (30-33)
6. The shepherds (false prophets) shall have no way to flee. (34-38)

Chapter 46—The Fall of Egypt Prophesied.
1. Nebuchadnezzar, king of Babylonia, will smite Pharaoh Necho of Egypt at Carchemish. (1-12)
2. Nebuchadnezzar will smite the land of Egypt. (13-26)
3. (30-31) Israel will be saved and will return from the lands of her captivity. (27-28) (Cf. Jer. 30:10-11)
   A. (35?) The Lord will make a full end of the nations where she has been driven. (28)
   B. (35) The house of Israel will not go wholly unpunished. (28)

Chapter 47—The Fall of the Philistines Prophesied.
1. The Philistines will be overpowered by a wave from the north. (Babylonia) (1-7)

Chapter 48—The Fall of Moab Prophesied.
1. The fall of Moab prophesied. (1-46)
2. (34)[1] The Lord will bring again (restore) Moab in the latter days. (47)

---

[1] Numbers in parentheses at the beginning of items refer to the fifty events of the last days listed in Chapter Four.

JEREMIAH—SECTION II   451

Chapter 49:1-33—**The Fall of Ammon, Edom, Damascus, and Kedar Prophesied.**
1. The Ammonites will be conquered. (1-5)
2. (34?) The Ammonites will be restored afterward. (6)
3. Edom will be conquered. (7-22) (Cf. the book of Obadiah)
4. Damascus is feeble and will fall. (23-27)
5. Kedar (Kĕ'-där) and Hazor (Hā'-zôr) will be made desolate by Nebuchadnezzar. (28-33)

Chapter 35—**The Example of the Rechabites.**
1. The Lord commanded Jeremiah to bring the Rechabites (Rĕ'-chăb-ītes) into the temple chambers and offer them wine. (1-2)
   Note: The Rechabites were a tribe which had adhered to the ascetic life of their forefathers since the time of Moses (See 1 Chron. 2:55; Num. 10:29-32; Judg. 1:16; 2 Ki. 10:15, 23)
2. When offered the wine, the Rechabites refused, saying that it was against the commandment of their fathers. (3-11)
3. Judah has not followed the example of the Rechabites: they have not followed the commandment of the Lord. (12-17)
4. Jeremiah's promise to the Rechabites: the tribe will continue forever. (18-19)

Chapter 36—**King Jehoiakim Burns Jeremiah's Revelations.**
1. In response to the Lord's commandment, Jeremiah wrote all his revelations in a book. (1-4)
2. He sent Baruch (Bâr'-uch) to read it in the temple. (5-10)
3. The princes called Baruch to read the book to them. When they heard it, they advised Baruch and Jeremiah to hide. (11-19)
4. The scroll was read to King Jehoiakim. He burned it and commanded that Jeremiah and Baruch be captured. The Lord hid them. (20-26)
5. The Lord commanded Jeremiah to rewrite the scroll, and many words were added. (27-32)

Chapter 45—**Jeremiah's Prophecy to His Scribe, Baruch.**
1. Jeremiah's prophecy to Baruch, his scribe.
   A. The Lord will break down the land of Judah. (1-4)
   B. Do not seek great things for yourself. You will be hunted. (5)

SECTION III

CHAPTERS OF JEREMIAH PERTAINING TO THE REIGN OF KING ZEDEKIAH

Chapter 29—Jeremiah's Letter to the Exiles in Babylonia.

1. Build houses and live in peace there. You will be there for seventy years. (4-10)
2. After seventy years the Lord will gather Judah from all the nations where they have been driven and bring them home. (10-15)
3. The Jews that are still left in Palestine will be persecuted with famine, sword, and pestilence. (16-19)
4. Prophecies of destruction concerning Ahab, Zedekiah, and Shemiah—three false prophets who have established themselves among the Babylonian captives. (20-32)

Chapter 32—Jeremiah Buys a Field to Show that Israel Will Be Restored.

1. Babylonia was besieging Jerusalem. (1-2)
2. Jeremiah had been shut up in the court house of the prison by Zedekiah because he had prophesied of Jerusalem's fall and Zedekiah's captivity. (3-5)
3. In answer to a command from the Lord, Jeremiah bought a field in Anathoth. (6-15)
4. **Jeremiah's prayer:** He recounts the powers and wondrous deeds of the Lord, then inquires why he was commanded to buy the field. (16-25)
5. **The Lord's Reply:**
    A. The Chaldeans will capture and burn Jerusalem because the people have rejected the Lord and practiced idolatry. (26-36)
       B. (30-31) God will gather the people back out of all countries and make them His people. (37-42)
          C. (30-31) Fields shall be purchased in the land. (43-44)

Chapter 49:34-39—The Fall of Elam Prophesied.

Note: Elam was Persia.
1. Elam will be destroyed. (34-38)
2. (34) Elam will be restored in the latter days. (39)

JEREMIAH—SECTION III 453

Chapter 50—The Fall of Babylon Prophesied.
1. Babylon will be defeated by a nation which will come upon her from the north. (1-3)
2. When Babylonia is defeated the children of Israel and Judah shall go and seek the Lord. (4-8)
3. An assembly of great nations from the north country shall spoil Chaldea. (9-10)
4. Babylon shall be a wilderness. (11-13)
5. Babylon will fall because of the vengeance of the Lord. He will punish the king of Babylon as He did the king of Assyria. (14-18)
6. (31, 38) The Lord will bring Israel to feed on Carmel and Bashan, Mount Ephraim and Gilead. The iniquity of Israel and Judah will not be found in that day. (19-20)
7. Prophetic description of the fall of Babylonia. (21-32)
8. The redeemer of Israel and Judah will plead their cause and disquiet Babylon. (33-34)
9. Prophetic description of the fall of Babylonia as it is attacked by people from the north. (35-46)

Chapter 51—The Fall of Babylon Prophesied.
1. The fall of Babylonia prophesied. (1-4)
2. Judah and Israel are to flee out of Babylon in the time of the Lord's vengeance. (5-10)
3. The king of the Medes has devised against Babylon, to destroy it. Babylon will fall because it has afflicted the house of Israel. (11-58)
4. Jeremiah sent this prophecy with an exile into Babylon. He was to read it and then cast it into the Euphrates, as a symbol that Babylon would sink. (59-64)

Chapter 24—The Jews of the First and Second Deportations Contrasted.
1. The symbol of two baskets of figs.
   A. The Lord showed Jeremiah two baskets of figs. The first had good, ripe figs. The figs of the second basket were bad and unedible. (1-3)
      B. Interpretation:
         (1). **The Good figs: The people of Judah who were carried away in the first deportation (with Jehoiachin, c. 598 B. C.) The Lord will bless them and return them to Palestine.** (4-7)

(2). **The Bad figs:** Zedekiah and his followers who remained in Judah. They will be visited by famine, sword, and pestilence, and be removed to all the kingdoms of the earth. (8-10)

Chapter 30—**The Restoration of Israel in the Last Days.**
This chapter is outlined in Section V.

Chapter 31—**The Restoration of Israel in the Last Days.**
This chapter is outlined in Section V.

Chapter 33—**The Branch, a Descendant of David, Will Rule Israel.**
This chapter is outlined in Section V.

Chapter 21—**Judah's Choice—Life in Captivity or Death.**
1. King Zedekiah sent messengers who asked Jeremiah to inquire the Lord's will as Nebuchadnezzar, king of Babylonia, made war on Judah. (1-2)
2. **The Lord's Reply:**
   A. The city will be smitten. Zedekiah and the people will be captured by Nebuchadnezzar. (3-7)
   B. The Lord would give the people a choice between life (in captivity), by going out and surrendering to the Babylonians, or death (by famine, sword and pestilence) by remaining in the besieged city. (8-10)
   C. The Lord will punish the house of Judah. (11-14)

Chapter 34—**Failure to Free the Slaves Brings Condemnation to Judah.**
1. During Nebuchadnezzar's siege of Jerusalem, the Lord sent Jeremiah to Zedekiah to prophesy the fall and burning of Jerusalem and the capture of Zedekiah. (1-7)
2. Zedekiah (apparently to win favor of the Lord) proclaimed that all the slaves who were Hebrews should be set free. The nobles complied, and then immediately made them slaves again. (8-11)
3. Jeremiah received the word of the Lord concerning these noblemen: Since they did not proclaim liberty to their servants they would have to suffer famine, sword, and pestilence. (12-22)

Chapter 37—**Jeremiah is Accused of Desertion and Is Imprisoned.**
1. The Egyptian army distracted the Babylonian army so their siege of Jerusalem was temporarily lifted. (5)

JEREMIAH—SECTION III 455

2. King Zedekiah sent messengers to Jeremiah to inquire the word of the Lord. (1-4)
3. Jeremiah's prophecy: The Egyptians will return to Egypt. The Babylonians (Chaldeans) will return and conquer Jerusalem and burn it. (6-10)
4. While the Chaldean siege was lifted, Jeremiah left Jerusalem to go into the land of Benjamin. He was arrested, accused of deserting to the Babylonians, and imprisoned in the house of Jonathan. (11-15)
5. King Zedekiah had him released after many days and then secretly inquired the word of the Lord. Jeremiah told him Jerusalem would fall. Jeremiah was imprisoned in the court of the prison in Jerusalem. (16-21)

Chapter 38—**Jeremiah Escapes Death in a Mire-Filled Dungeon.**

1. The temple officials came to Zedekiah and asserted that Jeremiah's prophecies were treasonable and that they were weakening Judah. King Zedekiah released Jeremiah into their custody. (1-5)
2. They put Jeremiah in a deep, mire-filled dungeon, and left him to die. (6)
3. An Ethiopian eunuch, Ebedmelech (ē'-bĕd-mĕl'-ĕch), spoke in behalf of Jeremiah to King Zedekiah, and secured Jeremiah's release. (7-13)
4. King Zedekiah met Jeremiah secretly. Jeremiah told him again that if he would surrender the city the people would live and the city would not be burned with fire. If he refused, the city would be captured and destroyed. (14-23)
5. The princes inquired of his encounter with the king and Jeremiah told them he had asked not to be returned to the prison at the house of Jonathan. (24-28)

Chapter 39—**The Fall of Jerusalem.**

1. Babylonia besieged Jerusalem a year-and-a-half, and conquered it. (1-3)
2. King Zedekiah attempted to escape by night but was captured and brought before Nebuchadnezzar. He saw his sons and the nobles of Judah slain, then his eyes were put out and he was taken to Babylon in chains. (4-7)

3. The Babylonians broke down the walls of Jerusalem, burned the homes, and carried all but the poorest Jews into captivity. (8-10)
4. Jeremiah was given special care by the Babylonians and was committed into the custody of Gedaliah, the provisional ruler. (9-14)
5. The Lord promised Ebedmelech (the Ethiopian eunuch who had saved Jeremiah's life) that his life would be spared and that he would not die by the sword. (15-18)

Chapter 52—**The Fall of Jerusalem Described.**
1. The siege and fall of Jerusalem described. (1-6)
2. King Zedekiah's flight and capture. (7-11)
3. Jerusalem is burned, the walls are broken down, and the people are carried into captivity. (12-16)
4. The articles of the temple are carried away. (17-23)
5. The leaders of Judah are slain. (24-27)
6. Nebuchadnezzar's deportations from Judah. (28-30)
7. Evil-merodach (ē'vil-mĕr'-ō-dăch), king of Babylon, brought Jehoiachin, king of Judah, out of prison after 37 years of captivity. (31-34)

SECTION IV

CHAPTERS OF JEREMIAH PERTAINING TO THE FINAL PERIOD OF THE PROPHET'S LIFE

Chapter 40—Gedaliah Is Made Governor.
1. Jeremiah was apparently taken by mistake with a group of captives to Ramah and then released by the Babylonians. (1-4)
2. Gedaliah was made provisional governor of Judah by the Babylonians. Many Jews who had fled to other countries returned to Judah. (5-14)
3. Gedaliah was advised that the king of the Ammonites had set a plot to kill him but he disregarded the report. (15-16)

Chapter 41—Gedaliah Is Slain.
1. Gedaliah and his supporters were slain by Ishmael and his followers. (1-9)
2. Ishmael attempted to carry many captives from Mizpah south. They were pursued and the captives were released by Johanan (Jō-hā'-năn) and settled near Bethlehem. (10-18)

Chapter 42—The Lord's Choice offered to Johanan.
1. Johanan and his followers came to Jeremiah for guidance, and pledged to follow the will of the Lord. (1-6)
2. **The Lord's Reply to Johanan:** If you stay in Judah you will prosper, but if you go to Egypt you will die by famine, sword and pestilence. (7-22)

Chapter 43—Jeremiah Is Carried into Egypt.
1. Johanan did not believe Jeremiah. He forced the prophet and all the remnant of the people of Judah to dwell in Egypt. (1-8)
2. **The symbol of the hidden stone:**
    A. Jeremiah was commanded to hide a stone in the brick kiln at the entrance to the house of Pharaoh in Tahpanes (Täh'-păn-hēs). (8-9)
    B. The stone was a symbol that the Babylonians under Nebuchadnezzar would conquer Egypt and burn the houses of the Egyptian gods. (10-13)

Chapter 44—**The Destruction of the Jewish Remnant in Egypt Prophesied.**
1. The Jews in Egypt have seen how Judah was destroyed for serving other gods. Now they are committing the same sin by worshipping the false gods of Egypt. (1-10)
2. **Jeremiah's prophecy:** The remnant of Judah which is in Egypt will die by famine, sword, and pestilence. (11-14)
3. **The people's reply to Jeremiah:** We will not listen to you. When we sacrificed to the queen of heaven (the moon) all was well. We fell by the sword and famine when we stopped worshipping her. (15-19)
4. **Jeremiah's prophecy:** The remnant of Judah in Egypt shall die by famine and sword. Only a small group will live to return to Judah to report the fulfillment of the prophecy. (20-28)
5. **The sign of the prophecy:** Pharaoh Hophra will fall into the hands of his enemies. (29-30)

SECTION V

CHAPTERS OF JEREMIAH PERTAINING TO THE LAST DAYS

Chapter 3—The Restoration of Israel in the Last Days.

1. Judah (the Lord's bride) has played the harlot (by worshipping false gods) but the Lord calls her to return unto him. (1-5)
2. Judah is following the path of religious whoredom that Israel walked. (6-11)
3. Jeremiah is sent to the north to proclaim the redemption of Israel in the last days. (12-25)

    A. Israel is invited to confess and return and partake of the Lord's mercy. (12-13)

    B. (30) The Lord will bring one of a family and two of a city back to Zion. They shall have righteous pastors and will not need to remember the ark of the covenant. (14-16)

    C. (41) Jerusalem shall be called the throne of the Lord, and all nations shall be gathered unto it. (17)

    D. (30-31) Judah and Israel will come together to the land of their inheritance. (18)

    E. (38) Judah and Israel shall call God "My Father," and shall not turn away from Him. (19)

4. The house of Israel have forgotten the Lord. Return, and He will heal your backslidings. (20-25)

Chapter 16—Judah's Approaching Destruction and Eventual Return.

1. Jeremiah is commanded not to marry or have children, for the children will die grievous deaths. (1-4)
2. Both the great and the small of Judah shall die and be left unburied. (5-9)
3. Because of following other gods and evil imaginings of their heart Judah will be cast out into an unknown land. (10-13)
4. (30-31) The children of Israel will be gathered back into their land.

    A. (30) They will be hunted (by missionaries?). (16)

B. (35) At first the Lord will recompense their iniquity double. (17-18)

C. (41) The gentiles will come and acknowledge that they had inherited lies (which had kept them from recognizing God). (19-20)

D. (35?) They shall know the Lord's hand and his might. (21)

Chapter 31—**The Restoration of Israel in the Last Days.**
1. (38) The Lord will be the God of all the families of Israel. (1)
2. (31) The Lord will build the people. They shall yet plant vines on the mountains of Samaria. (2-5)
3. (31) The watchmen upon Mt. Ephraim shall cry, "Arise ye, and let us go up to Zion unto the Lord our God." (6-7)
4. (22, 30-31) The Lord will gather them from the north country, and from the coasts of the earth. They shall walk by the rivers in a straight way. (8-9)
5. (30-31) They shall come and sing in the height of Zion, and shall flow together to the goodness of the Lord. (10-14)
6. (31) The Lord will remember Ramah and Ephraim and restore their children. (15-20)
7. (30, 31) Set up waymarks, and set thine heart toward the highway. (21)
8. (30) Judah shall be called the mountain of holiness. (22-26)
9. (30-31) Judah and Israel will be built up. Men shall be punished for their own iniquity, not another's. (27-30)
10. (38) God will make a new covenant with the house of Israel. He will put his law in their hearts. He will be their God, and they shall be His people. They all shall know the Lord. (31-37)
11. (30) The dimensions of the holy city in the last days are given. (38-40)

Chapter 30—**The Restoration of Israel in the Last Days.**
1. (35) The Lord will break the bonds off Israel and Judah in the time of Jacob's trouble. (1-8)
2. (32) They shall serve the Lord and David their King. (9)
3. (35?) The Lord will make a full end of the nations in which Israel is scattered but will not make a full end of Israel. (10-11) (Cf. Jer. 46:27-28)

JEREMIAH—SECTION V   461

4. (35?) The Lord will correct Israel and not leave her altogether unpunished. (11-12)
5. (30-31) At present, no one desires the house of Israel, but she shall be restored and Jerusalem will be rebuilt. (13-18)
6. (41) Israel will multiply, their rulers will draw near the Lord, and He shall be their God. (19-22)
7. (42?) The Lord will punish the wicked: in the latter days ye shall consider it. (23-24)

Chapter 23—**False Prophets Have Misled the People.**
1. Woe to the false prophets who have scattered the people of the Lord. (1-2)
2. (30-31) The Lord will gather the remnant of his flock. They shall increase and fear no more. (3-4)
3. (32) The Lord will raise up a righteous Branch. (5-6) (Cf. Jer. 23:15-18)
    A. A king who shall reign and prosper.
    B. He shall execute judgment and justice.
    C. In his days Judah shall be saved, and Israel shall dwell safely.
    D. He shall be called "The Lord Our Righteousness."
4. (22, 30-31) People will say, "The Lord liveth which led the tribes from the north and from all the countries." (7-8)
5. The false prophets have misled the people by prophesying peace. They shall be destroyed. (9-40)

Chapter 33—**The Branch, a Descendant of David, Will Rule Israel.**
1. The Lord will cause Israel and Judah to return. He will cleanse them from their iniquity. (4-8)
2. The Lord will bless his people with prosperity and joy. (9-14)
3. (32) The Lord will cause the Branch of righteousness to grow up unto David; David shall never want a man to sit upon the throne of the house of Israel. (15-18) (Cf. Jer. 23:5-6)
4. (32) The covenant that the seed of David will reign on the throne will not be broken unless the day and night cease to come in their order. (19-26)

Doctrinal Analysis of the Book of Jeremiah:

The Sins of the People:

—They have rebelled against Jehovah:
1. They have forsaken God. (1:16; 2:5; 2:17; 5:7; 5:19; 9:13)
2. They burned incense to other gods. (1:16; 2:25-28; 7:9, 18-20; 18:15; 19:4-5)
3. They worshipped the works of their own hands. (1:16)
4. They have forsaken me, the fountain of living waters. (2:13)
5. They have hewed them out broken cisterns (false gods) that can hold no water. (2:13)
6. The people say, We are Lords; we will come no more unto thee. (2:31)
7. My people have forgotten me days without number. (2:32; 3:21)
8. She hath been rebellious against me. (4:17)
9. They serve and worship other gods. (13:10; 17:2)
10. Thou hast forgotten me, and trusted in falsehood. (13:25)
11. He hath taught rebellion against the Lord. (29:32)
12. They have turned unto me the back and not the face. (32:33)

—They defile and pollute:
1. Ye defiled my land. (2:7)
2. They have set their abominations in the house which is called by my name, to pollute it. (7:30; 32:34)

—Their religious leaders err:
1. The priests said not, where is the Lord? (2:8)
2. The pastors transgressed against me. (2:8)
3. The prophets prophesied by Baal, and walked after things that do not profit. (2:8; 7:9; 23:13)
4. The prophets prophesy falsely, the priests bear rule by their means, and my people love to have it so. (5:31; 20:6; 23:11)
5. The pastors are become brutish, and have not sought the Lord. (10:21)
6. Many pastors have destroyed my vineyard. (12:10-11; 23:1-2)
7. The prophets lie in my name. (14:13-16)
8. Prophets prophesy falsely. (23:16-17, 21-22, 25-40; 27:9-10, 14-18; 28:1-17; 29:8-9)

JEREMIAH—SECTION V

—They break covenants:
1. They have broken my covenant which I made with their fathers. (11:10)
2. They transgressed God's covenant. (34:18)
3. They have not walked in the Lord's law, statutes, or testimonies. (44-10)

—They are morally depraved:
1. Harlotry. (2:20; 3:1, 6)
2. They committed adultery with stones and with stocks. (3:9)
3. Adultery: they assembled themselves by troops in the harlots' house, everyone neighed after his neighbor's wife. (5:8; 7:9; 13:27; 23:10, 14; 29:23)
4. They were not ashamed when they had committed abominations. (6:15; 8:11)
5. They walk with slanders. (6:28)
6. They are all corruptors. (6:28)

—They are treacherous and deceitful:
1. Ye have dealt treacherously with me. (3:20; 5:11)
2. They set a trap: they catch men. (5:26)
3. Their houses are full of deceit. (5:27)
4. Everyone dealeth falsely. (6:13; 23:14)
5. They say peace when there is no peace. (6:14; 8:11)
6. They swear falsely. (7:9; 23:10)
7. Truth is perished, and is cut off from their mouth. (7:28)
8. They hold fast deceit, they refuse to return. (8:5)
9. They bend their tongues like their bow for lies. (9:3; 9:5; 29:23)
10. Through deceit they refuse to know me. (9:6)
11. One speaketh peaceably to his neighbor with his mouth, but in heart he layeth his wait. (9:8)
12. Woe to him that useth his neighbor's service without wages, and giveth him not for his work. (22:13)

—They are guilty of theft and murder:
1. They are murderers. (4:31; 7:9)
2. They steal. (7:9)

—They are generally evil:
1. Thou hast spoken and done evil things as thou couldest. (3:5)
2. They proceed from evil to evil. (9:3)

3. They weary themselves to commit iniquity. (9:5)
4. Woe to him that buildeth his house by unrighteousness, and his chambers by wrong. (22:13)
5. Thine eyes and thine heart are but for thy covetousness, and to shed innocent blood, and for oppression and violence. (22:17)
6. They strengthen also the hands of evildoers, that none doth return from his wickedness. (23:14)

—**They are obstinate and disobedient:**
1. We have not obeyed the voice of the Lord. (3:25; 9:13)
2. They have refused to receive correction. (5:3)
3. The word of the Lord is unto them a reproach. (6:10)
4. No man repented of his wickedness. (8:6)

—**They are head-strong, self-righteous and self-justified:**
1. They claim to be delivered to do all these abominations. (7:10)
2. They did not heed the prophet. (18:18; 19:15; 44:16)
3. I spake unto thee in thy prosperity but thou saidst, I will not hear. (22:21)
4. They have not hearkened to receive instruction. (32:33; 37:2; 44:23)
5. They are not humbled, neither have they feared. (44:10)
6. Thou hast trusted in thy works and in thy treasures. (48:7)
7. He magnified himself against the Lord. (48:26)

—**They are selfish and worldly:**
1. Everyone is given to covetousness. (6:13)
2. They walk in the imagination of their heart. (13:10)

—**They are unwise and without understanding:**
1. My people is foolish, they have none understanding. (4:22; 5:21)
2. They are wise to do evil, but to do good they have no knowledge. (4:22)
3. They have not known me. (4:22; 9:3)

—**The political leaders err:**
1. They that handle the law knew me not. (2:8)
2. They overpass the deeds of the wicked. (5:28)
3. They do not judge the rights of the needy and fatherless. (5:28)

JEREMIAH—SECTION V   465

—Other sins:
1. They offer their children as human sacrifices. (7:21; 19:4-5; 32:35)
2. They are not valiant for the truth upon the earth. (9:3)
3. They tell the prophets to prophesy not. (11:21)
4. They ate human flesh during the siege. (19:9)
5. They brought servants and handmaidens into slavery. (34:11-16)
6. Israel was a derision unto thee. (48:27)
7. We have heard the pride of Moab, his loftiness, his arrogancy, and the haughtiness of his heart. (48:29)
8. Thy terribleness hath deceived thee, and the pride of thine heart. (49:16)

Judgment of God:

—God knows man's thoughts and acts:
1. In thy skirts is found the blood of the souls of the poor innocents; I have not found it by secret search, but upon all these. (2:34)
2. O Lord, are not thine eyes upon the truth. (5:3)
3. Thou, O Lord, knowest me: thou hast seen me, and tried mine heart toward thee. (12:3)
4. Mine eyes are upon all their ways: they are not hid from my face, neither is their iniquity hid from mine eyes. (16:17)
5. I have set my face against this city for evil, and not for good, saith the Lord. (21:10)
6. Can any hide himself in secret places that I shall not see him? Do I not fill the heaven and the earth? (23:24)
7. They have committed adultery and have spoken lying words, even I know, and am a witness, saith the Lord. (29:23)
8. Thine eyes are open upon all the sons of men; to give every one according to his ways and the fruit of his doings. (32:19)

—Punishment is Certain:
1. I will utter my judgments against them touching all their wickedness. (1:16)
2. Thou wash thee with nitre, and take thee much soap, yet thine iniquity is marked before me. (2:22)
3. Now also will I give sentence against them. (4:12)
4. Thou hast stricken them, but they have refused to receive correction. (5:3)

5. They are foolish, for they know not the way of the Lord, nor the judgment of their God. (5:4)
6. He will now remember their iniquity, and visit their sins. (14:10)
7. I will pour their wickedness upon them. (14:16)
8. I will destroy my people, since they return not from their ways. (15:7)
9. I will recompense their iniquity and their sin double. (16:18; 17:18)
10. I will cause them to know mine hand and my might. (16:21)
11. Surely shalt thou be ashamed and confounded for all thy wickedness. (22:22)
12. And this shall be a sign unto you, that I will punish you in this place, that ye may know that my words shall surely stand against you for evil. (44:29)
13. The Lord God of recompenses shall surely requite. (51:56)

—**Punishment May Be Avoided Through Repentance:**
1. If that nation, against whom I have pronounced, turn from their evil, I will repent of the evil that I thought to do unto them. (18:7-10)
2. Amend your ways and your doings, and obey the voice of the Lord, and the Lord will repent him of the evil that he hath pronounced against you. (26:13)
3. I will forgive their iniquity, and I will remember their sin no more. (31:34)
4. I will pardon all their iniquities, whereby they have sinned and transgressed against me. (33:8)

—**God Will Smite Man:**
1. In vain have I smitten your children; they received no correction. (2:30)
2. Now also will I give sentence against them. (4:12)
3. I will bring evil upon this people, even the fruit of their thoughts. (6:19)
4. The animals know their time, but my people know not the judgment of the Lord. (8:7)
5. O Lord, that trieth the reins and the heart. (11:20; 20:12)

—**Man Judged for His Own Deeds:**
1. I the Lord search the heart, I try the reins, even to give

JEREMIAH

every man according to his ways, and according to the fruit of his doings. (17:10)
2. I will punish you according to the fruit of your doings. (21:14)
3. I will recompense them according to their deeds, and according to the works of their own hands. (25:14)
4. Every one shall die for his own iniquity. (31:30)
5. Cursed be he that doeth the work of the Lord deceitfully. (48:10)

—Oft-times Wickedness Brings Its Own Punishment:
1. Thine own wickedness shall correct thee, and thy backslidings shall reprove thee. (2:19)
2. Your iniquities have turned away these things, and your sins have withholden good things from you. (5:25)
3. Our iniquities testify against us. (14:7)
4. He that getteth riches, and not by right, shall leave them in the midst of his days, and at his end shall be a fool. (17:11)
5. I will make thee a terror to thyself, and to all thy friends. (20:4)
6. Every man's word shall be his burden, for ye have perverted the words of the living God. (23:36)

—Man Has a Choice:
1. I set before you the way of life, or the way of death. (21:8)

The Nature of God:

—Attributes of God:
1. I remember thee, the kindness of thy youth, the love of thine espousals. (2:1)
2. Thou shalt call me "My Father" and shalt not turn away from me. (3:19)
3. I am the Lord which exercise loving kindness, judgment, and righteousness, for in these things I delight. (9:24)
4. The Lord is the true God, he is the living God, and an everlasting king. (10:10)
5. Thou, O Lord, art in the midst of us. (14:9)
6. Am I a God at hand, and not a God afar off? (23:23)
7. I will cure them, and will reveal unto them the abundance of peace and truth. (33:6)

—**Qualities and Emotions of God:**
1. Anger, Angry: (3:12; 4:26; 7:18-20; 8:19; 12:13; 18:23; 21:5; 23:20; 25:7, 37-38)
2. Astonished: (8:21)
3. Avenge, Avenging: (5:9; 5:29; 9:9; 50:15)
4. Brings joy: (33:9)
5. Comforts: (31:13)
6. Compassion: (12:15)
7. Fury: (4:4; 6:11; 25:15-16; 44:6)
8. Grief: (10:19)
9. Hurt: (8:21; 10:19)
10. Love, loving: (31:3; 32:18)
11. Merciful: (3:12; 31:20; 33:11; 42:12)
12. Pain, pained: (4:19)
13. Praise: (33:9)
14. Righteous, Righteousness: (4:2; 12:1)
15. Savior and Redeemer: (14:8)
16. True, truth: (4:2)
17. Weary: (6:11)

—**God Controls the Elements:**
1. [because of whoredoms] Therefore the showers have been withholden, and there hath been no latter rain. (3:3)
2. God has placed the sand for the bound of the sea by a perpetual decree, that it cannot pass it. (5:22)
3. Our God, that giveth rain, both the former and the latter, in his season: he reserveth unto us the appointed weeks of the harvest. (5:24)
4. At his wrath the earth shall tremble. (10:10)
5. He hath made the earth by his power, he hath established the world by his wisdom, and hath stretched out the heavens by his discretion. (10:12)
6. When he uttereth his voice there is a multitude of waters in the heavens, he maketh vapours, lightnings with rain, and bringeth forth the wind. (10:13)
7. Are there any among the vanities of the Gentiles that can cause rain? Art thou not he, O Lord? Thou hast made all these things. (14:22)
8. I have made the earth, man and beast, and have given it unto whom it seemeth meet to me. (27:5)
9. Thou hast made the heaven and the earth, and there is nothing too hard for thee. (32:17)
10. Behold, I am the Lord, the God of all flesh: is there anything too hard for me? (32:27)

JEREMIAH

11. God has appointed the ordinances of the heaven and earth. (33:25)
12. Upon Elam I will bring the four winds from the four quarters of heaven and will scatter them. (49:36)

—God Controls the Nations:
1. I will bring a nation upon you from far. (5:15-17)
2. Be thou instructed, lest I make thee desolate, a land not inhabited. (6:8)
3. Amend your ways and I will cause you to dwell in this place. (7:3-7)
4. The sword of the Lord shall devour from one end of the land to the other. (12:12)
5. If they will not obey, I will utterly pluck up and destroy that nation. (12:17)
6. I will consume them by famine, sword, and pestilence. (14:12)
7. I will cause them to be removed into all the kingdoms of the earth. (15:4)
8. I will cause them to fall by the sword before their enemies. (19:7)
9. I will deliver the strength and precious things of this city into the hand of their enemies. (20:5)
10. I will turn back your weapons, and I myself will fight against you with an outstretched hand and with a strong arm. (21:4-6)
11. I will deliver Zedekiah and the people of Jerusalem into the hand of Nebuchadnezzar. (21:7)
12. I will prepare destroyers against thee, every one with his weapons. (22:7)
13. I will bring all the families of the north, and Nebuchadnezzar, and bring them against this land. (25:9)
14. I will punish the king of Babylon. (25:12)
15. I have given all these lands into the hands of Nebuchadnezzar. (27:6-8)
16. I give this city into the hand of the king of Babylon, and he shall take it. (32:3)
17. I will punish the people of Egypt and deliver them into the hands of those that seek their lives. (46:25-26)

—When People Become Sufficiently Wicked, God will No Longer Hear Them:
1. Pray not for this people, for I will not hear thee. (7:16; 11:14)

2. Pray not for this people for their good. (14:11)
3. Though Moses and Samuel stood before me, yet my mind could not be toward this people; cast them out of my sight. (15:1)

Functions of a Prophet:

—Go Where Sent and Speak What the Lord Commands:
1. Thou shalt go to all that I send thee, and whatsoever I command thee thou shalt speak. (1:7)
2. Behold, I have put my words in thy mouth. (1:9)
3. Speak unto them all that I command thee: be not dismayed at their faces lest I confound thee before them. (1:17)
4. The word of the Lord came unto me, saying Go and cry in the ears of Jerusalem, saying, Thus saith the Lord; [message] (2:1)
5. Stand in the gate of the Lord's house, and proclaim there this word, and say, Hear ye the word of the Lord: [message] (7:2; 11:2-3, 6; 27:1-2)
6. Take an earthen bottle and go forth unto the valley. (19:1-2)
7. Thus saith the Lord; Go down to the house of the king of Judah, and speak there this word, and say, Hear the word of the Lord: [message] (22:1-2)
8. Speak all the words that I command thee to speak unto them; diminish not a word. (26:2)

—God's Special Envoy to Do His Work:
1. I have set thee over the nations to root out and to destroy, to build and to plant. (1:10)
2. I have made thee a defensed city: they shall not prevail against thee. (1:18-19)
3. I will make my words in thy mouth fire, and this people wood, and it shall devour them. (5:14)
4. I will bring upon that land all my words, even all that is written in this book, which Jeremiah hath prophesied. (25:13)

—Receiver of Visions and Revelations:
1. (God shows vision and asks) What seest thou? . . . Thou hast well seen: for I will hasten my word to perform it. (1:12)
2. I will give you pastors according to mine heart, which shall feed you with knowledge and understanding. (3:15)

JEREMIAH

3. Thy words were found, and I did eat them; and thy word was unto me the joy and rejoicing of mine heart. (15:16)
4. I have not hastened from being a pastor to follow thee: that which came out of my lips was right before thee. (17:16)
5. Arise, and go down to the potter's house: and there I will cause thee to hear my words. (18:2-5)
6. I said I will not speak any more in his name, but his word was in mine heart as a burning fire shut up in my bones, and I was weary with forbearing, and I could not stay. (20:9)
7. Call unto me, and I will answer thee, and shew thee great and mighty things, which thou knowest not. (33:3)

—**Writer and Compiler of Revelations:**
1. Thus speaketh the Lord God of Israel, saying, Write thee all the words that I have spoken unto thee in a book. (30:2)
2. Take thee a roll of a book, and write therein all the words I have spoken unto thee. (36:2, 28)

—**God's Messenger to the People:**
1. Since the day that your fathers came out of Egypt I have even sent unto you all my servants the prophets, daily rising up early and sending them. (7:25)
2. The Lord hath sent unto you all his servants the prophets, rising early and sending them; but ye have not hearkened. (25:4; 26:5)
3. When the word of the prophet shall come to pass, then shall the prophet be known, that the Lord hath truly sent him. (28:9)
4. I will bring upon that land all my words, even all that is written in this book, which Jeremiah hath prophesied. (25:13)

—**Channel Through Which People May Inquire of the Lord:**
1. Requests of the priests and Kings: Pray now unto the Lord our God for us. (21:2; 37:3; 37:17; 42:2)

Pre-Mortal Life:
1. Before I formed thee in the belly I knew thee; and before thou camest forth out of the womb I sanctified thee, and I ordained thee a prophet unto the nations. (1:4-5)

The Last Days:
Shown in the chapter outline above.

Counsel for Righteous Living:

1. It is an evil thing and bitter, that thou hast forsaken the Lord thy God, and that His fear is not in thee. (2:19)
2. Acknowledge thine iniquity, that thou hast transgressed against the Lord. (3:13)
3. Thou shalt swear, The Lord liveth, in truth, in judgment, and in righteousness. (4:2)
4. Wash thine heart from wickedness, that thou mayest be saved. How long shall thy vain thoughts lodge within thee? (4:14)
5. Be thou instructed, . . . lest my soul depart from thee. (6:8)
6. Amend your ways and your doings . . . (7:3)
7. Trust ye not in lying words . . . (7:4)
8. Amend your ways, execute judgment, oppress not, shed not innocent blood, do not walk after other gods. (7:5-6)
9. Obey my voice, and walk ye in all the ways that I have commanded you. (7:23)
10. Let him that glorieth glory in this, that he understandeth and knoweth me. (9:23-24)
11. The way of man is not in himself. O, Lord, correct me, but with judgment; not in thine anger. (10:23-24)
12. If thou hast run with the footmen, and they have wearied thee, then how canst thou contend with horses? (12:5)
13. If they will diligently learn the ways of my people, to swear by my name, the Lord liveth; then shall they be built in the midst of my people. (12:16)
14. Give glory to the Lord your God, before he cause darkness, and before your feet stumble. (13:16)
15. May ye also do good, that are accustomed to do evil. (13:23)
16. We acknowledge, O Lord, our wickedness. (14:20-21)
17. Cursed be the man that trusteth in man, and whose heart departeth from the Lord. (17:5)
18. Blessed is the man that trusteth in the Lord, and whose hope the Lord is. (17:7-8)
19. Heal me, O Lord, and I shall be healed; save me, and I shall be saved. (17:14)
20. Be not a terror unto me: thou art my hope in the day of evil. (17:17-18)
21. Hallow the Sabbath day. (17:21-24)
22. Execute judgment in the morning, and deliver him that is spoiled out of the hand of the oppressor. (21:12; 22:3)

23. Do not worry. Do no violence to the stranger, the fatherless, nor the widow; neither shed innocent blood. (22:3)
24. Thy father judged the cause of the poor and needy; was not this to know me? (22:16)
25. I will give them an heart to know me, that I am the Lord. (24:7)
26. Seek the peace of the city, and pray unto the Lord for it: for in the peace thereof shall ye have peace. (29:7)
27. Call upon me, ye shall go and pray unto me. Ye shall seek me and find me when ye shall search for me with all your heart. (29:12-13)
28. Thy work shall be rewarded. (31:16)
29. After I was turned, I repented; and after that I was instructed. I was ashamed because I did bear the reproach of my youth. (31:19)
30. Will ye not receive instruction to hearken to my words? (35:13)
31. Obey the voice of the Lord, so it shall be well unto thee, and thy soul shall live. (38:20)
32. Whether it be good or evil, we will obey the voice of the Lord, that it may be well with us, when we obey the voice of the Lord. (42:6)
33. Seekest thou great things for thyself? seek them not. (45:5)
34. Come, and let us join ourselves to the Lord in a perpetual covenant that shall not be forgotten. (50:5)
35. Flee out of the midst of Babylon, and deliver everyman his soul. (51:6, 45)

Author and Date of Authorship:

According to the book of Jeremiah, the Lord commanded the prophet to write down the words which had been revealed to him previously. This took place in the fourth year of the reign of Jehoiakim (c. 604 B. C.) and approximately twenty-two years after Jeremiah had begun his ministry. The prophet called his scribe, Baruch, and dictated his prophecies. The book was then read before some of the Jewish nobles and finally before Jehoiakim, the king. Jehoiakim cut up the book and threw it in the fire. Jeremiah then dictated the revelations once again to Baruch and "there were added besides unto them many like words." (Jer. 36) The prophecies were not written down in chronological order at that time or else they have since been disturbed.

Some critics assert that the book contains three types of writings: the words written or dictated by Jeremiah himself, a biography of Jeremiah which supposedly was written by Baruch, and miscellaneous additions by later authors and commentators.

Style of the Book:
1. The book is partly in prose and partly in poetry. The poetry sections are as follows:
    1:4-10.
    2:2-7.
    3:1-5, 12-14, 19-23.
    4:1-8, 13-31.
    5:1-17, 20-31.
    6:1-30.
    8:4-22.
    9:1-11, 17-22.
    10:2-10, 12-25.
    11:18-20.
    12:1-13.
    12:15-27.
    14:2-10, 17-22.
    15:2, 5-9, 15-21.
    17:5-18.
    16:19-20.
    18:13-17, 19-23.
    20:7-18.
    21:11-14.
    22:6-7, 10, 13-23, 28-30.
    23:9-15, 18-22.
    25:30-32, 34-38.
    26:18.
    30:5-7, 10-24.
    31:1-22, 35-37.
    46:3-12, 14-24, 27-28.
    47:2-7.
    48:1-9, 11, 14-20, 28-33, 40-47.
    49:1-11, 14-16, 23-33.
    50:2, 11-16, 21-27, 31-32, 35-38, 41-43.
    51:1-23, 25-58.
2. The poetry shows distinctive originality but is not regarded as being on a par with that of Amos or Isaiah.
3. The prose is considered dull. It is repetitious and uses many stereotyped expressions.

JEREMIAH

4. Jeremiah's writing shows a love of people and of children.
5. The imagery is drawn from rural and uninhabited areas rather than from urban scenes. He shows a close acquaintance with animals.
6. He dwells on death and macabre subjects.
7. His writing reflects the gloom, melancholy and despair of his day.
8. He reveals more of his own personality and attitudes than does any of the other prophets. His relationship with God is depicted as being more intimate than that of other prophets.
9. His language at times lacks energy and tenseness. His sentences are often long and drawn out.
10. His writing does not show the artistry of some of the other prophets.

Textual transmission: It appears that the book of Jeremiah has been greatly altered by scribes and those who have transmitted it. There are a great many repetitions and glosses. Many of these repetitions have been omitted in the Greek Septuagint version, and that version is about one-eighth (about 2700 words) shorter than the Hebrew text.

Bible Criticism:

Most of the critical comment revolves around hypotheses concerning how much of the book was written by Baruch. It is asserted that he rewrote the book of Jeremiah and added much of the historical data. Much of the dull and uninteresting prose is attributed to him. The many differences between the Hebrew and Greek texts are cited as indications that the book underwent later alterations.

Changes Made in the Inspired Version of the Bible—Book of Jeremiah

King James Translation	Inspired Version
2:24—... All they that seek her will not weary themselves; in her month they shall find her.	2:24—... all they that seek her **will weary** themselves; in her month they shall **not** find her.
3:2—... and see where thou hast not been lien with ... ... with thy whoredoms and with thy wickedness.	3:2—... and see where thou hast not been **lain** with ... ... with thy whoredoms and wickedness.

476 PROPHETS AND PROPHECIES OF THE OLD TESTAMENT

King James Translation	Inspired Version
3:3—Therefore the showers have been withholden, . . .	3:3—Therefore **thy** showers have been withholden, . . .
17:5—. . . and whose heart departeth from the Lord.	17:5—. . . and **the man** whose heart departeth from the Lord.
18:8—. . . I will repent of the evil that I thought to do unto them.	18:8—. . . I will **withhold** the evil that I thought to do unto them.
18:14—Will a man leave the snow of Lebanon which cometh from the rock of the field? or shall the cold flowing waters that come from another place be forsaken?	18:14—Will **you not** leave the snow of **the fields** of Lebanon; shall **not** the cold flowing waters that come from another place **from the rock,** be forsaken?
26:3—If so be they will hearken, and turn every man from his evil way, that I may repent me of the evil, which I purpose to do unto them because of the evil of their doings.	26:3—If so be they will hearken, and turn every man from his evil way, **and repent, I will turn away** the evil which I purpose to do unto them because of the evil of their doings.
26:5—. . . the prophets, whom I sent unto you, both rising up early, and sending them, . . .	26:5—. . . the prophets, whom I sent unto you, **commanding them to rise up early,** and sending them;
26:6—. . . and will make this city a curse to all the nations of the earth.	26:6—. . . and will make this city a curse to all the nations of the earth; **for ye have not hearkened unto my servants the prophets.**
26:13—. . . and obey the voice of the Lord your God; and the Lord will repent him of the evil that he hath pronounced against you.	26:13—. . . and obey the voice of the Lord your God, **and repent, and the Lord will turn away** the evil that he hath pronounced against you.
26:18—. . . and the mountain of the house as the high places of a forest.	26:18—. . . and the mountain of the house **of the Lord** as the high places of a forest.
26:19—. . . did he not fear the Lord, and besought the Lord and the Lord repented him of	26:19—. . . Did he not fear the Lord and **beseech** the Lord **and repent?** and the

JEREMIAH 477

King James Translation

the evil which he had pronounced against them? Thus might we procure great evil against our souls.

26:20—And there was also a man that prophesied in the name of the Lord, Urijah the son of Shemaiah of Kirjath-jearim, who prophesied against this city . . .

27:7—. . . until the very time of his land come: and then many nations and great kings shall serve themselves of him.

27:11—. . . those will I let remain still in their own land, . . .

29:19—. . . my servants the prophets, rising up early and sending them; . . .

30:12—. . . Thy bruise is incurable, and thy wound is grievous.

30:13—There is none to plead thy cause, that thou mayest be bound up: thou hast no healing medicines.

30:14—All thy lovers have forgotten thee; they seek thee not; . . .

30:15—. . . thy sorrow is incurable for the multitude of thine iniquity: because thy sins were increased, I have done these things unto thee.

Inspired Version

Lord **turned away the evil** which he had pronounced against them. Thus **by putting Jeremiah to death** we might procure great evil against our souls.

26:20—But there was a man **among the priests, rose up and said,** that, Urijah the son of Shemaiah of Kirjath-jearim, prophesied in the name of the Lord, who **also** prophesied against this city . . .

27:7—. . . until the very time of **their end come; and after that** many nations and great kings shall serve themselves of **them.**

27:11—. . . those will I let **still remain** in their own land, . . .

29:19—. . . my servants the prophets, **commanding them to rise early,** and sending them; . . .

30:12—. . . thy bruise is **not** incurable **although thy wounds are** grievous.

30:13—**Is there** none to plead thy cause, that thou mayest be bound up? **Hast thou** no healing medicines?

30:14—**Have all thy lovers forgotten thee, do they not seek thee?** . . .

30:15—. . . **Is thy sorrow incurable? It was for the multi**tude of thine iniquities, **and** because thy sins **are** increased I have done these things unto thee.

King James Translation	Inspired Version
30:16—Therefore all they that devour thee shall be devoured; . . .	30:16—**But** all they that devour thee shall be devoured; . . .
31:15—. . . Rahel weeping for her . . .	31:15—. . . Rachel weeping for her . . .
33:11—. . . his mercy endureth for ever: and of them that shall bring the sacrifice of praise into the house of the Lord.	33:11—. . . his mercy endureth for ever **unto them** that shall bring the sacrifice of praise into the house of the Lord.
34:15—And ye were now turned . . .	34:15—**But** ye were now turned . . .
35:14—. . . I have spoken unto you, rising early and speaking; . . .	35:14—. . . I have spoken unto you, **commanding you to rise early,** and speaking to you, . . .
35:15—. . . my servants the prophets, rising up early and sending them . . .	35:15—. . . my servants the prophets, **commanding them to rise up early,** and sending them . . .
37:16—When Jeremiah was entered into the dungeon, and into the cabins, and Jeremiah had remained there many days;	37:16—**And** Jeremiah was entered into the dungeon, and into the cabins, and **he remained** there many days.
42:10—If ye will still abide in this land, then will I build you, and not pull you down, and I will plant you, and not pluck you up: for I repent me of the evil that I have done unto you.	42:10—If you will still abide in this land, then will I build you, and not pull down; I will plant you, and not pluck up; **and I will turn away the evil** that I have done unto you.
42:14—. . . nor have hunger of bread, . . .	42:14—. . . nor have hunger **for want** of bread; . . .
42:21—. . . I have this day declared it unto you; but ye have not obeyed the voice of the Lord your God, . . .	42:21—. . . I have this day declared it unto you, **that** ye have not obeyed the voice of the Lord your God, . . .

JEREMIAH 479

King James Translation	Inspired Version
44:4—. . . my servants the prophets, rising early and sending them, . . .	44:4—. . . my servants the prophets, **commanding them to rise early,** and sending them, . . .
50:6—My people hath been lost sheep: . . .	50:6—My people **have** been lost sheep; . . .

Summary:

After studying the book of Jeremiah the student should know:
1. More is known about the life of Jeremiah than any of the other prophets. His life story is important because it reflects the history of the fall of Judah.
2. The main deportations to Babylonia:
    A. c. 598 B.C. (Jehoiachin)
    B. c. 586 B.C. (Zedekiah)
3. Important kings of this period:
    Judah
    A. Josiah—brought about reforms.
    B. Jehoiachin ⎫
    C. Zedekiah   ⎬ —taken into captivity.
    Egypt
    A. Necho—Pharaoh who killed Josiah.
    Babylonia
    A. Nebuchadnezzar—captured Judah and destroyed Jerusalem.
4. The four major messages of the book:
    A. Judah's wickedness will bring about her punishment.
    B. Judah's choice: submit to captivity and live; resist and die.
    C. Babylonia will eventually be destroyed for its wickedness.
    D. Judah will be restored in the last days.
5. Jeremiah gives penetrating insight into doctrinal areas, particularly—
    A. The nature of God's judgments upon man.
    B. The nature of God.
    C. The nature of prophets and prophecy.
    D. Counsel for Christian living.

CHAPTER XVIII

LAMENTATIONS

Date: 586 B.C.

Subject: A lament over the fall of Jerusalem.

Historical Background: Jerusalem fell to Nebuchadnezzar, king of Babylon, after a siege of a year-and-a-half. (Jer. 52) The siege brought great suffering to the population of Jerusalem. Many starved to death, and the book of Lamentations tells how some even ate their own children to escape that fate. King Zedekiah finally attempted to escape but was captured. His stronghold fell and was destroyed. The king and the upper classes were deported to Babylon. The book describes the short period between the fall of the city and the deportation of the people.

Chapter 1—Judah is Punished for Rebelling Against the Lord.
1. The city which was once full now sits as a widow and weeps. (1-2)
2. Jerusalem has gone into captivity because the Lord afflicted her for the multitudes of her transgressions. (3-6)
3. Because of her sin Jerusalem stands naked before her enemies. (7-9)
4. The pleasantries of life have been destroyed. The enemy spoiled the temple and they sold their personal belongings for bread. (10-11)
5. Judah's suffering was sent by the Lord in His fierce anger. (12-14)
6. Judah weeps because there is no one to comfort her. (15-17)
7. Judah has rebelled against the Lord's commandments. (18-20)
8. The Lord is asked to see the wickedness of Judah's enemies and punish them also. (21-22)

Chapter 2—The Lord Destroyed Jerusalem in His Anger.
1. The Lord was as an enemy against Judah and destroyed her in His anger. (1-10)
2. The children faint in the streets for lack of food. (11-13)

LAMENTATIONS

3. False prophets misled the people with foolish and vain teachings. (14)
4. Judah's enemies mock when they see the ruins of Jerusalem. (15-16)
5. The Lord fulfilled his word when He threw down Jerusalem. (17)
6. Arise and weep. (18-19)
7. Lord, consider to whom thou hast done this. (20-22)

Chapter 3—God Gives Man A Choice Between Good and Evil.
1. Jeremiah recounts his great suffering. (1-20)
2. Hope in the Lord. It was through His mercy that they were not completely destroyed. (21-26)
3. God does not willingly afflict the children of men. He gives them a choice between evil and good. (27-41)
4. Judah transgressed and rebelled so the Lord punished them. (42-47)
5. Jeremiah recounts his sorrow and suffering. (48-55)
6. The Lord has heard Jeremiah's prayers. (56-63)
7. Jeremiah's plea for justice: punish his enemies. (64-65)

Chapter 4—Judah's Suffering and Starvation.
1. Judah's suffering is prolonged. They are starving. (1-10)
2. The false prophets and priests have been brought down. They did not receive preferential treatment. (11-16)
3. The people have been hunted and seized because they mistakenly awaited help from Egypt. (17-20)
4. Edom will also be punished. (21-22)

Chapter 5—Lord, Remember Judah's Suffering.
1. Lord, remember the many things which Judah has suffered. (1-18)
2. Lord, turn us unto thee and renew our days of old. (19-22)

Doctrinal Analysis

Counsel for Righteous Living:
1. My soul remembers my afflictions and is humbled in me. This I recall to my mind, therefore I have hope. (3:20-21)
2. The Lord is my portion, saith my soul; therefore will I hope in him. (3:24)
3. The Lord is good unto them that wait for him, to the soul that seeketh him. (3:25)

4. It is good that a man should both hope and quietly wait for the salvation of the Lord. (3:26)
5. Wherefore doth a living man complain for the punishment of his sins? Let us search and try our ways, and turn again to the Lord. (3:39-40)
6. Let us lift our heart with our hands unto God in the heavens. (3:41)
7. I called upon thy name, O Lord, out of the low dungeon. Thou hast heard my voice. (3:55-56)

The Nature of God:

1. The Lord hath afflicted Judah for the multitude of her transgressions. (1:5)
2. The Lord hath afflicted Judah in the day of His fierce anger. (1:12)
3. The Lord is righteous. (1:18)
4. The Lord hath swallowed up all the habitations of Jacob, and hath not pitied. (2:2)
5. The Lord hath despised in the indignation of his anger the king and the (wicked) priest. (2:6)
6. It is of the Lord's mercies that we are not consumed, because his compassions fail not. They are new every morning. (3:22-23)
7. Though the Lord cause grief, yet will he have compassion according to the multitude of his mercies. (3:32)
8. He doth not afflict willingly nor grieve the children of men. (3:33)
9. Out of the mouth of the most High proceedeth not evil and good? (3:38)
10. We have transgressed and rebelled: thou hast not pardoned. (3:42)
11. Thou drewest near in the day that I called upon thee. (3:57)
12. Thou hast pleaded the causes of my soul; thou hast redeemed my life. (3:58)
13. O Lord, thou hast seen my wrong; judge thou my cause. (3:59)
14. Render unto them a recompense, O Lord, according to the work of their hands. (3:64)
15. The Lord hath accomplished his fury; he hath poured out his fierce anger. (4:11)
16. Thou, O Lord, remainest for ever; thy throne from generation to generation. (5:19)

LAMENTATIONS 483

17. Thou hast utterly rejected us; thou art very wroth against us. (5:22)

Author and Date of Authorship:

There is no statement in the Old Testament as to the authorship of the book. The tradition that the Lamentations were written by Jeremiah can be traced back to the Septuagint. There the book is prefaced with these words:

> "And it came to pass, after Israel was led into captivity, and Jerusalem laid waste, that Jeremiah sat weeping, and lamented with this lamentation over Jerusalem, and said . . ."

If this tradition is correct, then the book was probably composed in 586 B.C. during the three months between the destruction of Jerusalem and the removal of the captives to Babylonia.

Style:

1. The book is composed of five independent poems.
2. Chapters 1, 2, 3, and 4 are each acrostics. This means that each verse of the poem begins with a letter of the Hebrew alphabet, in alphabetical sequence. Chapters 1, 2, and 4 each have twenty-two verses—a verse for each letter of the Hebrew alphabet. Chapter 3 is also acrostic, but three English verses comprise one Hebrew verse. Chapter 5 has twenty-two verses but is not acrostic.
3. The rhythm of the poetry is, apparently, peculiar to Hebrew elegy. Each line of the verse is divided into two parts. The first is usually of normal length, the second is noticeably shorter.[1] For instance:

> (2:3) He has cut down in fierce anger
>   all the might of Israel;
>   he has withdrawn from them his right hand
>   in the face of the enemy;
>   he has burned like a flaming fire in Jacob,
>   consuming all around.
>
> (3:1-3) I am the man who has seen affliction
>   under the rod of his wrath;

---

[1] In normal Hebrew poetry each of the two halves of the line has four stress accents. In the elegaic meter the first half has four accents, the second half has three. Actually a rest replaces the last foot of the verse.

> he has driven and brought me
> into darkness without any lights;
> surely against me he turns his hand
> again and again the whole day long.[2]

Bible Criticism:

Only internal criticism can be used to determine if the Septuagint tradition of Jeremiah's authorship is correct or not, and the critics are divided in their opinions. In accordance with the current trend of Bible scholarship, most of the critics deny the authorship of Jeremiah.

Summary:

After studying the book of Lamentations the student should know:
1. The book is a lament over the fall of Jerusalem.
2. The three major lessons of the book:
   A. God offers man a choice between the paths of good and evil. He will reward the righteous but punish the wicked.
   B. Judah fell because of its rebellion against God.
   C. When man is being punished for wickedness, God may withdraw His Spirit and refuse to hear his prayers until the punishment is over.
3. Jerusalem was destroyed by Babylonia in 586 B.C.
4. Some of the poetry of Lamentations constitutes acrostics in which each verse begins with the letters of the Hebrew alphabet in order.
5. Hebrew poetic meters:
   A. Normal meter—each line has two parts with four stresses each.
   B. Elegaic meter—each line has two parts. The first has four stresses and the second has three.

---

[2]These passages are cited from the Revised Standard Version of the Bible. When the King James Translation was made the translators did not understand the nature of Hebrew poetry and did not preserve the poetic form.

PART IV

The History
- The Rise of Persia
- The Fall of Babylonia
- The Jewish Exile
- The Panorama of World Empires

The Prophets
- Daniel
- Ezekiel

The Doctrine
- The Sins of Judah
- God's Communication with His Prophets
- Israel's Redemption in the Last Days
- Important Events of the Last Days

CHAPTER XIX

HISTORICAL SUMMARY
THE FALL OF BABYLONIA, THE RISE OF MEDIA AND PERSIA AND THE BABYLONIAN EXILE OF THE JEWS

The Decline and Fall of Babylonia

The glory of Babylonia was short lived. The Babylonian empire existed for only 86 years, from 625 to 539 B.C. It never reached the height of its predecessor, Assyria, nor the glory of its successors, the Medes and the Persians. Throughout its existence it was overshadowed by the successes and relentless expansion of Media. Babylonia had only six kings. The glory of the empire was centered in the first two, Nabopolassar and Nebuchadnezzar. (Review Nabopolassar and Nebuchadnezzar in chapter XII.)

1. **Evil-Merodach** (Amil-Marduk)—c. 562-560 B.C.
   A. Nebuchadnezzar's son.
   B. Killed by his sister's husband, Neriglissor.
2. **Neriglissor**—c. 560-556 B.C.
   A. An officer in Nebuchadnezzar's army who married his daughter.
   B. At peace with neighboring countries.
   C. Spent most of his time building a new palace.
3. **Labashi-Marduk**—c. 556-555 B.C.
   A. Son of Neriglissor.
   B. He was placed on the throne as a young boy but was assassinated after nine months.
4. **Nabonidus**—c. 555-538 B.C.
   A. He was one of the conspirators who had Labashi-Marduk murdered.

B. He was interested in the history and archaeology of Babylon and left important archaeological records.

   C. He was so interested in his building programs that he withdrew many of his troops from foreign lands to aid in the construction projects. This weakened the kingdom.

   D. He spent eight years in North Arabia, leaving his son(?), Belshazzar, in control.

   E. While Belshazzar was in control the kingdom was conquered by Cyrus the Persian.

   F. Cyrus made Nabonidus the governor of one of the provinces.

5. The city of Babylon remained intact under Persian rule for twenty-five years. In 514 B.C. the people revolted against Darius the Great. Because of their revolt the city's walls were destroyed. The city gradually declined in the Hellenistic period and was abandoned and desolate before the time of Christ.

6. **Description of Babylon**

   "Ancient historians said that its wall was 60 miles around, 15 miles on each side, 300 ft. high, 80 ft. thick, extending 35 ft. below the ground so that enemies could not tunnel under; built of brick 1 ft. square and 3 or 4 inches thick; ¼ mile of clear space between the city and wall all the way around; the wall protected by wide and deep moats (canals) filled with water; 250 towers on the wall, guard rooms for soldiers; 100 gates of brass. The city was divided by the Euphrates into two almost equal parts; both banks guarded by brick walls all the way, with 25 gates connecting streets, and ferry boats; one bridge, on stone piers, ½ mile long, 30 ft. wide, with drawbridges which were removed at night. A tunnel under the

THE FALL OF BABYLONIA, THE RISE OF MEDIA AND PERSIA

river, 15 ft. wide, 12 ft. high. Excavations of recent years have, to large extent, verified the seemingly fabulous accounts of ancient historians.

"The Great Temple of Marduk (Bel), adjoining the Tower of Babylon (Babel?), was the most renowned sanctuary in all the Euphrates valley. It contained a golden image of Bel and a golden table which together weighed not less than 50,000 pounds. At the top were golden images of Bel and Ishtar, 2 golden lions, a golden table 40 ft. long and 15 ft. wide, and a human figure of solid gold 18 ft. high. Truly Babylon was a "city of gold," Isa. 14:4. The city was very religious: It had 53 temples; and 180 altars to Ishtar.

"It may have been in the plain between Tower of Babylon and Palace of Nebuchadnezzar that the "image of gold" was set up, [Dan.] 3:1.

"Nebuchadnezzar's Palace, into which Daniel often went, was one of the most magnificent buildings ever erected on earth. Its vast ruins were uncovered by Koldewey, 1899-1912. The south walls of the Throne Room were 20 ft. thick ... The north side of the palace was protected by three walls. Just north of them were more walls 50 ft. thick. A little further on still more massive walls. And about a mile further out was the Inner Wall of the city, which consisted of two parallel walls of brick, each about 20 ft. thick, 40 ft. apart, the space between filled with rubble, making a total thickness of 80 ft., with a deep and wide moat (canal) on the outside. Further on was the Outer Wall, built in the same manner. In the days of ancient warfare the city was simply impregnable!"[1]

---
[1] Halley, Henry H., *Bible Handbook*, (Grand Rapids, Mich., Zondervan Publishing House, 24th edition) pp. 336-337.

"The city was built in a square, divided diagonally by the Euphrates. A surrounding wall, twenty-five yards in width, with a cavalry fort every twenty yards, enclosed it like impenetrable armour; the fortifications of Constantinople, that so much impressed the Crusaders, or the Great Wall of China, must have borne resemblance to this gigantic military structure. It would have taken a man fifteen hours to walk all over it. Where the Sacred Way, reserved for processions and triumphs, entered the city, the "Gate of Ishtar" raised its massive portals, decorated with nearly six hundred fantastic animal figures. The river was spanned by a bridge of five arches. The seven piles are still visible, great brick structures, encased in stone, whose angles cleave the current. In the colossal temples, the Ziggourats, towers built in stages, proudly carried once more the ancient names of "House of the lofty brow" and "house that upholds heaven and earth." On terraces faced with sandstone, limestone and basalt, the palaces covered acres with their buildings and courtyards. And descending by terraces to the banks of the Euphrates, were the "hanging gardens," with their avenues of rare trees acclimatized from distant countries, their flights of steps, and their cascades, while in the shelter of the arches that supported them, cool rooms gave shelter from the summer heat."[2]

The Rise and Fall of Media

Little is known of Media until the ninth century B.C., when its inhabitants are known to have paid tribute to Assyria. Sargon II (c. 721-705 B.C.) conquered Media and made it a vassal state to Assyria. Media had four kings of importance:

---

[2] Daniel-Rops, *Israel and the Ancient World*, (Eyre and Spottiswoode, London) p. 210.

1. **Deioces**
   A. He was one of the Median rulers who was carried off as an Assyrian prisoner in 715 B.C.
   B. He founded the Median kingdom on an independent basis and established Ecbatana as its capital.
2. **Phraortes**—(647?-625? B.C.)
   A. He extended the Median empire by subjugating Persis (southeast of Media).
   B. He conquered other parts of Asia.
   C. He died in an unsuccessful attempt to conquer Nineveh.
3. **Cyaxares**—(c. 625-585 B.C.)
   A. He raised Media to its greatest power and importance.
   B. He advanced against Nineveh but had to return to protect his kingdom against the advancing Scythians.
   C. The Scythians overpowered Media but Cyaxares negotiated with them and saved his throne. He finally slew all their chiefs when they became drunk at a feast.
   D. He formed an alliance with Nabopolassar of Babylonia and together they overthrew the Assyrians.
   E. The Assyrian dominions were partitioned between Media and Babylonia with Media receiving the northern possessions and Babylonia receiving the southern portion of the Assyrian kingdom.
   F. Cyaxares gave his daughter in marriage to Nabopolassar of Babylonia.
   G. Media waged war against Lydia for five years. On May 28, 585 B.C., while their forces were engaged in battle, there was a total eclipse

of the sun. This terrified the soldiers and led to a peace agreement.
4. **Astyages**—(c. 584-550 B.C.)
   A. He was the last independent king of Media.
   B. In 550 B.C. Media was conquered by Cyrus the Persian and the Median empire became the base for further Persian conquests.

The Rise of Persia

The birthplace of Persia was the tiny kingdom of Elam at the northern end of the Persian gulf. Elam was conquered by the Assyrians under Ashurbanipal and ceased to exist. A vassal king of Parsumash, a small section of northeastern Elam, began to reunite the people of Elam and founded the Persian or Archaemenean Empire. The Persian Empire rose from a tribal estate to the role of a major world power under two kings:

1. **Cambyses**—(c. 600-559 B.C.)
   A. He founded the Persian state.
   B. His territory was overrun by Media and Persia became a vassal state to the Medes.
   C. Cyaxares the Mede entrusted him with the administration of the territories Media had conquered in the vicinity of Persia.
   D. Cambyses married the daughter of the Median king, Astyages, and they were the parents of Cyrus II (Cyrus the Great).
2. **Cyrus II, The Great**—(c. 558-529 B.C.)
   A. He conquered Media in 550 B.C. and it became the center of his territorial conquests.
   B. He conquered the Lydian kingdom in 546 B.C.
   C. He annexed the Greek colonies in Asia Minor.
   D. He conquered Babylon in 539 B.C.

The Fall of Babylonia, The Rise of Media and Persia 493

    E. It was Cyrus who allowed the Jews in Babylon to return to their homeland.

    F. He was killed while leading an expedition in the eastern portion of his kingdom in 529 B.C.

    G. At the time of his death Persia had conquered all the great powers except Egypt.

Judah during the Babylonian Captivity

1. During the early period of the captivity most of the exiled Jews apparently lived in various cities or concentration camps, such as the home of Ezekiel (Tel-a-bib on the river Chebar[3]). They served as slave labor for the construction of buildings, for agricultural work, etc. Many, no doubt, aided in Nebuchadnezzar's extensive building projects in Babylon itself.
2. Some of the Jews, such as Daniel and his three friends, found places within the royal palace and rose to positions of importance and trust.
3. The early years of the exile were harsh and cruel. The Jews, however, worked hard and eventually found a happier way of life. After fifty years of the captivity had passed, the lot of exiled Judah had become much improved.

    A. Many of the Jewish settlements on the middle Euphrates (in the Nippur district) had greatly prospered.

    B. Many of the Israelites actually had slaves themselves and had acquired great wealth.

    C. Their wealth had brought them political influence and favor with the Babylonian government. For instance, Jehoiachin, the Jewish king who had gone into captivity at the age of eight, was released and given the freedom of the royal court.

---

[3] The River Chebar was actually a canal which passed through Nippur and connected the ship traffic of the Euphrates and Tigris Rivers.

D. A Jewish remnant had clung to the proper observance of their religion as their ray of hope during the dark days of the captivity and now the Jewish colonies were faithfully heeding the tenets of their laws. The priests were respected, and they formed groups of the faithful around themselves. With no temple available, other types of worship were instituted and synagogues were established.

Summary:

While studying the period of the Babylonian exile, the student should know:

Babylonia

1. The period of the Jewish captivity in Babylonia was one of great building programs. They required so much attention that the empire was allowed to shrink and decay.
2. Babylonia never did gain the great power of Assyria because of the strength and growth of its ally, the Medes.
3. Two Babylonians are important to Bible history:
    A. Nebuchadnezzar, who established Daniel in the Babylonian palace.
    B. Belshazzar—a temporary substitute for Nabonidus, who allowed Babylon to fall to Persia.

Media

4. The Median empire only had four kings. Cyaxares overthrew Assyria with the help of Babylonia.
5. Media was conquered by Cyrus and the Persians.

Persia

6. The Persians rose to power by conquering first Media and then Babylonia.
7. Persia's second king, Cyrus the Great, allowed the Jews to return to Jerusalem.

The Fall of Babylonia, The Rise of Media and Persia

The Jewish Exiles
8. They were slaves at the beginning of the captivity.
9. By the end of the captivity many of them had risen to positions of wealth and influence.

Important Dates
10. 550 B.C.—Media was conquered by Persia.
11. 539 B.C.—Babylonia was conquered by Persia.

Important Places
12. Babylon—capital of Babylonia.
13. Ecbatana—capital of Media.
14. Susa (Shushan) } —capitals of Persia.
15. Persepolis
16. The extent of the Babylonian Empire.
17. The extent of the Median Empire.

CHAPTER XX

DANIEL

Prophet's Name: Daniel means "A Judge Is God." His Babylonian name was Belteshazzar, meaning "Protect His Life."

Scriptural Information About the Prophet:
1. He was apparently of the royal lineage of Judah. (1:3-4)
2. He was taken into Babylonia c. 606 B. C. This was a minor deportation of chosen Jewish children who were selected to serve in the Babylonian court. Many historians, however, mark the beginning of the seventy years of captivity (see Jer. 25:11-14; 29:10; 2 Chron. 36:21) from this deportation.
3. He had knowledge and skill in all learning and wisdom, and had understanding in all visions and dreams. (1:17)
4. Nebuchadnezzar made him a ruler over the whole province of Babylon, and chief of the governors over all the wise men of Babylon. (2:48)
5. He continued in prominence in the Babylonian court throughout the period of the captivity, until the third year of Cyrus, king of Persia. (10:1) The majority of the book is a record of his experiences during this period.

Date of Daniel's Mission: c. 606-536 B. C. This is determined by calculating from the dates of accession of kings Jehoiakim and Cyrus. (see 1:1, 10:1)

Prophesied To: The kings of Babylonia and Persia.

Contemporary Prophets:
Jeremiah (c. 626-586 B. C.) To Judah, from Judah.
Ezekiel (c. 593-571 B. C.) To Judah, from Babylonia.

Contemporary Prophets Contrasted:

Daniel came to Babylon eight years earlier than Ezekiel and was a younger man. He rose to prestige and power in the Babylonian court and lived in comfort there. Much of Daniel's ministry involved the receiving and interpreting of difficult dreams and visions. His ministry was primarily con-

DANIEL

cerned with the affairs of state and the rise and fall of empires.

Ezekiel lived the life of a captive and labored among the Jewish exiles and slaves in Babylonia. Like Jeremiah, he was commanded to perform symbolic actions. Like Jeremiah, he struck out at the sins of Judah and gave the reason for God's rejection of His chosen people. Though of upper class heritage before going into captivity, he was forced to live a life of poverty and despair. He ministered to the common people while Daniel ministered to the royalty.

Jeremiah had no political connections and was not influential in the affairs of the royal court during king Josiah's time. The recorded ministry of Jeremiah extended over fifty years and during the reign of five kings of Judah. Jeremiah was of an introspective and emotional temperament.

Contemporary Kings:

Babylonia:

1. **Nebuchadnezzar.** (c. 604-562 B. C.) He took Jehoiachin and the Jews to Babylon (**First Deportation** c. 598 B. C.), then Zedekiah and more Jews to Babylon (c. 586 B. C.) and then destroyed Jerusalem. (c. 586 B. C.)
2. **Evil-Merodach.** (c. 562-560 B. C.)
3. **Neriglissor.** (c. 560-556 B. C.)
4. **Labashi-Marduk.** (c. 556-555 B. C.)
5. **Nabonidus.** (c. 555-538 B. C.) He spent eight years in North Arabia, leaving his son(?), Belshazzar, in control.
6. **Belshazzar.** (c. 546-538 B. C.) He was not actually a Babylonian king but presided over Babylon during its final years.

Judah:

1. **Jehoiakim.** (c. 609-598 B. C.) Daniel was deported to Babylon during his rule.
2. **Jehoiachin.** (c. 598 B. C.) He and Judah's upper class were deported to Babylonia. This was the **first major deportation of the Jews.**
3. **Zedekiah.** (c. 598-587 B. C.) Jerusalem fell to Babylonia during his reign. He and many of his people were deported to Babylon. This was the **second major deportation of the Jews.**

Media:
1. **Cyaxares.** (c. 625-585 B. C.) He formed an alliance with Babylonia and together they overthrew the Assyrians. Media reached its greatest heights during his rule.
2. **Astyages.** (c. 584-550 B. C.) Media fell to Cyrus the Persian in 550 B. C.

Persia:
1. **Cambyses II.** (c. 600-559 B. C.) He founded the Persian state.
2. **Cyrus II, the Great.** (c. 558-529 B. C.) He conquered Media c. 550 B. C. and Babylonia c. 539 B. C. It was Cyrus who allowed the Jews to return to Jerusalem.

Another ruler plays an important role in the book of Daniel. He is

Darius The Mede (Dă-rī'-us) (see Dan. 5:30-31; 6:1-28; 9:1-2; 11:1)

There is no further information at present known about him beyond what Daniel records. Bible scholars have suggested two theories as to his identity:
1. He was a provisional governor of Babylon who ruled for about three years after the fall of Babylon to Persia and then relinquished control to Cyrus. This belief has merit because it extends the period of the Babylonian exile to a full seventy years (from Daniel's deportation, 606 B. C. past the supposed three-year rule of Darius the Mede, 539-537 B. C. to the coming of Cyrus the Persian in 536 B. C.) in fulfillment of Jeremiah's prophecy.
2. Darius is another name for Astyages, the final king of Media. There is no reason to believe that Astyages ruled in Babylon, however, and Darius is not a Median name.

National Conditions—Babylonia:

Daniel was associated with the Babylonian court for almost the entire period of Babylonia's existence. This was an era of great building programs, and Daniel undoubtedly saw many of his people used as slaves in the great construction program. He apparently rose to positions of honor and gained control over many of the activities of the kingdom, which may, in part, account for the happier lot of the Jews toward the end of the exilic period.

DANIEL   499

Outline of the Book:

Chapter 1—Daniel Rises To Favor in the Babylonian Court.
1. Nebuchadnezzar took tribute from Jehoiakim, king of Judah, and carried some of the children of royal blood into Babylon. (1-4)
2. Daniel and three of his friends insisted on obeying the Hebrew food laws. They fared better than their companions who accepted the rich Babylonian foods without question. (5-16)
3. Daniel and his three friends found favor in the sight of Nebuchadnezzar because they had greater wisdom and understanding than the Babylonian magicians and astrologers. (17-21)

Chapter 2—Nebuchadnezzar's Dream of the Coming of the Kingdom of God.
1. Nebuchadnezzar had an important dream which he wanted to have interpreted. He forgot the details of the dream, however, and told his wise men to both reveal the dream and interpret it on threat of death. They were unable to do so and the king set the date for their execution. (1-13)
   Note: Nebuchadnezzar saw his dream in the second year of his reign, or about 603 B. C. This was during Daniel's third or fourth year in Babylon.
2. Daniel went to the king and requested time to receive the interpretation. He and his companions then sought revelation from the Lord. The dream and its interpretation was revealed to Daniel, who went before the king to explain it. (14-30)
3. The dream: (31-35)
   A. A great image in the form of a man with a
      (1). Head of fine gold,
      (2). Breast and arms of silver,
      (3). Belly and thighs of brass,
      (4). Legs of iron,
      (5). Feet of part iron and part clay.
   B. A stone was cut out without hands and hit the image on its feet.
   C. The image broke into pieces and became as chaff, and the wind blew it away.
   D. The stone became a great mountain, and filled the earth.

4. Daniel's interpretation: (36-45)
   A. The image is like a calendar, and the parts represent kingdoms which will arise. Nebuchadnezzar is the head of Gold.
   B. (3, 18)[1] The stone is a kingdom which shall be set up by the God of heaven.
      (1). It will come in the time of the divided kingdoms of the image's feet.
      (2). It shall never be destroyed.
      (3). The kingdom shall not be left to other people.
      (4). (29) The kingdom shall break in pieces and consume all the other kingdoms.
      (5). (50) The kingdom shall stand forever.
      (6). The dream is certain, and the interpretation thereof sure.

Note 1: The Latter-day Saint understanding of this passage is as follows:

1. The image represents the major kingdoms of the western world since the time of Babylonia. Its purpose is to indicate the exact period in which the kingdom will be established by the Lord.
   A. The head = The Babylonian Empire c. 625-539 B. C.
   B. The breast and arms = The Persian Empire c. 539-331 B. C.
   C. The belly and thighs = The Macedonian (Greek) Empire c. 331-161 B. C.
   D. The legs = The Roman Empire c. 161 B. C.-431 A. D.
   E. The feet = The variety of strong and weak kingdoms which formed after the collapse of the Roman empire.
2. The stone represents the restored Gospel kingdom of Jesus Christ and the political kingdom which will be established from it in the last days.[2] (see D & C 65:2)
3. The major messages of the prophecy:
   A. The time when God would set up his kingdom upon the earth was to be in the last days, not during Christ's ministry in the first century A. D.

---

[1]Numbers in parentheses at the beginning of items refer to the fifty events of the last days listed in Chapter Four.
[2]For a discussion of the dual nature of the kingdom of God and a reporting of substantiating statements pertaining to this theme, see *Prophecy—Key to the Future*, chapters V and XV.

Daniel

      B. The prophecy makes it clear that no Church has a valid claim to being Christ's kingdom if it maintains that it has continued in an unbroken succession since Christ's earthly ministry, for such a belief violates the many Biblical prophecies of the apostacy. On the contrary, the prophecy shows that Christ's kingdom was to be re-established in a later era—the last days.

4. Other messages of the prophecy:

    A. Christ's kingdom will be a great kingdom which will fill the whole earth. (2:35)

    B. Christ's kingdom will break in pieces and consume earthly kingdoms. (2:44)

    C. Christ's kingdom shall never be destroyed or left to another people; it shall stand forever.

    D. The prophecy is not only religious but political in nature. Christ's kingdom will be both religious and political.

Note 2: Other interpreters, who do not understand the nature of the restored Church and Biblical prophecies pertaining to it, attempt to interpret this as a prophecy of Christ's coming in the meridian of time by disregarding the feet as a separate portion of the image and then asserting that Christ came in the period of the Roman Empire. Such an interpretation, of course, would be in complete disregard of the many Biblical prophecies concerning the apostacy.

Note 3: Many critics assign the authorship of the book of Daniel to the Maccabean period. In their efforts to nullify any element of prophecy, they cite the image as a historical passage. To thus interpret it, however, they make the second kingdom Media, the third kingdom Persia, and the fourth kingdom the Macedonians. They completely disregard the most important aspect of the prophecy: the kingdom to be established by God. Such an interpretation is untenable not only because of its omission of the major portion of the prophecy (the stone), but because it is historically inaccurate. Media did not follow Babylonia but existed concurrently with it and was conquered before Babylonia by Persia. There never was a Median empire following the fall of Babylonia.

5. Nebuchadnezzar made Daniel a ruler and a great man. (46-49)

Chapter 3—Shadrach, Meshach and Abednego Escape the Fiery Furnace.

1. Nebuchadnezzar made an image of gold and commanded that all his kingdom should fall down and worship it. (1-7)
2. Shadrach (Shā'-drăch), Meshach (Mē'-shăch) and Abednego (ă-bĕd'-nĕ-gō), Daniel's three friends, refused to bow before the image. (8-13)
3. Nebuchadnezzar had them thrown into a fiery furnace. (14-23)
4. They were joined in the furnace by a fourth being. They were all protected and emerged unharmed. (24-27)
5. Nebuchadnezzar promoted them and decreed that no one should speak anything amiss about their God. (28-30)

Chapter 4—Nebuchadnezzar's Insanity and Recovery.

1. Nebuchadnezzar saw a dream, but his soothsayers could not interpret it for him. (1-7)
2. Nebuchadnezzar called for Daniel and described his dream to him. (8:18)

   A. He saw a great tree which had many leaves, and gave shade to the animals.

   B. A watcher and an holy one came down from heaven and commanded that the trees be hewed down.

   C. The stump and roots were to be left in the earth.

      (1). It was to have a band of iron and brass.

      (2). It was to be wet with the dew of heaven.

      (3). It was to eat grass.

      (4). Its heart was changed from a man's to a beast's heart.

      (5). Seven times passed over him.

   Note: "Times" are generally interpreted as years or seasons. Some have asserted that in Babylonia only winters and summers were counted, so that seven seasons would be three-and-one-half years.

3. Daniel's interpretation: The tree was Nebuchadnezzar. He would be driven from men and eat grass in the kingtimes till he knew that the most High ruleth in the kingdom of men. His kingdom would remain secure to him during his madness. (19-27)

DANIEL

4. The prophecy was fulfilled. (28-37)
   Note: No other record gives indication of Nebuchadnezzar's madness. Many critics have speculated that the madness came upon Nabonidus, rather than Nebuchadnezzar, which would explain his long absence while Belshazzar ruled the kingdom.

Chapter 5—Belshazzar's Feast and The Fall of Babylon.

1. Belshazzar gave a great feast. The revelers drank out of the temple vessels taken from the temple in Jerusalem. (1-4)
   Note: Belshazzar was definitely not the son of Nebuchadnezzar. He is believed to be the son of Nabonidus. He was probably a co-regent rather than the sole king. There are many unanswered questions concerning his identity.
2. A hand appeared and wrote upon the wall. The wise men could not interpret the message so Daniel was called. (5-16)
3. His message to Belshazzar: Thou hast not humbled thine heart. (17-23)
4. The handwriting on the wall: Mene, Mene, Tekel, Upharsin. Its interpretation: (25-28)
   A. Mene (Mē'-nē)—God hath numbered thy kingdom, and finished it.
   B. Tekel (Tē'-kĕl)—Thou art weighed in the balances, and art found wanting.
   C. Peres (Pē'-rĕs)—Thy kingdom is divided, and given to the Medes and Persians.
5. Belshazzar made Daniel the third ruler of the kingdom. (29)
6. That night Belshazzar was slain and the kingdom was taken over by Darius the Mede. (30-31)

Chapter 6—Daniel Is Protected From the Lions.

1. Darius set Daniel as one of the three presidents who ruled over one hundred and twenty princes of the kingdom. (1-3)
2. A plot was made against Daniel. Darius was persuaded to issue a decree that anyone who asked a petition of any god or man except king Darius would be cast into the den of lions. (4-9)
3. Daniel continued to pray to the Lord. He was reported, apprehended, and cast into the lion's den. (10-17)

4. The king came to the lion's den the following day and found that the Lord had delivered Daniel from the lions. (18-22)
5. Daniel was released, Darius issued a decree that the people should fear before the God of Daniel, and Daniel's enemies were thrown among the lions. (23-28)

Chapter 7—Daniel's Vision of the Four Beasts and the Council at Adam-ondi-Ahman.
1. Daniel's dream in the first year of the reign of Belshazzar:
    A. Four great beasts came up from the sea:
        (1). The first—like a lion, with eagle's wings. Its wings were plucked, and it was lifted up from the earth, and made to stand upon the feet as a man, and a man's heart was given to it. (3-4)
        (2). The second—like a bear. It had three ribs in its mouth. They said thus unto it, Arise, devour much flesh. (5)
        (3). The third—like a leopard; with four wings of a fowl on its back, and four heads. Dominion was given to it. (6)
        (4). The fourth—dreadful and terrible and strong exceedingly—and it had great iron teeth and nails of brass. It devoured and brake in pieces the whole earth, and stamped the residue with the feet of it. (7, 19, 23)
            a. It had ten horns. (7, 20)
            b. (25) There came up among them another little horn. (8, 20)
                1. Before the little horn three of the first horns were plucked up by the roots. (8, 20)
                2. In this horn were eyes like the eyes of man, and a mouth speaking great things, whose look was more stout than his fellows. (8, 20)
                3. (25) The little horn made war with the saints, and prevailed against them until the Ancient of days came. (21-22)

4. (25) He shall speak great words against the most High. (25)
5. (25) He shall wear out the saints of the most High. (25)
6. (25) He shall think to change times and laws. (25)
7. (25) The saints shall be given into his hand until a time and times and the dividing of time. (25)

B. (26) Thrones were cast down. (9)

C. (26) The (fourth) beast was slain, and his body destroyed, and given to the burning flame. (11)

D. (26) The rest of the beasts had their dominion taken away, yet their lives were prolonged for a season and a time. (12)

E. (27) The Ancient of days did sit and judgment was given to the saints of the most High. (9, 22)

(1). Ten thousand times ten thousand (100,000,-000) stood before him. (10)
(2). The judgment was set, and the books were opened. (10)
(3). (28?) The judgment shall sit, and the saints will take away the dominion of the little horn, to consume and destroy it unto the end. (26)
(4). (27) The Son of man came to the Ancient of days, and they brought him near before Him. There was given Him dominion, and glory, and an everlasting kingdom. (13-14)

F. (50) The saints of the most High shall take the kingdom, and possess the kingdom for ever. (18, 27)

2. Daniel's clues to interpretation:

A. These great beasts, which are four, are four kings, which shall arise out of the earth. (17)

B. The fourth beast shall be the fourth kingdom upon earth, and shall devour the whole earth. (23)

C. The ten horns out of this kingdom are ten kings that shall arise. (24)

D. Another king shall arise after them (the little horn); and he shall be diverse from the first, and he shall subdue three kings. (24)

Note 1: The prophecies of Daniel are extremely difficult to interpret. Extensive calculations of eschatological events have been made by numerous individuals from various churches during the last several centuries; time has already proven many of their calculations to be false. Bible students must approach their interpretation with caution. Yet they are not to be ignored! Certainly the Lord does not expect man to ignore and shun His word and to refuse to seek an understanding of it. There is no official meaning or interpretation for Daniel's prophecies which can be ascribed to the Church of Jesus Christ of Latter-day Saints. Consequently there is some difference which can be found in the interpretations made by various L. D. S. scriptorians. Certain keys for interpretation are available, however, which provide enlightenment for the Mormon student. These are:

1. Daniel's interpretative clues.
2. The coming of the Ancient of days, and the coming of the Son of man are definitely regarded as being last days events which are still future.

    A. They have not happened yet.

    B. A revelation in the D & C identifies the location and the future nature of the event: "Adam-ondi-Ahman, because, said he, it is the place where Adam shall come to visit his people, or the Ancient of Days shall sit, as spoken of by Daniel the prophet." (D & C 116)

    C. Adam is the Ancient of Days. (see B. above.)

3. The end of the fourth beast, the casting down of thrones, the removal of the dominion of the other three beasts, the end of the oppression of the little horn, the giving of judgment to the saints, and the everlasting kingdom being given to the saints, are all connected with the coming of the Ancient of Days in the prophecy and can thus be regarded as last days events which are yet future.

With these items as keys, the following clues to interpretation are suggested for consideration:

1. The four beasts:

    A. **The first beast** = The Babylonian Empire.
The plucking of the wings and the giving of a man's heart could possibly be references to the humbling process to which Nebuchadnezzar and Belshazzar were subjected. (2:46-47; 3:29; 4:25, 27, 34-37; 5:18-23)

DANIEL

B. **The second beast** = The Persian Empire.
"It devoured much flesh." The Persian conquests were far more extensive than the Assyrian, Babylonian, Median, and Egyptian conquests which preceded them.

C. **The third beast** = The Greco-Macedonian Empire. "The beast had four heads." After the death of Alexander the Great, in 323 B. C., his empire was divided among his generals and soon broke into four sections:

(1). The Seleucid Empire.
(2). The Ptolemaic Empire.
(3). The Macedonian Empire.
(4). Greece.

D. **The fourth beast** = The Roman Empire.

(1). It had great iron teeth (note the similarity to the description of the Roman empire in Nebuchadnezzar's dream image, see 2:40)
(2). It was diverse because it became associated with Christianity and adopted it as the official religion.

2. **The ten horns of the fourth beast** = Ten kings that shall arise out of it.

Note: Bible commentators have struggled with the identity of these kings for centuries, and still have not been able to clearly identify them. No interpretation seems to fit. The areas for consideration are as follows:

A. Those who regard the prophecy as having reference to the Maccabean period regard the ten kings as either Alexander the Great and nine of the Seluecid kings or ten of the Seluecid kings. Such an interpretation is completely unacceptable to Latter-day Saints because

(1). It does not fit the pattern of the kings of that period,
(2). It does not conform to the latter-days interpretation of the coming of the Ancient of Days which is asserted in the D & C.

B. Many protestant commentators have assumed these kings to be individuals who lived during or following the collapse of the Roman Empire from 400 to 800 A. D.

C. The fourth beast could conceivably be extended to include not only the Roman empire but also the Holy

Roman Empire, which was solidified by Charlemagne and ended shortly after 1800 A. D. Again the ten kings or kingdoms remain unidentified, yet it moves the time of the interpretation to the last days, in conformance with the latter portion of the prophecy.

3. **The Little Horn =**

   A. Those who attempt to find fulfillment of the prophecy during the Maccabean period assert that this was Antiochus IV Epiphanes, who ruled from 175-164 B. C. in Syria and attempted to crush Jewish worship and nationality.

   B. Most protestants have interpreted the little horn as the Catholic papacy and find the prophesied oppression in the struggles of the inquisition and the protestant reformation.

   C. Latter-day Saint commentators have never attempted to fix the identity of the little horn with certainty, nor is any real clue provided from other L. D. S. scriptures. Yet his role is important and will have a definite bearing upon the future of the Church. The following clues should be noted in particular.

   (1). Though the beginning of his influence cannot be clearly determined from Daniel's prophecy, the period of his dominion can be:

   a. **He oppresses the saints of the most High.** (25) This clearly implies that he functions in a period when the saints are on the earth. To Latter-day Saints this means either the first century A. D. (preceding the apostacy) or since 1830 A. D. (since the restoration of the Church.)

   b. **He makes war against the saints and prevails against them until the Ancient of Days comes and sits in judgment.** (21-22) This places the period of his activity, or at least the termination of his activity, clearly in the future; just before the coming of the Ancient of Days to the council at Adam-ondi-Ahman. (see D & C 116)

   c. It would seem that the Saints he oppresses will be members of the Church rather than the people of Palestine, who apparently will not yet be converted to Christ. This, however, is not indicated with absolute clarity.

(2). He will have power over the saints which will be ended at the Council of Adam-ondi-Ahman. (25-26) This period of oppression will last for "a time and times and the dividing of a time." (Most Bible interpreters understand this to be 3½ years.)

(3). He will apparently be in a position of authority in which it will be possible to "change times and laws." (25)

4. **The three horns who are plucked up by the little horn =** They are unknown, except that they are three of the ten kings or kingdoms. It is not clear whether they lived in the past or whether they are still future.

A. Those who attempt to find fulfillment of the prophecy during the Maccabean period regard them as either Seleucus IV, Heliodorus, and Demetrius Sotor; or Heliodorus, Demetrius, and Ptolemy VI. Again, their case is vague and indefinite.

B. Those who attempt to find fulfillment of the prophecy in the rise of papal authority hold that these are the Lombards, Ravenna, and Rome, which were handed over to the popes as the papacy achieved temporal dominion in 754 A. D.

5. **Thrones are cast down, the fourth beast is destroyed, and the dominion of the other three beasts is taken away =** This is obviously a major international calamity which affects the nations. The following observations should be noted:

A. These are clearly last days events which take place at approximately the same time as the Council at Adam-ondi-Ahman (9-14) as indicated by the interwoven context.

B. The beasts represented empires which were terminated long ago, yet the beasts continue to function in a last days context. It would seem that the only interpretation possible is that the destructions indicated would take place with the modern decendants of those empires. Thus the fourth beast would seem to include most of Europe. The combined first, second, and third kingdoms would seem to include Turkey, Syria, Iraq, Iran, Afghanistan, Pakistan, Saudia Arabia, Egypt and their smaller neighbors.

C. A brief interlude of "a season and time" is said to take place in which the other beasts find their life prolonged but are without dominion. That this happens to the three beasts together indicates that they are to be regarded as a unit and that they meet their fate jointly. Could this interlude be the time between the fourth world war and the Battle of Armageddon?[2]

6. **The Ancient of Days is clearly understood by Latter-day Saints to be Adam.** (see statements by Joseph Smith to this effect in HC 3:386-87 and HC 4:207-09)
7. **The Council at Adam-ondi-Ahman is understood to be the time when Christ will receive His earthly kingdom and the responsibility of world government will pass into the hands of the Saints.** (see statements by Joseph Smith to this effect in HC 3:386-87 and HC 4:207-09)
8. **Summary of the important lessons of Daniel's prophecy of the Four Beasts.** Although much is not yet clear concerning this prophecy, certain understandings may be gleaned from it, as follows:

    A. A great council will be held at Adam-ondi-Ahman in which

    (1). Christ will receive the earth as His dominion and kingdom.
    (2). The Saints will inherit His everlasting kingdom.
    (3). Judgment will be held upon the nations of the world.
    (4). Persecution by the "little horn" against the Saints will be ended.

    B. The council at Adam-ondi-Ahman will take place in close proximity in time to the destruction of Europe and the removal of the dominion of the nations of Asia minor.

    C. There will be a period of extensive persecution against the saints by some great individual or power.

Chapter 8—**Daniel's Vision of the Ram and the He-Goat.**
1. The vision was given to Daniel in the third year of the reign of Belshazzar. (1)

---

[2]See *Prophecy—Key to the Future*, pp. 159-195.

DANIEL 511

2. In his vision Daniel saw himself at Shushan (the Persian capital) and then at the nearby river of Ulai. (2)
3. Daniel's vision:
    A. A ram. (1) It had two horns of different height. The higher horn came up last. (3) It pushed north, south, and west, and nothing could stand before it. (4)
    B. A He-Goat. It came from the west. (5) It had a notable horn between its eyes. (5)
    C. The he-goat smote the ram and broke its two horns. (6-7)
    D. The he-goat waxed strong. Then his horn was broken and four other notable horns came out. (8)
    E. Out of one of the four horns came a little horn which waxed exceedingly great toward the south, toward the east, and toward the pleasant land. (9)
    F. He took the daily sacrifice away and cast down the place of the sanctuary. (10-11)
    G. The sanctuary was to be desolated for 2300 days and then cleansed. (13-14)
4. The interpretation to the vision was given by Gabriel. (15-19)
    A. The ram is the kings of Media and Persia. (20)
    B. The goat is the king of Greece. (21)
    C. The horn is the first king. (21)

Note: This would seem to be Alexander the Great, although he was not the first king.

   D. Four kingdoms of lesser strength came out of his kingdom.

Note: Upon the death of Alexander, his kingdom was divided among his generals.
    (1). Ptolemy—Egypt.
    (2). Selecus—Syria.
    (3). Lysimachus—Thrace.
    (4). Cassander—Macedonia.

   E. (35?) A king of fierce countenance will be raised up. (23)
        (1). His power shall be mighty, but not by his own power. (24)
        (2). He shall prosper and practice. (24)
        (3). He shall destroy the mighty and the holy people. (24)

(4). He shall cause craft to prosper in his hand. (25)
(5). He shall magnify himself in his heart. (25)
(6). By peace (marginal note: prosperity) shall destroy many. (25)
(7). He shall stand up against the Prince of princes. (25)
(8). He shall be broken without hand. (25)

Note: This king of fierce countenance is generally interpreted to be Antiochus IV Epiphanes who

 a. Ruled Palestine from Syria, 175-164 B. C.
 b. Replaced the Jewish leader in Jerusalem, Onias III, with his brother, Jason, who promised to pay large sums of Judah's wealth into the royal treasury. He also established a gymnasium in the shadow of the temple and caused the priests to leave their temple duties for the games.
 c. Sold a large portion of the population of Jerusalem as slaves.
 d. Destroyed the walls of Jerusalem.
 e. Plundered Jerusalem and the temple.
 f. Converted the temple into a shrine for the Olympian god Zeus.
  1. An image of Zeus was set up on the altar December 15, 168 B. C.
  2. A sow was sacrificed in its honor ten days later.
  3. He made Jewish observance of heathen festivals compulsory.
 g. Prohibited the practice of Judaism completely.
  1. Those who read or even possessed the Torah were put to death.
  2. Circumcision and Sabbath observance were forbidden.

A revolt was led against Antiochus by Mattathias, an old Jewish priest. The cause soon fell upon the shoulders of his son Judas, who was nick-named Maccabeus ("the hammer"). In a short but effective campaign Judas defeated the Syrians, expelled them from Jerusalem, and cleansed the temple. When news of his army's defeat reached Antiochus he was apparently so shocked that he died soon thereafter.

Note 2: While the history of Antiochus and the Maccabean revolt seems to fulfill the details of Daniel's prophecy, the interpretation given by Gabriel seems to allude to another personage in the last days. Can this be a reference to the Battle of Armageddon, when the army of Gog will wage war on the people of Palestine and against David the prince, and then be cut off by the power of the Lord? Note the clues which he gives to such an interpretation:

a. For at the time of the end shall be the vision. (17)
b. I will make thee know what shall be in the last end of the indignation: for at the time appointed the end shall be. (19)
c. And in the latter time of their kingdom, when the transgressors are come to the full, ... (23) (The Battle of Armageddon is often regarded as a time of judgment upon the wicked).
d. His power shall be mighty, but not by his own power. (24) (Does he come by the Lord's power? see Zeph. 3:8)
e. He shall destroy the mighty and the holy people. (24)
f. He shall also stand up against the Prince of princes. (25) (Who was this in Antiochus' day? The Savior? If this were the Battle of Armageddon would this be David the prince? Or the Savior?)
g. He shall be broken without hand. (25) (It was Judas who broke Antiochus' hold by fighting. If this were the Battle of Armageddon would not Gog be broken by the appearance of the Lord upon the mount of Olives?)

It must be admitted that the passage seems to carry allusions which may find applications in the Battle of Armageddon. This is especially true if this prophecy follows the same pattern as all of Daniel's other prophecies of world events: he speaks of the kingdoms of his time and then skips to the last days. On the other hand, strong evidence can also be shown that the prophecy was fulfilled in Antiochus Epiphanes. It would seem that the matter should be left open for further study and contemplation.

Chapter 9—Daniel's Prophecy of the Coming of Christ.

1. The prophecy was given in the first year of Darius the Mede. (1)
2. Daniel understood that the seventy years of captivity was almost completed. (2)
3. Daniel's prayer, in which he confesses the wickedness of Israel and seeks the mercies of the Lord upon His people. (3-19)
4. Gabriel came to give him skill and understanding. (20-23)
5. Gabriel's prophecy:

    A. Seventy weeks are determined upon thy people and upon the holy city (24)

        (1). To finish the transgression.
        (2). To make an end to sins.
        (3). To make reconciliation for iniquity.
        (4). To bring in everlasting righteousness.
        (5). To seal up the vision and prophecy.
        (6). To anoint the most Holy.

    B. From the going forth of the commandment to restore and build Jerusalem to the Messiah shall be seven weeks, and threescore and two weeks. (69 weeks) (25)

    C. The street and the wall (of Jerusalem) shall be built again in troublous times. (25)

    D. After threescore and two weeks shall Messiah be cut off, but not for Himself. (26)

    E. The people of the prince that shall come shall destroy the city and the sanctuary; and the end thereof shall be with a flood. (26)

DANIEL   515

F. Unto the end of the war desolations are determined. (26)

G. He shall confirm the covenant with many for one week. (27)

H. In the midst of the week He shall cause the sacrifice and the oblation to cease. (27)

Note 1: This prophecy deals with three identifiable items:
   (1). The rebuilding of Jerusalem after the Babylonian exile. (B & C above)
   (2). The dating of the ministry of Christ. (A, B, G, H above)
   (3). The destruction of Jerusalem by the Romans. (E & F above)
Item D with the 62 weeks is not clearly understood.

Note 2: The seventy weeks is generally understood to mean seventy weeks of years (or seventy sevens of years, or 7 x 70 = 490 years). This is the "year-day theory," in which a day is understood to equal a year. (see Ezekiel 4:4-5) The date when the seventy weeks was to begin was when the decree would be issued by a Persian king to return and rebuild Jerusalem. This would be either the decree to Zerubabbel (Ezra 1) c. 536 B. C. or the decree to Ezra (Ezra 7) in c. 457 B. C. It would appear that the latter is the pertinent date for the calculation of the prophecy.

   (1). It was to be 69 weeks or 483 years from the commandment to restore Jerusalem to the time of the Messiah.

   457 B. C. (the year of the commandment to Ezra to rebuild Jerusalem.)
   +483 years (69 weeks)
   ─────────
   26 A. D. (This is the year generally accepted as the time Christ began His public ministry.)

   (2). Christ was to put an end to sacrifice and oblation in the midst of a week. His ministry was approximately 3½ years, or half of a seven-year "week." His death on the cross fulfilled the law of Moses which specified the Israelite sacrifices.

(3). The Romans destroyed the sanctuary and the city of Jerusalem after a five-month siege in 70 A. D. They then flooded over into Caesarea and killed more than a million Jews.

Chapter 10—Heavenly Beings Prepare To Show Daniel What Will Befall His People in the Latter Days.

1. The vision was given in the third year of Cyrus the Persian. (1)

   Note: This was two years after his decree to return to Jerusalem had been issued.

2. Daniel had fasted three weeks, then he saw the vision by the river Hiddekel. (2-4)
3. A heavenly being appeared to him and said that God had heard Daniel's words. (5-12)
   A. The prince of the kingdom of Persia withstood the visitor twenty-one days, but Michael helped him. (13)
4. The being came to make Daniel understand what should befall his people in the latter days, for yet the vision is for many days. (14)
5. Daniel was without strength but two angels strengthened him. (15-19)
6. The angel said he must return to fight with the prince of Persia, and when he has gone, the prince of Grecia shall come. (20)
7. The angel said that he would show Daniel what was noted in the scripture of truth. (21)
8. The angel said that there was none that held with him in these things but Michael your prince. (21; 11:1)

Chapter 11—The Conflict Between the Seleucids and Ptolemies—The Last Days.

1. There will yet be four kings of Persia. The fourth shall be far richer than the rest. Through his strength and riches he shall stir up all against the realm of Grecia. (2)

   Note: The four kings of Persia were

   A. Cyrus.
   B. Cambyses II.

DANIEL 517

C. Darius.

D. Xerxes (Ahasuerus) He invaded Greece in 480 B. C. but was defeated at Salamia.

Seven other kings ruled Persia, however, before it actually fell to Greece: Artaxerxes, Xerxes II, Darius II, Artaxerxes II, Artaxerxes III, Arses, and Darius III.

2. A mighty king shall rule with great dominion. (3)

   Note: Alexander the Great.

3. His kingdom shall be broken, and shall be divided toward the four winds of heaven, and not to his posterity. (4)

   Note: Alexander's Empire was divided by his four generals:

   A. Ptolemy.
   B. Seleucus.
   C. Lysimachus.
   D. Cassander.

4. The king of the south shall be strong. (5-12)

   Note: The king of the south was Ptolemy who ruled Egypt.

   A. One of the princes will be strong above him and have dominion. (5)

   Note: Seleucus, after helping Ptolemy defeat Antigonus at Gaza in 312 B. C., became the master of Mesopotamia and Syria.

   B. They will join themselves together, for the king's daughter of the south shall come to the king of the north to make an agreement. (6)

   Note: Berenice, the daughter of Ptolemy II, married the Seleucid king, Antiochus II. He divorced his wife, Laodice, to marry her.

   C. She shall not retain the power of the arm; neither shall he stand, nor his arm. (6)

   Note: Laodice had Antiochus II, Berenice, and their son murdered.

   D. Out of the branch of her roots shall one come with an army and shall prevail against the king of the north. (7-9)

   Note: Ptolemy III, Berenice's brother, defeated Seleucus II, son of Laodice.

   E. The sons of the king of the north shall assemble

a multitude of great forces, and pass through, and return to his fortress. (10-17) The king of the south shall attack the king of the north with multitude, but the attacking king will lose. (11-12) The king of the north will attack after certain years with a great army.

Note: Seleucus II counterattacked, and a truce was signed. He was followed by two sons: Seleucus III and Antiochus III. The latter was successful in war, defeating the Egyptians at Gaza in 201 B. C. and Banias in 199 B. C.

F. A prince shall cause his reproach to cease when he turns his face to the isles. He shall turn to his own land, but he shall stumble and fall and not be found. (18-19)

Note: Antiochus III tried to conquer Pergamon and Greece but was defeated in 190 B. C. by the Roman Lucius Cornelius Scipio. Antiochus died suddenly three years later.

G. A raiser of taxes will be raised up in the northern kingdom but will be destroyed in a few days. (20)

Note: Seleucus IV sent out a tax collector, Heliodorus, to replenish the treasury but the tax collector assassinated the king.

H. A vile person shall gain the kingdom by flatteries. He shall slay the prince of the covenant and shall scatter and spoil for a time. (21-24)

Note: Antiochus IV Epiphanes came to the throne illegally, slew the Jewish high priest, Onias III, and looted in Palestine and Egypt.

I. He shall come against the king of the south with a great army and shall conquer, for the king of the south shall not stand. (25-28)

Note: Antiochus IV Epiphanes looted Egypt in his first campaign in 170 or 169 B. C.

J. He shall again come toward the south, but shall not be successful, for the ships of Chittim shall come against him. (29-30)

Note: The second campaign of Antiochus against Egypt was prevented by the Romans under Gaices Popilius Laenas. Chittim is Cyprus.

DANIEL

K. He shall be grieved and have indignation against the holy covenant, and shall take away the daily sacrifice, and shall place the abomination that maketh desolate. (30-31)

Note: Antiochus desecrated the Jewish temple by setting up idols and abolishing the temple rituals.

L. The people shall know their God, shall be strong, and do exploits. Yet they shall fall by the sword, flame, and captivity many days. (32-35)

Note: The Maccabean Wars between Syria and Judah continued from 168-129 B. C.

M. The king will exalt himself and shall prosper till the indignation be accomplished. He shall acknowledge a strange god. (36-39)

Note: Antiochus magnified himself by calling himself "god manifest" (Epiphanes) and substituted the god Zeus for Apollo, which had been the patron god of the Seleucid dynasty.

At this point Daniel's vision ceases to foretell the history of the conflict between the Seleucid and Ptolemaic dynasties of Greece. No fulfillment can be found for these events in the history of that time, and the context of chapter 12 places them in a last days setting:

N. The remaining events of the chapter take place "at the time of the end." (40)

Note: Various commentators have tried to find fulfillment in Antiochus Epiphanes, the Mohammedan possession of the Holy Land, the Papacy, etc.

O. (26?) The king of the south shall push at the north. (40)

P. (26?) The king of the north shall come against him with chariots, horsemen, and with many ships. He shall enter into the countries, overflow, and pass over.

    (1). He shall enter into the glorious land. (41)
    (2). Many countries shall be overthrown. (41)
    (3). Edom, Moab, and Ammon shall escape. (41)
    (4). Egypt shall not escape. He shall possess Egypt's precious things. The Libyans and the Ethiopians shall be at his steps. (42-43)
    (5). Tidings out of the east and north shall trouble him. He shall go forth to destroy, and utterly to make away many. (44)

(6). He shall plant the tabernacles of his palace between the seas in the glorious holy mountain. (45)
(7). He shall come to his end, and none shall help him. (45)
(8). It shall be at the time when
  a. Michael shall stand up. (12:1) (Adam [see D & C 27:11] at the Council of Adam-ondi-Ahman?)
  b. There shall be a time of trouble worse than any previous. (12:1)
  c. Thy people shall be delivered. (12:1)
  d. Many that sleep in the dust shall awake, both righteous and wicked. (12:2)

Chapter 12—Universal Conflict and The Council at Adam-ondi-Ahman.

1. (27) Michael shall stand up. (1)

   Note: Michael is Adam. (See D & C 27:11.) This seems to be a reference to the Council at Adam-ondi-Ahman.

2. (26) There shall be a time of trouble such as never there was since there was a nation even to that same time. (1)
3. (28?) At that time thy people shall be delivered. (1)
4. (27) Many of them that sleep in the dust of the earth shall awake, some to everlasting life and some to shame and everlasting contempt. (2-3)

   Note: This seems to be a resurrection of both the righteous and the wicked which takes place in connection with the Council of Adam-ondi-Ahman. (see Joseph Smith's comments which would seem to explain the reason for the resurrection at this time in HC 3: 386-87.)

5. Daniel was to seal up the book, even to the time of the end. (4)
6. (26) Daniel saw heavenly beings and one inquired, "How long shall it be to the end of these wonders?" The reply was "It shall be for a time, times, and an half; and when he shall have accomplished to scatter the power of the holy people, all these things shall be finished." (5-7)

   Note 1: This seems to be another allusion to the "little horn" who will persecute the Saints "for a time and times and the dividing of time." (7:21-22, 25-26)

DANIEL

Note 2: A time is usually interpreted as a year, times as two years, and a half as six months. There is no evidence, however, that such an interpretation is correct. Assuming its correctness, however, would give this period of persecution a length of 3½ years or 1290 days. (see also Rev. 11:2) There is no indication of what will begin this period, but both Daniel's references to it seem to indicate that it will end with the war during which the Council at Adam-ondi-Ahman is held.

7. The words are closed up and sealed till the time of the end. None of the wicked shall understand but the wise shall understand. (8-10)
8. (26) From the time that the daily sacrifice shall be taken away and the abomination that maketh desolate set up, there shall be a thousand two hundred and ninety days. (11)

    Note: Is this a clue to the event that marks the beginning of the period of persecution of Dan. 7:21-22, 25-26? (see also JS 2:32)

9. (27?) Blessed is he that waiteth, and cometh to the thousand three hundred and five and thirty days. (12)

    Note: This seems to be an important event 45 days after the end of the 1290 days, above.

10. But go thou thy way till the end be: for thou shalt rest, and stand in thy lot at the end of the days. (13)

Doctrinal Analysis:

The Sins of the People:

1. Thou hast not humbled thine heart, but hast lifted up thyself against the Lord of heaven. (5:22-23)
2. Thou hast praised the gods of silver and gold. (5:23)
3. The God in whose hand thy breath is, and whose are all thy ways, hast thou not glorified. (5:23)
4. We have rebelled, even by departing from thy precepts and from thy judgments. (9:5)
5. Neither have we hearkened unto thy servants the prophets. (9:6)
6. Neither have we obeyed the voice of the Lord our God, to walk in his laws, which he set before us by his servants the prophets. (9:10)

The Nature of God:

1. He changeth the times and the seasons. (2:21)
2. God knoweth what is in the darkness, and the light dwelleth with him. (2:22)
3. The form of the fourth individual in the fiery furnace was like the Son of God. (3:25)
4. His kingdom is an everlasting kingdom, and his dominion is from generation to generation. (4:3)
5. I praised and honoured him that liveth for ever, whose dominion is an everlasting dominion, and his kingdom is from generation to generation. (4:34)
6. He is the living God, and steadfast for ever, and his kingdom that which shall not be destroyed, and his dominion shall be even unto the end. He delivereth and rescueth, and he worketh signs and wonders in heaven and in earth. (6:26-27)
7. The Lord is the great and dreadful God, keeping the covenant and mercy to them that love him, and to them that keep his commandments. (9:4)
8. O Lord, righteousness belongeth unto thee. (9:7)
9. To the Lord our God belong mercies and forgivenesses, (9:9)
10. The Lord our God is righteous in all his works which he doeth. (9:14)

Appearances and Visions of God and Heavenly Beings:

1. A fourth being walked in the fiery furnace. (3:25)
2. A hand wrote on the wall. (5:5)
3. An angel closed the lions' mouths. (6:22)
4. One like the Son of man came with the clouds of heaven and came to the Ancient of days. (7:13-14)
5. The coming of Gabriel. (9:20-27)
6. The appearance of a heavenly messenger. (10:5-7)
7. Heavenly beings strengthen Daniel. (10:10-21)

God Controls the Fate of Individuals:

1. Now God had brought Daniel into favour and tender love with the prince of the eunuchs. (1:9)
2. God gave them knowledge and skill in all learning and wisdom: and Daniel had understanding in all visions and dreams. (1:17)

DANIEL

3. Thou, O King, art a king of kings: for the God of heaven hath given thee a kingdom, power, and strength, and glory. (2:37)
4. This decree is to the intent that the living may know that the most High ruleth in the kingdom of men, and giveth it to whomsoever he will. (4:17)
5. The most High ruleth in the kingdom of men and giveth it to whomsoever he will. (4:25, 32)

God Governs The Fate of Nations:

1. The Lord gave Jehoiakim king of Judah into the hand of Nebuchadnezzar. (1:1-2)
2. God removeth kings, and setteth up kings. (2:21)

Men May Change the Outcome of Prophecy By Repentance:

1. Break off thy sins by righteousness, and thine iniquities by showing mercy to the poor; if it may be a lengthening of thy tranquility. (4:27; see context)

Prophets and Revelation:

1. Daniel and his companions desired the mercies of God in revealing the king's secret. Then was the secret revealed unto Daniel in a night vision. (2:18-19)
2. God gives wisdom unto the wise and knowledge unto them that know understanding. He revealeth the deep and secret things. (2:20-22)
3. There is a God in heaven that revealeth secrets. (2:28)
4. He that revealeth secrets maketh known to thee what shall come to pass. (2:29)
5. The dream is certain, and the interpretation thereof sure. (2:45)
6. An excellent spirit, and knowledge, and understanding, interpreting of dreams, and showing of hard sentences, and dissolving of doubts were found in Daniel. (5:12)
7. Light and understanding and excellent wisdom were found in Daniel. (5:14)
8. The Lord set before us his laws by his servants the prophets. (9:10)

The Last Days:

Outlined in the text above.

Counsel for Righteous Living:
1. He purposed in his heart that he would not defile himself. (1:8)
2. They desired the mercies of the God of heaven concerning this secret. (2:18)
3. Break off thy sins by righteousness, and thine iniquities by showing mercy to the poor, if it may be a lengthening of thy tranquility. (4:27)
4. He kneeled upon his knees three times a day, and prayed, and gave thanks before his God. (6:10)
5. Thy God whom thou servest continually, he will deliver thee. (6:16)
6. We make prayer before the Lord our God, that we might turn from our iniquities, and understand thy truth. (9:13)
7. We do not present our supplications before thee for our righteousness, but for thy great mercies. (9:18)
8. From the first day that thou didst set thine heart to understand, and to chasten thyself before thy God, thy words were heard. (10:12)

Author and Date of Authorship:

Daniel claims to be the author of the book. (see 7:1, 12:4) This is the traditional view. However, his very existence is denied by some Bible critics today, who assert that the book was written about 165 B. C. by some "pious Jew" to strengthen the people during the persecutions of Antiochus Epiphanes.

The evidence for the historicity of Daniel is far stronger than for many of the other Old Testament Prophets:
1. He is called a prophet by the Savior. (Mt. 24:15)
2. He is regarded as a righteous man by Ezekiel. (Ezek. 14:14, 20[3])
3. References in the D & C refer to him as a prophet and allude to his teachings. (D & C 116; 65:2)

The book is not classified among the "prophets" but among the "writings" in the Hebrew Old Testament. The Greek Septuagint placed the book between the major and minor prophets and thus established its present position in the Bible.

Style of the Book:
1. The book is written in two languages, Hebrew and Ara-

---

[3]Some critics regard this as an allusion to the Daniel mentioned in the Ras Shamya tablets rather than to the Biblical Daniel.

maic. The Aramaic section is in the middle, from 2:4b to 7:28.[4] It is considered to be better written than the Hebrew portion.
2. His writing does not show the polish and ornate quality of some of the other Old Testament prophets. He is writing an account of his visions and history rather than a literary work.
3. The chapters tend to be disconnected, but individual episodes are explained in detail.
4. His prophecies are more detailed and comprehensive than those of the other prophets.
5. Daniel is more definite in his prophecies than most other prophets.
6. He does not only foretell history, but also interprets it and sets it forth as a religious philosophy.

Bible Criticism: Bible critics have attempted to prove three theories in connection with Daniel.
1. Daniel was a fictitious person and the book is not history but fiction.
2. The book was not written by Daniel but by an anonymous author during the reign of Antiochus IV Epiphanes.
3. The book was not written by one author but by two.

The various critics have assumed a variety of positions in connection with these theories.

Most of the criticism has centered in attempts to prove a late authorship. The evidence includes:
1. The prophetic element is discounted. The assumption is made that the book was written as a history, after the events took place, rather than a prophecy before the events happened.
2. The book uses many Persian words, which supposedly indicates a date of authorship long after the Persian influence had become prevalent.
3. The book contains at least three Greek words, which supposedly indicates the book was written after the conquests of Alexander the Great.
4. The Aramaic of Daniel is a western Aramaic dialect of the type spoken in and about Palestine.
5. The Hebrew seems to be of the style followed after the time of Nehemiah.

---

[4] Aramaic passages also appear in Ezra 4:8-6:18; 7:12-26; Jer. 19:11 and Gen. 31:47.

6. The theology of the book supposedly comes from a period later than the exile.

Much of the criticism of the book is based on the work of Porphyry, a Neo-Platonic philosopher of the late third century, who attempted to use the book of Daniel in his fight against Christianity.

Changes Made in the Inspired Version of the Bible:

King James Translation	Inspired Version
5:28—PERES; . . .	5:28—UPHARSIN; . . .
6:5—. . . the law of his God.	6:5—. . . the law of God.
10:11—And he said unto me, . . .	10:11—And said unto me, . . .

Summary: After studying the book of Daniel the student should know:

1. Daniel and Ezekiel were contemporary prophets who preached in Babylonia during the Jewish captivity.
2. Several historical events from the book are important for their moral:
    A. Daniel's refusal to break the health laws.
    B. The deliverance of Shadrach, Meshach, and Abednego from the fiery furnace.
    C. Daniel's delivery from the lions' den.
3. Daniel's Visions and Interpretations Have Important Messages:
    A. Nebuchadnezzar's dream of the image and the stone cut out without hands.
    Meaning: The kingdom of God was not established for the last time in Christ's day, but was to come forth in the last days.
    B. The four beasts and the coming of the Ancient of days.
    Meaning: Three future events.
        (1). Persecution against the Saints.
        (2). The Council at Adam-ondi-Ahman.
        (3). The destruction of the kingdoms of Europe and the loss of dominion of the nations of Asia minor.
    C. The ram and the he-goat.

DANIEL 527

    Meaning:
        (1). The future of Persia and Greece.
        (2). The persecution of the Jews during the Maccabean period.
        (3). A possible reference to the Battle of Armageddon.
    D. The seventy weeks.
    Meaning:
        (1). The rebuilding of Jerusalem.
        (2). The time of the Savior's ministry.
        (3). The destruction of Jerusalem by the Romans.
    E. The vision of the future.
    Meaning:
        (1). Details of the Seleucids and Ptolemies until the time of Antiochus IV Epiphanes.
        (2). A great time of trouble at the time of the Council at Adam-ondi-Ahman.
        (3). The resurrection.
4. Prophetic time is usually interpreted as follows, although the correctness of the interpretation is unsure.
    A. A time = one year.
    B. Times = two years.
    C. Half a time = one-half year.
    D. A Season = one-half year.
    E. The day-year theory = one day of prophetic time equals one year.
5. The student should review and thoroughly understand the history of Persia, Greece, and the Maccabees to be able to grasp the message of Daniel.
6. The student should have a general understanding of the major prophecies of Daniel and the variety of interpretations which have been placed on them.
7. The words of Daniel are "closed up and sealed till the time of the end." Until God sees fit to reveal more about them some of his writing cannot be interpreted with certainty.

CHAPTER XXI

EZEKIEL

Prophet's Name: Ezekiel (ē-zēk'-iĕl) means "God Will Strengthen."

Scriptural Information About the Prophet:
1. He was the son of Buzi. (Bū'-zī) (1:3)
2. He is spoken of as "the priest." (1:3)
3. He was among the group carried to Babylon in c. 598 B. C. with king Jehoiachin. His being taken in this deportation implies that he was of the upper class among the people of Judah. (see 2 Ki. 24:10-14)
4. He was placed among the captives of Judah along the river Chebar (Chē'-bär). (1:1) This river was actually a large canal and passed through Nippur and connected the Tigris and Euphrates rivers.
5. He was married, and had a home which the elders of Judah visited. (3:24; 8:1)
6. His wife died during the Babylonian captivity. (24:16-18)
7. If the assumption that 1:1 is a reference to his age is correct, Ezekiel was about 25 or 26 years old when he was taken to Babylonia.

Date of Ezekiel's Mission: (c. 593-571 B. C.)

Ezekiel gives the date of his call as the "thirtieth year, in the fourth month, in the fifth day of the month . . ." It is uncertain, however, just what event marked the beginning of the period from which he reckoned. It is generally assumed that this was a reference to his age, for the age of thirty was when men usually began their service to the Lord (see Nu. 4:3). It is known that Ezekiel's thirtieth year was the fifth year of king Jehoiachin's (and Ezekiel's) captivity. (1:2) He carefully dated his visions and they can be listed as follows:

EZEKIEL   529

| Year | Month | Day | Month as in modern calendar | Year of modern reckoning | Reference |

Chapters 1-23—Before the Siege of Jerusalem

1. 5th	4th	5th	July	c. 593 B. C.	1:2
2. 6th	6th	5th	September	c. 592 B. C.	8:1
3. 7th	5th	10th	August	c. 591 B. C.	20:1

Chapters 24-25; 29:1-16—During the Siege of Jerusalem

4. 9th	10th	10th	January	c. 588 B. C.	24:1
5. 10th	10th	12th	January	c. 587 B. C.	29:1

Chapters 26-28; 29:17-21; 30-48—After the Fall of Jerusalem
(Jerusalem fell the 11th year, 4th month, 9th day)

6. 11th	(?)	1st	(?)	c. 587 B. C.	26:1
7. 11th	1st	7th	April	c. 587 B. C.	30:20
8. 12th	10th	5th	January	c. 585 B. C.	33:21
9. 12th	12th	1st	March	c. 585 B. C.	32:1
10. 12th	(?)	15th	(?)	c. 585 B. C.	32:17
11. 25th	1st(?)	10th	April(?)	c. 573 B. C.	40:1
12. 27th	1st	1st	April	c. 571 B. C.	29:17

Prophesied To: The Jews in captivity in Babylonia.

Contemporary Prophets:

| Jeremiah | (c. 626-586 B. C.) | To Judah, from Judah. |
| Daniel | (c. 606-536 B. C.) | To Babylon and Persia, from Babylon. |

Contemporary Prophets Contrasted:

Ezekiel lived the life of a captive and labored among the Jewish exiles and slaves in Babylonia. Like Jeremiah, he was commanded to perform symbolic actions. Like Jeremiah, he struck out at the sins of Judah and gave the reason for God's rejection of his chosen people. Though of an upper class heritage before going into captivity, he was forced to live a life of poverty and despair. He ministered to the common people while Daniel ministered to the royalty.

Jeremiah had no political connections and was not influential in the affairs of the royal court during king Josiah's time. The recorded ministry of Jeremiah extended over fifty years and during the reign of five kings of Judah. Jeremiah was of an introspective and emotional temperament.

Daniel was younger than Ezekiel and came to Babylon eight years earlier. He rose to prestige and power in the Babylonian court and lived in comfort there. Much of Daniel's ministry involved the receiving and interpreting of difficult dreams and visions. His ministry was primarily concerned with the affairs of state and the rise and fall of empires.

Contemporary Kings—Babylonia:

Nebuchadnezzar (c. 604-562 B. C.)

1. Took Jehoiachin and the Jews to Babylon. **First Deportation**—(c. 598 B. C.)
2. Took Zedekiah and more Jews to Babylon. **Second Deportation**—(c. 586 B. C.)
3. Destroyed Jerusalem. (c. 586 B. C.)

National Conditions:

The exiles had begun an extended period of slavery and servitude, during which they gradually improved their status and living conditions.

Most of Ezekiel's prophecy, however, is concerned with the conditions in Judah between the first major deportation of the Jews and the fall of Jerusalem.

(Review the discussion of National Conditions in the chapter on Jeremiah, pp. 439-440.)

Outline of the Book:

The book of Ezekiel divides into four parts:
Section I—Ezekiel's Call to the Ministry and Introductory Visions. (Chapters 1-3)
Section II—Prophecies Against Judah and Jerusalem. (Chapters 4-24)
Section III—Prophecies Against Surrounding Nations. (Chapters 25-32)
Section IV—Prophecies Concerning the Last Days. (Chapters 33-48)

SECTION I

EZEKIEL'S CALL TO THE MINISTRY AND INTRODUCTORY VISIONS:

Chapter 1—Ezekiel's Vision of the Four Creatures, the Four Wheels, And the Lord.

1. Description of the four creatures:
    - A. They came out of an amber-colored fire. (4)
    - B. They had the likeness of a man. (5)
    - C. Each creature had four faces and four wings. (6)
    - D. Their feet were straight, with soles like a calf's foot and sparkled like burnished brass. (7)
    - E. They had the hands of a man under their wings on their four sides. (8)
    - F. Their wings were joined one to another. They did not turn, but went straight forward. Two wings of each one were joined together, and two wings covered their bodies. Their wings were stretched upward. (9, 11-12, 23)
    - G. The four beings had the faces of a man, a lion, an ox, and an eagle. (10)
    - H. Light, fire, and lightning came out of them. (13)
    - I. They ran and returned like flashes of lightning. (14)
    - J. The likeness of the firmament upon the heads of the living creature was as the color of the terrible crystal. (22)
    - K. The noise of their wings was as the noise of great waters and the voice of the Almighty.
    - Note: These four creatures resemble the four beasts of Rev. 4:6-8. Of those beasts the D & C gives this information:

    Q. What are we to understand by the four beasts, spoken of in the same verse?

    A. They are figurative expressions, used by the Revelator, John, in describing heaven, the paradise of God, the happiness of man, and of beasts, and of creeping things, and of the fowls of the air; that which is spiritual being in the likeness of that which is temporal; and that which is temporal in the likeness of that which is spiritual; the spirit of man in the likeness of his person, as also the spirit of the beast, and every other creature which God has created.

Q. Are the four beasts limited to individual beasts, or do they represent classes or orders?

A. They are limited to four individual beasts, which were shown to John, to represent the glory of the classes of beings in their destined order or sphere of creation, in the enjoyment of their eternal felicity.

Q. What are we to understand by the eyes and wings, which the beasts had?

A. Their eyes are a representation of light and knowledge, that is, they are full of knowledge; and their wings are a representation of power, to move, to act, etc. (D & C 77:2-4)

These four creatures are again described in chapter 10, in which they are referred to as cherubims.

2. Description of the Four Wheels:
    A. They were the color of a beryl. (16)
    B. They had one likeness, or looked the same. (16)
    C. They had a wheel in the middle of a wheel. (16)
    D. In moving they went upon their four sides, without turning. (17)
    E. They had rings which were so high they were dreadful. The rings were full of eyes. (18)
    F. The wheels moved in conjunction with the four creatures. (19)
    G. The spirit of the living creature was in the wheels. (20-21)

3. Description of the Lord and His throne:
    A. The throne had the appearance of a sapphire stone. (26)
    B. God was the likeness as the appearance of a man. (26)
    C. He was surrounded in fire of an amber-hue. (27)
    D. His brightness had the appearance of a rainbow. (28)

Chapter 2—Ezekiel's Call: To Be a Prophet To A Rebellious Nation.

1. Ezekiel stood on his feet and the spirit entered him. (1-2)

EZEKIEL

2. Ezekiel is called to be a prophet to a rebellious nation. (3-5)
3. Be not afraid of them. (6-8)
4. A book was sent to him on which was written lamentations, and mourning, and woe. (9-10)

Chapter 3—**Ezekiel's Preparation and Instruction for His Prophetic Mission.**

1. Eat the roll and speak unto the house of Israel. (1-3)
2. The house of Israel will not hearken unto thee, for they will not hearken unto me. (4-7)
3. The Lord has made Ezekiel strong against them. (8-9)
4. All my words that I shall speak unto thee receive in thine heart. (10-11)
5. The spirit took him away. He returned to his people. (12-15)
6. A week later he again received the word of the Lord. A prophet is responsible for his people. If he does not warn them, their blood is required at his hand. (16-21)
7. Ezekiel saw the Lord and His glory upon the plain. (22-23)
8. Ezekiel was not to speak his own words of reproof, but was to speak the word of the Lord. (24-27)

SECTION II

PROPHECIES AGAINST JUDAH AND JERUSALEM

Chapter 4—Three Symbolic Acts. The Fate of Jerusalem.
1. **First Symbolic Act:** The siege of Jerusalem.
    Note: This is the first of four symbolic acts performed by Ezekiel which are found in chapters four and five.
    A. Ezekiel drew a picture of Jerusalem on a tile, laid siege against it and set an iron upon it to represent a wall of iron between him and that city. (1-3)
2. **Second Symbolic Act:** A representation of the length of the iniquity of Israel and Judah.
    A. Ezekiel lay on his left side for 390 days to represent 390 years of Israel's iniquity. (4-5)
    B. Ezekiel lay on his right side for 40 days to represent 40 years of Judah's iniquity. (6-8)
3. **Third Symbolic Act:** The famine in Jerusalem.
    A. Ezekiel eats short food and drink rations to represent the famine which will take place in Jerusalem. (9-17)

Chapter 5—Fourth Symbolic Act: Thirds of Jerusalem to Die by Fire and Famine, The Sword, and a Third Shall Be Scattered.
1. **Fourth Symbolic Act:** The Destruction of Jerusalem.
    A. Ezekiel cut his hair. He burned a third of it, stabbed another third with a knife, and scattered the remaining third in the wind. (1-4)
    B. Explanation: This is what will happen to the people of Jerusalem. (5-17)

Chapter 6—Judah Will Be Destroyed by Famine, Sword, and Pestilence.
1. The people of Judah will be destroyed on all the mountains and valleys. (1-7)
2. A remnant will escape and go into captivity. They shall know that I am the Lord. (8-10)
3. The house of Israel shall fall by famine, sword and pestilence. (11-14)

EZEKIEL 535

Chapter 7—The Lord Will Shortly Pour Out His Fury upon Judah.
1. An evil end has come upon the four corners of the land. (1-6)
2. The Lord will shortly pour out his fury and recompense them for all their abominations. (7-15)
3. Those that escape will be covered with horror and shame. (16-19)
4. Robbers shall pollute the Lord's secret place. (20-22)
5. The worst of the heathen shall possess their houses. The law shall perish from the priests, and counsel from the ancients. (23-27)

Chapter 8—A Vision of The Sinfulness of Judah.
1. A heavenly being transported Ezekiel to the Jerusalem temple in a vision. (1-3)
   Note: This vision comprises chapters eight through eleven.
2. Ezekiel saw the Lord and his glory. (4)
3. The Lord showed Ezekiel the idolatry and abominations of the house of Israel. (5-16)
4. The Lord said that because of their abominations, he will also deal in fury. (17-18)

Chapter 9—A Vision of Heavenly Beings Destroying Jerusalem.
1. A heavenly being marked the righteous people of Jerusalem. Then other heavenly beings destroyed the remainder of the people, beginning at the sanctuary. (1-8)
2. The Lord said he hath forsaken the earth and will not have pity, but recompense their way upon their head. (8-11)

Chapter 10—A Vision of the Cherubim.
1. Ezekiel again saw the cherubim (see chapter one). (1-5, 8-22)
2. The Lord commanded a heavenly being to take fire from between the cherubims. (6-7)

Chapter 11—Israel's Princes Will Be Judged in the Borders of Israel.
1. The spirit carried Ezekiel to the east gate of the temple, where he was shown twenty-five of the princes of Jerusalem. He was told that it was they who gave wicked counsel to the people. (1-4)

2. Ezekiel's prophecy to them: They will be delivered into the hands of strangers and will be judged in the border of Israel. (5-12)
3. Ezekiel inquired if the Lord would make a full end of Israel. (13-14)
4. (30-31) The Lord will gather the people and assemble them out of the countries where they have been scattered, and give them the land of Israel. (17-20)
   A. They shall take away the detestable and abominable things.
   B. The Lord will put a new heart and spirit within them, and they shall keep his statutes and ordinances.
5. The glory of the Lord went up from the city and stood upon the mountain on the east side. (22-23)
6. The spirit returned Ezekiel to Chaldea (Babylonia). (24-25)

Chapter 12—Two Symbolic Acts: Captivity and Famine.

1. **Fifth Symbolic Act:** Removing Goods for the Captivity.

   Note: For Ezekiel's previous symbolic acts see chapters four and five.

   A. Ezekiel was commanded to dig through the side of his house and remove his goods in the sight of his neighbors with his eyes covered. (1-7)
   B. His action symbolized Zedekiah's removal from Judah after he was blinded. (8-13) (see Jer. 52:7-11)
2. The Lord will scatter most of Judah. He will only leave a few from the famine, sword and pestilence to declare their abominations among the heathen. (14-16)
3. **Sixth Symbolic Act:** They shall eat with Care and Astonishment.
   A. Ezekiel was to eat bread with quaking and to drink water with trembling and astonishment, and then tell the people that is how the inhabitants of Jerusalem shall eat. (17-20)
4. The words of the Lord shall come to pass, and shall no longer be prolonged. (21-28)

Chapter 13—False Prophets Will Be Punished For Prophesying Peace.

1. False prophets and prophetesses have led Israel astray by prophesying lies of peace. The Lord's hand is against them. (1-23)

EZEKIEL 537

Chapter 14—The People are So Wicked Even Noah, Daniel, and Job could not Save Them.

1. Certain men who had turned to idolatry came to Ezekiel for counsel. The Lord refused to let them inquire of Him. (1-5)
2. Such men must repent or the Lord will cut them off from the midst of His people. (6-8)
3. If the prophets attempt to aid these wicked people they shall also share in their punishment. (9-11)
4. The people are so wicked that even Noah, Daniel and Job would only be able to save themselves and no one else. (12-21)
5. A remnant will be left which will go into captivity. When Ezekiel sees them he will know that the Lord has not done without cause all that He has done. (22-23)

Chapter 15—Allegory of the Vine Tree: Jerusalem Will Be Burned.

1. Jerusalem has become like a vine tree that is useless for work. It is fit only for fuel so it will be burned. (1-8)

Chapter 16—Allegory of the Unfaithful Wife: Jerusalem Has Betrayed the Lord.

1. The Lord saved Israel when she was born. He raised her and cared for her. When she came of age He covenanted with her and she became His. (1-8)
2. The Lord gave her beautiful things, and she was known for her beauty. (9-14)
3. Now Jerusalem has played the harlot with every one that passed by. She worshipped idols and sacrificed her children to them. She has committed harlotry with Egypt, Assyria, and the Chaldeans. She has given gifts to hire lovers. (15-34)
4. Her lovers will discover her nakedness. They will burn her houses with fire and execute judgments. (35-41)
5. Jerusalem has been as her sisters: Samaria and Sodom, yet she is more wicked than they were. (42-52)
6. (30-31) When Sodom and Samaria shall return to their former estate, then Jerusalem will return to its former estate. (53-55)
7. Just as Jerusalem looked down on Sodom in the days when she was righteous, Jerusalem shall also be despised. (56-59)

8. (30-31) The Lord will remember His covenant with Jerusalem when she receives her sisters (Samaria and Sodom). Then Jerusalem shalt know that He is the Lord. (60-63)

Chapter 17—Allegory of the Two Eagles And The Cedar Tree.

1. A great eagle came unto Lebanon, and took the highest branch of the cedar, and carried it into a land of traffick. (1-4)

   Note: This passage is generally understood by Bible scholars in this manner:
   A. The eagle = Nebuchadnezzar, king of Babylonia.
   B. The highest branch = Jehoiachin, king of Judah.
   C. The land of traffick = Babylonia.

   Ezekiel's explanation: (12)

   Summary: These verses have reference to the first major deportation of the Jews to Babylonia. They, along with king Jehoiachin, went into captivity c. 598 B. C.

2. A spreading vine of low stature bent her roots toward another eagle that he might water and strengthen her. (5-8)

   Note:
   A. The spreading vine of low stature = Zedekiah, king of Judah.
   B. The other eagle = Egypt.

   Ezekiel's explanation: (13-15)

   Summary: Zedekiah broke his covenant with Babylonia and sought for aid from Egypt.

3. The Vine shall not prosper. It shall wither. (9-10)
   Ezekiel's explanation: (16-21)

   Summary: Egypt will not come and fight for Judah. Zedekiah will be captured and taken to Babylon. His followers will fall by the sword and be scattered.

4. A tender one will be cropped off of the young twigs of the cedar. The Lord will plant it upon an high mountain and it shall bring forth boughs, and bear fruit, and be a goodly cedar. (22-24)

   Note: In this passage L. D. S. interpretation differs from that of other Bible scholars. The tender one is regarded as a reference to Mulek, a son of king Zedekiah, who came to the Americas and prospered here.

EZEKIEL 539

> The Book of Mormon gives account of him in Omni 15-17; Mos. 25:2; Hel. 6:10 and 8:21.[1]

Chapter 18—**The Doctrine of Repentance and Punishment.**

> Note: Ezekiel also sets forth these principles of repentance and punishment in 3:18-21 and 33:8-20.

1. A man will die for his own sins, and not for his father's. (1-4)
2. An illustration: a comparison of three generations:
     A. A man lives righteously—he shall surely live. (5-9)
     B. His son is wicked—he shall surely die. (10-13)
     C. His son turns away from his father's wickedness and lives righteously—he shall surely live. (14-20)
3. If the wicked will turn from all his sins and do what is right, he shall surely live, and his sins shall not be mentioned. (21-23)
4. If the righteous will turn from his righteousness and commit iniquity, he shall die, and his righteousness shall not be mentioned. (24)
5. God's ways are equal. It is man's ways that are unequal. (25-29)
6. Repent, and turn from all your transgressions; so iniquity shall not be your ruin. The Lord hath no pleasure in the death of the wicked. (30-32)

Chapter 19—**Allegories of the Lioness and Her Whelps and the Vine and Its Branch: Laments for the Mother of Zedekiah.**

1. A lioness had whelps which grew into young lions. One was captured and taken into Egypt. Another was captured and was taken into Babylon. (1-9)

   Note:
     A. The lioness = Hatmutal, the mother of Kings Jehoahaz and Zedekiah (2 Ki. 23:31; 24:18)
     B. The whelp taken to Egypt = King Jehoahaz (Shallum) who was taken into Egypt by Pharaoh Necho in c. 609 B. C. (2 Ki. 23:30-34)
     C. The whelp taken to Babylonia = King Zedekiah, who was taken captive to Babylonia. c. 587 B. C. (2 Ki. 25:1-7)

---

[1]This interpretation was set forth and explained by Orson Pratt. See *Orson Pratt's Works*, 1899 ed. pp. 209-210.

Two kings with different mothers reigned between Jehoahaz and Zedekiah.
2. A vine was fruitful and had strong rods. She was plucked up in fury and cast down. Her strong rods were broken and withered. (10-14)
Note: The vine is again Hatmutal, and the rods her sons.

Chapter 20—Israel's Iniquity and Promised Redemption.

1. Certain elders came to inquire of Ezekiel but the Lord refused to hear their inquiry, and said they should be shown the iniquity of their fathers. (1-4)
2. A history of Israel, its iniquity and idolatry is given. (5-30)
3. (30)[2] The Lord will gather His people out of the countries where they are scattered with a mighty hand and with fury poured out. (33-44)
    A. (30) He will plead with them face to face in the wilderness.
    B. (38) He will bring them into the bond of the covenant.
    C. (30) He will purge out the rebels from among them. He will bring them out of the country where they sojourn, and they shall not enter into the land of Israel.
    D. (38) In His holy mountain shall all of them in the land serve the Lord, and He will accept them.
    E. (35) The Lord will be sanctified in them before the heathen.
    F. (30) Ye shall know He is the Lord when He brings you into the land of Israel.
    G. (38) Ye shall remember your doings wherein ye have been defiled, and ye shall loathe yourselves.
4. (35?) Fire will devour every green tree in the south forest, and all faces from the south to the north shall be burned therein. And all flesh shall see that I the Lord have kindled it: it shall not be quenched. (45-48)

Chapter 21—The Sword of the Lord Will Smite Judah and Ammon.

1. The Lord will draw His sword against all flesh from the north to the south. It shall be upon all the princes of Israel. (1-17)

---

[2]Numbers in parentheses at the beginning of items refer to the fifty events of the last days listed in Chapter Four.

Ezekiel

2. The king of Babylon will use divination to decide whether he should attack Jerusalem or Rab-bath, capital of the Ammonites. The decision will be made to attack Jerusalem. Though the Jews will regard the divination as false, they will be taken. (18-24)
3. The profane, wicked prince of Israel (Zedekiah) will be abased. (25-26)
4. (32?) The Lord will overturn Israel and it shall be no more, until he come whose right it is; the Lord will give it to him. (27)
5. The Lord's judgment will also come upon the Ammonites. (28-32)

Chapter 22—**The Sins of Jerusalem.**
1. Ezekiel was to judge the city of Jerusalem and show her all her abominations. (1-2)
2. Numerous sins of Jerusalem are listed, including idolatry, oppressing the poor, murder, Sabbath desecration, adultery, incest, usury, extortion, etc. For these sins she will be judged and punished. (3-31)

Chapter 23—**Aholah and Aholibah: An Allegory of the Wickedness of Samaria and Jerusalem.**
1. There were two sisters who committed whoredom in Egypt. Aholah (ă-hō′-lăh) is Samaria Aholibah (ă-hōl′i-băh) is Jerusalem. (1-4)
2. Aholah doted on her lovers from Assyria and Egypt, so the Lord delivered her into the hands of her lovers, the Assyrians, who slew her. (5-10)
3. Aholibah was more corrupt than her sister. She doted upon the Assyrians, but when she saw the Babylonians she sent to them and they also defiled her. Yet she multiplied her wickedness by renewing her affair with Egypt. (11-21)
4. The Lord will raise up Aholibah's lovers against her. The Babylonians and their allies will judge her and deal furiously with her. (22-35)
5. The sins of Aholah and Aholibah are listed. They will be removed and spoiled because of them. (36-49)

Chapter 24—**Allegory of the Boiling Caldron and the Death of Ezekiel's Wife.**
1. The siege of Jerusalem began this same day. (1-2)

2. Utter a parable unto the rebellious house: (3-14)
    A. Set on a pot and pour water into it.
    B. Fill it with choice bones and seethe them therein.
    C. The Lord will make the pile for fire great.
    D. The Lord will let the bones be burned to destroy the scum.
    Note:
    (1). The pot = Jerusalem.
    (2). The bones = The inhabitants of Jerusalem.
    (3). The fire = The purging of the people.
    (4). The scum = wickedness.
    The people of Jerusalem will have to suffer greatly to purge their wickedness from among them.
3. The Lord suddenly took Ezekiel's wife, but the prophet was forbidden to weep and mourn for her. (15-18)
4. The people will also have to pine without visible mourning as Ezekiel has done when their families are destroyed by the sword. (19-27)

SECTION III

PROPHECIES AGAINST SURROUNDING NATIONS

Chapter 25—**The Fall of Ammon, Moab, Edom, and the Philistines Foretold.**

1. Because Ammon said Aha when Israel and Judah went into captivity, the Lord will deliver her into the possession of the men of the east. (1-7)
2. Because Moab said the house of Judah is like unto all the heathen, the Lord will deliver her into the possession of the men of the east with the Ammonites. (8-11)
3. Because Edom took vengeance on the house of Judah, the Lord will make Edom desolate. (12-14)
4. Because the Philistines have dealt by revenge the Lord will take vengeance upon them and destroy the remnant of the sea coast. (15-17)

Chapter 26—**Nebuchadnezzar to Destroy Tyre.**

Note: Chapters 26, 27, and 28 were given the year Jerusalem fell.

1. Tyre will be destroyed by the king of Babylon. Her walls and towers will be broken down. Her riches and merchandise will become a prey and a spoil. (1-21)
Note: The year after Jerusalem fell, Nebuchadnezzar began a thirteen year siege of Tyre which finally brought about its capitulation.

Chapter 27—**A Dirge Over Tyre.**

1. Tyre is depicted as a beautiful ship which is filled with fine treasures. She has done commerce with many countries but she will be destroyed and lamented. (1-36)

Chapter 28—**Tyre and Zidon Will Be Destroyed.**

1. The King of Tyre has claimed to be a God because of his riches and the beauty of his goods. Strangers will defile his brightness and he shall die. (1-19)
2. Zidon will also be destroyed by pestilence and the sword, and she will cease to be a pricking brier to the house of Israel. (20-24)

3. (30-31) When the Lord has gathered the house of Israel from the people among whom they are scattered they will dwell safely in their land. They will build houses and plant vineyards. (25-26)
4. (35) The Lord will be sanctified among His people in the sight of the heathen and will execute judgments upon all those that despise His people round about them. (25-26)
5. (38) His people shall know the Lord is their God. (26)

Chapter 29—Nebuchadnezzar Will Conquer Egypt.
1. Egypt is compared to a crocodile that will be thrown out on the land. It will be destroyed because it was a staff of reed to (it failed to support) the house of Israel. It will be desolate for forty years, then the people will return and it will be the basest of the kingdoms. They shall no more rule over the nations. (1-16)

   Note:
   A. This section was revealed six months before the fall of Jerusalem.
   B. When the Persians conquered Babylonia, they allowed all the conquered peoples to return to their lands.
2. Nebuchadnezzar will conquer Egypt. (17-21)

   Note: This section (29:13-30:19) was revealed sixteen years after the fall of Jerusalem. Tyre had been besieged for thirteen years, and the booty was disappointing in comparison to the time expended.

Chapter 30—Nebuchadnezzar Will Conquer Egypt.
1. Egypt and her allies, Ethiopia, Libya, Lydia, and Chub, shall fall by the sword before Nebuchadnezzar. (1-19)
2. The Lord has broken Pharaoh's arms and strengthened the arms of the king of Babylon. (20-26)

   Note: This section was given three months before the fall of Jerusalem. It probably refers to the prior defeat of Pharaoh's army at Carchemish. c. 605 B. C.

Chapter 31—The Egyptians Will Fall As Did Assyria.
1. The Egyptians are compared to the greatness of Assyria. Assyria was high and lofty, yet it was brought down and delivered unto death. (1-17)
2. Pharaoh and also his multitude will be brought down in like manner. (18)

EZEKIEL 545

Chapter 32—**Egypt Will Join the Fallen Nations In Hell.**
1. The sword of the king of Babylon shall come upon Egypt. The people will be destroyed and the land of Egypt will be laid desolate. The daughters of the nations shall lament her. (1-16)
2. Egypt shall be slain and shall go down into the pit. In hell she will bear her shame before Assyria, Elam, Meshech, Tubal, Edom, the princes of the north, and all the Zidonians, who will have preceded her to the grave. (17-32)

Note: These two revelations were given a year and eight months after the fall of Jerusalem.

SECTION IV

PROPHECIES CONCERNING THE LAST DAYS

Chapter 33—The Doctrine of Repentance and Punishment.
1. A watchman has the responsibility of warning the people. If he fails to warn them, the Lord will require his blood. Ezekiel is called as a watchman to warn the house of Israel. (1-8)
2. Turn ye from your wicked ways. (9-11)
3. The righteousness of the righteous shall not deliver him in the day of his transgression. As for the wickedness of the wicked, he shall not fall thereby in the day that he turneth from his wickedness. (12-20)

    Note: Ezekiel also sets forth these principles of repentance and punishment in 3:18-21 and 18:1-32.
4. Ezekiel receives the report that Jerusalem has fallen. (21)
5. The Lord will destroy those that have escaped from the siege. (22-29)
6. The people come to hear Ezekiel's words, but they will not do them. When judgment comes, then shall they know that a prophet hath been among them. (30-33)

Chapter 34—The Lord Will Gather His People, and David Shall Rule Over Them.
1. The shepherds of Israel have failed to care for their sheep. The Lord is against them, and will require His flock at their hand, and cause them to cease from feeding the flock. (1-10)
2. (30-31) The Lord will seek out His sheep, and will deliver them out of all places where they have been scattered, and bring them to their own land, and feed them upon the mountains of Israel. (11-15)
3. (35?) The Lord will judge His flock. He will judge between cattle and cattle. He will destroy the fat and the strong and feed them with judgment. (16-22)
4. (32) The Lord will set His servant, David, over them: (23-24)
    A. He shall feed them and be their shepherd.
    B. The Lord will be their God.
    C. His servant David will be a prince among them.

EZEKIEL 547

5. (41) The Lord will make them a covenant of peace. The shower will come down in its season and the earth shall yield her increase. (25-27)
6. (35) They shall be safe in their land when the Lord has broken the bands of their yoke, and delivered them out of the hand of those that served themselves of them. They shall no more be a prey to the heathen. (27-28)
7. (38) They shall no more be consumed with hunger. Thus shall they know that the Lord their God is with them. (29-31)

Chapter 35—**Edom Will Be Desolate.**
1. The Lord will make Edom desolate because she thought to occupy the conquered territories of Israel and Judah. (1-15)

Chapter 36—**Israel Will Be Multiplied and Will Rebuild the Waste Places.**
1. The Lord has spoken against the residue of the heathen who thought to occupy the conquered territories of the house of Israel. (1-7)
2. (30-31) The Lord will multiply man upon the mountains of Israel. The cities shall be inhabited and the waste places shall be builded. (8-12)
3. (35) The mountains shalt devour men no more, neither will the Lord cause men to hear in thee the shame of the heathen any more. (13-15)
4. When the house of Israel dwelt in their own land they defiled it. When they were scattered among the heathen they profaned the Lord's holy name. (16-20)
5. (35) The Lord will sanctify His great name which was profaned among the heathen and the heathen shall know that I am the Lord, when He shall be sanctified in Israel before their eyes. (21-23)
6. (38) The Lord will give Israel a new spirit and a new heart, and He will be their God. (24-28)
7. (41) The Lord will multiply the food, and there will be no more famine. (29-31)
8. (41) In the day that I shall have cleansed you from all your iniquities, I will also cause you to dwell in the cities, and the wastes shall be builded and the desolate land shall be tilled. Then the heathen that are left round about you shall know that I the Lord build the ruined places. (32-36)

9. (38) The waste cities shall be filled with flocks of men: and they shall know that I am the Lord. (37-38)

Chapter 37—**The Dry Bones and The Two Sticks.**
1. (30-31) Ezekiel was shown a valley of dry bones. He saw them regain their flesh and life and become an exceeding great army. The Lord said the bones are the whole house of Israel. They will know that He is the Lord when He causes them to come out of their graves and places them in their own land. (1-14)

    Note: It would appear that Ezekiel was not talking about the doctrine of resurrection of the body here, but of the restoration of the nation of Israel. Yet it is clear that Ezekiel understood the doctrine of the resurrection (see verses 12-14), a fact which many Bible critics challenge. Isaiah had spoken of the doctrine long before Ezekiel's time. (see Is. 26:19)

2. Ezekiel was commanded to take two sticks and write upon them, on one stick for Judah, and for the children of Israel his companions, and the other for Joseph, the stick of Ephraim, and for all the house of Israel his companions. They shall be joined one to another into one stick, and they shall become one in thine hand. (15-17)

    Note: Most Bible commentators see here only a prophecy of the reuniting of the nations of Israel and Judah. Latter-day Saints find a much deeper meaning. They recognize the sticks to be scrolls, or sticks wrapped with papyrus, and believe that Ezekiel's prophecy should be literally interpreted as a prophecy of actual books which will be joined together. The Bible is easily recognized as the stick of Judah, and the Book of Mormon is asserted to be the stick of Joseph (to which the Lord seemingly made reference as the "stick of Ephraim" in D & C 27:5). Missionaries have long asserted the similar mission of the two books as dual representatives for Christ.

    The author feels that certain elements of the prophecy have been overlooked by many Latter-day Saints, however, which greatly add to the meaning and interpretation of the passage. First of all, many individuals fail to read the full context of the prophecy (verses 15-28) and therefore fail to note that seven clues are provided as to the **time** when the prophecy is to be fulfilled. The books are to come together when

A. The children of Israel will be gathered from among the heathen and restored to the land of Palestine. (21)

B. The two kingdoms, Judah and Israel, will have combined and will have been established as one nation in that land. (22) This means that the Ten Tribes will have, in that period, already returned to Palestine.

C. They shall be ruled by a king. (22)

D. The Lord will have cleansed them from sin. (23)

E. Their king shall be named David. (24-25)

F. The Lord's sanctuary (temple?) will have been built in the land of Palestine. (26-27)

G. The Heathen nations will have been taught that God sanctifies and protects Israel. (28)

Because the careful description Ezekiel gives of the time when the two sticks will be joined clearly indicates that the event is yet future, the present joint role of the Bible and Book of Mormon should be regarded as only the beginning of the prophecy's fulfillment. One other aspect of the prophecy is worthy of note and should not be overlooked. Ezekiel describes the stick of Joseph as being of a dual nature: the record is to be "the stick of Ephraim" and it must also be "for all the house of Israel his companions." Then Ezekiel adds that the stick of Joseph is to be "in the hand of Ephraim, and the tribes of Israel his fellows." Ephraim, of course, was the leading tribe among the tribes which were carried away captive by Assyria and which are now known as the Ten Lost Tribes. Is the stick of Joseph, then, to be one record, or two, or several? The Book of Mormon neither fulfills nor claims to fulfill Ezekiel's stipulations that the stick of Joseph must speak for all the house of Israel who are the companions to Ephraim, nor that it has been in the hands of the tribes of Israel. It is a record of a few descendants of Manasseh (Lehi and his family were of Manasseh, see Alma 10:3) of Judah (the Mulekites were descendants of the Jewish king Zedekiah), and of Ephraim. (Erastus Snow quoted the prophet Joseph Smith as saying that "Ishmael was of the lineage of Ephraim" see **Journal of Discourses** XXIII, p. 184). Certainly the lineage for the Book of Mormon people would be counted through Lehi and his sons (not their wives), which makes the Book of Mormon primarily a record of the descendants of the tribe of Manasseh rather than of Ephraim. It would therefore seem that more than the Book of Mormon is needed to fulfill Ezekiel's prophecy completely. Other records of the Ten Tribes, records which are representative of all of them, are also needed. Perhaps Ezekiel's prophecy will see complete fulfillment when the Bible and Book of Mormon are joined by the records of the lost tribes of Israel, in fulfillment of a Book of Mormon prophecy:

> Wherefore, because that ye have a Bible ye need not suppose that it contains all my words; neither need ye suppose that I have not caused more to be written.
>
> For I command all men, both in the east and in the west, and in the north, and in the south, and in the islands of the sea, that they shall write the words which I speak unto them; for out of the books which shall be written I will judge the world, every man according to their works, according to that which is written.
>
> For behold, I shall speak unto the Jews and they shall write it; and I shall also speak unto the Nephites and they shall write it; and I shall also speak unto the other tribes of the house of Israel, which I have led away, and they shall write it; and I shall also speak unto all nations of the earth and they shall write it.
>
> **And it shall come to pass that the Jews shall have the words of the Nephites, and the Nephites shall have the words of the Jews; and the Nephites and the Jews shall have the words of the lost tribes of Israel; and the lost tribes of Israel shall have the words of the Nephites and Jews.**
>
> **And it shall come to pass that my people, which are of the house of Israel, shall be gathered home unto the lands of their possessions; and my word also shall be gathered in one.** And I will show unto them that fight against my word and against my people, who are of the house of Israel, that I am

EZEKIEL 551

       God, and that I covenanted with Abraham that I would remember his seed forever. (2 Ne. 29:10-14)

3. (30-31) Ezekiel's explanation of the prophecy of the two sticks: The sticks will be **in thine hand before their eyes,** (therefore tangible objects.) (18-20)
4. (30-31) The children of Israel will be gathered from among the heathen to their own land. (21-22)
5. (30-31) The Lord will make them one nation, neither shall they be divided into two kingdoms any more at all. (22)
6. (32) One king shall be king to them all: David. (22-25)
7. (38) They shall be my people, and I will be their God. (23)
8. (33) The Lord will place His sanctuary and tabernacle in the midst of them for evermore. (26-27)
9. (40) The heathen shall know that the Lord sanctifies Israel. (28)

Chapter 38—**The Battle of Armageddon.**

1. (35) The general, Gog, is identifed:

    A. From the land of Magog. (2)
    B. The chief prince of Meshech and Tubal. (2, 3, 39:1)

Note: These are the ancient terminologies for the Biblical lands. Magog is located just north of the Caspian Sea in what is now Russia. The identifying feature which is repeated, however is that Gog will be the chief prince of Meshech and Tubal, which are both located in present-day Turkey. With the anticipated shifting and devastation of nations which is expected to precede the Battle of Armageddon, it is not safe to assert any nationality for him with finality at the present time.

2. (35) The Lord will turn back his (Gog's) army of horses and horsemen, bucklers, shields and swords. (3-4)
3. (35) Persia, Ethiopia, Libya, Gomer, Togarmah and many people will be with him. (5-6)
4. (35) Israel is to be prepared when it is brought forth out of the nations. (7-8)
5. (35) They shall come to take a spoil. (9-13)
6. (35) They will come on horseback from the north parts, a great company. (14-16)

552   PROPHETS AND PROPHECIES OF THE OLD TESTAMENT

7. (35) The Lord will bring them against His land that the heathen may know Him when He is sanctified in Gog before their eyes. (16)
8. (35) When Gog comes against Israel there will be a great shaking in that land, and the mountains and walls shall be thrown down. (17-20)
9. (35) The Lord will call for a sword against him throughout the mountains. (21)
10. (35) The Lord will rain pestilence, rain, hailstones, fire and brimstone upon them. Thus He will magnify and sanctify Himself before the heathens. (22-23)

Note: See D & C 29:16-21.

Chapter 39—The Battle of Armageddon.

1. (35) The Lord will turn Gog back and leave but a sixth part of his army. (1-2)
2. (35) Gog will come up from the north parts to the mountains of Israel. (2)
3. (35) Gog will fall with his bands upon the open field. (3-5)
4. (35) The Lord will send fire on the army of Magog so the heathen shall know that He is the Lord. (6-8)
5. (35) The people from the cities of Israel shall burn their weapons for seven years and shall spoil and rob those that robbed them. (9-10)
6. (35) The valley of the passengers on the east of the sea will be the burial place for Gog and his multitude. It will take seven months to bury them. (11-16)
7. (35) The fowls and beasts will devour the dead. (17-20)

Note: See D & C 29:18-20.

8. (38) The heathen will see the judgment the Lord has executed. The house of Israel shall know the Lord is their God from that day forward. (21-24)
9. (38) When the Lord has gathered His people out of their enemies' lands, and is sanctified in them in the sight of many nations, then shall they know that He is the Lord their God. (25-28)
10. (39) The Lord will not hide His face from them any more, for He has poured out His spirit upon the house of Israel. (29)

EZEKIEL 553

Chapter 40—The Temple in Jerusalem.
1. Ezekiel was carried in vision to the land of Israel to a very high mountain, where he saw a man measuring the temple to be built in the latter-days. (1-2)
2. (33) The dimensions and description of the latter-day temple are given. (3-49)

Chapter 41—The Temple in Jerusalem.
1. (33) The dimensions and description of the latter-day temple are given. (1-26)

Chapter 42—The Temple in Jerusalem.
1. The dimensions and description of the latter-day temple are given. (1-20)

Chapter 43—The Temple in Jerusalem.
1. Ezekiel saw the Lord come to His temple. (1-6)
2. The Lord will dwell in the midst of the children of Israel for ever. (7-9)
3. Ezekiel was told to write the information concerning the temple so that all Israel would know its form and its ordinances and laws. (10-12)
4. (33) More dimensions are given. (13-17)
5. (33) The ordinances for offering sacrifices are given. (18-27)

Chapter 44—The Ordinances for the Temple in Jerusalem.
1. (32) The east gate of the sanctuary will be reserved for the prince. (1-3)
2. (33) The rules and ordinances for the temple are given. (4-31)

Chapter 45—The Division of Land for the Temple and the Prince.
1. (33) The division of the land for the temple and priests is defined. (1-5)
2. (33) The division of the land for the city is defined. (6)
3. (33) The division of the land for the prince is defined. (7-8)
4. (33) The measuring system is defined. (9-13)
5. (32) The sacrifices to be offered by the prince are defined. (14-25)

   Note: These sacrifices correspond to the feast of the Passover and the Feast of Tabernacles.

Chapter 46—Regulations For The Prince.

1. (32) The prince shall worship at the threshold of the east gate of the inner court. (1-3)
2. (32) Regulations regarding the prince are given. (4-18)
3. Ezekiel was shown special areas that shall be for the priests. (19-24)

Chapter 47—Israel's Borders in the Last Days.

1. (33) Water will come out from the temple, and will flow into the Dead Sea, and fish will flourish there. (1-12)
2. (30-31) The borders of Israel in the last days are given. (13-23)

Chapter 48—The Areas of Inheritance for the Tribes of Israel.

1. The areas of inheritance for the tribes in the last days are given. (1-29)
2. The gates of the city of Jerusalem are described. (30-35)

Doctrinal Analysis:

Sins of the People:

—They Are Rebellious:

1. They are a rebellious nation that hath rebelled against me. (2:3)
2. They rebelled against me in the wilderness. (20:13, 16)

—They Are Hard-hearted:

1. They are impudent children, and stiffhearted. (2:4)

—They Will Not Hearken:

1. The house of Israel will not hearken unto thee; for they will not hearken unto me. (3:7)
2. They have eyes to see, but see not, they have ears to hear, and hear not: for they are a rebellious house. (12:2)

—They Deny the Lord:

1. They say, the Lord seeth us not; the Lord hath forsaken the earth. (8:12)
2. The city is full of perverseness, for they say, the Lord hath forsaken the earth, and the Lord seeth not. (9:9)
3. Thou hast forgotten me, saith the Lord God. (22:12)
4. Thou hast forgotten me, and cast me behind thy back. (23:35)

EZEKIEL   555

—They Are Irreverent:
1. They have defiled the sanctuary. (5:11)
2. Your fathers have blasphemed me. (20:27)
3. Her priests have violated my law and have profaned mine holy things. They have put no difference between the holy and profane, neither have they showed difference between the unclean and the clean, and have hid their eyes from my sabbaths, and I am profaned among them. (22:26)
4. They have defiled my sanctuary, and have profaned my sabbaths. (23:38)
5. Thou hast defiled thy sanctuaries. (28:18)
6. They defiled the land by their own way and by their doings. (36:17)
7. Ye have profaned my name in the midst of the heathen. (36:23)

—They Worship Idols and False Gods:
1. The people worshipped idols. (8:12-16)
2. Thou madest images of men and worshipped them. (16:17-19)
3. Thou hast accepted the gods of the Egyptians, the Assyrians, and the Chaldeans. (16:26-29)
4. With their idols they have committed adultery. (23:37)
5. Ye lift up your eyes toward your idols, and shed blood. (33:25)

—They Sacrifice Children:
1. Thou hast slain my children, and delivered them to pass through the fire. (16:20-21)
2. They have also caused their children, whom they bare unto me, to pass for them through the fire, to devour them. (23:37)

—They Have Changed the Statutes:
1. They have changed my judgments into wickedness. (5:6)
2. They have refused my judgments and my statutes, they have not walked in them. (5:6)
3. Ye have not walked in my statutes, neither executed my judgments, but have done after the manners of the heathen that are round about you. (11:12)
4. They walked not in my statutes, and they despised my judgments. (20:13, 16)

—The Prophets Prophesy Falsely:

1. The prophets prophesy out of their own hearts and follow their own spirit, and have seen nothing! (13:2-4)
2. False prophetesses lie to the people. (13:19)
3. With lies they have made the heart of the righteous sad. (13:22)
4. Her prophets have divined lies unto them, saying, Thus saith the Lord God, when the Lord hath not spoken. (22:28)

—They Give Wicked Counsel:

1. These are the men that devise mischief, and give wicked counsel in this city. (11:2)

—They Have Strengthened the Wicked:

1. They have strengthened the hands of the wicked, that he should not return from his wicked way. (13:22)

—They Speak Falsely:

1. She hath wearied herself with lies. (24:12)
2. With their mouth they show much love, but their heart goeth after their covetousness. (33:31)

—They Have Broken the Covenant:

1. Thou hast despised the oath in breaking the covenant. (16:59)

—They Break the Sabbath:

1. My sabbaths they greatly polluted. (20:13, 16)
2. They have defiled my sanctuary, and have profaned my sabbaths. (23:38)

—They Commit Murder:

1. The land is full of bloody crimes, and the city is full of violence. (7:23)
2. They have taken gifts to shed blood. (22:12)

—They Commit Adultery and Fornication:

1. Thou didst trust in thine own beauty, and playedst the harlot because of thy renown. (16:15)
2. One hath committed abomination with his neighbour's wife, another hath lewdly defiled his daughter-in-law, and another hath humbled his sister. (22:11)
3. They have committed adultery. (23:37)

EZEKIEL 557

4. With their idols they have committed adultery. (23:37)
5. Ye work abomination, and ye defile every one his neighbour's wife. (33:26)

—**They Oppress the Poor:**
1. Neither did she strengthen the hand of the poor and needy. (16:49)
2. Thou hast taken usury and increase. (22:12)
3. Thou hast greedily gained of thy neighbours by extortion. (22:12)
4. Her princes are like wolves ravening the prey, to shed blood, to get dishonest gain. (22:27)
5. The people of the land have used oppression, and exercised robbery, and have vexed the poor and needy: yea, they have oppressed the stranger wrongfully. (22:29)
6. The shepherds (leaders) feed themselves instead of their flocks. (34:2-4, 8)
7. With force and with cruelty have ye ruled them. (34:4)

—**There is Violence:**
1. The land is full of bloody crimes, and the city is full of violence. (7:23)
2. With force and with cruelty have ye ruled them. (34:4)

—**They Are Filled With Pride:**
1. Thou didst trust in thine own beauty, and playedst the harlot because of thy renown. (16:15)
2. Pride, fulness of bread, and abundance of idleness was in her. (16:49)
3. The king has said he is a God. His heart is lifted up. (28:2-6)
4. Thine heart was lifted up because of thy beauty; thou hast corrupted thy wisdom by reason of thy brightness. (28:17)

—**They Do Not Care for the Welfare of Others:**
1. My sheep (people) wandered through all the mountains, and none did search or seek after them. (34:6)

The Nature of God:
1. Like the noise of great waters, as the voice of the Almighty. (1:24)
2. A description of the Lord on His throne. (1:26-28)

3. I shall execute judgments in thee in anger and in fury and in furious rebukes. (5:15)
4. I will send mine anger upon thee, and will judge thee according to thy ways. (7:3)
5. Mine eye shall not spare thee, neither will I have pity. (7:4)

Visions and Appearance of God and Heavenly Beings:
1. The heavens were opened, and I saw visions of God. (1:1)
2. The vision of the four creatures and the four wheels. (1:4-25)
3. A vision of the Lord. (1:26-28)
4. The glory of the Lord stood there, as the glory which I saw by the river. Then the spirit entered into me . . . (3:23-24)
5. A being with the appearance of fire carried him in vision to Jerusalem. (8:1-3)
6. The Lord showed visions of the destruction of Jerusalem to Ezekiel. (8:4-11:24)

Judgment:
1. I will do unto them after their way, and according to their deserts will I judge them. (7:27)
2. I will recompense their ways upon their own heads. (11:21)
3. When ye see their ways and their doings, ye shall know that I have not done without cause all that I have done in it, saith the Lord God. (14:23)
4. Some people are so wicked the Lord will not allow them to inquire of Him. (20:1-3, 31)
5. Their own way have I recompensed upon their heads, saith the Lord God. (22:31)
6. According to thy ways, and according to thy doings, shall they judge thee, saith the Lord. (24:14)
7. They shall bear their iniquity, and they shall bear their shame, and their abominations which they have committed. (44:12-13)

The Lord Controls the Fate of Individuals:
1. Son of man, behold, I take away from thee the desire of thine eyes with a stroke. Forbear to cry, make no mourning for the dead. . . . and at evening my wife died. (24:16-18)

EZEKIEL   559

The Lord Controls the Fate of Nations:

1. The Lord gave Israel statutes and judgments which were good, and by which they should live, but Israel rejected them. Then he gave them also statutes that were not good, and judgments whereby they should not live; that He might make them desolate, to the end that they might know He is the Lord. (20:18-26)
2. I will give the land of Egypt unto Nebuchadnezzar king of Babylon. (29:19)
3. I will scatter the Egyptians among the nations, and I will strengthen the arms of the king of Babylon. (30:23-24)
4. I will bring Gog and Magog against my land, that the heathen may know me, when I shall be sanctified in thee, O Gog, before their eyes. (38:16)
5. I am against thee, O Gog, and I will turn thee back, and leave but the sixth part of thee. (39:1-2)

God's Dealings With His Prophets:

1. The word of the Lord came expressly unto Ezekiel the priest, and the hand of the Lord was there upon him. (1:3)
2. I do send thee unto them; and thou shalt say unto them, Thus saith the Lord God. (2:4)
3. They shall know that there hath been a prophet among them. (2:5)
4. Thou shalt speak my words unto them, whether they will hear, or whether they will forbear. Be not afraid of them. (2:6-7; 3:11)
5. When I say unto the wicked, Thou shalt surely die; and thou givest him not warning, the same wicked man shall die in his iniquity; but his blood will I require at thine hand. Yet if thou warn the wicked, and he turn not from his wickedness, he shall die in his iniquity, but thou hast delivered thy soul. (3:18-21)
6. The hand of the Lord was there upon me; and he said unto me, Arise, go forth into the plain, and I will there talk with thee. (3:22)
7. The Lord closed Ezekiel's mouth and prohibited him from reproving the house of Israel without inspiration, but told him, when I speak with thee, I will open thy mouth, and thou shalt say unto them, Thus saith the Lord God. (3:26-27)

8. When destruction cometh, then shall they seek a vision of the prophet. (7:25-26)
9. The land is so wicked that if Noah, Daniel, and Job were in it, they should deliver but their own souls by righteousness, saith the Lord. (14:14-20)

The Lord Fulfills His Revelations:
1. They shall know that I the Lord have spoken it in my zeal, when I have accomplished my fury in them. (5:13)
2. I am the Lord: I will speak, and the word that I shall speak shall come to pass. It shall no longer be prolonged. In your days will I say the word, and will perform it. (12:21-25)

Guidance of the Holy Ghost:
1. Whither the spirit was to go, they went. (1:12, 20)
2. The spirit entered me when the Lord spoke to me. (2:2)
3. The spirit took me up. The spirit lifted me up and took me away. (3:12-14)
4. The spirit lifted me up, and brought me. (8:3; 11:1; 11:24)
5. The Lord in vision, said, Therefore prophesy against them, prophesy, O son of man. And the Spirit of the Lord fell upon me, and said unto me, Speak; Thus saith the Lord . . . (11:4-5)
6. The hand of the Lord was upon me, and carried me out in the spirit of the Lord. (37:1)

The Lord Will Not Hear the Wicked:
1. For every one of the house of Israel which separateth himself from me, and setteth up his idols in his heart, and putteth the stumbling block of his iniquity before his face, and cometh to a prophet to inquire of him concerning me, I will set my face against that man, and I will cut him off from the midst of my people. (14:7-8)
2. And if the prophet be deceived when he hath spoken a thing, I the Lord have deceived that prophet, and I will stretch out my hand upon him, and will destroy him from the midst of my people Israel. (14:9; See Inspired Version.)

Repentance:
1. When a righteous man doth turn from his righteousness, and commit iniquity, his righteousness which he hath done shall not be remembered. (3:18-21)

EZEKIEL

2. The son that sees the sins of his father and does not do them, he shall not die for the iniquity of his father, he shall surely live. (18:1-18)
3. If the wicked will turn from all his sins that he hath committed, he shall surely live, and his transgressions shall not be mentioned to him. But when a righteous man turneth away from his righteousness, and committeth iniquity, he shall surely die, and all his righteousness shall not be remembered. (18:20-29)
4. The righteousness of the righteous shall not deliver him in the day of his transgressions: as for the wickedness of the wicked, he shall not fall thereby in the day that he turneth from his wickedness. (33:8-20)

The Spirit World:
1. The Assyrian was cast down to hell with them that descend into the pit. (31:16-17)
2. The vanquished shall speak from the midst of hell and the pit. (32:21-31)

Counsel for Righteous Living:
1. Be not thou rebellious like that rebellious house. (2:8)
2. All my words that I shall speak unto thee receive in thine heart, and hear with thine ears. (3:10)
3. Hear the word of the Lord God. (6:3)
4. Ye shall know that I am the Lord. (6:7)
5. They shall know that I am the Lord, and that I have not said in vain. (6:10)
6. Thus saith the Lord God: Repent, and turn away your faces from all your abominations. (14:6)
7. A man that is just, and does that which is lawful and right,
    A. Hath not lifted up his eyes to idols,
    B. Hath not defiled his neighbour's wife,
    C. Hath not come near to a menstruous woman,
    D. Hath not oppressed any,
    E. Hath restored to the debtor his pledge,
    F. Hath spoiled none by violence.
    G. Hath given his bread to the hungry,
    H. Hath covered the naked with a garment,
    I. Hath not given forth upon usury,
    J. Hath not taken any increase,
    K. Hath withdrawn his hand from iniquity,

       L. Hath executed true judgments between man and man,
       M. Hath walked in my statutes,
       N. Hath kept my judgments, to deal truly,
    He is just, he shall surely live, saith the Lord God. (18:5-9)

8. Repent, and turn yourselves from all your transgressions; so iniquity shall not be your ruin. Make you a new heart and a new spirit: for why will ye die? (18:30-32)
9. I gave them my sabbaths, to be a sign between me and them, that they might know that I am the Lord that sanctify them. (20:12)
10. I am the Lord your God; walk in my statutes, and keep my judgments, and do them; (20:19)
11. Hallow my sabbaths; and they shall be a sign between me and you, that ye may know that I am the Lord your God. (20:20)
12. Son of man, I have set thee a watchman unto the house of Israel. (33:1-7)
13. They shall teach my people the difference between the holy and profane, and cause them to discern between the unclean and the clean. (44:23)
14. They shall keep my laws and my statutes in all mine assemblies; and they shall hallow my sabbaths. (44:24)
15. Remove violence and spoil, and execute judgment and justice, take away your exactions from my people, saith the Lord God. (45:9)
16. Ye shall have just balances. (45:10)

Author and Date of Authorship:

    Until very recently the book was almost universally regarded as being the writing of Ezekiel and as having been written during the Babylonian captivity.

Style of the Book:
1. The book is in prose except for the poetry of chapters 15; 16:3-14; 17:3-10, 19-20, 22-24, 32-34; 24:3-5; 26:2-6, 3-14, 17-18; 27:3-9, 25-36; 28:1-23; 29:3-7; 30:2-4, 6-8, 10-19; 31:3-9; 32:2-8, 12-15. There is lack of agreement on the poetical nature of some of these verses.
2. His moods are varied and sometimes contradictory.
3. His poetry is lively and vivid, in contrast with his dull and often monotonous prose.

Ezekiel

4. He makes extensive use of parables and allegories, and he develops and explains them carefully.
5. His poetry often takes the rhythmical form used in lamentations.
6. He uses many stereotyped expressions and repeats them frequently.
7. He was not a skilled orator but expresses profound conviction. His writing reveals him to be an individual with a keen mind and many eccentricities.

Textual Transmission: The book shows clear signs of modification and corruption during transmission.

Bible Criticism:

During the last several decades the critics have advanced more and more divergent theories which lead to irreconcilable conclusions and have covered the authorship of the book of Ezekiel with a cloud of uncertainty. Some have even challenged the actual existence of Ezekiel! There still appears to be no theory which can be effectively substantiated which can alter the assertion that the book is written by Ezekiel. Some critics regard him as a prophet to Samaria or Jerusalem, others debate whether he was in Babylonia or Palestine. Some question whether he was a poet or a writer of prose. Some debate whether his book is fiction or history. In short, recent criticism has spread in a multitude of directions with little good being accomplished.

Changes Made in the Inspired Version of the Bible—Book of Ezekiel

King James Translation	Inspired Version
14:9—And if the prophet be deceived when he hath spoken a thing, I the Lord have deceived that prophet, and I will stretch out my hand upon him, and will destroy him . . .	14:9—And if the prophet be deceived when he hath spoken a thing, I the Lord have **not** deceived that prophet; **therefore** I will stretch out my hand upon him, and will destroy him . . .
18:32—. . . wherefore turn yourselves, and live ye.	18:32—. . . wherefore **turn ye and live.**
19:10—Thy mother is like a vine in thy blood, planted by the waters:	19:10—Thy mother is like a vine, planted by the waters;

King James Translation	Inspired Version
20:30—. . . Are ye polluted after the manner of your fathers? and commit ye whoredom after their abominations?	20:30—. . . **Ye are** polluted after the manner of your fathers, and **ye commit** whoredom after their abominations.
23:17—. . . and her mind was alienated from them.	23:17—. . . and her mind was alienated **from me** by them.
23:22—. . . I will raise up thy lovers against thee, from whom thy mind is alienated, and I will bring them . . .	23:22—. . . I will raise up thy lovers against thee, by **whom** thy mind is alienated **from me,** and I will bring them . . .
23:28—. . . into the hand of them from whom thy mind is alienated . . .	23:28—. . . into the hand of them **by** whom thy mind is alienated.
23:34—. . . break the sherds . . .	23:34—. . . break the shreds . . .
31:8—. . . nor any tree in the garden of God . . .	31:8—. . . **not** any tree in the garden of God
35:6—. . . sith thou hast not hated blood . . .	35:6—. . . **since** thou has not hated blood . . .
47:11—. . . marishes . . .	47:11—. . . **marshes** . . .
48:35—. . . and the name of the city from that day shall be, The Lord is there.	48:35—. . . and the name of the city from that day shall be called, Holy; for the Lord shall be there.

Summary: After studying the book of Ezekiel the student should know:

1. Ezekiel was carried into Babylon with the first major deportation of the Jews, c. 598 B. C.
2. His contemporary in Babylon was Daniel. In Judah, it was Jeremiah.
3. The major portion of his book was written between the first deportation of the Jews and the fall of Jerusalem. It is mostly concerned with the fall of Jerusalem.
4. Ezekiel gives important teachings on
    A. The nature of repentance, (chapters 18 and 33)
    B. The duty of prophets and religious leaders to warn their people, (chapter 33) and

EZEKIEL 565

      C. The relationship of the Bible to other scripture. (chapter 37)
5. Ezekiel's writing includes details and significant contributions to the doctrines of the last days, including:
      A. The Battle of Armageddon.
      B. The Jerusalem temple.
      C. The functions of David the Prince.
      D. The role of sacrificial worship.
      E. The borders of Israel.
      F. The inheritances of the twelve tribes.
6. Ezekiel was privileged to see the Lord on several occasions and also saw the cherubim which dwell in the heavens with Him.

PART V

The History
> Persia
> Judah Following the Return from Exile

The Historical Books
> Ezra
> Esther
> Nehemiah

The Prophets
> Haggai
> Zechariah
> Malachi
> Joel

The Doctrine
> The Nature of God
> Counsel for Righteous Living
> Directions for Worship and Religious Covenants
> Important Events of the Last Days

CHAPTER XXII

HISTORICAL SUMMARY
PERSIA AND JUDAH FOLLOWING THE BABYLONIAN CAPTIVITY

Persia.

The Persian empire had risen to great heights under the rule of its first two kings, Cambyses and Cyrus II. It was Cyrus who issued the proclamation which allowed the captive Jews to return and rebuild their homeland. Under his rule the Persian empire overcame every major power except Egypt. With his death in 529 B.C., the rule of the kingdom passed to his son, Cambyses II.

At this point the student should review Cambyses I and Cyrus II in Chapter XIX. The Persian kings who followed were:

1. **Cambyses II**—(c. 529-521 B.C.)

    A. He continued to extend the Persian empire and conquered Egypt.

    B. He is believed to be the Artaxerxes who stopped work on the temple in Jerusalem. (See Ezra 4:7, 11, 23)

    C. He committed suicide in the face of a revolt which later proved unsuccessful.

2. **Darius (Hystaspes)**—(c. 521-485 B.C.)

    A. The Persian empire reached its greatest extent under his rule. It was even larger than the empire established by the Romans four centuries later.

    B. He crossed the Bosphorus and penetrated into Europe to the area of the Danube in combatting the Scythians. On his return he pacified Thrace and Macedonia.

C. He turned eastward to India and conquered portions of the Punjab and Sind.

D. He attacked the Greek mainland to suppress a revolt of the Ionian Greeks. The Greeks defeated the Persian army in the battle of Marathon in 490 B.C.

E. He was responsible for the engraving of the famous Behistun Rock. These inscriptions, which describe his conquests, were recorded in Persian, Elamite, and Babylonian. The rock is significant because it provided the key to the previously undecipherable Babylonian language.

F. He authorized the completion of the Jerusalem temple. (Ezra 6)

3. **Xerxes (Ahasuerus)**—(c. 485-466 B.C.)

A. During his reign the Persian army and fleet were defeated at Salamis, Thermopylae, and Plataea.

B. Xerxes was the husband of the Jewish queen, Esther.

C. He was assassinated.

D. The Persian empire began its rapid decline during his reign.

4. **Artaxerxes (Longimanus)**—(c. 466-425 B.C.)

A. He suppressed an Egyptian revolt which temporarily halted the decline of the empire.

B. He authorized Nehemiah, the cupbearer, to return to Palestine and rebuild the Jerusalem wall.

During the rule of the remaining six kings, the Persian empire continued to decline until it collapsed under the military might of Alexander the Great.

5. **Xerxes II**—(c. 424 B.C.)

6. **Darius II (Nothius)**—(c. 423-405 B.C.)
7. **Artaxerxes II (Mnemon)**—(c. 405-358 B.C.)
8. **Artaxerxes III (Ochus)**—(c. 358-338 B.C.)
9. **Arses**—(c. 338-335 B.C.)
10. **Darius III (Codomanus)**—(c. 335-331 B.C.)

    A. He was defeated and killed by Alexander the Great at the battle of Arbela.

    B. With this defeat Persia fell and became part of the Macedonian empire.

Judah, Following the Babylonian Captivity.

1. **The returns**

   A. 536 B.C.—Led by Zerubbabel.

   B. 457 B.C.—Led by Ezra.

2. **Construction**

   A. 536-516 B.C.—The temple was rebuilt.

   B. 444 B.C.—The wall of Jerusalem was rebuilt.

3. **Diminished territory**—The returning Jews found their territory vastly reduced by the encroachment of new and old neighbors and foes. The territory they returned to was about 25 by 35 miles, or less than one-fourth the territory originally assigned to the tribe.

4. **Government**

   A. For two centuries Judah remained under Persian domination. The governor was nominated at Susa by the Persians but he was chosen from among the Jewish people.

   B. The Jews also appointed their own national leader, whom they regarded as the real authority. He was the High Priest. This position became one of great importance from this period forward.

   C. An aristocracy of priests gradually formed around the high priest. This aristocracy grew into a senate which later became the Sanhedrin.

5. **Lack of freedom**

    A. The Jews were constantly annoyed and persecuted by their enemies, who resisted their efforts to strengthen their position. The Samaritans were particularly active in their efforts to prevent the rebuilding of the temple and the walls of Jerusalem.

    B. The growth and restoration of Judah was dependent on the whims of the Persian rulers.

6. **Religion**

    A. Evil practices immediately began to creep back into the Jewish way of life. Foreign women were taken to wife, the priests were making fortunes by collecting taxes for the Persians, and outrageous rents and interest rates were being charged.

    B. Important reforms were undertaken by Nehemiah and Ezra.

7. **Language**—By this time the people were growing accustomed to speaking Aramaic—the international language of the times. Hebrew came to be regarded as a literary or classical language. It soon became necessary for the Hebrew scripture to be accompanied by an Aramaic translation, or "Targum," in order that the common people could understand it.

8. **Canonization of scripture**—The fifth to the first century B.C. was the period when the Old Testament canon was established.

Following the return from captivity, Judah was never able to emerge from the status of a conquered vassal state. It lived in a small, self-centered world of its own, which finally dissolved with the Roman destruction of Jerusalem and the complete dispersion of the Jews throughout the Roman Empire.

PERSIA AND JUDAH FOLLOWING BABYLONIAN CAPTIVITY 573

Summary:

While studying the post-exilic period, the student should know:

Persia

1. Persia had twelve kings. Its empire reached its greatest extent under the fourth king and then degenerated.
2. Five Persian kings are important in Bible history; they reigned in consecutive order as indicated:
    A. Cyrus—Sent the Jews back to Palestine.
    B. Cambyses II—stopped work on the Jerusalem temple.
    C. Darius—authorized completion of the Jerusalem temple.
    D. Xerxes (Ahasuerus)—made Esther queen.
    E. Artaxerxes—authorized Nehemiah to rebuild the Jerusalem wall.

Post-exilic Judah

3. There were two major groups which returned to Judah:
    A. Group one—with Zerubbabel.
    B. Group two—with Ezra.
4. Reconstruction:
    A. Zerubbabel, Haggai, and Zechariah rebuilt the temple.
    B. Nehemiah rebuilt the wall of Jerusalem.
5. Judah returned to an area less than one-fourth its original size.
6. Judah remained a vassal state.
7. The language of Judah changed from Hebrew to Aramaic.
8. The era between the Old and the New Testaments is the period in which the Old Testament canon was set.

CHAPTER XXIII

EZRA

Date: This book describes the return of two groups of Jews from Babylonia to Palestine:
    A. 536 B.C. Led by Zerubbabel. (Chapters 1-6)
    B. 457 B.C. Led by Ezra. (Chapters 7-10)

Subjects:
    A. The Return of the Jews.
    B. The Building of the Temple in Jerusalem.
    C. The Cleansing of Judah from Racial and Religious Intermarriage.

Historical Background: Under the Babylonians' policy of deporting conquered peoples from their home lands, the Jews had been carried from Judah to Babylonia. After being in captivity for seventy years, the Jews saw their Babylonian foes suddenly overthrown by the Persians under Cyrus. The Persians reversed the scorched-earth policies of the Assyrians and Babylonians and returned the conquered peoples to their homelands.

Outline of the Book:

Chapter 1—The Proclamation of Cyrus.
1. Cyrus decreed that the temple be built in Jerusalem. (1-4)
2. The temple vessels were returned to Sheshbazzar (Shĕshbăz'-zär)—(the Persian or Babylonian name for Zerubbabel?) (5-11)

Chapter 2—The List of Those Who Returned to Jerusalem.
1. The registry (by groups) of those who were to return: a total of 42,360 plus 7,337 servants. (1-67)[1]
2. The removal from the priesthood of those who were not found in the genealogy. (61-63)
3. The return, and donations to the temple building fund. (68-70)

---

[1] Josephus shows the number of returned exiles as 4,628,000.

EZRA

Chapter 3—The Restoration of Sacrifice and the Laying of the Temple Foundation.
1. The beginning of sacrifices in the seventh month following the return. (1-7)
2. The laying of the foundation of the temple in the second year, second month. (8-11)
3. The weeping of the ancient men. (12-13)

Chapter 4—Work on the Temple Halted By Deceit.
1. The enemies of Judah weakened the work on the temple until Cyrus died (about six years). (1-5)
2. In the beginning of the reign of Artaxerxes (är-tă-xĕrx'-ēs—also known as Cambyses) Judah's enemies wrote a letter of accusations against the Jews to the Persian king which caused the work on the temple to be halted for about eight years, until the second year of the Persian king Darius. (6-24)

Chapter 5—Haggai and Zechariah Start Building the Temple Again.
1. Haggai and Zechariah prophesied to the people and started work on the temple again. (1-2)
2. Opposition to the work again developed in the form of a letter to King Darius complaining that the work had been resumed. (3-17)

Chapter 6—The Temple Is Completed.
1. Darius commanded that the temple be built and forced Judah's enemies to aid in its construction. (1-12)
2. The temple was completed. (13-15)
3. Feasts and ceremonies of rejoicing were held. (16-22)

— 59 years pass —

Chapter 7—Ezra Comes From Babylon to Judah.
1. Ezra, a descendant of Aaron, the brother of Moses, returned to Judah from Babylon. (1-10)
2. Ezra's letter of authorization from King Artaxerxes (är-tă-xĕrx'-ēs) allowed him to regulate the worship of Judah. (11-28)

Chapter 8—Ezra's Journey to Jerusalem.
1. A list of those who returned with Ezra is given. (1-20)
2. Ezra proclaimed a fast so they would be protected in their travel without an escort. (21-23)

3. The journey and arrival in Jerusalem is described. (24-36)

Chapter 9—The Sin of Intermarriage.
1. Ezra learned of the intermarriage of the Judeans. (1-4)
2. Ezra prayed and confessed the sin of Judah.

Chapter 10—The Men Separate Themselves From Their Strange Wives.
1. The Jewish people covenanted to put away all their foreign wives and the children of these marriages. (1-5)
2. Ezra proclaimed that all who would not keep the covenant would have to leave Judah and forfeit their possessions. (6-8)
3. A meeting was held in which the people agreed to put away their strange wives in an orderly manner. (9-17)
4. A list of the men who had taken foreign wives is given. (18-44)

Doctrinal Analysis

God's Dealings With His Prophets:
1. That the word of the Lord by the mouth of Jeremiah might be fulfilled, the Lord stirred up the spirit of Cyrus that he make a proclamation . . . (1:1)
2. The people prospered through the prophesying of Haggai the prophet and Zechariah . . . (6:14)

Priesthood Authority:
1. The children of Habaiah sought their register among those that were reckoned by genealogy, but they were not found: therefore were they put from the priesthood. (2:61-63) (See D & C 85:11-12)

The Nature of God:
1. He is good, for his mercy endureth forever toward Israel. (3:11)
2. The Lord had made them joyful, and turned the heart of the king of Assyria unto them, to strengthen their hands in the work of the house of God. (6:22)
3. The king granted Ezra all his request, according to the hand of the Lord his God upon him. (7:6)

Ezra 577

4. We were bondsmen; yet our God hath not forsaken us in our bondage, but hath extended mercy unto us . . . (9:9)
5. O Lord God of Israel, thou art righteous. (9:15)

Counsel for Righteous Living:

1. Ezra had prepared his heart to seek the law of the Lord, and to do it, and to teach in Israel statutes and judgments. (7:10)
2. And thou, Ezra, after the wisdom of thy God, that is in thine hand, . . . judge all that know the laws of thy God; and teach ye them that know them not. (7:25)
3. I was strengthened as the hand of the Lord my God was upon me. (7:28)
4. I proclaimed a fast, that we might afflict ourselves before our God, to seek of him a right way for us. (8:21)
5. Ye are holy unto the Lord. (8:28)
6. They furthered the people, and the house of God. (8:36)
7. The importance of proper marriage discussed. (Chapters 9 and 10)
8. He had prayed and confessed, casting himself down before the house of God. (10:1)
9. Let us make a covenant with our God according to the counsel of my Lord and of those that tremble at the commandment of our God; and let it be done according to the law. (10:3)
10. Make confession unto the Lord God of your fathers, and do his pleasure. (10:11)

Author and Date of Authorship:

The books of Ezra and Nehemiah were regarded as being only one book in the Hebrew Bible until they were separated in 1448. Their separation had been made more than a thousand years earlier in Greek and Latin texts.

In both books the material changes from the **first** to the **third** person. It is believed that the two books were written from "memoirs" of Ezra and Nehemiah (the first person sections) many years later by the author of Chronicles. (Note that 2 Chron. 36:22-23 is repeated as an introduction in Ezra 1:1-3a.) According to Jewish tradition, Ezra was the author of Chronicles, Ezra and Nehemiah.

Bible Criticism:

Several problems exist when the books of Ezra and Nehemiah are compared with the existing secular records of the time. Bible scholars have considered them and have reached a variety of different and conflicting conclusions. Many scholars have concluded that the Persian documents cited are Jewish forgeries, that the edicts of the Persian kings were never given, that many of the details regarding chronology are imaginary, that the powers and funds given to Ezra were extraordinary and unrealistic, etc.

Summary:

After studying the book of Ezra, the student should know:
1. The Book of Ezra tells about two groups of Jewish exiles who returned from Babylonia to Judah.
2. The two leaders of these expeditions were:

    A. Zerubbabel   536 B.C.   Rebuilt the temple.
    B. Ezra   457 B.C.   Stopped intermarriage.

3. The three major lessons of the book:
    A. The Lord fulfills His promises to man.
    B. The Lord influences people and events to aid his people when they are attempting to achieve righteous objectives.
    C. Religious intermarriage is displeasing to the Lord.
4. The Old Testament books of Ezra and Nehemiah were originally one book.
5. Bible scholars have challenged the historical veracity of the book with serious accusations.

CHAPTER XXIV

ESTHER

Date: 478-473 B.C. This is between the times of Zerubbabel and Ezra.

Subject: The Jews' Deliverance from Extermination throughout the Persian Empire.

Historical Background: Persian inscriptions have revealed that Xerxes, the great Persian ruler, held a great feast in preparation for his expedition[1] against Greece in 482 B.C. It was apparently at this time that he deposed Queen Vashti. He did not take Esther to wife until four years later, in 478 B.C., after his return from the expedition. Esther's actions constituted one of the most important events in Jewish history, for she saved the entire nation from annihilation.

Outline of the Book:

Chapter 1—**Queen Vashti Is Deposed.**
1. King Ahasuerus (ă-hăs-u-ē'-rus, or Xerxes) gave a great feast. (1-9)
2. During the feast he sent for Queen Vashti but she refused to come. (10-12)
3. Queen Vashti's rebellious nature was considered a bad influence for the women of the empire. It was decided that an example would be made of her so she was deposed. (13-22)

Chapter 2—**Esther is Made Queen.**
1. It was decided that the fair young virgins of the kingdom would be brought to the palace. From them the king would choose a new queen. (1-4)
2. Mordecai (Môr-dĕ-cā'-ī) was a Jew whose great-grandfather had come to Babylon in the first deportation. He had raised Esther, his uncle's daughter. (5-7)
3. Esther was taken to the palace where she underwent a year long period of purification. She found favor there

---
[1]In which he fought the battles of Salamis and Thermopylae in 480 B.C.

and was given preferential treatment. She did not reveal that she was Jewish. (8-14)
   4. Esther was chosen queen. (15-20)
   5. While waiting at the palace gate for news of Esther, Mordecai learned of a plot to kill the king. He reported to Esther, who sent word to the king, and the would-be assassins were hanged. (21-23)

Chapter 3—**Haman Secures a Decree of Death for the Jews.**

1. Haman was promoted and everyone bowed down to him. Mordecai refused to bow to him on religious grounds. (1-4)
2. Haman was angry with Mordecai and, since Mordecai was a Jew, Haman proposed to the king that all the Jews in the empire be slain. The king decreed that all the Jews should be killed. (5-15)

Chapter 4—**Esther Prepares to See the King.**

1. Mordecai and the Jews mourned. (1-4)
2. Mordecai requested that Esther go in and plead for their nation before the king. (5-9)
3. Since anyone who went to see the king without an appointment might be put to death if the king didn't hold out his sceptre, Esther asked that all the Jews in Shushan fast for three days in her behalf. (10-17)

Chapter 5—**Haman's Plan to Hang Mordecai.**

1. Esther went to see the king and was received. She requested that the king and Haman attend a banquet she had prepared. (1-8)
2. As Haman left the king's presence, he was again angered by Mordecai. (9)
3. Haman told his wife and friends about Mordecai. It was suggested that he have a tall gallows made and then ask the king to have Mordecai hanged. (10-14)

Chapter 6—**The King Honors Mordecai.**

1. That night the king read in his records of the deed Mordecai had performed in saving his life. He found that Mordecai had not been rewarded. (1-3)
2. Just then Haman came to ask for Mordecai's death. The king asked Haman for his suggestion as to how to reward a man the king might choose to honor. Haman, thinking the honor would come to himself, suggested that the man

ESTHER 581

      should be dressed in the king's apparel and led through the streets on horseback by one of the nobles. (4-9)
3. The king sent Haman to honor Mordecai in this manner. (10-11)

Chapter 7—**Haman Is Hanged.**
1. The king and Haman came to Esther's banquet. (1)
2. Esther told the king that she and her people were to be killed because of Haman. (2-6)
3. The king had Haman hanged on the gallows which had been prepared for Mordecai. (7-10)

Chapter 8—**The Jews Are Commanded to Defend Themselves.**
1. The king gave Haman's house to Esther, who gave it to Mordecai. (1-2)
2. Esther again requested that the king spare her people. The king's proclamation could not be reversed but he gave Esther and Mordecai permission to write any proclamation they wanted. (3-8)
3. Mordecai proclaimed that the Jews were to defend themselves and spoil their attackers. (9-17)

Chapter 9—**The Feast of Purim is Established.**
1. On the appointed day the Jews defended themselves and slew their enemies. (1-11)
2. In answer to Esther's request, the king had the ten sons of Haman hanged. (12-14)
3. The total slain by the Jews was 75,800. (6, 15-16)
4. The Jews established an annual time of feasting in remembrance of the great event. This is called the feast of Purim. (17-32)

Chapter 10—**Mordecai Becomes the King's Lieutenant.**
1. Mordecai stood second to the king in greatness. (1-3)
    Note: Ahasuerus (Xerxes) died thirteen years after his marriage to Esther. There is little doubt that Esther lived on into the reign of her step-son, Artaxerxes. She may have been instrumental in bringing about the favorable attitudes shown to Ezra and Nehemiah by the Persian court.

Examples for Living:
1. The importance of women rendering obedience to their husbands. (1:10-18)

2. The loyalty of Mordecai in reporting treachery to the king. (2:21-23)
3. Mordecai's religious obedience in refusing to bow to Haman. (3:1-5, 5:9)
4. The fasting of the Jews to seek divine aid. (4:3, 16)

Author and Date of Authorship: Unknown.

Bible Criticism:

Bible critics have rejected the idea of Esther being an actual person. They regard the book as a book of fiction (a classification to which they also relegate Jonah, Daniel, and Ruth) and treat it as a story designed to glorify the Jewish race. They attribute its authorship to an unknown "ardent Jew."

Summary:

After studying the book of Esther the student should know:
1. The story of the book, including the identity of Esther, Mordecai, and Haman.
2. The two major lessons of the book:
    A. God foresees the needs of His people and prepares to meet them.
    B. God may choose any worthy individual to accomplish his purposes.
3. The incidents described in the book take place about 478-473 B.C. in Shushan, the capital of Persia.
4. The location of Persia and Shushan.
5. Esther became queen between the time of the journeys to Judea of Zerubbabel and Ezra.
6. The salvation of the Jews is the basis for the Jewish feast of Purim.
7. Some critics reject the actuality of the book of Esther and regard it only as a novel with a moral.

CHAPTER XXV

NEHEMIAH

Date: 444-432 B.C.

Subject: The Rebuilding of the Wall of Jerusalem.

Historical Background: Nehemiah was a cupbearer to King Artaxerxes in the Persian court. He was appointed to return to Jerusalem and rebuild the wall so that the city would be fortified. His calling was different from that of Ezra, for he was a civil governor while Ezra was a teacher of religion. Ezra had labored for thirteen years in Jerusalem before Nehemiah came.

Outline of the Book:

Chapter 1—**Nehemiah's Prayer that God Would Influence the King.**
1. Nehemiah learned of the afflictions of the Jews in Jerusalem and that the walls of that city had not yet been rebuilt. (1-3)
2. Nehemiah prayed that he might have mercy in the sight of the king, that the king would honor his request. (4-11)

Chapter 2—**Nehemiah's Journey to Jerusalem.**
1. Nehemiah sought and was given permission to journey to Jerusalem and rebuild its walls. (1-8)
2. He arrived in Jerusalem, surveyed the situation, and began the work on the walls. (9-20)

Chapter 3—**Work on the Wall is Organized.**
1. A list of those who undertook to repair each section of the wall is given. (1-32)

Chapter 4—**A Plot to Halt the Work.**
1. Sanballat and Tobiah mocked the Jews. (1-3)
2. A prayer that the enemies of Judah might be punished for their sins. (4-5)
3. Judah's enemies conspired to come and fight against Jerusalem. (6-8)

4. The Jews learned of the plot and had half the people stand guard while the other half worked. The people moved into Jerusalem to protect it. (9-23)

Chapter 5—Nehemiah Stops the Crime of Usury.

1. The people complained because of their poverty, the high taxes, and the high price of food, that they were having to borrow money at unfair interest. They were losing their property. (1-5)
2. Nehemiah made the rich covenant to give back the lands and goods they had obtained through usury. (6-13)
3. Nehemiah spent twelve years as governor, during which his expenses were not charged to the people. (14-19)

Chapter 6—The Wall Is Completed.

1. Judah's enemies attempted to get Nehemiah to come out of Jerusalem so they could harm him. He refused to come. (1-4)
2. Judah's enemies said they were going to tell the Persian king that Nehemiah was going to rebel and set himself up as king. (5-9)
3. Judah's enemies hired a false prophet to tell Nehemiah to flee for his life into the temple. (10-14)
4. The wall was finished in fifty-two days. (15)
5. There was correspondence between the Jewish nobles and their enemies. (16-19)

Chapter 7—The Genealogy of the Exiles.

1. Nehemiah established control of the city gates. (1-4)
2. Nehemiah repeats the genealogy of the people who had previously returned to Judah. (See Ezra Ch. 2.) (5-73)

Chapter 8—The Law is Read.

1. Ezra read the law of the Lord to the people and it was explained to him. (1-8)
2. The people were joyful on the holy day. (9-12)
3. The feast continued seven days. They read the law of the Lord and made booths as the law commanded them. (13-18)

Chapter 9—The People Worship God.

1. A fast meeting was held in which they read the law, confessed their sins, and worshipped God. (1-3)

NEHEMIAH 585

2. The sermon of the Levites is recorded, in which they called to mind the Lord's wondrous deeds, and the rebelliousness of their fathers. (4-37)
3. The people made a covenant with God. (38)

Chapter 10—**The Covenant With God.**
1. A list of those who sealed themselves in the covenant is given. (1-27)
2. The covenant into which they entered was—(28-39)
   A. To obey the law of Moses.
   B. To keep the Lord's commandments, laws, and statutes.
   C. To keep their children from marrying those that were not of their people.
   D. Not to buy or sell on the Sabbath.
   E. To keep the Sabbath of years and the debt laws.
   F. To contribute for the maintenance of the temple.
   G. To take their turn in providing the labor for the needs of the temple.
   H. To pay tithes of their produce, and
   I. To not forsake the house of God.

Chapter 11—**The People Move to Jerusalem and Other Villages.**
1. The people cast lots to see who would live in Jerusalem. (1-2)
2. The list of those who lived in Jerusalem is given. (3-24)
3. A list of the villages settled by the Jews is given. (25-30)
4. A list of the villages settled by the Benjaminites is given. (31-36)

Chapter 12—**The Wall Is Dedicated.**
1. A list of the priests and Levites is given. (1-26)
2. The wall of Jerusalem was dedicated. (27-43)
3. The temple activities were organized. (44-47)

Chapter 13—**Nehemiah Revisits Jerusalem and Initiates Reforms.**
1. The Ammonites were separated from the house of Judah. (1-3)
2. Eliashib the priest had allowed Tobiah (an enemy of Judah) to use a chamber in the temple. (4-5)
3. Nehemiah again visited Jerusalem. He corrected several evils:

A. He cast Tobiah out of the temple. (7-9)
B. He restored the Levites and had the people resume the payment of their tithes. (10-13)
C. He made the people observe and honor the Sabbath day. (14-22)
D. He rebuked them for intermarrying with those who were not their people. (23-31)

Doctrinal Analysis

The Nature of God:

1. The Lord God of heaven is the great and terrible God. (1:5)
2. God keeps covenants and has mercy for them that love him and observe his commandments. (1:5)
3. The God of heaven, he will prosper us. (2:20)
4. Our God shall fight for us. (4:20)
5. Thou hast made heaven, the earth, the seas, and thou preservest them all. (9:6)
6. Thou hast performed thy words, for thou art righteous. (9:8)
7. Thou didst divide the sea for Moses' people so that they went through the midst of the sea on dry land. (9:11)
8. Thou art a God ready to pardon, gracious and merciful, slow to anger, and of great kindness. (9:17)
9. Thou art a gracious and merciful God. (9:31)
10. God is great, mighty, and terrible, and keeps covenant and mercy. (9:32)
11. Thou art just in all that is brought upon us, for thou hast done right. (9:33)

God's Dealings With His Prophets—Revelation:

1. Thou spakest with them from heaven, and gavest them right judgments, and true laws, good statutes and commandments. (9:13-14)
2. Thou gavest also thy good spirit to instruct them. (9:20)
3. Thou testified against them by thy spirit in thy prophets. (9:30)

Examples for Living:

1. Nehemiah's mourning and desire for the well-being of his people. (1:1-11)
2. The people put away usury. (5:1-13)

3. Nehemiah supports himself as governor. (5:14-19)
4. Nehemiah avoids a compromising situation in which he could be accused of sin. (6:10-13)
5. Unauthorized persons were denied the rights of the priesthood. (7:64-65)
6. Group scripture reading. (8:1-8)
7. Instructions for keeping a day holy. (8:9-12)
8. A description of a day of fasting and worship. (9:1-3)
9. A dedication service. (12:27-43)
10. Nehemiah reproved the nobles for profaning the Sabbath day. (13:15-22)
11. Nehemiah reproved the people for marrying outside of the Church. (13:23-29)

Counsel for Righteous Living:

1. Nehemiah confesses his sins and the sins of his people. (1:6-7)
2. O Lord, I beseech thee, to hear the prayer of thy servants who desire to fear thy name. (1:11)
3. So I prayed to the God of heaven (for immediate help during a conversation). (2:4)
4. Neither told I any man what my God had put in my heart to do. (2:12)
5. Remember the Lord, and fight for your brethren, your sons, and your daughters, your wives and your houses. (4:14)
6. Ought ye not to walk in the fear of our God because of the reproach of our enemies? (5:9)
7. Think upon me, my God, for good, according to all that I have done for this people. (5:19)
8. He was a faithful man, and feared God above many. (7:2)
9. The ears of all the people were attentive unto the book of the law. (8:3)
10. They caused the people to understand the law. (8:7-8)
11. We make a sure covenant. (9:38)
12. The covenant of righteousness is explained. (10:29-39)
13. Then brought all Judah the tithe. (13:12)
14. Remember me, O my God, concerning this, and wipe not out my good deeds that I have done. (13:14)
15. They should cleanse themselves and should come and keep the gates, to sanctify the sabbath day. (13:15-22)

588   Prophets and Prophecies of the Old Testament

Author and Date of Authorship:

The books of Ezra and Nehemiah were regarded as being only one book in the Hebrew Bible until they were separated in 1448. Their separation had been made more than a thousand years earlier in Greek and Latin texts.

In both books the material changes from the **first** to the **third** person. It is believed that the two books were written from "memoirs" of Ezra and Nehemiah (the first person sections) many years later by the author of Chronicles. (Note that 2 Chron. 36:22-23 is repeated as an introduction in Ezra 1:1-3a.) According to Jewish tradition, Ezra was the author of Chronicles, Ezra and Nehemiah.

Bible Criticism:

Several problems exist when the books of Ezra and Nehemiah are compared with the existing secular records of the time. Bible scholars have considered them and have reached a variety of different and conflicting conclusions. Many scholars have concluded that the Persian documents cited are Jewish forgeries, that the edicts of the Persian kings were never given, that many of the details regarding chronology are imaginary, that the powers and funds given to Ezra were extraordinary and unrealistic, etc.

Changes Made in the Inspired Version of the Bible—
Book of Nehemiah

King James Translation	Inspired Version
6:11—And I said, Should such a man as I flee? and who is there, that, being as I am, would go into the temple to save his life? I will not go in.	6:11—And I said, Should such a man as I flee? and who is **mine enemy, that such a man as I** would go into the temple to save his life? I will not go in.
6:13—Therefore was he hired, that I should be afraid, and do so, and sin, and that they might have matter for an evil report, that they might reproach me.	6:13—Therefore **should I be afraid of him he hired, and do so as he said, and sin; and that they might have me for an evil report,** that they might reproach me?
7:10—The children of Arah, six hundred fifty and two.	7:10—The children of Arah, **seven hundred seventy and five.**

NEHEMIAH 589

King James Translation	Inspired Version

7:11—. . . two thousand and eight hundred and eighteen.

7:13—The children of Zattu, eight hundred forty and five.

7:15—The children of Binnui, six hundred forty and eight.

7:16—The children of Bebai, six hundred twenty and eight.

7:17—The children of Azgad, two thousand three hundred twenty and two.

7:18—The children of Adonikam, six hundred threescore and seven.

7:19—The children of Bigvai, two thousand threescore and seven.

7:20—The children of Adin, six hundred fifty and five.

7:22—The children of Hashum, three hundred twenty and eight.

7:23—The children of Bezai, three hundred twenty and four.

7:24—The children of Hariph, an hundred and twelve.

7:32—The men of Bethel and Ai, an hundred twenty and three.

7:37—. . . seven hundred twenty and one.

7:38—. . . three thousand nine hundred and thirty.

7:44—The singers: the children of Asaph, an hundred forty and eight.

7:45—. . . an hundred thirty and eight.

7:11—. . . two thousand and eight hundred and **twelve.**

7:13—The children of Zattu, **nine** hundred forty and five.

7:15—The children of **Bani,** six hundred forty and **two.**

7:16—The children of Bebai, six hundred twenty and **three.**

7:17—The children of Azgad, **a** thousand **two** hundred twenty and two.

7:18—The children of Adonikam, six hundred **sixty and six.**

7:19—The children of Bigvai, two thousand **fifty and six.**

7:20—The children of Adin, **four** hundred fifty and **four.**

7:22—The children of Hashum, **two** hundred twenty and **three.**

7:23—The children of Bezai, three hundred twenty and **three.**

7:24—The children of **Jorah,** a hundred and twelve.

7:32—The men of Bethel and Ai, **two** hundred twenty and three.

7:37—. . . seven hundred twenty and **five.**

7:38—. . . three thousand **six** hundred and thirty.

7:44—The singers **of** the children of Asaph, **a** hundred **twenty** and eight.

7:45—. . . a hundred thirty and **nine.**

King James Translation	Inspired Version
7:62—. . . six hundred forty and two.	7:62—. . . six hundred **fifty** and two.
10:29—They clave to their brethren, their nobles, and entered into a curse, and into an oath, to walk in God's law, which was given by Moses the servant of God, and to observe and do all the commandments of the Lord our God, and his judgments and his statutes;	10:29—They clave to their brethren, their nobles, and entered into **an oath, that a curse should come upon them if they did not** walk in God's law, which was given by Moses the servant of God, and to observe and do all the commandments of the Lord **their God**, and his judgments and statutes.
10:30—And that we would not give our daughters unto the people of the land, nor take their daughters for our sons.	10:30—And that **they** would not give **their** daughters unto the people of the land, nor **take the daughters of the people for their** sons.

Summary:

After studying the book of Nehemiah the student should know:
1. Nehemiah was a cupbearer to King Artaxerxes in the Persian court.
2. The three major lessons of the book:
    A. The enthusiasm and determination of one individual can cause a group of people to accomplish miracles through organized activity.
    B. It is important that people covenant with God.
    C. The religion of that day was very similar to the program of the Church today.
3. The 9-point covenant made by the people in that day outlines the basic responsibilities of the followers of God in all eras:
    A. Obedience to the established law of the Church.
    B. Obedience to current commandments and policies.
    C. Marriage within the Church only.

Nehemiah

    D. Observance of the Sabbath Day.
    E. Frugality[1] and integrity.
    F. Budget contributions.
    G. Labor contributions and service.
    H. Tithing contributions.
    I. Church attendance.

---

[1] The law regarding a Sabbath of years every seven years was actually a conservation measure which enabled the land to be more productive. Frugality through proper use and conservation of our means is a good application of this principle today.

CHAPTER XXVI

HAGGAI

Prophet's Name: The meaning of the name Haggai (Hăg'-gai) is uncertain. It comes from a Hebrew root word which means "festival" or "feast."

Scriptural Information About the Prophet:
1. He prophesied in the second year of Darius (Hystaspes), the fourth king of Persia. (Hag. 1:1)
2. He was a contemporary of the prophet Zechariah. (Ezra 5:1)
3. The prophecies of Haggai and Zechariah were instrumental in bringing about the completion of the temple in Jerusalem. (Ezra 6:14)

Date of Haggai's Mission: 520 B. C. This date is derived from its relationship to the ascension of Darius to the throne of Persia.

Prophesied to: The Jews who had returned from the Babylonian captivity.

Contemporary Prophet: Zechariah—520-518 B. C.—To the Jews who had returned from the Babylonian captivity.

Contemporary Prophets Contrasted:

Haggai was a plain-speaking individual who worked actively to achieve a specific objective. His message is matter-of-fact and specific. It is presented in a reasoning manner designed to anticipate and counter any objections which might be raised to it.

Zechariah's writing reveals a more complex individual than was Haggai. He saw a variety of visions and centered much of his comment on the events of the last days. His prophecies are profound and are extremely difficult to interpret. While Haggai's message is forthright and plain, Zechariah's writing uses much apocalyptic imagery.

Contemporary Kings and Rulers:

Judah: Zerubbabel 536-516? B.C.

He was the first governor appointed by the Persians to lead the Jews in their return to their homeland. By the time of Haggai's mission he had governed for about eighteen years.

Persia: Darius (Hystaspes) 521-485 B. C.

The Persian Empire reached its greatest extent under his rule.

National Conditions in Judah:

Political:
1. Judah was still a vassal state to Persia.
2. The Jews had been allowed to return to their homeland and rebuild their temple by Cyrus; the first group had returned to Judah eighteen years previous to Haggai's mission.
3. The Jews were unable to claim more than about one-fourth of their original territory. During their captivity other groups, primarily the Samaritans,[1] had expanded and had occupied their territories.
4. Intense resistance had been exerted by the Samaritans against the rebuilding of the temple. Their deceit had brought the work to a halt eight years before Haggai's mission. (See Ezra 3, 4)

Economic:
1. As yet Judah did not have an established economy. Her people were still living on a temporary, unsettled basis.
2. They had wealth which they had brought from Persia but there was little opportunity to use it without the established forms of trade being available.
3. As their religious fervor diminished and work on the temple halted, the people began to rebuild their own homes and to work to meet their personal needs. Their work was relatively unproductive.

Religious:
1. The people had restored the practice of offering sacrifices shortly after their return.
2. Those who returned to Judah were primarily the devout men of Judah who had come back to re-establish their

---

[1] A group made up of Jews who had escaped the Babylonian captivity and remained in the land. They had intermarried with deported refugees from other lands who had been moved into the area formerly occupied by Israel. Thus the group was part Jew and part Gentile.

religious life. Their situation is somewhat comparable to the Pilgrims, Puritans, and the Saints during the early days of the Utah period.

3. Their failure to rebuild the temple in the early days of the return, however, had brought about a spirit of religious indifference which was retarding the progress of the people.

Outline of the Book: The book of Haggai is a summary of five revelations, with accompanying historical notes.

Section I—An Exhortation to Build The Temple. (1:2-11) (Given the first day of the sixth month of the second year of Darius the king, Sept. 1, 520 B. C.)

1. The people say the time is not come for the Lord's house to be built. (2)
2. The people work for themselves and not for the Lord. Therefore their work is unproductive. (3-6)
3. Go bring wood and build the house. (7-8)
4. There is drought and the land is unproductive because the temple lies wasted. (9-11)

Section II—Work on the Temple Is Begun. (1:12-15) (Given the 24th day of the sixth month; three weeks later.)

1. The people repented and began to work on the temple. (12, 14-15)
2. The Lord's revelation to them: "I am with you." (13)

Section III—The Glory of the Temple In the Latter-days Will Be Greater Than Its Present Glory. (2:1-9) (Given the 21st day of the seventh month, or October 21st; almost a month later.)

1. Compare the present temple to the former temple. The temple being built is insignificant in comparison. (1-3)
2. Be yet strong. My spirit remaineth among you. (4-5)
3. (14)[2] I will shake the heavens and the earth, and the sea, and the dry land, and all nations. (6-7)
4. (41) The desire of all nations shall come. (7)

   Note: Some commentators interpret the "desire" as being Christ.

---

[2]Numbers in parentheses at the beginning of items refer to the fifty events of the last days listed in Chapter Four.

HAGGAI   595

5. (39) I will fill this house with glory, and in this place I will give peace. (7-9)

Section IV—Unclean Offerings Are Not Acceptable To The Lord. (2:10-19) (Given the 24th day of the ninth month; December 24th, two months later)

1. If an offering touch unholy materials, is it unclean? (10-13)
2. This nation is unclean before the Lord, and that which they offer is polluted. (14)
3. Consider that before the temple construction began their supplies were limited and nature opposed them. Now that construction has begun the Lord will bless them. (15-19)

Section V—Zerubbabel Compared To The Future King David? (2:20-23) (Given the same day)

1. (14) The Lord will shake the heavens and the earth. (21)

   Note: Some commentators regard this shaking as political upheaval. Others understand it to be physical upheavals in nature.

2. (26?) The Lord will overthrow thrones, and destroy the strength of the kingdoms of the heathens. Their horsemen will come down, every one by the sword of his brother. (22)
3. (32?) In that day, I will take thee, O Zerubbabel, and will make thee as a signet, for I have chosen thee. (23)

   Note: A signet is a seal-ring used in signing documents. It is a symbol of authority.

   This passage is controversial in its nature and is open to differing interpretations. Some regard it as a tribute to Zerubbabel in his day. They are unable to show any recorded evidence of any change in Zerubbabel's position to indicate his special calling before the Lord. Such a calling may have existed, but Bible history does not show it.

   Other interpreters regard the prophecy as an allusion to the great destruction which will reduce the power and dominion of the heathen nations in the last days. (See Dan. 7:9, 11-12[3]) It is understood that the calling of David the Prince will take place

---

[3]For a number of explanatory statements regarding this period see *Prophecy—Key to the Future*, chapter X.

shortly after that destruction. If Zerubbabel is regarded as a prophetic type of the future David, the interpretation fits the order of the passage. (See also Zech. 3, 4)

The interpretation of this passage, like that of many other prophetic allusions in the Bible, should be left open until more information is available.

Doctrinal Analysis:

The Nature of God:

1. Build the temple. I will take pleasure in it, and I will be glorified. (1:8)

Judgment:

1. Ye have not built my house; therefore the heaven over you is stayed from dew, and the earth is stayed from her fruit. (1:10)
2. I smote you with blasting and with mildew and with hail in all the labours of your hands; yet ye turned not to me. (2:17)

Personal Revelation:

1. The Lord stirred up the spirit of the people so that they came and did work on the Temple. (1:14)
2. My spirit remaineth among you. (2:5)

The Last Days:

Outlined in the text above.

Counsel for Righteous Living:

1. Consider your ways. Ye have sown much and bring in little, ye eat but have not enough. Consider your ways. (1:5-7)
2. The people obeyed the voice of their God and the words of their prophet. (1:12)
3. Be strong, all ye people of the land, saith the Lord, and work: for I am with you. (2:4)

Author and Date of Authorship: The authorship of Haggai at the time of his mission is generally accepted.

Style of The Book:
1. The book is entirely in prose, although Haggai at times shapes his statements in the parallel form of Hebrew poetry.
2. His writing is simple and plain.
3. He frequently asks questions and then answers them himself.
4. Most critics depreciate the book as literature because of its simplicity, but praise it for its historical value.

Textual Transmission: The Hebrew text, in spite of some apparent corruptions, seems to have been transmitted well.

Bible Criticism:

The book is regarded as a valid account of the beginning of the rebuilding of the temple: Its historicity is not generally challenged. Critics regard 2:18, the laying of the foundation, as evidence that the temple was begun in 520 B. C., however, and challenge Ezra's account of the edict of Cyrus and the return of the Jews in 538 B. C. as fictitious.

Summary: After studying the book of Haggai, the student should know:
1. Haggai and Zechariah were the two prophets whose message and leadership brought the work on the temple to completion.
2. The Temple was constructed, in the main, from 520 to 516 B. C.
3. The three messages of the book:
    A. Man does not prosper when he ignores the work of the Lord to work for his own selfish ends.
    B. The Lord aids man when man labors in His work.
    C. The temple in the latter days will be glorious.

CHAPTER XXVII

ZECHARIAH

Prophet's Name: Zechariah (Zĕch-ă-rī'-ăh) means "Jehovah remembers."

Scriptural Information About the Prophet:
1. He was the son of Berechiah (Bĕr-ē-chī'-ăh), the son of Iddo (id'dō) the prophet. (1:1; Ezra 5:1; 6:14) Iddo apparently returned from the exile with Zerubbabel. (Neh. 12:4)
2. He prophesied with Haggai to bring about the construction of the Jerusalem temple. (Ezra 5:1; 6:14)
3. He prophesied in the second (1:1) and fourth (7:1) years of the reign of the Persian king Darius.

Date of Zechariah's Mission: c. 520-518 B. C.

This date is derived from its relationship to the reign of king Darius.

Prophesied To: The Jews who had returned from the Babylonian captivity.

Contemporary Prophet: Haggai 520 B. C. To the Jews who had returned from Babylonian captivity.

Contemporary Prophets Contrasted:

Zechariah's writing reveals a more complex individual than was Haggai. He saw a variety of visions and centered much of his comment on the events of the last days. His prophecies are profound and are extremely difficult to interpret. Zechariah's writing uses much apocalyptic imagery while Haggai's message is forthright and plain.

Haggai was a plain-speaking individual who worked actively to achieve a specific objective. His message is matter-of-fact and specific. It is presented in a reasoning manner designed to anticipate and counter any objections which might be raised to it.

ZECHARIAH

Contemporary Kings and Rulers:

Judah: Zerubbabel

He was the first governor appointed by the Persians to lead the Jews in their return to their homeland. By the time of Zechariah's mission he had governed for about eighteen years.

Persia: Darius (Hystaspes) 521-485 B. C.

The Persian Empire reached its greatest extent under his rule.

National Conditions in Judah:

—Political:

1. Judah was still a vassal state to Persia.
2. The Jews had been allowed to return to their homeland and rebuild their temple by Cyrus; the first group had returned to Judah eighteen years previous to Zechariah's mission.
3. The Jews were unable to claim more than about one-fourth of their original territory. During their captivity other groups, primarily the Samaritans, had expanded and had occupied their territories.
4. Intense resistance had been exerted by the Samaritans against the rebuilding of the temple. Their deceit had brought the work to a halt eight years before Zechariah's mission. (See Ezra 3, 4)

—Economic:

1. As yet Judah did not have an established economy. Her people were still living on a temporary, unsettled basis.
2. They had wealth which they had brought from Persia but there was little opportunity to use it without the established forms of trade being available.
3. As their religious fervor diminished and work on the temple halted, the people began to rebuild their own homes and to work to meet their personal needs. Their work was relatively unproductive.

—Religious:

1. The people had restored the practice of offering sacrifices shortly after their return.

2. Those who returned to Judah were primarily the devout men of Judah who had come back to re-establish their religious life. Their situation was somewhat comparable to the Pilgrims, Puritans, and the Saints during the early days of the Utah period.
3. Their failure to rebuild the temple in the early days of the return, however, had brought about a spirit of religious indifference which was retarding the progress of the people.

Outline of the Book:

The book is often divided into two sections: Zechariah's dated prophecies (1-8) and his undated prophecies (9-14).

Chapter 1—The Lord Will Restore Judah and Punish Its Enemies.

1. The Lord has been sore displeased with their fathers because they would not turn from evil and hearken unto Him. They are admonished not to be as their fathers were. (1-6)
2. **First Vision:** The Lord Will Have Mercy on Jerusalem.

   Note: This is the first of a series of eight visions which Zechariah saw all in one night.

   A. A man was riding up on a red horse, followed by other horses which were red, speckled, and white. (8)
   B. The angel said they were those whom the Lord had sent to walk to and fro through the earth. (9-11)
   C. The angel asked the Lord how long would he not have mercy on Jerusalem and Judah. (12-13)
   D. The Lord is displeased with the heathen that are at ease. (15)
   E. (33?)[1] The Lord is returned to Jerusalem with mercies: his house shall be built in it. (16)
   F. (39?) His cities through prosperity shall yet be spread abroad. The Lord shall yet comfort Zion and shall yet choose Jerusalem. (17)
3. **Second Vision:** The Four Horns and the Four Carpenters.

   A. Zechariah saw four horns which had scattered Judah, Israel, and Jerusalem. (18-19)
   B. Zechariah saw four carpenters who came to fray them and cast out the horns of the Gentiles. (20-21)

---

[1]Numbers in parentheses at the beginning of items refer to the fifty events of the last days listed in Chapter Four.

ZECHARIAH 601

> Note: It is difficult to specify the four horns (although Egypt, Syria, Assyria, Babylon, and Persia are often mentioned). It is even more difficult to identify the carpenters. Yet the meaning is clear: God will bring His judgment upon those who have afflicted His people Israel.

Chapter 2—**The Redemption of Judah and the Battle of Armageddon.**
1. **Third Vision**: The Redemption of Judah and the Battle of Armageddon.
    A. A man with a measuring line came to measure Jerusalem. (1-2)
    B. (39) Jerusalem shall be inhabited as towns without walls for the multitude of men and cattle therein, for the Lord will be a wall of fire around about, and will be the glory in the midst of her. (3-5)
    C. (30-31) Israel is to flee from the land of the north and deliver herself from Babylon. (6-7)
    D. (35) The Lord will shake His hand upon the nations that spoil Israel, and they shall be a spoil to the servants, and ye shall know that the Lord of hosts hath sent me. (8-9)
    E. (39) The Lord will come and dwell in the midst of Israel. (10)
    F. (40) Many nations shall be joined to the Lord in that day. (11)
    G. (30) The Lord shall inherit Judah his portion in the holy land, and shall choose Jerusalem again. (12)

Chapter 3—**Joshua Compared to the Branch of the Last Days.**
1. **Fourth Vision**: Joshua Compared to the Branch of the Last Days.
    A. The Lord rebuked Satan, who was resisting Joshua, the high priest. (1-2)
    B. The Lord had Joshua remove his filthy garments as a symbol that the sins of the people would be removed. (3-5)
    C. Joshua was told if he would walk in the Lord's ways, he would judge the Lord's house. (6-7)
    D. The Lord will bring forth His servant the Branch. (8)

Note: Some commentators have understood Joshua to be the branch, but that does not appear to be the correct interpretation. Rather, Joshua is compared to a ruler, David the prince, who will also walk in God's ways but will rule in the last days when the iniquity of the land is removed. (see verses 9 & 10)

   E. (42) The Lord will remove the iniquity of that land in one day. (9)

   F. (44) In that day shall ye call every man his neighbor under the vine and under the fig tree. (10)

Chapter 4—Zerubbabel Will Build the Temple.
1. **Fifth Vision:** The Golden Candlestick and the Two Olive Trees.

   A. Zechariah saw a golden candlestick and two olive trees. (1-3)

   B. The word of the Lord unto Zerubbabel: (5-10)

   (1). Not by might, nor by power, but by my spirit, saith the Lord. (6)

   (2). Before Zerubbabel the great mountain shall become a plain. His hands have laid the foundation of this house, and His hand shall also finish it. (7-10)

   C. (35) The two olive branches are the two anointed ones, that stand by the Lord of the whole earth. (12-14)

   Note: These two olive trees are understood to represent the two prophets who will fall and be resurrected in Jerusalem during the Battle of Armageddon. (see Rev. 11:4)

Chapter 5—Visions of Judgment and the Removal of Sin.
1. **Sixth Vision:** The Flying Roll.

   A. Zechariah saw a flying roll, twenty cubits long and ten cubits wide. (1-2)

   B. (42) The roll is a record of those that steal and swear. Those that commit those crimes shall be cut off. (3-4)

2. **Seventh Vision:** Sin Taken to Shinar.

   A. Zechariah saw an ephah (ē'-phäh) and a talent of lead which was compared to a woman. (5-7)

   Note: An ephah was a measuring basket a bit larger than a bushel basket. A talent weighed either 100 or 200 pounds.

   B. This is wickedness. He cast the lead into the midst of the ephah. (8)

ZECHARIAH 603

    C. Two women with wings like a stork carried the ephah of wickedness to the land of Shinar. (9-11)

    Note: The land of Shinar is the land of Babylonia.

Chapter 6—Joshua: A type for the Branch of the Last Days.

1. **Eighth Vision:** The Four Chariots.

   A. Four chariots pulled by different-colored horses came out from between two mountains. (1-3)

   B. The chariots were the four spirits of the heavens, which go forth from standing before the Lord of all the earth. (4-7)

   C. The chariots that went to the north country quieted the Lord's spirit in the north country. (8)

2. Crowns were taken and set upon the head of Joshua, the high priest. (9-11)

3. (32) Speak unto Joshua saying, (12-13)

   A. Behold the man whose name is The Branch,

   B. He shall grow up out of his place,

   C. He shall build the temple of the Lord,

   D. He shall bear the glory, and shall sit and rule upon His throne.

   E. He shall be a priest upon His throne,

   F. The counsel of peace shall be between them both.

   Note: It would appear that once again Zechariah uses Joshua as a type and symbol for the Branch in the last days. While he was a type, he did not fulfill the details of the prophecy as the prince of the last days is expected to do.

4. The crowns were to be left as a memorial in the temple. (14)

5. (33) They that are far off shall come and build in the temple of the Lord. (15)

Chapter 7—The Nature of True Religion.

1. The people raised the question as to whether or not they should continue their religious fasts. (1-3)

2. Did they fast for the Lord, or did they eat and drink for themselves? (5-6)

3. The former prophets said to execute true judgment, show mercy, and imagine no evil. (7-10)

4. The people refused to hearken to the former prophets, so the Lord refused to hear their cries, and scattered them among the nations. (11-14)

Chapter 8—**The Glory of Jerusalem in the Last Days.**
1. (39) The Lord will return to Zion, and will dwell in the midst of Jerusalem. It will be called the city of truth; and the mountain of the Lord of hosts, the holy mountain. (3)
2. (41) Old people and young children will dwell happily in Jerusalem. (4-6)
3. (30-31) The Lord will save His people from the east and the west and will bring them to Jerusalem. (7-8)
4. (38) They shall be the Lord's people, and He shall be their God. (8)
5. Be strong, for the Lord will no longer afflict His people. Now the crops will be fruitful, and the Lord will no longer punish His people. (9-15)
6. Speak the truth to your neighbor and imagine no evil. (16-17)
7. The fasts of Judah shall be joy and gladness. (18-19)
8. (41) People from many cities and nations will come to seek the Lord in Jerusalem. (20-22)
9. (41) Ten men of all nations shall take hold of a Jew, saying, we will go with you, for we have heard that God is with you. (23)

Chapter 9—**Prophecies of Future Combat With Greece; the Coming of the Savior**
1. A list of cities from Syria, Phoenicia and Philistia which were to fall (to the Greeks, both to Alexander the Great and to the Seleucids.) (1-8)
2. Rejoice, O daughter of Jerusalem: behold thy king cometh unto thee: He is just, and having salvation; lowly, and riding upon an ass, and upon a colt the foal of an ass. (9)
   Note: This prophecy of Christ in the meridian of time is quoted and its fulfillment is shown in Mt. 21:1-9.
3. (44?) The Lord will speak peace to the heathen, and His dominion shall be from sea even to sea, and from the river even to the ends of the earth. (10)
4. (43?) As for thee also, by the blood of thy covenant I have sent forth thy prisoners out of the pit wherein is no water. The Lord will render double unto thee. (11-12)
   Note: This may be a vague allusion to the doctrines of resurrection and salvation for the dead. (See D & C 128:22; Is. 14:15; 24:22; Ezek. 31:16; 32:21-30; etc.)

ZECHARIAH 605

5. The Lord will defend the sons of Zion against the sons of Greece. (13-17)

Chapter 10—**The Gathering of Ephraim.**
1. The Lord will make bright clouds, and give them showers of rain. (1)
2. The idols have spoken vanity and the diviners have seen a lie. The Lord's anger was kindled against the shepherds, and He punished the goats. (2-3)
3. (35) The Lord has made Judah as His goodly horse in the battle, and they shall be as mighty men. They shall fight, because the Lord is with them. (3-5)
4. (30-31) The Lord will strengthen the house of Judah, and will save the house of Joseph, and will bring them again to place them. (6)
5. (31) They of Ephraim shall be like a mighty man. The Lord will gather them, and they shall increase as they have increased. They shall remember the Lord in far countries and turn again. (7-9)
6. (31) The Lord will gather Ephraim out of Egypt and Assyria and they will settle in Gilead and Lebanon, and place shall not be found for them. (10)
7. (31) Ephraim shall pass through the sea with affliction, and shall smite the waves in the sea, and all the deeps of the river shall dry up. (11-12)
8. (35) The pride of Assyria shall be brought down, and the sceptre of Egypt shall depart away. (11)

Chapter 11—**The Allegory of the Foolish Shepherd: The Past History of Israel.**
1. Lebanon, Bashan and Jordan is spoiled. (1-3)
2. The flock is delivered every man into his neighbor's hand, and into the hand of his king. Their shepherds feed the flock of the slaughter and pity them not. (4-6)
3. The Lord fed the flock and cut off three of the wicked shepherds, but the flock loathed Him. (7-8)
4. The Lord left the people to themselves and broke off His staff, Beauty, meaning His covenant with them. (9-11)
5. They weighed for the Lord's price thirty pieces of silver. They were cast to the potter in the house of the Lord. (12-13)

Note: This passage is quoted in the New Testament as a prophecy concerning the Savior in the meridian of time. (See Mt. 26:14-16; 27:3-10) Matthew, however, attributed the prophecy to Jeremiah.

6. The Lord broke His other staff, Bands, meaning the brotherhood between Judah and Israel. A foolish shepherd would eat the flesh of the fat, and tear their claws in pieces. (14-17)

Chapter 12—The Battle of Armageddon.
1. (35) They will lay siege both against Judah and against Jerusalem. (1-2)
2. (35) All that burden themselves with Judah in that day shall be cut in pieces, though all the people of the earth be gathered together against it. (3)
3. (35) In that day the Lord will smite every horse with astonishment and blindness and his rider with madness. (4)
4. (30) The governors of Judah shall say in their heart, The inhabitants of Jerusalem shall be my strength in the Lord. In that day the governors of Judah shall devour the people round about, and Jerusalem shall be inhabited again. (5-6)
5. (35) The Lord shall save the tents of Judah first, that the glory of the house of David and the inhabitants of Jerusalem do not magnify themselves against Judah. (7)
6. (35) In that day shall the Lord defend the inhabitants of Jerusalem; and he that is feeble among them at that day shall be as David. The Lord will seek to destroy all the nations that come against Jerusalem. (8-9)
7. (38) The Lord will pour upon the house of David and upon the inhabitants of Jerusalem the spirit of grace and of supplication, and they shall look upon me whom they have pierced. (10)
   Note: John applied this passage in reference to the crucifixion of Christ. (see Jn. 19:37)
8. (35) In that day shall there be a great mourning in Jerusalem, as the mourning of Hadadrimmon in the valley of Megiddon. (11-14)

Chapter 13—The Battle of Armageddon and Christ's Appearance to the Jews.
1. (30-31) In that day there shall be a fountain opened to the house of David and to the inhabitants of Jerusalem for sin and for uncleanness. (1)

ZECHARIAH 607

2. (30-31) False prophets will be thrust through when they prophesy. (2-5)
3. (37, 38) One shall say unto Him, What are these wounds in thine hands? Then He shall answer, Those with which I was wounded in the house of my friends. (6)

Note: See also D & C 45:48-54.

4. (35) In all the land, two parts therein shall be cut off and die; but the third shall be left therein and shall be refined as silver is refined. (7-9)

Chapter 14—**The Battle of Armageddon.**
1. (35) The spoil will be divided in the midst of thee. (1)
2. (35) The Lord will gather all nations against Jerusalem to battle. The city shall be taken, and half the city shall go into captivity, and the residue of the city shall not be cut off from the city. (2)
3. (37) The Lord shall stand in that day upon the mount of Olives and the mount shall cleave in the midst thereof toward the east and toward the west, and there shall be a very great valley. (4)

Note: See D & C 45:48-49; 133:20.

4. (35) Ye shall flee to the valley of the mountains. (5)
5. (37) The Lord my God shall come, and all the saints with thee. (5)
6. (35) It shall come to pass in that day that the light should not be clear, nor dark, not day, nor night; at evening time it shall be light. (6-7)
7. (41) Living waters shall go out from Jerusalem; half of them toward the former sea, and half of them toward the hinder sea. (8)
8. (37) The Lord shall be king over all the earth in that day. (9)
9. (35) The land shall be turned as a plain from Geba to Rimmon. (10)
10. (30) Jerusalem shall be inhabited from Benjamin's gate unto the place of the first gate, unto the corner gate, and from the tower of Hananeel unto the king's winepresses. (10-11)
11. (35) This will be the plague wherewith the Lord will smite all the people that have fought against Jerusalem: Their flesh, eyes and tongue shall consume away. (12)
12. (35) A great tumult from the Lord shall be among them, and Judah also shall fight at Jerusalem. (13-14)

13. (35) The wealth of all the heathen round about shall be gathered together. (14)
14. (35) And so shall be the plague of the horse, mule, camel, ass, and all the beasts that shall be in these tents, as this plague. (15)
15. (41) Everyone that is left of all the nations which came against Jerusalem shall even go up from year to year to worship the King. Upon those that do not come up to worship, there shall be no rain. (16-17)
16. (41) If Egypt does not come up to worship there shall be the plague. (18-19)
17. (41) In that day shall there be upon the bells of the horses, Holiness Unto the Lord. The pots shall be like the bowls before the altar. All they that sacrifice shall come and take of them, and seethe therein. (20-21)
18. (41) In that day there shall be no more the Canaanite in the house of the Lord of hosts. (21)

Doctrinal Analysis:

The Sins of the People:

1. They did not hear, nor hearken unto me, saith the Lord. (1:4)
2. They refused to hearken, and pulled away the shoulder, and stopped their ears, that they should not hear. (7:11)
3. The idols have spoken vanity, and the diviners have seen a lie, and have told false dreams; they comfort in vain. (10:2)

The Nature of God:

1. I am returned to Jerusalem with mercies. (1:16)
2. I will be their God, in truth and in righteousness. (8:8)
3. How great is his goodness, and how great is his beauty! (9:17)
4. Mine anger was kindled against the shepherds, and I punished the goats. (10:3)
5. The Lord stretcheth forth the heavens, and layeth the foundation of the earth, and formeth the spirit of man within him. (12:1)

The Lord Governs the Fate of Man:

1. I set all men every one against his neighbor. (8:10)

ZECHARIAH

Prophecies of Christ in the Meridian of Time:
1. Rejoice greatly, O daughter of Zion; shout, O daughter of Jerusalem: behold, thy King cometh unto thee: he is just, and having salvation; lowly, and riding upon an ass, and upon a colt the foal of an ass. (9:9)
2. They weighed for my price thirty pieces of silver. And I took the thirty pieces of silver, and cast them to the potter in the house of the Lord. (11:12-13)

Prophets and Revelation:
1. Not by might, nor by power, but by my spirit, saith the Lord of hosts. (4:6)
2. The Lord sent the law and words in his spirit by the former prophets. (7:12)

Judgment:

—Man's Attitude Toward God Determines God's Attitude Toward Man:
1. Turn ye unto me, saith the Lord of hosts, and I will turn unto you. (1:3)
2. I am very sore displeased with the heathen that are at ease; for I was but a little displeased, and they helped forward the affliction. (1:15)
3. They made their hearts as an adamant stone, lest they should hear the law; therefore came a great wrath from the Lord of hosts. (7:12)
4. Therefore it is come to pass, that as he cried, and they would not hear; so they cried, and I would not hear, saith the Lord of hosts: (7:13)

—God Tries Man:
1. I will bring the third part through the fire, and will refine them as silver is refined, and will try them as gold is tried. (13:9)

—Records are Kept:
1. The flying roll had the names of those who steal and swear. They will be cut off. (5:1-4)

—Punishment Is Based on Actions:
1. Like as the Lord of hosts thought to do unto us, according to our ways, and according to our doings, so hath he dealt with us. (1:6)

—God Knows Men's Thoughts and Actions:

1. They are the eyes of the Lord, which run to and fro through the whole earth. (4:10)

The Last Days:

Indicated in the outline above.

Satan:

1. Satan was seen resisting an angel. (3:1-2)

Counsel for Righteous Living:

1. Be silent, O all flesh, before the Lord: for He is raised up out of His holy habitation. (2:13)
2. If thou wilt walk in my ways, and if thou wilt keep my charge, then thou shalt also judge my house, and shalt also keep my courts, and I will give thee places to walk among these that stand by. (3:7)
3. When ye fasted and mourned, did ye at all fast unto me, even to me? (7:5)
4. Should ye not hear the words which the Lord hath cried by the former prophets? (7:7)
5. Execute true judgment, and show mercy and compassions every man to his brother: and oppress not the widow, nor the fatherless, the stranger, nor the poor; and let none of you imagine evil against his brother in your heart. (7:9-10)
6. Fear not, but let your hands be strong. (8:13)
7. Speak ye every man the truth to his neighbour; execute the judgment of truth and peace in your gates: and let none of you imagine evil in your hearts against his neighbour; and love no false oath. (8:16-17)
8. Love the truth and peace. (8:19)
9. Let us go speedily to pray before the Lord, and to seek the Lord of hosts. (8:21)
10. Ask ye of the Lord rain in the time of the latter rain. (10:1)
11. Their heart shall rejoice in the Lord. (10:7)

Style of the Book:

1. The book is in prose, except for 9:1-11:3; 11:17; 13:7-9.
2. The prose is usually simple and straightforward.

ZECHARIAH

3. The symbols and imagery of the book are quite complicated and usually require explanation.
4. His poetry is often lacking in rhythm, and many of his parallelisms lack symmetry.
5. His style tends to change to suit his topic more than the other prophets.

Textual Transmission: The Hebrew text is corrupt and has a number of passages where the corruptions make the meaning obscure. It appears, also, that certain portions of the text have been moved from their original location and the order is altered.

Author and Date of Authorship:

Most critics regard Zechariah as the author of chapters 1-8 only. The remainder is attributed either to an anonymous author writing before the fall of Israel to Assyria or else to an anonymous author writing between 333 and 280 B. C.

Bible Criticism:

Bible criticism is centered mainly in efforts to show a dual authorship for the book and establish a case for either early or late authorship of chapters 9-14. As is the case with most of the apocalyptic prophecies of the Old Testament, many of the scholars regard Zechariah's prophecies of the last days as imaginative story telling rather than revelation.

Changes Made in the Inspired Version of the Bible—
Book of Zechariah

King James Translation	Inspired Version
4:10—. . . they are the eyes of the Lord, which run to and fro . . .	4:10—. . . they are the **servants** of the Lord, which run to and fro . . .
4:14—. . . These are the two anointed ones, that stand by the Lord of the whole earth.	4:14—. . . These are the two anointed ones, that stand **before** the Lord of the whole earth.
6:5—. . . These are the four spirits of the heavens, which go forth . . .	6:5—. . . These are the four **servants** of the heavens, which go forth . . .
8:7—. . . Behold, I will save my people from the east country, . . .	8:7—. . . Behold, I will **gather** my people from the east country . . .

King James Translation	Inspired Version
8:13—. . . so will I save you, and ye shall be a blessing . . .	8:13—. . . so will I **gather** you, and ye shall be a blessing . . .

Summary: After studying the book of Zechariah the student should know:
1. Zechariah and his contemporary prophet Haggai prophesied about eighteen years after the beginning of the return from the Jewish exile.
2. They were instrumental in the completion of the Jerusalem Temple.
3. The major themes of Zechariah are concerned with the last days:
    A. The restoration of Israel.
    B. The gathering of Ephraim (the ten tribes).
    C. The Branch (compared to the high priest, Joshua).
    D. The battle of Armageddon.
    E. Christ's appearance on the mount of Olives.
4. Zechariah adds certain teachings not found in the writings of the other Old Testament prophets:
    A. Christ will appear on the mount of Olives. That mount will split and provide an avenue of escape for the Jews during the battle of Armageddon.
    B. Christ will reveal His wounds to the Jews to prove His identity.
    C. Two-thirds of Israel will perish in the Battle of Armageddon.
    D. Half of Jerusalem shall go into captivity.
    E. Those that fight against Jerusalem shall be smitten with plague.

CHAPTER XXVIII

MALACHI

Prophet's Name: Malachi (Măl'-ă-chī) means "my messenger."

Scriptural Information About the Prophet: Nothing is known, nor is the name used elsewhere in the Old Testament.

Date of Malachi's Mission: c. 460 B.C.
1. The three abuses which he criticizes are the degeneracy of the priesthood, intermarriage with foreign women, and failure to meet financial obligations to the Lord. These are the abuses of the days of Ezra and Nehemiah (See Ezra 9:2; 10:1-44; Neh. 10:30, 32-39; 13:4-14, 23-31.)
2. He ministered in a time when Judah was ruled by a governor. (1:8) It is a time when the priests have attended to temple duties for so long they have grown weary of them. (1:13)

Prophesied to: Judah.

Contemporary Prophets: None.

National Conditions:

—Political
1. Judah was still a vassal state to Persia.
2. A spirit of discontent existed among the people. They had come to realize that theirs was not the glorious return of which the prophets had spoken.

—Economic
1. Bad harvests had added to the feeling of disappointment and lack of concern for religion.

—Religious
1. A spirit of religious indifference and moral laxity existed.
2. People had come to doubt the divine justice of the Lord.
3. Priests and temple workers performed their rites in a disinterested, ineffective manner. Improper sacrifices were being offered.

4. Mixed marriages were common and there was an increasing divorce rate.
5. The people were failing in the payment of their tithes and offerings.

Outline of the Book:

Chapter 1—The Sins of Judah: Ritual Neglect.
1. The Lord has loved Israel. The proof: Israel's enemy, Edom, has been laid waste. (2-5)
2. The people have not feared and honored God. The proof: (6)
    A. They offer polluted bread upon the Lord's altar. (7)
    B. They offer blind and sick animals for sacrifice. (8)
    C. They have profaned the Lord's table. (12)
    D. They have been weary of serving the Lord. (13)
3. The Lord has no pleasure in the people and will not accept their offerings. (9-10)
4. (41)[1] The Lord's name will be great among the Gentiles and among the heathen. (11)

Chapter 2—The Sins of Judah: A Degenerate Priesthood, Intermarriage, and Divorce.
1. A commandment for the priests. (1-10)
    A. If ye will not hear and lay it to heart, I will send a curse upon you. I will corrupt your seed. (2-3)
    B. The Lord had a covenant with Levi. The Lord gave him life and peace. Levi feared the Lord, walked with God in peace and equity, and turned many away from iniquity. (4-6)
    C. The priest's lips should keep knowledge. He is the Lord's messenger. (7)
    D. The priests have caused many to stumble at the law and have shown partiality. Therefore the Lord has made them contemptible before all the people. (8-9)
    E. Why do we deal treacherously against our brothers by profaning the covenant of our fathers? (10)
2. Judah has married foreign women who serve strange gods. The Lord will cut off the man that doeth this. (11-13)

---
[1] Numbers in parentheses at the beginning of items refer to the fifty events of the last days listed in Chapter Four.

MALACHI 615

3. Ye have dealt treacherously with the wife of your youth. The Lord hates "putting away" or divorce. (14-16)
4. Ye have wearied the Lord by saying "Everyone that doeth evil is good in the sight of the Lord," and "Where is the God of judgment?" (17)

Chapter 3—A Messenger Will Prepare For the Lord's Coming; Tithing and A Book of Remembrance.

Note: This chapter is quoted in 3 Ne. 24.

1. (3) A messenger will prepare the way before the Lord suddenly comes to His temple. When the Lord comes He will be like a refiner's fire to purify the sons of Levi. (1-3)

    Note 1: Moroni quoted a portion of Malachi Chapter three to Joseph Smith among the passages he said were about to be fulfilled. Although it is not recorded what part he quoted, it seems probable that he quoted verses 1-3 or 1-6. The remainder of the chapter seems to pertain to Malachi's time, with the exception of verses 16-18. (See JS 2:36, 40.)

    Note 2: The time of the coming of the messenger is determined from Moroni's statement that it was about to be fulfilled in Joseph Smith's day. The passage itself also makes the time of its fulfillment clear. The messenger is to precede a coming of the Lord in which He comes like a refiner's fire (an extremely hot fire) and like fuller's soap (a strong lye soap which is too powerful to be handled without protective clothing). This coming, then, is His appearance in glory, when He will purge the righteous and destroy the wicked.

    Note 3: The identity of the messenger was explained by the Saviour Himself. While speaking of John the Baptist He said,
    This is he, of whom it is written, Behold, I send my messenger before thy face, which shall prepare thy way before thee.
    For I say unto you, Among those that are born of women there is not a greater prophet than John the Baptist . . . (Lu. 7:27-28)
    Yet the prophecy speaks of John's coming in a last days setting, not during the meridian of time.

Note 4: When John the Baptist came he was functioning in the office of a forerunner. A person who is called to perform such work is said to be possessed with the spirit and calling of Elias. This was the meaning of Jesus' statement when his disciples asked him—

... Why then say the scribes that Elias must first come?

And Jesus answered and said unto them, Elias truly shall first come, and restore all things.

But I say unto you, That Elias is come already, and they knew him not, but have done unto him whatsoever they listed. Likewise shall also the Son of man suffer of them.

Then the disciples understood that he spake unto them of John the Baptist. (Mt. 17:10-13)

Some difficulty exists because Bible scholars have not been able to differentiate between the **title** Elias and the proper name Elias. The title refers to one who has the calling to prepare the way before another individual. (See also D & C 110:12, 27:6; HC 6:250.)

Note 5: The prophecy seems to find fulfillment in the appearance of John the Baptist to Joseph Smith and Oliver Cowdery on May 15, 1829. (See JS 2:68-73; D & C 13; D & C 27:7-8, 128:24, 88:31-34.)

2. (38) Then shall the offering of Judah and Jerusalem be pleasant unto the Lord. (4)
3. (42) The Lord will come in judgment upon the wicked, but the sons of Jacob will not be consumed. (5-6)
4. The people have robbed God of tithes and offerings. (7-12)
   A. Robbing God has cursed the whole nation. (9)
   B. The blessings promised for tithing payment:
      (1). The Lord will pour out a blessing that there shall not be room enough to receive it. (10)
      (2). The devourer shall be rebuked so the fruits of your land shall not be destroyed, neither shall your vine cast her fruit before the time in the field. (11)
      (3). All nations shall call you blessed. (12)
      (4). Ye shall be a delightsome land. (12)
5. Your words against the Lord have been stout. Ye have said, "It is vain to serve God: and what profit is it that

MALACHI   617

we have kept his ordinance . . . they that tempt God are
even delivered." (13-15)
6. (43) A book of remembrance was kept for them that
feared the Lord. They will be spared when the Lord
makes up his jewels. Then shall ye return, and discern
between the righteous and the wicked. (16-18)

> Note: In Biblical times the meritorious service rendered
> by individuals was written down so the individual
> could be rewarded at a future time. (See Esther 2:23;
> 6:1-11. See also Moses 6:5-6.)

Chapter 4—The Coming of Elijah and The Destruction of the Wicked.

Note: This chapter is quoted in 3 Ne. 25.

1. (42) The day cometh when all that do wickedly shall be as stubble. (1)

> Note: Chapter four of Malachi was also quoted by Moroni
> with the understanding that it was about to be ful-
> filled. (See JS 2:36-37, 40.) A significant change was
> made in this verse, however. Moroni explained the
> source of the fire that destroys the wicked when Christ
> comes. Instead of saying "The day that cometh shall
> burn them up . . ." as the Malachi text reads, he said,
> "**They** that come shall burn them . . ." (JS 2:37)
> (See also D & C 29:9, 24, and 133:64.)

2. (35?) The Sun of righteousness shall arise with healing in his wings, and ye shall tread down the wicked. (2-3)
3. Remember the statutes and judgments of the law of Moses. (4)
4. (3) Elijah the prophet shall come before the coming of the great and dreadful day of the Lord. He shall come and turn the hearts of the fathers to the children and the hearts of the children to the fathers, lest I come and smite the earth with a curse. (5-6)

> Note 1: When Moroni quoted this passage he made cer-
> tain alterations in it as follows:
>
>> Behold, I will **reveal unto you the Priesthood, by
>> the hand of** Elijah the prophet, before the coming of
>> the great and dreadful day of the Lord.
>> And he shall **plant in the hearts of the children
>> the promises made to the fathers, and the hearts of
>> the children shall turn to their fathers. If it were**

not so, the whole earth would be utterly wasted at his coming. (JS 2:38-39)

The alterations in the text of Mal. 3:1-3 and 4:5-6 which Moroni made must have been paraphrasing designed to increase Joseph Smith's understanding, for the Savior quoted the passages to the Book of Mormon peoples as they stand in Malachi's Old Testament text.

Note 2: Elijah appeared with Moses to Peter, James and John on the mount of transfiguration. (See Mt. 17: 1-9; D & C 63:20-21.) Some difficulty exists because Bible scholars have not been able to differentiate between the names of Elias and Elijah.

Note 3: Malachi's prophecy was fulfilled with the appearance of Elijah to Joseph Smith and Oliver Cowdery in the Kirtland Temple on April 3, 1836. Elijah committed the keys of this dispensation to the two Church leaders. (D & C 110:13-16)

Note 4: Joseph Smith gave this explanation of the keys which Elijah restored:

... The spirit, power, and calling of Elijah is, that **ye have power to hold the key of the revelation, ordinances, oracles, powers and endowments of the fullness of the Melchizedek Priesthood and of the kingdom of God** on the earth; and **to receive, obtain, and perform all the ordinances belonging to the kingdom of God,** even unto the turning of the hearts of the fathers unto the children, and the hearts of the children unto the fathers, even those who are in heaven.

... Now comes the point. What is this office and work of Elijah? **It is one of the greatest and most important subjects that God has revealed.** He should send Elijah to seal the children to the fathers, and the fathers to the children.

... I wish you to understand this subject, for it is important; and if you will receive it, **this is the spirit of Elijah, that we redeem our dead, and connect ourselves with our fathers which are in heaven,** and seal up our dead to come forth in the first resurrection; and here we want the power of Elijah to seal those who dwell on earth to those who dwell in heaven.

MALACHI 619

This is the power of Elijah and the keys of the kingdom of Jehovah.

... **What you seal on earth, by the keys of Elijah, is sealed in heaven; and this is the power of Elijah,** and this is the difference between the spirit and power of Elias and Elijah; for while the spirit of Elias is a forerunner, **the power of Elijah is sufficient to make our calling and election sure;** and the same doctrine, where we are exhorted to go on to perfection, not laying again the foundation of repentance from dead works, and of laying on of hands, ressurection (sic) of the dead, &c.

We cannot be perfect without the fathers, &c. We must have revelation from them, and we can see that the doctrine of revelation far transcends the doctrine of no revelation; for one truth revealed from heaven is worth all the sectarian notions in existence.

This spirit of Elijah was manifested in the days of the apostles, in delivering certain ones to the buffetings of Satan, that they might be saved in the days of the Lord Jesus. They were sealed by the spirit of Elijah unto the damnation of hell until the day of the Lord, or revelation of Jesus Christ. (HC 6:251-252)

In summary:

A. **The power of Elijah:** The power to make what is sealed on earth be also sealed and binding in heaven.

B. **The spirit of Elijah:** The desire to redeem our dead and connect ourselves with our forefathers which are in heaven.

Doctrinal Analysis:

Sins:

1. Ye offer polluted bread upon mine altar. (1:7)
2. Ye said, Behold, what a weariness is it (of worshipping the Lord.) (1:13)
3. Ye have caused many to stumble at the law. Ye have corrupted the covenant of Levi. (2:8)
4. Each man deals treacherously against his brother. (2:10)
5. Judah hath profaned the holiness of the Lord. (2:11)
6. Judah hath married the daughter of a strange god. (2:11)

7. Ye have wearied the Lord with your words. (2:17)
8. Ye say, Everyone that doeth evil is good in the sight of the Lord and He delighteth in them. (2:17)
9. Ye are gone away from mine ordinances, and have not kept them. (3:7)
10. Ye have robbed God in tithes and offerings. (3:8)
11. Your words have been stout against me. (3:13)
12. Ye have said it is vain to serve God. (3:14)
13. They call the proud happy, and say that they that work wickedness are set up and delivered. (3:15)

Judgment:
1. I have no pleasure in you, saith the Lord, neither will I accept an offering at your hand. (1:10)
2. If ye will not hear, and if ye will not lay it to heart, to give glory unto my name, saith the Lord, I will even send a curse upon you, and I will curse your blessings. (2:2)
3. I will spare them, as a man spareth his own son that serveth him. (3:17)

The Nature of God:
1. I loved Jacob, and I hated Esau. (1:2-3)
2. A son honoureth his father, and a servant his master: if then I be a father, where is mine honour? and if I be a master, where is my fear? (1:6)
3. Hath we not all one father? hath not one God created us? (2:10)
4. I am the Lord, and I change not. (3:6)

Counsel for Righteous Living:
1. Beseech God that he will be gracious unto us. (1:9)
2. My covenant was with him of life and peace; and I gave them to him for the fear wherewith he feared me, and was afraid before my name. (2:5)
3. The law of truth was in his mouth, and iniquity was not found in his lips: he walked with me in peace and equity, and did turn many away from iniquity. (2:6)
4. The priest's lips should keep knowledge, and they should seek the law at his mouth. (2:7)
5. Take heed to your spirit. (2:15)
6. Bring ye all the tithes into the storehouse, and prove me now herewith, if I will not open you the windows of heaven. (3:10-12)

MALACHI

7. A book of remembrance was written before him for them that feared the Lord. (3:16)

Author and Date of Authorship:

Some Bible critics believe the term Malachi was not actually a person's name, but that the title of the book was taken from "my messenger" in 3:1. Their assertion is that the book may have been written by Ezra or by the individual who compiled the volume of the twelve prophets.

This explanation is untenable to Latter-day Saints, who know of the Savior's words to the Nephites:

> And it came to pass that he commanded them that they should write the words which the Father had given unto Malachi, ...
>
> And these are the words which he did tell unto them, saying: Thus said the Father unto Malachi ... (3 Ne. 24:1)

The exact time of his writing is not known. It is clear that he lived in the post-exilic period. Synagogue tradition makes him a contemporary of Nehemiah.

Style of the Book:

1. The book is written entirely in prose.
2. Malachi adopted an unusual literary form, in which he
    A. briefly states his message,
    B. gives the contradiction or objection which it will probably provoke, and
    C. gives his reply to the opposition and reinforces his position. Examples of this technique are found in 1:2-5; 1:6-8; 2:13-16; 3:7-12; 3:13-15. This dialectic treatment eventually became the major method of exposition for the Jewish schools.
3. His arguments are not profound, yet they are simple and realistic.
4. His writing shows vigor and forcefulness.
5. Like the book of Haggai, the book of Malachi is regarded as unimportant as a literary piece but valuable as a historical source.

Textual Transmission: The text has been transmitted well.

Bible Criticism:

Almost all criticism centers around the dating of the book.

Summary:

After studying the book of Malachi, the student should know:
1. Malachi labored to overcome three evils:
    A. Neglect of the proper forms of worship.
    B. Intermarriage among the Gentiles.
    C. Non-payment of tithes and offerings.
2. The book has two significant prophecies of the restoration:
    A. The messenger who will prepare the way before the Lord's coming: John the Baptist.
    B. The coming of Elijah the prophet.
3. References showing the fulfillment of these prophecies:
    A. John the Baptist: Lk. 7:27-28—He is the messenger. JS 2:68-73—He restored the Priesthood.
    B. Elijah: D & C 110:13-16—He restores the keys. HC 6:251-252—Joseph Smith's explanation of the power and spirit of Elijah.
4. Powers and missions defined:
    A. The spirit of Elias—to be a forerunner.
    B. The spirit of Elijah—the desire to redeem our dead and connect ourselves with our forefathers which are in heaven.
    C. The power of Elijah—the power to make what is sealed on earth be also sealed and binding in heaven. This power pertains to all ordinances.
5. Malachi contains important passages on two other doctrinal subjects:
    A. The covenant of the priesthood. (2:1-10)
    B. The importance of tithes and offerings. (3:8-13)
6. The four blessings of tithing payment:
    A. The Lord will pour out a blessing that there shall not be room enough to receive it.
    B. The devourer shall be rebuked so the fruits of your land shall not be destroyed, neither shall your vine cast its fruit before the time in the field.
    C. All nations shall call you blessed.
    D. Ye shall be a delightsome land.

CHAPTER XXIX

JOEL

Prophet's Name: Joel (Jō'-ĕl) means "Jehovah is God."

Scriptural Information About the Prophet:
1. He was the son of Pethuel (Pĕ-thū'-ĕl). (1:1)

Date of Joel's Mission:
   There is no unity of scholarly opinion on the dating of the book of Joel. Lack of external evidence makes the dating dependent upon internal clues only. Since the internal evidence is subject to widely divergent interpretations, scholars generally date the book either very early or very late. Those who date it early usually place it during the reigns of the Jewish kings Joash (c. 837-797 B.C.), or Uzziah (c. 792-740 B.C.). Those who date it late usually place it after the time of Nehemiah, from 400 to 350 B.C. The major reason for placing it late in Judah's history is that it carries the apocalyptic spirit which is believed to have been characteristic of the later period.

Prophesied to: Judah.

Contemporary Prophets:

   Not known because of the indefinite period of his mission.

Outline of the Book:

Chapter 1—Suffering From Famine and Drought as An Army Devastates the Land.

1. Old men, hath this been in your days, or even in the days of your fathers? Tell your children of it and have them teach their children. (1-3)

   Note: The answer to this question governs the interpretation of this chapter of the book of Joel. If the answer is yes, the devastation already happened, then chapter one of Joel is history. If the answer is no, and the elders are being told to remember and transmit Joel's prophecy, then the event is a happening of

the last days and is related to the latter portion of the book.
2. Locusts have cut off the food and drink of the nation. (4-5)

Note: Palmerworms, cankerworms and caterpillars are all representations of locusts in different stages of development.

3. (35)¹ A strong nation has come and laid the countryside bare. (6-7)
4. (35) The offering is cut off from the house of the Lord and the priests mourn. (8-9)
5. (35) The field is wasted and the harvest is perished. (10-12)
6. (35) The priests howl for the drink offering is withheld. Call a solemn assembly and gather the elders into the house of the Lord. (13-14)
7. (35) The day of the Lord is at hand. As a destruction from the Almighty shall it come. (15)
8. (35) Fire hath devoured the wilderness and the rivers of water are dried up. (16-20)

Note: Many critics interpret chapter one and 2:1-17 as a description only of the ravages of locusts. An unbiased reading reveals clues which make it readily apparent that the locusts, the burning and the lack of food are only the aftermath of an attacking army which has devastated the land. These clues include,

A. A nation is come upon my land, strong, and without number . . . (1:6)
B. A great people and a strong . . . (2:2)
C. They shall run like mighty men . . . (2:7)
D. When they fall upon the sword, they shall not be wounded . . . (2:8)
E. Give not thine heritage to reproach, that the heathen should rule over them . . . (2:17)
F. I will remove far off from you the northern army . . . (2:20)

Do locusts comprise a nation? Are locusts heathens? Do people fight locusts with a sword?

---

¹Numbers in parentheses at the beginning of items refer to the fifty events of the last days listed in Chapter Four.

Rather than interpret the passage as a description of locusts being represented metaphorically as a human army, shouldn't the figure be placed in reverse? Isn't this a clear-cut description of an organized human army that has been compared to locusts? With this understanding all major problems of interpretation disappear. No longer must one search in vain for supporting prophecy of attacking locusts. It becomes clear that chapters one and two describe the same event as chapter three: the Battle of Armageddon.

Chapter 2—The Battle of Armageddon

1. (35) Blow the trumpet and sound the alarm in Zion, the holy mountain, for the day of the Lord is nigh at hand. (1)

   Note: Some L. D. S. commentators have asserted that the term "day of the Lord" is an indication that the passage in which it is used refers to the final coming of Christ in glory. Such an assertion does not hold true in the light of scripture. The term "day of the Lord" is used 24 times in the Bible. In a third of these instances the passage clearly refers to instances of the Lord's retribution in times other than events of the last days. Another third makes such ambiguous reference to the term as to be useless for interpretation. The remaining third is divided between references to the Battle of Armageddon and the Lord's final coming in glory. While the phrase "day of the Lord" is often a key that a passage should refer to latter-day happenings, it is unsafe to relegate the term to a single interpretation. It can be interpreted as a reference to any of several times when the Lord has poured out His wrath upon the wicked.

2. (35) A day of darkness, gloominess, clouds, and thick darkness in the morning. (2)
3. (35) A great people and a strong. There shall not be another people like it for many generations. (2)
4. (35) A flame burns before and behind them. They leave the land desolate. (3)
5. (35) A description of the approaching army: (4-9)

A. As horsemen, so shall they run. (4)
B. Like the noise of chariots in the tops of mountains shall they leap. (5)
C. They shall run like mighty men. (7)
D. They shall climb the wall like men of war. (7)
E. They shall not break their ranks. (7)
F. When they fall upon the sword they shall not be wounded. (8)
G. They shall run to and fro in the city. They shall enter in at the windows like a thief. (9)

6. (35) The earth shall quake before them; the heavens shall tremble. (10)
7. (35) The sun and the moon shall be dark, and the stars shall withdraw their shining. (10)

Note: D & C 29:14 alludes to this passage and places this time in a proper chronological order. The context has described the final coming of the Lord in glory with all the hosts of heaven and the calling forth of the righteous dead (D & C 29:8-13).

Then the passage lists a series of events which will precede His final coming: But, behold, I say unto you that **before this great day shall come, ...**

A. The sun shall be darkened, the moon shall be turned to blood, and the stars shall fall from heaven. (D & C 29:14)
B. A great hailstorm shall destroy the crops of the earth. (D & C 29:16)
C. The Lord will take vengeance upon the wicked. (D & C 29:17)
D. Flies will eat the flesh of the inhabitants of the earth. (D & C 29:18)
E. Men's flesh shall fall from their bones. (D & C 29:19)
F. The beasts and fowls shall devour them up. (D & C 29:20)
G. The great and abominable church shall be cast down by devouring fire. (D & C 29:21)

Thus it becomes clear that this is an event which will precede the final coming of Christ in glory (as does the Battle of Armageddon) rather than accompany His final coming. (See also D & C 45:42.)

JOEL   627

8. (35) The Lord shall utter his voice before his army: for his camp is very great: for he is strong that executeth his word. (11)
9. (35) The day of the Lord is great and very terrible; and who can abide it? (11)
10. (35) Repent and read your hearts. (12-14)
11. (35) Let the priests pray that the heathen shall not rule over them. (15-17)
12. (35) Then the Lord will pity his people and send them corn. (18-19)
13. (35) The Lord will remove far off the northern army and drive him to a barren land where his face is toward the east sea and his back toward the utmost sea. (20)

> **Note:** The East sea is the Salt Sea or Dead Sea (cf. Ezek. 47:18). The utmost sea is the Mediterranean.

14. (35) The army's stink and ill savour shall come up. (20)
15. (35) The Lord will restore the rain and the food which has been lost. (21-26)
16. (35) The Lord will be in the midst of Israel, and His people will know He is their God. (27)
17. (41) It shall come to pass **afterward** that the Lord will pour out His spirit on all flesh. Your sons and daughters shall prophesy, old men will dream dreams and young men shall see visions. (28-29)

> **Note:** This passage is often interpreted by Latter-day Saints as referring to the Church at the present time. Yet the prophecy definitely refers to a time following the Battle of Armageddon and the conversion of the Jews. It should also be pointed out that while the passage makes general reference to the Spirit being poured out upon all flesh, the prophecy is directed specifically to the people who will be living in Palestine during that era.
>
> The temptation to take prophecies of future events and claim fulfillment by present situations has long been present. Is it possible that Peter did just that as he quoted this passage to explain the actions of the early disciples? (See Acts 2:14-21.) It would appear that such was the case. There can be no doubt that this passage pertains to the last days, however, for Moroni quoted it to Joseph Smith and told him

"this was not yet fulfilled, but was soon to be." (J.S. 2:41)

It is recognized, of course, that the gifts of the Spirit exist within the Church today and that prophecy, dreams and visions are presently manifested among the Saints. Yet the prophecy still seems to speak of a time yet future.

18. (35) The Lord will show wonders in the heavens and in the earth: blood, and fire, and pillars of smoke. The sun shall be turned into darkness and the moon into blood, before the great and terrible day of the Lord come. (31)
19. (41) Deliverance shall be in Mount Zion and in Jerusalem and in the remnant whom the Lord shall call.

Chapter 3—The Battle of Armageddon.

1. (35) In that time when the Lord shall bring again the captivity of Judah and Jerusalem the Lord will gather all nations and bring them down into the valley of Jehoshaphat and will plead with them there. (1-2)

    Note: To "bring again" means "to end."

2. (35) The nations have sold and scattered Israel. The Lord will recompense His enemies and Judah will sell their children to the Sabeans. (3-8)
3. (35) Proclaim war among the Gentiles, and beat your plowshares into swords. (9-10)
4. (35) Assemble the heathen. Let them come up to the valley of Jehoshaphat, for there the Lord will sit to judge all the heathen round about. (11-13)
5. (35) Multitudes, multitudes in the valley of decision. (14)
6. (35) The day of the Lord is near in the valley of decision. (14)
7. (35) The sun, moon, and stars shall be darkened. (15)
8. (39) The Lord also shall utter his voice out of Jerusalem. So shall ye know that He dwells in Zion. (16-17)
9. (41) The hills shall flow with milk, the rivers of Judah shall flow with waters, and a fountain shall come forth of the house of the Lord and shall water the valley of Shittim. (18)
10. (34) Egypt shall be a desolation, and Edom shall be a desolate wilderness. (19)

JOEL 629

11. (39) Judah shall dwell forever, for the Lord dwelleth in Zion. (20-21)

Doctrinal Analysis:

The Nature of God:

1. He is gracious and merciful, slow to anger, and of great kindness. (2:13)
2. Then will the Lord be jealous for his land, and pity his people. (2:18)
3. The Lord will do great things. (2:21)
4. God hath given you the former rain, and he will cause to come down for you the rain. (2:23)
5. The Lord will be the hope of his people, and the strength of the children of Israel. (3:16)

Personal Revelation:

1. I will pour out my spirit on all flesh; and your sons and daughters shall prophecy, your old men shall dream dreams, your young men shall see visions. (2:28-29)

The Last Days:

Outlined in the text above.

Counsel for Righteous Living:

1. Tell your children of it, and let your children tell their children, and their children another generation. (1:3)
2. Sanctify ye a fast, call a solemn assembly, gather the elders and all the inhabitants of the land into the house of the Lord and cry unto the Lord. (1:14)
3. O Lord, to thee will I cry. (1:19)
4. Saith the Lord, turn ye even to me with all your heart, and with fasting, and with weeping, and with mourning, and rend your heart, and not your garments, and turn unto the Lord your God. (2:12-13)
5. Sanctify a fast, call a solemn assembly: gather the people, sanctify the congregation. (2:15-16)

Author and Date of Authorship:

Joel is accepted as the author. The book was probably written between 400 and 350 B.C. Some scholars place it 450 years earlier.

Style of the Book:

1. The book is almost entirely in poetry, with the exception of the superscription and 2:30-38.
2. He uses vivid imagery and description.
3. His poetry is rhythmic and his parallelisms are regular.
4. His organization is smooth and careful. He makes few abrupt changes of subject.
5. His language is lofty and polished.
6. His book reveals taste and skill in writing. It is regarded as one of the best written of the Old Testament.

Textual Transmission: The Hebrew text has been transmitted well.

Bible Criticism:

Criticism for Joel is limited, and centers mostly in the date of the book and in discussions of whether chapters one and two are historical description, allegory, or prophetic descriptions of events of the last days. Some critics have pointed to the parallels between Joel and more than half of the prophetic books. These parallels stem from the common references to the Battle of Armageddon.

**Changes Made in the Inspired Version of the Bible—
Book of Joel**

King James Translation	Inspired Version
1:6—. . . whose teeth are the teeth of a lion, . . .	1:6— . . . whose teeth are **as** the teeth of a lion, . . .
2:13— . . . slow to anger, and of great kindness, and repenteth him of the evil.	2:13— . . slow to anger, and of great kindness, and **he will turn away the evil from you.**
2:14—Who knoweth if he will return and repent, and leave a blessing behind him; even a meat offering and a drink offering unto the Lord your God?	2:14—**Therefore repent, and** who knoweth but he will return and leave a blessing behind him; **that you may offer** a meat offering, and a drink offering, unto the Lord your God.

JOEL

Summary:

After studying the book of Joel the student should know:
1. It is uncertain whether Joel was the earliest or the latest of the writing prophets of the Old Testament.
2. There is controversy concerning whether chapter one is a description of an unknown event of the past or a prophetic description of a future happening.
3. There is controversy concerning whether chapters one and two describe an invasion of locusts or an invading army.
4. The major lesson of the book: God will judge the heathen in the Battle of Armageddon.
5. Moroni quoted a portion of the book to Joseph Smith, saying that it was about to be fulfilled.

INDEX

This index is limited to names, places, and major listings. Specific scriptural passages should be sought with the aid of a Bible concordance. Major references are shown in bold type.

A

Aaron: 295, 575.
Abednego: 502, 526.
Abiathar: 434.
Abijah: 45, 46, 47, 48, **71, 181, 232.**
Abijah (Son of Jeroboam): 188.
Abijam: See Abijah.
Abraham: 36, 37, 356, 551.
Absalom: 45.
Accept Counsel: 91.
Achor, Valley of: 135, 144, 153, 276.
Acrostic: 423, 424, 483, 484.
Adad-nirari II: 173.
Adad-nirari III: 173, 247, 253, 260, 273, **303.**
Adam (Michael, Ancient of Days): **130-131,** 504-510, 516, 520, 522.
Adam-ondi-Ahman: **131,** 504, 506, 508, 509, 520, 526.
Adoram: See Hadoram.
Afghanistan: 510.
Agency of Man: 77, 88-89, 228-233, 245.
Ahab (False Prophet): 452.
Ahab (King of Israel): 51, 52, 53, 54, 55, **71,** 177-178, **182, 183, 185,** 196, 197, 198, 199, 200, 202, 203, 204, 205-208, 218, 219, 230, 248, 295.
Ahasuerus: See Xerxes.
Ahaz: 64, 65, 66, **72, 184, 186,** 270, 272, 282, 283, 297, 299, 300, **303,** 307, 308, 309, **319,** 337, 425.
Ahaziah (Azariah, Jehoahaz, King of Judah): 55, 56, 57, **71, 178, 182, 183,** 198, 200-201, **303.**
Ahaziah (King of Israel): 53, 54, **71, 178, 182,** 209.
Ahijah: 44, 47, 49, **187-189.**
Ahikam: 449.
Aholah: 541.
Aholibah: 541.
Aid the Afflicted and Oppressed, Help Others: 91-92.
Alexander the Great: 429, 507, 511, 517, 525, 571, 604.
Alexandria: 310.

Amaziah: 60, 61, **72,** 179, **183,** 219, 220, 231, 299, 425.
Amenophis IV: 253.
America: **122, 123, 124, 125, 131,** 292, 324, 348, 349, 350, 353, 373, 376.
Amil-Marduk: See Evil Merodach.
Amitai: 62, 247.
Ammon, Ammonites: 53, 63, 64, 69, 130, 143, **182,** 184, 208-209, 232, 260, 269, 408, 418, 419, 451, 457, 519, 540, 541, 543, 585.
Amon: 68, 69, **73, 303,** 407, 413, 414.
Amos: 179, 181, 183, 247, **257-269,** 270, 271, 278, 284, 419, 474.
Amoz: 297.
Anata: 434.
Anathoth: 434, 436, 445, 452.
Ancient of Days: See Adam.
Anthon, Professor: 349.
Antigonus: 517.
Antiochus II: 517.
Antiochus III: 518.
Antiochus IV (Epiphanes): 508, 512, 513, 514, 518, 519, 525, 527.
Aphek: 217.
Apollo: 519.
Apostacy: 117-118, 261, 363, 501.
Arabia, Arabians, Arabs: 53, 63, 176, 182, 183, 325, 326, 425.
Arbela, Battle of: 571.
Archaemenean Empire: See Persia.
Ariel: See Jerusalem.
Armageddon, Battle of: 128, 142, 143-151, 155, 156, 157, 169, 276, 277, 281, 316-317, 324, 356-358, 359, 360, 373, 510, 513, 514, 527, 551, 552, 565, 601, 602, **607-608,** 612, 623-629, 630, 631.
Armenia: 174, 175.
Arses: 517, 570.
Artaxerxes (Longimanus): 517, 570, 573, 575, 581, 583, 590.
Artaxerxes II (Mnemon): 517, 571.
Artaxerxes III (Ochus): 517, 571.
Articles of Faith: 116.
Asa: 48, 49, 50, 51, **71, 181,** 193, 194.
Ashdod: 311.
Asher: 38, 411.
Ashtoreth: 260, 273.
Ashur-nasirpal II: 173, 249.
Ashurbanipal: **176,** 249, **403,** 413, 421, 492.

Asia Minor: 510, 526.
Asmonaeans: 41.
Asshur: 177, 403, 435.
Asshur-Lush: 174, 258, 260, 272, 273.
Assur-Dayan III: 174, 260, 272, 273, **303**.
Assyria, Assyrians: 39, 40, 63, 65, 66, 67, 68, 135, 139, 143, 148, **173-177**, 178, 180, 181, 184, **185**, 186, 189, 202, 230, 231, 233, 247, 248, 249, 250, 253, 254, 256, 258, 259, 260, 267, 272, 273, 274, 275, 277, 283, 284, 285, 286, 287, 294, 295, 297, 300, **303**, 307, 308, 309, 310, 311, 312, 314, 315, 316, 317, 319, 320, 321, 325, 326, 328, 330, 336, 338, 403, 404, 405, 406, **410**, 413, 414, 419, 421, 422, 432, **435**, 439, 442, 453, 487, 490, 491, 492, 494, 498, 507, 537, 541, 544, 545, 555, 574, 576, 601, 605, 611.
Astarte: 260, 273.
Astral Cults: 406.
Astyages: **492**, 498.
Athaliah: 57, 58, 72, 182, 183.
Author and Date of Authorship: listing explained, 8, Jonah 252-253, Amos 267, Hosea 279, Micah 294, Isaiah 376-380, Zephaniah 418, Nahum 420, Obadiah 427, Habakkuk 432, Jeremiah 473-474, Lamentations 483, Daniel 524, Ezekiel 562, Ezra 577, Esther 582, Nehemiah 588, Haggai 596, Zechariah 611, Malachi 621, Joel 629.
Avoid Evil: 92.
Azariah (King of Judah): See Ahaziah. See also Uzziah.
Azariah (Son of Oded): 50, **193-194**, 235.
Azias: See Uzziah.

B

Baal: 51, 52, 65, 68, 69, 177, 178, 179, 197, 207, 233, 260, 273, 279, 461.
Baalzebub: 200.
Baasha: 49, 50, **71**, 177, 188, 194, 195.
Babylon, Babylonia, Babylonians (See also Chaldea, Chaldeans): 39, 40, 41, 67, 68, 69, 70, 110, 122, 173, 174, 175, 176, 222, 230, 231, 249, 285, 287, 294, 295, **303**, 320, 321, 322, 324, 325, 326, 327, 328, 336, **403-405**, 406, 409, **410**, 411, 413, 415, 419, 421, 422, 424, 425, 430, 433, 435, 436, 438, 439, 442, 443, 445, 447, 448, 449, 450, 452, 453, 454, 455, 456, 457, 469, 479, 480, 483, 484, 485, **487-490**, 492, 493, 494, 495, 496, 497, 500, 506, 507, 526, 528, 529, 530, 538, 539-540, 541, 545, 559, 562, 563, 570, 574, 575, 592, 593, 598, 601, 603.
Banias: 518.
Baruch: 435, 451, 473, 474.
Bashan: 138, 153, 422, 453, 605.
Battle of Gog and Magog: 166.
Be Courageous and Strong: 92-93, 373.
Be Diligent: 93.
Be Humble: 93-94, 372.
Beeri: 270.
Beersheba: 198.
Behistun Rock: 570.
Bel: 326, 489.
Belshazzar: **303**, 488, 494, 497, 503, 504, 506, 510.
Belteshazzar: See Daniel.
Benhadad: 49, 52, 56, 177, 198, 202, 204, 215, 216, 219.
Benhadad (Son of Hazael): 59, 60, 179.
Benjamin: 38, 44, 434, 455, 585.
Ben-Sirach, Jesus: 379.
Berechiah: 598.
Berenice: 517.
Bethel: 45, 48, 190-191, 192, 193, 210, 211, 218, 258, 261, 264, 281.
Bethlehem: 257, 457.
Bible Criticism: listing explained 8-9, 12, 34, **190-191**, Jonah 253-256, Amos 267, Hosea 279-280, Micah 294-295, Isaiah 376-380, 400, Zephaniah 419, Nahum 424, Obadiah 427-428, Habakkuk 432, Lamentations 484, Daniel 525-526, Ezekiel 563, Ezra 578, Esther 582, Nehemiah 588, Haggai 597, Zechariah 611, Malachi 621, Joel 630.
Book of Mormon: 75, 118-119, 126, 128, 132, 133, 145, 153, 167, 288, 292, 296, 298, 307, 309, 311, 322, 323, 324, 325, 328, 338, 342, 348-349, 350, 351, 352, 353, 354, 355, 361, 373, **376-380**, 399, 400, 539, 548-551, 617, 621.
Book of the Law of the Lord: 69, 434.
Bosphorus: 569.
Buzi: 528.

INDEX

C

Caesarea: 516.
Calah: 174, 175, 248, 267.
Cambyses I: 569.
Cambyses II: 303, 492, 498, 516, 569, 573, 575.
Canaan, Canaanites: 160, 317, 608.
Capernaum: 339.
Carchemish, Battle of: 39, 303, 404-405, 410, 411, 435, 438, 439, 450, 544.
Carmel, Mt. Carmel: 138, 153, 197, 211, 212, 263, 353, 422, 453.
Caspian Sea: 551.
Cassander: 511, 517.
Caucasus Mountains: 176.
Chaldea, Chaldeans: 69, 176, 232, 233, 234, 321, 430, 432, 452, 453, 455, 536, 537, 555.
Charlemagne: 508.
Chebar River: 493, 528.
Chemarims: 415.
Chenanah: 205.
Cherith, brook: 196.
Chiun: 263.
Christ, Jesus: 128, 152, 160-163, 167, 169, 247, 255, 277, 285, 288, 293, 303, 311, 318, 337-346, 349, 354, 355, 358, 373, 378, 488, 500, 509, 514, 515, 532, 594, 604, 606, 607, 609, 612.
Chronicles, 2nd: 3, 36, 39, 43-70, 74, 187-246, 577, 588.
Chub: 544.
Cimmerians: 176.
Contemporary Kings: listing explained 7, Jonah 247, Amos 258, Hosea 271, Micah 283, Isaiah 300, Zephaniah 413, Jeremiah 438, Lamentations 480, Daniel 497-498, Ezekiel 530, Haggai 592-593, Zechariah 599.
Contemporary Prophets: listing explained 7, Jonah 247, Amos 258, Hosea 270, Micah 282, Isaiah 299, Zephaniah 413, Nahum 421, Obadiah 425, Habakkuk 429, Jeremiah 437, Daniel 496, Ezekiel 529, Haggai 592, Zechariah 598.
Contemporary Prophets Contrasted: listing explained 7, Amos 258, Hosea 271, Micah 282-283, Isaiah 299, Zephaniah 413, Habakkuk 429, Jeremiah 437, Daniel 496-497, Ezekiel 529-530, Haggai 592, Zechariah 598.
Counsel for Righteous Living: 91-114, 1 & 2 Ki., 2 Chron. 235-241, Jonah 251, Amos 266, Hosea 278, Micah 293, Isaiah 318-319, 335, 345, 370-373, Zephaniah 418, Habakkuk 431-432, Jeremiah 472-473, Lamentations 481-483, Daniel 524, Ezekiel 560-562, Ezra 577, Nehemiah 586-587, Haggai 596, Zechariah 610, Malachi 620-621, Joel 629.
Covenant: 94-95.
Criticism, Bible—See Bible Criticism.
Cushan: See Ethiopia.
Cushi: 412.
Cyaxares: 176, 404, 491-492, 494, 498.
Cyprus (Chittim): 518.
Cyrus II (Cyrus the Great): 41, 70, 191, 231, 235, 287, 303, 324, 326, 327, 336, 377, 488, 492-493, 494, 496, 498, 516, 569, 573, 574, 575, 576, 593, 597, 599.
Danube River: 569.
Damascus: 65, 66, 174, 180, 216, 260, 264, 273, 308, 309, 310, 316, 451.
Dan: 38, 45, 281.
Daniel: 130, 437, 485, 493, 494, 496-527, 537, 560, 564, 582.
Darius I: (Hystaspes, the Great): 303, 488, 517, 569-570, 573, 575, 592, 593, 594, 598.
Darius II (Nothius): 517, 571.
Darius III (Codomanus): 517, 571.
Darius the Mede: 498, 503, 504, 514.
Date of Mission: listing explained—7, Jonah 247, Amos 257-258, Hosea 270, Micah 282, Isaiah 299, Zephaniah 412, Nahum 421, Habakkuk 429, Jeremiah 436-437, Daniel 496, Ezekiel 528-529, Haggai 592, Zechariah 598, Malachi 613, Joel 623.
David (King of Israel): 38, 104, 149, 154, 165, 190, 224, 230, 232, 239, 265, 267, 338, 434, 461, 606.
David (Prince in Latter Days): 132, 135, 139-141, 155, 169, 276, 353-354, 356, 357, 373, 454, 460, 461, 513, 546-547, 549, 551, 553, 554, 565, 595-596, 601-602, 603.
Day of the Lord: 625.
Dead Sea: 554, 627.
Dedanim: 325.
Deioces: 491.
Demetrius Sotor: 509.
Do what is Right: 95-97.
Doctrinal Analysis: listing explained—8, 75-170, Jonah 251-

252, Amos 263-266, Hosea 274-278, Micah 285-293, Isaiah Section I 315-319, Section II 328-336, Section III 344-345, Section IV 365-373, Zephaniah 417-418, Nahum 423, Obadiah 427, Habakkuk 431-432, Jeremiah 462-473, Lamentations 481-483, Daniel 521-524, Ezekiel 554-562, Ezra 576-577, Nehemiah 586-587, Haggai 596, Zechariah 608-610, Malachi 619-620, Joel 629.
Doctrine and Covenants: D & C: 9, 30, 118, 119, 120, 121, 122, 123, 127, 128, 133, 144, 148, 150, 152, 153, 154, 161, 162, 163, 164, 166, 167, 168, 192, 325, 340, 352, 354, 355, 357, 364, 365, 416, 426, 429, 506, 507, 520, 524, 531, 532, 548, 576, 607, 616, 618, 622.
Dodavah: 209, 626.
Dothan: 214.
Dumah: See Edom.
Dur-Sharrukin: See Khorsabad.

E

Ebedmelech: 455, 456.
Ecbatana: 490, 495.
Edom, Edomites: 55, 61, 65, 130, 142, 143, 157, 182, 183, 208-209, 211, 219, 220, 229, 259, 260, 265, 267, 269, 272, 302, 308, 325, 326, 364, 425, 426, 427, 428, 451, 481, 519, 543, 545, 547, 613, 628.
Egypt, Egyptians: 38, 39, 40, 41, 43, 63, 67, 69, 130, 139, 143, 144, 148, 156, 160, 176, 181, 189-190, 229, 253, 259, 272, 275, 277, 287, **303**, 308, 310, 311, 312, 314, 316, 317, 357, 404, **405**, 408, 410, 411, 419, 432, 435, 436, 438, 439, 442, 450, 454, 455, 457, 458, 469, 471, 481, 493, 507, 510, 518, 519, 537, 538, 539, 540, 541, 544, 545, 555, 559, 569, 601, 605, 608, 628.
Ekron: 200.
Elah: 50, 66, 71, 177, 181, 195.
Elam, Elamites: 143, 175, **176**, 325, 436, 452, 469, 492, 545, 570.
Elath: 183.
Eli: 434.
Eliakim (Ruler in Jerusalem): 312, 314, 315.
Eliakim: See Jehoiakim.
Elias: 616, 618, 619, 622.
Eliashib: 585.
Eliezer: 209.
Elijah: 51, 52, 53, 54, 55, 56, 119, 178, 181, 185, **196-202**, 207, 210, 218, 233, 234, 252, **617-619**, 622.

Elisha: 52, 54, 55, 56, 57, 58, 60, 178, 181, 198, 202, **210-217**, 218, 225, 234, 252.
Elkosh: 421.
El-Meshed: 247.
Eltekeh: 310.
Ephraim: 38, 139, 219, 275, 308, 312, 316, 354, 460, 548-549, 605, 612.
Esaias: See Isaiah.
Esarhaddon: 173, 175, **176**, 310, 403.
Esau: 143, 166, 426.
Esdraelon: 197, 276, 281.
Esther: 3, 10, 567, 570, **579-582**.
Ethbaal: 51, 177.
Ethiopia, Ethiopians: 48, 130, 147, 159, 163, 266, 311, 315, 349, 417, 418, 419, 430, 436, 455, 456, 519, 544, 551.
Euphrates River: 404, 405, 435, 445, 453, 488, 489, 490, 493, 528.
Europe: 509, 510, 526, 569.
Evil-Merodach: **303**, 409, 456, **487**, 497.
Ezekiel: 118, 137, 378, 437, 485, 493, 496, 497, 524, 526, **528-565**.
Ezra: 3, 10, 107, 114, 325, 515, 567, 571, 572, 573, **574-578**, 579, 582, 583, 584, 588, 597, 613, 621.

F

Fast: 97-98.
Fear and Acknowledge God: 98-99, 370-371.

G

Gabriel: 511, 513, 514, 522.
Gad: 38.
Gadi: 62, 180.
Gain Knowledge: 99-101.
Galilee: 311, 338, 339, 345, 421.
Gath: 282.
Gath-hepher: 247, 248.
Gathering: 132-139.
Gaza: 267, 517, 518.
Geba: 149, 607.
Gedaliah: 73, 181, **303**, 406, **409-410**, 436, 438, 456, 457.
Gehazi: 213-214.
Gilead: 138, 139, 153, 453, 605.
Gilgal: 210, 212, 258, 264, 281.
Ginath: 50.
Give Glory to God: 101.
Goal of Scripture Study: 12, 22-23.
God, Godhood (See also Nature of God): 76-80, 89-91.
Gog: 144-151, 513, 551-552, 559.
Gog, Battle of: See Battle of Gog and Magog.

INDEX 637

Gomer (location): 147, 551.
Gomer (wife of Hosea): 273, 274, 279, 280.
Great and Abominable Church: 131-132.
Great Zab River: 248.
Greece, Greeks: 41, 500, 507, 511, 516, 517, 525, 527, 570, 571, 579, 604, 605.

H

Habaiah: 576.
Habakkuk: 10, 421, 428, **429-433**, 437.
Hadadrimmon: 149, 606, 621.
Hadoram: 43.
Haggai: 10, 567, 573, 575, 576, **592-597**, 598.
Haman: 580, 581, 582.
Hamath: 180, 221, 264, 267.
Hanani: 49, 194.
Hananiah: 445, 449-450.
Haran: 177, 403, 411, 435.
Hassuna ware: 249.
Hatmutal: 539-540.
Have Faith: 101-102, 373.
Have Mercy: 103.
Hazael: 52, 56, 59, 60, 178, 179, 183, 198, **216**.
Hazor: 451.
He-Goat: 510-514, 526-527.
Heleodorus: 509, 518.
Heliopolis: 310.
Herod: 277, 278.
Herodotus: 255, 315.
Hezekiah: 66, 67, 68, **73**, 107, 175, 184-185, 186, 229, 270, 272, 282, 283, 284, 294, 297, 299, 300, 301, 302, **303**, 314, 315, **319**, 324, 406, 412, 413, 437.
Hiddekel River: 516.
Higher Criticism: term explained—8, 253, 254, 279, 280, 294-295.
Hilkiah: 222, 407, 434.
History of the Church: 9, 123, 124, 131, 141, 166, 427, 510, 520, 616, 618-619.
Holy Roman Empire: 507-508.
Hope: 103.
Hophra: 458.
Hosea: 179, 181, 183, 258, 262, 267, **270-281**, 282, 283, 295, 299, 319, 399.
Hoshea: 66, 67, **73**, 175, 180, 181, 185, 271, 283, 300, **303**.
Huldah: 222-223, 407.

I

Iddo: 598.
Idols, Idolatry: 45, 48, 61, 67, 68, 69, 84, 184, 187, 188, 220, 225, 258, 273, 274, 275, 284, 285, 301, 313, 321, 406, 407, 414, 417, 444, 446, 458, 555.
Idumea: See Edom.
Imlah: 205, 282.
India: 570.
Inspired Version of the Bible: 6, history of—9-10, minor changes explained—10, 1 & 2 Ki., 2 Chron. 241-244, Jonah 256, Amos 268, Hosea 280, Isaiah 380-399, Nahum 424, Jeremiah 475-479, Daniel 526, Ezekiel 563-564, Nehemiah 588-590, Zechariah 611-612, Joel 630.
Iran: 510.
Iraq: 249, 510.
Isaac: 37.
Isaiah: 31, 68, 75, 179, 181, 183, 184, 185, 191, 222, 257, 267, **270**, 271, 282, 283, 287, 288, 294, 295, 296, 297-400, 406, 414, 416, 419, 474.
Isaiah, Literary Problem of: 377-380, 400.
Ishmael: 457.
Ishtar: 249, 489, 490.
Israel, House of: 153-154, 155, 158, 159.
Israel (Jacob): 38.
Israel (Northern Kingdom): 38, 43-67, 126, 132-139, 153, 173, 174, 175, 177-181, 182, 183, 184, 185, 186, 188, 189, 193, 195, 196, 198, 200, 202, 203, 205, 211, 216, 219, 220, 221, 231, 232, 233, 234, 236, 240, 245, 247, 248, 252, 257, 258, 259, 260, 261, 262, 264, 265, 266, 268, 269, 270, 271, 272, 273, 274, 275, 276, 279, 280, 282, 283, 284, 285, 288, 290, 291, **294**, 295, 296, 297, 298, 300, 301, 302, **303**, 307, 308, 309, 310, 312, 313, 317, 319, 320, 322, 323, 324, 325, 327, 328, 331, 332, 337, 339, 341, 350, 352, 353, 356, 358, 360, 362, 370, 413, 414, 415, 417, 418, 419, 425, 428, 437, 447, 453, 459, 460, 461, 465, 536, 537, 540, 541, 543, 544, 547, 549, 550, 551, 552, 554, 559, 560, 577, 600, 601, 606, 611, 612, 614.
Issachar: 38.

J

Jabash: 62.
Jabesh: 180.
Jacob: 37, 38, 92, 153, 163, 290, 291, 295, 320, 331, 333, 336, 341, 349, 370, 380, 381, 426, 482, 620.
Jahaziel: 208-209, 235.
James: 618.
Jason: 512.
Jehoahaz (Son of Jehu; King of Israel): 59, 72, 179.
Jehoahaz (Son of Joram; King of Judah): See Ahaziah.
Jehoahaz (Son of Josiah; King of Judah): 39, 69, 73, 407, 408, 409, 411, 419, 435, 438, 442, 448, 539-540.
Jehoash: See Joash.
Jehoiachin (Jeconiah, Joachin, Coniah): 40, 70, 73, 303, 405, 406, 408-409, 411, 419, 425-426, 435, 438, 448, 449, 453, 456, 479, 493, 497, 528, 530, 538.
Jehoiada: 57, 58, 59, 183, 219.
Jehoiakim (Eliakim): 39, 40, 69, 70, 73, 303, 408, 409, 411, 419, 435, 438, 448, 451, 473, 496, 497, 499, 523.
Jehoram (King of Israel): 54, 55, 56, 57, 71, 178, 198, 199.
Jehoram (King of Judah): 54, 55, 56, 71, 182, 200, 425.
Jehoshaphat: 51, 53, 54, 71, 178, 181-182, 186, 195, 205-208, 209, 211, 231.
Jehoshaphat, Valley of: 151, 628.
Jehosheba: 57.
Jehu (King of Israel): 52, 56, 57, 58, 62, 72, 178-179, 182, 198, 217, 218, 248, 259, 272.
Jehu (prophet): 49, 50, 194-195.
Jeremiah: 31, 39, 40, 41, 69, 70, 223, 234, 235, 258, 271, 283, 299, 408, 409, 413, 419, 421, 425, 427-428, 429, 434-484, 496, 497, 529, 564, 576, 606.
Jericho: 210, 211, 218, 221.
Jeroboam: 43, 44, 45, 46, 47, 48, 49, 71, 177, 187, 188, 190-191, 194, 195, 232, 234.
Jeroboam II: 61, 62, 72, 179-180, 185, 221, 247, 253, 257, 258, 261, 264, 268, 270, 271, 303.
Jeruel: 209.
Jerusalem: 43, 44, 45, 59, 61, 65, 70, 133-138, 141-142, 145, 148, 149, 153, 154, 155, 158, 159, 160, 165, 167, 168, 169, 183, 184, 185, 187, 190, 194, 300, 303, 309, 312, 314, 315, 320, 321, 322, 327, 329, 330, 339, 348, 352, 353, 357, 358, 360, 361, 363, 370, 405, 406, 408, 409, 411, 413, 416, 417, 425, 427, 434, 439, 443, 444, 455-456, 459, 460, 470, 479, 480, 481, 484, 497, 512, 514, 515, 516, 527, 529, 530, 534-542, 543, 544, 545, 553, 563, 564, 570, 572, 574, 576, 583, 585, 598, 600, 601, 602, 604, 606, 607, 608, 609, 612, 616, 628.
Jesse: 119, 140, 165, 354, 355.
Jezebel: 51, 52, 53, 57, 177, 178, 196, 198, 199, 207, 218.
Jezreel: 56, 134, 144, 197, 199, 218, 274, 275, 276, 281.
Jezreel (Son of Hosea): 274.
Joash (Jehoash; King of Israel): 60, 61, 72, 179, 182, 183, 217, 623.
Joash (Jehoash; King of Judah): 57, 58, 59, 60, 72, 183, 219.
Job: 537, 560.
Joel: 567, 623-631.
Johanan: 436, 457.
John the Baptist: 340, 345, 416, 615, 616, 622.
John the Revelator: 531, 532, 618.
Jonah: 62, 173, 174, 179, 181, 183, 192, 221, 247-256, 260, 273, 424, 582.
Jonathan: 436, 455.
Joppa: 250.
Joram: See Jehoram.
Jordan River: 202, 210, 213, 214, 219, 338, 339, 605.
Joseph (Father of Jesus): 277, 337.
Joseph (Son of Israel): 38, 354, 355, 605.
Josephus: 257, 379, 574.
Joshua: 141, 601, 612.
Josiah: 39, 69, 73, 190-191, 222, 223, 231, 295, 303, 404, 407, 408, 409, 411, 412, 413, 414, 419, 434-435, 437, 438, 442, 444, 479, 497, 529.
Jotham: 63, 64, 66, 72, 184, 270, 272, 282, 283, 297, 299, 300, 303.
Journal of Discourses: 120, 122, 123, 124, 125, 126, 128, 129, 131, 132, 138, 141, 144, 163, 166, 167, 168, 549.
Judah (Son of Jacob): 38.
Judah (Southern Kingdom): 38, 43-70, 71-73, 107, 132-138, 153, 154, 157, 173, 175, 178, 179, 181-186, 189, 190, 191, 193, 198, 200, 211, 219, 221, 222, 230, 232, 233, 234, 237, 257, 260, 267, 269, 270, 271, 272, 273, 276, 280, 282, 283, 284, 285, 287, 294, 295, 297,

INDEX

299, 300, 301, **303**, 307, 308, 309, 310, 311, 312, 314, 315, 316, 320, 321, 322, 323, 328, 336, 337, 356, 361, 364, 405, **406-411**, 412, 413, 414, 415, 416, 418, 419, 421, 422, 425, 426, 427, 429, 430, 433, 435, 437, 438, 439, 443, 444, 445, 446, 447, 448, 453, 454, 455, 457, 458, 459, 460, 471, 479, 480, 481, 496, 497, 499, 519, 528, 530, 534-542, 543, 547, 549, 550, 571, 573, 574, 575, 583, 587, 592, 593, 599, 600, 601, 605, 606, 613, 614, 616, 619, 623, 628, 629.
Judas Maccabeus: 512, 513.
Judges: 38.
Judgment, Final: 167.
Judgments, God's; 89-91, 1 & 2 Ki., 2 Chron. 228-229, Amos 263-265, Hosea 275-276, Micah 286-287, Isaiah Section I 316-318, Section II 330-331, Section III 344, Section IV 366, Habakkuk 432, Jeremiah 465-467, Ezekiel 558, Haggai 596, Zechariah 609-610, Malachi 620.

K

Karkar, Battle of: 248.
Kedar: 326, 451.
Keep Records: 103.
Keep the Sabbath: 103-104.
Khalule: 175.
Khorsabad: 175, 248.
Kingdom of God: 124-125.
Kings, 1st: 3, 36, **43-54**, 74, 187-246, 295.
Kings, 2nd: 3, 36, 39, 40, 54-70, 74, **187-246**, 411.
Kirtland Temple: 618.
Knowledge: 85.
Koldewey: 249.
Kuyunjik: 249.

L

Labashi-Marduk: 487, 497.
Lachish: 183, 220, 314.
Laenas, Gaices Pompitius: 518.
Lamanites: 126, 288, 292, 293, 349, 354.
Lamentations: 3, 10, 480-484.
Laodice: 517.
Last Days: 115-168, Amos 265, Hosea, 276-277, Micah 287-293, 295, Isaiah 301, **303**, 316-317, 347-365, Zephaniah 417, 418, Nahum 421-422, Obadiah 426-427, Habakkuk 430-431, Jeremiah 441, 454, 458-461, Daniel 499-501, 504-510, 513-514, 520-521, Ezekiel 530, 546-554, Haggai 594-595, Zechariah 604-608, Malachi 615-619, Joel 623-629.
Layard, Sir Austin Henry: 249.
Learn of God and Seek Him: 104-106, 370, 371.
Lebanon: 135, 139, 141, 349, 353, 359, 422, 476, 538, 605.
Lehi: 549, 550.
Levi, Levites: 38, 45, 58, 119, 585, 614, 615, 619.
Libnah: 182, 229.
Library, Recommended Basic: 18-19.
Libya, Libyans: 130, 519, 544, 551.
Literary Problem of Isaiah: 377-380, 400.
Live Harmoniously: 106.
Live Religion From the Heart, Not Ritualistically: 106-107.
Loammi: 274.
Lombards: 509.
Loruhamah: 274.
Lower Critics: term explained—8, 254-255, 280, 427-428.
Lucifer: 325, 336.
Lydia, Lydians: 404, 491-492, 544.
Lysimachus: 511, 517.

M

Maachah: 45, 48.
Maccabees: 426, 501, 509, 512, 513, 519, 527.
Macedonia: See Greece.
Magog: 144-151, 551-552, 559.
Maher-shalal-hash-baz: 297, 309.
Malachi: 10, 202, 567, **613-622**.
Manasseh (King of Judah): 68. 73, 222, 229, 231, 232, 294, 295, 300, **303**, **405**, **406**, 407, 417.
Manasseh (Son of Joseph): 38, 549, 550.
Marathon, Battle of: 570.
Marduk, temple of: 489.
Marry According to God's Law: 87, 107.
Mary: 277, 337-338.
Masistius: 255.
Mattaniah: See Zedekiah.
Mattathias: 512.
Matthew: 338-339.
Media, Medes: 173, 174, 176, 177, 249, **303**, 320, 324, 326, 336, 403, 404, 422, 439, 453, 487, **490-492**, 494, 495, 498, 501, 503, 507, 511.
Mediterranean Sea: 627.
Megiddo, Megiddon: 69, 143, 149, 231, 407, 435, 438, 606.

Melchizedek Priesthood: 618.
Memphis: 176.
Menahem: 62, 63, 72, 180, 271, 283, 300, 303.
Merodach-baladan: 68, 175, 324.
Meshach: 502, 526
Meshech: 147, 545, 551.
Micah: 10, 179, 181, 183, 270, 271, 282-296, 299, 319, 324, 399, 449.
Micaiah: 53, 178, 205-208, 282.
Michael: See Adam.
Midian, Midianites: 163, 430.
Millennium: 157, 164-166, 170, 355, 356, 361, 364, 365, 374.
Missouri: 123, 125, 126, 131, 323, 350, 351.
Mizpah: 457.
Moab, Moabites: 53, 54, 60, 69, 130, 143, 178, 182, 208-209, 211, 230, 232, 260, 309, 365, 408, 418, 419, 450, 465, 519, 543.
Moloch: 263, 295.
Monsul: 249.
Moreshath: 282.
Mordecai: 579, 580, 581, 582.
Moroni: 354, 615, 617, 618, 627, 631.
Moses: 38, 255, 260, 273, 277, 451, 469, 516, 575, 585, 586, 618.
Mt. Carmel: See Carmel, Mt. Carmel.
Mt. Ephraim: 44, 138, 139, 153, 453, 460.
Mt. Horeb: 210.
Mt. of Olives: 144-151, 152, 276, 513, 607, 612.
Mulek: 538-539, 549.

N

Naaman: 57, 213.
Nabonidus: 303, 487-488, 494, 497, 503.
Nabopolassar: 176, 303, 403, 404, 410, 413, 438, 487, 491.
Naboth: 53, 178, 199.
Nabu: 249.
Nadab: 48, 49, 71, 177.
Nahum: 421-424, 428, 437.
Naphtali: 38, 311, 338, 339.
National Conditions: listing explained—7, Jonah 248, Amos 258-260, Hosea 272, Micah 284, Isaiah 300-301, Zephaniah 413-414, Nahum 421, Obadiah 425, Jeremiah 439-440, Daniel 498, Ezekiel 530, Ezra 574, Esther 579, Nehemiah 583, Haggai 593-594, Zechariah 599-600, Malachi 613-614.

Nature of God and Godhood: 76-80, 1 & 2 Ki., 2 Chron. 224-225, 228-233, Jonah 251-252, Amos 265-266, Hosea 277, Micah 293, Isaiah 300-301, 317-318, 331-335, 344-345, 366-369, Zephaniah 418, Nahum 423, Obadiah 427, Habakkuk 431, Jeremiah 467-470, Lamentations 482-483, Daniel 522-523, Ezekiel 557-559, Nehemiah 586, Haggai 596, Zechariah 608, Malachi 620, Joel 629.
Nazareth: 247, 339, 343.
Nazarites: 263, 266.
Nebi Yunus: 248, 249.
Nebo: 326.
Nebuchadnezzar: 40, 41, 69, 70, 303, 321, 404, 405, 408, 410, 425, 436, 438, 443, 450, 451, 454, 456, 469, 470, 480, 487, 489, 493, 494, 469, 479, 480, 487, 489, 493, 494, 526, 530, 538, 543, 544, 559.
Necho: 39, 69, 231, 404, 405, 407, 408, 435, 438, 450, 479, 539-540.
Negroes: 266.
Nehemiah: 3, 92, 107, 111, 254, 525, 567, 570, 572, 577, 578, 583-591, 613, 621, 623.
Nephi, Nephites: 75, 288, 298, 348, 350, 550.
Neriglissor: 487, 497.
Nero: 41.
New Jerusalem: 125, 126, 128, 132, 168, 292, 293, 323, 350, 351, 358, 361, 373.
New Testament: 34, 118, 122, 128, 132, 144, 145, 148, 151, 152, 160, 166, 167, 168, 183, 247, 255-256, 261, 277-278, 311, 325, 338, 339, 340, 342, 343, 344, 346, 363, 378, 416, 524, 531, 606, 615, 616, 618, 622, 627.
Nimshi: 178.
Nineveh: 68, 109, 177, 221, 248-249, 250, 251, 252, 253, 254, 255, 256, 303, 403, 411, 415, 421, 422, 423, 424, 435, 491.
Nippur: 493, 528.
Noah: 537, 560.
No-Amon: See Thebes.

O

Obadiah (Governor): 52.
Obadiah (Prophet): 10, 425-428, 437, 451.
Obadiah (Servant of Ahab): 196, 207.
Oded: 50, 65, 184, 221, 308.
Omri: 50, 51, 71, 177, 295.

INDEX

Onias III: 512, 518.
Orontes River: 248.
Outline of the Book: listing explained—7, Jonah 250-251, Amos 260-262, Hosea 273-274, Micah 284-285, Isaiah Section I 307-319, Section II 320-336, Section III 337-344, Section IV 347-365, Zephaniah 415-417, Nahum 421-423, Obadiah 426-427, Habakkuk 429-431, Jeremiah 440-462, Daniel 499-521, Ezekiel 530-554, Ezra 574-576, Esther 579-581, Nehemiah 583-586, Haggai 594-596, Zechariah 600-608, Malachi 614-619, Joel 623-629.

P

Pakistan: 510.
Parsumash: 492.
Pashur: 435, 447.
Passengers, Valley of the: 148.
Paul: 30, 31, 416.
Pay Tithing: 107.
Pearl of Great Price: 116, 118, 119, 120, 121, 123, 160, 163, 164, 256, 354, 520, 615, 616, 617, 618, 622, 628.
Pekah: 64, 65, 66, 72, 174, **180**, 184, 185, 271, 283, 297, 300, **303**, 307.
Pekahiah: 63, 72, 180, 271, 283, 300, **303**.
Penuel: 44.
Pergamon: 518.
Persecution: 121-122.
Persepolis: 495.
Persia: 41, 70, 147, 176, **303**, 320, 324, 325, 326, 336, 452, 485, 487, 492-493, 494, 495, 496, 498, 500, 501, 507, 511, 516, 525, 527, 544, 551, 567, **569-573**, 574, 578, 579, 582, 583, 584, 588, 590, 592, 593, 598, 599, 601, 613.
Persis: 491.
Peter: 30, 31, 339, 618, 627.
Pethuel: 623.
Philistia, Philistines: 53, 63, 65, 67, 182, 183, 184, 200, 260, 269, 308, 311, 325, 425, 450, 543, 604.
Phoenicia, Phoenicians: 196, 260, 269, 604.
Phraortes: **491**.
Plataea: 570.
Poetry: 483, 484.
Porphyry: 526.
Pray and Seek Guidance: 108-109.
Pre-Mortal Life: 370, 442, 471.
Prepare the Heart: 107.
Priesthood: 111.

Prophecy: 82.
Prophesied to: listing explained—7, Jonah 247, Amos 258, Hosea 270, Micah 282, Isaiah 299, Zephaniah 413, Nahum 421, Obadiah 425, Habakkuk 429, Jeremiah 437, Ezekiel 529, Haggai 592, Zechariah 598, Malachi 613, Joel 623.
Prophet's Name: listing explained —7, Jonah 247, Amos 257, Hosea 270, Micah 282, Isaiah 297, Zephaniah 412, Nahum 421, Obadiah 425, Habakkuk 429, Jeremiah 434, Daniel 496, Ezekiel 528, Haggai 592, Zechariah 598, Malachi 613, Joel 623.
Prophets; Prophetic Functions: 81-83, 1 & 2 Ki., 2 Chron. 233-235, 245-246, Jonah 252, Amos 266, Isaiah 318, 334-335, 345, Habakkuk 431, Jeremiah 470-471, Daniel 523, Ezekiel 559-560, Ezra 576, Nehemiah 586, Zechariah 609.
Ptolemy, Ptolemies: 507, 511, 516-520, 527.
Ptolemy II: 517.
Ptolemy III: 517.
Ptolemy VI: 509.
Pul: See Tiglath Pileser III.
Punjab: 570.
Purim: 581, 582.

R

Rab-bath: 541.
Rabshakeh: 314, 315.
Ram: 510-514, 526-527.
Ramah: 139, 194, 436, 457, 460.
Ramoth-gilead: 53, 56-57, 178, 182, 198, 204, 205, 206, 208, 216, 218, 230.
Raphia: 310.
Ravenna: 509.
Rechabites: 435, 451
Red Sea: 259, 272.
Rehoboam: 43, 44, 45, 46, 47, 71, 181, 188, 189, 190, 232.
Remaliah: 180.
Reorganized Church of Jesus Christ of Latter Day Saints: 9.
Repent: 109-111.
Respect Authority: 111.
Restoration of the Church: 119.
Resurrection (first): **163-164**.
Resurrection (second): **166**.
Reuben: 38.
Rezin: 64, 65, 180, 184, 297, **307**.
Rimmon: 149, 607.

Rising of Slaves Against Their Masters: **121**.
Rod: 354-356.
Rome, Romans: 36, 41, 151, 500, 501, 507, 509, 515, 516, 518, 527, 572.
Russia: 551.
Ruth: 582.

S

Sabeans: 151, 628.
Salamia: 517.
Salamis: 570, 579.
Salt Lake City, Temple: 287-288, 361.
Samaria: 58, 137, 139, 175, 185, **186**, 199, 200, 202, 211, 214, 215, 221, 248, 281, 283, 286, 294, 300, **303**, 308, 309, 311, 316, 320, 460, 537, 538, 541, 563.
Samaritans: 572, 593, 599.
Sammuramat: 173.
Samuel: 469.
Sanballat: 583.
Sanhedrin: 571.
Sarah: 356.
Sarduris: 174.
Sargon II: 39, **175**, 181, 184, 185, 283, 294, 300, **303**, 309, 310, 325, 326, 424, 490.
Satan: 601, 610, 619.
Saudi Arabia: 510.
Saul: 38.
Saviors on Mt. Zion: 426, 427.
Scipio, Lucius Cornelius: 518.
Scriptural Information About the Prophet: listing explained 7, Jonah 247, Amos 257, Hosea 270, Micah 282, Isaiah 297, Zephaniah 412, Nahum 421, Obadiah 425, Habakkuk 429, Jeremiah 434-436, Daniel 496, Ezekiel 528, Haggai 592, Zechariah 598, Malachi 613, Joel 623.
Scythians: 412, 414, 415, 434, 442, 443, 491, 570.
Seir: See Edom.
Seleucus, Seleucids: 507, 511, 516-520, 527, 604.
Seleucus II: 518.
Seleucus III: 518.
Seleucus IV: 509, 518.
Sennacherib: 67, 68, **175**, 184, 185, **186**, 249, 272, 283, 295, 297, 300, **303**, 309, 312, **314**, 315, 319, 325, 376, 424.
Septuagint: 378, 419, 475, 483, 484, 524.
Servant Songs: 340-343, 346.

Serve and Obey God: 111-113.
Shadrach: 502, 526.
Shallum (King of Israel): 62, **72**, 180, 271, **303**.
Shalmaneser III: 173, 178, 248.
Shalmaneser IV: 174, 303.
Shalmaneser V: 39, 66, 67, **175, 181**, 283, 300, **303**, 424.
Shamash-shum-ukin: 176, 403.
Shamshi-Adad V: 173.
Shapat: 210.
Sharon: 353.
Shear-jashub: 297.
Shebna: 312.
Shechem: 43, 44, 281.
Shemaiah (False Prophet): 452.
Shemaiah (Man of God): 44, 46, **189-190**, 477.
Sheshbazzar: 574.
Shiloh: 188, 443.
Shinar: 603.
Shishak: 46, 47, 189-190.
Shittim: 160, 628.
Shunem: 212, 216.
Simeon: 38.
Shushan: 511, 580, 582.
Sin: 83-88, 1 & 2 Kings, 2 Chronicles 225-228, Amos 263, Hosea 274-275, Micah 285-286, Isaiah Section I 315, Section II 328-330, Section III 344, Section IV 365-366, Zephaniah 417-418, Nahum 423, Obadiah 427, Habakkuk 431, Jeremiah 462-465, Daniel 521, Ezekiel 554-557, Zechariah 608, Malachi 619-620.
Sind: 570.
Sinim: 127:351.
Smith, Joseph: 9, 10, 29, 340, 349, 354, 355, 356, 380, 427, 510, 520, 549, 615, 616, 618, 627, 631.
Snow, Erastus: 549.
Sodom: 137, 537, 538.
Solomon: 36, 38, 43, 44, 47, 187, 188, 224, 230, 434.
Sons of the Prophets: 217-219.
Style of the Book: listing explained 8, Jonah 252, Amos 267, Hosea 278-279, Micah 293-294, Isaiah 374-376, Zephaniah 419, Nahum 423-424, Obadiah 427, Habakkuk 432, Jeremiah 474-475, Lamentations 483-484, Daniel 524-525, Ezekiel 562-563, Haggai 597, Zechariah 610-611, Malachi 621, Joel 630.
Summary: listing explained 10, This Book and How To Use It

INDEX 643

12-14, How To Study and Interpret Scripture 34-35, Understanding Bible History and Chronology 74, Six Major Doctrines 168-170, Historical Summary: Assyria—Fall of Israel 185-186, The Early Prophets and Their Messages 245-246, Jonah 256, Amos 268-269, Hosea 280-281, Micah 295-296, Isaiah Section I 319, Section II 336, Section III 345-346, Section IV 373-374, Isaiah 399-400, The Rise of Babylonia and The Fall of Judah 410-411, Zephaniah 419, Nahum 424, Obadiah 428, Habakkuk 432-433, Jeremiah 479, The Fall of Babylonia, The Rise of Media and Persia 494-495, Daniel 526-527, Ezekiel 564-565, Persia and Judah Following the Babylonian Captivity 573, Ezra 578, Esther 582, Nehemiah 590-591, Haggai 597, Zechariah 612, Malachi 622, Joel 631.
Susa: 571.
Syria: 49, 52, 53, 56, 57, 58, 59, 60, 64, 65, 69, 173, 174, 175, 178, 179, 182, 183, 184, 194, 195, 198, 202-203, 204, 205-208, 213, 214-215, 216, 217, 221, 232, 233, 247, 248, 259, 260, 269, 271, 272, 273, 283, 300, 307, 308, 309, 310, 337, 404, 405, 408, 508, 510, 512, 513, 517, 519, 601, 604.
Syro-Ephraimite War: 185, 194, 221, 231, 297, **303**, **307-308**, 319, 337.

T

Tahpanes: 457.
Talmud: 299.
Targum: 572.
Tarshish: 209, 250.
Tartessus: See Tarshish.
Tartan: 311.
Teach and Warn Others: 113-114, 372.
Tekoa: 257.
Tel-a-bib: 493.
Textual Transmission: listing explained 8, Jonah 252, Amos 267, Hosea 279, Micah 294, Isaiah 380, Zephaniah 419, Nahum 424, Obadiah 427, Habakkuk 432, Jeremiah 475, Ezekiel 563, Haggai 597, Zechariah 611, Malachi 621, Joel 630.
Thebes: 421, 422.

Thermopylae: 570, 579.
Thrace: 511, 570.
Tibni: 50.
Tiglath-pileser III (Pul): 63, 65, 174, 175, 180, 184, 185, 260, 271, 272, 273, 283, 300, **303**, 308, 309, 310, 325, 424.
Tigris River: 248, 249, 528.
Times of the Gentiles: 120-122.
Tobiah: 583, 585, 586.
Togarmah: 147, 551.
Tools for Bible Study: 15-19.
Tribes, Ten Tribes of Israel: 122, **126-128, 132-139**, 175, 187, 189, 283, 293, 300, 320, 341, 350, 351, 373, 550, 554, 565, 612.
Tubal: 147, 544, 551.
Tukulti-Ninurta II: 173.
Turkey: 510, 551.
Tyre: 267, 321, 405, 543, 544.

U

Ulai River: 511.
United Kingdom: 38.
Urartu: See Armenia.
Urijah: 408, 449, 477.
Utah: 353, 594, 600.
Uzziah (Azariah): 61, 62, 63, 64, 72, 174, **183-184**, 231, 247, 257, 258, 270, 272, 297, 299, 300, **303**, 623.

V

Vashti: 579.

W

War: poured out on all nations 120, preparatory wars 120, third world war 121, wars of total destruction 123-124, 128-129, fourth world war 129-130.
Witnesses: 30, 31, 105, 319.
Work: 114.

X

Xerxes (Ahasuerus): 517, **570**, 573, 579, 581.
Xerxes II: 517, **570-571**.

Z

Zachariah (Son of Jeroboam II: 62, 72, 180, 271, **303**.
Zaraphath, Widow of: 51, 196-197.
Zebulun: 38, 247, 311, 338.
Zechariah (Father of Jahaziel): 208.

Zechariah (Prophet): 294, 567, 573, 575, 576, 592, 597, **598-612**.
Zechariah (Son of Jehoiada): 59, 219, 235.
Zedekiah (Mattaniah): 40, 41, 70, 73, 230, **303**, 405, 406, **409**, 411, 419, 425, **436**, 438, 452, 454, 455, 456, 469, 479, 480, 497, 530, 536, 538, 539, 541.
Zephaniah: 10, 223, **412-420**, 421, 428, 437.
Zerah: 48.
Zeus: 512, 519.
Zidon: 51, 177, 196, 543, 545.

Ziggourats: 490.
Zimri: 50, 71, 177, 195.
Zerubabbel: 141, 515, 571, 573, 574, 578, 579, 582, 592, 595-596, 598, 599, 602.
Zion, Mt. Zion: 114, 116, 127, 128, 133, 135, 136, 141, 144, 145, 150, 152, 153, 154, 155, 157, 160, 165, 166, 266, 286, 287, 288, 289, 297, 311, 313, 316, 317, 322, 326, 329, 331, 335, 339, 350, 352, 353, 356, 358, **361-362**, 363, 364, 368, 370, 372, 426, 459, 460, 600, 604, 605, 625, 628, 629.